AF781838

How to design and develop COBOL programs

A practical approach to design, coding, testing, and documentation

Paul Noll
Mike Murach

GoTo's CAUSE CANCER
Paul Noll

Mike Murach & Associates, Inc.
4222 West Alamos, Suite 101
Fresno, California 93711
(209) 275-3335

Development Team

Originator/author:	Paul Noll
Director/writer:	Mike Murach
Writer/editor:	Anne Prince
Production director:	Steve Ehlers
Cover design:	Michael Rogondino

Related program development products

A handbook called *The COBOL Programmer's Handbook*
Case Studies for *How to Design and Develop COBOL Programs*
Instructor's Guide for *How to Design and Develop COBOL Programs*
LISTMODS software for preparing structure listings from COBOL source programs

Related system development products

A textbook called *How to Design and Develop Business Systems*
Case Studies for *How to Design and Develop Business Systems*
Instructor's Guide for *How to Design and Develop Business Systems*

Related COBOL products

A textbook called *Structured ANS COBOL, Part 1*
A textbook called *Structured ANS COBOL, Part 2*
A textbook called *Report Writer*
Advisor's Guide for *Structured ANS COBOL*

© 1985, Mike Murach & Associates, Inc.
All rights reserved.
Printed in the United States of America

20 19 18 17 16 15 14 13 12 11 10 9 8 7 6 5 4 3 2 1

Library of Congress Catalog Card Number: 84-61556

ISBN: 0-911625-20-8

Contents

Preface

In 1977, we published a book by Paul Noll called *Structured Programming for the COBOL Programmer*. It presented a complete method of program development that included techniques for top-down design, structured coding, and top-down testing. Back then, we felt that this method would improve any programmer's productivity. We also felt that this method would help programmers improve the reliability and maintainability of their programs.

Since 1977, more than 35,000 people have bought this book in more than 12,000 different companies throughout the country and the world. In addition, as an independent consultant and trainer, Paul has taught his development method to more than 5,000 programmers in 100 different companies. Based on a survey that we conducted earlier this year, we estimate that Paul's complete method is now used in more than 3,000 companies. And ideas taken from his method are used in thousands of other companies.

Since 1978, when we installed our first computer system at Mike Murach & Associates, we have used the method presented in *Structured Programming* in our own COBOL shop. We have used it with four different kinds of compilers on four different kinds of computer systems. We have developed both batch and interactive systems with it. We have developed about one million lines of COBOL code with it. We have developed complete operational systems for four different companies with it. And now, we can say from experience that the program-development method in *Structured Programming* works...and it works better than any other method we've used, read about, or heard about.

What this book does

This book is a revised edition of *Structured Programming for the COBOL Programmer*. Its purpose is to show you how to improve the quality of your programs as well as your programming productivity. Whether or not you are using structured development techniques right now, we believe this book will show you a better way to develop COBOL programs.

If you check the contents of this book, you can see that it consists of four sections. In general, the first section presents background information that is designed to convince you that our method is the right one for you. The next two sections present the procedures and techniques that make up the method. And the fourth section presents related subjects that can help you make more effective use of the development method.

In section 1, you will find three chapters that present the status of structured programming as we see it today. In our opinion, structured programming has failed in most COBOL shops, and to a large extent it has failed due to the bewildering array of techniques and methods that have been promoted under the name of "structured programming." But that doesn't mean it has to fail in your shop. In fact, chapter 3 presents eight principles that can lead you to dramatic improvements in programmer productivity and program quality.

In section 2, you will learn about the nine-task procedure for program development that we recommend for any COBOL shop. Chapter 4 presents the nine-task procedure. And chapters 5 through 11 present the techniques you should use for each of the tasks in the procedure. To keep this section manageable, the examples used to present the techniques are all taken from batch programs.

Then, in section 3, you'll learn how to apply the procedures and techniques of section 2 to interactive programs. You'll also learn how interactive compilers can force you to modify the standards recommended in section 2. When you finish this section, you should be able to apply the method of this book to interactive programs using any COBOL compiler.

Finally, in section 4, you'll find seven chapters on subjects related to the method of this book. For instance, chapter 15 shows you how the 198X COBOL standards may affect the way you develop programs. And chapter 16 presents other common methods of structured program development so you can compare them with the one in this book. Overall, this section presents many ideas that you can use in conjunction with the development techniques recommended in this book.

For those of you who read the first edition of this book, I think you'll find four major areas of improvement in this second edition. First, the development method of the first edition is refined and improved; it is presented in section 2 of this book. Second, the interactive material in section 3 of this book is new material that we've had dozens of requests for over the last few years. Third, section 4 presents much new material that gives you more perspective on program development. And, fourth, throughout this book, we've made more of an effort to explain *why* our method is more effective than some of the other methods you are likely to be using. As a result, we expect this edition of the book to be more convincing than the first edition was.

As you can see from the contents, this is a lengthy book. But it doesn't have to be overwhelming. Keep in mind, then, that section 2 (chapters 4 through 11) presents the essential method of the book, while the other chapters only provide supporting information. As a result, you can skim or skip section 1 (chapters 1 through 3). You don't have to read section 3 until you're ready to apply the techniques of section 2 to interactive programs. And you only have to read the chapters in section 4 if they become of interest to you. If you read the book with this perspective, I think you'll find it quite manageable.

How we developed this book

When we wrote the first edition of this book, Paul Noll was the originator of the material and I was its writer and editor. Unfortunately, though, Paul Noll wasn't able to help with the development of this second edition of the book because he is teaching at Academia Sinica in Chengdu, China. However, Paul and I did meet for three days last February to compare notes and to agree on what the revision would contain.

So you're not confused when you read this book, I want you to realize now that Paul and I don't agree on everything related to the development of COBOL programs. Yes, we agree on the essential techniques of program design, structured coding, and top-down testing, but we don't agree on some of the related techniques like the use of HIPO diagrams and walkthroughs. This is understandable because Paul's experience has been primarily in large businesses and mine has been in small businesses. Throughout this book, then, I'll try to make clear who believes in what so you can draw your own conclusions. Remember, though, that I'm writing the book, and I'm trying to do my best to present both Paul's opinion and my opinion whenever they differ.

Who this book is for

At the present time, there are thousands of COBOL programmers who are *not* writing structured programs. And this is a preposterous waste of programming talent. So if you're one of these programmers, this book is for you.

But this is also for those programmers who are writing "structured" programs, but who aren't writing reliable programs that are easy to read and maintain and who aren't producing their programs at a professional rate of productivity. Unfortunately, as you'll learn in section 1, we feel that these programmers represent the majority of the programmers working today.

If you are a programming manager, you probably have more personnel problems than you care to think about. So this book is for you too. If you enforce the method in this book throughout your shop, we believe you'll experience dramatic improvements in programmer productivity and program quality in your shop. So a year from now, you should have fewer personnel problems than you have today.

If you read the first edition of this book, we think you'll find that it's worth reading this one too. In brief, this book presents improvements to the method of the first edition; it shows you how to apply the method to interactive programs; and it gives you more background and perspective on program development.

Why this book is effective

We think this book is effective for five main reasons. First, Paul Noll is a practical man who emphasized the practical side of program development in the first edition of this book. And that's what we've tried to do in the second edition too. So this is not a book of theory; it is a book of proven techniques.

Second, Paul Noll has presented the method of this book to hundreds of programmers over the last ten years. Since 1978 Paul has been an independent consultant and trainer who has taught more than 5000 programmers how to program more effectively. Before that, he was the director of technical training for Pacific Telephone in San Francisco at which time he developed more than 50 courses for a staff of more than 120 programmers. As a result of these experiences, Paul has been able to refine his educational approach and to increase its effectiveness. And we've used Paul's approach in this book.

Third, this book was developed with the belief that a method should never be presented without showing its application. In contrast to other books, then, this book presents complete and practical solutions for actual programming problems. Once you see how the development method is applied to these problems, you can see how it can improve your effectiveness.

Fourth, the fact that this book presents structured programming in the context of COBOL increases its effectiveness. In contrast to the many books that present structured programming without relating it to a specific language, you won't be told how to design a program without seeing how the design relates to the COBOL code. You won't learn what the three valid coding structures are without seeing them coded in COBOL. You won't be told what a program stub is without seeing several in COBOL. And you'll see all of the structured coding techniques in COBOL.

Finally, this book contains dozens of illustrations taken from all phases of structured programming...more than twice as many as there were in the first edition of the book. You'll see structure charts for the four types of batch programs common to most business systems. You'll see three different structure charts for the same interactive program as it's implemented using three different COBOL compilers. You'll see pseudocode for the key modules of these programs. You'll see many examples of COBOL coding. You'll see examples of other design and coding methods. And you'll see much more. In our opinion, these illustrations, more than any other factor, determine whether or not a methods course is effective...and they are the missing ingredient in other books on program development.

Some related products

If you want to run a course on the program-development method of this book, we offer a complete training package. It consists of this book, *Case Studies* that go with this book, and an *Instructor's Guide* that makes it easy for an instructor to administer a course using the case studies and text. This package not only teaches a student how to apply modern programming methods to the development of COBOL programs, but it also motivates experienced programmers to use these methods.

If you decide to adopt the method of this book throughout your shop, we offer a reference book called *The COBOL Programmer's Handbook*. This handbook presents standards for program development that conform to the recommendations made in this textbook. It also presents seven model programs, four batch and three interactive, that you can use as models for the development of your own programs. In addition, the *Handbook* can be used as a training aid in a course on program development.

If you're concerned about system design and development as well as program development, we offer a training package for system development too. It is called *How to Design and Develop Business Systems*. And it too consists of text, case studies, and advisor's guide. If you get this package, you will see that its methods for designing and developing business systems complement this book's methods for designing and developing COBOL programs.

Finally, if you train programmers in COBOL, we offer a complete package in *Structured ANS COBOL* that supports the development method presented in this book. It consists of three textbooks and an advisor's guide. If you get this package, you will see that it is closely coordinated with our package for designing and developing COBOL programs. So your COBOL students will learn to develop programs the right way from the start.

Conclusion

Quite frankly, we were disappointed with the sales of the first edition of this book even though we sold more than 35,000 copies of it. In fact, because the need for a better method of program development is so great, we see our experiences with the first edition as a failure in marketing. We were even more disappointed to discover through a survey that less than 50 percent of the people who bought the first edition actually adopted the method it presented. And we know from 17 years in the publishing business that it's much easier to sell a book on a specific skill like CICS or TSO than it is to sell a book on a method for developing systems or programs. It seems, in fact, that most programmers will do everything they can to get the technical training they need, but they won't take the time to get the methods training that is critical to their effectiveness.

As you can see, though, that hasn't stopped us from revising the first edition of this book. I guess we just felt compelled to revise it because we've learned so much in the last eight years. Maybe this time the book will be more convincing. And certainly the development method is more complete than it was in the first edition. Maybe this time more people will join us in reaching the high levels of programming fulfillment that are possible when you use an effective method of program development.

If you have any comments or questions about the method or this book, we'd love to hear from you. So please use the comment form in the back of this book. And thanks for being our customer.

Mike Murach
Fresno, California
October, 1984

Section 1

Introduction

This section is intended to give you some perspective on structured programming and the structured-programming movement. Specifically, this section tries to answer three questions that are important to any programmer or programming group: Has structured programming failed? If it has failed, why did it fail? And what can you do to make sure structured programming doesn't fail in your shop?

If by chance you're not interested in this introductory information, you can skip this section. In this case, you can go on to sections 2 and 3, which present the procedures and techniques you should use if you want structured programming to succeed in your shop. Section 2 presents the procedures and techniques you should use when you develop any business program using batch programs as examples. Section 3 shows you how to apply these procedures and techniques to the development of interactive programs.

Chapter 1

Has structured programming failed?

By the mid-1970s, it was clear that most companies that had computers were not doing an adequate job of developing COBOL programs. A study done in 1975 showed that the average COBOL programmer produced only 10 to 12 lines of tested code per day. In addition, the programs in a typical COBOL shop were generally unreliable, often requiring emergency repairs in order to get basic jobs done. And each year the cost of maintaining old programs went up so it wasn't unusual for a company to spend more than half of its programming budget on program maintenance rather than on new program development.

With these problems, it was natural that the users of most computer systems were something less than satisfied. In a typical shop, more than half the new programs were delivered behind schedule and over budget. And if a user made a request for a new program, he was likely to wait many months before the programming department even started it.

Into this situation, growing more desperate each day, came the promise of "structured programming." If we were to change our methods of developing programs, we were told, we could make dramatic improvements in both programmer productivity and program quality. Then, the computer users would be satisfied because programs would be delivered on time and within budget. And the programming backlog, the jobs waiting to be done by the programming department, would eventually be reduced to reasonable proportions.

By the late 1970s, the structured programming movement had gained considerable momentum. For several years, it was one of the primary subjects of conversation and training. Countless articles and several books were published on the subject. Almost all COBOL training took on a structured look. And most COBOL shops made a serious effort to "get structured."

But now it's the mid-1980s, and you don't hear much about structured programming anymore. If you read the major trade magazines, you rarely find an article on structured programming. Only an occasional book is published on the subject. And, overall, the subject seems quite dead. Microcomputers, networking, and fourth-generation languages seem to be far more important to the average data processing manager.

The questions we have to ask, then, are these: Has structured programming fulfilled its promise? Is that why the subject is dead? Or, has structured programming failed? After the articles were published, after the seminars were given, after the development standards were revised...did things improve or did most COBOL shops simply replace one set of ineffective development standards with a new set?

Before I try to answer these questions, I'm going to review the major changes in program development from 1965 to the present. Next, I'll point out the shortcomings of unstructured development methods and the promised benefits of structured methods. Then, I'll present the effect of the structured programming movement on programmer productivity and program quality. Last, I'll summarize the results of a COBOL survey we recently conducted. When you complete this chapter, I think you'll be able to decide for yourself whether or not structured programming has failed. Keep in mind, though, that the important question is not so much whether structured programming has failed, but whether structured programming has failed in *your* shop.

Changes in COBOL program development from 1965 to the present

Although the COBOL language was developed in the late 1950s, it wasn't used much until third-generation computer systems were introduced in the mid-1960s. As a result, the history of COBOL programming is a short one. The significant history runs from 1965 to the present.

In general, you can divide COBOL programming into three styles or eras. First, a typical shop in 1965 simply adapted assembler language techniques to the development of COBOL programs. The result was what I call *GOTO programming.* Second, in an attempt to improve programmer productivity and program quality, a typical COBOL shop experimented with *modular programming.* Finally, in an attempt to improve on modular programming, a typical COBOL shop converted to *structured programming.*

More important than this general history, though, is the history of program development in each COBOL shop. For instance, a well-run COBOL shop may have started with GOTO programming in 1965, moved to modular programming by 1970, and established structured programming by 1975. In contrast, a poorly-run shop may still be developing programs using GOTO programming.

If you've been in the data processing business for more than a short time, you probably know what I'm talking about when I mention GOTO, modular, and structured programming. But in case you don't, here's a brief introduction to each of these programming styles. Once you understand them, you'll have a better idea of why the promise of structured programming was so alluring.

GOTO programming In the GOTO era of program development, a programmer designed a program by developing a detailed program flowchart. Figure 1-1, for example, is a flowchart for a simple file-to-printer program that prepares a wage report. As you can see, the flowchart goes into so much logical detail that the programmer has used a flowcharting form to make it somewhat easier to follow. If you work in a well-run COBOL shop, it may be hard for you to believe that people ever created flowcharts like this. But ten years ago, they were quite common.

After a programmer completed a detailed flowchart, he began coding the program using the flowchart as a guide. When he reached a decision block like block J1, he continued with the processing for one of the conditions and coded the routines for the other conditions later on. After all routines were coded, a good programmer checked the code for completeness using the flowchart as a reference.

One of the characteristics of traditional COBOL coding was the extensive use of GOTO statements, because at least one GOTO was used for every decision block in a flowchart. To code the wage-report program based on the flowchart in figure 1-1, for example, a programmer would probably have used a dozen or more GOTO statements. But it is this branching from one paragraph to another within a COBOL program that makes the code difficult to read and modify. In actual practice, a traditional COBOL program that used 1000 different verbs in the Procedure Division was likely to use anywhere from 100 to 250 GOTO statements, so the code was extremely difficult to follow.

Modular programming As you can see in figure 1-1, a flowchart from the GOTO era had no identifiable structure. As a result, it was difficult to create, read, and maintain. And the resulting program was difficult to code, test, debug, and maintain. By the late 1960s, then, programmers in the better COBOL shops began to think in terms of modular programming.

The idea of modular programming was to divide a program into a number of independent modules—one mainline module and one or more subroutine modules. By so doing, the logic of a program was simplified, which in turn simplified coding and testing.

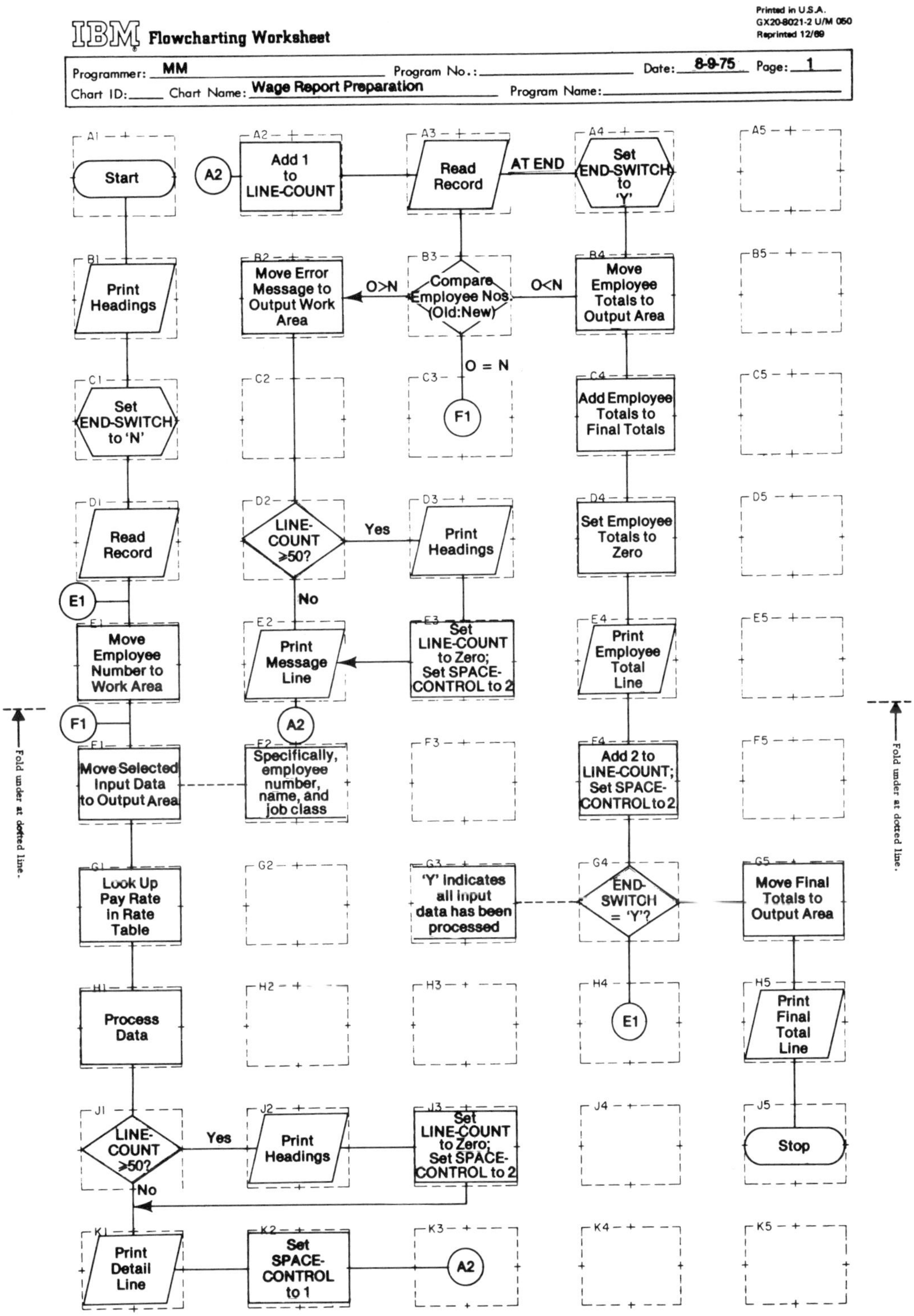

Figure 1-1 A program flowchart for a program that prepares a wage report

Figure 1-2, for example, is a flowchart for the mainline module of the same wage-report program that is flowcharted in figure 1-1. This module indicates all the major processing modules as well as the logical decisions required to direct the program to these modules. As you can see, each module has a stripe at the top of the symbol to indicate the name of the module. So the wage-report program consists of the mainline module plus eight other modules named HOUSEKEEPING, READ-RECORD, and so on.

After a programmer completed the flowchart for the mainline module, she flowcharted each of the subroutine modules, or at least the more complex modules. To continue the concept of modularity, she might divide a subroutine module into additional, more specific, modules, depending on the length and complexity of the module. Since the idea was to make each programming module manageable, the programmer tried to keep each module between 50 and 200 statements in length.

To code a modular program, the programmer started with the mainline module. Next, she coded each of the subroutine modules. In contrast to GOTO programming, then, the modular program was coded in a somewhat predictable sequence.

By using modules, the COBOL programmer cut down on her use of GOTO statements. Instead, to control the execution of subroutine modules, she used PERFORM statements. For instance, the code in figure 1-3 represents the mainline module flowcharted in figure 1-2. Notice that all the PERFORM statements are written with the THRU EXIT clause so the mainline routine won't have to be changed no matter how many paragraphs the subroutines contain. Notice also, however, that GOTO statements are still used extensively. In this 22-statement routine, five GOTO statements are used.

Structured programming When structured programming started to become popular in the mid-1970s, it was somewhat revolutionary. It said throw away your flowcharts and your GOTOs and do things differently. Because many people were aware of the problems they experienced using unstructured techniques, they were ready to make this revolutionary change. Then, when success stories were published showing the dramatic improvements possible when you used structured programming, more people became convinced that they should make this change to new methods. Eventually, so many people had changed their methods, were in the process of changing them, or were considering changing them, that it was clear structured programming was here to stay. In fact, so many people changed that it was fair to describe the change as an industry-wide movement, the structured programming movement.

When you develop programs using structured programming, you no longer use a program flowchart (although some people tried). Instead, you design a program using a design document like a structure chart, a

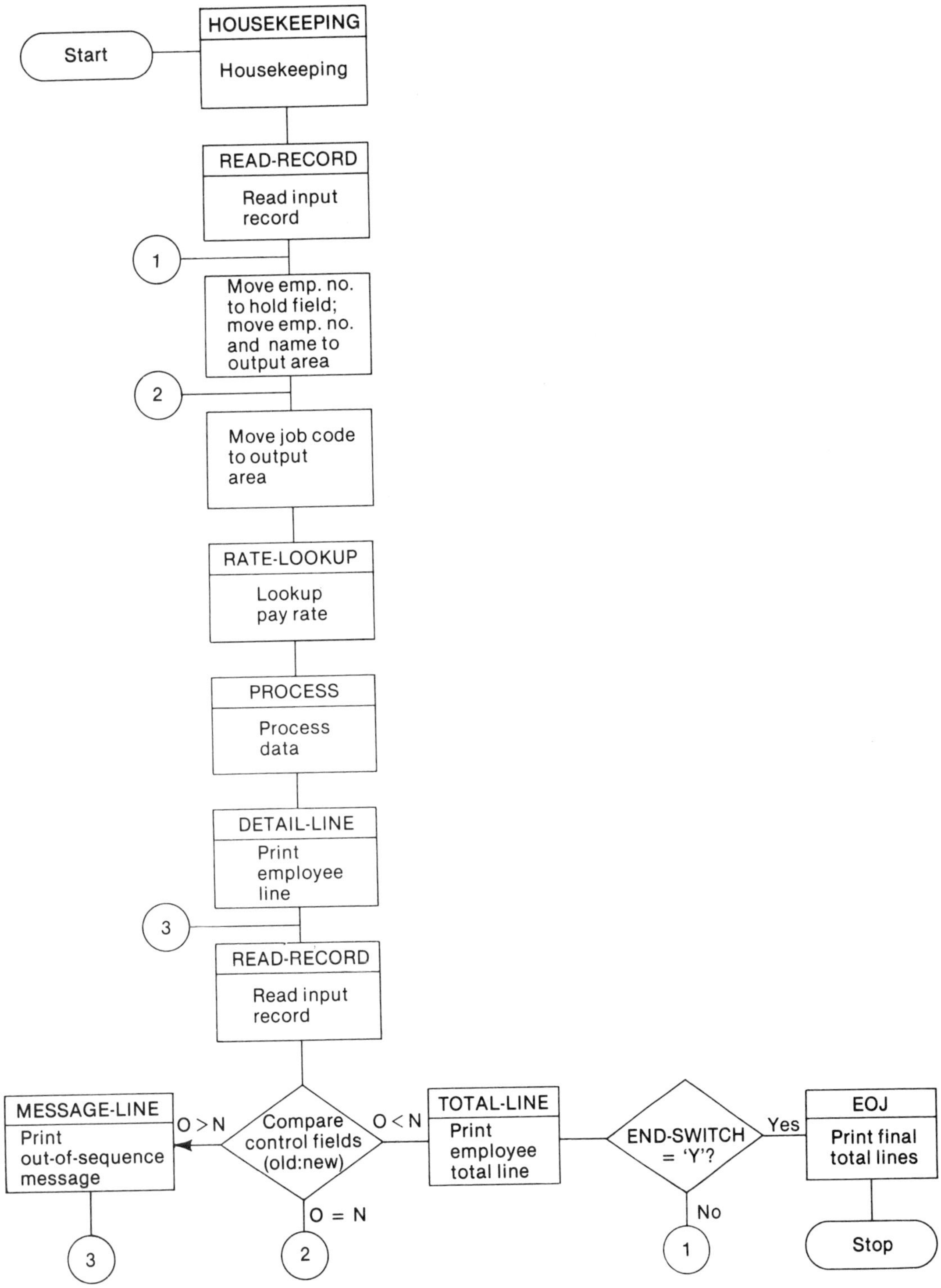

Figure 1-2 A modular flowchart for a program that prepares a wage report

```
PROCEDURE DIVISION.
MAINLINE SECTION.
    PERFORM HOUSEKEEPING-RT THRU HOUSEKEEPING-EXIT.
    PERFORM READ-RECORD-RT THRU READ-RECORD-EXIT.
NEW-CONTROL-NUMBER.
    MOVE EJ-EMP-NO TO WS-EMP-NO.
    MOVE EJ-EMP-NO TO WR-EMP-NO.
    MOVE EJ-EMP-NAME TO WR-EMP-NAME.
SAME-CONTROL-NUMBER.
    MOVE EJ-JOB-CODE TO WR-JOB-CODE.
    PERFORM RATE-LOOKUP-RT THRU RATE-LOOKUP-EXIT.
    PERFORM PROCESS-RT THRU PROCESS-EXIT.
    PERFORM DETAIL-LINE-RT THRU DETAIL-LINE-EXIT.
READ-ANOTHER-CARD.
    PERFORM READ-RECORD-RT THRU READ-RECORD-EXIT.
    IF WS-EMP-NO IS EQUAL TO EJ-EMP-NO
        GO TO SAME-CONTROL-NUMBER.
    IF WS-EMP-NO IS LESS THAN EJ-EMP-NO
        GO TO TOTAL-LINE-PROCESSING
    ELSE
        GO TO READ-ANOTHER-CARD.
TOTAL-LINE-PROCESSING.
    PERFORM TOTAL-LINE-RT THRU TOTAL-LINE-EXIT.
    IF END-SWITCH IS EQUAL TO 'Y'
        GO TO END-OF-JOB
    ELSE GO TO NEW-CONTROL-NUMBER.
END-OF-JOB.
    PERFORM END-OF-JOB-RT THRU END-OF-JOB-EXIT.
    STOP RUN.
```

Figure 1-3 Modular coding for the mainline module of a program that prepares a wage report

tree chart, or a Warnier/Orr diagram. In figure 1-4, for example, you can see a *structure chart* for the same wage-report program that is flowcharted in figures 1-1 and 1-2. In contrast to the flowcharts, the structure chart presents an identifiable, top-down structure. Also, since each of the blocks on the structure chart is one module of the COBOL program, the structure chart is an index to the COBOL code.

After you've designed a structured program, you code it using GOTOless COBOL (although some people refuse to give up GOTOs completely). Figure 1-5, for example, shows the first page of the Procedure Division of the wage-report program in structured COBOL. As you can see, the code uses no GOTO statements at all, and one paragraph of the program corresponds to one module in the structure chart. Instead of GOTO statements, the program makes extensive use of PERFORM statements and nested IF statements.

Although structured programming implies much more than just new techniques for program design and COBOL coding, let's leave it at that for now. Then, in the next chapter, I'll introduce all of the techniques that have come to be associated with structured programming.

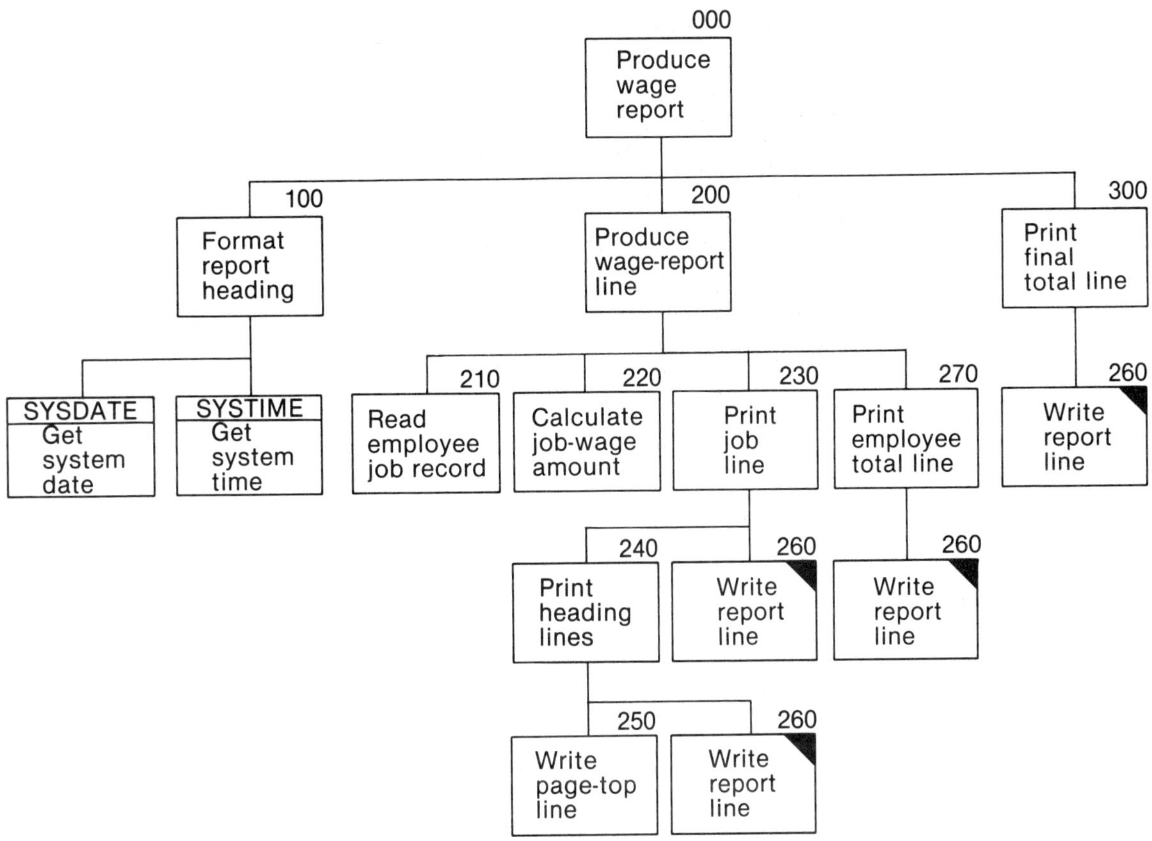

Figure 1-4 A structure chart for a program that prepares a wage report

The shortcomings of unstructured development methods

Before the structured programming era, the development procedures in most COBOL shops were inefficient and ineffective, to say the least. For the most part, whether or not modular programming was used, all phases of programming—design, coding, testing, documentation, and maintenance—were done on an unprofessional, unmanaged basis.

In the design phase, for example, the flowchart was difficult to create and once created was difficult to change. Most damning of all, however, the flowchart became less useful as the programming problem became larger and more complex. From a practical point of view, flowcharts were so ineffective that programmers tended to hurry through the design phase and begin coding before they had a reasonable programming plan.

```
 PROCEDURE DIVISION.
*
 000-PRODUCE-WAGE-REPORT.
*
     OPEN INPUT  EMPJOB
          OUTPUT WAGERPT.
     PERFORM 100-FORMAT-REPORT-HEADING.
     PERFORM 200-PRODUCE-WAGE-REPORT-LINE
         UNTIL EMPLOYEE-JOB-EOF.
     PERFORM 300-PRINT-FINAL-TOTAL-LINE.
     CLOSE EMPJOB
           WAGERPT.
     STOP RUN.
*
 100-FORMAT-REPORT-HEADING.
*
     CALL 'SYSDATE' USING TODAYS-DATE.
     MOVE TODAYS-DATE  TO HDG1-DATE.
     MOVE COMPANY-NAME TO HDG1-COMPANY-NAME.
     CALL 'SYSTIME' USING HDG2-TIME.
     MOVE 'PR1450'      TO HDG2-REPORT-NUMBER.
     MOVE REPORT-TITLE TO HDG2-REPORT-TITLE.
*
 200-PRODUCE-WAGE-REPORT-LINE.
*
     PERFORM 210-READ-EMPLOYEE-JOB-RECORD.
     IF NOT EMPLOYEE-JOB-EOF
         IF FIRST-RECORD
             MOVE EJ-EMPLOYEE-NUMBER TO OLD-EMPLOYEE-NUMBER
             PERFORM 220-CALCULATE-JOB-WAGE-AMOUNT
             PERFORM 230-PRINT-JOB-LINE
             MOVE 'N' TO FIRST-RECORD-SWITCH
         ELSE
             IF EJ-EMPLOYEE-NUMBER IS EQUAL TO OLD-EMPLOYEE-NUMBER
                 PERFORM 220-CALCULATE-JOB-WAGE-AMOUNT
                 PERFORM 230-PRINT-JOB-LINE
             ELSE
                 IF EJ-EMPLOYEE-NUMBER
                         IS GREATER THAN OLD-EMPLOYEE-NUMBER
                     PERFORM 240-PRINT-EMPLOYEE-TOTAL-LINE
                     MOVE EJ-EMPLOYEE-NUMBER
                         TO OLD-EMPLOYEE-NUMBER
                     PERFORM 220-CALCULATE-JOB-WAGE-AMOUNT
                     PERFORM 230-PRINT-JOB-LINE.
     IF EMPLOYEE-JOB-EOF
         PERFORM 240-PRINT-EMPLOYEE-TOTAL-LINE.
*
 210-READ-EMPLOYEE-JOB-RECORD.
*
     READ EMPJOB RECORD INTO EMPLOYEE-JOB-RECORD
         AT END
             MOVE 'Y' TO EMPLOYEE-JOB-EOF-SWITCH.
*
 220-CALCULATE-JOB-WAGE-AMOUNT.
*
```

Figure 1-5 Structured COBOL for a program that prepares a wage report

In the coding phase, programmers generally worked without standards or restrictions. They determined in what sequences they would code paragraphs and in what sequences they would place the paragraphs in the programs. As they coded, they created their own paragraph names and data names and used their own styles of indentation and coding. Is it any wonder that no two programmers did work that looked alike so there was no consistency in the work done in a typical COBOL shop? Is it any wonder that important details and required paragraphs of a program were often overlooked?

As for unstructured testing, it was too often a nightmare. In this stage, all of the mistakes made in design and coding come back to haunt you. And when a bug is detected, you have to determine the cause. But if the program lacks structure, how do you know where to look? Although modular program design helped to isolate certain types of program bugs, the use of GOTO statements still made it difficult to follow the flow of control during program execution. Using unstructured techniques, a program of several thousand source statements often contained hundreds of errors and took months to debug.

As you might guess, all of the problems just mentioned came into play again when it became necessary to change, or maintain, a program. And if the maintenance programmer wasn't the same person who created the program, the problems were compounded. In actual practice, the maintenance programmer was usually confronted by an incomplete set of flowcharts to guide her through the program changes (these flowcharts would have been difficult enough to follow if they had been complete). Then, when she confronted the source code, she was likely to find the "rat's nest" or "spaghetti" code that is characterized by the extensive use of GOTO statements. So when the maintenance programmer changed the procedure or module that she thought would bring about the desired program change, she was likely to create a new program bug. As a result, the cost of making a change to a program was many times the cost of coding the routine in the first place.

The promise of structured development methods

In contrast to unstructured methods, structured program development promises much. In brief, it can make dramatic improvements in programmer productivity and program quality. By designing a program from the top down using a structure chart or a similar design document, the programmer can shorten the design phase of programming. When finished, the structure chart shows all of the modules required by the program as well as the relationships between these modules. Furthermore, the chart can act as an index to the COBOL code. That is, each box on the structure chart can be coded in a single COBOL paragraph (or section). This helps during the testing and maintenance phases of program development.

If the structure chart is drawn properly, it gives the paragraph names, the sequence numbers for these paragraphs, and an indication of the sequence in which the modules should be coded. Then, if the programmer codes the modules without using GOTO statements, each module will only have one entry and one exit point. As a result, the entire program will only have one entry and one exit point. This means that you will be able to read the program listing from the top down with only a limited amount of flipping back and forth between the pages.

The benefits of structured programming are perhaps most obvious when it comes to testing. Because the program consists of independent modules and because these modules have only one entry and one exit point, the structured program is almost sure to have fewer bugs than an unstructured program. In addition, these bugs are likely to be simple clerical errors rather than complex logical errors. Finally, due to the structured design, the bugs will be relatively easy to find and correct.

When it comes to the documentation for a structured program, it should be an automatic by-product of the development procedure. In general, the primary pieces of documentation are the structure chart and the program listing. Because the structure chart for a program is relatively simple when compared to a detailed flowchart or a modular flowchart, it can be kept up-to-date more easily. So the chances are much better that a structure chart will be kept current than they are that a program flowchart will be kept current. In addition, because the structure chart is an index to the paragraphs or sections within the COBOL program, the documentation is easier to follow.

The benefits of structured programming are again obvious when it comes to program maintenance. Because the documentation is more current and easier to follow, a programmer can more easily identify the modules of a program that need to be changed. Because the COBOL code conforms to structured programming standards, it is easier to read and understand. And because the entire program is based on a structured design, a change to one module of a program isn't likely to create new problems in other modules of the program.

These improvements in design, coding, testing, documentation, and maintenance, of course, mean improvements in programmer productivity and program quality. In terms of productivity, the programmer spends less time designing, coding, testing, documenting, and maintaining a program, so his productivity improves. How much does it improve? When structured programming techniques first were introduced, nobody knew for sure what the results would be. So the promise was great. Certainly, you could increase your productivity by 50 percent. And perhaps by 100 percent...or 300 percent...or 500 percent.

Early studies done on productivity when using the new methods seemed to bear out this promise of structured programming. One study, for example, showed an average productivity per programmer of from 35 to 65 tested lines of code per day. That was a 300 percent or more increase in productivity when compared with the results of unstructured projects. Another study showed an average productivity per programmer of from 110 to 120 tested lines of code per day...that's a tenfold increase in productivity. A third study that had collected data on programming techniques for over four years showed an increase in productivity of 77 percent or more when the techniques of structured programming were used.

In terms of program quality, structured programs were definitely more reliable. Although it's hard to collect data on improvements in quality, it seemed clear to everyone that structured programs had fewer bugs after they were put into production. And they were certainly easier to maintain. In fact, the goal of 100 percent reliability seemed reasonable. And a reduction in maintenance costs of 50 percent or more seemed easily attainable.

In terms of user satisfaction, if a company converted to structured programming methods, users were sure to be more satisfied. Not only would the programs break down less often, but enhancements to the programs could be made more easily. Also, program development would be more manageable so programs could be delivered on time and within budget. And eventually, the programming backlog would be reduced so a user's request could be put into development within a reasonable period of time.

The effect of structured programming on programmer productivity and program quality

Now, some five years after the structured programming movement hit its peak of activity, we can try to compare the actual effect of the movement with its promised benefits of improved programmer productivity and program quality. As you might guess, the results are mixed.

Before I start this analysis, though, I'd like you to know what I mean when I talk about programmer productivity and program quality. I don't think there's much chance of misunderstanding when it comes to programmer productivity because we'd both agree that productivity has something to do with units of useful work. On the other hand, we would probably disagree on how productivity should be measured. Should it be the number of programs produced by a programmer, the number of program functions, the number of lines of COBOL code, the number of verbs in the Procedure Division, or what? In chapter 21, I'll give you some ideas on how to measure programmer productivity, but until then I'd just like you to think of productivity in terms of lines of COBOL code. I'm not saying that this is the best measurement, but it's one that we all understand.

When I speak of program quality in this book, I'm thinking of two specific qualities for a batch program: program reliability and program maintainability. For an interactive program, I also think of ease-of-use. To measure reliability, you can count the number of times a program blows up or requires repairs after the program is put into production. For maintainability, you must consider how easy a program is to maintain. So reliability is relatively easy to measure while maintainability is difficult to measure. As you can imagine, ease-of-use for an interactive program is also difficult to measure. As a result, program quality is far more difficult to measure than programmer productivity. Nevertheless, it is important, and you certainly don't want to increase programmer productivity at the expense of program quality.

With this as background, we can try to analyze the effect of structured programming on programmer productivity and program quality. And the results are mixed. On the one hand, some companies have reported dramatic improvements in productivity and program quality. On the other hand, hundreds of companies still develop programs as if it were the mid-1960s. In order to understand the effect of the structured-programming movement, then, I think we have to review the effect in the worst COBOL shops, the effect in the best COBOL shops, and the effect in the average COBOL shop.

The effect of structured programming in the worst COBOL shops Although it's hard for me to understand, thousands of COBOL shops in this country have never converted to structured development methods. Apparently, thousands of managers and programmers in this country decided that the methods they were using were just as effective as structured programming methods. So they left it at that. As I see it, however, the decision to stay with unstructured methods is the worst decision a programming manager can make.

One reason why managers make this decision is that they don't really understand what structured programming is. Over the years, I have reviewed many programs that were said to be structured only to find that the programs didn't even meet the development standards of the modular programming era. So perhaps simple ignorance is the main reason why the worst COBOL shops stick with unstructured development methods.

The effect of structured programming in the best COBOL shops At the other extreme, some shops did report dramatic improvements in programmer productivity and program quality over the last five years. One company, for example, reported that its programmers averaged 500 lines of code per week throughout the life of a project that used structured development methods. Furthermore, an average of only 3 bugs were discovered for each of the programs after they were put into production. Similarly, a consultant reports that productivity rates of 24,000 to 28,000 lines per programmer-year (or about 500 lines of code per week) are not unusual in large companies with efficient development practices.

I believe these reports because they are consistent with what we've experienced in our own shop. When we established a minimum production standard of 500 lines of tested code per week for our programmers, only a few of the more experienced programmers groaned. The younger programmers, those who had never known anything but structured programming, thought this was a perfectly reasonable minimum. Furthermore, our good programmers far surpassed this minimum with rates of well over 1000 lines of code per week, or 50,000 lines per year. And our two best programmers produced more than 100,000 lines of interactive code in a single year. All of this with no overtime in a 35-hour work week.

In terms of program quality, I think the best shops approach 100 percent reliability when they release a program for production; that is, no bugs at all after a program is put into production. But if maintenance is required, it can be done in a small fraction of the time it would have taken if the programs were unstructured.

In our own shop, we put the emphasis on productivity, not on reliability. So we expect a few bugs during the first two or three months after a program is put into production. After that, however, we expect our programs to run indefinitely without any problems. In terms of maintenance programming, one person in our shop does the maintenance for about 600,000 lines of COBOL code. She does it using less than two days per month of her time, and most of the maintenance she does is program enhancement, not debugging or fixing.

The effect of structured programming in the average COBOL shop If some shops don't know structured programming exists and some have had excellent results with it, what is happening in the average COBOL shop? Although it's always difficult to generalize, I think it's clear that the average shop either converted to some form of structured programming or made an attempt to convert. But I think it's also clear that many shops that did convert to structured programming showed little or no improvement in programmer productivity or program quality. One large company, for example, did a careful study of a project that covered 14 programmer-months of work using structured methods. To their surprise, the productivity rate in their shop was approximately the same as it had been before they converted to the new methods. On the other hand, they felt strongly that the reliability and maintainability of their programs had improved significantly.

In terms of programmer productivity, then, the improvements in the average shop seem to be marginal rather than dramatic. One extensive study, for example, showed a 100 percent improvement in productivity when structured programming was used. In terms of lines of code, though, that was only an improvement of about 1.5 lines of code per hour per programmer. But at a total of 3 lines of code per hour per programmer, or about 120 lines of code per week, a 120,000-line application requires 20 programmer-years to develop. At that rate, we're not going to make much reduction in the programming backlog. What we need to see are improvements of 300 percent or more...and they are possible. After all, unstructured programming methods were horribly inefficient.

In terms of program quality, I think it's clear that programs have improved in the average COBOL shop as a result of structured programming. Most companies report fewer bugs detected after a program has been put into production so reliability is up and maintenance time is down. But, here again, the improvements tend to be marginal. Although structured programs may have 50 percent fewer bugs than unstructured programs, what we really need are improvements that are far more dramatic than that. We need programs that have only one percent as many bugs as their unstructured predecessors. After all, unstructured programs were a maintenance nightmare.

When we look at some industry-wide data, it supports our feeling about the average COBOL shop. It seems, in fact, that we have almost as many programming problems now as we did before the structured programming movement ever got started. And that doesn't speak well for what's happening in the average COBOL shop. For instance, a recent study done of programs developed for the government showed that 60 percent were over budget and 50 percent were behind schedule. Meanwhile, the maintenance burden seems to be getting worse, not better, as 50 percent or more of a programming budget gets spent on maintaining old programs, rather than on developing new programs. And the programming backlog seems to have lengthened, rather than shortened, with a backlog of 18 months or more in 93 percent of the companies reviewed in an IBM study. In many Fortune 500 companies, in fact, programming backlogs of five to seven years are common.

Another indication that we haven't improved program development enough is the current emphasis on microcomputers and decision-support centers. What we are saying here is that we can't deliver the programs our users want right now. So until we can, why don't they develop their own programs using general-purpose programs like Visicalc and TKSolver! In fact, the programming backlog has been reduced somewhat because of the use of microcomputers. But that just highlights the ineffectiveness of the program development methods we use on large systems. Users have finally accepted the fact that they're better off with an inefficient program running on a microcomputer than they are with no program at all running on the company's mainframe.

When I asked Paul Noll what his feeling was about the status of program development in the average COBOL shop, he said it's dismal. Bear in mind that Paul consults in many large companies with extensive training budgets. And still the results are dismal.

In fact, in some of his training seminars, Paul gets the attention of the group by starting this way: "I don't have to tell you how bad things are around here. Most of you are developing only 10 or 20 lines of tested code each day, and you know you're capable of doing much more. The programs that you put into production are unmaintainable garbage, and you know it. Many of the older programs are so bad that they can no longer be maintained at all, and you know it. There isn't decent documentation for more than a handful of your production programs...." As he went on like this in one shop, all of the programmers were nodding their heads in agreement.

In this case, though, the vice-president of the company, who is also the information director, was sitting in the back of the room. Finally, when he could take no more, he stood up and said: "Will someone here please tell me that Paul is wrong? We've been writing structured programs for five years now." But no one came forward. They sat there sheepishly knowing full well that somehow, between the idea of structured programming and the reality of it, something had gone wrong.

When Paul and I met to discuss how we would develop this book, I asked Paul how people decide that they want to use his services as a consultant or a trainer. Did they realize that they could improve their programming productivity by using better methods? Did they realize that their program quality left something to be desired? "No" Paul said, "when people call me it's usually not because they have an identifiable problem in terms of productivity or program quality. They call because they have a chaotic mess." That may be overstating it a bit, but all the data we've assembled and all the experiences we've had point to the fact that program development in the average COBOL shop can be improved dramatically.

The results of our 1984 survey of COBOL shops

Before we started work on this book, we sent a questionnaire to 255 businesses that had purchased one or more of our COBOL books at sometime during the preceding two years. Our goal was to find out what methods people were using to develop COBOL programs and what their results were in terms of programmer productivity and program quality. The questionnaires that we received from 82 respondents helped give us a more precise idea of what people are doing in the average COBOL shop.

Unfortunately, the survey clearly indicates that most program development is being done on an unprofessional, unmanaged basis. For instance, only 23 percent of our respondents make any attempt to measure programmer productivity, and only 40 percent make any attempt to measure program quality. Worse, 63 percent of the respondents still use program flowcharts as a design tool, and 61 percent still use GOTO statements. And these results didn't come from small, unsophisticated COBOL shops...73 percent of the respondents were in shops using IBM mainframes.

But rather than present all of the data of this survey right now, let me simply say that it corroborates the other data that I've reported. Program development in most COBOL shops leaves much room for improvement. Please keep this survey in mind, though, because I will refer to it throughout this book.

Has structured programming failed?

In terms of its industry-wide effect on programmer productivity and program quality, I have to feel that structured programming has failed. But as far as you're concerned, that's not the important question anyway. The important question is: Has structured programming failed in your shop? And only you can answer that.

To answer this question, you should compare what you're doing with what the best COBOL shops are doing. Do you measure up to their standards? Do your programmers produce a minimum of 500 lines of tested COBOL code per week? Do your best programmers produce more than 50,000 lines of COBOL code per year and still have half their time left over for systems analysis and design? Do your programs approach 100 percent reliability after they are put into production? Can one of your programmers maintain 500,000 lines of code in as little as one day per week and have the rest of his time to develop new programs? If these seem like preposterous standards, structured programming has failed in your shop, and it's high time you do something about it.

Fortunately, structured programming doesn't have to fail in your shop. In the next chapter, I'll show you why structured programming has failed to fulfill its promise in the industry as a whole and in the average COBOL shop. Then, in chapter 3, I'll show you what you can do to make dramatic improvements in programmer productivity and program quality in your shop.

Terminology

GOTO programming
modular programming
structured programming
structure chart

Objectives

1. Describe the shortcomings of unstructured program development in terms of design, coding, testing, documentation, and maintenance.

2. Describe the promised benefits of structured program development in terms of programmer productivity and program quality.

3. Describe the effect of structured programming in the average COBOL shop.

Chapter 2

Why structured programming has failed

To understand why structured programming has failed in the average COBOL shop, you need to understand more about structured programming and the techniques that are associated with it. So in this chapter, I'll start by reviewing the theory of structured programming. Next, I'll introduce the primary techniques that are associated with this theory; these are often called the *improved productivity techniques*. Then, I'll present some of the disagreements programmers and programming managers have about the improved productivity techniques. By the time you finish this material, I think you'll be able to draw your own conclusions about why structured programming has failed.

I'll tell you right now, though, that structured programming doesn't have to fail in your shop just because it has failed in most shops. Whether you're just now thinking about trying the improved productivity techniques or whether you've been using structured programming techniques for several years, the potential of structured programming is still there. You just have to make sure that you select the right techniques. And the purpose of this book is to help you make these selections.

The theory of structured programming

Professor Edsger W. Dijkstra of the University of Eindhoven, Netherlands, has been given much of the credit for the development of *structured programming*. As far back as 1965 he suggested that the GOTO statement could and should be eliminated from programming languages. He felt that the more GOTO statements a program contained, the worse it was. He was convinced that a program was easiest to read and debug when it contained no GOTO statements at all.

To write a program without GOTOs, however, you must use other control statements. This led Professor Dijkstra and other computer scientists to give rigid definitions for the structures that are acceptable in a well-structured program. These efforts led to the theory of structured programming.

The basic theory of structured programming is that any program can be written using only three logical structures. These structures are summarized in figure 2-1. They are called the sequence, selection, and iteration structures.

The *sequence structure* is simply the idea that imperative program statements are executed in sequence. For instance, if the COBOL ADD, SUBTRACT, and MULTIPLY statements (without SIZE ERROR options) are coded in sequence in a program, they are executed one after the other. As a result, a sequence box can consist of one imperative statement or many. And two sequence boxes can be combined into one without changing the basic sequential structure.

The *selection structure* is a choice between two and only two actions based on a condition. If the condition is true, one function is done; if false, the other is done. Either one of the two actions may be null, or not expressly stated; in other words, an action may be specified for only one result of the condition test. Then, when the other result occurs, the program continues by executing the next statement in sequence. This structure is often referred to as the *IF-THEN-ELSE structure*, and many programming languages have code that closely approximates it.

The *iteration structure*, often called the *DO-WHILE structure*, provides for doing a function as long as a condition is true. When the condition is no longer true, the program continues with the next structure. A common alternate structure for iteration is the fourth one shown in figure 2-1, the *DO-UNTIL structure*. Logically related to the DO-WHILE, the DO-UNTIL does a function *until* a condition becomes true.

Although COBOL doesn't directly provide for either the DO-WHILE or DO-UNTIL structure, it does offer the PERFORM-UNTIL structure. This is the third iteration structure shown in figure 2-1. As you can see, it is closely related to the DO-UNTIL structure. In fact, it differs from the DO-UNTIL only in that the condition is tested before the function is done rather than after.

In actual practice, the PERFORM-UNTIL structure is often referred to as a DO-UNTIL structure since the difference is more academic than real. When I refer to a DO-UNTIL structure in this book, you can imagine coding it with the COBOL PERFORM-UNTIL statement.

Notice that all of the structures in figure 2-1 have only one entry and one exit point. As a result, a program made up of these structures will have only one entry and one exit. Thus, the program will be executed in a controlled manner from the first statement to the last. These characteristics make up a *proper program*.

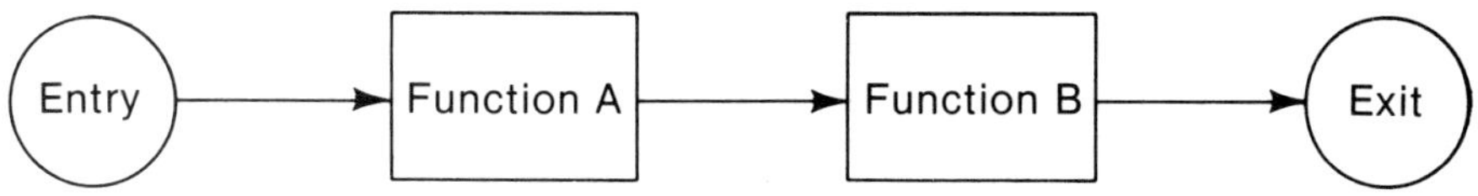

The sequence structure (DO)

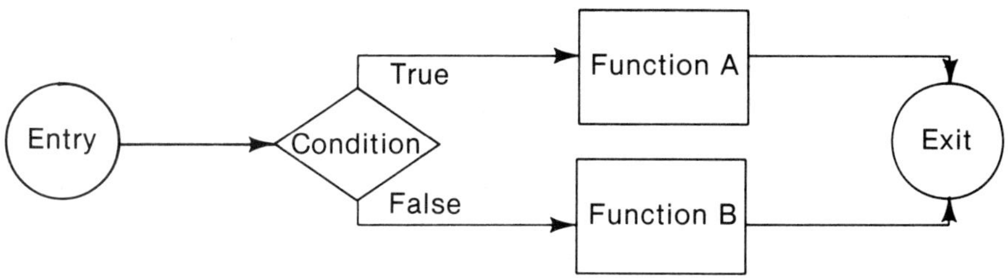

The selection structure (IF-THEN-ELSE)

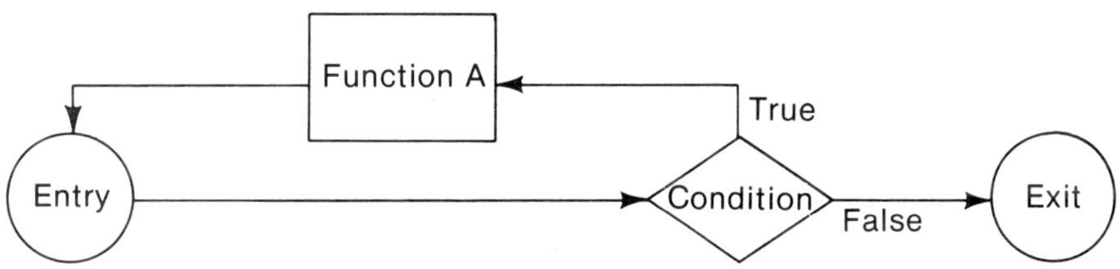

Variation 1 of the iteration structure (DO-WHILE)

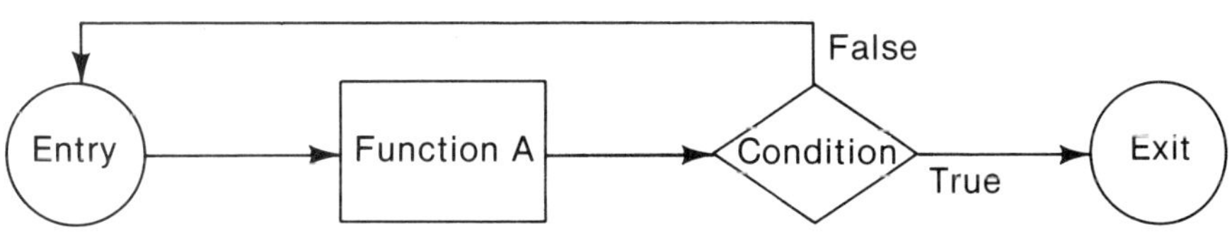

Variation 2 of the iteration structure (DO-UNTIL)

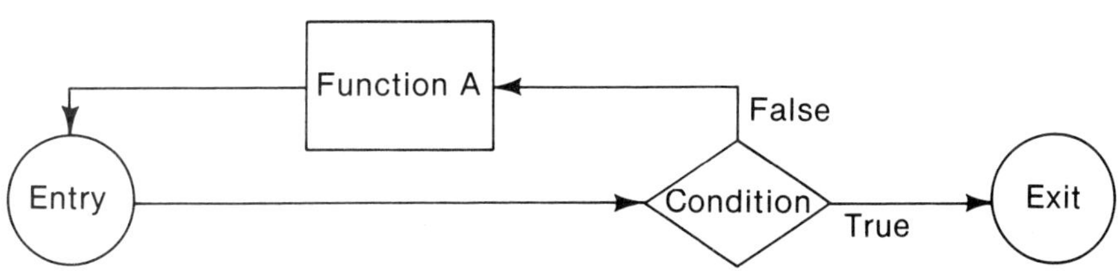

Variation 3 of the iteration structure (COBOL PERFORM-UNTIL)

Figure 2-1 The basic structures of structured programming

To create a proper program, any of the three basic structures can be substituted for a function box in any of the other structures. The result will still be a proper program. Similarly, two or more of the basic structures in sequence can be treated as a single function box. This means that structures of great complexity can be created with the assurance that they will only have one entry and one exit and that they will be executed in a controlled manner from start to finish.

To illustrate the use of substitution and combination, consider the proper program in figure 2-2. Here, a sequence structure, a selection structure, and another sequence structure are substituted for the function box of a DO-UNTIL structure. Note, however, that the program still has only one entry and one exit. Similarly, any of the basic structures can be substituted in function boxes A, B, C, or D and the program will still have but one entry and one exit.

This theory is an important contribution to the art of programming because it places necessary restrictions on program structure. As you can see, the GOTO statement that is so widely used in unstructured programs is illegal in structured programs. As a result, uncontrolled branching within a proper program is impossible. This in turn reduces the likelihood of program bugs and makes it easier to find errors when there are bugs. In addition, if handled correctly, the structured program is easier to read and understand than the unstructured program.

An introduction to the improved productivity techniques

Although the theory of structured programming was an important one, it dealt primarily with coding. But you can't just start off coding proper programs, except for trivial ones. In order to apply the theory of structured programming to business programs of 1000 lines of code or more, new techniques of program design were needed.

Unfortunately, it took many years before practical methods of applying the theory were developed. By the mid-1970s, for example, only about one-fourth of the COBOL shops were using structured programming at all. And most of these didn't use effective methods for applying the theory.

Eventually, however, the theory of structured programming helped bring important new techniques to program development. These techniques came to be known as the *improved productivity techniques*, or *IPTs*. Before we continue, then, I'd like to introduce you to the most widely-used IPTs: top-down design, structured module design, structured coding, top-down testing, structured walkthroughs, chief programmer teams, and development-support libraries.

Top-down design Although it is possible to draw flowcharts for structured programs, it isn't practical. You've already seen the shortcomings of the program flowchart. So it doesn't make much sense to

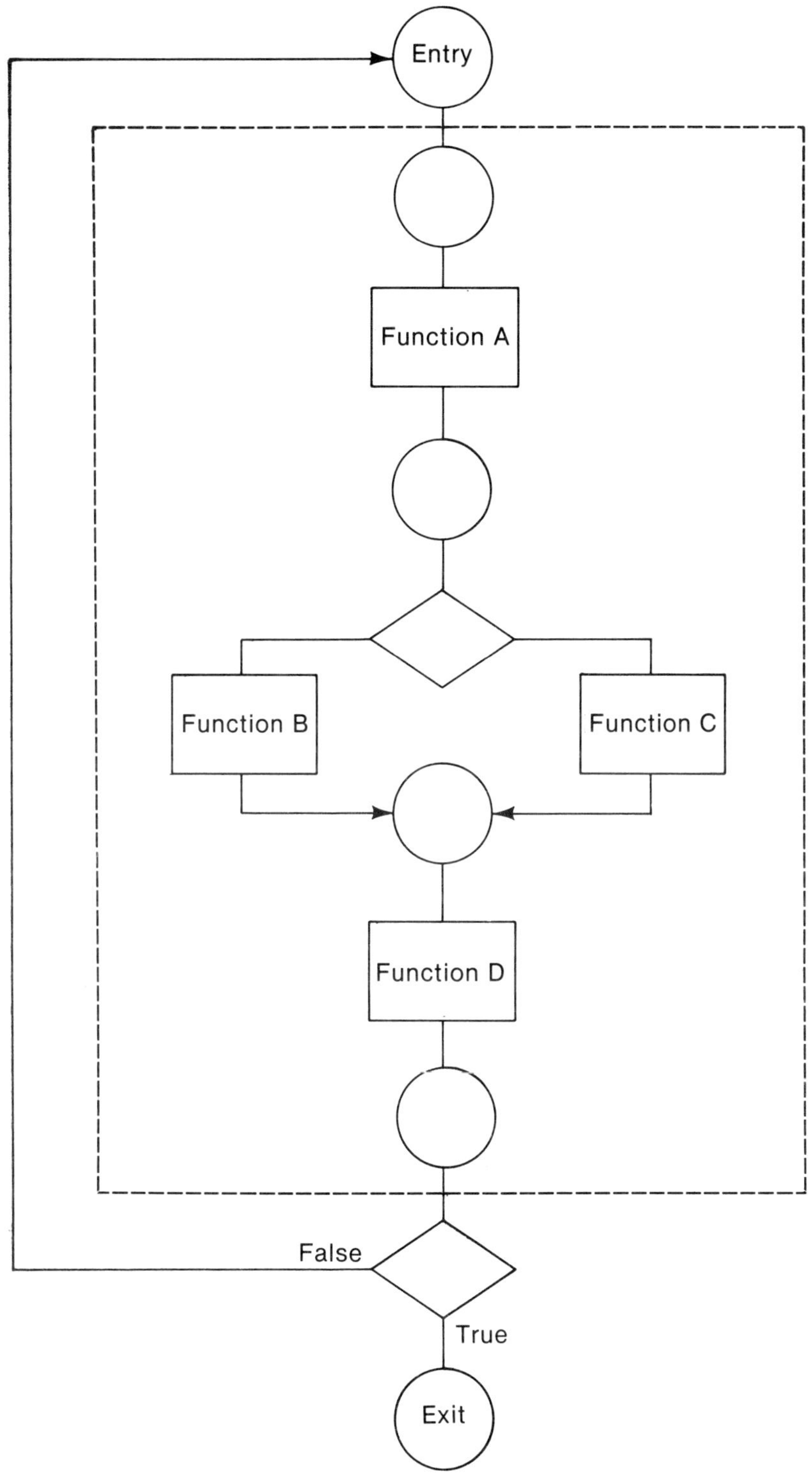

Figure 2-2 Substitution and combination: sequence and selection structures within a DO-UNTIL structure

use an ineffective design technique like flowcharting to implement a new theory of programming. But that's what some people did. They developed methods for drawing structured flowcharts and recommended that these be used for designing a structured program.

Others, however, realized that flowcharts would defeat the purposes of structured programming. So they experimented with new methods of design. Although the details vary from one method to another, they all attempt to design a program from the top down. This is referred to as *top-down design*, or *structured design*.

When you use top-down design, you design a program from the top down using a design document that shows structural levels. In figure 1-4, for example, you saw a structure chart for a program that prepared a wage report. In figure 2-3 you can see two other types of documents used for top-down design. One is a tree chart; the other is a Warnier-Orr diagram. Both documents show that the program is divided into five modules at three levels.

To design a program from the top down, the programmer first tries to divide the entire program into its major functional modules. These modules in turn are divided into their subordinate modules, and so forth. Note, then, that program design starts with the highest-level module and ends with the lowest-level modules. This is in sharp contrast to traditional methods of design in which trivial programming details must be dealt with in the early stages of design.

When the programmer is finished, the design document shows the modules required by the program as well as the relationships between these modules. Later on, these modules can be coded with one entry and one exit point using only the sequence, selection, and iteration structures. Thus, the complete program will be a proper program.

Structured module design Traditionally, the program flowchart has been used to design all of the modules of a program. It was natural, then, that people tried to use flowcharts to design the modules within a top-down design, no matter what type of design document they used for designing the entire program. Others, however, realized that better methods were needed to design the modules of a program.

In figure 2-4, for example, you can see two design documents for the modules of a program. The first one, called a HIPO diagram, is part of IBM's HIPO method of documentation. It shows the inputs and outputs of each module as well as the processing steps required by the module. The second one, called a Nassi-Schneiderman diagram, graphically illustrates the programming structures required by a module.

Structured coding When you code a structured program, you naturally use *structured coding*. This implies that the program only uses the constructs of structured programming, so it does not use GOTO statements. In addition, this implies the use of a number of techniques that make a program easy to read and understand. If you refer back to figure 1-5, you can see an example of structured coding that doesn't use GOTOs and that is easy to read and understand.

A tree chart

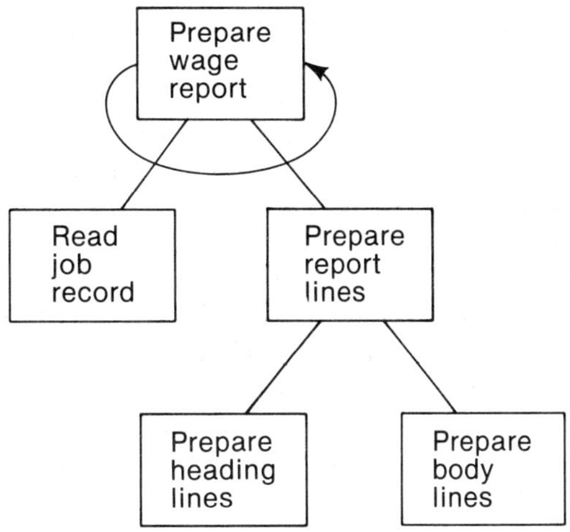

A Warnier/Orr diagram

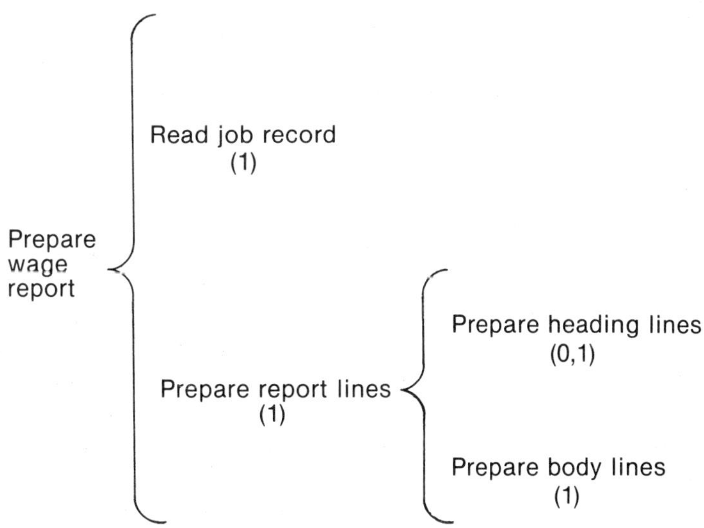

Figure 2-3 Two design documents that can be used for top-down program design

A HIPO diagram

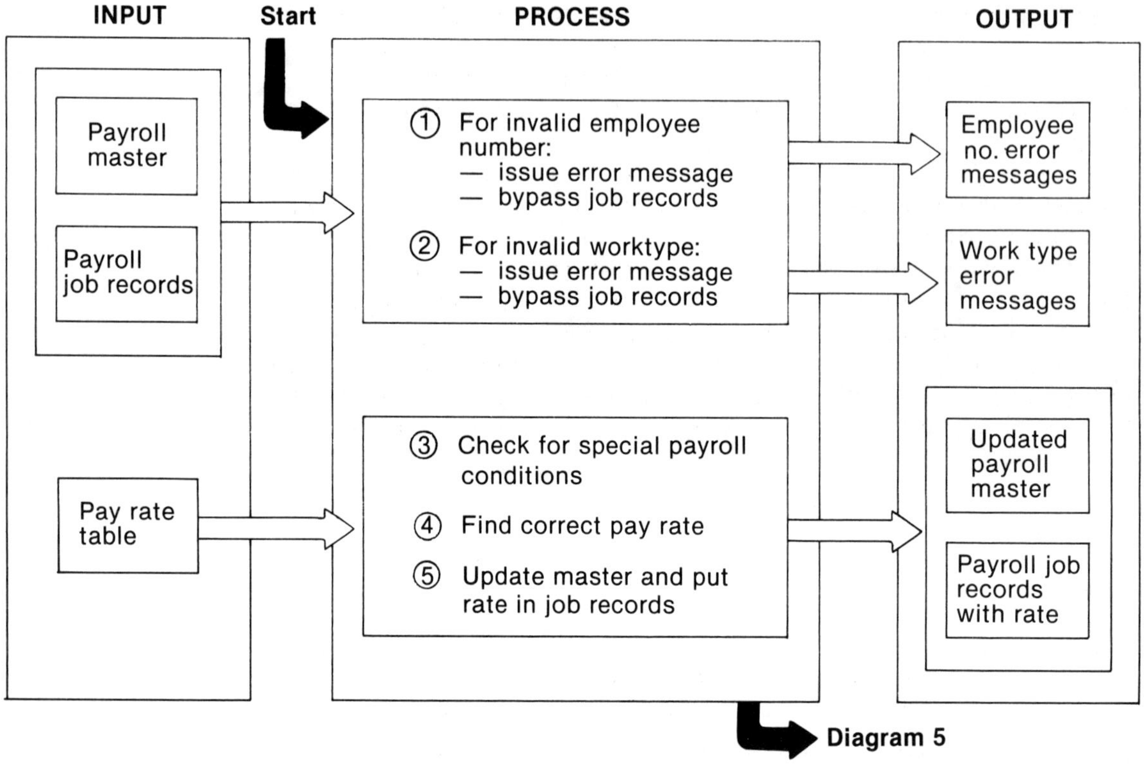

A Nassi-Schneiderman diagram

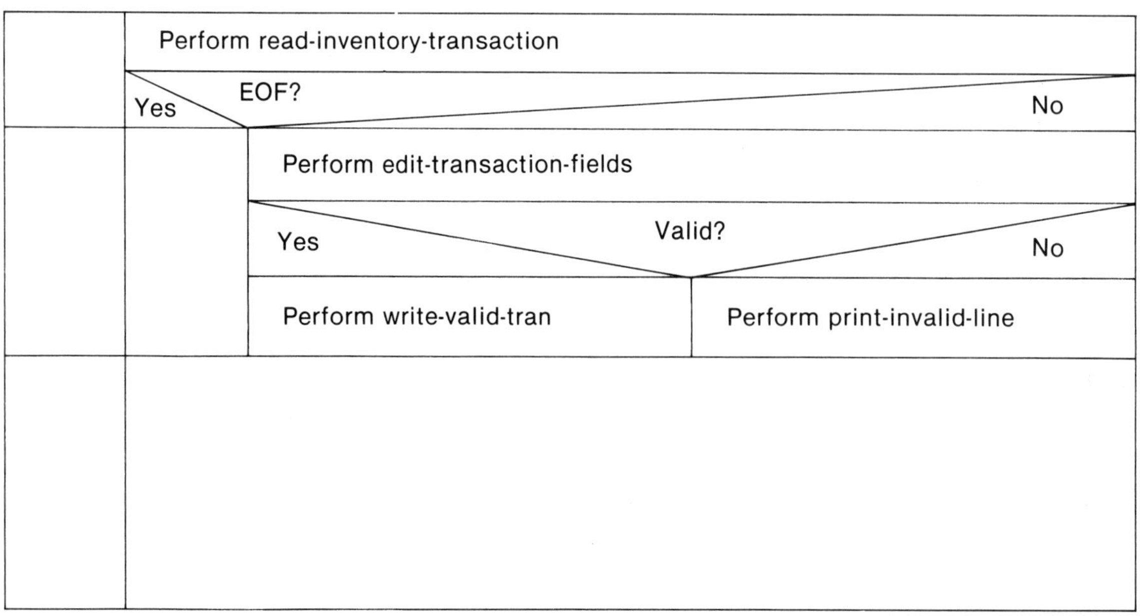

Figure 2-4 Two documents that can be used for designing the modules of a program

Top-down testing *Top-down testing* implies coding and testing a program a few modules at a time. For instance, the first test run for a program might test only the modules of the top two levels of the program's design document. Then, depending on the complexity of the program, all of the modules in the next level or only a few of these modules might be added to the program for the next test run. Eventually, the lowest-level modules will be tested in combination with all the other modules of the program.

The advantage of top-down testing is that testing is controlled. If a bug is detected when using the same test data as in the previous test run, it is clearly the result of the module or modules added since that run. Since these modules are independent, it is relatively easy to find the cause of the bug and correct it. Top-down testing sharply contrasts traditional test methods in which the entire program with its dozens or hundreds of bugs is tested at once.

Structured walkthroughs By improving design and documentation techniques, structured programming made *structured walkthroughs* possible. This means that it is practical to review or "walk through" a structured program in any of its stages of development. Thus, ineffective approaches and potential problem areas can be discovered in the design or coding stages, which is far more productive than realizing that a program is poorly conceived during testing. Repeated walkthroughs can improve the reliability of a program until it approaches 100 percent reliability.

A structured walkthrough is simply an informal review of a programmer's work with the intent of finding any problems the program might have. Normally, no managers are present during the walkthroughs so there is no attempt to evaluate a programmer's work in a walkthrough. In addition, there is normally no attempt to correct problems during a walkthrough. Instead, the problems are simply listed so they can be corrected by the programmer later on.

Chief programmer teams Because of the improved clarity of the design and coding of a structured program, structured programming makes it possible to use programming teams for the development of a single program. This usually implies a *chief programmer* with one or more specialists assigned to him. The chief programmer is likely to take responsibility for coordinating the project with user groups, for designing the program or programs required by the project, and for supervising the implementation of the programs. Members of the staff code, test, and document the programs and modules that the chief has designed.

Development support libraries The idea behind *development-support libraries* is to keep centralized libraries that contain the essential data for all programs that are being developed. This has the advantage of reducing the clerical load on each programmer, thus increasing productivity. It also brings a programmer's work out into the open ("from private art to public practice"). Although you can maintain development support libraries whether or not you use structured programming techniques, these libraries became associated with the IPTs during the structured programming movement.

Disagreements about the improved productivity techniques

By the late 1970s, everyone seemed to agree that the improved productivity techniques could help a COBOL shop make dramatic improvements in programmer productivity and program quality. But not many people agreed on how the techniques should be implemented. Yes, the improved productivity techniques were exciting. But what's the best way to design a program from the top down? What's the best way to design the modules of the program? What's the best way to code a structured program? And so on. For each question, six people gave you six answers.

Take the design documents for top-down design, for example. Certainly, some documents are better than others when it comes to top-down design. But as the documents in figures 1-4 and 2-3 illustrate, we can't even agree on the form a chart should take. One guy says it should look like an organization chart; another says it should look like a tree; another says we shouldn't use charts at all, we should use brackets; and some still believe you can design a structured program using a structured flowchart.

Beyond this, program designers can't agree on how modules should be named or numbered. And worse, they can't even agree on what the modules of the same program should be or what legitimate variations for a program design are. For instance, the charts in figure 1-4 and 2-3 are for the same program. But the chart in figure 1-4 has 13 different modules and the chart in figure 2-3 only has five. Furthermore, there's little similarity in the form of the structures. Now, certainly, for a program as simple as this, two different program designers should come up with similar solutions.

When it comes to designing the modules for a program, you run into the same type of problem. Should you use HIPO diagrams, Nassi-Schneiderman charts, Warnier-Orr diagrams, Chapin charts, pseudocode, or maybe nothing at all? As you will see in chapter 8, our most productive programmers use pseudocode for the critical modules of a program and nothing at all for most of the modules of a program (that is, the COBOL code itself documents the module). But the debate about what's best goes on.

As for structured coding, people can't agree on the most basic principles. For instance, they can't agree on whether a module of a program should be coded as a COBOL paragraph, a COBOL section, a series of COBOL paragraphs executed by a PERFORM THRU statement, or a separately-compiled subprogram. And there are those who say that a program can be structured even if it uses GOTOs as long they are used within specific limitations. Perhaps the worst assumption people make is that their programs are structured as long as they don't use GOTOs. But effective programming requires much more than that.

Not only can't people in our industry agree on standards for one of the improved productivity techniques, they can't agree on which techniques are most valuable. For instance, back in the mid-1970s, chief programmer teams received a lot of good publicity. As a result, some companies started by implementing chief programmer teams rather than more general methods like top-down design. Other companies started by implementing structured walkthroughs. But you can't use either of these techniques effectively until you've first implemented an effective method for designing and coding a structured program.

To compound the disagreements, the main promoters of structured programming techniques seem to insist on the use of high falutin vocabularies. For instance, one promoter has created dozens of new terms to describe aspects of structured programs...terms like program morphology, pathological connection, subcoroutine, and central transform. Although I respect many of the man's ideas, I have to ask: Who's kidding whom? Is programming so difficult that it requires its own vocabulary? I just don't think so. Terms like these only make it more difficult to analyze the essence of a developmental technique and to resolve the related disagreements.

When Paul Noll first started teaching structured programming, someone asked him what he called his method, because everyone else seemed to have a name for theirs. After Paul explained that he simply tried to borrow the best ideas from all of the methods and to integrate them to come up with a practical way to develop COBOL programs, the man complained that that just wasn't good enough. "Well," Paul said, "I guess you could say that I use a form of top-down design that says that all of the modules in the design should be functional." "In that case," said the man, "I've got it. You should call your book *Paul Noll's Functional Decomposition*." "Somehow," Paul says, "I can see myself rotting in a field every time I think of that book title."

No, we didn't use that title for Paul's first book on structured programming, because we didn't feel the industry needed more promoters of personal methods, more disagreement, and more confusion. In fact, if we could stop the zealous selling of personal methods, I think it would do the programming industry a lot of good. Instead of looking for one person's methods, we should be looking for the best methods currently available. And these methods shouldn't need a promoter; they should sell themselves.

Why structured programming has failed

I hope by now you can draw your own conclusions as to why structured programming failed. Certainly, it has something to do with the diversity of methods that have been promoted over the years along with the resulting disagreements and confusion. Although the best COBOL shops seem to have selected effective methods for program development, too many shops decided to stay with the methods they had rather than to take on others that they weren't sure of. Other shops selected structured methods that really weren't much more effective than the unstructured methods they were already using. And many large shops, rather than select one method for the entire shop, decided to let the individual project managers make their own decisions about structured programming methods. As a result, some of the projects in a shop like this are developed using efficient methods; and some are developed using inefficient methods. But, as Paul says, "Everyone has a method for developing COBOL programs; what you want is to have everyone in your shop using the same set of effective methods."

It's important that you realize, though, that structured programming failed due to the disagreement and confusion that surrounded it, not because its potential was overstated. Structured programming and the improved productivity techniques still have the potential to make dramatic improvements in programmer productivity and program quality in your shop. But you have to select and implement the right techniques. You have to look beyond the surface, beyond the charisma of the promoter, beyond the vocabulary and the three-piece suit, to find practical development techniques that fit your personality and style.

To help you find the right techniques, we're going to present the ones Paul and I feel are most critical to your development efforts. But as we go along, I'm also going to present the pros and cons of other methods. For instance, in the chapter on designing the modules of a program, I'm going to present two methods of design. Paul Noll strongly believes in the use of HIPO diagrams. But most of the people who work for me believe in using either pseudocode or nothing at all to design the modules of a program. So I'll present the pros and cons of each method and let you select the method that is right for you.

Then, in chapter 16, I'll present some of the techniques that we haven't covered in the main body of this book. Although we have borrowed an idea or two from some of these methods, we generally don't recommend using them as specified by their originators. And in this chapter, I'll explain why. Then, in case you don't quite agree with us, you can research these methods on your own. In most cases, however, I think you'll agree that the methods we recommend in this book are the best ones currently available.

That's why we say that structured programming doesn't have to fail in your shop. By the time you finish this book, you'll be able to decide for yourself whether a technique or method is practical for the development of business programs in your shop. To get you started in that direction, I will present the general style of programming that we recommend in the next chapter. And I will list the factors that I think are critical to the effectiveness of any method of program development.

Terminology

structured programming
sequence structure
selection structure
IF-THEN-ELSE structure
iteration structure
DO-WHILE structure
DO-UNTIL structure
proper program
top-down design
structured design
structured coding
top-down testing
structured walkthrough
chief programmer team
chief programmer
development-support library

Objectives

1. Name and describe the three programming structures that are legal in a proper program.

2. Name and describe four of the improved productivity techniques.

3. Describe the disagreements programmers have over the best methods for top-down design and structured coding.

Chapter 3

How to make sure that structured programming succeeds in your shop

If you use the methods recommended in this book, I'm confident that structured programming will succeed in your shop. As you will see in the next chapter, hundreds of companies already use these methods. And many have reported dramatic improvements in productivity and program quality as a result of using these methods.

But before I present the methods we recommend for designing and developing COBOL programs, I'd like to present a program that we developed using these methods. In particular, I'd like to show you the complete documentation for a simple edit program. Then, you can decide for yourself whether our style of programming is likely to lead to improvements in programmer productivity and program quality.

After I introduce you to this model program, I will present the eight principles that we believe are critical for effective program development in a COBOL shop. I'll also present some factors that we don't think are critical and two critical factors that can't be controlled by the COBOL programmer. When I finish this presentation, I'll give you an idea of what you can reasonably expect in terms of productivity and program quality if you convert to the methods of this book.

An effective COBOL program

Appendix A gives the complete documentation for a COBOL program that we developed using the methods recommended in this book. I know the documentation is lengthy, but I want you to know in advance what kind of programs you will be developing if you use the methods of this book. If you take a moment now to look at the program specifications, the structure chart, and the COBOL listing for this program, I think you'll find that they're quite easy to read and understand. Incidentally, any time you spend reviewing this program now won't be wasted, because this edit program is used as the basis for many of the examples in this book.

The program specifications The program specifications consist of a 3-page program overview, two pages of COPY members representing record formats, and a one-page print chart for a listing of invalid transactions. We call this program "the edit program" because it is a typical batch edit of the records in an input file. Naturally, we've simplified the program so it's more useful for illustration than a complete production program would be. But I think you can see that this program illustrates the essential design and code that any edit program requires.

Depending on your installation practices, a systems analyst may prepare the program specifications for a program like this. Or, he may pass this job onto the programmer who is going to develop the program. But someone has to develop the specifications. And if the systems analyst doesn't do an adequate job of developing them, the programmer has to fill in the gaps.

When you prepare program specifications, we recommend that you limit your use of forms and graphics. So in our shop, we prepare program overviews using our word processing system. The record layouts are COPY members. And we only use forms for items like report layouts and screen layouts.

The structure chart The structure chart, which we developed using top-down design, is an index to the paragraphs of the COBOL program. As you can see in the COBOL listing, the coding for the top-level module of the structure chart can be found in the first paragraph of the Procedure Division. It is named 000-EDIT-INVENTORY-TRANS so it corresponds to the number and name of the module on the structure chart. Similarly, every other paragraph in the COBOL listing corresponds to one module shown on the structure chart.

The COBOL listing The COBOL listing shows how COBOL can be used to create a program that is easy to read and understand. Because of its readability, a program like this is more likely to be reliable than a less readable program. And it's going to be easy to maintain. In fact, if you're an experienced COBOL programmer, I'll bet you could do some heavy maintenance to this program right now without much trouble at all...even before you read about the development methods that we used when creating it.

If you review the code in the Procedure Division, you can see that it

Eight critical principles

1. Limit your use of graphics in all phases of program development.
2. Design each program from the top down so each module represents one independent function that can be coded in a single COBOL paragraph.
3. Code each module on your design document as a single COBOL paragraph.
4. Code your programs so they're easy to read and understand.
5. Use the design and code from old programs as the basis for writing new programs.
6. Make effective use of COPY members and subprograms.
7. Use top-down testing for all programs that take more than one day to develop.
8. Make sure your program documentation is a by-product of your program development procedures.

Figure 3-1 Eight principles that are critical to effective program development

doesn't use GOTO statements. That's one reason why the program is easy to read from the top down. Another reason is that each module only calls the modules that are subordinate to it on the structure chart. Other reasons are the naming conventions used, the numbering conventions used, the way switches are used, the sequence of the paragraphs in the program, and so on.

Eight critical principles for effective program development

As I pointed out in the last chapter, it's not easy to select a development method when you first convert to structured programming. But it's also not easy to select a new method of structured programming after you've used an ineffective one for a few years. With so many different ways to design and develop a COBOL program, how do you know which method is best?

With this in mind, I'd like to present the eight principles that we think are critical to a program development method. They are listed in figure 3-1. If you agree with these, you'll have a basis for selecting the development techniques that are right for you. If you don't agree with all of the principles, you can modify the list so you end up with a list of your own. Then, you can choose new program-development methods based on the principles on your own list.

Principle 1: Limit your use of graphics in all phases of program development Some people love to draw boxes and circles and arrows. But drawing charts and diagrams is time-consuming. So you must limit your use of graphics throughout your program development efforts. In general, you should only use graphics when they definitely improve the documentation of a program or when they help you understand something that you couldn't understand without the graphics.

With this in mind, you shouldn't use record layout forms when you create program specifications (use COPY members instead). You shouldn't let your program design or module design documents get too fancy. And so on. In general, the more time you spend drawing graphic representations of what you're doing, the less productive you are.

Principle 2: Design each program from the top down so each module represents one independent function that can be coded in a single COBOL paragraph I think most of the promoters of structured programming methods agree with the first part of this statement. You have to design a program from the top down and each module on the structure chart (or other design document) should represent an independent function. Then, these functions can be divided into their subordinate subfunctions. And so on.

Although the promoters agree to this extent, they disagree about what independence is, what a function is, and when you should stop designing the program. As we see it, many of these promoters allow more than one function to be combined into a single module of the program. They don't create modules that are independent. And they don't design the program down to a low enough level.

To illustrate this point, compare the structure chart in appendix A with the structure chart in figure 3-2. Both are for the same program. Both designers think they have created modules that represent one independent function. And both designers think they have designed down to a low enough level. But each module in the structure chart in the appendix can be coded in a single COBOL paragraph, and some of the modules in the structure chart in figure 3-2 can't be. That in turn means that it will be more difficult to code, test, and maintain the program represented by figure 3-2. So which design is better? (Incidentally, the design in figure 3-2 was developed by a programming manager who feels he is an expert on program design; at present, he manages a staff of 200 programmers.)

Because it is impossible to develop an effective COBOL program based on the design in figure 3-2, Paul tries to give a specific guideline for knowing how far down to design a program. He says that a program should be designed from the top down until each module can be coded *in a single COBOL paragraph*. That way, you'll usually be able to code each module of the program in 50 statements or less. In addition, your structure chart will be an index to each paragraph of the COBOL program. In contrast, you can't begin to tell how many paragraphs the

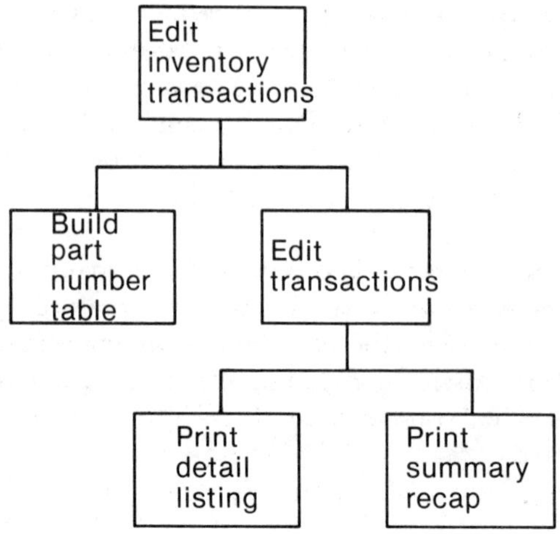

Figure 3-2 An unacceptable design for the edit program

design in figure 3-2 will require. And two of the modules of the program will do 80 percent or more of the program's work.

As we see it, this principle is absolutely essential to effective program development in a COBOL shop. But many promoters of structured methods do *not* insist that each design module be codable as a single COBOL paragraph. And that point by itself can have a serious effect on any improvements in programmer productivity or program quality that you might otherwise have experienced.

As you will see in a moment, just because you design your programs so each module can be coded as a single COBOL paragraph doesn't mean that you actually have to code them that way. Although we recommend that you do, there are other options. If, for example, you want to code each module as two paragraphs executed by a PERFORM-THRU statement and use GOTO statements in the first paragraph, you can do so and still not defeat your purposes entirely. In other words, designing down to a level that makes coding easy is more important than how you code the modules.

Naturally, there's room for some debate as to how a program should be designed. It's not all black and white, no matter what design method you use. But regardless of the method, most of your training should be focused on design. If you get the program design right, most of the subsequent development steps follow easily. But if the program design has shortcomings, you're in trouble from the start. As I see it, the average COBOL shop simply doesn't have adequate standards for program design. But Paul Noll has brought some important ideas to the task of program design that can help you make an immediate improvement in your development efforts.

Principle 3: Code each module on your design document as a single COBOL paragraph Some people say a module of the program should be coded as a section; some say it should be a series of paragraphs executed by a PERFORM-THRU statement; and some say it should be a separately-compiled subprogram. But as soon as you code the modules of a program in any one of these three ways, you start to defeat the purposes of structured programming.

The first two methods are bad because they make it harder for you to enforce effective coding standards. If you allow sections or PERFORM-THRUs, where do you draw the line? How many paragraphs are you going to allow in a section? How many paragraphs in a series that is PERFORMed THRU? And how many GOTOs in the implementation for one module of the structure chart? Furthermore, you usually don't gain anything by coding a module in either of these ways. It just means more code, which means reduced productivity.

Similarly, when you code each module as a separately-compiled subprogram, you don't gain anything that is worth the extra effort required for subprogram linkage. Although the idea of independent subprograms sounds good in theory, it doesn't work well in practice. You just end up writing more code and spending more time trying to debug the interfaces between the subprograms.

We realize, of course, that one of the ideas behind the use of subprograms is to develop modules that can be used in more than one program. And we have no objection to this when a module has a general purpose that is needed in more than one program. But otherwise, a COBOL paragraph is easier to reuse than a subprogram.

Unfortunately, it's not always possible to code each module of a program as a single COBOL paragraph. For instance, using the COBOL SORT statement forces you to use an EXIT paragraph and a GOTO statement within a COBOL section. And, if you use CICS on an IBM mainframe, you have to code some of the CICS modules as a sequence of paragraphs rather than as single paragraphs. That's why, for CICS programs, we recommend that all of the design modules be coded as sections as you will see in chapter 14. But these are exceptional cases. In most cases, you will be able to code each module of a program as a single COBOL paragraph, and the quality of your programs will be improved if you do so.

In case you feel that you have to use sections, PERFORM-THRUs, or GOTO statements in your programs, we'll show you how to use them without much loss in productivity or program quality. We'll do this because we feel that how you design a program is much more important than how you code it. We also know that it's sometimes easier for a person to convert to structured programming one task at a time. So if using GOTOs helps you get started using effective design methods, we'll show you how to get started that way. Eventually, though, we think you'll see the light and convert to GOTOless code. Remember, however, that whether or not you use GOTOs, it's essential that you design your programs so each module can be coded as a single COBOL paragraph if that's how you decide to code it.

Principle 4: Code your programs so they're easy to read and understand I don't think anyone is going to argue about this principle. The more readable a program is, the easier it is to test and maintain. Nevertheless, not enough has been said about how COBOL programs should be coded so they are as readable as possible within some practical limits. But here again, I think Paul Noll has brought some important ideas to the task. So if you adopt the coding standards presented in this book, I think you'll end up with more readable programs than you've ever had before.

In contrast to Paul, most of the promoters of structured programming methods don't talk too much about COBOL coding. And yet, the COBOL code can make or break the effectiveness of a company's program development procedures. If the code isn't readable, it's going to reduce programmer productivity and program quality even if your program modules meet all sorts of standards in terms of functionality, independence, and GOTOless code. I think this is an obvious point, but one that is overlooked in many COBOL shops.

To illustrate this point, look at the coding samples in figure 3-3. The first is taken from a production program that the programmer calls "structured." The second is taken from a program that is part of a software package for payroll. By our standards, both can be improved considerably. The first simply isn't structured; it is unmaintainable foolishness. The second isn't that bad, but it violates some of the standards that we feel are important for readability. If you compare either of these samples with the code in the edit program in the appendix, I think you'll see that our coding standards can lead to significant improvements in program readability.

Principle 5: Use the design and code from old programs as the basis for writing new programs One of the benefits of structured programming is that you don't have to start each program from scratch. For instance, since a sequential update for an inventory file is logically much the same as a sequential update for a customer file, the design and code for both programs should be similar. As a result, you can use the design and code from one program as the basis for writing similar programs.

This is a major point, because this is the principle that leads to increases in productivity of 300 percent or more. When we adopted our structured programming standards, for example, the biggest surprise we had was the dramatic improvement in productivity we were able to attain by reusing COBOL code. We found that we were able to reuse code from all four divisions of a COBOL program including large portions of code taken from the Data Division and the Procedure Division. As we see it, unless you are able to build each new program from a base of code taken from old programs, you will never realize the productivity increases that are possible with structured programming.

To get the maximum productivity gains from reusing code from one program to the next, you have to do three things. First, you have to design your programs so each module can be coded as a single COBOL

A coding sample from a "structured" production program

```
AA43.   PERFORM KK.
        IF ITMSTS20 = ' ' GO TO AAA43.
        IF ITMSTS20 = 'N' AND ITMSTS70 (A, SS) = 'N'
        PERFORM A54G THRU X54G GO TO B43
        IF ITMSTS20 = 'N' PERFORM CC43 PERFORM A54J
        MOVE '25' TO ACT40 MOVE ITMSTS20 TO ITMSTS40 GO TO B43.
        IF ITMSTS70 (A, SS) = 'N' GO TO CC43.
AAA43.  PERFORM EQCHEC.
        IF EQWORK1 = EQWORK2 GO TO QQ43.
        IF EQWORK2 = SPACES GO TO QQ43.
        GO TO CC43.
QQ43.   PERFORM EE THRU KK.
B43.    PERFORM A54D THRU X54D GO TO D42.
CC43.   MOVE '40' TO ACT40.
        .
        .
```

A coding sample from one program of a structured software package

```
LEVEL-1 SECTION.
MAIN-LOGIC.
    PERFORM OPENING-PROCEDURE.
    IF OPENING-PROCEDURE-SUCCESSFUL
        IF PR-CTL-USE-JOB-NUMBER-FLAG IS = 'N'
            PERFORM JOB-NOS-NOT-SELECTED-MESSAGE,
            MOVE UNSUCCESSFUL TO OPENING-PROCEDURE-STATUS,
        ELSE
            PERFORM ENTER-MENU-SELECTION,
            IF NOT END-KEY-PRESSED
                PERFORM JOB-FILE-MAINTENANCE UNTIL
                END-KEY-PRESSED.
    PERFORM CLOSING-PROCEDURE.
MAIN-LOGIC-EXIT.
    PERFORM WAIT-MESSAGE-ROUTINE.
    EXIT PROGRAM.
    STOP RUN.
LEVEL-2 SECTION.
OPENING-PROCEDURE.
    PERFORM OPEN-CRT-FILE.
    PERFORM OPEN-PR-CONTROL-FILE.
    IF PR-CONTROL-FILE-STATUS IS = I-O-OK
        MOVE FILE-IS-OPEN TO PR-CONTROL-FILE-OPEN-STATUS,
        PERFORM READ-PR-CONTROL-FILE,
    ELSE
        MOVE UNSUCCESSFUL TO OPENING-PROCEDURE-STATUS.
    .
    .
```

Figure 3-3 Two samples of COBOL code that are difficult to read

paragraph. Second, you have to code each module as a single COBOL paragraph. Third, you have to code each module so it is easy to read and understand. If you do these things, a programmer who is developing a new program can select the COBOL paragraphs that he wants from old programs with relative ease. Then, he can copy them into his new program at the appropriate points. And he can modify them so they are integrated with the other COBOL paragraphs. If your functional modules consist of more than one paragraph, if they're subprograms, or if they're not easy to read, it becomes much more difficult to reuse code from one program to the next.

When you think of it, many fourth-generation program-development tools are based on this principle of reusing COBOL code. A COBOL preprocessor, for example, generates many COBOL statements from a single programmer statement. Similarly, application generators create programs by linking the subprograms that the system requires. As a result, if you can create new programs by reusing large portions of COBOL code, you can reach productivity levels that make some of the fourth-generation tools less attractive. In truth, one of the vendors of a fourth-generation tool for the Wang VS system promises productivity levels that our programmers have already reached using standard COBOL. In addition, our programs do exactly what the users want them to do, while the generated programs are more limited.

Principle 6: Make effective use of COPY members and subprograms If you check the listing for the edit program in the appendix, you can see that it uses three subprograms and three COPY members. This goes along with the principle of reusing code whenever possible. Although I think most installations try to do this whether or not they use structured programming methods, you can certainly do this more effectively when your programs are divided into independent, functional modules. So some planning here can lead to significant gains in productivity and program quality.

Note, then, that we *do* recommend the use of subprograms; we just don't recommend that you code each module of a program as a subprogram. In other words, subprograms should be used for general-purpose functions that can be used without change from one program to the next. But they shouldn't be used for modules that must be modified before you can reuse them in another program.

Principle 7: Use top-down testing for all programs that take more than one day to develop In general, we recommend that all programs that take more than a day to code and test should be tested on a top-down basis. In other words, you should code and test a portion of a program each day. If you do this, you can simplify testing so much that it can make major contributions to your productivity. In addition, you are more likely to test all of the modules of your program so its reliability is likely to improve. In short, if you use structured programming, but you don't use top-down testing, you're not getting all of the benefits you should be getting.

Principle 8: Make sure your program documentation is a by-product of your program development procedures I don't think anyone likes to put together program documentation. It's tedious and time-consuming. So the more your documentation results from the program development process, the happier you'll be. And the more productive you'll be.

Using our methods, the primary pieces of program documentation are the program specifications, the structure chart, and the program listing...the items you see in the appendix. We have documented programs for several years now using only these documents, and we have never had a problem with program maintenance.

This method of documenting programs is the most productive one because all three items are by-products of our development methods. When you finish a program, you refine the program specifications and structure chart somewhat, put it together with the program listing, and you're done. The result: useful documentation in a minimum of time. In contrast, many COBOL shops require items of documentation that are time-consuming to produce and impossible to keep up-to-date.

If there's a problem with our method of documentation, it's that the structure charts don't always correspond to the COBOL code. This happens, for example, when a programmer changes the structure somewhat when he codes a program, but doesn't remember to change the structure chart. This can also happen during program maintenance.

To get around this problem and to appease the programmers who were sick of refining structure charts for final documentation, we developed a structure listing program to create the final documentation for a program's design. This program creates a structure listing, like the one in figure 3-4, from the COBOL source code; this structure listing corresponds to the structure chart of the edit program in the appendix. In recent years, we've used structure listings like this one in place of structure charts as final documentation, and we've found them to be more effective than structure charts. Structure listings may be a little harder to read than structure charts, but you know they correspond to the source code and they don't take any time to prepare.

Factors that aren't critical to effective program development

We think the principles I've just presented are critical to the successful implementation of structured programming in a COBOL shop. And we'll give added support to these principles as we present our development techniques throughout this book. But I think we should also ask: What factors aren't critical to the success of a program development method? This will help you focus on the critical factors as you go through this book and ignore the trivial ones. So let me list some of the factors that aren't critical.

The graphics you use in your program design documents There seems to be so much talk about the graphics of your program design documents. Most people agree that you should design from the top down. But one person says you should use a tree structure; another says you should use a

```
*
 000-EDIT-INVENTORY-TRANS
*
        100-FORMAT-REPORT-HEADING
        *
               'SYSDATE'
               'SYSTIME'
        *
        200-LOAD-PART-NUMBER-TABLE
        *
               210-READ-PART-NUMBER-RECORD
        *
        300-EDIT-INVENTORY-TRAN
        *
               310-READ-INVENTORY-TRAN
               320-EDIT-TRANSACTION-FIELDS
               *
                      330-EDIT-CODE-1-FIELDS
                      *
                             'DATEDIT'                          C
                             340-SEARCH-PART-NUMBER-TABLE       C
                      *
                      350-EDIT-CODE-2-FIELDS
                      *
                             'DATEDIT'                          C
                             340-SEARCH-PART-NUMBER-TABLE       C
                      *
               *
               360-PRINT-INVALID-TRANSACTION
               *
                      370-PRINT-HEADING-LINES
                      *
                             380-WRITE-PAGE-TOP-LINE            C
                             390-WRITE-REPORT-LINE              C
                      *
                      390-WRITE-REPORT-LINE             C
               *
               400-WRITE-VALID-TRANSACTION
        *
        500-PRINT-TOTAL-PAGE
        *
               380-WRITE-PAGE-TOP-LINE          C
               390-WRITE-REPORT-LINE            C
        *
*

C = COMMON MODULE
```

Figure 3-4 A structure listing for the edit program generated from the COBOL code in appendix A

structure like an organization chart; another says you should use nested brackets. One person says you should use arrows to show what data and switches are passed from one module to another; another says you should use symbols to show whether a module is executed only one time or repeatedly; another says you shouldn't put any of this extra information on the structure chart.

Well, I'm here to tell you that none of this has a significant effect on your program development results. Much more important is what your modules represent, whether they're independent, whether they can be coded as COBOL paragraphs, and so on. That's the real content of a design document, and that's what counts. So, although we'll recommend one type of design document, you should realize that the form of the document doesn't matter that much. In fact, we'll show you some other types of design documents that you may prefer to use.

The module design documents you use The only good documentation for a program module is the COBOL code for the module. So any design documents you use for a module are for your own use only; call them working papers. Once you have coded a module, you can throw your working papers away. In fact, most of our programmers don't believe that you need to design a module at all before you code it...if you develop your program design down to a low enough level.

With this in mind, it doesn't matter too much what you use to design your modules. Pseudocode, HIPO diagrams, Nassi-Schneiderman charts, you name it. Remember, however, that you should limit your use of graphics. The more you use graphics, the less efficient you are. So this leads you toward the use of pseudocode and away from the more graphic approaches to module planning and design.

The use of structured walkthroughs, programming teams, and development support libraries Walkthroughs, teams, and libraries are only related to structured programming in an indirect way; that is, structured programming makes it possible to use these techniques effectively. As a result, making use of these techniques should be your last priority. Although some companies have used these techniques effectively, they can also be more trouble than they're worth. So the place to start when you're improving your development methods is with effective methods for design, coding, testing, and documentation. Once you've succeeded in establishing effective standards for these tasks, you can decide whether you want to experiment with walkthroughs, teams, and libraries.

Critical factors the programmer can't control

When we talk of programmer productivity and program quality, you should realize that they can be significantly affected by factors other than your program development method. Often, neither the programmer nor the programming manager can control these factors. But you should still be aware of them.

The software and hardware of the development system In our shop, we've developed programs on four different computer systems during the last six years. So we can tell you that system differences can have dramatic effects on programmer productivity...and program quality too. In general, a good development system makes it easy to enter code into a system, modify the code, copy code from one program to another, correct diagnostics interactively, and test and debug programs interactively. In terms of productivity, I think a simple thing like converting from one computer system to another can increase productivity by 100 percent or more. In fact, that has happened in our shop.

So when I quote a productivity statistic from one of our programming projects, keep in mind that in recent years we have been developing programs on an outstanding development system, the Wang VS system. If your system isn't as good, your results may not be as good as ours, even if you adopt our methods in their entirety. If, for example, 1000 lines of code per week is reasonable on the Wang VS, maybe only 500 lines of code per week is reasonable on an IBM mainframe.

Although this factor is beyond the programmer's control, I think it's something that managers should think about. At the least, a programming manager should do everything she can to make sure that her programmers have a modern development system available to them.

The procedures for systems analysis and design This book tells you how to design and develop programs after the system has been designed and divided into programs. Keep in mind, however, that poor systems design can have a negative effect on program development. For example, what happens when you discover that a record in a system requires a few more fields? Or that a system requires a new file? Or that a file requires another access path? If half the programs in the system are already done, it means recompiling them with new COPY members at the least. And it can mean weeks or months of reprogramming, which in turn means reduced productivity and probably reduced program quality (you just don't revise a program as effectively as you write it in the first place).

With this in mind, I'd like to recommend a book called *How to Design and Develop Business Systems* by Steve Eckols. It shows you how to design a system from the top down so you can do it efficiently and so you don't lose track of details that cause reprogramming months after the development of a system has been started. When you use the methods in this systems book, you create a *system* structure chart that identifies the programs in a system just as a *program* structure chart identifies the modules within a program.

Here again, system analysis and design is usually beyond the control of the programmers. But if your programmers analyze and design their own systems, you should make sure they are using effective system development methods. And, if they don't design their own systems, you should make sure that late changes in systems design are recorded. Then, you can determine whether it's your programming methods that are at fault when a project fails or whether it's your systems methods.

Improvements you can expect when you use effective development methods

It's always difficult to say what you can expect in terms of improved productivity and program quality when you convert to new development methods. But we certainly have a much better idea about this now than we did in the mid-1970s. So let me give you some ideas about this.

Improvements in programmer productivity Six years ago, when we were using a Datapoint ARC system, we set a minimum standard of productivity of 500 lines of tested COBOL code per week, or 25,000 lines of code per year. Unfortunately, the Datapoint system just wasn't meant to be a COBOL system so editing was difficult and compiles typically took 20 minutes or more. Nevertheless, only a few programmers out of a staff of 12 had any difficulty producing 500 lines of tested code per week. And our best programmers produced at least 2,000 lines of code per week.

Now, on our Wang VS system, a minimum standard of 1,000 lines of code per week, or 50,000 lines of code per year, is reasonable. Recently, for example, because our staff was busy and I wasn't, I developed a short marketing program on my own. But even though I hadn't developed a program in more than 18 months and my skills were more than rusty, I developed the program (about 750 lines of code) in about a day and a half. At the other extreme, our two best programmer/analysts designed, developed, and installed complete interactive systems of more than 125,000 lines of code each in less than a year working by themselves. That's an average of about 2,500 lines of code per week per person for the year. But that doesn't take into consideration the months spent on analyzing and designing the systems. If that time were considered, I would say that each programmer actually averaged over 5,000 lines of tested code per week.

When it comes to developing programs for an IBM mainframe, you have to distinguish between batch and interactive programs. For batch programs, I see no problem with developing from 500 to 1,000 lines of code per week. But you have to consider the capabilities of your programmers. Perhaps they can do much more.

For instance, we just hired a first-year UCLA student as a summer employee to help with some development work we're doing on an IBM 4300 running under VSE. Before she started with us, she had taken a one-semester Pascal course in college and she had read our introductory COBOL text. Although she had no previous experience with the IBM 4300, she still managed to design, code, and test three COBOL case studies in her first week on the job. In other words, even though she had to learn how to use the 4300 to enter, compile, and test programs, and even though she had never before developed a COBOL program, she developed about 1000 lines of code her first week on the job. And just so you don't think the case studies were trivial, I'm including one in appendix B of this book. This is the second case study she did, about 400 lines of code, and it took her about two days to complete it. So how much more should an experienced programmer be able to do?

For interactive programs, most IBM shops use CICS. Since this reduces productivity, you have to adjust your productivity standards accordingly. Although we've never developed CICS production programs, we have worked quite a bit with CICS programs on our own 4300 under VSE. Based on this experience, we feel that a minimum standard of from 250 to 500 lines of CICS code per week is reasonable. But again, you must consider the capabilities of your programmers.

If you work in one of those companies that seems quite comfortable with programmers that average around 100 lines of tested code per week, you can see the productivity gains that are possible if you improve your development methods. In most cases, you can improve productivity by 300 percent or more. And in some cases, you'll improve productivity by 1000 percent or more!

With increases like this, your whole atmosphere changes. Overtime and job pressures diminish. The programming backlog shrinks. On time and within budget becomes the norm. I'm not promising you two cars in every garage and a chicken in every pot, but programming can be satisfying if you start to get results.

Improvements in program quality Although it's hard to measure improvements in program quality, there's no doubt in my mind that program quality improves dramatically when you use effective development methods. For instance, when you look at the edit program in the appendix, is there any doubt in your mind that it is more reliable and easier to maintain than any program developed using GOTO programming or modular programming? Some things you know even if you don't have the data to support it. It's like the guy who spent two years studying the effect of a mother's love on child development. When he was done, he wrote a 500-page book corroborating the fact that the intensity of a mother's love correlates with the mental health of the loved children. Aren't some things so obvious that they don't need to be proven?

Nevertheless, I'll try to give you the skimpy data we have on program quality. I've already told you that one of our programmers maintains about 600,000 lines of COBOL code in less than two days per month. Furthermore, most of the maintenance would more properly be called program enhancement. I think this by itself speaks for the improvements in program quality that are possible when you use effective development methods.

In contrast, think of the problems that unstructured programs had in terms of reliability and maintainability. When Paul worked for Pacific Telephone, for example, he analyzed the number of times programs were changed during testing and after they went into production. In the library of production programs, he found a 561-statement program that had been changed 45 times during the first two months that it was in production...that's about once every working day. He found many programs that had been changed from 25 to 50 times in the two years or so after they were put into production. And he found a 3146-statement program that had been changed 123 times in less than a year after it was put into production. That's ten times per month, and the program was supposedly "structured"! Now certainly something is wrong with programs that encounter maintenance problems of this magnitude. And what do you think the chances are that these programs will ever be completely reliable?

Yes, improving your methods can improve your program quality. Although it may be hard to measure the improvement, you'll know it when it happens.

Two objections to structured programming

As we see it, there's just no room for argument. Structured programming offers you the potential to make dramatic improvements in program quality and programmer productivity if you obey the eight critical principles presented in this chapter. Nevertheless, many people resist new methods. And some resist them with great emotion. So for those people who have not yet experimented with structured programming techniques, let me cover two of the more emotional objections right now.

"The use of all those PERFORM statements decreases object program efficiency" There is some truth to this statement. If, for example, you're working on a virtual storage system and the use of PERFORMs leads to excessive paging, this can degrade program efficiency quite a bit. But let's keep this in perspective.

First, the major problem in most data processing installations is programmer efficiency, not computer efficiency. Usually, the yearly cost of the programming staff is as much or more than the yearly cost of the computer system, and this ratio will get worse as hardware costs decrease relative to programming costs. So if you have a choice between increasing programmer productivity by 100 percent or increasing computer efficiency by 2 percent, what would you take?

Second, if hardware efficiency is a problem, structured program design helps you cope with it. If, for example, your program is running inefficiently due to excessive paging, you can easily rearrange the modules in a structured Procedure Division to reduce this problem. Similarly, if your program is running poorly due to an excessive number of I/O operations or due to an inefficient table-handling routine, it's easy for you to find the offending modules and improve them. In fact, it's relatively easy to fine tune a system made up of structured programs, while it's almost impossible to fine tune a collection of GOTO programs.

Finally, if efficiency is your concern, optimizers are your best solution. Paul has had considerable experience, for example, with the

Capex optimizer. And he feels that it will solve most efficiency problems more easily than any programmer efforts can.

"Structured programming makes you use switches" This objection goes back to the days of GOTO programming in which switches were considered to be "bad." They were considered bad because they made a program that was already a maze of complexity even more difficult to read and understand. Every time you used a switch, you needed another GOTO or two to branch one way if the switch was on and another way if the switch was off.

But you use switches in a controlled way when you use them in structured programs. A switch that is set in one module can only be used by its calling module or a module that calls its calling module. Also, as you'll see in the chapter on COBOL coding, switches should be coded in a rigidly prescribed way in a structured program. So when you use switches in this way, they can actually improve the readability of a program.

Yes, the use of too many switches can reduce readability. Yes, you should try to limit your use of them. But used properly, they present no problems.

How to make sure that structured programming succeeds in your shop

In this chapter, I've listed eight principles that we believe are critical to the success of structured programming in a COBOL shop. Although you may not accept all of the recommendations that we make in this book, I hope you will give some thoughtful consideration to these eight principles. If you're not getting the benefits from structured programming that you expected, it's probably because your methods aren't based on these principles.

If you question one or more of our eight principles, I ask you to do this. Compare the program in the appendix with a program that is based on other development principles: perhaps a program developed in your shop or a program developed by a promoter of a structured programming methodology. Then ask yourself questions like this: Which program is easier to read? Which program do you think is more likely to be reliable? Which program do you think is going to be easier to maintain? Unless you're convinced that our program is inferior in terms of reliability or maintainability, I recommend that you continue with this book...because there's no doubt in my mind that our methods are the most productive methods currently available.

If you still have doubts about our methods, take the time to develop and test the program specified by the case study in appendix B using your current methods. Or, ask one of your programmers to develop this program. Certainly, if a complete novice to COBOL programming could develop this 425-line program on her second and third day on the job, an experienced programmer should be able to develop it in an afternoon. But you won't be able to do so unless the development methods you're using are effective. In my opinion, if you can complete this program in four or five hours, it's okay for you to stick with the principles your current methods are based on. Otherwise, I ask you again to thoughtfully consider ours.

In summary, I'm convinced that structured programming will succeed in your shop if you adopt the principles presented in this chapter and the methods presented in this book. As you go through this book, you will at times be given a choice of methods for a certain programming task. Then, you can choose the one that seems right for you. But all of the methods that we recommend are based on the principles in this chapter.

Terminology

None

Objectives

1. Given any of the eight principles for effective program development that are presented in this chapter, explain its effect on programmer productivity and program quality.

2. List two critical factors for effective program development that the programmer can't control.

Section 2

Procedures and techniques

This section presents the procedures and techniques that you should use if you want to improve programmer productivity and program quality in your shop. After chapter 4 presents a nine-task procedure for developing COBOL programs, chapters 5 through 11 present the techniques that you should use when you do these tasks.

Although the examples used in this section are for batch programs, the procedures and techniques apply to the development of interactive programs too. Nevertheless, section 3 presents some specific techniques you should use when you develop interactive programs. In section 3, you'll also see many programming examples that apply the procedures and techniques of section 2 to interactive programs.

This is the most important section in this book because it presents the ideas that will help you develop programs more effectively. As a result, you should read it completely before you go on to section 3 or 4.

Chapter 4

A practical procedure for developing COBOL programs

In this chapter, I'm going to present a practical procedure for developing COBOL programs. Paul Noll developed this procedure back in the mid-1970s when he worked for Pacific Telephone. And we've used it ever since we installed our first computer back in 1978.

The nine tasks of our program development procedure

Figure 4-1 lists the nine tasks of our program development procedure. The first two make up the *analysis* phase of program development; the next two make up the *design* phase; and the last five make up the *implementation* phase.

Task 1: Get complete program specifications Sometimes the systems designer gives complete program specifications to the programmer; sometimes she doesn't. In either case, it's the programmer's responsibility to make sure the specifications are complete. If they aren't complete when the programmer gets them, he must complete them himself. In chapter 5, then, we'll show you how to get complete specifications.

Task 2: Get related programs, COPY members, and subprograms In the last chapter, I pointed out how reusing designs, coding, COPY

Analysis

1. Get complete program specifications.
2. Get related programs, COPY members, and subprograms.

Design

3. Design the program using a structure chart.
4. If necessary, plan the modules of the program using pseudocode or HIPO diagrams.

Implementation

5. Plan the testing of the program by creating a test plan.
6. If necessary, code the job-control procedures for the test runs.
7. If necessary, create the test data for the test runs.
8. Code and test the program using top-down testing.
9. Document the program.

Figure 4-1 The preferred sequence of tasks for developing a program

members, and subprograms can increase productivity. So the second task is to gather any of these items that you may be able to use in the program you're about to develop. Then, before you even start to design the program, you can select the items you think will be useful to you and use them in the subsequent development tasks. In chapter 6, we'll show you how to select the items that you should reuse.

Task 3: Design the program using a structure chart In chapter 7, we'll show you how to design an effective program using a structure chart like the one in appendix A. As I said, it's not the graphics that are important; it's the content of the chart that counts. You have to design a program so each module on the design document (in our method, on the structure chart) represents one independent function that can be coded in a single COBOL paragraph.

Task 4: If necessary, design the modules of the program using pseudocode or HIPO diagrams In chapter 8, we'll show you how to design the modules of a program in two ways. First, we'll show you how to use pseudocode. For example, the pseudocode in figure 4-2 represents a plan for the coding of the first seven modules of the edit program in appendix A. Second, we'll show you how to use HIPO diagrams. In figure 4-3, for example, you can see a HIPO diagram for the top-level module of the edit program. This is not the type of HIPO diagram that is recommended by IBM, one that makes extensive use of graphics; it is a simplified version that Paul developed.

```
000-edit-inventory-transactions.

     Open files.
     DO 100-format-report-heading.
     DO 200-load-part-number-table
          VARYING table-index from 1 by 1
          UNTIL part-number-eof.
     DO 300-edit-inventory-transaction
          UNTIL tran-eof.
     DO 500-print-total-page.
     Close files.
     Stop run.

100-format-report-heading.

     Format report heading.

200-load-part-number table.

     DO 210-read-part-number-record.
     IF NOT part-number-eof
          load table entry
     ELSE
          reduce table-index by 1
          set entry-count to table-index.

210-read-part-number-record.

     Read record
          AT END move "Y" to part-number-eof-sw.

300-edit-inventory-transaction.

     DO 310-read-inventory-transaction.
     IF NOT tran-eof
          DO 320-edit-transaction-fields
          IF NOT valid-tran
               DO 360-print-invalid-transaction
          ELSE
               DO 400-write-valid-transaction.

310-read-inventory-transaction.

     Read record
          AT END move "Y" to tran-eof-sw.
     IF NOT tran-eof
          add 1 to trans-processed-count.
```

Figure 4-2 Pseudocode for the first seven modules of the edit program

We're going to show you two ways of designing modules because Paul likes HIPO diagrams and we prefer pseudocode. In fact, our best programmers feel that structured COBOL is so easy to use that you don't need to design the modules at all. That's why we say task 4 is to design the modules "if necessary." In chapter 8, we'll present the pros and cons of using pseudocode, using HIPO diagrams, and not planning the coding at all.

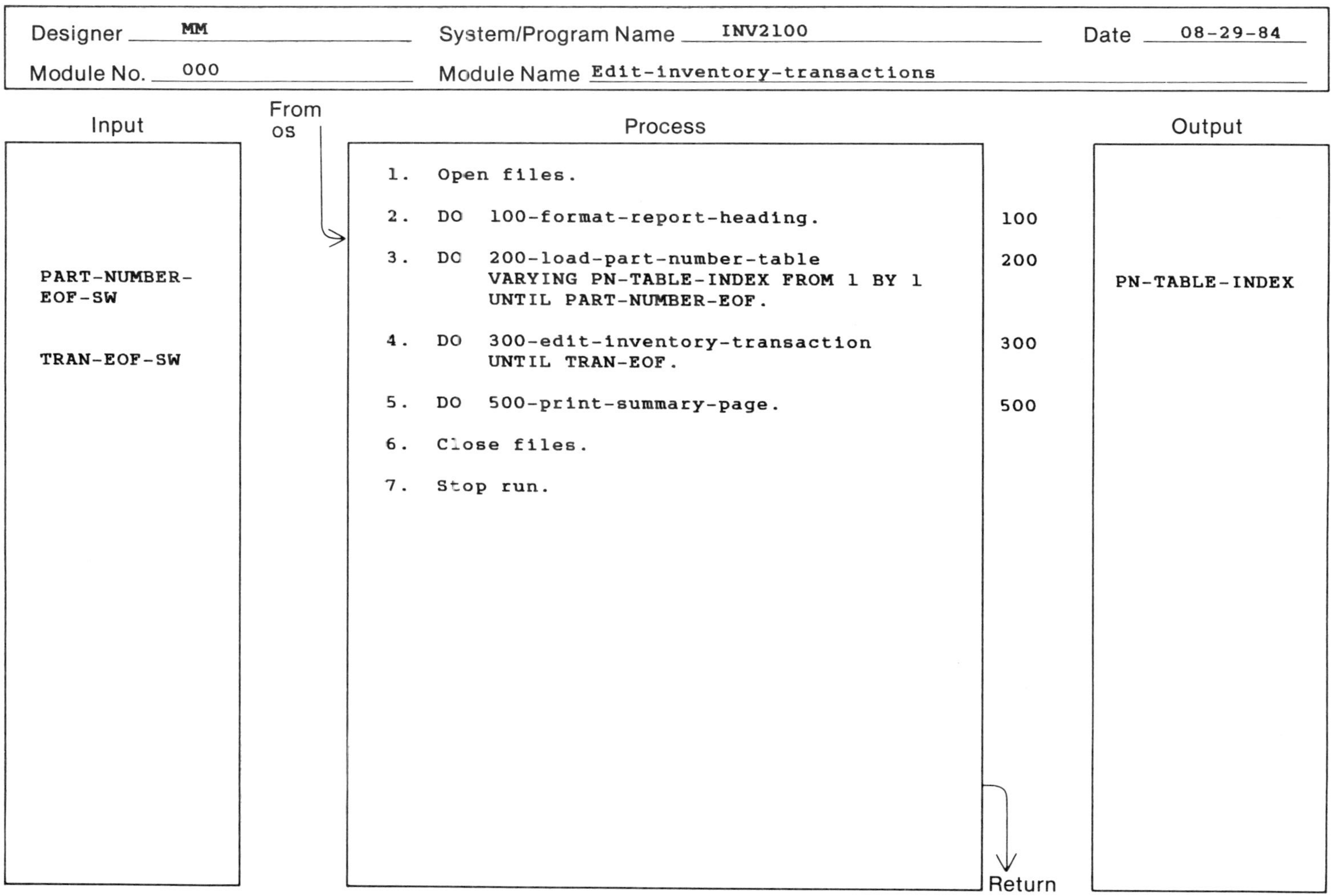

Figure 4-3 A HIPO diagram for module 000 of the edit program

Task 5: Plan the testing of the program by creating a test plan Before you even code a program, we feel that you should plan its testing. You should plan the sequence of modules to be coded and tested if you're using top-down testing. And you should plan the test runs you're going to need for the unit test. Figure 4-4, for example, shows a test plan for the edit program. The basic principles of planning a test run are presented in chapter 10 along with other ideas for improving your testing methods.

Task 6: If necessary, code the job-control procedures for the test runs On some systems, you can test your programs interactively so you don't have to develop job-control procedures for your test runs. But if you do, chapter 10, the chapter on testing, will give you some ideas on how to do this efficiently.

Task 7: If necessary, create the test data for the test runs For some programs, you won't have to create your own test data. When you're writing a simple file-to-printer program, for example, live data may be adequate for your test runs. Similarly, the output from other programs that are in development will sometimes be adequate for testing your program. But if you have to create your own test data, chapter 10, the chapter on testing, will give you some ideas on how to do it efficiently.

Task 8: Code and test the program using top-down testing Chapter 9 gives you detailed ideas for coding a program so it is readable and thus easy to test and maintain. Then, chapter 10 shows you how to code and test a program using top-down testing. As I mentioned in the last chapter, we recommend that you use top-down testing whenever it takes you more than a day to develop a program. So you'll probably use top-down testing for most of the programs you develop. That's why we specify top-down coding and testing in the procedure in figure 4-1.

Task 9: Document the program After your program has passed the system test and the acceptance test, you document it. In chapter 11, we'll give you some ideas on how to do this efficiently.

Some related ideas

The procedure shown in figure 4-1 probably isn't much different than the procedure you're using now. So the important thing is that you do the tasks efficiently and effectively. And that's basically what the next seven chapters are about. Before I continue, though, let me give you some additional perspective on the methods presented in this book.

Overlapping or rearranging the tasks in the development procedure Just because I've listed nine tasks in sequence in figure 4-1, doesn't mean that you should always do them in that sequence. For instance, you can reasonably overlap the two tasks in the analysis phase.

Program: INV2100 EDIT INVENTORY TRANSACTIONS	Page: 1
Designer: Anne Prince	Date: 08-18-84

Test phase	Data	Data source
1. Valid transactions	Three valid part-number records; two valid transactions, one for each transaction code, and one with the first part number in the table, one with the last part number	Self
2. Single error	Invalid transactions that will test all possible causes of invalid fields	Self
3. Contingencies	Mixed data from test runs 1 and 2; any new records that might cause a contingent error	Self
4. Page overflow and maximum table size	As many part-number records as the program is supposed to provide for; 150 transactions with enough invalid transactions to cause page overflow	Test data generator

Figure 4-4 A test plan for the edit program

While you're getting the complete specifications, you can also start to look for related programs, COPY members, and subprograms. Similarly, you can overlap the tasks in the design phase. It's natural, for example, to go back and forth to a limited extent between the design of the program and the design of some of its critical modules.

In the implementation phase, you can not only overlap the tasks somewhat, but you can rearrange them to some extent. Of course, you have to have the job-control procedure, the test data, and the COBOL code for any test run before you can run it. But that doesn't mean you always have to develop these items in that sequence. If, for example, you develop the code first, the test data second, and the procedure last, it shouldn't have much effect on your efficiency (if any). Yes, you should plan your testing first and document your program last, but otherwise the sequence of the implementation tasks isn't that important.

Although you may decide to overlap or resequence some of the development tasks, you must be sure to keep the phases separate. You should definitely analyze the program before you design it. And you should definitely design it before you implement it. Too often, though, I've seen programmers start to implement programs before they've finished designing them and without ever analyzing them.

How the methods in this book have evolved In chapter 2, I showed you a few of the many methods that people use for designing and developing COBOL programs. I said that was one of the reasons why structured programming hasn't fulfilled its potential in many COBOL shops. People just couldn't decide which methods were best so they didn't change at all or they selected methods that proved to be ineffective.

That's why I'd like you to know how the methods in this book have evolved. None of them were actually created by Paul Noll. He just borrowed the best ideas that were available in the mid-1970s and modified them to suit his purposes. Then, he coordinated them until they became one integrated system for the development of COBOL programs rather than a collection of methods that don't quite work together. At this time, then, I'd like to give credit where credit is due by telling you where the major methods of this book originated.

The structure chart we recommend is based on the Visual Table of Contents that is part of IBM's Hierarchical Input-Process-Output (HIPO) documentation system. In fact, Paul still calls his structure charts VTOCs, though we're going to call them structure charts throughout this book. To make them useful for COBOL programming, Paul had to develop a system for designing the modules in the charts, for naming the modules, for numbering the modules, and for relating the structure chart to the COBOL code. And I don't know of any other structured programming practitioner who has done a better job of this.

The module design documents Paul recommends are the HIPO diagrams, which are also taken from IBM's HIPO. But Paul simplified them so they don't make extensive use of graphics, and so you can create one in a few minutes.

The COBOL coding techniques recommended in this book are largely Paul's. From the start, of course, it was clear as to how the structured programming constructs were to be coded in COBOL. Everybody talked about that. But, as I think you've already seen, there's a lot more to readability and maintainability than writing GOTOless code. In terms of our own shop, we give Paul the credit for the effectiveness of our code because we've never seen more efficient methods for coding structured programs than the ones he recommends.

I don't really know who to give the credit to for top-down coding and testing. It's been around for ten years or more, and everyone seems to agree on the basic principles for its use. So Paul simply accepted it as one of the techniques that can help you improve programmer productivity and program reliability. Then, he tried to give specific guidelines for coding the dummy modules or program stubs that are required when you use top-down testing.

The acceptance of the methods in this book

Perhaps you would like to know how many companies use the methods presented in this book. Although I can't give you exact data, I can give you some ideas about this so you can draw your own conclusions.

To start, you should know that this book is a revised edition of a book we published in 1977 called *Structured Programming for the COBOL Programmer*. Since its publication, we have sold one or more copies to more than 12,000 businesses throughout the United States and the world. Based on our recent COBOL survey, from 30 to 40 percent of the companies that bought this book actually implemented the methods in their COBOL shops. And this leads us to believe that more than 3,000 COBOL shops use the methods presented in this book either in whole or in part.

In the last eight years, Paul and I have had many experiences that corroborate these statistical extrapolations. Dozens of people have written to tell me that they were adopting the methods of the book in their entirety. And Paul has consulted in many companies that changed their standards to conform with the development practices recommended in this book. In fact, I have standards manuals from a couple of companies as proof of the fact that they adopted our methods.

Our first book apparently convinced many of the writers of COBOL textbooks to change the methods they presented. So right now, three of the four best-selling COBOL texts for colleges teach the methods presented in this book. As a result, you can expect that most of the people you hire who have taken COBOL classes in college will be familiar with the methods of this book.

Then, in 1980, IBM Corporation replaced their COBOL Independent Study Program with a training package we developed. This package includes our COBOL texts, which teach the methods of this book, as well as *The Structured Programming Cookbook*, which presents development standards based on our methods. As of this writing, IBM still uses our package for customer and employee training in COBOL.

I present this information so you don't think that we're presenting a set of untried methods in this book. On the contrary, we believe that the methods presented in this book are the most widely-used methods for developing COBOL programs. If they aren't, we think they ought to be because we're confident that they're the most effective methods currently available for developing COBOL programs.

Conclusion

Although you're not likely to disagree with the development procedure recommended in this chapter, you may disagree with some of the methods we recommend for the tasks in the procedure. As a result, you should realize that you can use this book in two ways.

First, you can simply treat this book as an idea book. That is, you can see it as a collection of methods that you can adapt for use in your shop. If, for example, you like our ideas on program design but you don't agree with our thoughts about module design, you can use one technique but not the other. In you treat the book in this way, I'm confident that you'll get some ideas that will improve program development in your shop.

The other alternative is to accept our method in its entirety. As I've said earlier, our method works. In fact, I think it works better than any other development method I've seen. So if you do everything we recommend in this book, I believe you'll make dramatic improvements in programmer productivity at the same time that you improve the quality of your programs.

Terminology

None

Objective

List the three phases and the nine tasks of the program development procedure presented in this book.

Chapter 5

How to get complete program specifications

Today, as in the past, the specifications that come down to a programmer are likely to be heavy with detail, even though they omit one or more important aspects of the problem. Often, then, your first job as a programmer is to create an adequate program specification. To do this, you must wade through the pages of detail and create a program specification that accurately defines the program to be developed.

The other extreme is to receive specifications that are brief and sketchy. This often happens when you have a reputation for creating good program specifications. Then, the analyst in effect passes the job of creating the specifications on to you. In some cases, the analyst may just give you a verbal description of what your program is supposed to do or a few notes on yellow paper. He may even leave it up to you to figure out what files to use...so you have to refer to the systems documentation in order to create the program specification. In this case, of course, you are definitely doing systems design work rather than program development work.

In recent years, the trend is to make less distinction between programmer and systems analyst. So there are more programmer/analysts each year, and fewer programming or systems specialists. I think this trend is in the best interests of our industry because it is difficult to cleanly separate systems design and program development. For maximum efficiency, then, systems analysts should know more about programming and programmers should know more about systems analysis.

In any event, when you develop a program, you must make sure that you start with an adequate program specification. As you will see in the chapter on documentation, this specification will eventually become a part of the final program documentation. So it will be a permanent record of your work.

The components of a complete program specification

Most companies have standards for what a complete program specification must include. In general, a complete program specification should include at least three items: (1) some sort of program overview, (2) COPY members for at least the record layouts of all files used by the program, and (3) print charts for all printed output prepared by the program. For interactive programs, you should also have screen layouts for all terminal screens used by the program and screen flow diagrams if there's any doubt about how the screens are to be used. Since chapter 12 will show you how to use screen layouts and screen flow diagrams, I will only present the first three components of a complete program specification right now.

The program overview Most companies have standards for preparing program overviews. For instance, one of the companies Paul has worked with has a standard that says the program overview should be prepared on a HIPO diagram form like the one in figure 5-1. This example gives an overview for the edit program that is documented in appendix A. You'll become more familiar with the HIPO diagram form in chapter 8, but you can see that it provides for the input files, the output files, and a brief statement of the processing requirements of a program.

In an attempt to reduce our use of graphics, we use program overviews like the one in figure 5-2. In our experience, this is the most efficient document for summarizing the requirements of a program, both for the systems designer and for the programmer. Quite simply, the form provides for a listing of the input and output requirements of a program, plus a brief description of the processing requirements. Although we use the form shown in figure 5-2, I've seen variations of this form that will work just as well.

As you can see, the form in part 1 of figure 5-2 is divided into three parts. The top section is for identification. It gives the name and number of the program as specified by the system documentation. The middle part of the form lists and decribes all of the files (or database views) that the program requires. In addition, it tells what the program will do with each of those files: use them only for input, use them only for output, or use them for update.

The last section of the form is for processing specifications. It's this section, of course, that is the most critical. Here, you must make sure that all of the information you need to develop the program has been provided. If it isn't all there, you must develop it yourself.

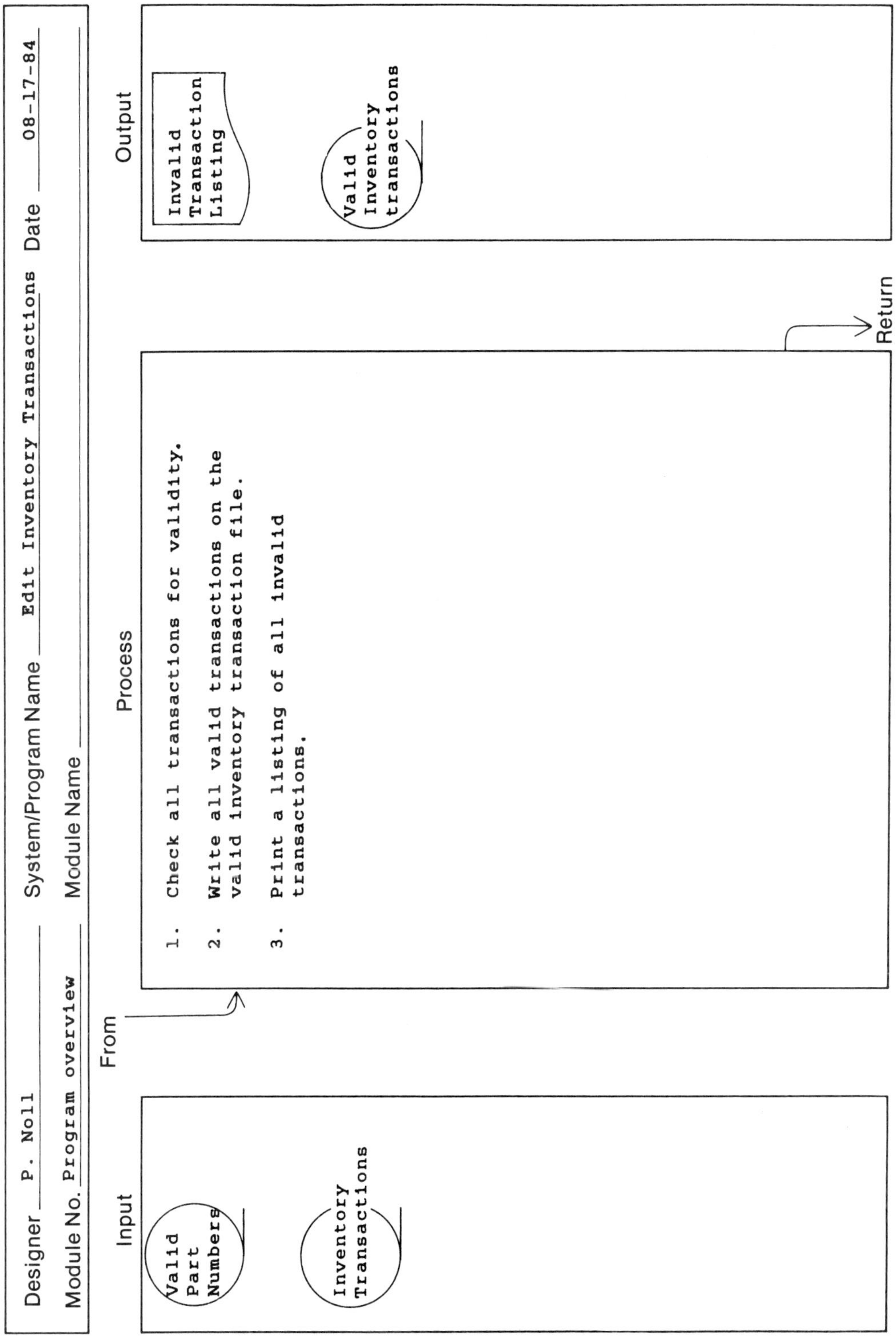

Figure 5-1 A program overview for the edit program on a HIPO diagram form

Program: INV2100 EDIT INVENTORY TRANSACTIONS	**Page:** 1
Designer: Anne Prince	**Date:** 08-17-84

Input/output specifications

File	Description	Use
INVTRAN	Inventory transaction file	Input
PARTNUM	Part number file	Input
VINVTRAN	Valid inventory transaction file	Output
IINVTLST	Print file: Invalid inventory transaction listing	Output

Process specifications

This program edits a file of transaction records consisting of two record types: sales transactions and return transactions. Althougn the formats for these records are similar, they are not exactly alike.

For efficiency, since the company has less than 100 inventory items, load a part-number table at the start of the program that can be used to check for valid part numbers throughout the program. The part numbers can be read from the part-number file. The records in this file are in order of transaction frequency; the first part number has the most activity, the last part number has the least.

Print the output listing in the same order that the transactions are read. And print the editing totals on a separate page on the invalid transaction listing.

The records in the valid transaction file have the same format as the records in the input transaction file.

Figure 5-2 A program overview for the edit program (part 1 of 2)

Program: INV2100 EDIT INVENTORY TRANSACTIONS	**Page:** 2
Designer: Anne Prince	**Date:** 08-17-84

Process specifications

The basic processing requirements follow:

Load the part-number table.

Do until the end of the inventory transaction file:

1. Read an inventory transaction record.
2. Edit the transaction fields.
3. If the transaction is invalid, print a line on the invalid transaction listing.
4. If the transaction is valid, write a record to the valid transaction file.

After all transactions have been processed, print the total page.

Figure 5-2 A program overview for the edit program (part 2 of 2)

```
 BKEND    C.INVTRAN

*
 01    INVENTORY-TRANSACTION-RECORD.
*
       05    ITR-TYPE-CODE.
             10    ITR-UPDATE-CODE         PIC X.
             10    ITR-TRAN-CODE           PIC X.
       05    ITR-REF-NO                    PIC X(10).
       05    ITR-REF-DATE                  PIC X(6).
       05    ITR-BRANCH-NO                 PIC XX.
       05    ITR-SALESMAN-NO               PIC XXX.
       05    ITR-CUSTOMER-NO               PIC X(5).
       05    ITR-QUANTITY                  PIC X(5).
       05    ITR-PART-NO                   PIC X(5).
       05    ITR-RETURN-CODE               PIC X(4).

 BKEND
```

Figure 5-3 A COPY member for the record layout of the inventory transaction file

If you have to create a program overview yourself, there are no firm rules to follow. For some applications, a form of pseudocode is efficient (more about pseudocode in chapter 8). For others, a simple narrative as shown on the first page of the program overview in figure 5-2 is effective. Often, you will want to combine two or more ways of giving processing requirements. Sometimes, for example, you will want to include decision tables or editing rules in your specifications.

As you can see by the two pages in figure 5-2, you can take as many pages as you need for a complete specification. The form you use for the first page should provide for input and output requirements as well as for processing requirements. But subsequent pages should provide only for processing requirements.

If you have access to a word processing system, you can create your program overviews with it. Since much of the work of creating program overviews is repetitive, word processing can improve your productivity dramatically. In our shop, we don't actually use preprinted overview forms anymore. Instead, the forms are part of our word processing documents, so the lines for the form print along with the specifications.

In general, you should avoid detailed descriptions of program logic when you create a program overview. Instead, you should try to present a complete list of the functional requirements in as brief a form as possible. You shouldn't think about program logic until you actually implement the program.

Listings of COPY members For each file used by a program, your specification should include listings of the COPY members for at least the record layouts of the file. For instance, figure 5-3 presents a listing of the COPY member for the inventory transaction record used by the inventory transaction file in the edit program. In addition, if they are available, your specification should include the COPY members for the SELECT statements and FD statements for all files used by the program.

If by chance you're still using some sort of record layout form for designing and documenting record layouts in your shop, you should switch to COPY members as soon as you can. They're easier to create and maintain. They're easier to understand. And they eliminate a development step, because you eventually have to create them anyway if you want to make maximum use of reusable code. More about the use of COPY members in the next chapter.

Print charts Figure 5-4 is a print chart for the invalid transaction listing of the edit program. Unless you're a complete novice to program development, you've probably created more of these than you care to remember. But in case you haven't created that many, you should know that you should use standard formatting practices when you design printed output. Standard formatting implies that report headings appear in the same places in all reports and that the heading data is clear. This makes it easier for the clerks who will distribute and file the reports as well as for the people who will read and use the reports.

The standard heading format we use is illustrated by the print chart in figure 5-4. All reports prepared in our shop have the same identifying data elements in the first three lines of the report. No matter how you format your reports, every report heading should include title, preparation date, preparation time (if appropriate), and some identifying number. In our shop, we use the program name to identify the reports it produces. In figure 5-4 for example, the transaction register is printed by program INV2100. If the program prepared more than one report, the first report would be identified as INV2100-1, the second as INV2100-2, and so on.

In some cases, it's desirable to assign serial numbers to reports to insure that all copies of it are accounted for. For instance, you might want to print serial numbers on all of the transaction registers prepared by the edit program. Then, if the register just printed is serial number 527 and the last one in the file of transaction registers is 525, it's apparent that register 526 is missing. The problem might be with clerical procedures or with the system, but the gap in serial numbers identifies the problem so it can be corrected. In any event, you should be aware that serial numbers may be a part of the standard heading for some documents.

Notice that all of the columns of the report in figure 5-4 are labelled. This is an obvious point, but all data elements on printed output should be identified. If the format of the report is non-columnar, you should use captions to identify data elements. As much as possible, then, each report you design should be self-explanatory. The user shouldn't have to ask what an item on a report means.

Some related ideas

After you have created or assembled the documents of the program specification, it's time to review it to make sure it's complete. In the case

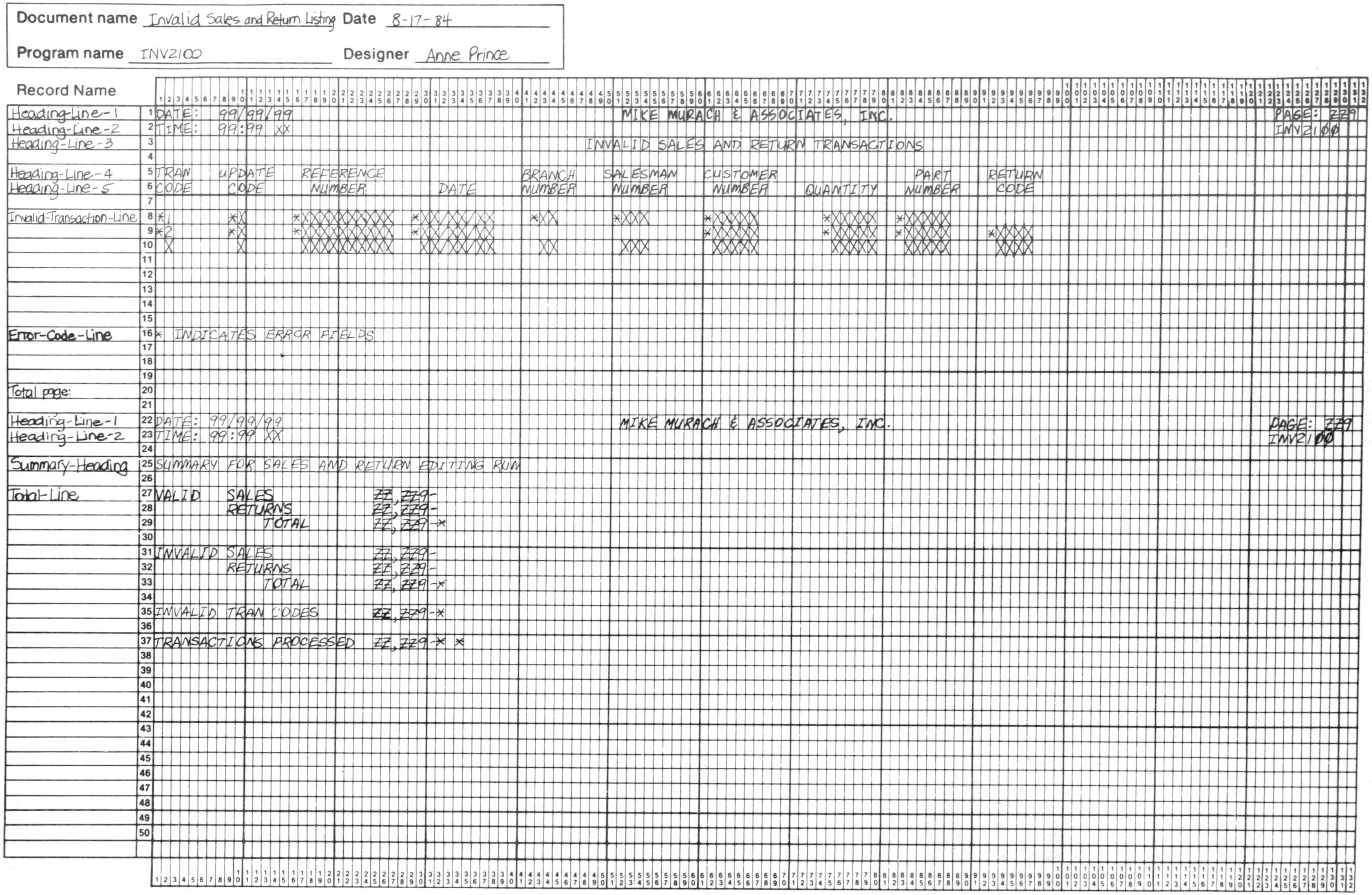

Figure 5-4 A print chart for the invalid inventory transaction listing prepared by the edit program

of the overview in figure 5-2, for example, do you have all the information you need to decide whether to do a sequential table search or a binary search? And what about the output file of valid transactions? Should it be in the sequence of the input file of transactions or should it be sorted into item number sequence so it can be used in a sequential update of the inventory master file later on?

My point is, look beyond the obvious. If you don't get specifications that give you a clear idea of what the problem is, you can't develop a program to meet the specifications. In fact, you will usually find that you can't create an adequate structure chart if the major functions of the program aren't clearly specified.

When to raise questions about the specifications In most cases, you should have questions about the program specifications that are given to you. It's simple enough for a systems designer to omit an important detail. And a good programmer should be able to raise questions that the designer might have missed.

When should you raise questions? Whenever you are sure that they are legitimate questions that haven't been answered anywhere in the materials you have been given. This means that you will normally ask some questions as soon as you've had time to review the specifications. In addition, you may need to ask other questions during the development of the program. Sometimes, for example, you may discover as you design the program that you can't do a required function without some additional input item. Sometimes, you may not discover an omission until you actually code the program. And sometimes, you won't discover an omission until your program becomes a part of the systems test.

Often, the blame for omissions is placed on the systems analyst, not the programmer. But you should still try to help the analyst discover omissions as early as possible. For maximum efficiency, the analyst should be able to depend on the programmer to find omissions. And the programmer should feel free to ask questions of the analyst whenever they arise.

To illustrate the type of detail that may not be discovered until you start to implement a program, consider a simple thing like putting serial numbers on the transaction listings for the edit program. Suppose, for example, that the analyst created the print chart for the program and showed the serial number on this chart, but didn't mention it in his program overview. In order to prepare the listing, of course, the program has to get the serial number (or the last serial number used) from somewhere (probably, from a control file of some sort). Often, however, the programmer will overlook this detail until he starts to code the heading for the report. Then, he will realize that he has no source for the serial number. So it's back to the analyst to clear up this omission.

Fortunately, this is a minor point, and a control file used just for this report will have no effect on the other programs of the system. So the late discovery of the omission won't have much impact on the development of the system. But, as any experienced programmer knows, worse discoveries are often made much later in the game. So the more conscientious the programmer is about discovering omissions early and raising questions about them, the better it is for the systems project.

What detail can be put off until later When I talk about detecting omissions, you should realize that I'm talking about the omission of major factors like files, data items, or functional requirements. In contrast, the details that are to be taken care of by the lower-level modules of a program can usually be put off until later. For instance, you can create the structure chart for the edit program without any details on what the specific editing rules are for each type of input transaction. In fact, it's often left to the programmer to figure out what the editing rules should be. So there's no point in making them part of the program specification.

On the other hand, if the analyst provides the editing rules, you can make them part of your specifications. For instance, figure 5-5 shows a third page for the program overview of the edit program that gives the editing rules for the two types of transaction records.

In other words, it's okay to have incomplete specifications when it comes to trivial details. Sometimes, you will get the information to complete these details when you design the program. Sometimes, you will put these details off until you actually code the program. As long as the details don't affect the design of the program, you can put them off until you need them. If you do, it may free your mind so you can develop a more complete specification in terms of the critical files and functions.

How to tell when your specifications are complete When you develop a program specification, it's natural to want to include more information than is necessary. So how do you know when your specifications are complete? Our answer is this: Your specifications are complete when a professional programmer could design the program using only the program overview and its supporting documents. That doesn't mean that the programmer won't have to find out some additional details as he implements the program. But he won't need any more information to do a complete design of the program.

With that in mind, is the program overview in figure 5-1 adequate as the basis for a complete specification? No. It doesn't say anything about how the part-number file is to be used. But what about the two parts of the overview in figure 5-2? Do they provide the basis for a complete specification when combined with the required COPY members and print chart? I think so. Using the overview and its supporting documents, a professional programmer should be able to design the program.

What should you do with the pages of specifications and notes that the analyst gave you that you don't need in your final specification? File them in a development folder for the program. Then, you can refer to them whenever questions arise as you implement the program. And when the implementation questions aren't answered by the documents in the file, it's back to the analyst to get the answers.

Program: INV2100 EDIT INVENTORY TRANSACTIONS		**Page:** 3
Designer: Anne Prince		**Date:** 08-17-84

Process specifications

Editing rules for a sales transaction:

ITR-UPDATE-CODE	Must be "C"
ITR-TRAN-CODE	Must be 1
ITR-REF-NO	No restrictions
ITR-REF-DATE	Use DATEDIT subprogram; must be a valid date in the form MMDDYY
ITR-BRANCH-NO	Numeric, greater than zero, and less than 25
ITR-SALESMAN-NO	Numeric and greater than zero
ITR-CUSTOMER-NO	Numeric and greater than zero
ITR-QUANTITY	Numeric and greater than zero
ITR-PART-NO	Must match with a number in the part-number table that is loaded at the start of the program
ITR-RETURN-CODE	Not used

Editing rules for a return transaction:

ITR-UPDATE-CODE	Must be "C"
ITR-TRAN-CODE	Must be 2
ITR-REF-NO	No restrictions
ITR-REF-DATE	Use DATEDIT subprogram; must be a valid date in the form MMDDYY
ITR-BRANCH-NO	Not used
ITR-SALESMAN-NO	Not used
ITR-CUSTOMER-NO	Numeric and greater than zero
ITR-QUANTITY	Numeric and greater than zero
ITR-PART-NO	Must match with a number in the part-number table that is loaded at the start of the program
ITR-RETURN-CODE	Alphabetic

Figure 5-5 An optional third page for the program overview of the edit program presenting detail that can be put off until later

Discussion

To develop a program effectively, you must start with complete program specifications. If you start to design a program without complete specifications, you'll pay for it later by having to revise your design and possibly your code too.

As obvious as this is, the urge to get on with design and implementation is strong. That's why, in our experience, too many programmers start to design and implement a program before they have complete specifications. As a result, most programmers can improve their productivity by simply making sure they start each programming project with complete specifications.

Terminology

program overview

Objectives

1. Describe the purpose of the program overview in a program specification.

2. Give a guideline that specifies how much detail you should include in a program specification.

Chapter 6

How to use related programs, COPY members, and subprograms

After you get complete program specifications for a program, you should get any related programs, COPY members, or subprograms that you may be able to use when you develop the program. The idea here is that you shouldn't start any program from scratch. For any program that you develop, you should be able to find an old program or two that you can derive the new program's design from. You should be able to pick up a major portion of the code for the new program from related old programs. And you should be able to pick up the equivalent of dozens of lines of code for the new program from COPY members and subprograms that are available to you.

Before you can understand how to get related programs, COPY members, and subprograms, however, you need to know how you are going to use them. In this chapter, then, I will try to introduce you to the use of these items. Later on, the chapters on program design and COBOL coding will expand upon these ideas.

How to use related programs

Using old programs as a basis for developing new programs is a critical development technique. To a large extent, how well you use old programs determines how much you can improve productivity and program quality in your shop. If, by chance, you're not making extensive use of old programs today, you have the potential to make dramatic improvements in program development by virtue of this technique alone.

Of course, you can't reuse old programs very well unless you developed them using effective methods for design and coding. For instance, it's difficult, if not impossible, to reuse code from a program written in the GOTO style of programming. And you don't gain much by reusing an old program's design if the design wasn't effective in the first place. So in order to get the maximum benefit from the reuse of old programs, you have to adopt effective development methods in the first place. Needless to say, the methods presented in this book will help you get the maximum benefit from the reuse of old programs.

Your library of model programs As we see it, all programmers should have their own libraries of model programs. At the least, each library should contain one program for each type of business program developed in a shop. For instance, each programmer in our shop keeps a library that contains model programs for at least four types of interactive programs: a file-maintenance program, a transaction-entry program, an inquiry program, and a selective report-preparation program. Since almost all of our interactive programs fall into one of these four categories, a library of just four programs can provide the basis for developing most of our interactive programs. Similarly, a library of just four or five batch programs can provide the basis for developing most batch programs.

When you first start using structured techniques, of course, you won't have a library of your own model programs. If possible, then, you should start by using someone else's library. But if you can't get access to an acceptable library, we recommend that you use the model programs in our reference book, *The COBOL Programmer's Handbook*. It provides model programs for four types of batch programs and one interactive program. And one or more of these programs can be used as a basis for developing most programs.

After you develop a new program based on someone else's program, you should replace the old model program with your own. Although both programs will have the same basic structure, each will probably have its own style. Because of this, it usually is easier to use your own program as a model for developing a new program than it is to use someone else's.

When I speak of a *model program*, I want you to realize that I just mean a production program that is one of your best efforts. I don't mean a program that is especially designed to be a generalized model for programs of a certain type. We've experimented with generalized models and have found that they're not worth the effort to develop. Production programs can be just as useful as generalized models when you design a new program. And production programs provide more opportunities for reusing code than generalized models do. So your model programs should simply be the best programs you've written. Then, when you write a better program for a certain type of business application than the model program you have been using, you replace the old model program with your new program.

When I speak of a *model program library*, I actually mean two libraries: an *external* library and an *internal* library. First, you should have a copy of the program documentation for each model program in your library. This can be thought of as an external library, and it should include both the structure chart and the COBOL listing for each program. Second, the source code for each model program should be available to you through the computer system. This can be thought of as an internal library. And this library can make it easy for you to reuse the COBOL code in your model programs.

How many programs should you have in your model program library? That depends on system resources and personal preferences. In our shop, for example, each programmer has access to the documentation and code for all production programs. Since all of our programmers use the standards presented in this book, all of our programs can be used as a starting point for new programs. Nevertheless, some of our programmers base their new programs on just a few model programs that they keep in a personal library. Others pick up design and code from any programs that are related to the program they're writing. Since there are advantages and disadvantages to both programming techniques, I have no recommendation one way or the other. As long as you're picking up a major portion of the design and code for each new program from old programs, it doesn't matter how many programs you keep in your model program library unless your system resources are limited.

How to reuse program structures Before you can reuse program structures effectively, you should be able to recognize the basic structure within a model program. To illustrate, I have reproduced the structure chart for the edit program of appendix A in figure 6-1. Can you see the basic structure in this structure chart?

If you leave out the modules that provide for the specific requirements of the edit program, you end up with the basic structure shown in figure 6-2. Here, I have used generalized module names to help illustrate the idea that this structure can be used as the basis for any program that edits transactions. Yes, the format of the invalid transaction listing may change from one edit program to another. And, yes, the editing rules may change. But this basic structure can be used in any batch edit program.

The structure charts of your model programs should provide you with the basic structures you will need for most of your new programs. Then, when you design a new program, you just make revisions to an old chart to provide for the specific requirements of the new program. If your new program requires structural elements from more than one model program, you combine the structures from the model programs into a single structure chart.

In chapter 7, you'll learn how to design programs from scratch using a structure chart. But you'll also be introduced to the basic structures for several different types of business programs. When you finish chapter 7, you'll have a better idea of how you can reuse program structures from one program to the next.

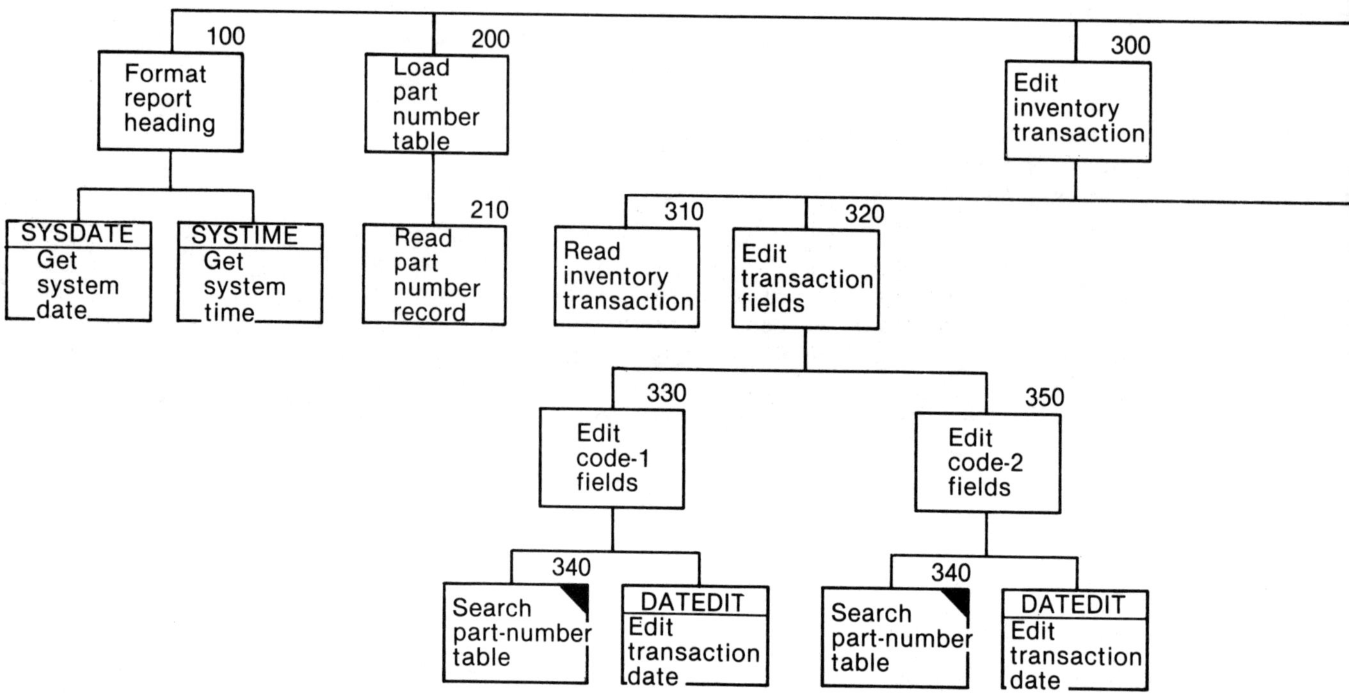

Figure 6-1 The structure chart for the edit program in appendix A

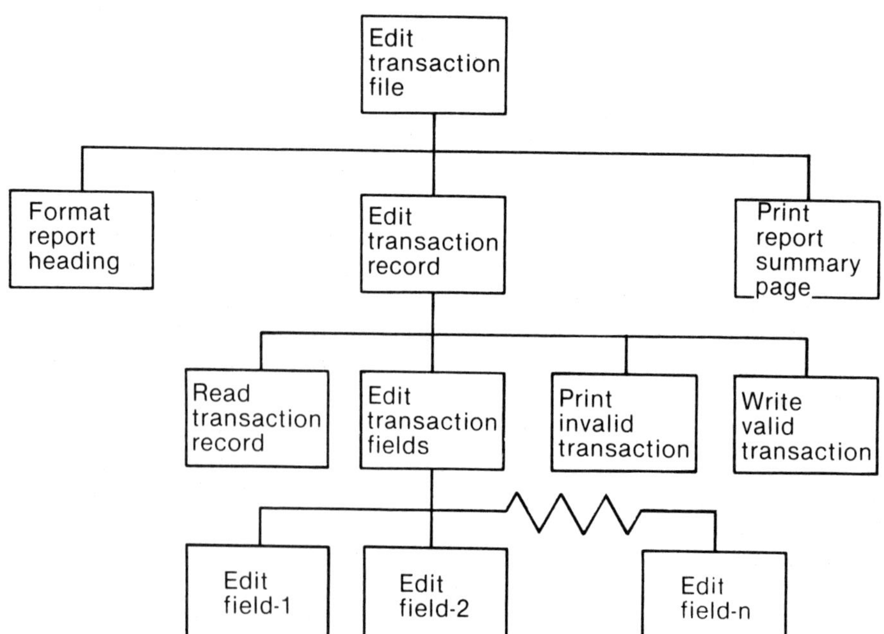

Figure 6-2 The basic structure of an edit program that can be reused in new edit programs

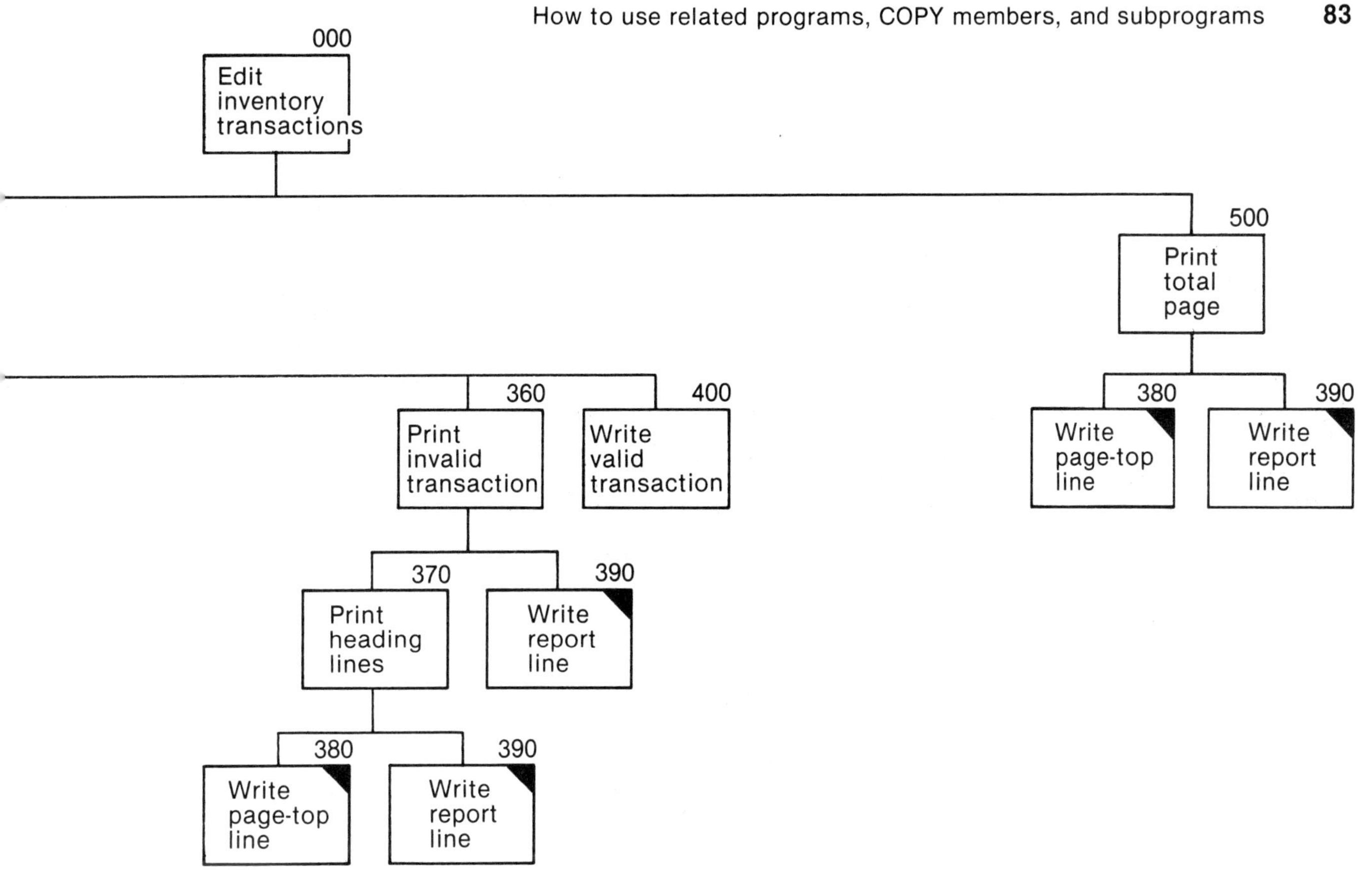

How to reuse COBOL code After you have created the structure chart for a new program based on the designs of one or more model programs, you have set the stage for reusing the code from these programs. For each module that you have reused in the new program's design, you should be able to reuse at least some of the COBOL code from the old program. If your new program consists of structures taken from more than one program, of course, you can reuse code from more than one program.

What kind of code can be reused from one program to the next? As we see it, more than 50 percent of the code in a typical business program can be reused with minor modifications in subsequent programs. This includes code in the Identification and Environment Divisions. It includes large portions of code in the Data Division. And it includes code in many of the modules of the Procedure Division. Even if the old code has to be modified extensively, this is usually more efficient than entering the code from scratch.

In topic 3 of chapter 9, I will present some detailed ideas on what kind of code you can reuse. As a result, you may not be able to appreciate the many ways in which code can be reused until you read that chapter. For now, though, let me just give you one illustration.

Figure 6-3 illustrates an edit module taken from the edit program in appendix A. The function of this module is to edit the fields within a code-1 transaction record. Although this code is closely related to this program's editing specifications, you can also see it as a general coding structure for any module that edits the fields in a transaction record. As a

```
330-EDIT-CODE-1-FIELDS.
*
     IF ITR-UPDATE-CODE NOT = 'C'
         MOVE 'N'                  TO VALID-TRAN-SW
         MOVE ERROR-INDICATOR TO ITL-UPDATE-CODE-ERR.
     CALL 'DATEDIT' USING ITR-REF-DATE, VALID-DATE-SW.
     IF NOT VALID-DATE
         MOVE 'N'                  TO VALID-TRAN-SW
         MOVE ERROR-INDICATOR TO ITL-REF-DATE-ERR.
     IF          ITR-BRANCH-NO NOT NUMERIC
              OR ITR-BRANCH-NO NOT GREATER ZERO
              OR ITR-BRANCH-NO NOT LESS 25
         MOVE 'N'                  TO VALID-TRAN-SW
         MOVE ERROR-INDICATOR TO ITL-BRANCH-NO-ERR.
     IF          ITR-SALESMAN-NO NOT NUMERIC
              OR ITR-SALESMAN-NO NOT GREATER ZERO
         MOVE 'N'                  TO VALID-TRAN-SW
         MOVE ERROR-INDICATOR TO ITL-SALESMAN-NO-ERR.
     IF          ITR-CUSTOMER-NO NOT NUMERIC
              OR ITR-CUSTOMER-NO NOT GREATER ZERO
         MOVE 'N'                  TO VALID-TRAN-SW
         MOVE ERROR-INDICATOR TO ITL-CUSTOMER-NO-ERR.
     IF          ITR-QUANTITY NOT NUMERIC
              OR ITR-QUANTITY NOT GREATER ZERO
         MOVE 'N'                  TO VALID-TRAN-SW
         MOVE ERROR-INDICATOR TO ITL-QUANTITY-ERR.
     PERFORM 340-SEARCH-PART-NUMBER-TABLE.
     IF NOT PART-NUMBER-FOUND
         MOVE 'N'                  TO VALID-TRAN-SW
         MOVE ERROR-INDICATOR TO ITL-PART-NUMBER-ERR.
     IF NOT VALID-TRAN
         ADD 1 TO INVALID-SALES-COUNT
     ELSE
         ADD 1 TO VALID-SALES-COUNT.
*
```

Figure 6-3 Code for an edit module that can be reused in new edit programs

result, you can reuse portions of this code in any new editing modules that you may write. For example, you can see from this coding that for every field that is invalid a switch must be set and the error must be indicated in the print line for the invalid-transaction listing. You can also see editing rules for specific types of fields such as dates and numeric fields. And, you can see that the count of valid and invalid transactions is kept in this module as well. So, although you may have to modify the code extensively, you at least have a basic coding structure to follow, which is better than starting from scratch.

Because some systems are more efficient than others when it comes to copying code from one program to another, the advantage of reusing code will vary depending on the type of system you are using. For example, our system allows us to copy segments of code from other programs while running the editor. In addition, the system makes it easy to modify the copied code. In contrast, other systems may not provide for easy copying and editing, in which case the benefits of reusing code are reduced somewhat.

As we see it, though, it is always more efficient to copy related code from another program than it is to create it from scratch, even if that means rekeying the copied code into the system yourself. When you reuse code, your code will be more consistent from one program to the next. And, since the code has already been tested in one program, it will probably work the first time you test it in your new program.

How to use related COPY members

You most likely use COPY members already in your shop. But chances are that you don't use them as much as you should. In general, you can use a COPY member for any segment of code that is required in more than one program and that doesn't need to be modified. In other words, you can use COPY members for code that has been standardized throughout a system.

Each time you use a COPY member, you reuse old code by writing only one COPY statement in the COBOL program. This, of course, can improve both programmer productivity and program quality. In addition, COPY members can make it easy for you to change specifications in all of the programs in a system. If, for example, you change a record format and the record format is a COPY member, you can change all programs that use the COPY member by recompiling them.

Your library of COPY members Perhaps the most common use of COPY members is for record descriptions. If you know that a file is going to be used in more than one program, you should always put the record description of that file in the COPY library. That way, any programmer that needs to use the file will have its record description available to him and the code will be consistent from one program to the next.

Depending on your system, you may also want to use COPY members for your SELECT and FD statements. If these statements are complex, using a COPY member for them will keep you from having to remember details like how the file is organized, what the keys are, or how many characters are in a record. And, again, they will help keep your code consistent.

COPY members can also be used for other items in the Data Division. For example, figure 6-4 illustrates a COPY member that we use in our shop for report headings. Because these heading lines are always the same, it makes sense to copy them into each program that prepares a report using a single COPY statement.

Although you can also use COPY members in the Procedure Division, we don't recommend it. The problem here is that the data names and the paragraph names used in the COPY member usually have to be modified if the code is to be consistent with the other modules of the program. As a result, it's better to copy the code from another program than it is to copy it from a COPY library. Then, you can edit the code so the names are appropriate for the new program. Yes, you can use a COPY-REPLACING statement to accomplish the same thing if the COPY member is simple enough, but this is often more trouble than it's worth.

```
 BKEND    C.RPTHDG14
*
 01  HEADING-LINE-1.
*
     05  FILLER                       PIC X(7)     VALUE 'DATE:'.
     05  HDG1-DATE                    PIC 99/99/99.
     05  FILLER                       PIC X(26)    VALUE SPACE.
     05  HDG1-COMPANY-NAME            PIC X(50).
     05  FILLER                       PIC X(31)    VALUE SPACE.
     05  FILLER                       PIC X(6)     VALUE 'PAGE:'.
     05  HDG1-PAGE-NUMBER             PIC ZZ9.
*
 01  HEADING-LINE-2.
*
     05  HDG2-TIME-DATA.
         10  FILLER                   PIC X(7)     VALUE 'TIME:'.
         10  HDG2-HOURS               PIC XX.
         10  FILLER                   PIC X        VALUE ':'.
         10  HDG2-MINUTES             PIC XX.
         10  FILLER                   PIC X        VALUE SPACE.
         10  HDG2-TIME-SUFFIX         PIC X(8).
     05  FILLER                       PIC X(101)   VALUE SPACE.
     05  HDG2-REPORT-NUMBER           PIC X(10).
*
 01  HEADING-LINE-3.
*
     05  FILLER                       PIC X(36)    VALUE SPACE.
     05  HDG3-REPORT-TITLE            PIC X(60).

 BKEND
```

Figure 6-4 A COPY member for a standard report heading

How to create a COPY member Have you ever been given a COPY member for a record description as part of a program specification and found that it was so unorganized that it was difficult to use? If so, you probably realize how important the structure of a record description can be. If the COPY member isn't easy to read and understand, it can reduce the quality of all of the programs in which it is used. And it can reduce the productivity of all the programmers who use it.

To create an effective COPY member, then, you need to organize it in a logical manner. This is particularly true when you are creating a COPY member for a record description. In general, the first part of the record description should contain all of the reference data including the record key if the file is indexed. After that, you should try to group all related fields. For each group, you should consider a group heading at a higher level that indicates the relationships between the fields in the group.

Figure 6-5 illustrates an effective record description for an invoice record. Notice how well-structured it is and how easy the group headings make it to find specific information. Also, notice how meaningful all of the data names are and how each has a two-character prefix to indicate that they are all from the same record. When you create COPY members like this one, you get the maximum benefit throughout your shop from the use of the COPY library.

```
*
 01  INVOICE-RECORD.
*
     05  IR-INVOICE-NUMBER              PIC X(6).
     05  IR-INVOICE-DATE.
         10  IR-INVOICE-MONTH           PIC 99.
         10  IR-INVOICE-DAY             PIC 99.
         10  IR-INVOICE-YEAR            PIC 99.
     05  IR-PURCHASE-ORDER-NUMBER       PIC X(10).
     05  IR-CUSTOMER-NUMBER             PIC X(6).
     05  IR-BILLING-ADDRESS.
         10  IR-BILL-NAME               PIC X(31).
         10  IR-BILL-ADDRESS            PIC X(31).
         10  IR-BILL-CITY               PIC X(18).
         10  IR-BILL-STATE              PIC XX.
         10  IR-BILL-ZIP-CODE           PIC X(5).
     05  IR-SHIPPING-ADDRESS.
         10  IR-SHIP-NAME               PIC X(31).
         10  IR-SHIP-ADDRESS            PIC X(31).
         10  IR-SHIP-CITY               PIC X(18).
         10  IR-SHIP-STATE              PIC XX.
         10  IR-SHIP-ZIP-CODE           PIC X(5).
     05  IR-PRODUCT-DATA                OCCURS 5 TIMES.
         10  IR-QUANTITY                PIC S9(3)      COMP-3.
         10  IR-PRODUCT-CODE            PIC X(5).
         10  IR-LIST-PRICE              PIC S9(5)V99   COMP-3.
         10  IR-NET-PRICE               PIC S9(5)V99   COMP-3.
     05  IR-TOTAL-DATA.
         10  IR-PRODUCT-TOTAL           PIC S9(5)V99   COMP-3.
         10  IR-CASH-DISCOUNT           PIC S9(5)V99   COMP-3.
         10  IR-SALES-TAX               PIC S9(5)V99   COMP-3.
         10  IR-FREIGHT                 PIC S9(5)V99   COMP-3.
         10  IR-INVOICE-TOTAL           PIC S((5)V99   COMP-3.
*
```

Figure 6-5 An effective COPY member for a record description

How to use related subprograms

Whenever a function is used in several programs or more, it makes sense to implement it as a subprogram. This is simply another way of reusing code so you don't have to write every routine from scratch. By coding only one CALL statement for each subprogram, you increase programmer productivity at the same time you improve program quality.

To illustrate, consider a subprogram for editing a date to make sure that its fields contain logical values. Although the function is simple, it still takes time to code and test the routine for it. So if each programmer codes the routine whenever it is required in a program, programmer productivity is reduced. In addition, there's a chance that the date-edit routines in some programs won't work correctly. In contrast, a tested subprogram means that the programmer can use the routine by writing only one CALL statement. It also means that the routine will work the first time it's tested.

Your library of subprograms Without much trouble, you can probably list several general functions that should be in your subprogram library.

Date- and time-handling functions:

- Convert a Gregorian date to a Julian date (and vice versa)
- Compute the elapsed time in days between two dates
- Determine the day of the week from the date
- Resequence the elements in a date
- Convert 24-hour time to a.m./p.m. time (and vice versa)
- Compute elapsed time

Editing functions:

- Validate a date
- Validate a state code
- Validate a zip code

Character-manipulation functions:

- Center a left-justified character string in a field
- Compress groups of spaces to a single space within a character string to create a new string that looks like a sentence

Figure 6-6 Some general subprograms that can be used in most COBOL shops

For instance, figure 6-6 lists some general functions that should be in most subprogram libraries. In fact, we use most of them regularly in our shop.

In addition to general-purpose subprograms, you should also consider using subprograms for special functions that must be done in several programs or more. In our order-processing system, for example, new customers and prospects are assigned keys by using a condensed version of their last names. Since there are several programs that allow a customer or prospect to be added to the system, we implemented the key-assignment function as a subprogram.

When you plan a new subprogram, you should make sure that it passes these tests. First, make sure that the subprogram is needed in more than one program. Otherwise, it makes no sense to write the routine as a subprogram. Second, be sure that the subprogram performs only one function. If it performs more than one function, you probably should make it into more than one subprogram. That way the subprograms are more likely to be used in new programs. Third, if the subprogram is to perform a general function, make sure that it is truly general-purpose. In other words, you shouldn't include any details in it that limit its usefulness. Usually, such details can be handled outside of the subprogram. If you use these guidelines, we think you'll end up with a library of subprograms that will be used in many programs throughout your shop.

In chapter 9, we'll discuss the use of subprograms as a way to implement modules that are going to be used in only one program. I'll tell you right now that we don't recommend this practice. But we'll show you why in detail in chapter 9.

How to create a subprogram Unless you have a solid reason for writing a subprogram in some other language, you should develop your subprograms in COBOL. As you do, you should follow the basic techniques for developing COBOL programs that are presented in this book. Then, the quality of your subprograms will be consistent with the quality of your programs themselves.

After you develop a subprogram, you should put it in a subprogram library that is accessible to all programmers who may want to use it. In addition, each programmer should have access to the documentation for all available subprograms. This programmer documentation should describe the subprogram function and show how it is invoked.

Figure 6-7 shows an acceptable programmer guide for a subprogram that edits a date field. In general, a one-page guide like this is adequate for most subprograms. And this page can be put in a binder that contains the guides for all of the subprograms in the installation.

How to get related programs, COPY members, and subprograms

Now that you have a general idea as to how you will use old programs, COPY members, and subprograms when you develop new programs, you should know what you have to do before you start the design and implementation of a new program. First, you should go through your library of model programs to find any programs that are related to the program you're about to develop. When you find a program that does some of the functions of the new program, pull out the documentation so you can refer to it when you design and develop your program. For each new program, you should be able to find at least one program that you'll be able to borrow structural elements and code from. And you may be able to find two or three related programs.

Second, get the COPY members that relate to your program. As part of the program specifications, you should have access to the COPY members for the record descriptions of the files your program is going to use. But after that you should look through the COPY library to see what else you might want to use. If the program is going to prepare a report, you should have a COPY member for a standard report heading. If the program uses interactive screens, you might have a COPY member for a standard screen heading. And so on.

Third, you should look through your subprogram library to see whether there are any subprograms your program may be able to use. If your program is going to edit fields, you should be able to find subprograms for functions like editing dates, editing state codes, and editing zip codes. If your program is going to prepare a report, you should be able to find subprograms for getting the date and time for the heading of the report. And so on.

Subprogram name:	DATEDIT
Programmer	Steve Eckols
Date:	6-30-83
Function:	This program evaluates a six-character date in the format MMDDYY (month-day-year) and sets a one-character switch field to "Y" if the date is logically valid or to "N" if it is not.

Processing:

All three fields within the date must be numeric.

The month field must have one of these values:
01, 02, 03, 04, 05, 06, 07, 08, 09, 10, 11, or 12.

If the month field has value 02, then the day field value must be between 01 and 28 if it is not a leap year (i.e., if the year field value is not evenly divisible by 4).

If the month field has value 02, then the day field value must be between 01 and 29 if it is a leap year (i.e., if the year field value is evenly divisible by 4).

If the month field has value 01, 03, 05, 07, 08, 10, or 12, then the day field value must be between 01 and 31.

If the month field has value 04, 06, 09, or 11, then the day field value must be between 01 and 30.

If all of these editing criteria are met, the switch field value is set to "Y". Otherwise, the switch field value is set to "N".

Use:

To use this program, code these (or similarly named) fields in the WORKING-STORAGE SECTION of your COBOL program:

```
05  VALID-DATE-SW      PIC X.
    88  VALID-DATE              VALUE 'Y'.
          .
          .
          .
05  CURRENT-DATE.
    10  CURRENT-MONTH  PIC XX.
    10  CURRENT-DAY    PIC XX.
    10  CURRENT-YEAR   PIC XX.
```

Then, code this CALL statement in your PROCEDURE DIVISION:

```
CALL 'DATEDIT' USING VALID-DATE-SW
                     CURRENT-DATE.
```

Figure 6-7 An acceptable programmer guide for a subprogram

After you get all of these items, you are ready to start the development of your program. True, you may not use everything you have assembled. And, true, you may discover as you design and implement the program that there are other old programs, COPY members, and subprograms that you can use. But at least you will have a starting point for the development of your program.

Discussion

One of the major benefits that you get from structured design and coding is the ability to reuse design and code taken from old programs, COPY members, and subprograms. The effective use of these items can lead to dramatic improvements in programmer productivity and program quality in your shop. Unfortunately, this is a benefit that only a minority of COBOL shops have taken advantage of.

In our own shop, the effective reuse of structure and code taken from old programs has led to high rates of programmer productivity and program reliability. The use of COPY and subprogram libraries has also helped, but in comparison it has had only a minor effect on our programming effectiveness. Although we have always used structured development methods, we didn't realize at first how important the reuse of old programs was. But once we started to develop all new programs based on design and code taken from old programs, our productivity more than doubled. Then, when we converted from one computer system to a more efficient one, we were able to double our productivity again, primarily because the new system made it easier to reuse code from old programs.

Terminology

model program
model program library
external library
internal library

Objectives

1. Describe the contents and purpose of each of these types of libraries: a model program library, a COPY library, and a subprogram library.

2. Describe an effective procedure for getting related programs, COPY members, and subprograms before you start to develop a new program.

Chapter 7

How to design a program using top-down design

I think the most important technique of an improved method for program development is the technique of top-down design. And I think Paul Noll has made some important contributions to the advancement of this technique. In particular, he has shown how to apply the technique to the development of COBOL programs so the COBOL programs are easy to create and maintain.

Because top-down design is so important, this chapter is divided into four topics. The first topic presents the basic principles of top-down design. The second topic shows you how to develop a structure chart that represents an effective program design. The third topic presents structure charts for typical business programs. And the fourth topic presents some other methods for designing programs along with ideas as to what you might want to try and what you definitely should avoid.

When you finish this chapter, you should be able to design an effective program using a structure chart. Then, as you will see, the structure chart becomes the basis for coding the program, planning the testing of the program, and so on. Since program design as represented by the structure chart is so critical to the effectiveness of any development method, this chapter is the most important one of the book.

Topic 1 The principles of top-down program design

In chapter 3, I introduced you to the edit program. Since I will use this edit program as a basis for illustration in this topic and the next topic, you may want to review this program right now. If so, you can find the program specifications, structure chart, and COBOL code for the program in appendix A.

So you don't have to do so much page flipping, figure 7-1 presents the structure chart for the edit program just as it is in the appendix. As you can see, it requires 24 boxes at five levels.

Some basic terminology

Since I will refer to structure charts throughout the rest of this book, I'd like to present some basic terminology right now. In particular, you should know what terms like *control module* and *subordination* mean. Rest assured, however, that this brief presentation of terminology will be the only one you will encounter in this entire book. Our methods do not require an extensive new vocabulary.

Structure charts and hierarchy charts We call a chart like the one in figure 7-1 a *structure chart*. But some people call them *hierarchy charts*. And in IBM's method of HIPO documentation (Hierarchy plus Input-Process-Output), a hierarchy chart can also be called a *visual table of contents*. Throughout this book, we'll call all such charts *structure charts*, but you should keep in mind that another term for the same thing may be used in your shop. In topic 4 of this chapter, I'll show you a variation of the structure chart, called a tree chart.

Subordinate modules and proper subordination When one module is at a lower level than another module and the modules are connected by lines, the lower-level module is said to be *subordinate* to the higher-level module. Thus, modules 100, 200, 300, and 500 are subordinate to module 000 in figure 7-1. Or, to say it another way, they are *subordinate modules*. Similarly, modules 310, 320, 360, and 400 are subordinate modules, and they are subordinate to module 300.

Subordination refers to all of the modules that are subordinate to another module. So when we speak of *proper subordination*, we mean that the subordinate modules are organized in a way that is acceptable

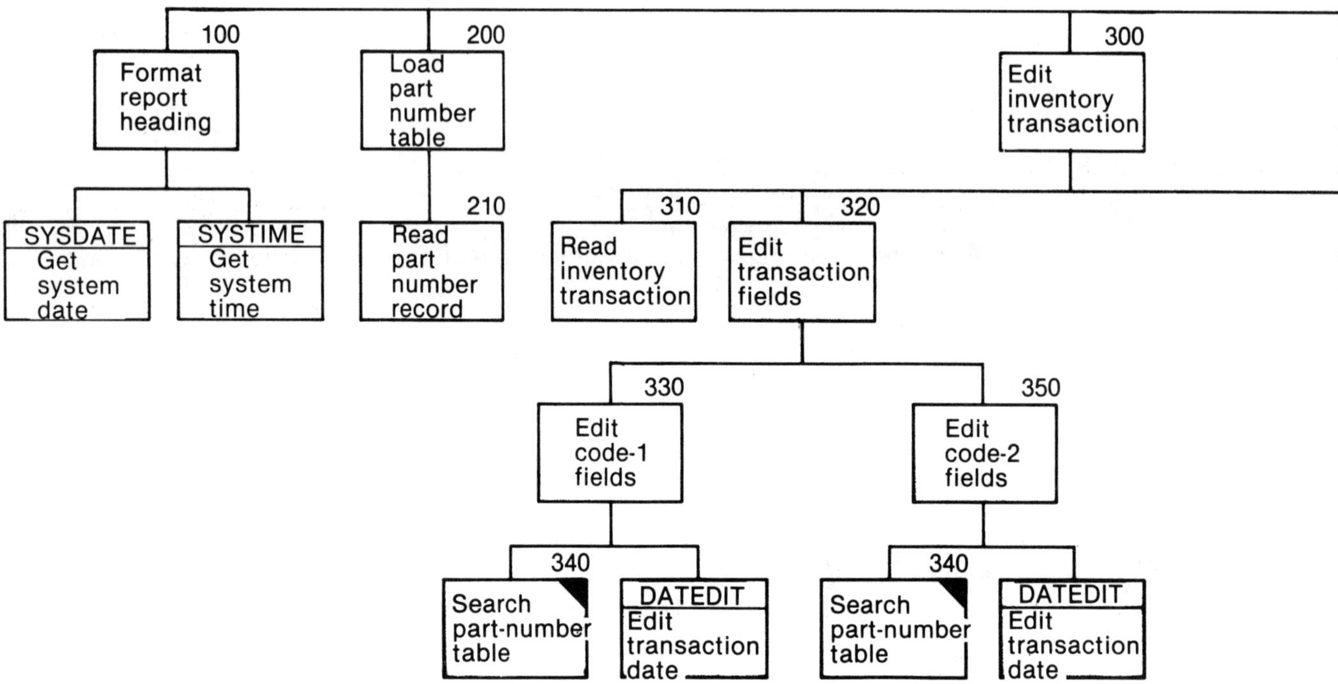

Figure 7-1 The structure chart for the edit program

when using our design method. More about proper subordination in topic 2 of this chapter.

Calling modules and called modules In a structured program, a module is said to *call* a subordinate module when it passes control to it. Thus, the subordinate module is the *called* module and the higher-level module is the *calling* module.

In a COBOL program, using the 1974 COBOL standards, you can call a module using a CALL statement, a PERFORM statement, or a PERFORM-UNTIL statement. All three of these statements are illustrated by the code in figure 7-2, which is the first page of the Procedure Division for the edit program. In module 000, for example, you can see how the PERFORM statement is used to call module 100 and how the PERFORM-UNTIL statement is used to call modules 200 and 300. Then, in module 100, you can see how the CALL statement is used to call the SYSDATE and SYSTIME subprograms.

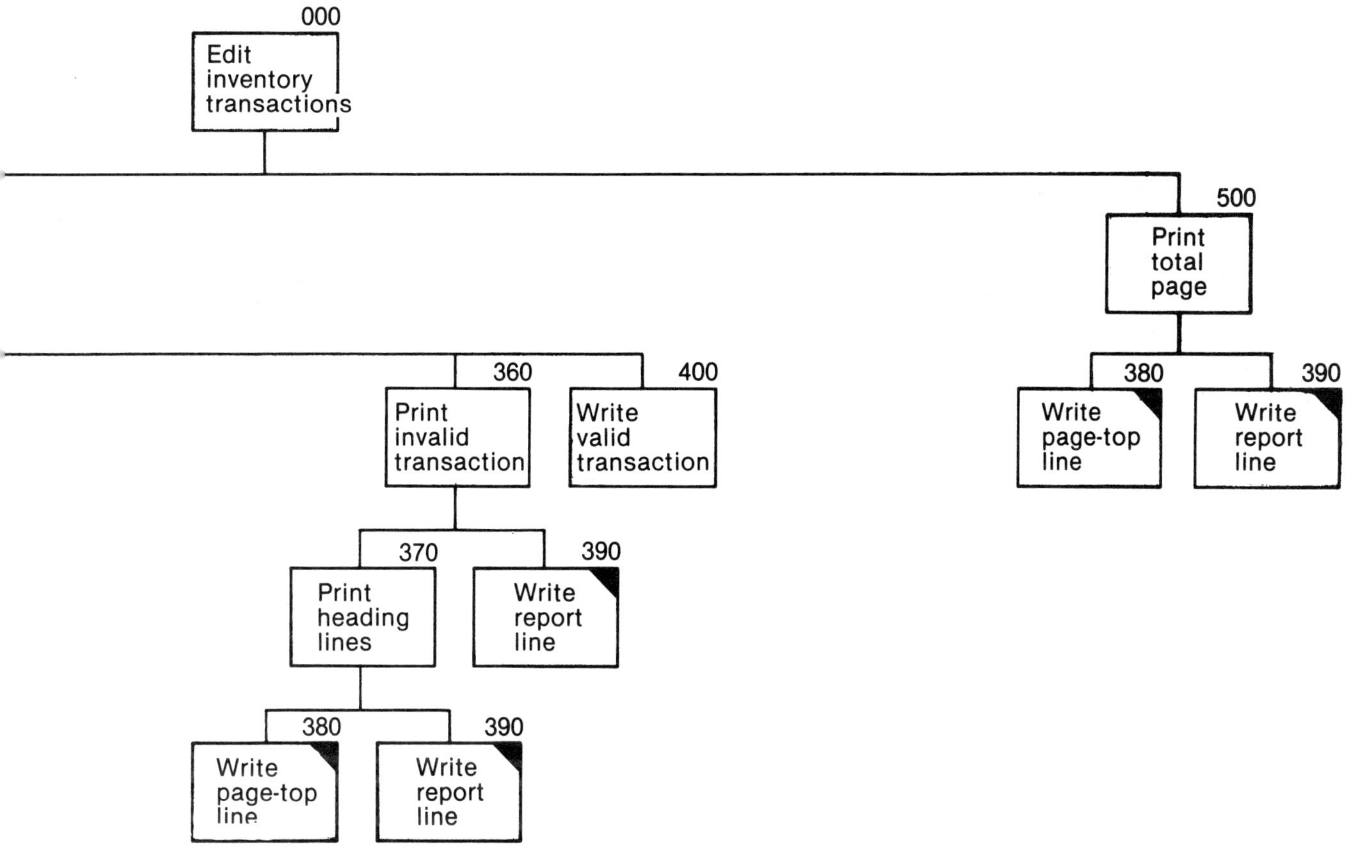

Control modules and work modules If a module calls one or more subordinate modules, it can be called a *control module* because it controls the execution of the modules it calls. Similarly, if a module doesn't call any subordinates, it can be called a *work module* because it should obviously do some work that contributes to the operation of the program. Using this terminology, modules 000, 100, 200, 300, 320, 330, 350, 360, 370, and 500 can be called control modules. And modules 210, 310, 340, 380, and 390 can be called work modules.

If you check the code for module 100 in figure 7-2, you can see that a control module can also do some work. In fact, this module does much of the work of formatting the report heading; it uses the subprograms only to get the date and time. Similarly, a module like module 360 will do much of the work of its named function in addition to controlling the execution of its subordinate modules. On the other hand, modules like module 000 or module 300 do little work since their primary function is to control the execution of their subordinates.

```
 000-EDIT-INVENTORY-TRANS.
*
     OPEN INPUT  PARTNUM
                 INVTRAN
          OUTPUT VINVTRN
                 IINVTLST.
     PERFORM 100-FORMAT-REPORT-HEADING.
     PERFORM 200-LOAD-PART-NUMBER-TABLE
         VARYING PN-TABLE-INDEX FROM 1 BY 1
         UNTIL PART-NUMBER-EOF.
     PERFORM 300-EDIT-INVENTORY-TRAN
         UNTIL TRAN-EOF.
     PERFORM 500-PRINT-TOTAL-PAGE.
     CLOSE PARTNUM
           INVTRAN
           VINVTRN
           IINVTLST.
     STOP RUN.
*
 100-FORMAT-REPORT-HEADING.
*
     CALL 'SYSDATE' USING TODAYS-DATE.
     MOVE TODAYS-DATE    TO HDG1-DATE.
     MOVE COMPANY-NAME   TO HDG1-COMPANY-NAME.
     CALL 'SYSTIME' USING   HDG2-TIME-DATA.
     MOVE 'INV2100'      TO HDG2-REPORT-NUMBER.
     MOVE REPORT-TITLE   TO HDG3-REPORT-TITLE.
*
 200-LOAD-PART-NUMBER-TABLE.
*
     PERFORM 210-READ-PART-NUMBER-RECORD.
     IF NOT PART-NUMBER-EOF
         MOVE PNR-PART-NO TO PN-TABLE-ENTRY (PN-TABLE-INDEX)
     ELSE
         SET PN-TABLE-INDEX DOWN BY 1
         SET PN-ENTRY-COUNT TO PN-TABLE-INDEX.
*
 210-READ-PART-NUMBER-RECORD.
*
     READ PARTNUM
         AT END
             MOVE 'Y' TO PART-NUMBER-EOF-SW.
*
 300-EDIT-INVENTORY-TRAN.
*
     PERFORM 310-READ-INVENTORY-TRAN.
     IF NOT TRAN-EOF
         PERFORM 320-EDIT-TRANSACTION-FIELDS
         IF NOT VALID-TRAN
             PERFORM 360-PRINT-INVALID-TRANSACTION
         ELSE
             PERFORM 400-WRITE-VALID-TRANSACTION.
*
```

Figure 7-2 The first page of the Procedure Division for the edit program

Common modules A *common module* is a module that is called by more than one calling module. In figure 7-1, the upper righthand corner of each common module is shaded. That makes it easy for you to tell that modules 340, 380, and 390 are common modules. As you can see, common modules are shown on the structure chart wherever they are needed. So module 340 appears in two places, and module 390 appears in three places. Wherever a common module appears, though, it has the same module number and name.

Subprogram modules When a module of a program is to be implemented in the form of a subprogram, it is called a *subprogram module*. Using our design technique, these modules are identified by a stripe at the top of the module that gives the actual subprogram name. In figure 7-1, then, the structure chart uses three subprograms named SYSDATE, SYSTIME, and DATEDIT. Notice that subprogram modules aren't numbered.

Legs of a structure chart The term leg (or a *leg of a chart*) is just programmer jargon that helps you talk about a chart. A leg is simply a series of connected modules progressing down a chart. Thus, modules 320 through 350 along with the DATEDIT module can be referred to as the edit-transaction-fields leg of the structure chart in figure 7-1. Similarly, the modules starting with module 500 can be referred to as the print-total-page leg of the chart. Practically speaking, a leg is simply a group of connected modules starting with one higher-level module.

The basic principles of program design

So much has been written about the proper design of a program that it's often hard to identify the basic principles of program design. Yes, you want to design the program from the top down, but is that a principle of design? Since you can easily design a poor program from the top down, I don't think it is. What follows, then, are the three principles that we think are essential to an effective program design.

Principle 1: Each module of a program design should represent one and only one function Do the modules in figure 7-1 meet this principle? I think so. "Edit inventory transactions" seems to be one function. "Edit inventory transaction" seems to be one function. "Print total page" is one function. "Write report line" is one function. In fact, every module in the entire chart seems to represent one function.

I don't want to get into the difference between a function and a subfunction right now, because that's not really the point. For instance, any subordinate function could be considered a subfunction, but that doesn't matter. The emphasis for now should be that each module should only do *one* function (or subfunction). If your program designs obey this principle, it will be easier to develop the resulting programs.

What kind of module doesn't represent one function? A module that does "housekeeping chores" or a module that does "termination processing." Usually, if you look at the code for modules like these, they

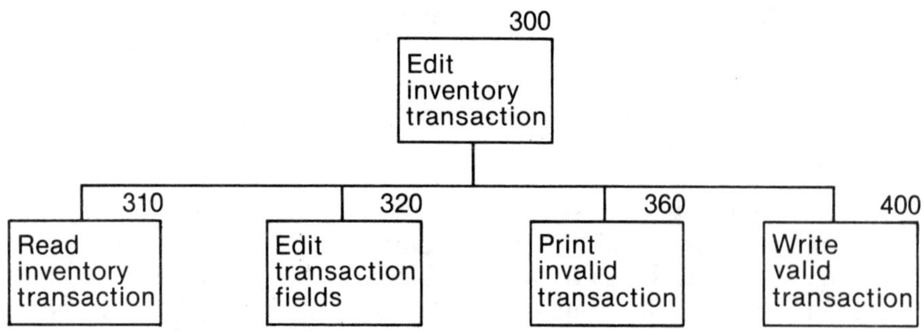

Figure 7-3 The edit-inventory-transaction module and its subordinates showing proper subordination

do several things so they don't represent a single function. Later on, I'll show you other examples of modules that don't represent one function.

Principle 2: The function of a called module must be logically contained in the function of its calling module To illustrate this principle, look at the portion of the structure chart for the edit program shown in figure 7-3. Are the functions of modules 310, 320, 360, and 400 logically contained in the function of module 300? Yes, because in order to edit an inventory transaction, module 300 must read an inventory transaction (module 310), edit the transaction fields (module 320), print a line on the report if the transaction is invalid (module 360), and write a record on the valid transaction file if the transaction is valid (module 400). So the subordinate modules are logically contained in the calling module. And you can refer to this as *proper subordination*.

In contrast, figure 7-4 presents a portion of a structure chart in which the subordinates aren't logically contained in the calling module. Here, the function of module 350 is "read inventory transaction," but this isn't logically a part of the function of the calling module, "edit transaction fields." As a result, this can be referred to as *improper subordination*. Although this may seem to be an extreme case, I can show you examples taken from production programs that are even worse.

If you check all of the modules in figure 7-1 for proper subordination, you can see that this is somewhat arbitrary. For instance, is the function of module 370, "print heading lines," logically contained in the function of its calling module, "print invalid transaction?" It is if we agree that one of the functions of any print module is to provide for page overflow and the printing of headings on the new page. You can think of this as a programming convention. Later on in this chapter, then, I'll present some common conventions for program design.

Principle 3: You must be able to code each module in a single COBOL paragraph Most of the practitioners of structured programming agree on the first two principles that I've presented. But this third principle is one that I credit Paul Noll with developing starting in the mid-1970s. As I

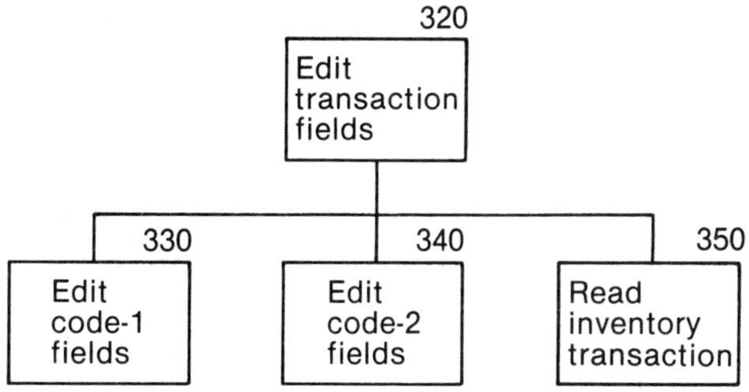

Figure 7-4 A portion of a structure chart showing improper subordination

see it, this principle is critical to an effective design method, but it is a principle that is not widely accepted in COBOL shops.

If you check the COBOL code for the edit program in figure 7-2, you can see that this principle is obeyed in the edit program. As a result, the structure chart is a directory or an index to the code of the program. For each module of the chart, there is one paragraph in the Procedure Division of the program. That's a major reason why programs that are based on our design method are easy to read and maintain.

In topic 4 of this chapter, I'll show you some designs that don't follow this principle. And I'll show you the effect of this on the maintainability of the resulting programs. So if you're not convinced right now that this is a principle that's essential to effective program design, I think you will be after you read topic 4.

Some practical considerations

If you follow the three principles I've just presented when you design programs, you'll improve your productivity and the quality of your programs. From a practical point of view, however, there are several other guidelines you should follow. At this time, then, I'll present some practical considerations you should be aware of.

How to name the modules of a program Can a simple thing like naming modules affect the quality of a program? We strongly believe it can. So we recommend that you name each module with a verb, one or two adjectives, and a noun. Thus, "edit inventory transactions" is an acceptable module name, and "write report line" is an acceptable module name.

To promote consistency in the module names used throughout a COBOL shop, we recommend the adoption of a verb list like the one in figure 7-5. This list, for example, is used in a number of the large shops that Paul does consulting in. Although this list doesn't cover every possibility, it should provide an adequate verb for more than 90 percent of the modules you name.

Input verbs	**Suggested meaning**
Accept	In interactive programs, physically accept the data from one field in a screen or from one full screen.
Get	Obtain an acceptable record or set of records. This can be used in a batch or an interactive program. In a batch program, subordinate modules might read a record, edit a record, and dispose of an invalid record. In an interactive program, subordinate modules might accept the data from a screen, edit it, and accept the operator's indication that the data is okay for processing.
Read	Physically read records from a file or database; count records if required.
Return	Sort language that means to make a record available in an output procedure; count records if required.
Output verbs	
Delete	Two related meanings: (1) Physically remove a record from a file or database; (2) Mark a record to indicate that it is deleted.
Display	In interactive programs, physically display the data in one field of a screen or in one full screen.
Print	Do everything associated with preparing a line to be printed on paper. This may include: (1) calling a module to read one or more related records that contain needed data for the print function, (2) formatting the output line or lines, (3) moving a proper spacing value into a space-control field before a line is printed, (4) calling a module to physically write a line, (5) resetting total fields to zero in preparation for the next group of records, and (6) setting up control or data fields in preparation for the next group of records.
Punch	Punch output cards; count records if required. This verb is becoming obsolete.
Put	Two meanings: (1) Format output record and call a module to physically write it on the output file or display it on an interactive screen; (2) Store an entry in a table; count entries if required.
Release	Sort language that means to make a record available in an input procedure; count records if required.
Rewrite	Physically write an output record in a file or database in the same location on a direct-access device from which the last record was read; count records if required.
Write	Physically write an output record on the output device; count records if required.
Processing verbs	
Accumulate	Develop totals by successive addition of intermediate totals.

Figure 7-5 A verb list (part 1 of 3)

Processing verbs (cont.)

Add	Add a record to a file. Subordinate modules might format the output record and physically write the record.
Apply	Apply a transaction to a record that is being updated or maintained without actually writing, rewriting, or deleting the record on the file. This verb is used in update and maintenance programs.
Calculate	Develop results by using any combination of arithmetic operations.
Change	Modify a record in a file. Subordinate modules might format the changed record and physically write the record.
Clear	In an interactive program, return data fields on a screen to blanks or zeros so the operator can enter the data for the next transaction.
Compare	Compare two fields or records.
Convert	Change something from one form to another.
Create	Develop a record, table, or file.
Determine	Find out; may include arithmetic computation.
Edit	Check one or more fields or records for validity.
Format	Prepare output records to be written, but this shouldn't include a call to a module that actually writes them.
Load	Read and store entries in a table; sort them if necessary.
Maintain	Add records to, change records in, or delete records from a master file based on maintenance transactions as opposed to operational transactions. (See **update**.)
Prepare	This is a general verb that should only be used in control modules. It means to prepare output by doing whatever needs to be done. Subordinate modules might read records, accumulate or calculate new data fields, and prepare the output.
Process	This is a general verb that should only be used in control modules. It means operate on the input fields to do whatever needs to be done. Subordinate modules might read records, accumulate or calculate new data fields, and prepare output. Avoid using this verb whenever you can use a more specific verb.
Produce	This is a general verb that should only be used in control modules. It means produce some output by doing whatever needs to be done. Subordinate modules might read records, accumulate or calculate new data fields, and produce output.

Figure 7-5 A verb list (part 2 of 3)

Processing verbs (cont.)	
Search	Look for in a table or a file.
Sort	Arrange records in a specified order.
Store	Place entries in a table or fields in storage.
Update	The primary meaning is to change records in a master file based on data in an operational transaction as opposed to a maintenance transaction. Sometimes, however, an update function will require adding records to a file or deleting records from a file based on operational data. (See **maintain**.)
Validate	In an interactive program, check the user's sign-on codes to make sure he or she is a valid user of the system.
Verify	In an interactive program, ask the user to give a response that indicates whether or not he or she has sight-verified the data on the screen and is ready to release it for processing.

Figure 7-5 A verb list (part 3 of 3)

When you use this method of naming modules, it helps you design modules that represent one and only one function (principle 1). In contrast, names that don't start with a verb don't specify a function as well. For instance, "transaction processing" is much less specific than "edit inventory transaction" so it's more likely to represent more than one function.

When you name control modules, particularly the higher-level control modules, your names tend to be more general. As a result, "prepare," "produce," and "process" are acceptable verbs in modules like this. As you get to the lower levels of your charts, however, your names should become more specific. And the names for all work modules should be specific.

If you check the suggested meanings in figure 7-5 for the verbs "get," "print," and "put," you can see that these are treated as generalized input and output verbs. As a result, they are allowed to mean more than their names may imply. For instance, we use the verb "print" to mean "do everything associated with preparing a line to be printed on paper." If you check the structure chart and code for the edit program, you can see that we used the verb "print" as suggested by the meaning in the verb list. Because the use of generalized input and output verbs helps you design effective programs, we suggest that you use verbs like this in your programs. In the next topic, you'll see more examples of the use of these verbs.

How to number the modules of a program Can a simple thing like numbering the modules of a program affect the quality of a program?

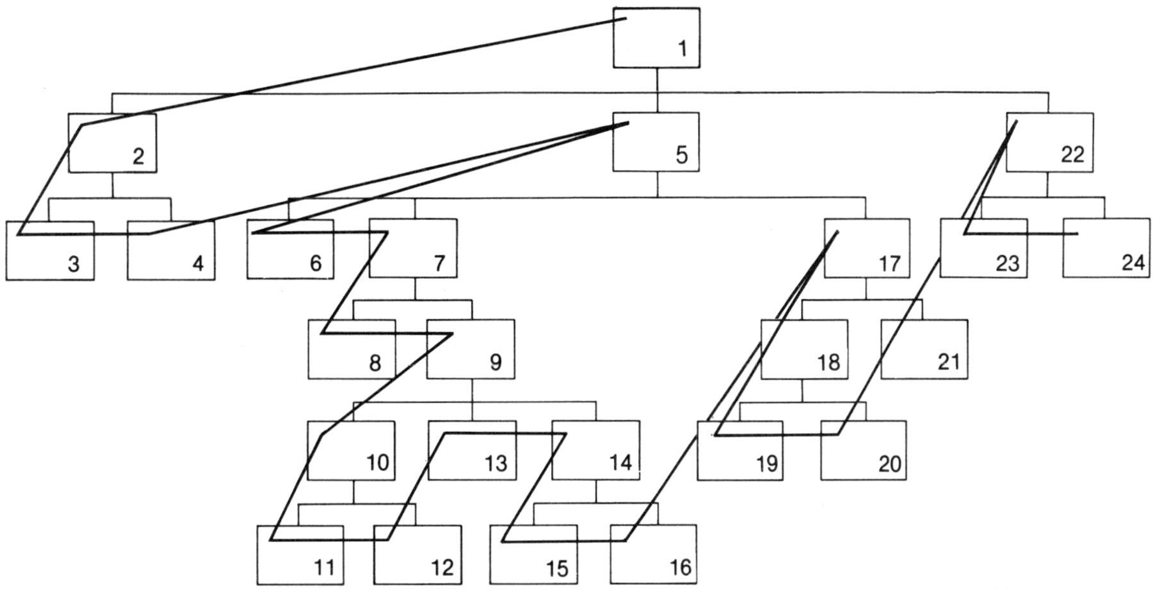

Figure 7-6 Numbering down the legs of a structure chart so the called COBOL paragraphs will follow the calling paragraphs in the COBOL listing

Yes, if you use the numbers as a guide to the sequence of the paragraphs in the COBOL program. If you compare the code in figure 7-2 with the structure chart in figure 7-1, you can see that the module number becomes a part of the paragraph name and that the paragraphs are in the same sequence as the module numbers. As a result, how you number the modules on the structure chart can have an effect on the readability of the program.

Figure 7-6 schematically illustrates our general recommendation for numbering the modules of a program. You start with the top-level module and you number down the legs of the chart on a left-to-right basis. That way, most of the called paragraphs in a COBOL program will be found immediately following the calling paragraph. This reduces the amount of page flipping you have to do when you read a program and it makes it easier to read a program listing from the top down.

So you can add modules to a completed structure chart without renumbering, we recommend that you leave gaps in the numbers. Thus, you can add module 125 between modules 120 and 130 if the need arises. With this in mind, we give the level-0 module the number 000 or 0000, depending on the expected size of the program (for a large program, start with 0000). Then, we number the level-1 modules with multiples of 100 or 1000, depending on whether we started with 000 or 0000. After this, all modules are numbered down the legs by tens or 100s, again depending on the size of the program.

This numbering system is flexible, so you can adapt it to the type of program you're writing. For instance, figure 7-7 shows another set of numbers for the edit program. Here, the programmer used multiples of

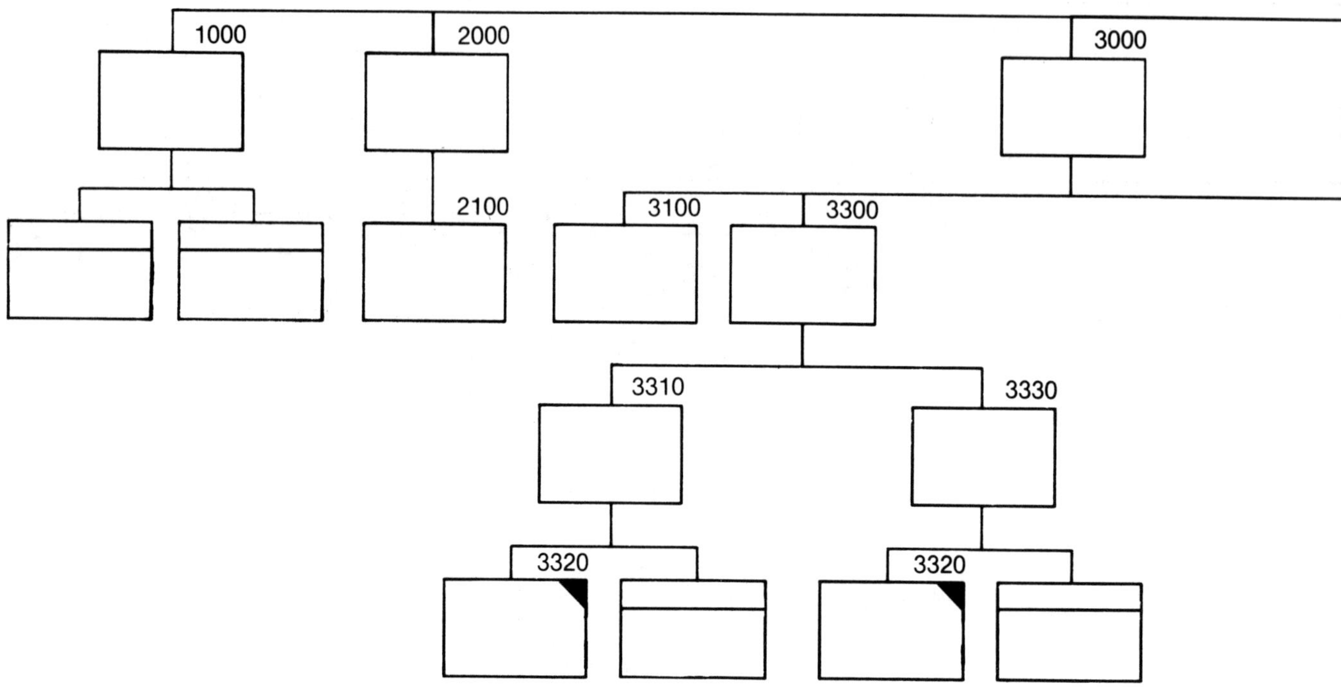

Figure 7-7 An alternate numbering scheme for the edit program

1000 in the top two levels of the chart, multiples of 100 at the third level, and multiples of tens at the fourth and fifth levels. Note, however, that the sequence of the modules is still the same as in figure 7-1.

To some extent, of course, the sequence of numbering is arbitrary. For instance, in the 3500 leg in figure 7-7, do you number sideways or down when you get to 3510. At these lower levels, it really doesn't matter. And this is true to a degree throughout the structure chart. As long as the modules are numbered in some sort of top-down sequence, you will be able to develop an effective COBOL program from the chart.

Note that the numbers do *not* indicate at what level a module can be found. This means that changes can be made to the structure chart without changing module numbers. In contrast, when more complex numbering systems are used, a change to the structure chart usually means a change to the module number, which in turn means a change to the module documentation, which in turn means a change in the COBOL source code.

For instance, some numbering systems use a number like 1.2.4 to indicate the fourth block under block number 1.2, which is the second

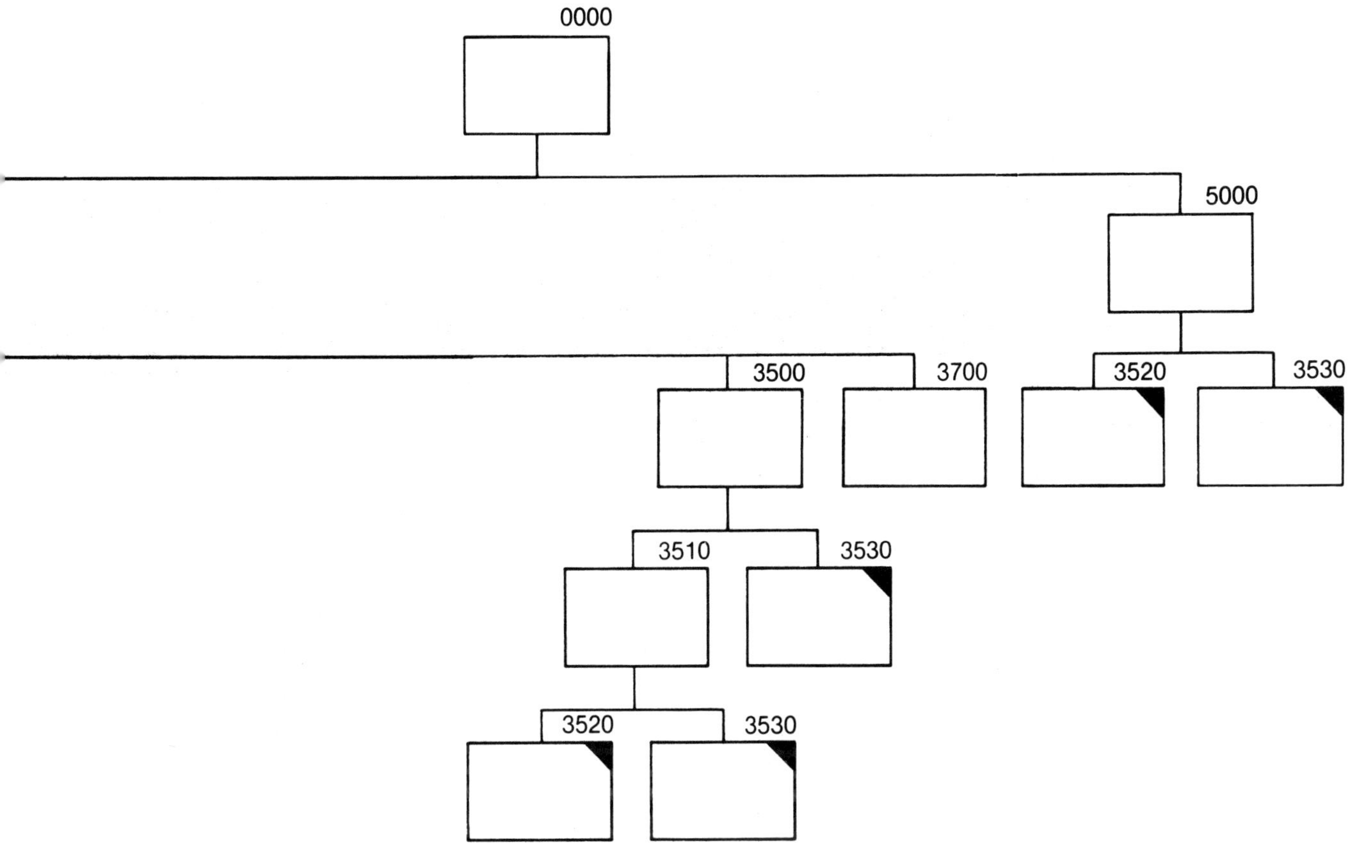

block under block number 1.0. If the chart is changed so block 1.2.4 should be the first block under block 3.1, its number must be changed to 3.1.1. As a result, you can easily become a slave to a numbering system like this.

Numbering by hundreds and tens makes it easy for you to add blocks to a structure chart after you think it's complete. For example, if you must add a subordinate to module 320 in figure 7-1, you can number it 355 without having to change any other module number. Likewise, if you need two subordinate modules for module 330, you can logically number them 341 and 342 without affecting the rest of the structure chart.

Incidentally, in some shops the numbers are placed inside the blocks themselves, in the lower righthand corner. However, by placing them outside the boxes as in figure 7-1, you have more room for the module description and the numbers are easier to locate.

Why you should use one I/O module for each READ or WRITE statement for a file In order to limit the number of READ and WRITE statements for each file, the READ and WRITE statements must be coded in separate read and write modules. These modules can then be performed whenever a record needs to be read or written. By isolating the READ and WRITE statements in this way, you end up with a more efficient program and one that is easy to modify.

In the structure chart in figure 7-1, for example, you can see that there is one I/O module for each READ and WRITE statement required by the program. If you check the code for these modules, you can see that the primary code in each I/O module is the READ or WRITE statement itself. In addition, you can count the number of records read or written in an I/O module. And, when you write a line on a printer, you can also increase the count of the number of lines on the page by adding the space-control field to the line-count field. If you check the verb list in figure 7-5, you can see that we suggest that you allow these counting operations in I/O modules. But that's all.

For the most part, you should only have one READ or one WRITE statement for each file. But this isn't always possible. For instance, COBOL print files usually require one WRITE statement that skips to the top of a page as well as one WRITE statement that spaces one or more lines based on the value in a space-control field. As a result, each print file will usually require two WRITE statements. Similarly, files with variable-length records often require several WRITE statements, one for each record size. If, for example, a file consists of 50-, 100-, and 200-byte records, the file will require three different WRITE statements.

Although there are a couple of other exceptions, such as when you use dynamic access of indexed files or reads with the intent to update in interactive programs, don't let the exceptions obscure the point. You should generally have only one READ or WRITE statement for each file. And each statement should be coded in its own I/O module. By so doing, your program will run more efficiently and you can easily do things like counting the number of records read or written. The alternative in a large program is to have several READ and WRITE statements for each file dispersed throughout the program.

How common modules should be shown on the structure chart To show that a module is used in more than one place in a chart, we recommend that you shade the upper righthand corners of these modules. As I mentioned before, you use the same module name and number for a common module and you repeat it wherever it is needed on the chart. Of course, you can indicate common modules in other ways, and the graphic convention that you use isn't important. For example, you could put an asterisk after the module number. We think, however, that the shaded corner is an effective graphic convention.

How subprograms should be shown on the structure chart To distinguish subprograms from modules that have to be coded in COBOL, we use a stripe at the top of subprogram modules. In this stripe, we give the actual name of the subprogram to be used so the programmer can use this name in his CALL statement when he codes the program. Below the

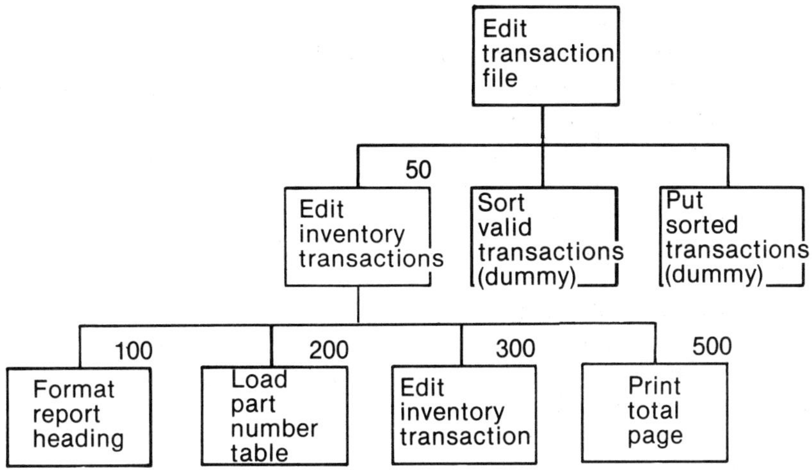

Figure 7-8 A structure chart for the edit program with an internal sort

stripe, we name the module just as we would name any other module in the chart using one verb, one or two adjectives, and a noun. You can see this convention used in the chart in figure 7-1.

How sort modules should be shown on the structure chart When you use a SORT statement in a COBOL program, it actually calls three subordinates: (1) the input procedure or USING module, (2) the sort module, and (3) the output procedure or GIVING module. As a result, if you use COBOL sorts in your shop, we recommend that you show these modules in your program design as illustrated in figure 7-8. Here, after the edit program edits the inventory transactions, it sorts the valid transactions in item-number sequence so they can be processed by a sequential update program.

In this case, module 000 contains the SORT statement, and module 50 is the top-level module of the input procedure, which is equivalent to module 000 in figure 7-1. (I numbered it 50 so the numbers for all of the other modules of the edit program could stay the same.) Then, the next level-1 modules are the sort module and the GIVING module. Since both of these modules are part of the sort program that is called by the SORT statement, they are marked "dummy" to show that they don't have to be coded in COBOL. On the other hand, if the SORT statement used an output procedure, the put-transaction-file module would be the top-level module of the output procedure. Then, it wouldn't be a dummy module so it would be numbered appropriately.

As you go through this book, you will see in more detail how you design and code a program with an internal sort. My point for now is to think of a SORT statement as a call to three subordinate modules. So you should show these modules on the structure chart. When you do, your program design is complete and logical.

Why declarative modules don't have much effect on program design Do you still use DECLARATIVE sections in your programs? For the most part, I think it's a dying practice. But if you do, you may wonder where these modules should be shown in your program design. Or, if they should be shown in your program design at all.

In general, you can use DECLARATIVES for three types of functions: (1) error processing functions for an I/O operation, (2) label processing functions for an I/O file, and (3) report writing functions that are not provided for by Report Writer. If you were to place these functions on your structure chart, you would have to show error-processing functions as subordinate to all modules that contain I/O statements for the named file. Similarly, you would have to show label-processing functions as subordinate to the modules that contain OPEN or CLOSE statements for the named file. And you would have to show report-writing functions as subordinate to the modules that contain the Report Writer verbs.

Since a declarative module is automatically called by the related I/O statement, it is correct to think of the statement itself as the calling statement. Furthermore, if you don't use GOTOs in your declarative modules, control is automatically returned to the next statement following the I/O statement once the declarative modules have been executed. So this is consistent with the principles of structured programming.

If you decide to show these modules on your charts, you can do so as shown in the chart in figure 7-9. This chart indicates that declarative modules are used for error processing on the part-number file. Since the declarative module can be called by the OPEN, CLOSE, or READ statement for this file, it is shown as a common module at two levels in the chart.

When you number a declarative module on a structure chart, we recommend that you give it a sequential number just as you would any other module. Then, because you know this module will actually be coded in the DECLARATIVES section of the program, we suggest that you give the number a prefix of D so it's obvious that it's a declarative.

Although you can show declarative modules on the structure chart as in figure 7-9, we think this is of questionable value. After all, label-processing and error-processing are normally transparent to the user. And their routines should be standard. So you don't gain much, if anything, by showing these modules on your structure charts. And you do take the chance of cluttering up your charts so much that they are difficult to read.

If there is a time to show a declarative module, it's in the case of report-writing functions since they do reflect user requirements. But most of the Report Writer processing is transparent to the programmer so it doesn't seem to matter much whether or not you show these subordinate functions. In fact, the programmer isn't likely to discover that he needs a declarative module until he actually codes the program. So again it seems that whether or not you show the declarative modules on your chart, it will have only a trivial effect on your resulting program.

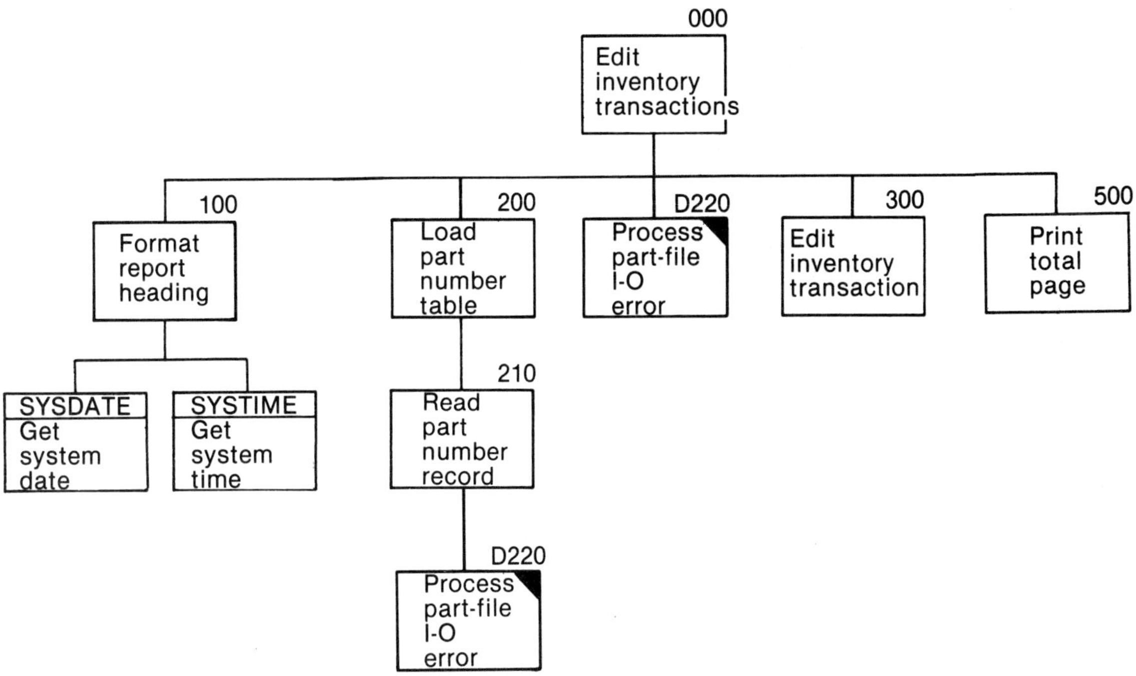

Figure 7-9 A structure chart for the edit program with declarative processing for I/O errors related to the part-number file

Discussion

This topic is designed to give you some preliminary terminology, principles, and guidelines for designing programs from the top down using structure charts. In the next topic, then, you'll learn how to design a program.

Perhaps the most critical principle that you should remember as you go through the next topic is that you must be able to code each module of a program as a single COBOL paragraph. If you can do this, you will improve your productivity dramatically at the same time that you improve the quality of your programs. This, perhaps more than anything else, is what distinguishes the design method we recommend from other methodologies.

Terminology

structure chart
hierarchy chart
visual table of contents
subordinate
subordinate module

subordination
proper subordination
called module
calling module
control module
work module
common module
subprogram module
leg of a chart
improper subordination

Objectives

1. List the three principles of program design.
2. Explain how you should name the modules of a structure chart.
3. Explain how you should number the modules of a structure chart.

Topic 2 How to design a program using a structure chart

Now that you know the basic principles of program design, I'd like to show you how to develop an acceptable program design using a structure chart. In this topic, then, I'll first give you a step by step example of program design. After that I'll present a basic procedure for developing structure charts, give you a checklist for analyzing your program designs, and present some practical considerations that you should be aware of.

By the time you complete this topic, you should understand the design process. Then, after you complete topic 3, you should be able to design effective structure charts of your own.

An example of top-down program design

To illustrate the thought processes that go into program design, I'll show you how I created the structure chart for the edit program.

The first two levels After studying the program specifications, I began by drawing the two modules shown in figure 7-10. These modules can be referred to as the level-0 module and the primary level-1 module of the program. Here, the level-0 module represents the entire program so the name I gave it, "edit inventory transactions," reflects this. I considered names like "edit inventory file" and "verify inventory transactions," but I ruled them out because you don't really edit the file, you edit the records, and because the program specifications refer to "editing," not "verifying."

After I completed the top-level module, I tried to identify the one functional module that will be performed repeatedly during the execution of the program. In figure 7-10, this is the edit-inventory-transaction module. When the program is coded, this module will be performed until all transactions have been read and processed. In other words, the top-level module represents the processing for the entire program. The primary level-1 module represents the processing for one input record or one set of input records.

After I decided on this primary level-1 module, I asked myself what functions needed to be performed before the program could repeatedly process this primary module. Then, I asked myself what modules needed to be performed after the program had finished executing the primary module. In figure 7-11, you can see my answers. The format-report-

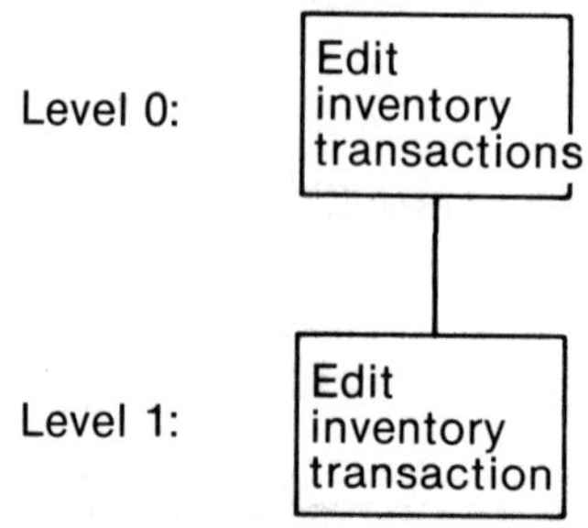

Figure 7-10 The start of the structure chart for the edit program

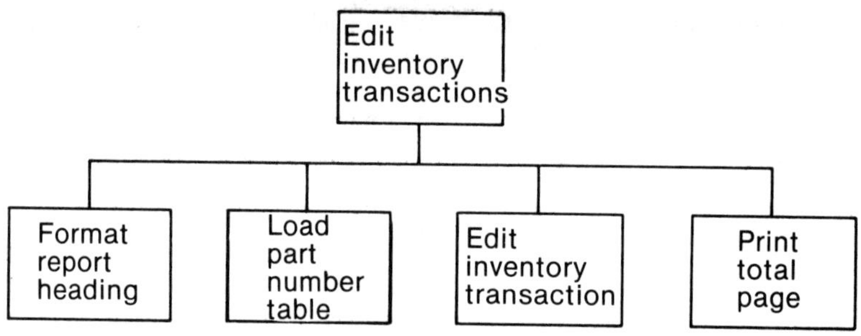

Figure 7-11 The first two levels of the structure chart for the edit program

heading and load-part-number-table modules need to be performed before the processing of the primary module; the print-total-page module needs to be performed after.

As you will see in topic 3, you can design the top levels of almost all business programs (if not all of them) using this same type of reasoning. Since business processing is repetitive, the top-level module of a business program performs the primary module at the next level until all sets of transactions have been processed. Thus, the first two levels of a program are relatively easy to design.

The format-report-heading leg Figure 7-12 shows the development of the format-report-heading leg of the program. To format a report heading, you normally move appropriate data into the fields of the heading lines. In this case, I found out that two subprograms were available when I checked the subprogram library before I started to design this program: one subprogram gets the current date from the system; the other one gets the current time. So I used these subprograms when I designed this leg of the program.

Since we use a leg like this whenever we format a standard report heading, I didn't have to think much to design this leg of the program. In

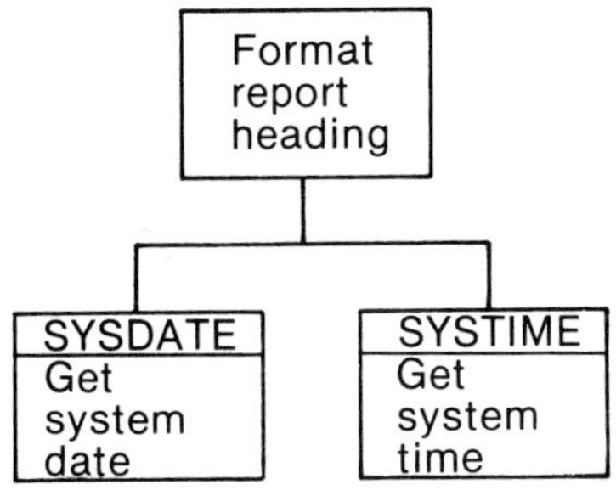

Figure 7-12 The development of the format-report-heading leg of the edit program

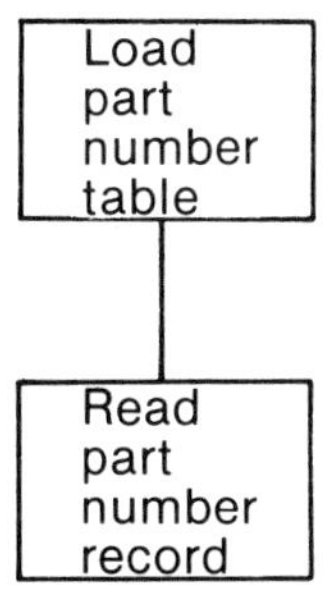

Figure 7-13 The development of the load-part-number-table leg of the edit program

fact, I could have taken this portion of the design from any program in our shop that uses a standard report heading. They're all done the same way.

The load-part-number-table leg Figure 7-13 shows the development of the load-part-number-table leg. To design it, I first asked myself how the level-1 module, "load part number table," was going to be called from the top-level module, by a PERFORM or a PERFORM-UNTIL statement. Since this module needs to read all of the records in a file and store the data from the records in a table, I decided it had to be a PERFORM-UNTIL. With that in mind, I decided that I could code the module in a single COBOL paragraph so no further subordination was required.

On the other hand, this leg did require a READ statement, and our shop standard is to put each READ statement in a separate I/O module. So that's what you see in figure 7-13. Although you don't really require a separate READ module in a case like this since this is the only portion of the program that will require a read of this file, it's best to follow this standard anyway. Then, if you decide later that you want to count the number of entries in the table, you've got a good module to do it in. Also, you can spot all of the I/O operations required by the program just by looking at the structure chart.

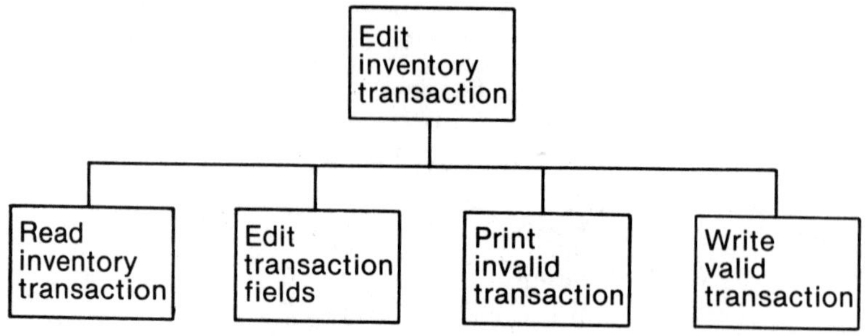

Figure 7-14 The start of the development of the edit-inventory-transaction leg of the edit program

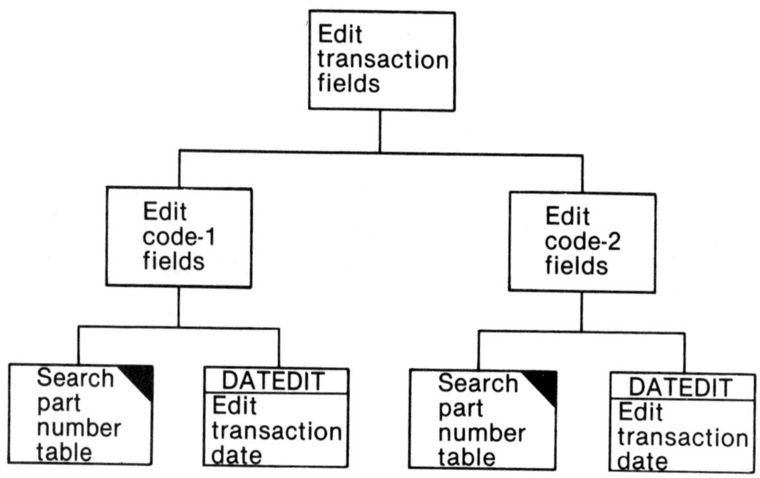

Figure 7-15 The development of the edit-transaction-fields leg of the edit program

The edit-inventory-transaction leg To edit a single transaction, you need to do four things: (1) read a transaction record, (2) edit the fields in the record, (3) print a line on the invalid transaction listing if the record is invalid, and (4) write a record in the valid transaction file if the record is valid. So those are the four modules I started with when I designed this leg of the program as shown in figure 7-14. There shouldn't be much room for disagreement here.

Since read and write modules are always work modules, you can't develop these modules down any further. But the edit-transaction-fields module and the print-invalid-transaction-line module require subordinates. In effect, this means that there are now two new legs to develop.

The edit-transaction-fields leg Figure 7-15 shows the complete development for this leg. I started by saying to myself that since this

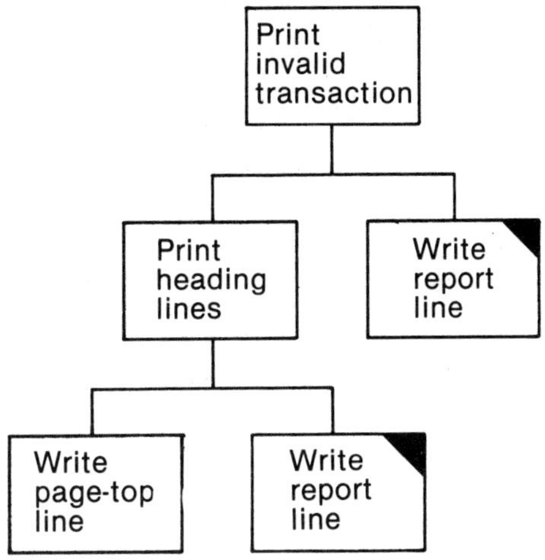

Figure 7-16 The development of the print-invalid-transaction leg of the edit program

program edits two types of transactions, there should be one module for one type of transaction and one module for the other. In figure 7-15, I refer to the fields in these two types of transactions as code-1 fields and code-2 fields, because the transaction types are identified by a 1 code and a 2 code. But I could have referred to them as receipt fields and issue fields or something like that, because that is what the transactions represent.

To edit the code-1 fields, I realized I needed to search the part-number table to find out whether the part-number field was valid. Also, I had checked the subprogram library before I started this program, so I knew that a subprogram for editing dates was available to me. In figure 7-15, then, I show two subordinates to the edit-code-1-fields module. Of course, when I started to develop the subordinates for the edit-code-2-fields module, I realized that it required the same subordinates so that's what you see in figure 7-15.

Incidentally, Paul says that you should always put a search-table function in its own module just as you put a READ or WRITE function in its own module. Since these modules are often called by more than one module in a program, this makes your programs easier to code and modify. And this is certainly the case for the edit program. If, at some future date, the program specifications are changed so the program edits a third type of transaction, the search function can easily be called by another control module.

The print-invalid-transaction leg Figure 7-16 shows the development of this leg of the edit program. In our shop, the print verb means to do everything required to print a line on a report or other document. This includes detecting when page overflow is required and printing headings on the next page of the report. So, to start, the print-invalid-transaction

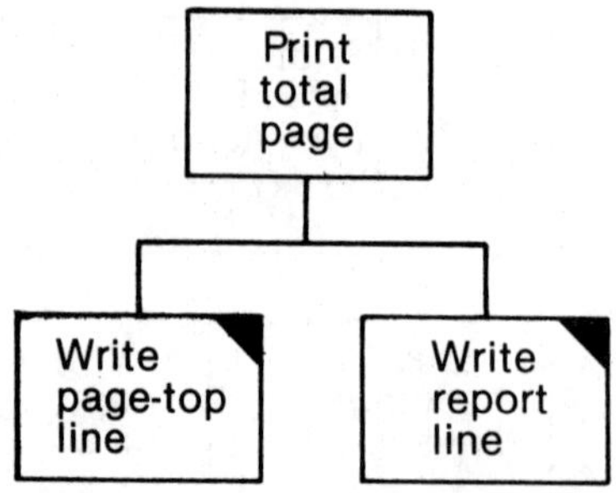

Figure 7-17 The development of the print-total-page leg of the edit program

module requires a subordinate that will print the headings when page overflow takes place. In addition, to print an invalid transaction line, the module requires a WRITE statement. But since each WRITE statement should have its own functional module, this means the print-invalid-transaction module requires a subordinate module that will actually write a line on the listing.

Going down a level, to print the report headings requires two subordinates, both of them for WRITE statements that require their own functional modules. First, a module is needed that will write a line at the top of a page. This will be used to write the first heading line on each page. Second, a module is needed to write all other report lines. But since this module already exists in this leg in the level above it, it becomes a common module. Later on, you'll see that the write-page-top-line module is a common module too, but you don't know this at this stage of the design.

The print-total-page leg Figure 7-17 shows the development of this leg of the edit program. Can you tell why its subordinates are different than those of the print-invalid-transaction module? After all, both modules must be able to skip to the top of the next page, print headings, and then print detail lines. So check the print chart in appendix A and see if you can explain the difference.

The answer is that the heading lines on the total page are somewhat different than those on the other pages of the listing. Specifically, the total-page heading is a 3-line heading, while the other pages require a 5-line heading. As a result, you can't use one common module for printing both headings without complicating the code in the module.

With this in mind, I decided to treat the printing of the total page as an unrelated function; that is, to code it from scratch. Then, the only subordinates that the print-total-page module needs are the modules (1) for writing a line at the top of a page and (2) for writing any other line. Since both of these modules are already available in the print-invalid-transaction leg of the program, the modules I show in figure 7-17 are common modules. I also mark the write-page-top-line module in the print-invalid-transaction leg as a common module at this time.

A basic procedure for developing structure charts

I hope you have followed the thought processes for designing the edit program that I just presented. If you haven't, you may want to study the structure chart and COBOL code in appendix A until you get a better idea of how the program works. I know I had trouble with these design concepts when Paul Noll first introduced me to structured programming. But now, the concepts and techniques seem far more natural to me than those we used in the days of GOTO programming.

In any event, I'd now like to give you a basic procedure for developing structure charts. In general, you design a program using a four-step procedure like this:

1. Create a rough draft of the structure chart for the program design using the thought processes I just illustrated.

2. Analyze the structure chart for the design to see whether you can improve it, and revise it if necessary.

3. Number the modules on the rough draft of the structure chart.

4. Redraw the structure chart in final form.

Although these steps should be easy to follow, let me make some brief comments about each of them.

Step 1: Create a rough draft of the structure chart The question here is, how rough is rough? To give you some idea, look at the rough draft in figure 7-18. That's about how my first draft of a structure chart usually looks. Notice that I don't even bother to use a template to make the boxes or draw the lines on my chart. And if the program is complicated, the chart might even be messier. Since the rough draft is simply one of your working papers, you do it as neatly or as messy as seems practical to you. No, the charts don't spring completely to your mind so you can draw them neatly the first time.

Step 2: Analyze and revise the rough draft This is an important step, because the first design of almost any program can be improved by some careful analysis. In a moment, then, I'll give you some detailed ideas for analyzing a program's design. If you decide to make changes, you simply modify your rough draft. So the more modifications you make, the messier it gets. At some point, it may get so messy that you need to start another rough draft. But you'll develop your own guidelines for this.

Step 3: Number the modules of the rough draft Once you're sure that your design is solid, you number the modules in the structure chart. In topic 1, I showed you how to number the modules of a chart. So this step is trivial.

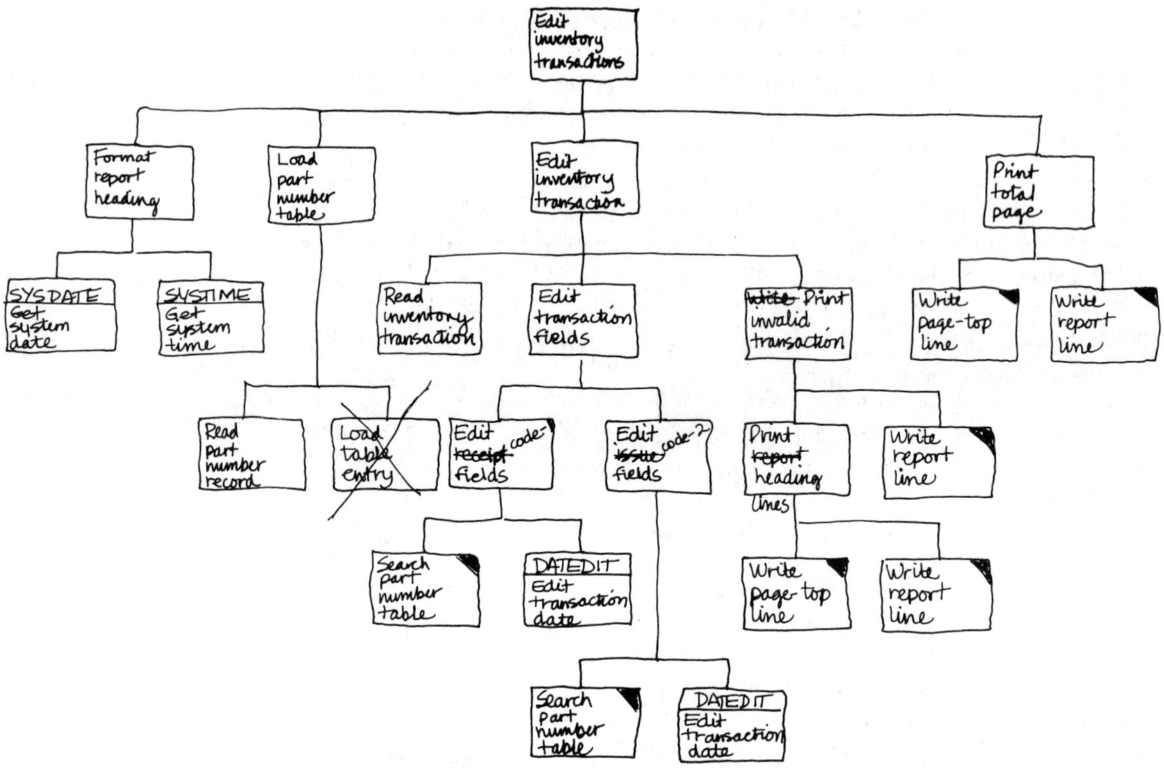

Figure 7-18 A rough draft of the structure chart of the edit program

Step 4: Redraw the rough draft in final form This is simply a time-consuming clerical step. If your rough draft isn't too messy and you have clerical help available to you, you can delegate this step. Otherwise, you have to do it yourself. This time, of course, you use a programming template so your lines are straight and your boxes are rectangular.

In our shop, one of our programmers wrote a program that allows you to enter a chart into the system after you've made a rough draft of it. Then, you can print the final chart on the printer. And if you discover that you need to make changes to the chart as you implement the program, you can quickly enter the changes and reprint a refined chart.

A checklist for analyzing a program's design

As I said, step 2, the analysis and revision step, is a critical one, because almost all first attempts at a design can be improved. At this time, then, I would like to give you a checklist of things to look for during your analysis.

Is the structure chart complete? Your first question after you've completed the rough draft of the design for a program should be this:

Does the structure chart provide for all functions that must be done by the program? To answer this question, you should review the program specifications to make sure you've provided for everything. But when a structure chart consists of several dozen modules or more, this can be a difficult question to answer.

The way to approach this question is one level at a time, from the top down. In figure 7-1, for example, you should first ask whether the four level-1 modules do everything implied by their boss, module 000. In other words, does editing the inventory transactions consist only of formatting the report headings (module 100), loading the part-number table (module 200), editing the individual transactions (module 300), and printing the total page (module 500)? Or should there be other level-1 functions (modules)? In my opinion, level 1 is complete as shown.

After you have analyzed one level for completeness, you continue with the next level down. For instance, does module 210 represent every subordinate function that module 200 requires? Do modules 310, 320, 360, and 400 provide for everything module 300 requires? And so on.

Since this analysis seems to give a lot of people trouble, Paul tells his students to jot down what they mean by a certain module description on a piece of scratch paper. In figure 7-1, for example, what does load part-number table (module 200) mean to you? To me it means (1) reading the table records and (2) loading the entries taken from the records into a working-storage table. As a result, the only subordinate that module 200 seems to need is the I/O module for reading the records in the part-number file. But if you have doubts about how you're going to code module 200, you may prefer to design its subordinates as shown in alternative 1 of figure 7-19. And if the program required a binary search of the table (which it doesn't), you would also include sorting the table in your list of subordinate modules as shown in alternative 2 of figure 7-19.

The point is, you develop a leg of a program by creating the subordinate modules you feel are required by a higher-level function. True, you may find out later that you don't need some of the subordinate modules. But it's easier to drop them out when you implement a program than it is to add new modules.

With that in mind, look again at the structure chart in figure 7-1 and tell me if you think the design for the print-invalid-transaction leg is complete? Before you can print a line on a listing, you first have to arrange the fields in the print area, don't you? So maybe this leg of the program should be shown as in figure 7-20. Here, the format-transaction-line module is used to arrange the transaction fields for printing.

As we see it, the design in figure 7-20 is a good one for this print leg of the program. In fact, it is more complete than the design in figure 7-1, and it will lead to COBOL code that is easy to read and modify. However, we know from experience that the format module will consist of only one MOVE statement for each field required in the transaction line. So these statements can easily be coded in the print-invalid-transaction module itself. That's why we don't normally use a format module as a subordinate for a print module. But it's okay to use one. And

Alternative 1

Alternative 2

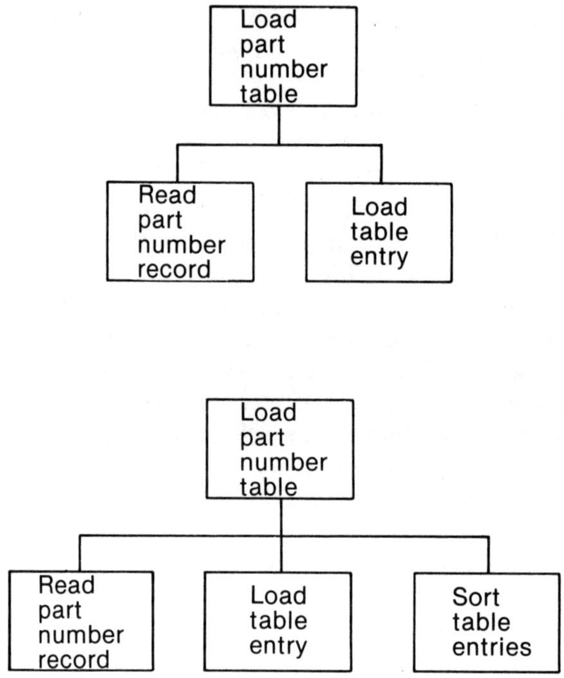

Figure 7-19 Two other ways to develop the load-part-number-table leg of the edit program

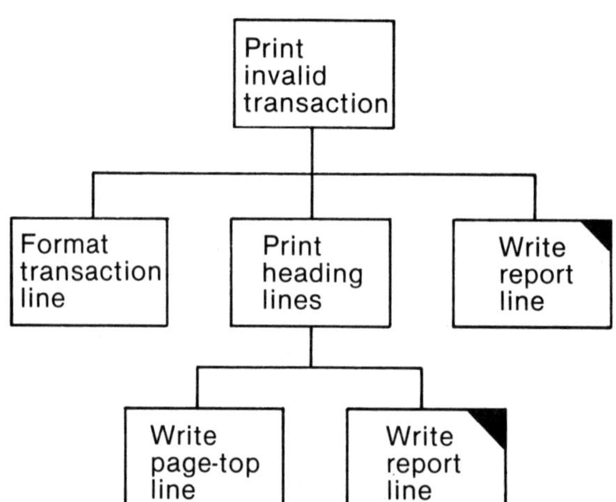

Figure 7-20 Another way to develop the print-invalid-transaction leg of the edit program

if the formatting is complex or extensive, we recommend that you use a format module.

In any event, you can use this scratch-pad idea whenever you have doubts about completeness. It is particularly useful when reviewing a structure chart with another person. As questions arise, you can list the subordinate functions that you think a module requires. Then, you can discuss the items on the list to determine (1) whether all functions are accounted for and (2) whether all functions contribute to the objective of the calling module. If you decide that all functions are not accounted for, you simply add the required modules and continue your analysis.

When you do a scratch-pad analysis, you will often discover problems with the verbs used in module descriptions. The major problem seems to be verbs that are too general. For example, it's tempting to name a module "process transaction data" when you're not quite sure what it's going to do. What you really mean is that the module should do everything that is required—but you don't know what that is—or that the module should do everything that isn't done by other modules at that level. In either case, you probably won't be able to list the functions required by the module. Only after you change the module description so it has a more precise meaning will you be able to continue your analysis.

Does each module name represent one function? Perhaps you've noticed my emphasis on function as I described how structure charts are created. This, of course, relates to the first principle of program design. Each module must represent one and only one program function.

You can be sure your modules are functional if you can describe them in a single imperative sentence such as "print the heading lines," "update the records in the master file," or "search the customer table." This, of course, is what you do when you name the module by using one verb, one or two adjectives, and an object. If you can't describe your modules in this way, they probably aren't functional and your program design is probably faulty.

One type of module that isn't functional is a module that refers to time. Thus, "perform end-of-file processing" isn't a functional description. The elements in a module like this are only related by the fact that they are done *after* all records have been processed. Similarly, "do housekeeping" or "perform initialization" modules aren't functional. Their elements are only related because they are done *before* the main processing routines. They too are related by time instead of by function.

Another type of module description to watch out for is one that refers to a class of data. Traditionally, for example, programs have contained "process input data" modules. The elements in these modules were only related insofar as they operated upon the same type of data (input data). In other words, these modules were simply a conglomeration of all the functions that had to do with any part of the input data. So watch out for modules built around classes of data—they aren't likely to be functional.

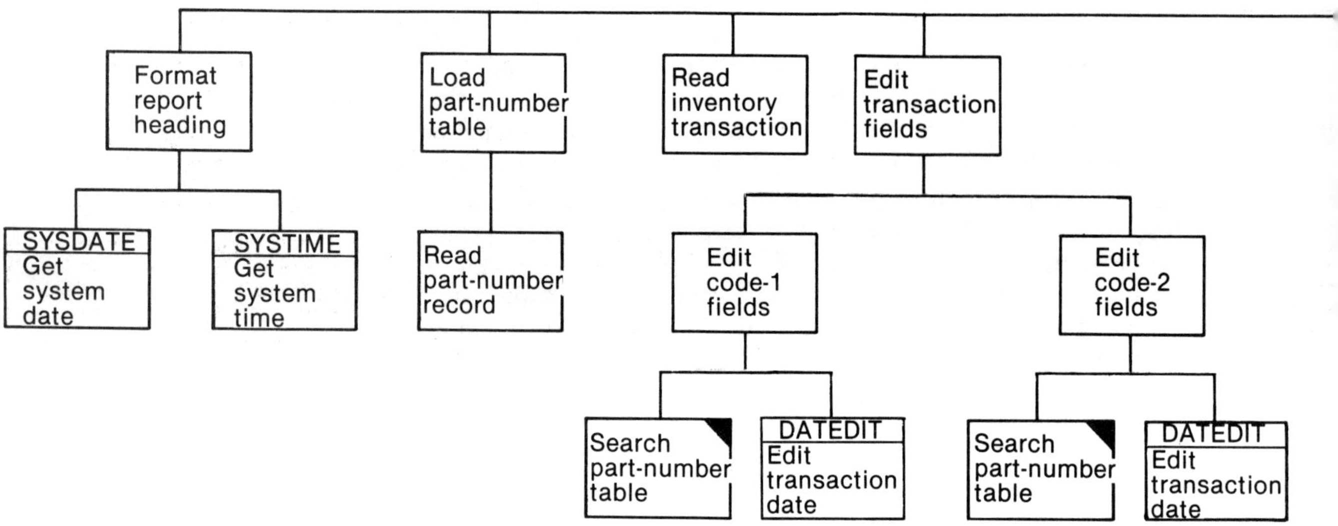

Figure 7-21 A design for the edit program in which the top-level module can't be coded as a single COBOL paragraph

Also, watch out for module names like "match input records" and "compare control fields." These tend to represent data processing *procedures* rather than data processing functions. In terms of the requirements of a program, though, matching records and comparing control fields are not legitimate functions.

If your module description requires the use of the word *and* or *or*, it is a good indication that the module contains more than one function. Thus, a "read and sort table records" module should be divided into two functional modules. And a "print valid or invalid message" module should be two modules.

In any event, try to make sure that each module in your design represents only one function. Test all module functions to see whether they can be described in a single imperative sentence. Test all of these sentences to see whether they represent a single specific function rather than several functions or a collection of elements related by time or class of data. If your modules represent one function, they will be relatively easy to document, code, and test. If they don't, you will run into problems as you develop the program.

Is proper subordination shown? When we refer to *proper subordination*, it means that called modules are related to the correct calling module. This goes back to the second principle of program design that I talked about in topic 1. Often, when you check your structure

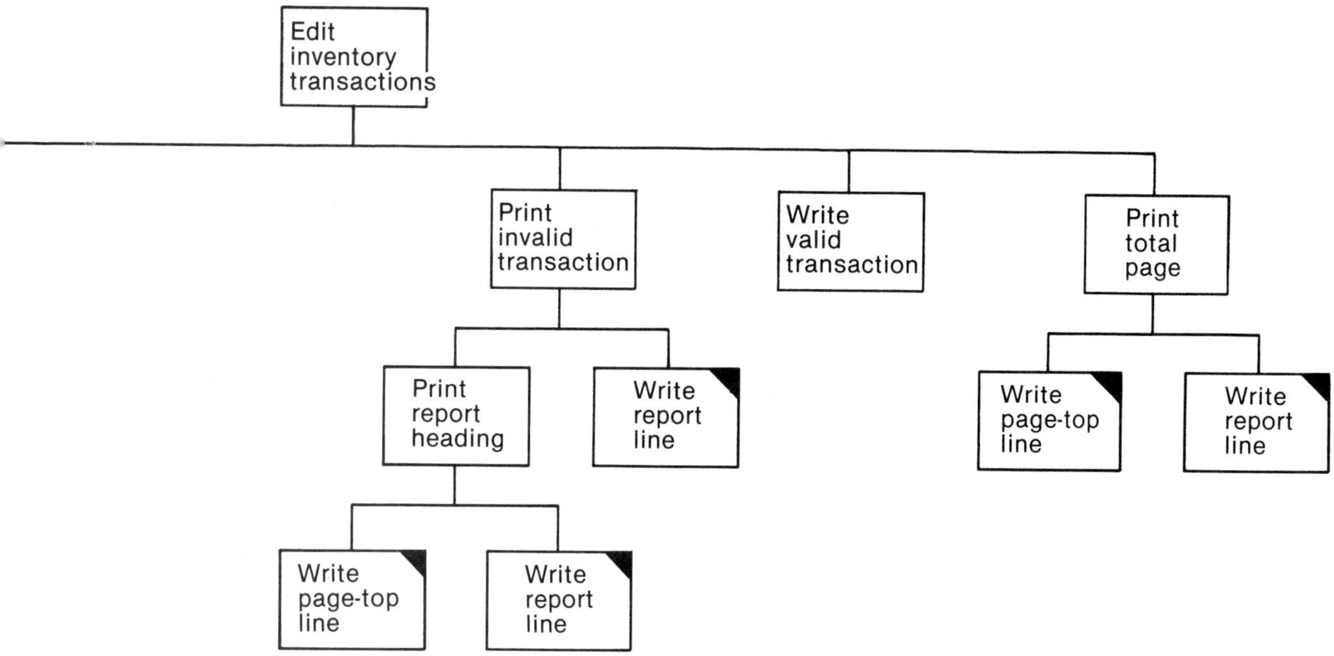

chart for completeness, you will also check to make sure that all of the modules called by another module are logically related to the calling module. But if you didn't, it's worth taking the time to review your structure chart again just to check this point.

Can each module be coded in a single COBOL paragraph? If a module can't be coded in a single COBOL paragraph, the design must be modified. Otherwise, both productivity and program quality will suffer. This goes back to the third principle of program design I discussed in topic 1.

To illustrate, look at the structure chart in figure 7-21. It is a design for the edit program. Here, the program designer has decided on seven level-1 modules. Unfortunately, with this design, you can't code the top-level module as a single COBOL paragraph. If you don't understand why, try to code it. Or check the code of the edit program in figure 7-1; it will give you some idea of how the high-level control modules must be coded. Yes, you could code the top-level module in figure 7-21 as a section that contained two paragraphs. Or, you could code it as just two paragraphs. But as soon as you do either of these alternatives, program quality and programmer productivity start to deteriorate.

So be sure that you can code each module of a program as a single COBOL paragraph. And if you didn't check this as you checked for other design qualities, it's worth taking a separate look at the structure chart to make sure all of the modules pass this test.

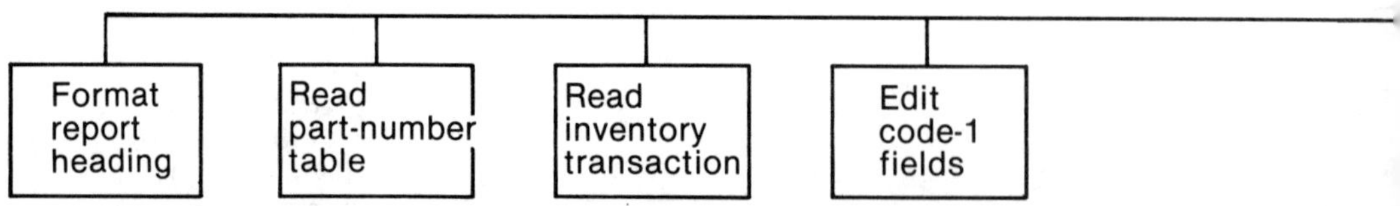

Figure 7-22 Improper subordination in a design for the edit program reflected by a broad span of control

Are the control spans reasonable? If a module has three other modules subordinate to it, its *span of control*, or *control span*, is 3. In other words, it controls the operation of three modules. Span of control is useful because it can indicate problems in program design.

As a rule of thumb, the span of control for a module shouldn't be more than nine...and seven or less is even better. If, for example, the edit program was charted as in figure 7-22, the span of control for the top-level module would be 9. This large span of control, then, could indicate that the modules were not designed with proper subordination. Also, it could indicate that the module that calls the nine subordinates will require so many levels of nested IF statements that it will be very difficult to follow once it is coded. On the other hand, if the called modules are simply executed in sequence (that is, the top-level module consists of one simple PERFORM statement after another), the large span of control may not indicate any problem at all.

The other extreme is illustrated in figure 7-23. Here the structure chart has several modules that have a span of control of one. Although there's usually no problem with an occasional module with a span of control of one, it is likely that the structure chart in figure 7-23 could be improved.

Span of control, then, is simply a measure that can indicate design problems. Although perfectly proper programs can have modules that have a span of control of ten or more, they deserve a second look. Similarly, though some programs may require a structure like the one in figure 7-23, it isn't common and it could indicate design flaws.

Are the modules independent? Structured programming depends on the use of independent modules. In other words, you should be able to code one module without knowing how any of the other modules are coded. If you have to refer to the code in one module as you code another one, the modules probably aren't independent.

To maintain independence, control codes created in a called module should only be used by the calling module. To say it another way, codes created in a subordinate module should only be *passed* to the calling

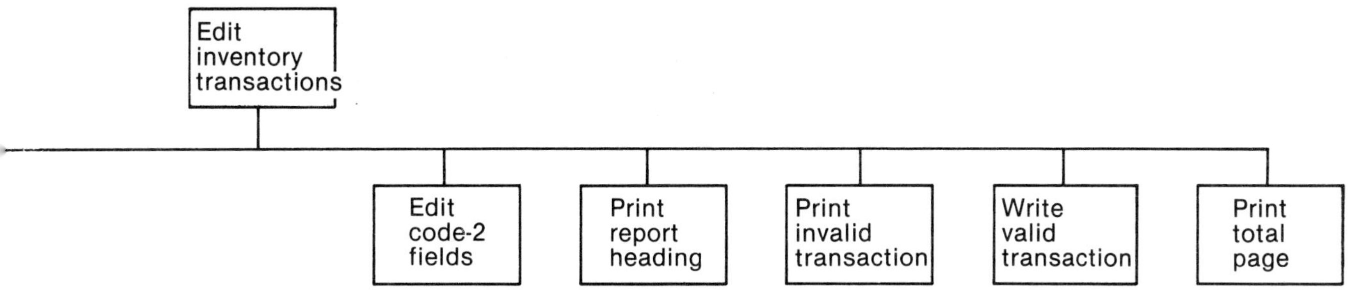

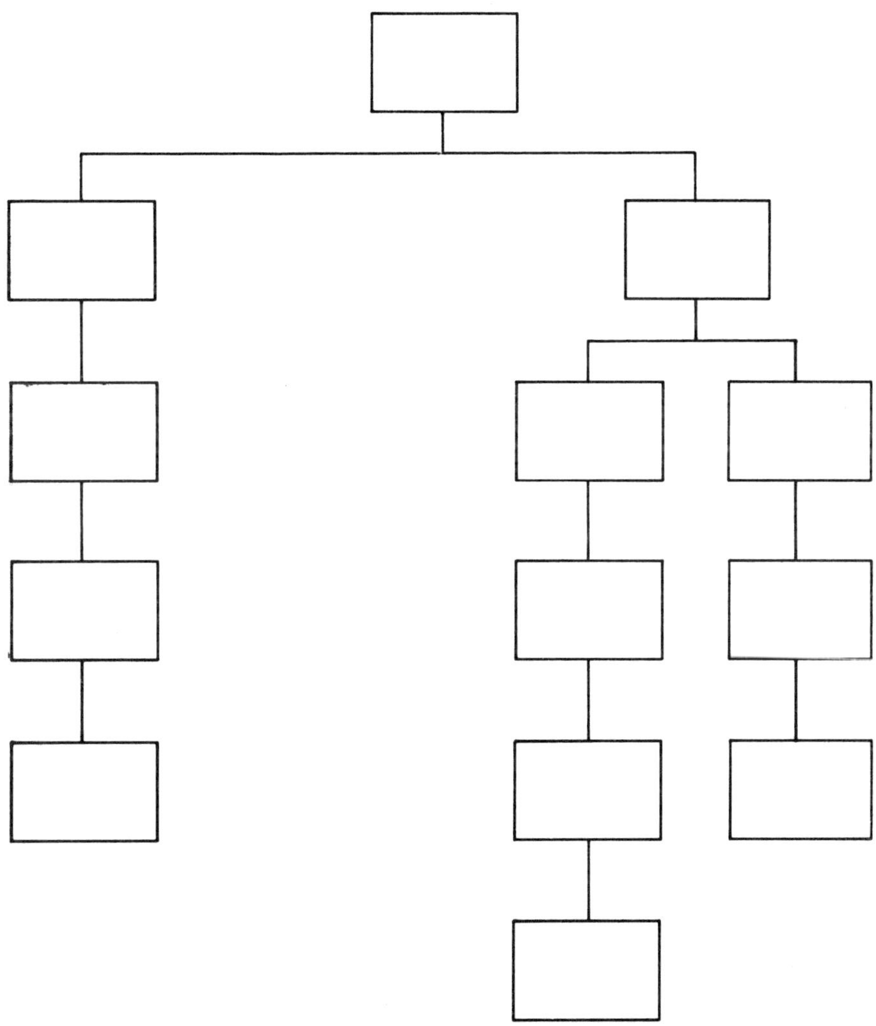

Figure 7-23 A structure chart with questionable control spans

module. For example, the validity code that must be created by module 320 in figure 7-1 should only be passed to module 300. If the code is required by the print-invalid-transaction-line module, module 360, this latter module isn't properly independent.

Although a code should only be required by the calling module, it is okay to pass a code from one calling module to another. In figure 7-1, for example, module 310 sets an end-of-file switch for the transaction file. This code is passed to and tested by module 300, which is module 310's calling module. Module 300 in turn passes the code up to the next calling module, module 000, which also tests the code. In other words, it's okay to pass a code up the line, from one calling module to another. But a code created in one module should *not* be required by modules at the same level or at lower levels in the structure chart; if it is, it indicates that the modules aren't independent.

Note here that I said *control codes* shouldn't be passed erratically from one module to another. I said nothing about data. On the contrary, it is perfectly all right for data that is created in one module to be used in modules other than the calling module. In figure 7-1, for example, data read by the read-inventory-transaction module (module 310) is used in modules 320, 330, 340, 350, and 360. Similarly, data created in a computational module is likely to be used in print modules at the same level or at lower levels.

Often, it is difficult or impossible to decide whether a module is independent by looking at a structure chart. This is particularly true when you first start to use structured development methods. Nevertheless, you should keep this goal of module independence in mind as you design a program. As you get more experience with these methods, you will be able to spot module dependencies before you start to code them.

Are the verbs consistent? Besides using precise verbs in your module descriptions, you should try to use them consistently. In other words, one verb should mean the same thing throughout a structure chart and, if possible, throughout a programming department. For instance, we use the word *get* to mean (1) reading a record, (2) editing the record, and (3) doing something with the invalid records; we use the word *read* to mean physically reading the record from the input device (as in the COBOL READ statement).

Quite frankly, the way we use these words can be debated. However, we are consistent throughout our shop, and I am consistent throughout this book. So once you understand what I mean by the verbs I use, you will be able to understand the module descriptions in figure 7-1 as well as in all of the other structure charts in this book. If you refer back to the verb list I presented in figure 7-5, you can find out how we use verbs in our shop. And you can use this verb list as a starting point for developing your own verb list.

Some practical considerations

At this point, you should have a basic understanding of how to create an acceptable program design. In the next topic, I'll show you several more program designs, so you'll get an even better idea about what an acceptable design should be. But before we go on to other designs, let me present a few practical considerations that are related to the technique of top-down design.

When to be concerned about processing details One of the benefits of top-down design is that you don't have to know all of the details of a program specification in order to design the program. In fact, our advice is to put off the concern with details as long as you can. In other words, don't worry about the details of a program until you need to use them. By delaying your concern for details, you can concentrate on the problem and design a better solution for it.

For instance, you don't have to know the editing rules for the edit program until you actually code the edit-fields modules. So after you study the program specification to the point that you understand that the program is going to be doing a field-by-field edit, you can forget about the detailed editing rules until you have to use them. On the other hand, you do have to know enough about the rules to realize that you have to search the part-number table to edit the item numbers and call the DATEDIT subprogram to edit the date.

Unfortunately, details often come into your mind as you design a program. If they bother you, Paul suggests that you keep a "worry list" as you develop a program. Then, whenever a concern comes up that isn't relevant to the task at hand, you can add it to this list. Later on, as you move into other phases of program development, you can check this list to make sure that you have provided for all of your concerns. By using the list, you help to clear your mind for the task you're working on.

When to stop designing subordinate modules I hope that my narrative on how I designed the edit program has given you some insight as to when you can stop designing subordinate modules. If you review the bottom modules in each leg of the structure chart in figure 7-1, I hope you can see that it would be pretty hard to develop subordinate modules from them. All of them are work modules implemented as subprograms, I/O modules, or search modules.

The answer, then, is to stop designing when you can't divide any of your lowest-level modules into subordinate functions. When you reach this point, your work modules will usually be of the three types I just named. And you will be able to code each module as a single COBOL paragraph.

How to handle the trivial subfunctions of a program In almost every program there are some trivial functions that you don't know what to do with. They seem to be too small to justify their own modules. But they don't seem to fit logically in any of the modules you've designed for the program. Counting transactions is one example of a trivial subfunction like this. Accumulating grand totals for reports is another example.

In our shop, we handle many of the common subfunctions by agreeing on conventions for handling them. For instance, we let a read or write module count an input or output transaction. And we let a print or a more general prepare, produce, or process module accumulate totals.

If you don't have conventions like this, however, you should create separate modules for these subfunctions. These extra modules won't have much effect on your design. But they will clearly identify the location of the subfunctions in your COBOL code. In contrast, if you decide to put a subfunction in a module that it doesn't logically belong in, it can make your program difficult to read and understand. In short, it's better to have a few extra modules than it is to put a subfunction in a module where it will be difficult to find later on.

For the most part, however, this is a coding question that you don't have to contend with when you design a program. So if you discover a required subfunction as you code a program, you can decide then whether or not it requires its own module. Since the design method I've presented is easy to modify, you can defer a decision like this without any penalty in terms of productivity or program quality. I'll talk more about the handling of subfunctions in the next chapter.

What the left-to-right placement of modules means In general, you should draw your modules from left to right in the sequence you think they will be called by the calling module. Keep in mind, however, that when you code the calling module you may decide to call the subordinates in a sequence different from the left-to-right sequence. I guess you can say, then, that the left-to-right placement of modules implies a logical sequence. But this sequence doesn't have to be adhered to when coding the program.

When to be concerned about module size I haven't really talked about module size yet. But I will talk about it in some detail in the chapter on COBOL coding. For now, you should be aware that part of the theory of structured design says that each module should be small enough to be manageable. For COBOL programs, this means that a module should be around 50 statements or less (50 statements is about the number that will fit on one page of a source listing). Studies have shown that the larger a module is, the more difficult it is to read and understand. Furthermore, the difficulty does not increase in direct proportion to the size of the module. Instead, a 100-statement module may be four or five times as difficult to read and understand as a 50-statement module.

Needless to say, you can't tell how large a module will be by looking at a structure chart. As a result, you may have to make changes to the structure chart when coding the program. If, for example, you code a module that requires 500 statements, you should divide it into some subordinate modules.

The simplest rule to go by in the design stage, then, is to develop your structure chart down to the lowest functional level. Although some books on structured design recommend that modules range from 10 to 50 statements, I think this is unrealistic. If a module requires only one statement but it is a clearly defined function, there is no point in combining it with some other function just to increase the module size. On the other hand, a 100-statement module may be perfectly acceptable if it consists primarily of imperative statements executed in sequence. In general, if you design down to the lowest functional level, relatively few modules will require more than 50 lines of COBOL code.

How to draw charts that use more than one page Figure 7-24 shows you how to draw charts that require more than one page. It shows how the edit program could be charted on two pages instead of just one. Quite simply, you put the number of the continuation page at the bottom of a module that is continued on a later page. Then, you repeat this module on the continuation page; above it, you put the number of the page it came from.

When to shorten module names so they lead to valid COBOL names As you can see by studying the chart in figure 7-1 and the COBOL code in figure 7-2, the COBOL paragraph names are created from the module number and name taken from the chart. Thus, module 000 named "edit inventory transactions" leads to a COBOL name of

```
000-EDIT-INVENTORY-TRANSACTIONS
```

Unfortunately, this is an invalid COBOL name since it has more than 30 characters. As a result, it is shown as

```
000-EDIT-INVENTORY-TRANS
```

in the COBOL listing. The question, then, is when to shorten your module names so they lead to valid COBOL names.

Paul says that you should shorten the module names during the design stage. In other words, after you number the modules, you should inspect the module names to make sure that they're not too long. In general, you will only have to be careful when two of the words in the module description are long like *inventory* and *transaction* or when a four-word module description is used. Then, if the paragraph name will turn out to be over 30 characters, you should shorten the description by abbreviating one or more words. Make every effort, however, to keep the module name on the structure chart meaningful.

The people in our shop, however, don't feel that it's worth their time to count the characters in their module names. So they don't deal with

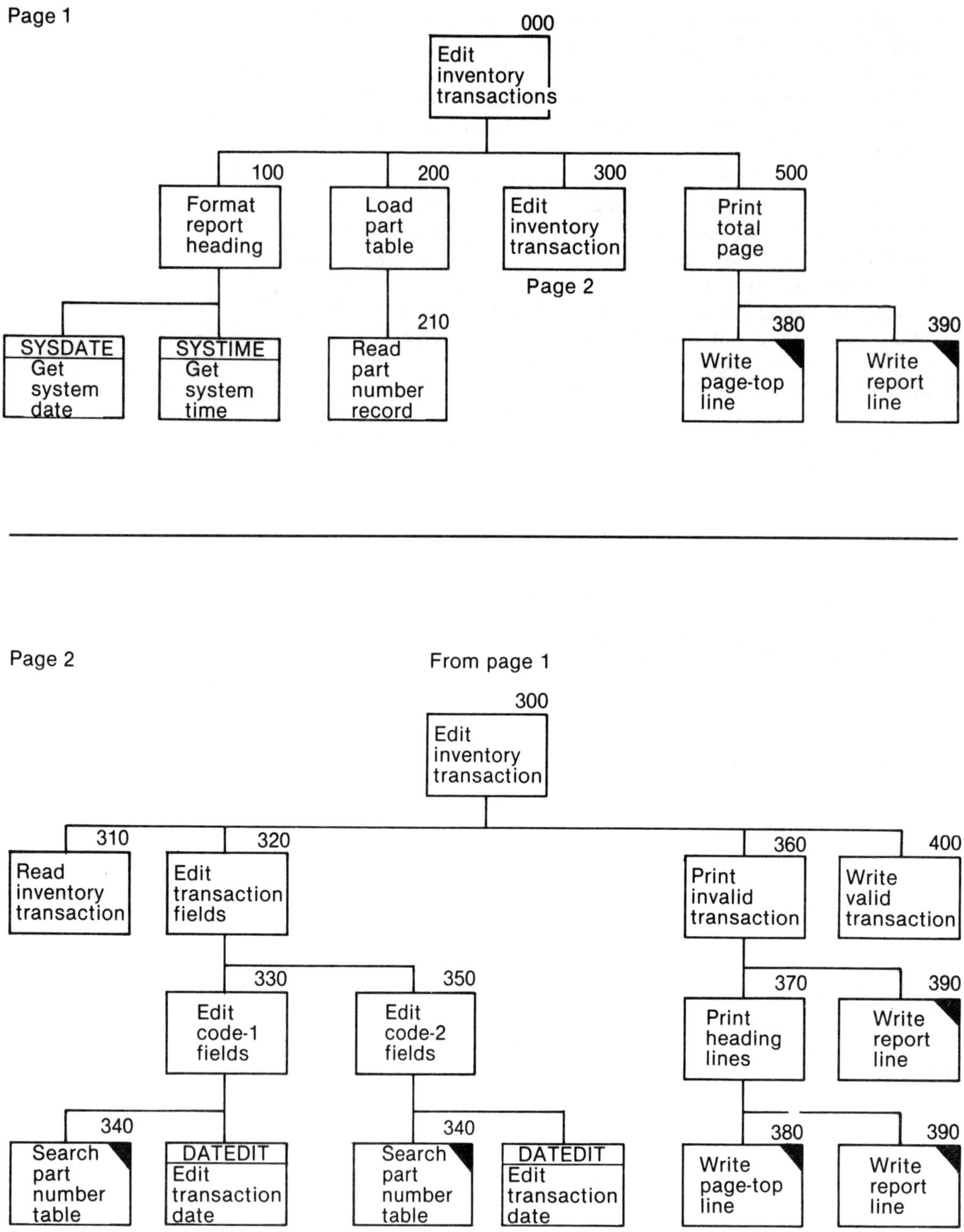

Figure 7-24 A two-page structure chart for the edit program

this problem until they code the program. In fact, they often let the computer identify any names that are too long in the first diagnostic listing. Then, they do a global replacement of the invalid names they used with shorter versions. Since it's easy to relate the design modules to the COBOL paragraphs using the module numbers, our programmers don't bother to change the names on their structure charts either. As a result, in the final documentation, the names in the COBOL listing may not agree exactly with the names on the structure chart. In fact, that's the way we left the documentation for the edit program in the appendix. We think this approach maximizes productivity with no loss in program quality.

Discussion

In this topic, I showed you how to design a program starting from scratch. Keep in mind, however, that most business programs repeat structural patterns. That's why you can often develop the design for one program from the design for another, similar program, or from parts of programs that do similar functions. That's really where the tremendous increase in productivity that is possible through structured programming comes from. First, you can reuse designs, and, second, you can reuse code.

One of the benefits of the method I've just shown you is that it is quite specific about how a program should be designed. As a result, based on the specifications for the edit program, all of the programmers in our shop would design a structure like the one in figure 7-1. In fact, there wouldn't be much variation in the names our programmers would use for the modules in this structure. More than once I have asked two members of my staff to design independent solutions for the same problem and the results have been markedly similar.

In the case of the edit program, there would probably be some variation as to how different programmers would handle the print legs of the chart. There might be some variations as to how the loading of the part-number table would be handled. And the numbers assigned to the modules would vary quite a bit. But all of these variations are trivial. In terms of the critical functional modules and in terms of subordination, all of our programmers would come to the same design conclusions.

Understand, however, that the edit program is unrealistically simple when compared with most business programs. Furthermore, the more complex a program is, the more ways it can be designed and still be effective. So, I'm not saying that two different programmers should always design the same structure for the same program specification. But I am saying that they should develop similar designs, particularly at the higher levels of the charts. And once a programmer has developed an effective design for one type of business program, he should be able to reuse that design for new programs of the same type.

Terminology

span of control
control span
passing a switch or code

Objectives

1. List the four steps you should follow when designing a structure chart.

2. Given any of the questions of this topic's checklist for analyzing a program's design, explain how to use it when you analyze a structure chart.

Topic 3 Some typical program structures

In the last topic, I showed you how to design a program from scratch. But you shouldn't design programs from scratch. One of the benefits of structured development techniques is that you can reuse old designs when you design new programs. And this can improve programmer productivity dramatically.

In this topic, then, I'm going to show you the design and some of the code for three more model programs. These should show you how the techniques of topic 2 apply to most business programs. Once you're familiar with these, I will show you the basic structures that these model programs contain. Last, I'll show you how you can use the model programs as a basis for designing new programs. By the time you complete this topic, you should be able to design structure charts of your own.

Three more model programs

As we see it, there are four classes of programs common to all batch business systems. They are (1) edit programs that check source data for validity; (2) report preparation (or extract) programs that prepare printed reports from one or more transaction or master files; (3) sequential update or file-maintenance programs for updating or maintaining master files; and (4) random update or file-maintenance programs. Since I've already shown you an example of an edit program, I'd like to now show you examples of the other three types of batch programs.

For each program, I will present the structure chart for the entire program and the COBOL code for the first several modules of the program. You should realize, however, that you don't have to know how you're going to code the modules when you design a program. I'm only presenting the code to you now in case you're not familiar with structured programming. By analyzing both the program design and the COBOL code, you can see the relationships between the design and the code. And once you understand these relationships, you can design most programs with little or no concern for the resulting code.

If you have our *COBOL Programmer's Handbook*, you can refer to it for additional information about the model programs. If, for example, you want to see the complete COBOL code for the model programs, you can find it in the *Handbook*. Similarly, you can find design alternatives in the *Handbook*. For now, I just want to show you one way of designing a program for each of the four classes of batch programs. But you should realize that there are other ways to design the programs.

To save space, I'm not going to give you complete specifications for each of the model programs. Instead, I'm just going to give you the first page of the program overview for each program. However, that should give you all the information you need to design each of the programs. Yes, you would need additional information to code each of the programs. But you don't need more information to design them. Here again, if you have the *Handbook*, you can find complete specifications for each of the model programs in it.

For illustrative purposes, it was tempting to give specifications for the model programs that kept their designs and code simple. But we didn't do that because production programs are rarely without complication. As a result, you'll find some realistic complications in each of the model programs. Although this doesn't have much effect on any of the program designs, it does make the code for some of the modules more complicated. And it gives you a better idea of how production programs should be designed and coded.

Because of these complications, you may be bothered by the complexity of the code for some of the modules in the model programs. This is likely to be true if you're not accustomed to using nested IFs and condition names. In chapter 9, though, you'll learn more about structured coding so this code should make more sense to you then.

For now, let me make this point about the coding of the model programs. It is true that most structured programs require a couple of critical modules that are logically complex. Quite frankly, you can't completely avoid programming complexity just by using structured development techniques. But once you get the coding for the critical modules right, the development of the rest of a structured program is routine. In a 2000 line program, for example, you may struggle with 200 of the coding lines. But you'll be able to develop the other 1800 lines of the program at a high rate of speed with much of it picked up from old programs.

Model program 1: A report-preparation program that prepares a multilevel report A *multilevel report* gives totals at two or more levels. For example, a sales report might give totals by customer, salesman, and branch. It would then be a three-level report. A report like this will also have one or more final totals. Because multilevel reports are common in industry, programs that prepare these reports are common. And, historically, this type of program has caused many programming difficulties, particularly, in the GOTO era of programming.

When intermediate totals must be accumulated in a report-preparation program, the input file must be in sequence based on the data in a *control field*. For instance, customer number is the control field if totals must be accumulated by customer number, so the input file that drives the program must be in customer-number sequence. Similarly, a file must be in sequence by a control field within a control field if totals are to be accumulated at two different levels.

In order to print one level of intermediate totals, the control field from one record must be compared with the control field from the previous record. If the new control field is greater than the old control field, it indicates that an intermediate total line should be printed. If the control fields are equal, it means that the data from the new record should be applied to the group being processed, so no total line should be printed. And if the new control field is less than the old control field, it indicates that the input file is not in sequence (an error condition). Needless to say, if more than one level of intermediate totals must be printed, the problem is complicated because comparisons must be done based on more than one control field (like customer number and salesman number).

Figure 7-25 gives the program overview for our model report-preparation program. And figure 7-26 gives a sample of the printed output that is to be prepared by the program. You can consider this a two-level report because the program must accumulate totals by salesman and by branch. In contrast, the customer totals are taken from the customer master records. Although most of the report's data is derived from the customer master file, the program must read one salesman record for each salesman group in order to print the salesman's name.

Figure 7-27 presents an acceptable structure chart for this program. So you can see how this design relates to the COBOL code for the modules, you will find the code for the first six modules of the program in figure 7-28. Although this is a relatively simple program, let me point out some highlights for you:

1. If you look at the structure chart, you would expect modules 200 and 220 to be the most complicated because they have the largest spans of control. Then, if you look at the code for these modules, you can see that this is true. But these are the only complicated modules in this entire program.

2. The code for module 220 is only complicated because the print chart requires that branch number, salesman number, and salesman name *only* be printed on the first line of each branch or salesman group. As a result, the module starts with a lengthy nested IF statement that is designed to make sure that these three fields are printed properly. Without this printing requirement, the coding for this module would be trivial. As I said earlier, though, I am presenting model programs with realistic complications so you can better understand how you can apply the methods of this book to production programs.

Program: MKTG1200 Produce Sales Report	Page: 1
Designer: Anne Prince	Date: 08-24-84

Input/output specifications

File	Description	Use
CUSTMST	Customer master file	Input
SALESMN	Salesman master file	Input
SALESRPT	Print file: Sales report	Output

Process specifications

The customer master file is in sequence by customer number within salesman number within branch number. This file should be read sequentially, and one line should be printed for each record in the file.

The year-to-date sales for the current and previous year are contained in each customer record, and the change amount and change percent are calculated from these values.

The salesman master file is indexed by salesman number within branch number. This file should be read randomly by the program, and the salesman records should be used to get the salesman's names for the sales report.

Totals should be printed for each salesman and branch. At the end of the report, a grand total of all sales should be printed.

Figure 7-25 The program overview for the report-preparation program

DATE: 09/12/84 MIKE MURACH & ASSOCIATES, INC. PAGE: 1
TIME: 3:31 PM MKTG1200

YEAR-TO-DATE SALES REPORT

BRANCH NO	SALESMAN NO	SALESMAN NAME	CUSTOMER NO	CUSTOMER NAME	SALES THIS YTD	SALES LAST YTD	CHANGE AMOUNT	CHANGE %
01	01	LINDA HUGHES	1	GEORGE DONALDSON	456.38	235.49	220.89	93
			2	BONNIE BRENDT	52.39	425.39	373.00-	87-
			5	YOLANDA PEREZ	129.38	0.00	129.38	N/A
			7	CELIA PRICE	0.00	253.49	253.49-	100-
			12	GEORGE THOMAS	1,253.39	538.49	714.90	132
				SALESMAN TOTALS:	1,891.54	1,452.86	438.68	30
	02	WILLIAM YOUNG	3	KENNY WRIGHT	389.38	629.39	240.01-	38-
			8	ALEX JONAS	0.00	0.00	0.00	N/A
			13	JOHN JOHNSON	35.38	74.39	39.01-	52-
				SALESMAN TOTALS:	424.76	703.78	279.02-	39-
	03	ANTHONY LUND	1	PATTI LANGE	545.39	235.49	309.90	131
			4	INEZ WHITE	45.29	125.39	80.10-	63-
			9	FARRIN LONG	0.00	35.28	35.28-	100-
			17	TINA RANDALL	37.49	58.54	21.05-	35-
			19	THOMAS RICE	254.39	386.39	132.00-	34-
				SALESMAN TOTALS:	882.56	841.09	41.47	4
	04	PETER PIPPIN	4	LARRY UPTON	59.38	0.00	59.38	N/A
				SALESMAN TOTALS:	59.38	0.00	59.38	N/A
	05	TRICIA REED	7	LINDA WENDT	39.49	564.39	524.90-	93-
			9	JOHN KELLY	465.39	253.39	212.00	83
			21	PATRICIA HARRISON	49.30	69.38	20.08-	28-
				SALESMAN TOTALS:	554.18	887.16	332.98-	37-
				BRANCH TOTALS:	3,812.42	3,884.89	72.47-	1-
02	01	PAUL JOHNSON	11	KELLY FLOYD	90.39	154.29	63.90-	41-
			13	SONYA SIMPSON	75.39	153.29	77.90-	50-
			17	HENRY HART	69.30	523.39	434.09-	82-
				SALESMAN TOTALS:	255.08	830.97	575.89-	69-

Figure 7-26 Page 1 of some sample output for the report-preparation program

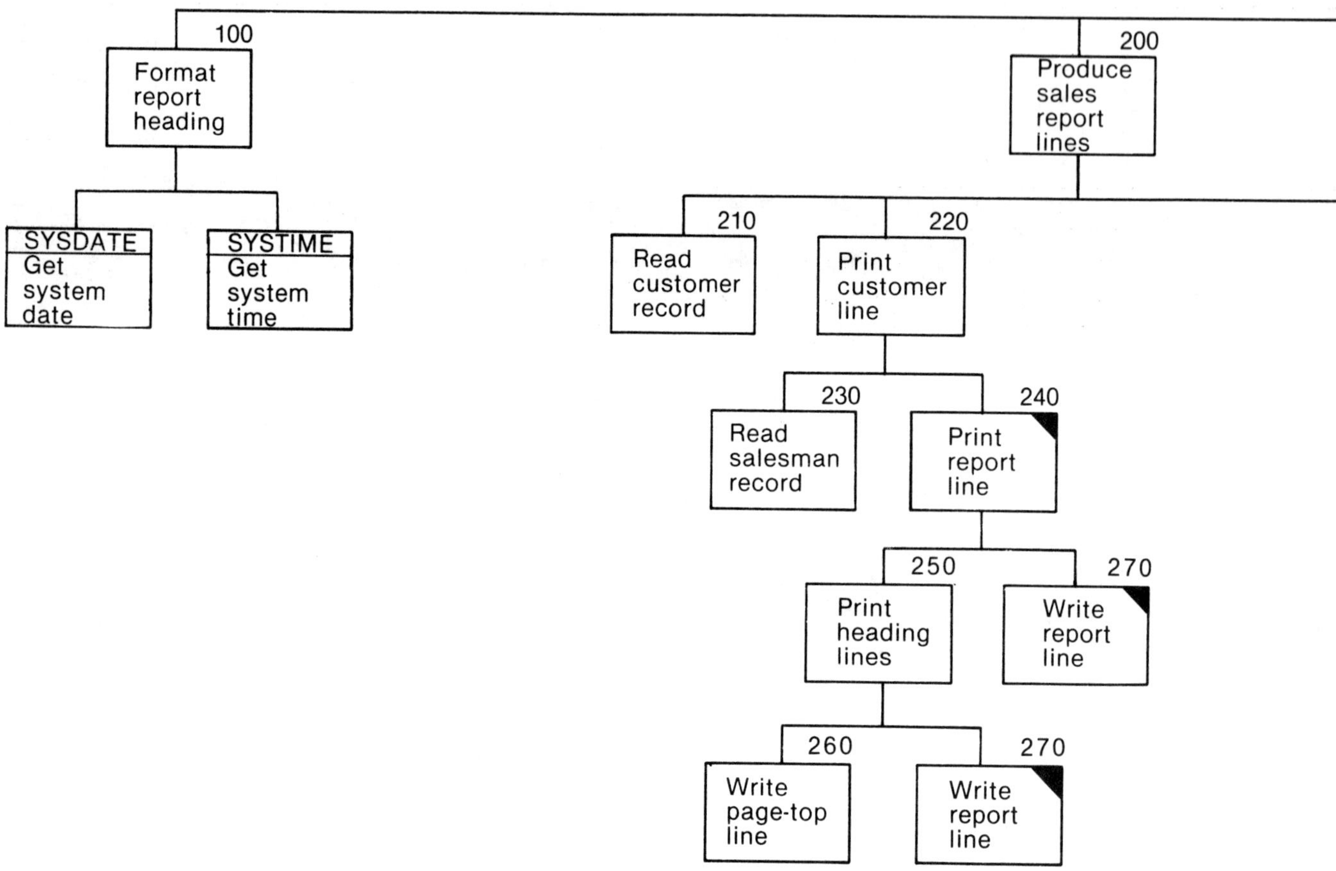

Figure 7-27 The structure chart for the report-preparation program

3. This program uses a general print routine (modules 240 through 270) to print all of the lines of the report. When you use a routine like this, you assume that it's okay to skip to the next page of the report at any point in the printing of the report. In some programs, however, you may not want to skip between the printing of related total lines. In this program, for example, you may not want to skip between the printing of a customer total line and a salesman total line or between a salesman total line and a branch total line. In other words, you may not want the last customer line for a salesman on one page and the salesman total on the next. And you may not

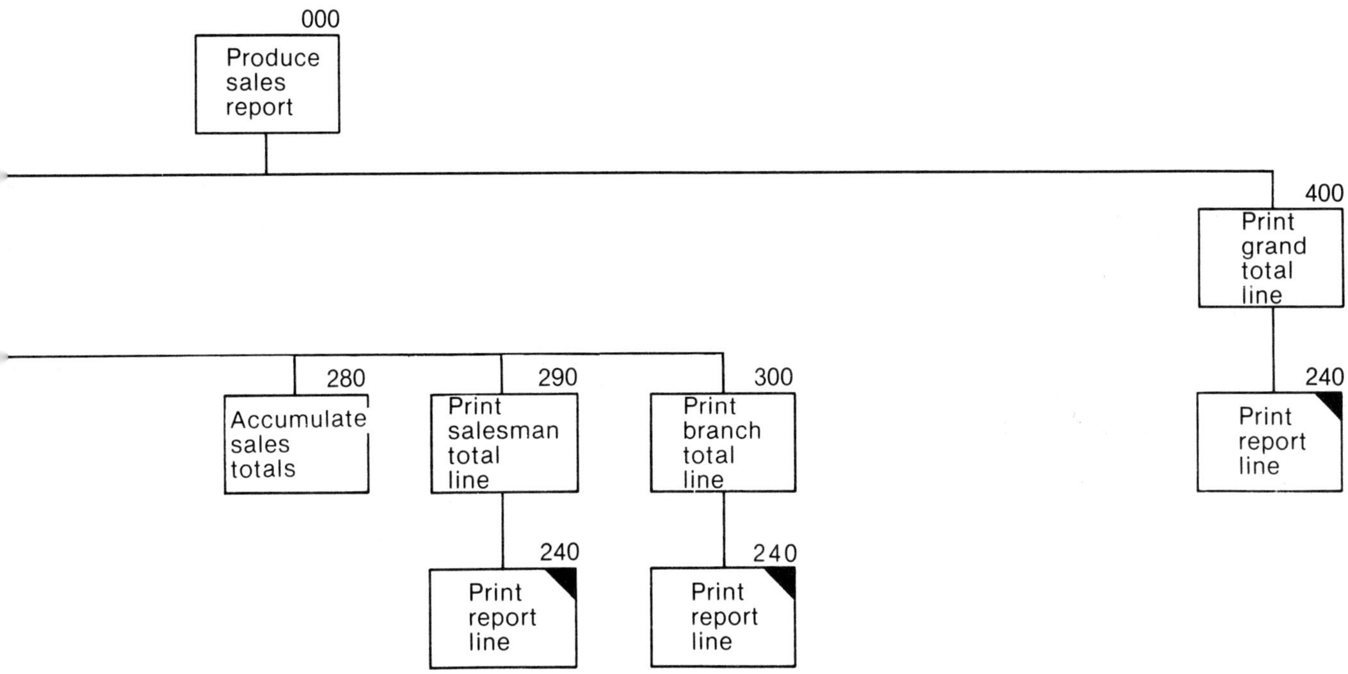

want a salesman total on one page and the branch total on the next. In cases like these, of course, you can adjust the page overflow by making only a minor change to the structure chart.

4. Rather than show modules 250 through 270 every time module 240 appears on the structure chart, we omit them after we've shown them once. This makes the structure chart easier to read and change. Understand, however, that module 240 will always call modules 250 and 270 and that module 250 will always call modules 260 and 270 even when they're not shown.

```
 000-PRODUCE-SALES-REPORT.
*
       OPEN INPUT  CUSTMST
                   SALESMN
            OUTPUT SALESRPT.
       PERFORM 100-FORMAT-REPORT-HEADING.
       PERFORM 200-PRODUCE-SALES-REPORT-LINES
           UNTIL CUSTOMER-EOF.
       PERFORM 400-PRINT-GRAND-TOTAL-LINE.
       CLOSE CUSTMST
             SALESMN
             SALESRPT.
       STOP RUN.
*
 100-FORMAT-REPORT-HEADING.
*
       CALL 'SYSDATE' USING TODAYS-DATE.
       MOVE TODAYS-DATE   TO HDG1-DATE.
       MOVE COMPANY-NAME  TO HDG1-COMPANY-NAME.
       CALL 'SYSTIME' USING HDG2-TIME-DATA.
       MOVE 'MKTG1200'    TO HDG2-REPORT-NUMBER.
       MOVE REPORT-TITLE  TO HDG3-REPORT-TITLE.
*
 200-PRODUCE-SALES-REPORT-LINES.
*
       PERFORM 210-READ-CUSTOMER-RECORD.
       IF NOT CUSTOMER-EOF
           IF FIRST-RECORD
               PERFORM 220-PRINT-CUSTOMER-LINE
               PERFORM 280-ACCUMULATE-SALES-TOTALS
               MOVE CM-SALESMAN-KEY TO OLD-SALESMAN-KEY
               MOVE 'N'             TO FIRST-RECORD-SW
           ELSE
               IF CM-SALESMAN-KEY NOT GREATER OLD-SALESMAN-KEY
                   PERFORM 220-PRINT-CUSTOMER-LINE
                   PERFORM 280-ACCUMULATE-SALES-TOTALS
               ELSE
                   IF CM-BRANCH-NUMBER GREATER OLD-BRANCH-NUMBER
                       PERFORM 290-PRINT-SALESMAN-TOTAL-LINE
                       PERFORM 300-PRINT-BRANCH-TOTAL-LINE
                       PERFORM 220-PRINT-CUSTOMER-LINE
                       PERFORM 280-ACCUMULATE-SALES-TOTALS
                       MOVE CM-SALESMAN-KEY TO OLD-SALESMAN-KEY
                   ELSE
                       PERFORM 290-PRINT-SALESMAN-TOTAL-LINE
                       PERFORM 220-PRINT-CUSTOMER-LINE
                       PERFORM 280-ACCUMULATE-SALES-TOTALS
                       MOVE CM-SALESMAN-NUMBER
                           TO OLD-SALESMAN-NUMBER
       ELSE
           PERFORM 290-PRINT-SALESMAN-TOTAL-LINE
           PERFORM 300-PRINT-BRANCH-TOTAL-LINE.
*
 210-READ-CUSTOMER-RECORD.
*
       READ CUSTMST
           AT END
               MOVE 'Y' TO CUSTOMER-EOF-SW.
*
```

Figure 7-28 COBOL code for the first six modules of the report-preparation program (part 1 of 3)

```
220-PRINT-CUSTOMER-LINE.
*
     IF FIRST-RECORD
         MOVE CM-BRANCH-NUMBER    TO CL-BRANCH-NO
         MOVE CM-SALESMAN-NUMBER  TO CL-SALESMAN-NO
         MOVE CM-SALESMAN-KEY     TO SM-SALESMAN-KEY
         MOVE 'Y'                 TO RECORD-FOUND-SW
         PERFORM 230-READ-SALESMAN-RECORD
         IF RECORD-FOUND
             MOVE SM-SALESMAN-NAME TO CL-SALESMAN-NAME
         ELSE
             MOVE 'SALESMAN RECORD NOT FOUND'
                 TO CL-SALESMAN-NAME
     ELSE
         IF CM-SALESMAN-KEY GREATER OLD-SALESMAN-KEY
             IF CM-BRANCH-NUMBER GREATER OLD-BRANCH-NUMBER
                 MOVE CM-BRANCH-NUMBER    TO CL-BRANCH-NO
                 MOVE CM-SALESMAN-NUMBER  TO CL-SALESMAN-NO
                 MOVE CM-SALESMAN-KEY     TO SM-SALESMAN-KEY
                 MOVE 'Y'                 TO RECORD-FOUND-SW
                 PERFORM 230-READ-SALESMAN-RECORD
                 IF RECORD-FOUND
                     MOVE SM-SALESMAN-NAME TO CL-SALESMAN-NAME
                 ELSE
                     MOVE 'SALESMAN RECORD NOT FOUND'
                         TO CL-SALESMAN-NAME
             ELSE
                 MOVE SPACE               TO CL-BRANCH-NO
                 MOVE CM-SALESMAN-NUMBER  TO CL-SALESMAN-NO
                 MOVE CM-SALESMAN-KEY     TO SM-SALESMAN-KEY
                 MOVE 'Y'                 TO RECORD-FOUND-SW
                 PERFORM 230-READ-SALESMAN-RECORD
                 IF RECORD-FOUND
                     MOVE SM-SALESMAN-NAME TO CL-SALESMAN-NAME
                 ELSE
                     MOVE 'SALESMAN RECORD NOT FOUND'
                         TO CL-SALESMAN-NAME
         ELSE
             MOVE SPACE TO CL-SALESMAN-NAME
                           CL-SALESMAN-NO
                           CL-BRANCH-NO.
     MOVE CM-CUSTOMER-NUMBER TO CL-CUSTOMER-NO.
     MOVE CM-CUSTOMER-NAME   TO CL-CUSTOMER-NAME.
     MOVE CM-SALES-THIS-YTD  TO CL-SALES-THIS-YTD.
     MOVE CM-SALES-LAST-YTD  TO CL-SALES-LAST-YTD.
     COMPUTE CHANGE-AMOUNT = CM-SALES-THIS-YTD
                           - CM-SALES-LAST-YTD.
     MOVE CHANGE-AMOUNT TO CL-CHANGE-AMOUNT.
     IF CM-SALES-LAST-YTD NOT EQUAL ZERO
         COMPUTE CHANGE-PERCENT ROUNDED = CHANGE-AMOUNT
                                        / CM-SALES-LAST-YTD
                                        * 100
         MOVE CHANGE-PERCENT TO CL-CHANGE-PERCENT
     ELSE
         MOVE 'N/A' TO CL-CHANGE-PERCENT-R.
     MOVE CUSTOMER-LINE TO NEXT-REPORT-LINE.
     PERFORM 240-PRINT-REPORT-LINE.
     MOVE 1 TO SPACE-CONTROL.
*
```

Figure 7-28 COBOL code for the first six modules of the report-preparation program (part 2 of 3)

```
230-READ-SALESMAN-RECORD.
*
     READ SALESMN
         INVALID KEY
             MOVE 'N' TO RECORD-FOUND-SW.
*
```

Figure 7-28 COBOL code for the first six modules of the report-preparation program (part 3 of 3)

5. If you check the code in module 220, you can see that I've used the verb print to mean this: Print the line and do everything else associated with printing the line. As a result, the code in this module (1) calls module 230 to read the associated salesman record, (2) arranges the output data in working storage, (3) computes two of the fields to be printed, and (4) moves the proper forms-control character into a space-control field for use by the WRITE statement. This use of print is consistent with the recommendations in the verb list in figure 7-5.

6. If you have written programs like this using traditional methods, you know that the first record read by the program has to be treated differently than the records that follow. As a result, the traditional program normally reads and processes the first record in an initialization module. In this program, however, you can see that the processing of the first record in the file is handled by IF statements in modules 200 and 220. To us, it's logical that these modules should process *all* input records; it's illogical to process the first record in some other module.

Although a report-preparation program can be designed in many different ways, I think the best thing to do is to find a structure that you like, settle on it, and use it as a model for all of the report-preparation programs that you write. Once you have a good model, it can save you many hours of development time.

Model program 2: A sequential file-maintenance program In this book, we distinguish between update and file-maintenance programs, although many people don't make this distinction. We use the term *update* when a program changes the records in a file based on operational data such as sales, hours worked, or receipts to inventory. We use the term *file maintenance* when the transactions contain maintenance rather than operational data.

The next model program, then, is a sequential file-maintenance program. To illustrate this type of program, consider the program overview in figure 7-29. Here, there are two input files: an inventory master file and a maintenance transaction file. And there are three output files: a maintained, or new, master file; a listing of the records that were maintained; and an error file of matched addition transactions and unmatched change and deletion transactions.

Program: MNT1500	MAINTAIN INVENTORY FILE	**Page:** 1
Designer: Anne Prince		**Date:** 08-30-84

Input/output specifications

File	Description	Use
OLDMAST	Old inventory master file	Input
MNTTRAN	Maintenance transaction file	Input
NEWMAST	New inventory master file	Output
ERRTRAN	Maintenance transaction error file	Output
MNTLIST	Print file: Inventory maintenance listing	Output

Process specifications

Use the transaction records to maintain the master records. A transaction record may change, add, or delete a master file record. There may be none, one, or several transactions for each master. Since the fields in the transaction record have already been edited, this program does **not** have to do any field editing.

The master file is in sequence by item number. The transaction file is in sequence by action code within item number. That means that for any one item number, the types of transactions are in this sequence: delete, add, changes. So it is possible to delete an item number, add a new record with the same item number to the file, and then update the new record.

The maintenance listing is to be printed with one line for each valid transaction record as shown on the print chart. The totals for the program are to be printed on a separate output page.

If an unmatched deletion or change transaction, or a matched addition transaction is detected, write a record in the error file. The error record should have the same format as the transaction record.

Figure 7-29 The program overview for the sequential file-maintenance program

The logic in a program like this is based on a comparison of the *control fields* in the master and transaction records that are read. In this program, the control field is the inventory item number. In order for the program to work, both files must be in sequence by the control field because a sequential file-maintenance program reads all input files in sequence.

As the program reads the records in the input files, if the control field of a transaction record and the control field of a master record are equal, it means that the transaction record should be either a deletion or a change record, and processing continues accordingly. Similarly, if the control field of the transaction record is less than that of the master record, it means that the transaction didn't have a matching master record, so the transaction should represent an addition record which should be added to the master file.

In contrast to a random update or maintenance program, a sequential program forces procedural thinking like this upon you. And to a large extent, this thinking goes back to the days of computing when most files were kept on magnetic tapes rather than direct-access devices. That's why it's usually more difficult to develop a sequential update or maintenance program than it is to develop a random program for the same purpose. Instead of concentrating on the functions that the sequential program requires, you have to be aware that the files are being read one record at a time and that you can't get a master record back once you've written it.

With this as background, figure 7-30 presents an effective structure chart for this program. And figure 7-31 gives the COBOL code for the first nine modules of the program. If you have written one or more file-maintenance programs at some time during your career, I think you will appreciate the simple logic of this program.

Some highlights follow:

1. Since modules 300 and 350 have the largest spans of control, they will probably be the most difficult in terms of COBOL code. So, when you code the program, you can concentrate on these modules. However, since no module has a span of control over four, all of the modules should be quite manageable. If you check the COBOL code in figure 7-31, I think you'll agree that none of the modules is that complicated.

2. Actually, the two most complicated modules in figure 7-31 are modules 320 and 350. Both are complicated by the requirement to process a deletion, an addition, and one or more changes for the same item number. As a result, the program can't just read the next master record when a record is deleted from the file. And it can't just write the new master record, when a record is added to the file. This accounts for the use of the MASTER-DELETED and the MASTER-HELD-FOR-ADDITION switches that are used in these

modules. Without this requirement, these modules would be quite straightforward.

3. The new verbs in this program are used as we've recommended in the verb list in figure 7-5. *Get* means at the least to read a record from a file, but it can also mean to edit the fields in each record and to do something with (dispose of) the invalid records. In this program, the get-inventory-master module calls modules to write a new master record and read an old master record, because the writing of the new file is related to the reading of the old file. In contrast, *apply* in this program means "process the transaction in working storage but don't actually write the updated record on the file." As a result, the program can apply more than one transaction to a single master record. Then, when no more transaction records are related to a master record, the program can actually write the master record.

4. If you have written programs like this using traditional methods, you know that the first record of the old master file is usually read before getting into the main processing modules of the program. As a result, the traditional program normally reads and processes the first record in an initialization module. In this program, however, you can see that the processing of the first record in the file is handled by an IF statement in module 320. To us, it's logical that this module should get all master records; it's illogical to get the first record in some other module.

Although a sequential file-maintenance program can be designed in many different ways, I think the best thing to do is to find a structure that you like, settle on it, and use it as a model for all of the file-maintenance programs that you write. And you should do the same thing for a sequential update program. Once you have good models for each type of program, they can save you many hours of development time. In fact, you can usually use the modules in the top three or four levels of the structure chart in all the file-maintenance and update programs you develop. The primary changes from one program to the next will be in the work modules, not the control modules, and these changes are usually routine.

Model program 3: A random update program with an internal sort Another typical business program is a random update program. In this type of program, the *key field* in each transaction is used to directly access the related master record. If the master record is found, it is updated based on the transaction data, after which it is rewritten on the file. If the master record can't be found, it indicates an error condition. If the transactions haven't been edited in a previous run, they should be edited in the update program so invalid records won't be used to update master records.

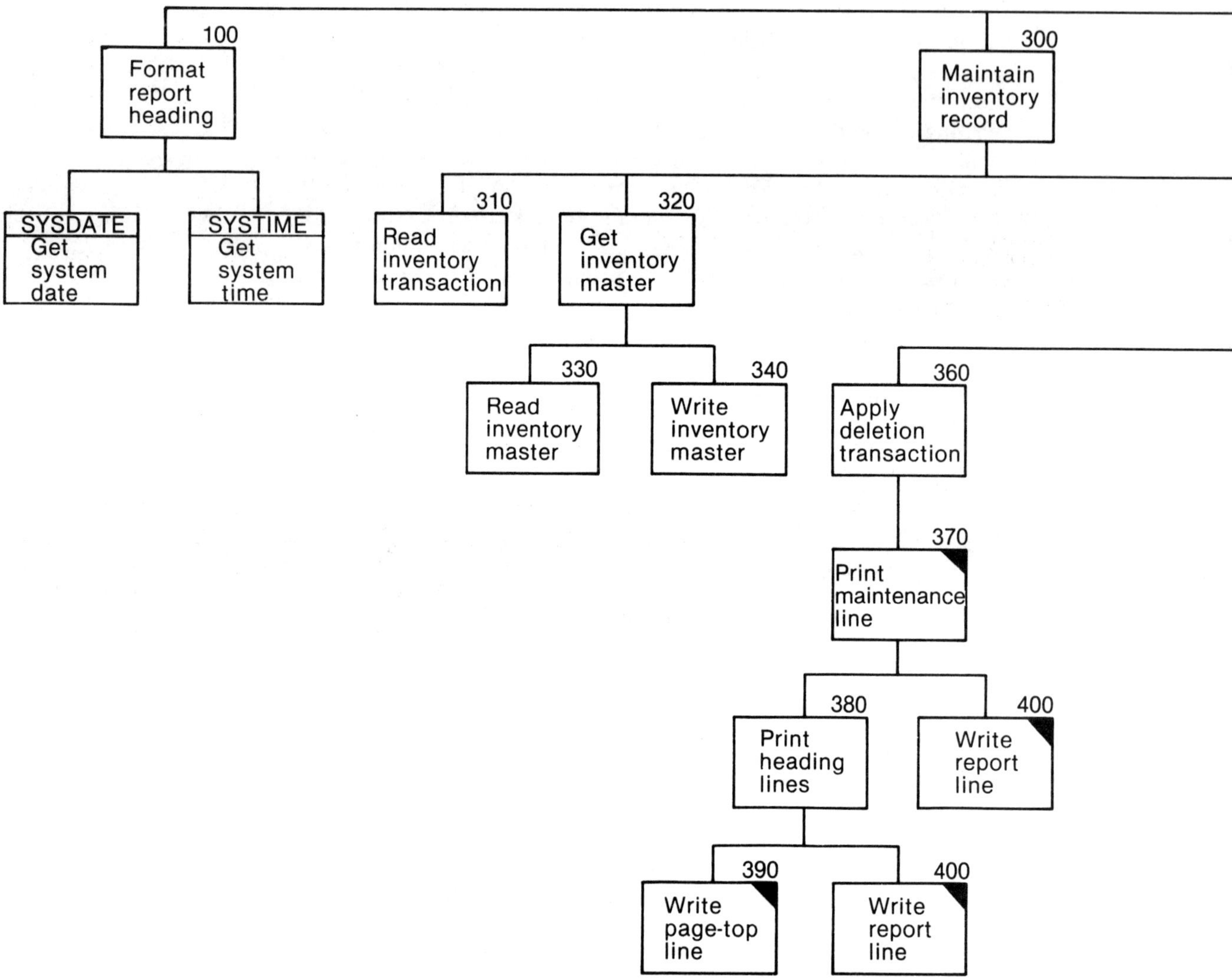

Figure 7-30 The structure chart for the sequential file-maintenance program

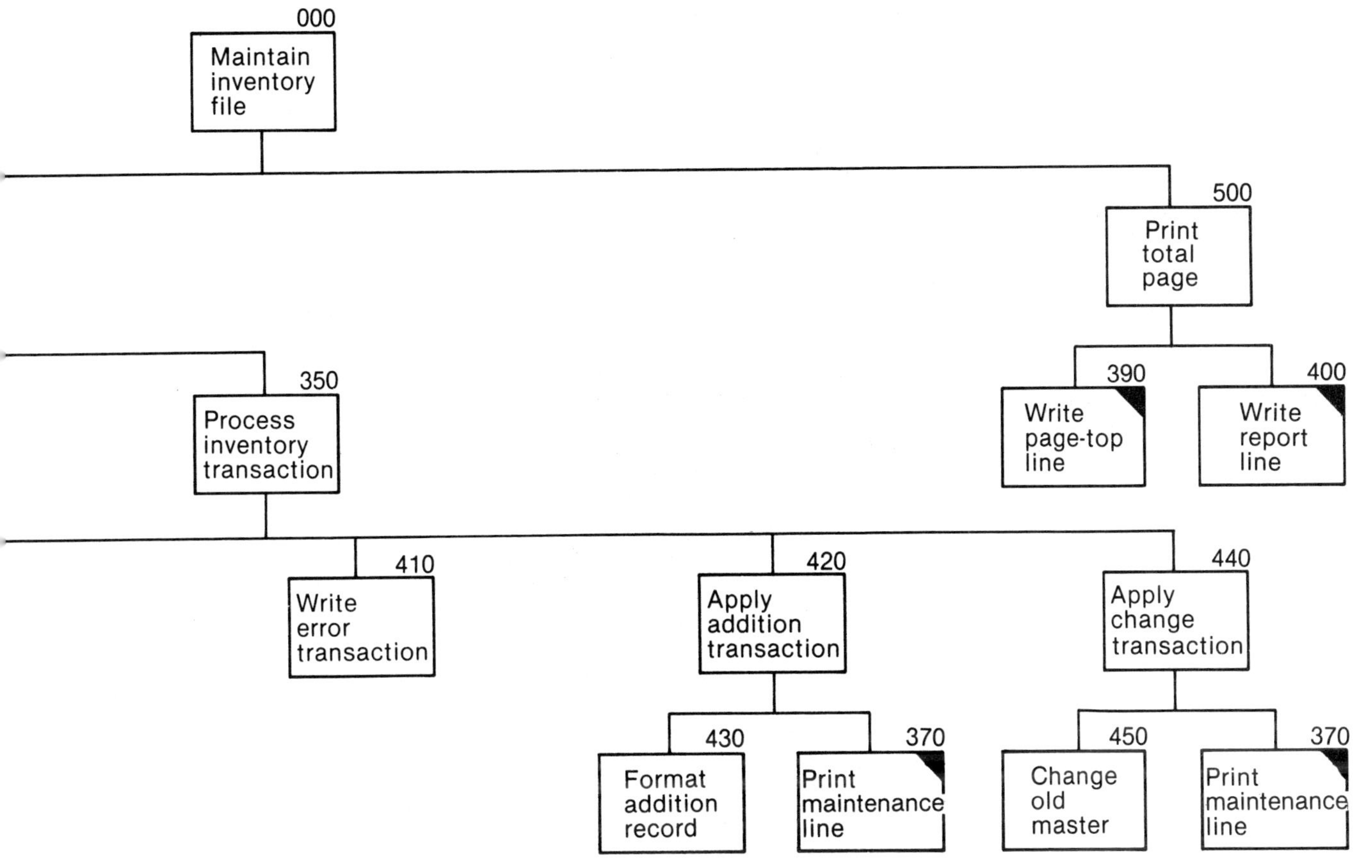
000
Maintain inventory file
500
Print total page
390
Write page-top line
400
Write report line
350
Process inventory transaction
410
Write error transaction
420
Apply addition transaction
440
Apply change transaction
430
Format addition record
370
Print maintenance line
450
Change old master
370
Print maintenance line

```
 000-MAINTAIN-INVENTORY-FILE.
*
     OPEN INPUT  OLDMAST
                 MNTTRAN
          OUTPUT NEWMAST
                 ERRTRAN
                 MNTLIST.
     PERFORM 100-FORMAT-REPORT-HEADING.
     MOVE LOW-VALUE TO IM-ITEM-NUMBER.
     PERFORM 300-MAINTAIN-INVENTORY-RECORD
         UNTIL ALL-RECORDS-PROCESSED.
     PERFORM 500-PRINT-TOTAL-PAGE.
     CLOSE OLDMAST
           MNTTRAN
           NEWMAST
           ERRTRAN
           MNTLIST.
     STOP RUN.
*
 100-FORMAT-REPORT-HEADING.
*
     CALL 'SYSDATE' USING TODAYS-DATE.
     MOVE TODAYS-DATE  TO HDG1-DATE.
     MOVE COMPANY-NAME TO HDG1-COMPANY-NAME.
     CALL 'SYSTIME' USING HDG2-TIME-DATA.
     MOVE 'MNT1500'    TO HDG2-REPORT-NUMBER.
     MOVE REPORT-TITLE TO HDG3-REPORT-TITLE.
*
 300-MAINTAIN-INVENTORY-RECORD.
*
     PERFORM 310-READ-INVENTORY-TRANSACTION.
     PERFORM 320-GET-INVENTORY-MASTER
         UNTIL IM-ITEM-NUMBER NOT LESS MT-ITEM-NUMBER.
     IF          MT-ITEM-NUMBER = HIGH-VALUE
             AND IM-ITEM-NUMBER = HIGH-VALUE
         MOVE 'Y' TO ALL-RECORDS-PROCESSED-SW
     ELSE
         PERFORM 350-PROCESS-INVENTORY-TRAN.
*
 310-READ-INVENTORY-TRANSACTION.
*
     READ MNTTRAN INTO MAINTENANCE-TRANSACTION
         AT END
             MOVE HIGH-VALUES TO MT-ITEM-NUMBER.
     IF MT-ITEM-NUMBER NOT = HIGH-VALUES
         ADD 1 TO TOTAL-COUNT.
*
```

Figure 7-31 COBOL code for the first nine modules of the sequential file-maintenance program (part 1 of 3)

On large systems, you often code a sort within an application program like an edit or a random update program. This is usually more efficient than sorting in one run and editing or updating in a separate run. To show you how the use of a COBOL sort affects a program's design, this next model program requires an internal sort in combination with a random update.

```
 320-GET-INVENTORY-MASTER.
*
     IF FIRST-EXECUTION
         PERFORM 330-READ-INVENTORY-MASTER
         MOVE 'N' TO FIRST-EXECUTION-SW
     ELSE
         IF NOT MASTER-DELETED
             PERFORM 340-WRITE-INVENTORY-MASTER
             IF MASTER-HELD-FOR-ADDITION
                 MOVE HELD-MASTER-RECORD
                     TO INVENTORY-MASTER-RECORD
                 MOVE 'N' TO MASTER-HELD-FOR-ADDITION-SW
             ELSE
                 PERFORM 330-READ-INVENTORY-MASTER
         ELSE
             MOVE 'N' TO MASTER-DELETED-SW
             IF MASTER-HELD-FOR-ADDITION
                 MOVE HELD-MASTER-RECORD
                     TO INVENTORY-MASTER-RECORD
                 MOVE 'N' TO MASTER-HELD-FOR-ADDITION-SW
             ELSE
                 PERFORM 330-READ-INVENTORY-MASTER.
*
 330-READ-INVENTORY-MASTER.
*
     READ OLDMAST INTO INVENTORY-MASTER-RECORD
         AT END
             MOVE HIGH-VALUES TO IM-ITEM-NUMBER.
*
 340-WRITE-INVENTORY-MASTER.
*
     WRITE NEW-MASTER-RECORD FROM INVENTORY-MASTER-RECORD.
*
```

Figure 7-31 COBOL code for the first nine modules of the sequential file-maintenance program (part 2 of 3)

Look, then, at the program overview in figure 7-32. Here, a master inventory file is to be updated based on receipts to inventory. Although the master file is specified as having indexed file organization, some other type of direct organization could be used without affecting the design process. To improve the efficiency of this program, the transactions are to be sorted into the master-file sequence before they are processed. Then, this program is supposed to be written so each updated master record will only be read and written once no matter how many transactions apply to it.

Figure 7-33 is a structure chart for this program. If you're not familiar with the COBOL SORT statement, the top two levels of this chart may seem awkward to you. As I explained earlier, however, the COBOL SORT statement forces this structure upon you.

```
 350-PROCESS-INVENTORY-TRAN.
*
     IF MT-DELETION
         IF IM-ITEM-NUMBER = MT-ITEM-NUMBER
             IF NOT MASTER-DELETED
                 PERFORM 360-APPLY-DELETION-TRANSACTION
             ELSE
                 PERFORM 410-WRITE-ERROR-TRANSACTION
         ELSE
             PERFORM 410-WRITE-ERROR-TRANSACTION
     ELSE
         IF MT-ADDITION
             IF IM-ITEM-NUMBER = MT-ITEM-NUMBER
                 IF MASTER-DELETED
                     PERFORM 420-APPLY-ADDITION-TRANSACTION
                 ELSE
                     PERFORM 410-WRITE-ERROR-TRANSACTION
             ELSE
                 PERFORM 420-APPLY-ADDITION-TRANSACTION
         ELSE
             IF MT-CHANGE
                 IF IM-ITEM-NUMBER = MT-ITEM-NUMBER
                     IF NOT MASTER-DELETED
                         PERFORM 440-APPLY-CHANGE-TRANSACTION
                     ELSE
                         PERFORM 410-WRITE-ERROR-TRANSACTION
                 ELSE
                     PERFORM 410-WRITE-ERROR-TRANSACTION.
*
 360-APPLY-DELETION-TRANSACTION.
*
     MOVE 'Y'               TO MASTER-DELETED-SW.
     MOVE DELETE-MESSAGE    TO ML-ACTION.
     ADD 1                  TO DELETION-COUNT.
     PERFORM 370-PRINT-MAINTENANCE-LINE.
*
```

Figure 7-31 COBOL code for the first nine modules of the sequential file-maintenance program (part 3 of 3)

Figure 7-34 gives the COBOL code for the first eight modules of this program. As you can see, module 000 contains this SORT statement:

```
SORT SORTFILE
     ON ASCENDING KEY SF-ITEM-NUMBER
     USING RCPTTRAN
     OUTPUT PROCEDURE IS 300-PROCESS-SORTED-
         TRAN-FILE.
```

In other words, the SORT statement itself will read the transaction file (a dummy module), sort it (another dummy module), and then transfer control to the output-procedure module. If an input procedure was used in the SORT statement, the get-transaction-file module wouldn't be a dummy module, but the sort module will always be a dummy module.

Some highlights follow:

Program: INV2300 UPDATE INVENTORY FILE	**Page:** 1
Designer: Anne Prince	**Date:** 08-23-84

Input/output specifications

File	Description	Use
RCPTTRAN	Receipt transaction file	Input
INVMAST	Inventory master file	Update
VRCPTRN	Valid receipt transaction file	Output
IRCPTLST	Print file: Invalid inventory receipt listing	Output
SORTFILE	Sorted inventory receipt transaction file	Output

Process specifications

The inventory master file has indexed file organization. It is a large file with low receipt activity.

The input file of receipt transactions is in a random order. Before the transactions are processed, they should be sorted into item-number sequence.

For object-program efficiency, the program should only read and write a master record once for each group of transactions that affect the master record.

The receipts must be edited and only valid receipts should be used to update the master records. The error code on the invalid listing will indicate only the first field that is invalid in each invalid record.

The totals for the update run should be printed on a separate page of printer output.

Figure 7-32 The program overview for the random update program

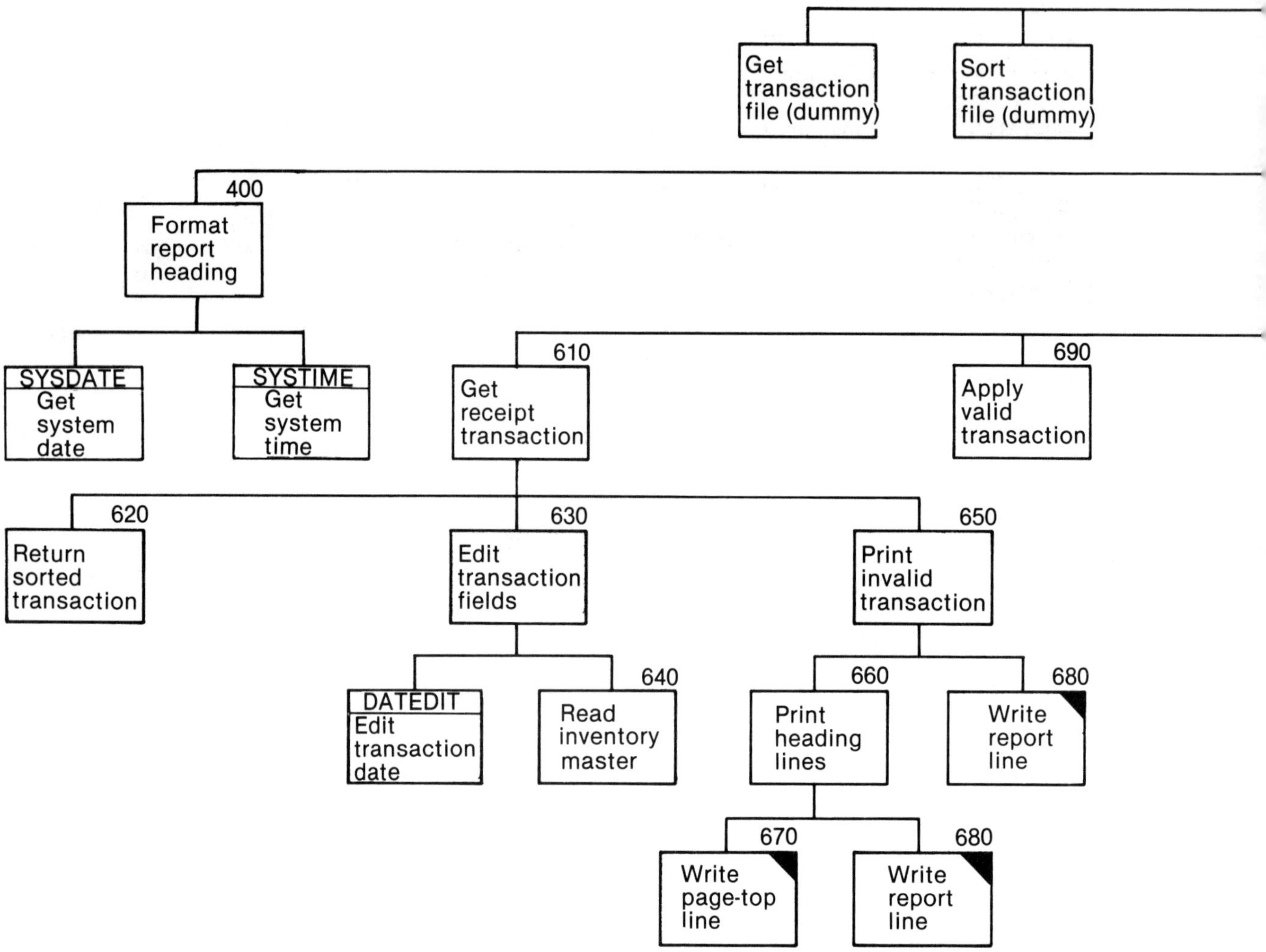

Figure 7-33 The structure chart for the random update program

1. Based on span of control, you would expect module 600 in the program to be most complicated. And, if you check the COBOL code, it is. Nevertheless, the program is quite easy to read and understand. The second most complicated module in this program is module 630, which edits the transaction records.

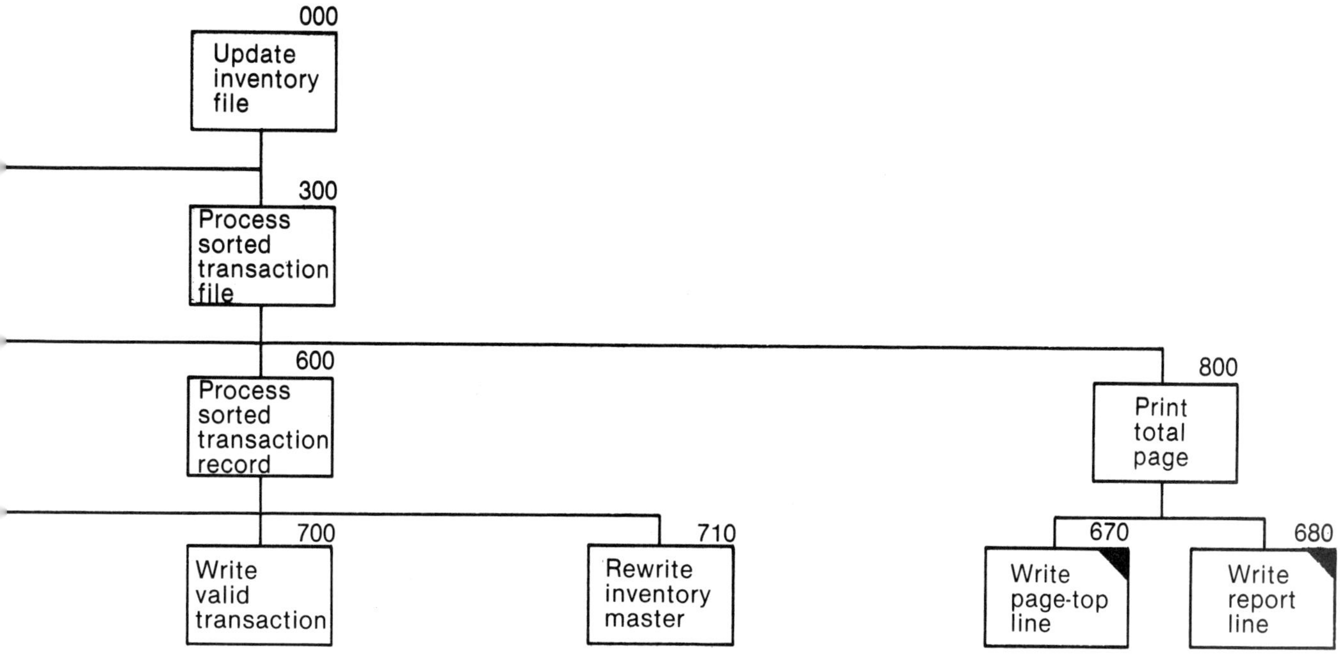

2. Part of the complexity in both modules 600 and 630 has to do with the requirement to read and write each updated master record only once so object-program efficiency is improved. Without this requirement, the COBOL code would be much simpler.

```
*
 000-UPDATE-INVENTORY-FILE    SECTION.
*
     OPEN I-O     INVMAST
          OUTPUT VRCPTRN
                 IRCPTLST.
     SORT SORTFILE
         ON ASCENDING KEY SF-ITEM-NUMBER
         USING RCPTTRAN
         OUTPUT PROCEDURE IS 300-PROCESS-SORTED-TRAN-FILE.
     IF SORT-RETURN IS NOT ZERO
         DISPLAY 'SORT FAILED'.
     CLOSE INVMAST
           VRCPTRN
           IRCPTLST.
     STOP RUN.
*
 300-PROCESS-SORTED-TRAN-FILE     SECTION.
*
     PERFORM 400-FORMAT-REPORT-HEADING.
     PERFORM 600-PROCESS-SORTED-TRAN-RECORD
         UNTIL TRAN-EOF.
     PERFORM 800-PRINT-TOTAL-PAGE.
     GO TO 300-EXIT.
*
 400-FORMAT-REPORT-HEADING.
*
     CALL 'SYSDATE' USING TODAYS-DATE.
     MOVE TODAYS-DATE  TO HDG1-DATE.
     MOVE COMPANY-NAME TO HDG1-COMPANY-NAME.
     CALL 'SYSTIME' USING HDG2-TIME-DATA.
     MOVE 'INV2300'    TO HDG2-REPORT-NUMBER.
     MOVE REPORT-TITLE TO HDG3-REPORT-TITLE.
*
 600-PROCESS-SORTED-TRAN-RECORD.
*
     MOVE 'N' TO VALID-TRAN-SW.
     PERFORM 610-GET-RECEIPT-TRANSACTION
         UNTIL VALID-TRAN.
     IF NOT TRAN-EOF
         IF FIRST-RECORD
             MOVE RT-ITEM-NUMBER          TO OLD-ITEM-NUMBER
             MOVE NEXT-INVENTORY-RECORD TO INVENTORY-MASTER-RECORD
             MOVE 'N'                     TO FIRST-RECORD-SW.
     IF NOT TRAN-EOF
         IF RT-ITEM-NUMBER EQUAL OLD-ITEM-NUMBER
             PERFORM 690-APPLY-VALID-TRANSACTION
             PERFORM 700-WRITE-VALID-TRANSACTION.
     IF RT-ITEM-NUMBER GREATER OLD-ITEM-NUMBER
         PERFORM 710-REWRITE-INVENTORY-MASTER
         IF NOT TRAN-EOF
             MOVE NEXT-INVENTORY-RECORD TO INVENTORY-MASTER-RECORD
             MOVE RT-ITEM-NUMBER          TO OLD-ITEM-NUMBER
             PERFORM 690-APPLY-VALID-TRANSACTION
             PERFORM 700-WRITE-VALID-TRANSACTION.
*
```

Figure 7-34 COBOL code for the first eight modules of the random update program (part 1 of 2)

```
 610-GET-RECEIPT-TRANSACTION.
*
     MOVE 'Y' TO VALID-TRAN-SW.
     PERFORM 620-RETURN-SORTED-TRANSACTION.
     IF NOT TRAN-EOF
         ADD 1 TO TRANSACTION-COUNT
         PERFORM 630-EDIT-TRANSACTION-FIELDS
         IF NOT VALID-TRAN
             PERFORM 650-PRINT-INVALID-TRANSACTION.
*
 620-RETURN-SORTED-TRANSACTION.
*
     RETURN SORTFILE INTO RECEIPT-TRANSACTION
         AT END
             MOVE HIGH-VALUE TO RT-ITEM-NUMBER
             MOVE 'Y' TO TRAN-EOF-SW.
*
 630-EDIT-TRANSACTION-FIELDS.
*
     MOVE 'Y' TO MASTER-FOUND-SW.
     IF RT-ITEM-NUMBER GREATER OLD-ITEM-NUMBER
         MOVE RT-ITEM-NUMBER TO IR-ITEM-NUMBER
         PERFORM 640-READ-INVENTORY-MASTER.
     IF NOT MASTER-FOUND
         MOVE FIELD-1 TO ITL-ERROR-CODE
         MOVE 'N'     TO VALID-TRAN-SW
     ELSE
         IF           RT-VENDOR-NUMBER NOT NUMERIC
                   OR RT-VENDOR-NUMBER NOT GREATER THAN ZERO
             MOVE FIELD-2 TO ITL-ERROR-CODE
             MOVE 'N'     TO VALID-TRAN-SW
         ELSE
             CALL 'DATEDIT' USING RT-RECEIPT-DATE, VALID-DATE-SW
             IF NOT VALID-DATE
                 MOVE FIELD-3 TO ITL-ERROR-CODE
                 MOVE 'N'     TO VALID-TRAN-SW
             ELSE IF RT-RECEIPT-YEAR NOT EQUAL TODAYS-YEAR
                 MOVE FIELD-3 TO ITL-ERROR-CODE
                 MOVE 'N'     TO VALID-TRAN-SW
             ELSE IF RT-RECEIPT-QUANTITY NOT GREATER THAN ZERO
                 MOVE FIELD-4 TO ITL-ERROR-CODE
                 MOVE 'N'     TO VALID-TRAN-SW.
*
 640-READ-INVENTORY-MASTER.
*
     READ INVMAST INTO NEXT-INVENTORY-RECORD
         INVALID KEY
             MOVE 'N' TO MASTER-FOUND-SW.
*
```

Figure 7-34 COBOL code for the first eight modules of the random update program (part 2 of 2)

3. The get-valid-transaction module uses the verb *get* as recommended in the verb list in figure 7-5. As you can see, it has three subordinate modules that (1) return a record from the sort, (2) edit the record, and (3) dispose of it if it's invalid.

4. Although our general recommendation is to avoid the use of the verb *process*, I've used it twice in this structure chart. Both times, I've used it in high-level control modules, one of which is forced upon me by use of the SORT statement. Perhaps you can find better verbs for these modules, but no matter what you do your choice of verbs in high-level modules like these is somewhat artificial.

Although a random update program can be designed in many different ways, I think the best thing to do is to find a structure that you like, settle on it, and use it as a model for all of the update programs that you write. And you should do the same thing for a random file-maintenance program. Once you have good models for each type of program, it can save you many hours of development time. In fact, you can usually use the modules in the top three or four levels of the structure chart in all the update and file-maintenance programs you develop. The primary changes from one program to the next will be in the work modules, not the control modules, and these changes are usually routine.

Four basic program structures

In chapter 6, I told you to use production programs as your model programs. That's why the programs I've just presented aren't generalized abstractions. I wanted each of them to have some realistic elements that complicated the code because that's the way production programs are.

In order to reuse a production program, though, you must be able to see the basic structure that underlies the specific programming requirements. It is this basic structure that you can reuse from one program to the next. And it is the lower-level work modules that change from one program to the next.

At this time, then, I'd like to show you the basic structures of the four model programs I've presented in this book. These structure charts don't show the lower-level modules that you'd have in a production program. And they use general module names. This should make it easier for you to see how one model program applies in a general way to all programs of its type.

The basic structure of the edit program Figure 7-35 shows you the basic structure of an edit program that you can derive from the structure chart in figure 7-1. This design is for one type of record in a single transaction file. But with minor modifications it can be used for editing two or more different types of records in one or more files.

The basic structure of the report-preparation program Figure 7-36 gives the basic structure of a report-preparation program that you can derive from the structure chart in figure 7-27. With little effort, it can be modified so it will produce reports with no intermediate totals, only one

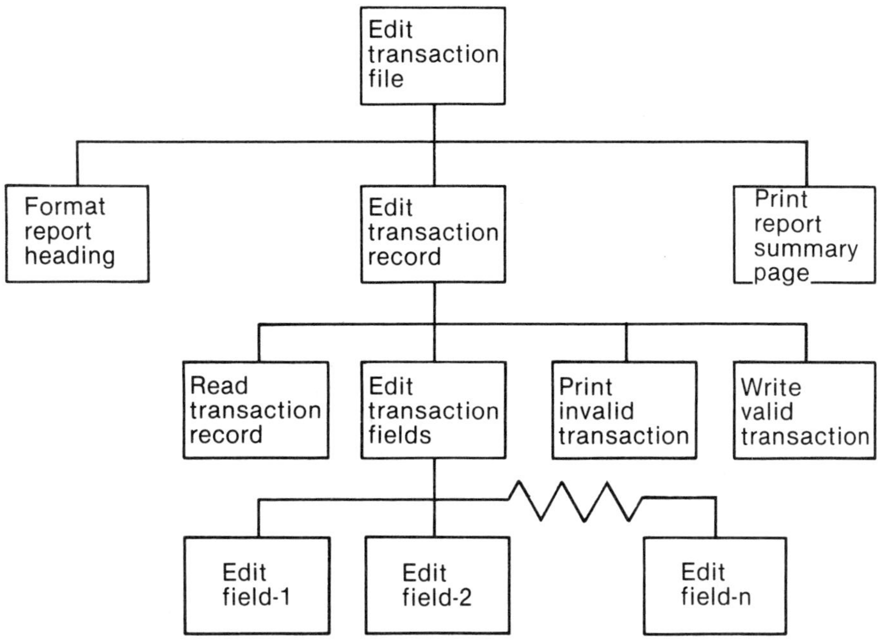

Figure 7-35 The basic structure of an edit program

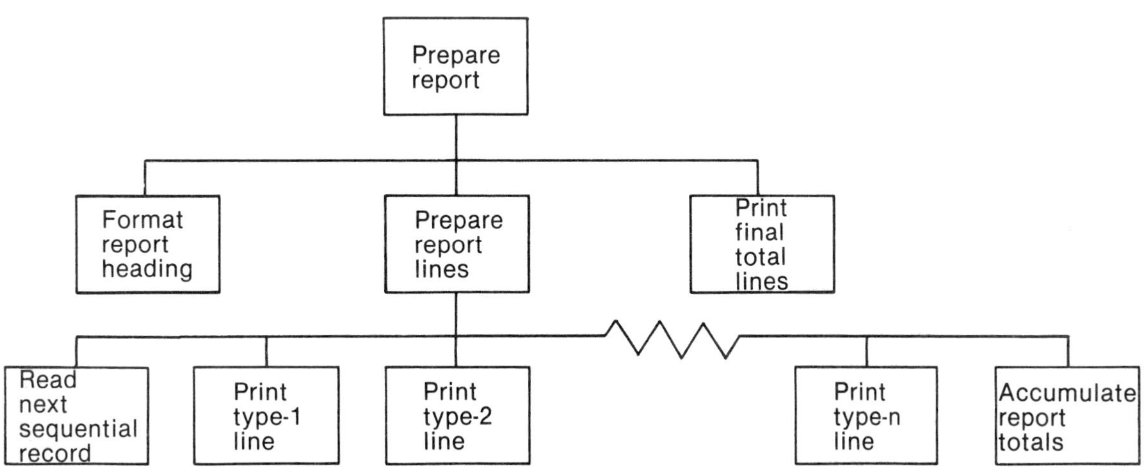

Figure 7-36 The basic structure of a report-preparation program

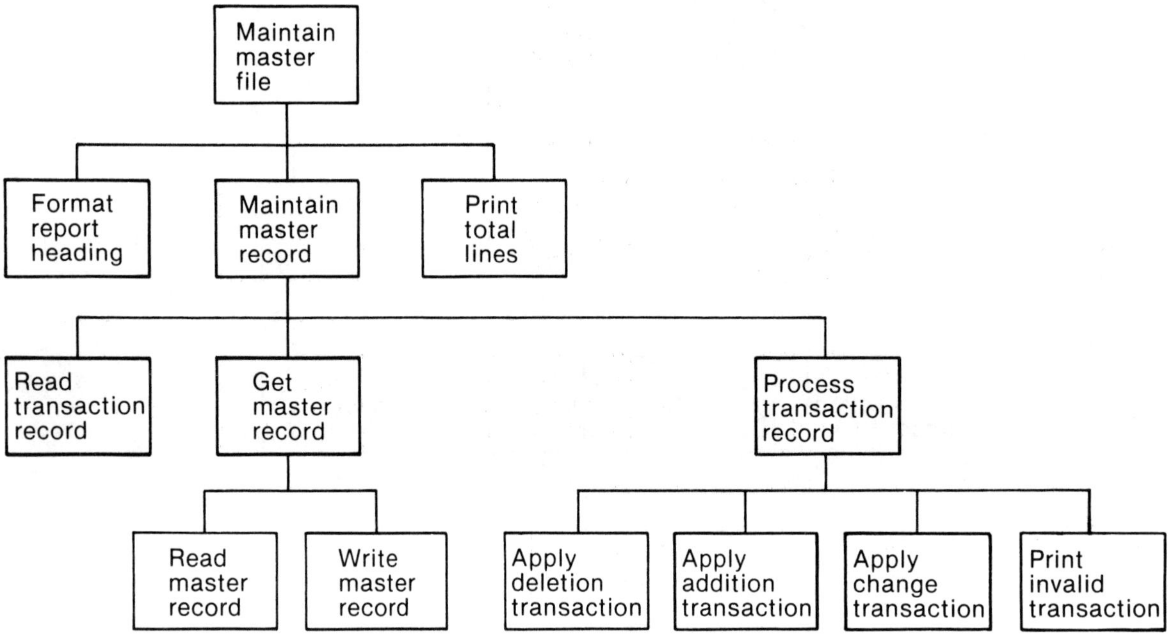

Figure 7-37 The basic structure of a sequental file-maintenance program

level of totals, or with 3 or more levels of totals. Similarly, it can be modified so it extracts data from more than one input file.

The basic structure of the sequential file-maintenance program Figure 7-37 gives the basic structure of a sequential file-maintenance program that you can derive from the structure chart in figure 7-30. It can easily be modified so it updates a master record based on one or more transactions. In fact, an update program has a simpler structure than a file-maintenance program.

The basic structure of the random update program Figure 7-38 gives the basic structure of a random update program that you can derive from the structure chart in figure 7-33. It can easily be modified so that it becomes a file-maintenance program that provides for changes, deletions, and additions.

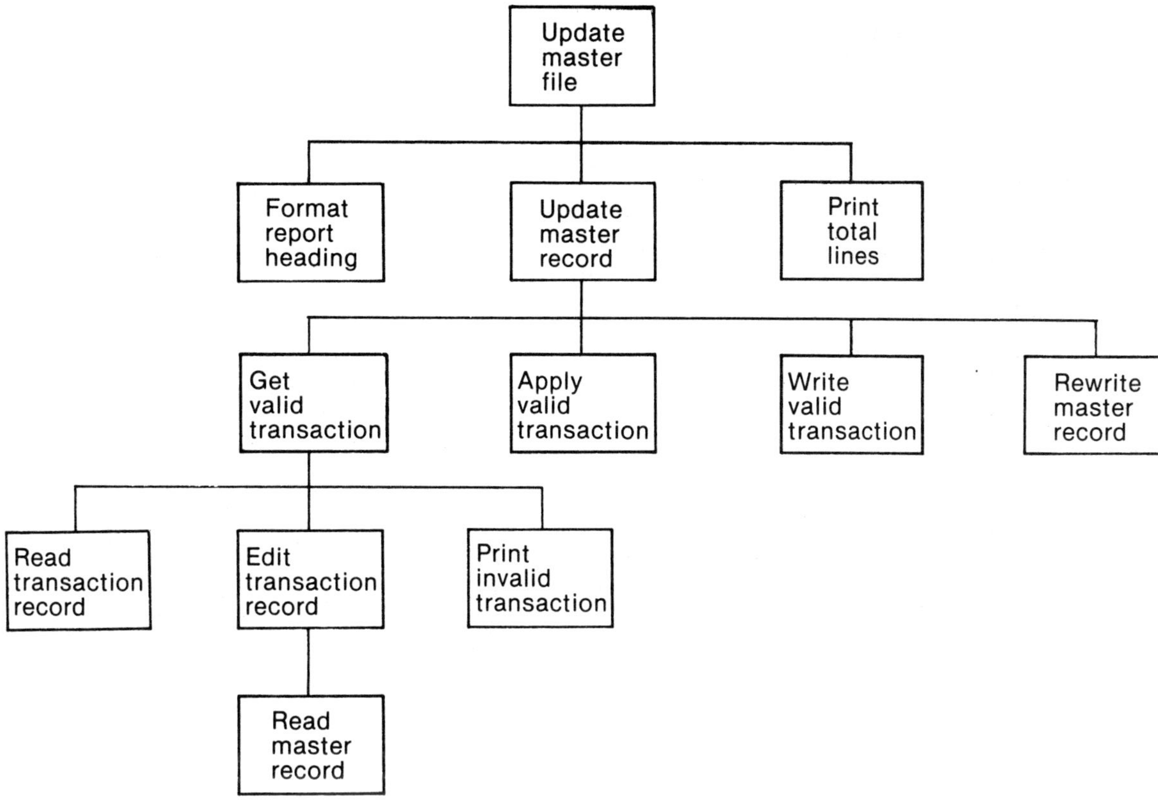

Figure 7-38 The basic structure of a random update program

Reusing the model programs

Once you understand the basic structures that the model programs contain, you can use their designs as the basis for many different programs. Not only can you use one structure chart as the basis for designing a similar program, but you can combine elements taken from two or more structure charts to create the design for a new program. To give you a better idea about this, let me present a few examples.

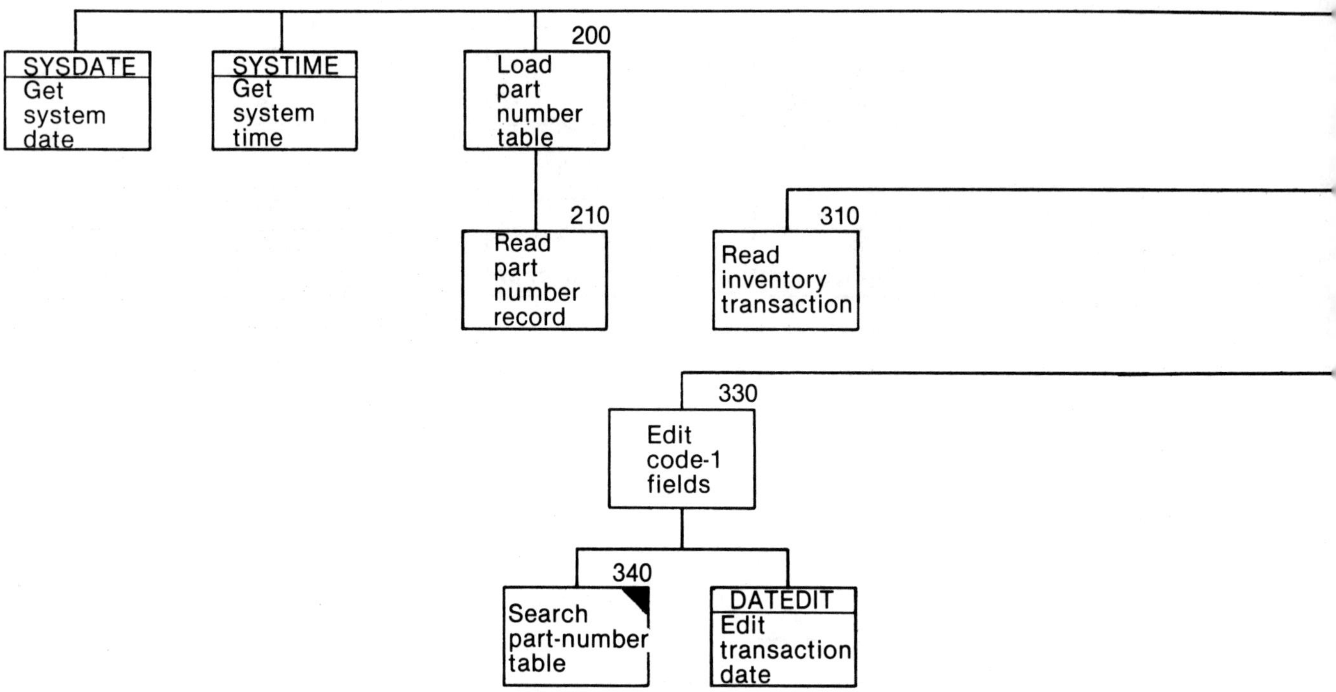

Figure 7-39 A structure chart for an edit program that uses Report Writer

An edit program that uses Report Writer Can you reuse the design of a model program when you want to develop a program that uses a special programming feature like Report Writer? You bet. For instance, the structure chart in figure 7-39 shows the design for the edit program when you use the Report Writer feature of COBOL to prepare the invalid-transaction listing. Because one Report Writer statement prints all of the lines of a report, all of the print modules are replaced by one Report Writer generate module. This module contains only one statement, the GENERATE statement. Otherwise, the structure of the edit program is left intact.

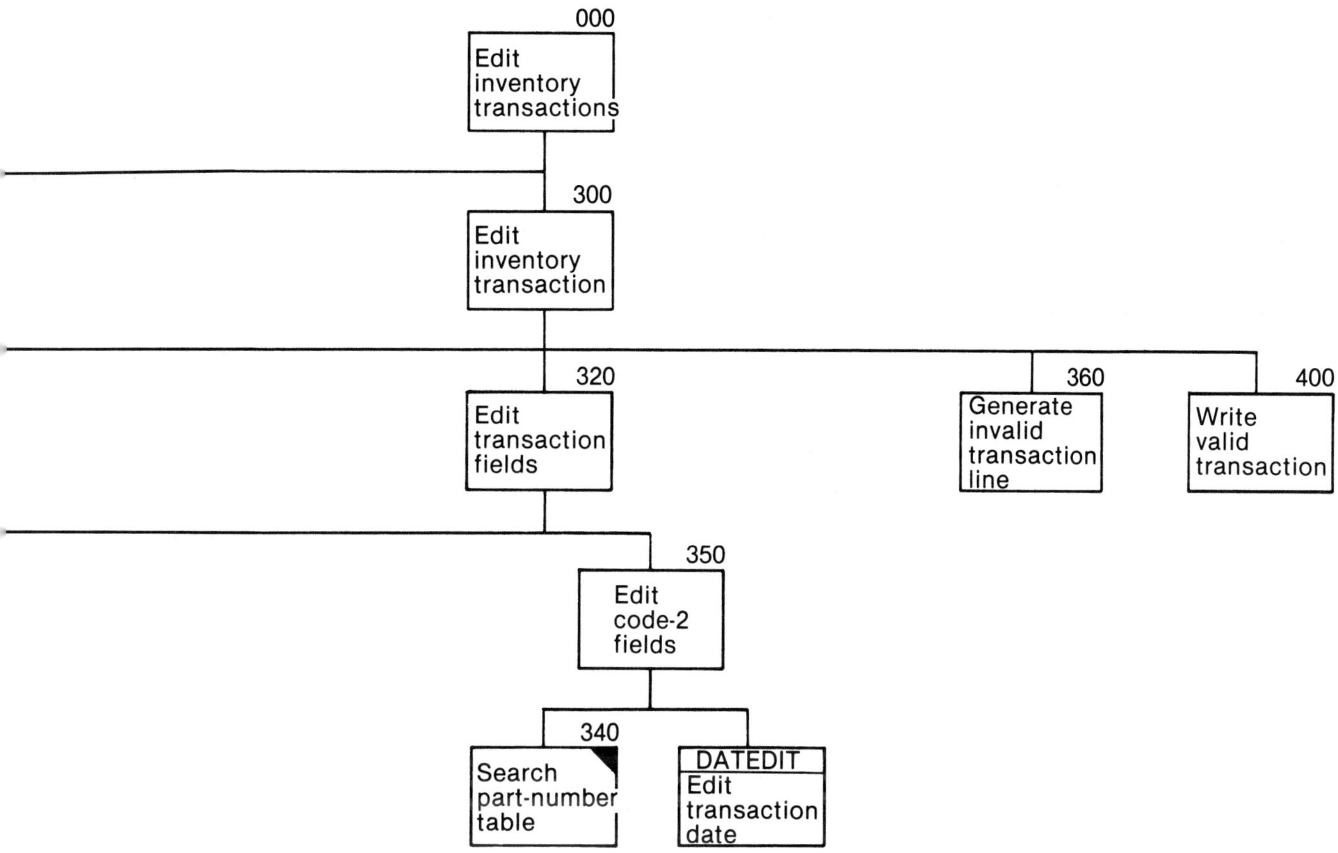

Because several modules of the original edit program are replaced by one Report Writer module, the edit program is simplified when you use Report Writer. That's why we feel that Report Writer is a valuable aid to productivity for the COBOL programmer. Nevertheless, it appears now that Report Writer will be dropped when the 198X COBOL standards are released, so we can't recommend that you continue to use it. I present this example to show that a model program can usually be modified to make use of a special programming feature.

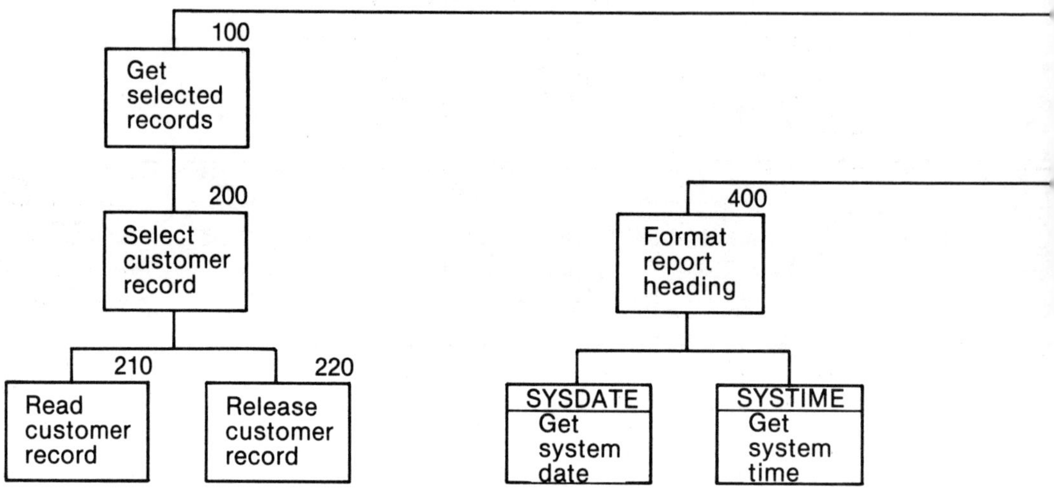

Figure 7-40 A structure chart for a report-preparation program that lists selected customer records after sorting them in descending sequence by year-to-date sales

A report-preparation program for a selective listing with an internal sort Suppose you have to prepare a listing of customers who have bought more than $10,000 worth of your products this year-to-date. In addition, this listing is to be in descending sequence by year-to-date sales; in other words, the listing starts with the best of the selected customers and ends with the worst. Can you use the model programs I've presented in this topic as a basis for designing this new program?

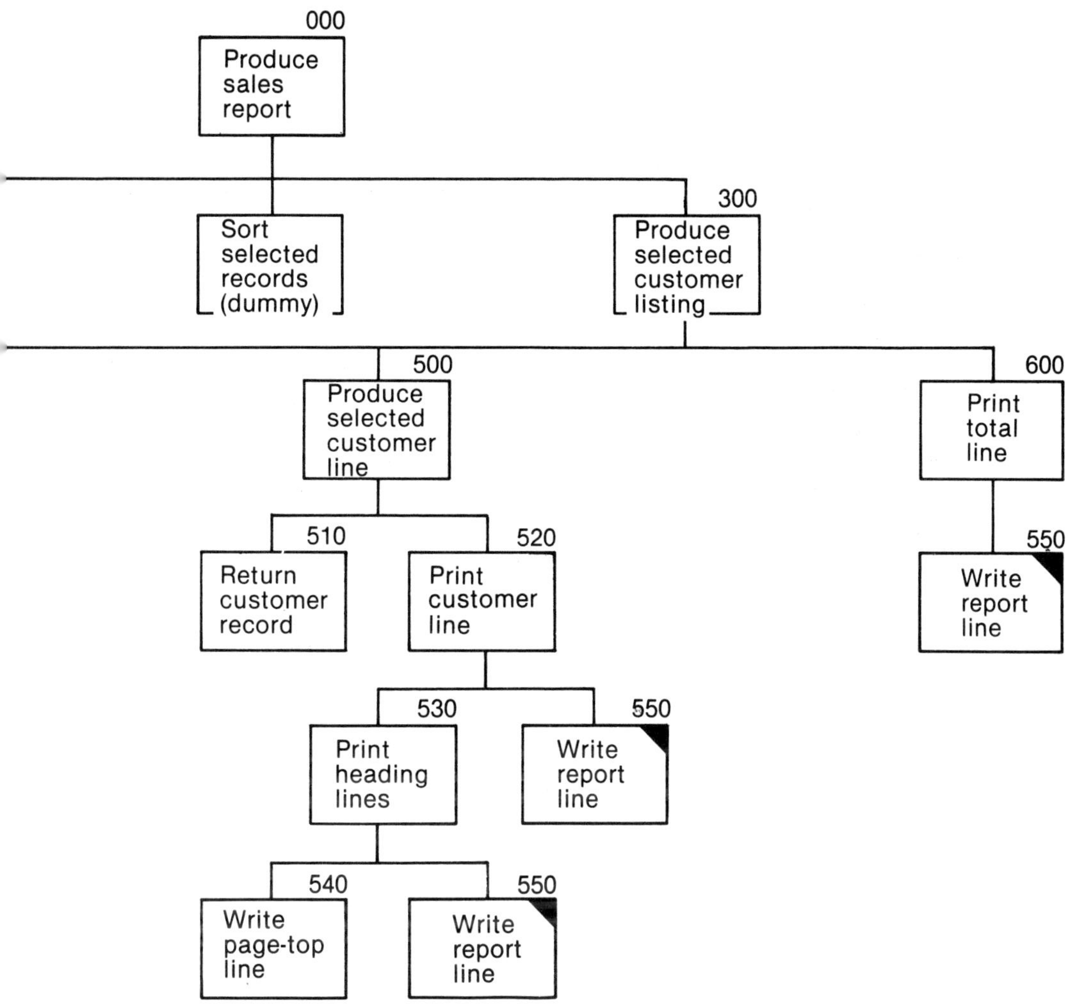

Of course, you can. But in this case you must combine the sort structure in the random update program (figure 7-33) with the structure of the report-preparation program (figure 7-27). An acceptable solution derived from these structure charts is shown in figure 7-40. In brief, the get-selected-records leg of the program is the input procedure for the sort statement. The produce-selected-customer-listing leg is the output procedure. And since the program prints only one line per selected record, the structure of the report-preparation leg is quite simple.

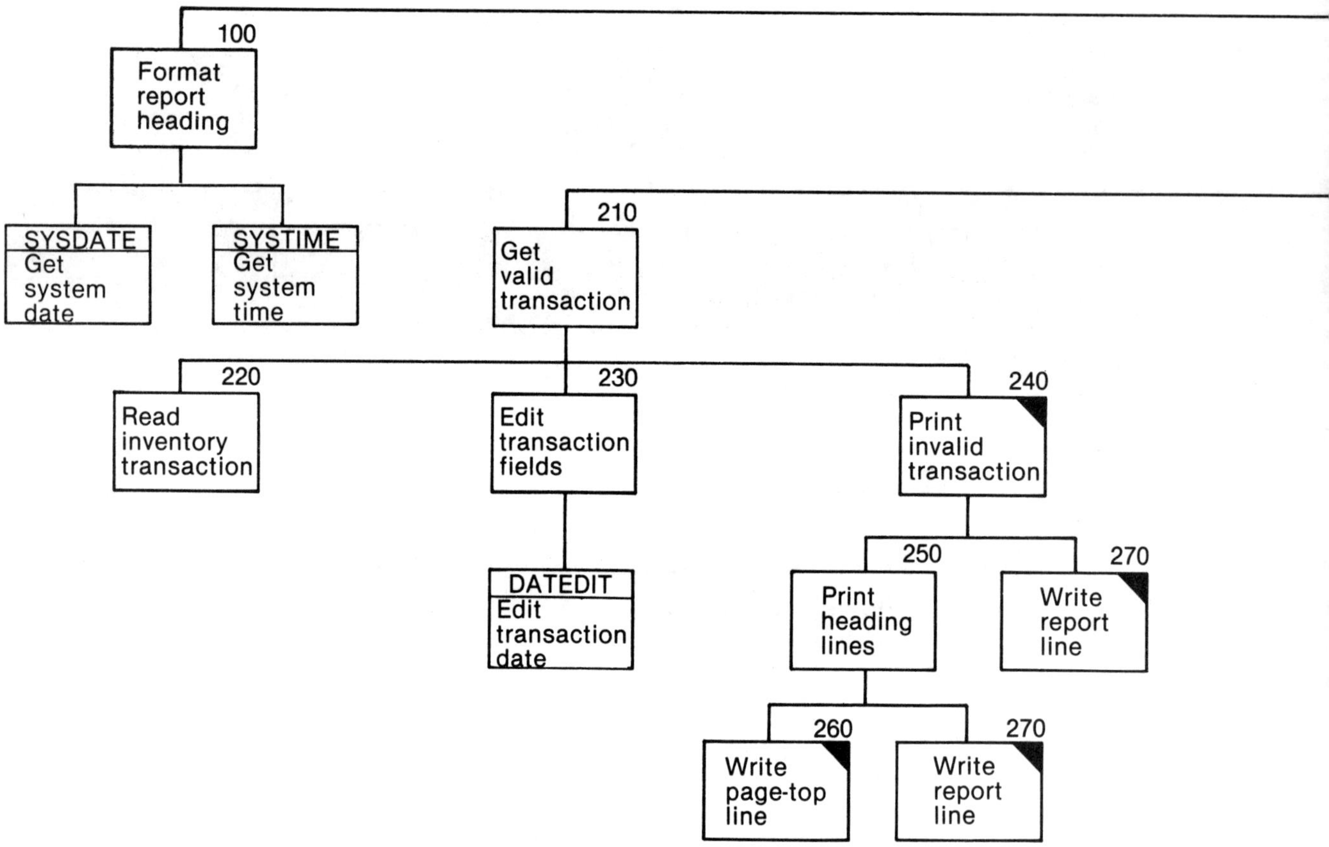

Figure 7-41 A structure chart for a sequential update program that edits the transaction records

A sequential update program with editing If you have to write a program that combines sequential file-updating with editing, you can combine portions of the structure chart in figure 7-1 with portions of the structure chart in figure 7-30. For instance, the structure chart in figure 7-41 is for a program that edits transaction records and then uses the

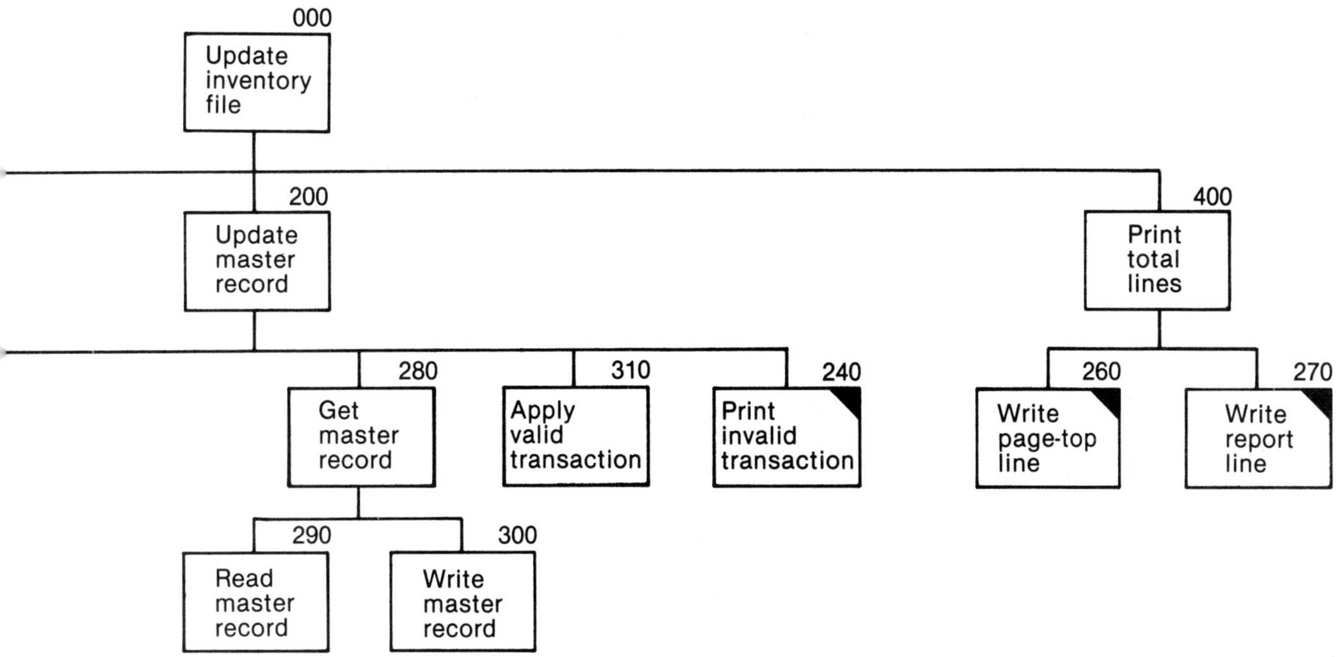

valid records to update records in an inventory master file. Since this program doesn't provide for adding records to a file and deleting records from it, the update portion of the structure is simpler than the one in figure 7-30. Similarly, since the program edits only one type of transaction, the edit portion of the program is simpler than the one in figure 7-1.

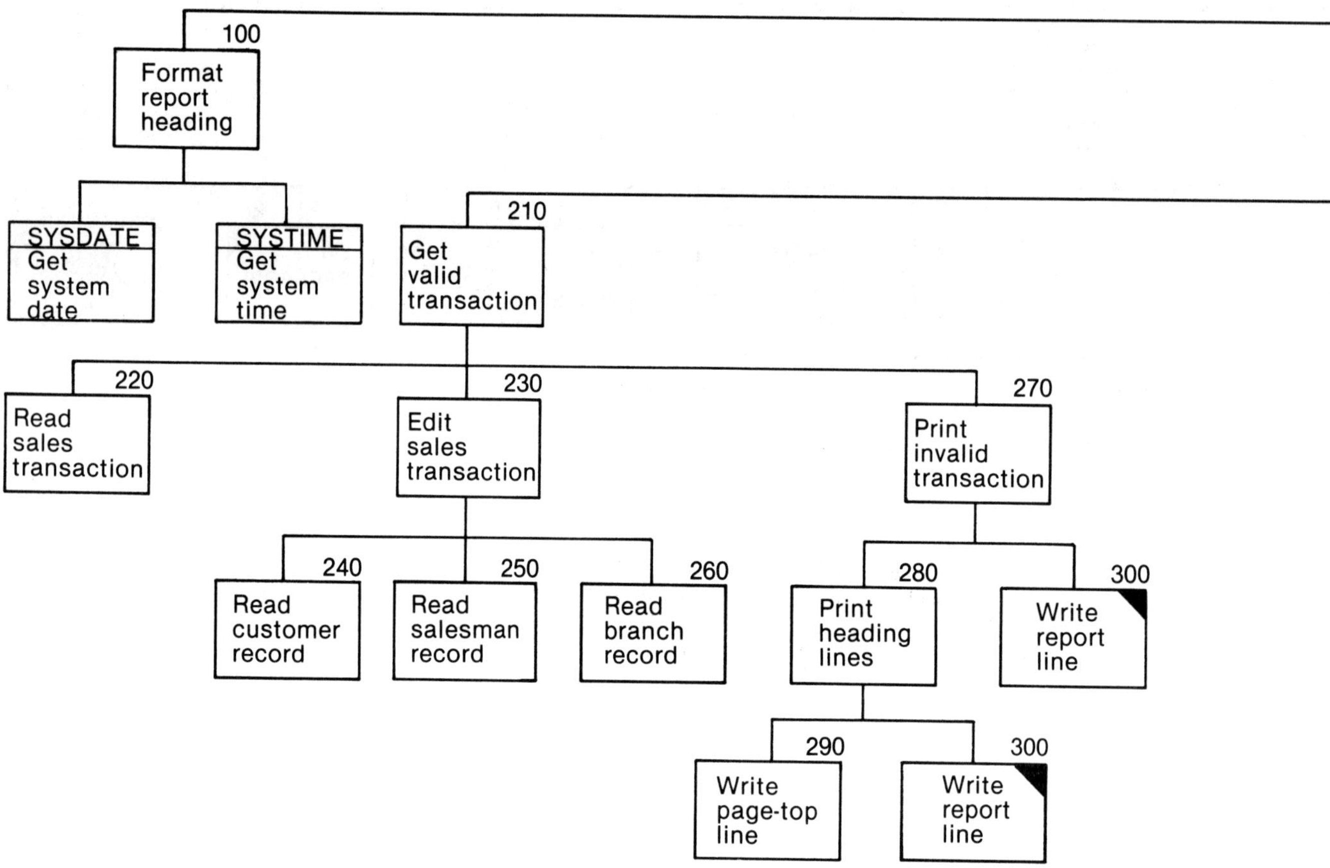

Figure 7-42 A structure chart for a random update program that updates three master records for each valid transaction

A random update program that updates three master files Figure 7-42 presents a structure chart for a random update program that updates three master files for each valid sales transaction. In this case, the transaction file is in sequence by customer number so for object-program efficiency the program should only read and write one customer master record for each group of transactions with the same customer number. On the other hand, the transaction file isn't in sequence by salesman number or branch number so these master records can be read and written once for each transaction. Can you see how you can derive this structure chart from the model program in figure 7-33?

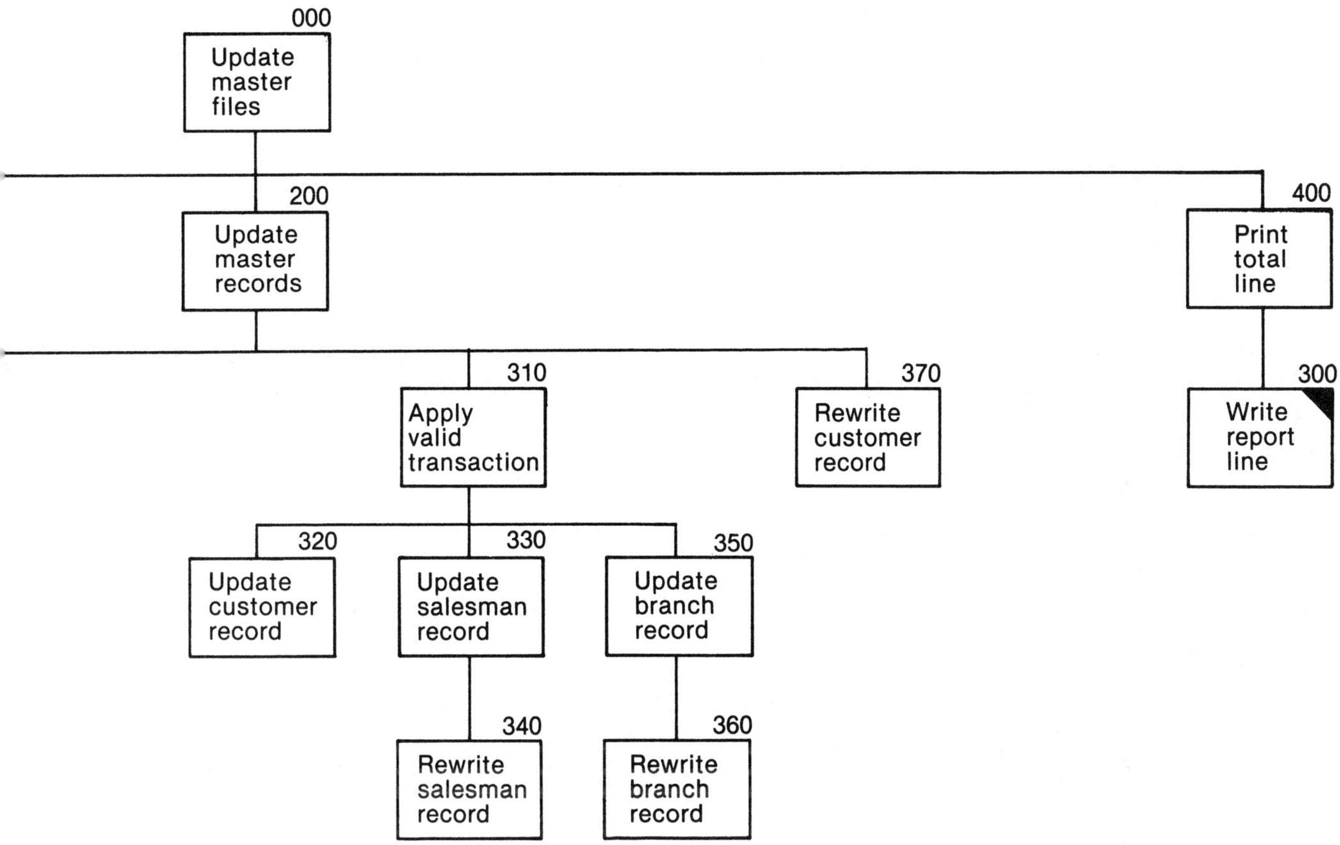

In the get-valid-transaction leg of the program, the edit leg calls modules that read three master records for each transaction. This helps determine whether the transaction is valid. If the edit leg finds the related record in each file, the transaction is considered valid and processing continues. Otherwise, this leg of the program prints a line on the invalid transaction listing.

In the apply-valid-transaction leg of the program, the transaction is applied to the three master records read in the edit leg. For object-program efficiency, the customer record is updated in storage in this leg, but it isn't rewritten on the master file until all of its transactions have been processed. That's why module 370 isn't in this leg of the program. In contrast, the update modules for the salesman and branch records call rewrite modules so the master records are rewritten on the master files each time they are updated.

The benefits of this design method

I hope by now you can see the benefits of this design method. Once you have your own library of model programs, you can start to reuse portions of the designs from one program to the next. And often you can reuse entire structure charts, deleting modules that you don't need and adding modules that you do need.

Although this by itself can lead to a significant increase in programming productivity, this also means that you can reuse COBOL code from one program to another. The code in control modules, for example, can often be used by changing only a few of the data or procedure names. And the code in many edit, search, and I/O modules can also be used with only minor modifications. In fact, you should code few modules from scratch. And this can lead to a dramatic increase in your productivity.

The presentation in this topic should also indicate how easy it is to modify a structured program if enhancements are requested. If, for example, the edit program is supposed to be changed so it edits a third type of record, you add a few modules to the program, change one of the control modules, and the enhancement is done. Since you don't have to change any of the other modules in the program, you can make an enhancement like this with maximum efficiency. Similarly, it's easy to modify programs when editing rules change, print formats change, and so on.

When you plan the code for the modules of a program or when you actually try to code them, you will sometimes find that you want to change the design. For instance, you may want to add another module to a chart. Or you may want to combine two or more modules into a single module. In some cases, if you find that a control module is extremely difficult to code, you may want to add some subordinate modules to the structure chart. When you decide to make one of these changes, you simply modify the structure chart and continue. That too is a benefit of structured programming. You can make changes to the design of a program as you implement it without paying a price in terms of reduced productivity.

Discussion

At this point, you should be able to create structure charts of your own. When you create new charts, you should base them on the model programs and basic program structures presented in this chapter. After you do this for a while, you will get a better appreciation for our design method. Then, you can develop your own library of model programs, one for each type of program you write.

At first, of course, you should expect to struggle a bit when you design a new program using the methods presented in this chapter. Before you will be able to design a program with maximum efficiency, you need to study the model programs, the basic structures, and the other structures presented in this topic. You need to understand the COBOL code for the critical modules of each program (which you may not be able to do until you read chapter 9). And you need to get some experience with these methods by applying them to your own production programs.

To speed up the learning process, we recommend that you use our *COBOL Programmer's Handbook*. It presents the complete documentation of the four model programs including the COBOL listings. It presents design and coding alternatives. It presents standards for program development ...and much more. By studying the materials in this *Handbook*, you can quickly see how all the tasks of structured program development fit together.

As you get more experience with structured programming, you'll find that you will make fewer modifications to your program designs as you code and test your programs. This is natural because you'll have a better idea from the start as to how a module will actually be coded using structured COBOL. In other words, since design and coding are to some extent related, you'll be able to design better structure charts after you learn how to code the modules of a design. So let's get on with the chapters on planning the code for the modules of a program and actually coding them. But first, the next topic gives you a quick look at some other ways to design programs.

Terminology

multilevel report
control field
update program
file-maintenance program
key field

Objectives

1. Given program specifications for any batch program, design an effective structure chart for its implementation.

2. Given the documentation for a program and specifications for a program modification, change the structure chart so it provides for the required modifications.

Topic 4 Other design methods

As I said in chapter 4, Paul's design methods are used in hundreds of COBOL shops throughout the country. Three of the four leading COBOL texts present his methods. And there's no doubt in my mind that his methods lead to improved programmer productivity and program quality.

Nevertheless, Paul's methods aren't used in a majority of the COBOL shops. In fact, several other methods of top-down design are in common use. And I think this helps explain why structured programming hasn't lived up to its potential in most COBOL shops.

In this topic, then, I'd like to introduce you to some other design methods. I'd like to show you what you might want to use...and what you should avoid. When you first see some of these other methods, you'll be struck by the differences in the graphic conventions. But these are only trivial differences. What you must watch out for are the differences in substance.

Graphic alternatives

I would say that there is general agreement in the industry that you should design a program using some sort of structure chart. About 50 percent of the people who responded to our COBOL survey said they used them. But the form of these charts may vary considerably from one designer to another. Also, some designers will put programming notation on their charts, while others won't.

Although 10 percent of the people who responded to our survey said they used Warnier/Orr diagrams for program design, I'm not going to present them in this topic. I will, however, present them in a larger context in chapter 16.

Tree charts Some people distinguish between tree charts and structure charts. For instance, figure 7-43 presents a tree chart for the edit program. All of the modules are the same as in figure 7-1, it's just that they are connected by straight lines ending in arrowheads. Also, you can see that a common module isn't repeated each time it is needed in the chart; instead, one line is drawn to a common module from each module that calls it.

Frankly, it doesn't matter much whether you use tree charts or structure charts. I think it's a little easier to draw structure charts and to repeat common modules wherever they are needed. And I can see no purpose at all for the arrowheads. But if you prefer to use tree charts, that should have little or no effect on the results you get from structured programming.

Charts that show programming detail Some designers like to show some of the important programming details of a program on the structure chart or tree chart. This is illustrated by the design in figure 7-44, another design for the edit program. In this case, the circle around the rightmost three lines leading from the top-level module indicates that these modules are executed repeatedly. In contrast, the leftmost module in level 1 is executed only once.

The little circles with arrows indicate data and switches that are passed between the modules of the program. The solid circles represent switches; the other circles represent data. For instance, the load-part-number-table module passes the table data and the end-of-file (EOF) switch for the part-number file to the top-level module. Similarly, the top-level module passes the transaction data to the invalid-print module and the write-valid-record module.

In my opinion, this type of information should be omitted from the structure chart. Not only does it make the structure chart more difficult to create and understand, it makes it more difficult to change. Furthermore, some of this information is difficult to develop without actually documenting the modules. Finally, it forces the programmer to think in terms of procedures and details...just the type of thinking you should try to avoid when you're designing a program.

Here again, though, I don't think this is a critical factor. If showing some of these programming details helps you keep things in perspective, go ahead and do it. I don't think it will have much effect on your productivity or the quality of your programs. Eventually, I think you'll realize that you don't need to be concerned about this detail when you design a program.

Common problems with other design methods

At this time, I'd like to present some problems with other methods that do make a difference. I'll present them in order of importance. The first one is critical to the success of your structured-programming efforts. The others are less critical, but they do make a difference.

Modules that can't be coded with a single COBOL paragraph I've already mentioned the importance of being able to code each module of a program's design in a single COBOL paragraph. Now, let's look at a design that doesn't provide for this. Look, for example, at the design in figure 7-44. Forget the graphic differences and imagine how the modules of the program must be coded.

Obviously, you can't code the top-level module as a single paragraph. The normal way that a module like this is coded requires at least two

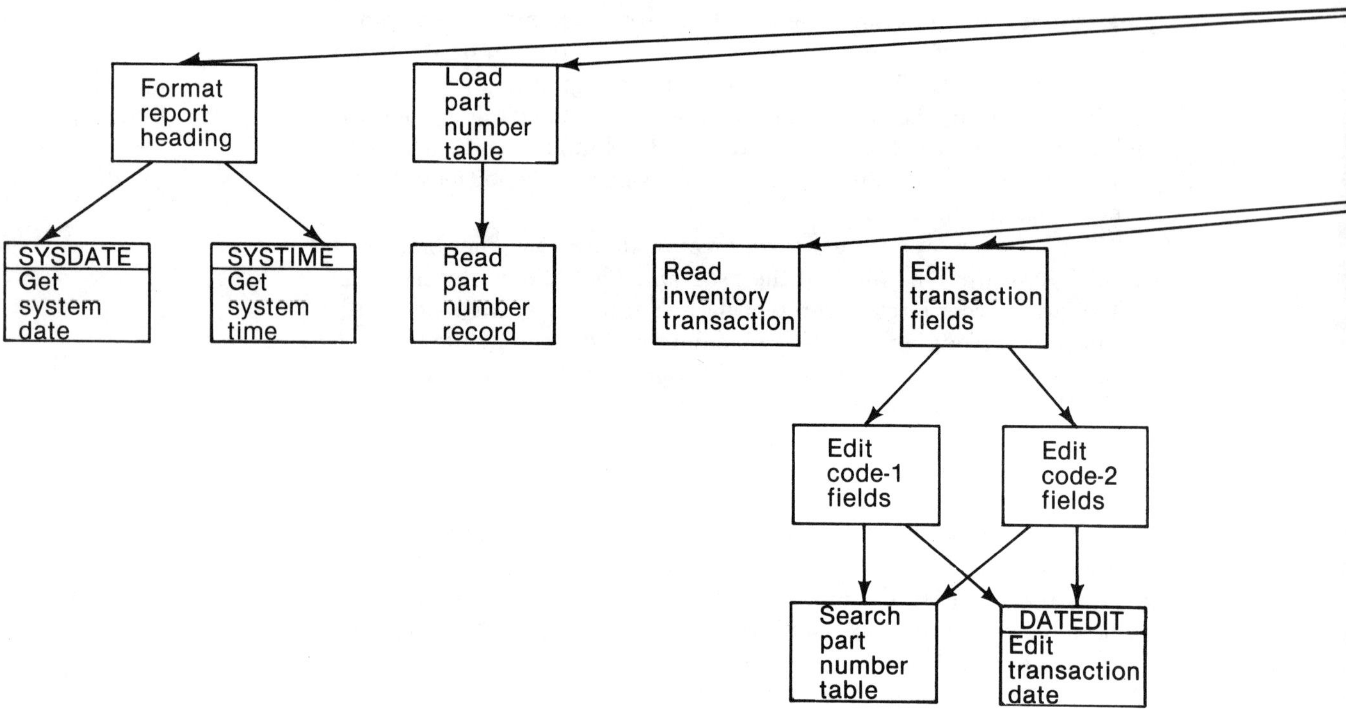

Figure 7-43 A tree chart for the edit program

paragraphs, the equivalent of our top-level module and the primary level-1 module. But a module like this may be coded as four or more paragraphs with at least one paragraph for initialization functions and another for termination functions.

Now look at the invalid-print module. Because we have presented the complete code for this function in appendix A, we know that it requires at least four paragraphs if you isolate the I/O statements in their own modules as you should. Even if you don't isolate the I/O statements, it should take two or more paragraphs. The problem is that you don't know how many paragraphs a module on the structure chart in figure 7-44 will require.

Since the edit program is a simple program that requires a total of only 16 paragraphs, violating the rule of one paragraph per module isn't that critical. But what if a program requires several dozen paragraphs and the structure chart only shows 10 or 12 modules. That means that each of the modules on the structure chart becomes a programming problem in itself consisting of several pages of COBOL code. So the

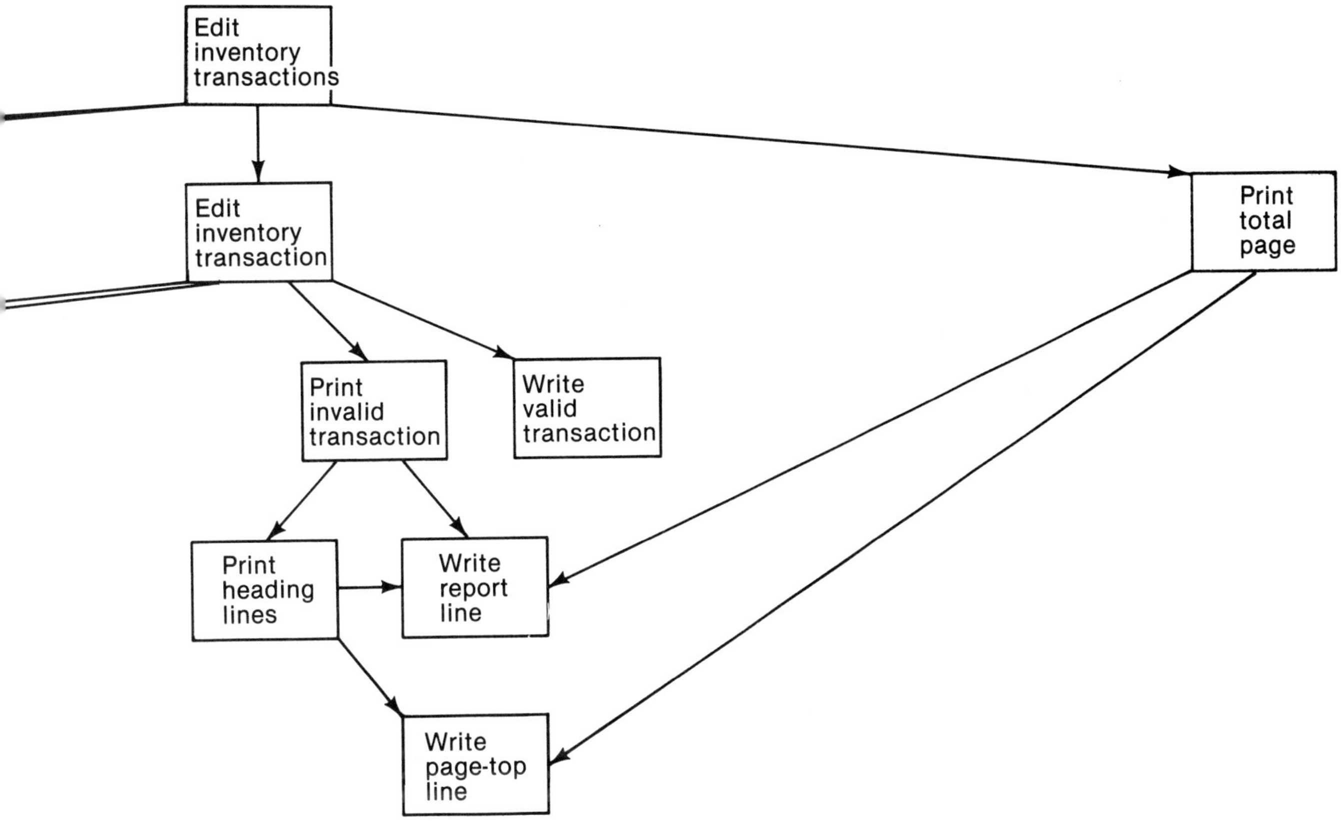

programmer is back to where he was before he took up structured programming...he's coding without a clear guide to the paragraphs he's going to write.

So there's no missing the point, we think that this is the most important single issue in a structured design method. If the design doesn't provide an index to all of the paragraphs of the COBOL program, you can't reuse old structure charts in new programs as easily. And you can't reuse paragraphs from one program to the next as easily. So both program quality and programmer productivity suffer.

In fact, I'll make this statement. *The more paragraphs you require per module on the structure chart, the worse your program is.* So a program that averages five paragraphs per module is significantly worse than a program that averages two paragraphs per module. And your goal should be one paragraph per module.

Questionable naming conventions Naming modules on a structure chart may seem rather trivial at first, but it has a significant effect on the

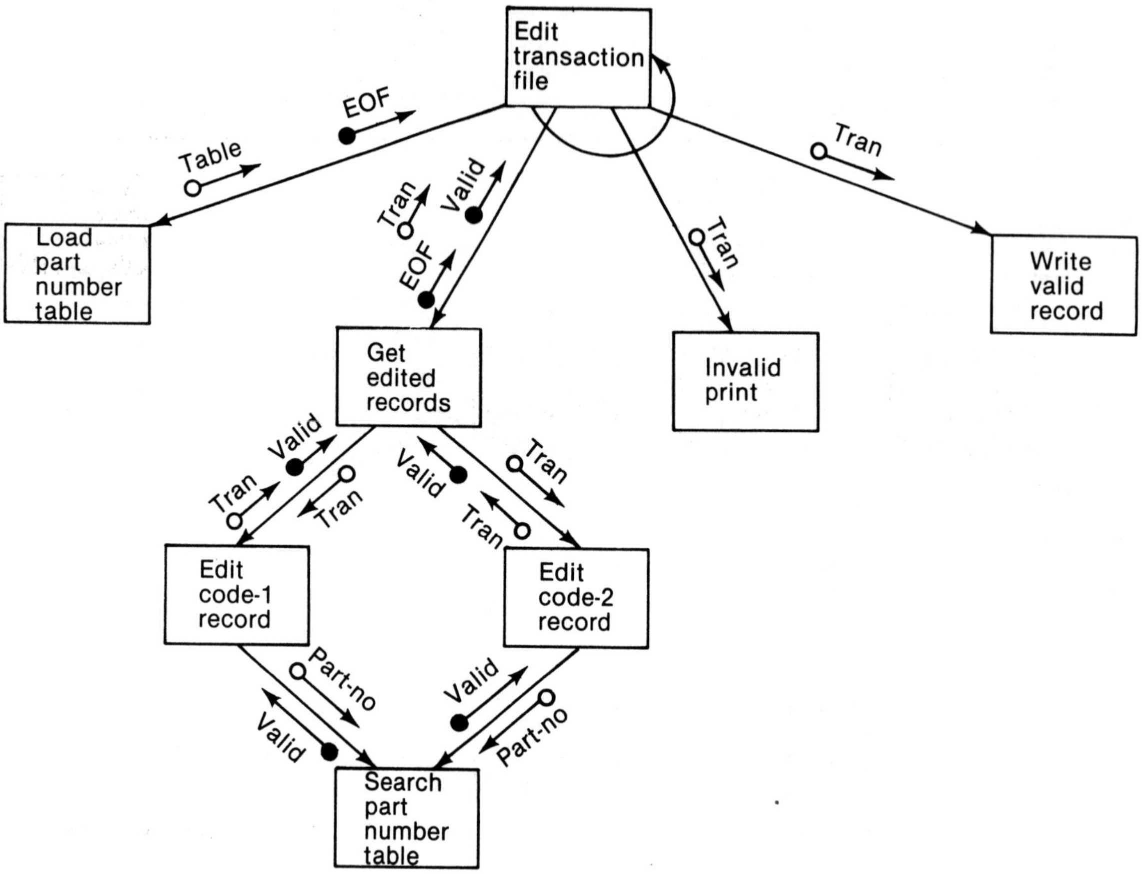

Figure 7-44 A tree chart for the edit program with some coding detail (and some design weaknesses)

quality of the resulting program. As I said earlier, our goal is to name a module with a verb, one or two adjectives, and a noun so it specifies one program function. As soon as you start to deviate from this goal, program quality suffers.

To illustrate, look at the names in the chart in figure 7-44. The top-level module says "edit transaction file." Then, one of the next-level modules says "get edited records." But does it get one record or more than one record? I assume it only gets one record, but I can't really tell unless I look at the COBOL code. A minor point, maybe a simple clerical error, but it detracts from readability and maintainability in the long run.

Next, look at the "invalid print" module. This name ends with a verb, instead of starting with a verb. Again, a minor point, but now I don't know if the module prints a message, a line, or an entire report. So isn't something like "print invalid transaction" more meaningful? And doesn't consistency in a company's naming conventions lead to improved program quality? On the plus side, the names in the chart in figure 7-44 seem to represent single functions. And that is the most important criterion that names should fulfill.

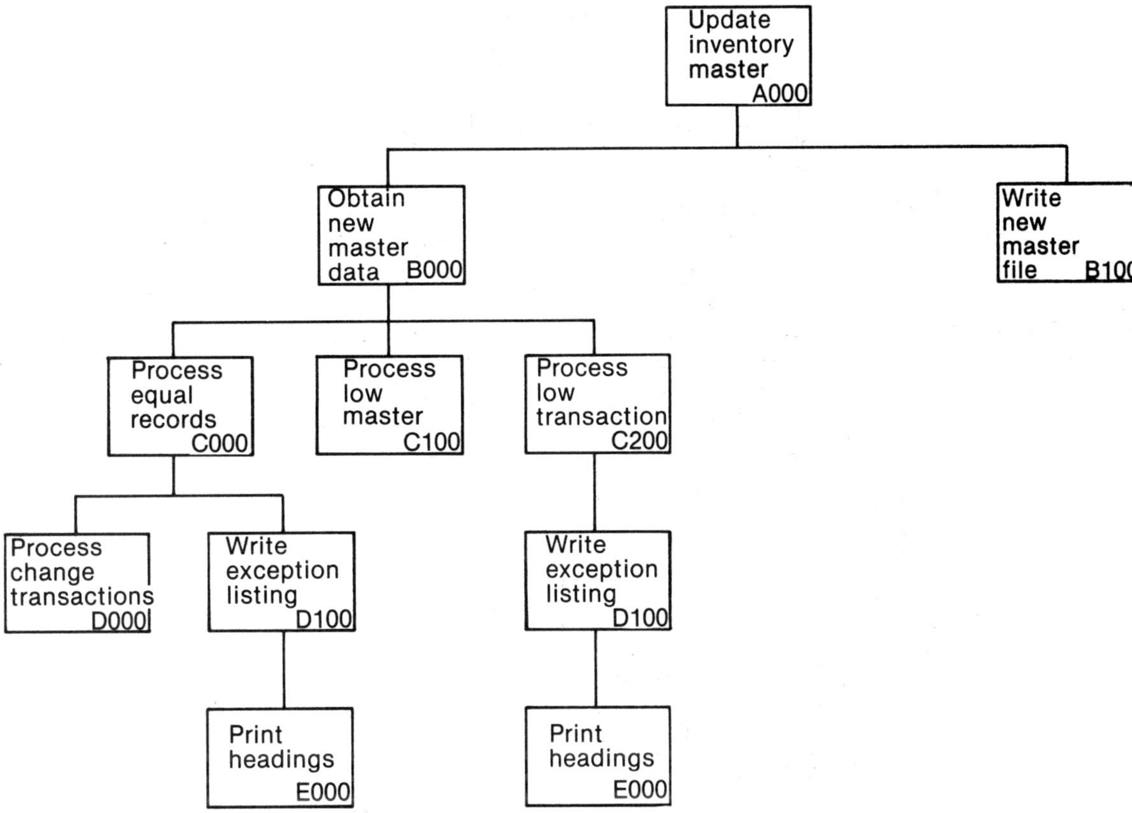

Figure 7-45 A structure chart for a sequential file-maintenance program with some design weaknesses

Now look at the names in the chart in figure 7-45. This is a chart for a sequential file-maintenance program. I created it based on the examples presented in a leading COBOL textbook. Look specifically at the names in the level-2 modules. Are these functional names? What, for example, does "process equal records" mean? Or, what does "process low master" mean? These names do not represent functions; they represent steps in a programming procedure. As a result, you can't really tell what these modules are going to do in terms of functions required by the program. Instead, you have to figure out what they're going to do by analyzing the subordinate modules shown for them or by studying the COBOL code for them.

In summary, we don't think naming conventions are trivial. If the module names in a structure chart don't clearly indicate the functions the modules are going to perform, the structure chart isn't a good index to the COBOL code. Then, the programmer has to look at the COBOL listing instead of the structure chart to find out what a module does. Then, both program quality and programmer productivity suffer.

Counterproductive numbering schemes In our system, the numbers on the structure chart indicate the sequence of the COBOL paragraphs in the resulting program. It's a simple numbering system that makes it easy for you to add a module to a structure chart as you implement a program. And, you can move a module from one place in the chart to another without changing the COBOL code.

The first problem with numbering schemes, then, is to not have any at all. The chart in figure 7-44 illustrates this. But this implies that the modules can be placed in the COBOL program in any sequence the programmer desires. So when you have to modify or maintain a program like this, you either use the cross-reference listing or page through the Procedure Division to find what you're looking for. How much simpler it is when the structure chart helps you locate the paragraph you're looking for by paragraph number.

The second problem with numbering schemes is to attempt to have the number indicate which level a module is on. For instance, the chart in figure 7-45 numbers the modules with the prefixes A for level 0, B for level 1, and so on. There are several reasons why this is counterproductive, though. First, you don't gain anything by knowing what level a module is on when you're working with the code, so the letter prefixes are unnecessary. Second, numbering like this usually means that the paragraphs in the COBOL code are in sequence by level. But a program is easier to read if the paragraphs are in calling sequence. Then, the modules called by another module can be found right after it. Finally, when a module number indicates a level, you can't move the module from one level to another without either changing the module number or violating the principles of the numbering scheme. But if you change the module number, you have to change your COBOL code (and you probably should resequence it too).

In short, you don't want to become a slave to your numbering system. You definitely should have one. But it should be a simple numerical system that doesn't indicate chart levels.

The prime-read syndrome and other carryovers from GOTO programming Since the chart in figure 7-45 doesn't isolate I/O statements in their own modules, you can't tell which module reads the old master file. In actual practice, though, you'll often find that READ statements are issued from more than one module in a program like this. The top-level module will read the first record in the file; the primary level-1 module will read the other records in the file.

Paul refers to this as the "prime-read syndrome" because reading the first record of a file before you enter the main processing loop of the program reminds him of "priming" a pump. In the GOTO era of programming, prime reads were often done in an initialization module. Then, the program went into its mainline loop, which processed the data in those records and ended by reading the next records in the files. When you're coding with GOTOs, there are strong reasons for using prime reads.

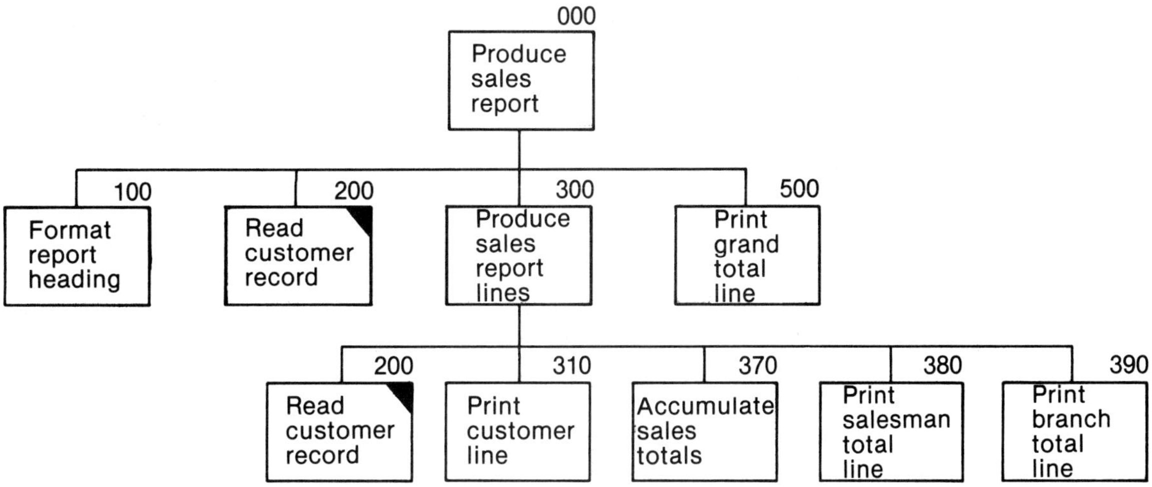

Figure 7-46 An unacceptable structure for the report-preparation program because modules 000 and 300 aren't independent of each other

Unfortunately, when you carry over this procedural logic into the design of a structured program, which should consist of functional modules, you decrease the quality of the resulting program. Since the READ statements are not functionally a part of the top-level module, they shouldn't be there. Instead, they should be in the modules they functionally relate to. Unfortunately, in the design in figure 7-45, there isn't a module that a read-transaction or a read-master module functionally relates to. And this indicates serious problems in the design of this program.

If you isolate all I/O statements in their own modules, of course, it's easier to spot the prime-read syndrome. For instance, the chart in figure 7-46 uses a prime read in a design for the model report-preparation program. Because of this, the read-customer-record module is a common module that appears at two different levels of the program. In this case, although the chart is easier to read, the prime-read syndrome still indicates a design problem. Specifically, if you use a prime read, the two modules that call the read module are dependent on each other. In other words, you can't write the code for module 300 unless you know how far module 000 went in the processing of the first record. And this in turn means that the program will be more difficult to code, test, and maintain.

In any event, program quality is reduced as we carry over habits from our GOTO days of programming to the development of structured programs. In the program in figure 7-45, the "process equal," and "process low" modules are carryovers from GOTO programming. And the sooner we can drop these carryovers, the better our programs will be.

Compared to other aspects of structured design, however, this isn't that important. If each of the modules of your programs is functional, if each can be coded in a single COBOL paragraph, and if you use meaningful naming conventions and practical numbering schemes, you will definitely increase your productivity and the quality of your programs. Then, quite frankly, a prime-read here or a match-master-and-transaction there isn't going to hurt your results that much. On the other hand, why not do everything you can to develop the best programs possible? Why not put the GOTO era of programming behind you?

Discussion

In chapter 16, I'll present some other methods of developing structured programs. But I wanted you know what's wrong with some of the common approaches to top-down design right now. As I see it, Paul's approach to top-down design is one of his major contributions to the improvement of COBOL programming. Although it isn't used in all COBOL shops, I think it should be.

Terminology

tree chart

Objectives

None. This topic is for information only.

Chapter 8

How to plan the modules of a program

After you create the structure chart for a program, you plan the coding for the modules of the program. How you do this depends a lot on your shop standards as well as your personal preferences. At the one extreme, your shop may require you to plan the code for all of the modules using a formal documentation form like the HIPO diagram. At the other extreme, your shop may not have any standards for module documentation and you may decide to skip this planning step. In that case, you code the COBOL program directly from the structure chart.

In this chapter, I will give you many ideas about how you can plan the modules of a program. In topic 1, I'll show you how to use pseudocode for this purpose. In topic 2, I'll show you how to use a simplified form of HIPO diagrams. In topic 3, I'll present some general principles of planning that apply no matter what planning documents you use. In topic 4, I'll present the two most common alternatives to simplified HIPO diagrams and pseudocode, and I'll point out the problems with them. By the time you complete this chapter, you'll not only know how to plan the modules of a program, but you'll also know which modules (if any) you should plan.

Topic 1 How to use pseudocode to plan the modules of a program

In our COBOL survey, we found that 34 percent of the COBOL shops use pseudocode for planning the modules of a program. That means that pseudocode is the most widely used method of module planning in structured shops. It is also the method that we feel is most useful for this purpose.

You should know, however, that Paul Noll still feels that HIPO diagrams are more suitable than pseudocode in a large shop because they are more formal than pseudocode. But more about that in the next topic. After you read this topic and the next, you can decide for yourself which method you prefer.

The language of pseudocode

Figure 8-1 presents three forms of *pseudocode* for module 000 of the edit program. In the simplest form of pseudocode, you capitalize all structure words such as DO, UNTIL, IF, THEN, and ELSE. These words, of course, indicate the logic of the module. In contrast, all functions are described as clearly as possible in English. These words are written in lower-case letters.

Although some people go out of their way to avoid the use of COBOL words in their pseudocode, I think there is little point in this. If a program is definitely going to be written in COBOL, why not use COBOL verbs and and even COBOL data names? In fact, for short modules, there is nothing wrong with using COBOL itself.

A combination of pseudocode and COBOL is shown in the second example in figure 8-1. Here, the COBOL PERFORM verb is used instead of the word DO. And all COBOL verbs and names are capitalized. As you can see, there's little difference between this and the simpler form of pseudocode shown above it.

In practice, some programmers prefer to use all capitals in their pseudocode. So this is shown in the third example in figure 8-1. Since this is as easy to understand as either of the examples above it, this is okay too.

As in COBOL, you should use indentation to make your pseudocode easy to read and understand. For instance, the clauses in nested IF

Simple pseudocode

```
Open files.
DO 100-format-report-heading.
DO 200-load-part-number-table
    UNTIL all part numbers are loaded in table.
DO 300-edit-inventory-tran
    UNTIL all transaction records have been read.
DO 500-print-total-page.
Close files.
Stop run.
```

Pseudocode plus COBOL

```
OPEN files.
PERFORM 100-FORMAT-REPORT-HEADING.
PERFORM 200-LOAD-PART-NUMBER-TABLE
    VARYING PN-TABLE-INDEX FROM 1 BY 1
    UNTIL PART-NUMBER-EOF.
PERFORM 300-EDIT-INVENTORY-TRAN
    UNTIL TRAN-EOF.
PERFORM 500-PRINT-TOTAL-PAGE.
CLOSE files.
STOP RUN.
```

Pseudocode plus COBOL using all capital letters

```
OPEN FILES.
PERFORM 100-FORMAT-REPORT-HEADING.
PERFORM 200-LOAD-PART-NUMBER-TABLE
    VARYING PN-TABLE-INDEX FROM 1 BY 1
    UNTIL PART-NUMBER-EOF.
PERFORM 300-EDIT-INVENTORY-TRAN
    UNTIL TRAN-EOF.
PERFORM 500-PRINT-TOTAL-PAGE.
CLOSE FILES.
STOP RUN.
```

Figure 8-1 Different forms of pseudocode for module 000 of the edit program

structures should be indented and aligned. Similarly, the UNTIL phrase should be indented from the start of the DO phrase as shown in figure 8-1. As you will see in the next chapter, this corresponds closely to the proper use of indentation in your COBOL coding.

The most important thing that you should remember about pseudocode is that it is a personal language. So use the form of pseudocode that is easiest for you to create and understand. Use any one of the forms in figure 8-1. Or develop your own version. As you will see later, pseudocode should never be used as documentation for a program, so your pseudocode papers are your working papers only. After you've coded your program using the pseudocode as a guideline, you can throw your pseudocode away.

```
000-edit-inventory-transactions.

    Open files.
    DO 100-format-report-heading.
    DO 200-load-part-number-table
        VARYING table-index from 1 by 1
        UNTIL part-number-eof.
    DO 300-edit-inventory-transaction
        UNTIL tran-eof.
    DO 500-print-total-page.
    Close files.
    Stop run.

100-format-report-heading.

    Format heading lines.

200-load-part-number-table.

    DO 210-read-part-number-record.
    IF NOT part-number-eof
        load table entry
    ELSE
        reduce table-index by 1
        set entry-count to table-index.

210-read-part-number-record.

    Read record
        AT END
            move "Y" to part-number-eof-sw.

300-edit-inventory-transaction.

    DO 310-read-inventory-transaction.
    IF NOT tran-eof
        DO 320-edit-transaction-fields
        IF NOT valid-tran
            DO 360-print-invalid-transaction
        ELSE
            DO 400-write-valid-transaction.

310-read-inventory-transaction.

    Read record
        AT END
            move "Y" to tran-eof-sw.
    IF NOT tran-eof
        add 1 to trans-processed-count.
```

Figure 8-2 Pseudocode for the edit program (part 1 of 3)

Pseudocode for the edit program

Figure 8-2 presents pseudocode for the entire edit program so you can compare it with the COBOL code in appendix A. As you can see, the pseudocode is close to the COBOL code in the control modules, because you express logic in pseudocode in much the same way that you do in

```
320-edit-transaction-fields.

    Move "Y" to valid-tran-sw.
    Move space to invalid-transaction-line.
    IF transaction-code = 1
        DO 330-edit-code-1-fields
    ELSE IF transaction-code = 2
        DO 350-edit-code-2-fields
    ELSE
        move "N" to valid-tran-sw
        move error-indicator to type-code-error
        add 1 to invalid-tran-code-count.

330-edit-code-1-fields.

    Edit all code-1 fields for validity.
    DO 340-search-part-number-table to check the validity
        of the part-number.
    CALL "DATEDIT" to check the validity of the date.
    Mark the fields that are in error.
    IF any fields are in error
        move "N" to valid-tran-sw.
    IF NOT valid-tran
        add 1 to invalid-sales-count
    ELSE
        add 1 to valid-sales-count.

340-search-part-number-table.

    Search table.
    IF the part-number is in the table
        move "Y" to part-number-found-sw
    ELSE
        move "N" to part-number-found-sw.

350-edit-code-2-fields.

    Edit all code-2 fields for validity.
    DO 340-search-part-number-table to check the validity
        of the part-number.
    CALL "DATEDIT" to check the validity of the date.
    Mark the fields that are in error.
    IF any fields are in error
        move "N" to valid-tran-sw.
    IF NOT valid-tran
        add 1 to invalid-return-count
    ELSE
        add 1 to valid-return-count.
```

Figure 8-2 Pseudocode for the edit program (part 2 of 3)

COBOL. For instance, with the exception of the OPEN and CLOSE statements, the pseudocode in module 000 parallels the COBOL code on a line for line basis.

On the other hand, the pseudocode for the work modules is not like the COBOL code. For instance, in module 100, I've just written "format heading lines," because I know this module will consist of MOVE

```
360-print-invalid-transaction.

    IF page-overflow
        DO 370-print-heading-lines.
    Format the invalid-transaction-line.
    DO 390-write-report-line.
    Move 1 to space-control.

370-print-heading-lines.

    Print the heading lines using modules 380 and 390 to
        actually write the lines.

380-write-page-top-line.

    Write a page-top line.
    Move one to line-count.

390-write-report-line.

    Write a line after advancing space-control lines.
    Add space-control to line-count.

400-write-valid-transaction.

    Write valid-inventory-transaction.

500-print-total-page.

    Format total lines and print them on the total page
        using module 390 to write the lines.
```

Figure 8-2 Pseudocode for the edit program (part 3 of 3)

statements and two CALLS to subprograms. Since this is trivial code, there's no sense in going into more detail in the pseudocode. Similarly, the pseudocode for module 500 says "format total lines and print them on the total page." In comparison, the COBOL code consists of 63 lines of MOVEs and PERFORMs.

For a module like 330, "edit code-1 fields," you have a lot of leeway as to how you present it in pseudocode. From experience, you should know that an edit module can be quite complex. But that doesn't mean that you have to go through it on a line for line basis as you would in COBOL. In figure 8-2, I've used pseudocode to remind myself what this module must do when I code it in COBOL.

Module 340 in figure 8-2 shows that you can use pseudocode even when you don't know the proper syntax of the COBOL code. Here, I've shown the logic of what I want this module to do, but there is no COBOL code that corresponds to my pseudocode. At this stage of program development, though, you don't have to be concerned with COBOL syntax. If you're confident that the function you've presented can be coded in COBOL, you can find out what the proper syntax is later. In fact, you shouldn't worry about COBOL details until you actually code a module.

Some related ideas

At this point, you should realize that it's easy to use pseudocode. It's your own personal language, and you can use it as you see fit to plan the modules of your program. In fact, you can think of pseudocode as an abbreviated version of COBOL that helps you identify the critical portions of a COBOL program. But before I go on, I'd like to present some related ideas.

Which modules you should plan Once you start to use pseudocode, you will quickly realize that the pseudocode for many of the modules is trivial. As a result, you may ask yourself whether it's worth the trouble to record the pseudocode for these modules. If you look at the pseudocode for modules 360 through 500 in figure 8-2, for example, you can see that the pseudocode tells you little that the structure chart and the module names didn't tell you already. Similarly, the pseudocode for modules 100, 200, and 210 doesn't tell you much that you didn't already know. So is it worth the trouble to develop pseudocode for all of the modules of a program? Unless you are required to, I don't think so.

Our general recommendation, then, is to develop pseudocode for only those modules that are critical to the operation of your program or for those modules that you aren't sure about. For the most part, these modules will only include the major control modules and the modules that set the critical switches of the program.

Figure 8-3, for example, gives the pseudocode for only those modules in the edit program that I would develop pseudocode for. This includes the major control modules plus the read-inventory-transaction module that sets the switch used by the major control modules. After I develop the pseudocode for these modules, I can study my pseudocode to make sure that all of the modules work together. Once I'm sure that they do, I can start coding the program in COBOL with the confidence that I won't encounter any significant coding problems.

How detailed your should pseudocode be The pseudocode in figure 8-2 consists of 96 lines, and the COBOL code in the Procedure Division in appendix A for these same modules consists of 239 lines. So you can see that you don't want to overdo the detail you put in your pseudocode. Otherwise, you end up coding the program twice: once in pseudocode, once in COBOL.

With this in mind, we recommend this simple rule: Code as much detail as you need to convince yourself that you can code the module in COBOL. For instance, I'm sure that I can code modules 330 and 350 of the edit program based on the pseudocode in figure 8-2. I'm not quite sure how I'll end up coding them, but I know I can do it. On the other hand, a less experienced programmer might develop the pseudocode in figure 8-4 for module 330. That way he can be sure that he can code all the editing rules in a single COBOL paragraph. On the other hand, this gets awfully close to COBOL itself, so as soon as you get more experience you should use less pseudocode for a module like this.

```
000-edit-inventory-transactions.

    Open files.
    DO 100-format-report-heading.
    DO 200-load-part-number-table
        VARYING table-index from 1 by 1
        UNTIL part-number-eof.
    DO 300-edit-inventory-transaction
        UNTIL tran-eof.
    DO 500-print-total-page.
    Close files.
    Stop run.

300-edit-inventory-transaction.

    DO 310-read-inventory-transaction.
    IF NOT tran-eof
        DO 320-edit-transaction-fields
        IF NOT valid-tran
            DO 360-print-invalid-transaction
        ELSE
            DO 400-write-valid-transaction.

310-read-inventory-transaction.

    Read record
        AT END
            move "Y" to tran-eof-sw.
    IF NOT tran-eof
        add 1 to trans-processed-count.

320-edit-transaction-fields.

    Move "Y" to valid-tran-sw.
    Move space to invalid-transaction-line.
    IF transaction-code = 1
        DO 330-edit-code-1-fields
    ELSE IF transaction-code = 2
        DO 350-edit-code-2-fields
    ELSE
        move "N" to valid-tran-sw
        move error-indicator to type-code-error
        add 1 to invalid-tran-code-count.
```

Figure 8-3 Pseudocode for the critical modules of the edit program

When you should type and when you should handwrite your pseudocode This is based on your personal preferences and the equipment available to you. Most programmers handwrite their pseudocode, so it's often intelligible only to them. On the other hand, some programmers type their pseudocode or enter it into a word processing system. In this case, they can usually record the code faster than they can handwrite it, and it's easy to read. Since pseudocode is simply your plan for coding, how you develop it should be up to you.

```
IF ITR-UPDATE-CODE is invalid
     move 'N' to VALID-TRAN-SW
     move '*' to mark error field.

CALL 'DATEDIT'.
IF ITR-REF-DATE is invalid
     move 'N' to VALID-TRAN-SW
     move '*' to mark error field.

IF ITR-BRANCH-NO is invalid
     move 'N' to VALID-TRAN-SW
     move '*' to mark error field.

IF ITR-SALESMAN-NO is invalid
     move 'N' to VALID-TRAN-SW
     move '*' to mark error field.

IF ITR-CUST-NO is invalid
     move 'N' to VALID-TRAN-SW
     move '*' to mark error field.

IF ITR-QUANTITY is invalid
     move 'N' to VALID-TRAN-SW
     move '*' to mark error field.

DO 340-SEARCH-PART-NUMBER-TABLE.
IF not PART-NUMBER-FOUND
     move 'N' to VALID-TRAN-SW
     move '*' to mark error field.

IF not VALID-TRAN
     add 1 to INVALID-SALES-COUNT
ELSE
     add 1 to VALID-SALES-COUNT.
```

Figure 8-4 Expanded pseudocode for module 330 of the edit program

Why you shouldn't use pseudocode for final documentation I've mentioned this before so I won't dwell on it. The only documentation you can be sure of is the actual COBOL listing of the working program or documents generated from the COBOL listing. So there's no point in trying to update your pseudocode when you modify your plans or program.

When you should use COBOL instead of pseudocode Quite frankly, we rarely use pseudocode, or any other form of module planning, in our shop. We used it when we first started structured programming. But we eventually came to the conclusion that it's just as easy to code a COBOL program as it is to develop the pseudocode for it. So why do things twice?

On the other hand, I think pseudocode is useful when you first start to use the techniques of structured programming. When you first use topdown design, for example, I think it's hard to see how the modules of the structure chart will be related by the COBOL code. So pseudocode for the critical modules of a program, like the pseudocode shown in figure

8-3, can help you see these relationships more clearly than COBOL code can. Then, once you see these relationships, you can code the program in COBOL with the confidence that all the modules will work together properly.

Our recommendation, then, is to use pseudocode as long as you feel you need it. As you get more experience, you should use it less and less. And eventually, you should get to the point where you don't need it at all. But even then, you may want to use it occasionally to help you plan the modules of a complicated program.

For maximum productivity, we feel that you can code a program directly from the structure chart almost as easily as you can create the pseudocode for it. So by going directly from program design to COBOL code, you can eliminate a step. And this in turn can increase your productivity.

Discussion

Although pseudocode is useful for planning the modules of a program, it's probably overused in most businesses. A couple of the leading texts on COBOL programming recommend that you develop pseudocode for all of the modules of a program, and we don't agree with that. Some also recommend that pseudocode be used as part of a program's final documentation. And we certainly don't agree with that.

In fact, we believe that you should experiment with coding your programs in COBOL directly from the structure chart once you get experience with structured programming techniques. If you do, we think you'll find that you can code your programs quite easily without using pseudocode.

Terminology

pseudocode

Objective

Given the logic for a program module, express it in pseudocode.

Topic 2 How to use HIPO diagrams to plan the modules of a program

Figure 8-5 shows a *HIPO diagram* for module 000 of the edit program. If you look in the process box of this form, you can see that it presents the processing requirements of the module using a form of pseudocode. As a result, you can think of the use of HIPO diagrams as a formal method for planning the modules of a program, but one that is closely related to the use of pseudocode.

Although HIPO diagrams started as a part of IBM's HIPO (Hierarchy plus Input-Process-Output) system of documentation, the form of HIPO diagram that we recommend in this topic is a simplified version of IBM's. As we see it, this simplification is a necessary one, because IBM's method is just too cumbersome to be practical. I'll explain this in more detail in topic 4.

HIPO diagrams can also be called *IPO diagrams*, or *IPOs*. Paul Noll, for example, routinely calls them IPOs. In this book, however, I'll always refer to them as HIPO diagrams.

As you will see, HIPO diagrams aren't much more difficult to develop than pseudocode, because their major element is pseudocode. However, they take more time to create than pseudocode, because they require a special form and because you have to record more than just the pseudocode. As a result, you should make sure that you derive some benefits from using HIPO diagrams that justify this extra development time.

Paul Noll believes in the use of HIPO diagrams, particularly in large companies that have difficulty controlling the quality of their programs. Because the HIPO diagrams formally document the functions of program modules, they can be reviewed by management or by development teams, whereas pseudocode is usually too informal for this purpose. By reviewing the HIPO diagrams, problems can be detected before a line of COBOL code is ever written.

As you read this topic, then, you should realize that you will normally use HIPO diagrams in a shop that has a formal development environment. In our COBOL survey, 18 percent of the shops said they used simplified HIPO diagrams for module documentation. So quite a few shops must have this kind of environment. On the other hand, if you don't work in this kind of environment, you can consider skipping this topic altogether.

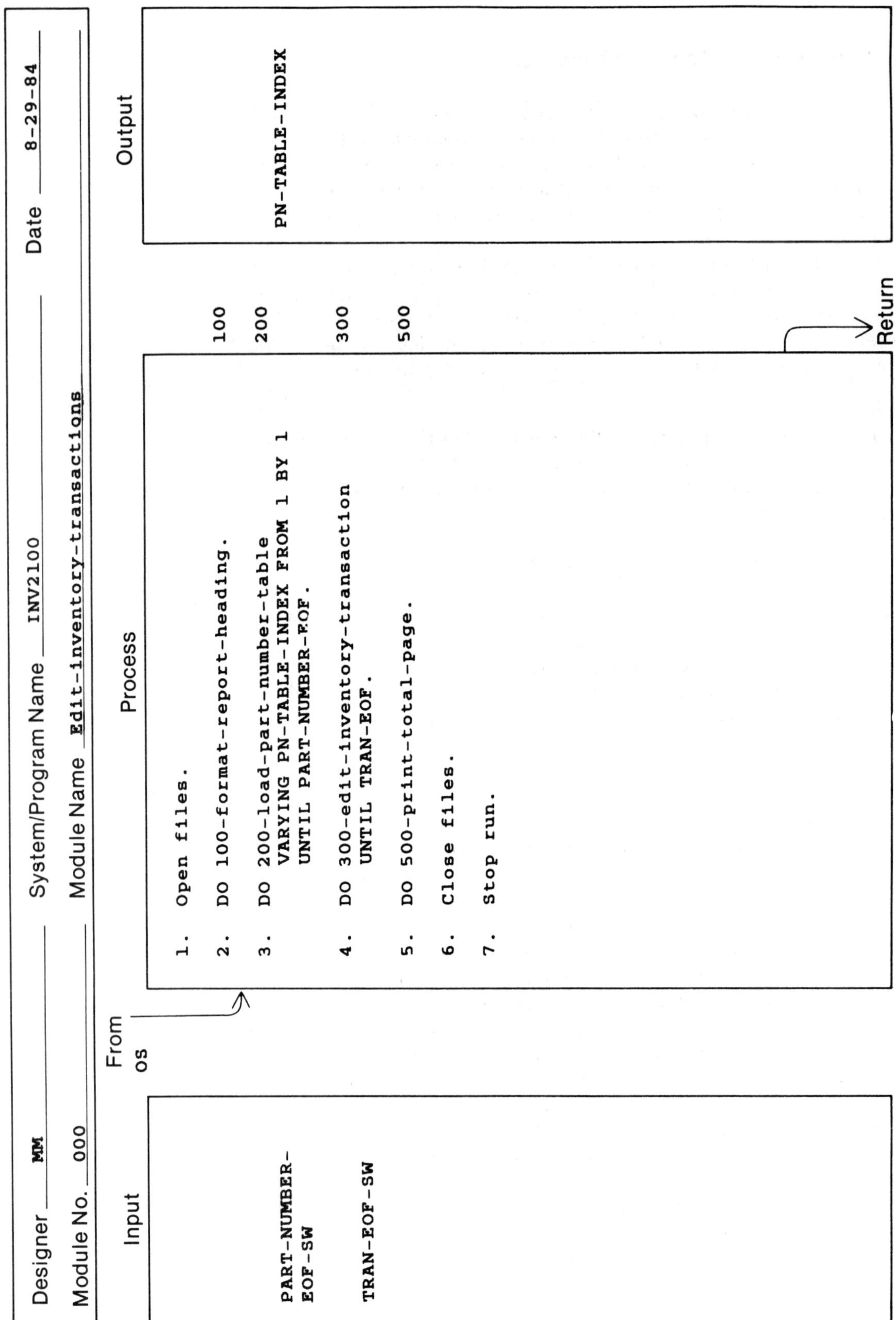

Figure 8-5 A HIPO diagram for module 000 of the edit program

Six steps for preparing HIPO diagrams

To create HIPO diagrams, you follow six basic steps. First, you complete the heading. Second, you record the processing requirements in the process box. Third, you record the input and output requirements in the input and output boxes. Fourth and fifth, you indicate the called modules and the calling modules. And sixth, you use extended descriptions whenever necessary.

A number of forms are available for HIPO diagrams; ours is shown in figure 8-5. All of the forms, however, have the same basic components: heading area plus input, output, and process boxes. So to plan a module, you fill in the portions of the HIPO form. Although this is usually quite simple, let me go through the six steps for completing the form as quickly as I can.

Step 1: Complete the heading In the heading of the HIPO form, you record your name, the program name, and the date. If your form has room for page numbers, I suggest leaving them blank since the module numbers will be used to keep the HIPO diagrams in order. Then, for the module number, you use the module number from the structure chart. Similarly, for the module name, you use the name given in the structure chart with the words separated by hyphens. You can see this in the diagram in figure 8-5.

Step 2: Record the processing requirements When the heading is complete, you begin the actual module documentation. In general, you will record the processing requirements first, although you will sometimes start with the input and output requirements. In this latter case, of course, you switch steps 2 and 3. When you record the processing requirements, you simply list the requirements of the module using pseudocode as illustrated in the previous topic.

Because switches are common in structured programming, they should always be used in a standard way. So here are the standards used in this book. First, all switch-field names will end in SW. Second, the condition represented by the switch should be self-explanatory if you drop the SW. Thus, TRAN-EOF means the end of the transaction file, and PART-NUMBER-EOF means the end of the part-number file. Similarly, a switch named VALID-TRAN-SW will be used for the condition named VALID-TRAN, which indicates a valid transaction. Third, a switch is off if it contains a value of N (for "no") and on if it contains a value of Y (for "yes"). Finally, all switches will be initialized to their proper starting values in working storage. This use of switches will be illustrated in COBOL in the next chapter, but you need to know it now since switches are used in many of the HIPO diagrams in this chapter.

Step 3: Record the input and output requirements In figure 8-5, you can see the input and output requirements that I recorded for module 000 of the edit program. For input, I've shown that two switches will be used by the module. For output, I've shown that a table-index will be used when the part-number table is loaded.

Although I don't put boxes around the I/O items that I show on a HIPO diagram, many programmers draw boxes around each I/O item or around related I/O items. And some use notations like WS above an I/O box to show that the item will be in working storage. As I see it, though, graphics and notations like these are optional. Most of the time, your HIPO diagrams will be just as clear whether or not you use the boxes and the WS indications. And you'll be able to create the diagrams more quickly.

If you look ahead to figure 8-7, you can see an I/O symbol for a tape file used in the input box in the HIPO diagram for module 310 of the edit program. Here again, I think the use of the symbol should be optional, because a HIPO diagram is usually just as clear without the graphic symbol.

Step 4: Set off the numbers of the called modules In figure 8-5, I've recorded the module numbers for all modules called by module 000 between the process and the output boxes, to the right of the step that called each module. As a result, it is easy to see that module 000 calls four other modules. I've set these numbers off in this way, because it makes them easy to find. Then, you can check them against the structure chart to make sure that all subordinate modules have been called.

Is this worth doing? I think it's debatable. Paul feels that it is since it takes only a few seconds. But it's a minor point.

Step 5: List the calling modules In figure 8-5, I've recorded OS (for Operating System) below the word "From" to show that module 000 of the edit program is called by the operating system. Similarly, in figure 8-6, I've recorded 000 in this area to show that module 300 is called by module 000. For a common module, you list the numbers of all the modules that call it in this area.

Since the structure chart indicates all the modules that will call other modules, you don't really have to list the numbers of the calling modules next to the incoming arrow. This documentation can be useful, however, because it allows you to refer to the HIPO diagrams of the calling modules without referring to the structure chart. As a result, each HIPO diagram is complete in itself.

Step 6: Use extended description when necessary When the requirements of a module are complicated, the *extended description* form is useful. In this case, the HIPO diagram should indicate the overall logic of the module, and the extended description form should be used to document the details.

To illustrate, consider the HIPO diagram in figure 8-8. It is for module 330 of the edit program. Basically, it says to move N into VALID-TRAN-SW if any field in the transaction record is invalid. It also says to mark each invalid field. But what determines whether a field is valid or invalid?

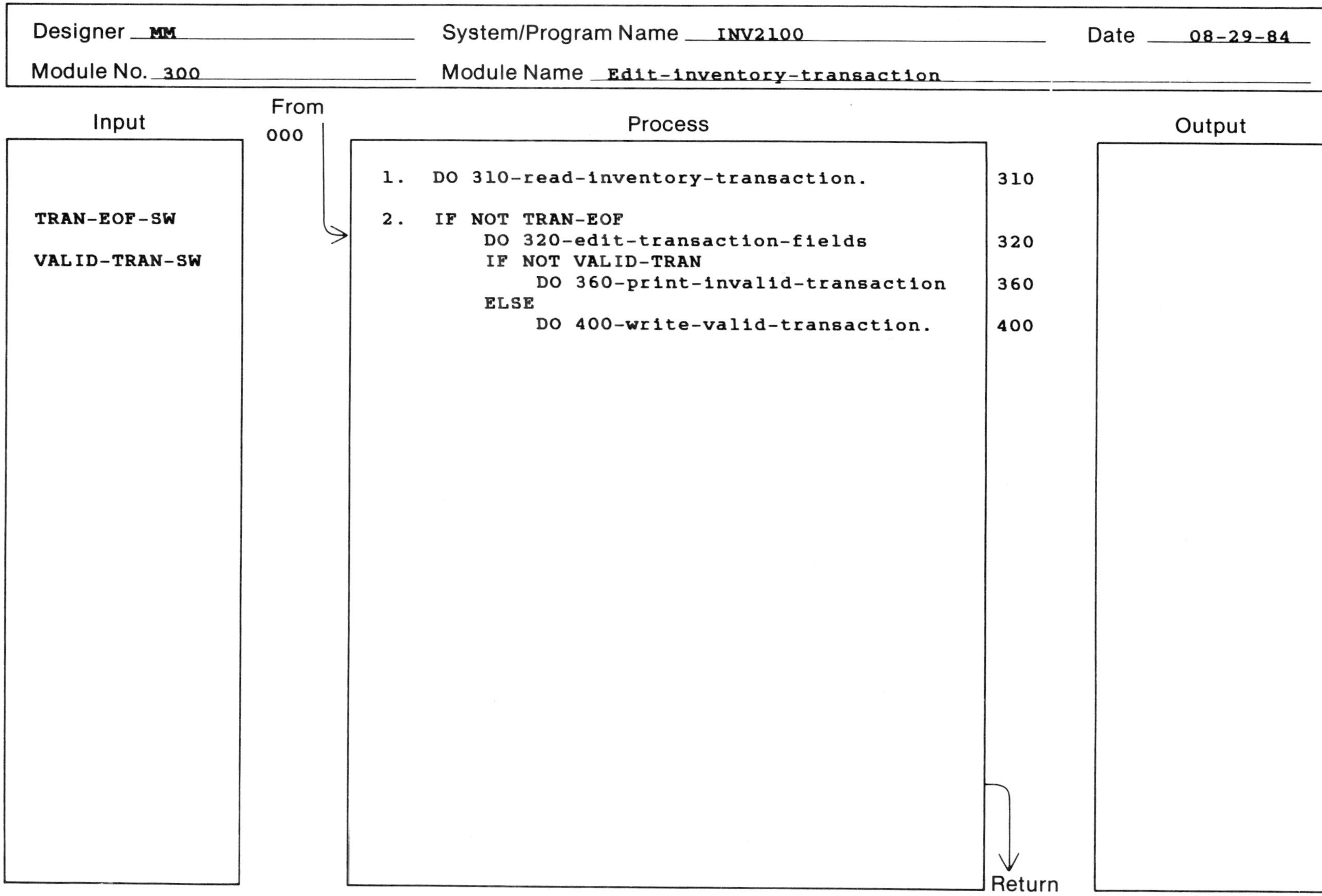

Figure 8-6 A HIPO diagram for module 300 of the edit program

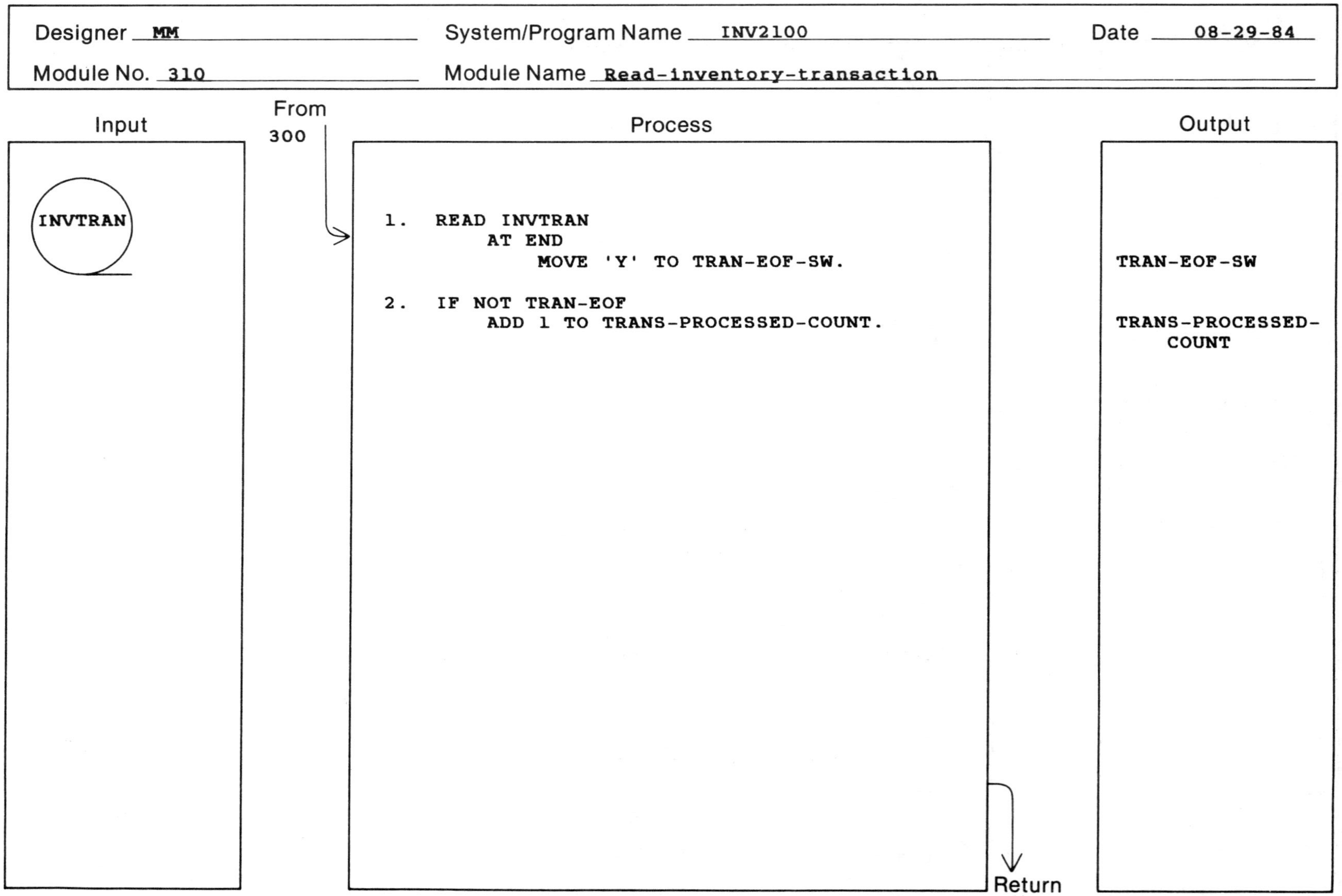

Figure 8-7 A HIPO diagram for module 310 of the edit program

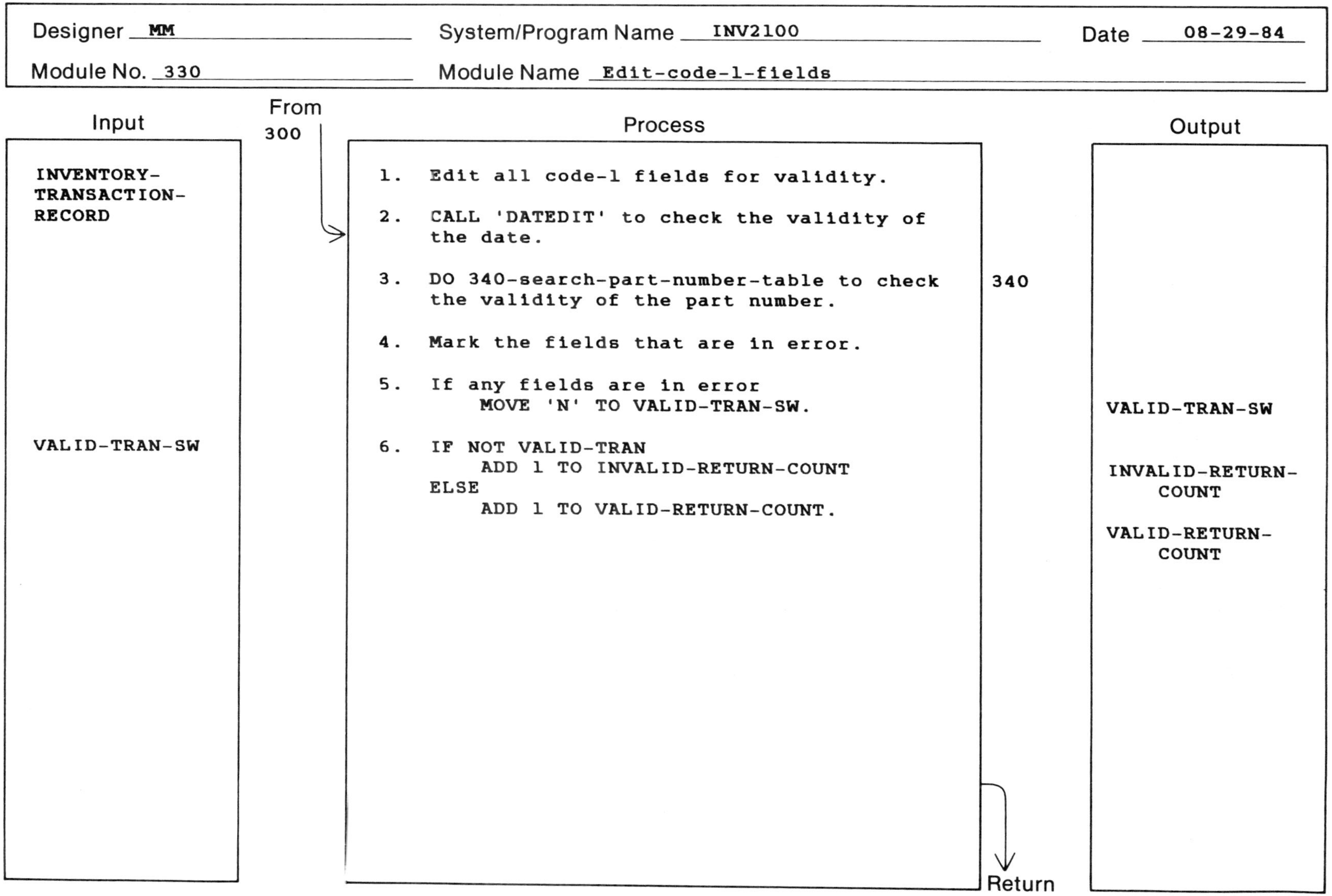

Figure 8-8 A HIPO diagram for module 330 of the edit program

Now, it may be that the program specifications provide all of the editing rules that you need for coding the program. On the other hand, maybe you don't have this information yet, and you want to record it now. If so, you can use an extended description form as shown in figure 8-9 for this purpose. This says, for instance, that ITR-BRANCH-NO should be greater than zero and less than 25. In the reference column for this item, 1 is specified, meaning that this information pertains to step 1 in the processing box of the HIPO diagram. Similarly, step 3 is specified next to the information for the part-number field. By using reference numbers, it is easy to relate the extended descriptions to the steps in the HIPO diagram.

As you can see from figure 8-9, the extended description consists of areas for notes and areas for reference numbers. As a result, you can use it for whatever you want. Sometimes you will give a narrative description of processing requirements. Sometimes you will use it to record a table or to refer to a table. For instance, you might say, "Refer to the decision table labelled 'Credit Rules' for detailed logical requirements." In short, you can use this form to record or refer to any documentation that will help clarify the requirements of the module.

Some HIPO diagrams for the edit program

Figures 8-5 through 8-8 give HIPO diagrams for some of the primary modules of the edit program. They should give you some idea of what a set of HIPO diagrams for a program will look like. Since there is one HIPO diagram (with or without extended descriptions) for each module on the structure chart, you end up with 16 HIPO diagrams for a simple program like the edit program. As you can imagine, then, HIPO documentation can get quite cumbersome for a large program.

If you go through the HIPO diagrams in this topic, you can see that the programmer has considerable freedom when she creates HIPO diagrams. In this case, the programmer has used the actual COBOL names taken from the COPY members in her pseudocode. Furthermore, she has created the actual COBOL names for switches and work fields that she will use when she codes the program. Paul recommends that you use this much COBOL when you create HIPO diagrams that will be reviewed by your peers. That way there's less room for doubt about what your pseudocode means or how it will actually be coded.

Otherwise, the ideas presented in the topic on pseudocode apply when it's used in the process box of a HIPO diagram. Indent as you would when you code COBOL statements. Capitalize the structured-programming words and the COBOL words. And if you want to capitalize all of the words in your pseudocode, that's okay too.

I think these few diagrams illustrate the advantage that the use of HIPO diagrams has over pseudocode. It's simply a more formal way of planning the modules of a program. So you end up with a neater package

Extended Description

Designer: MM | System/Program Name: INV2100 | Date: 08-29-84

Module No.: 330 | Module Name: Edit-code-1-fields

Notes		Ref.	Notes	Ref.
Editing rules for a sales transaction:				
ITR-UPDATE-CODE	Must be 'C'	1		
ITR-TRAN-CODE	Must be 1	320		
ITR-REF-NO	No restrictions	1		
ITR-REF-DATA	Use 'DATEDIT'	2		
ITR-BRANCH-NO	> zero and <25	1		
ITR-SALESMAN-NO	> zero	1		
ITR-CUSTOMER-NO	> zero	1		
ITR-QUANTITY	> zero	1		
ITR-PART-NO	Must be in table	3		
ITR-RETURN-CODE	Not used	1		

Figure 8-9 An extended description for module 330 of the edit program

of program documentation, one that can easily be reviewed by your manager or peers before you start to code your program.

Some related ideas

When you start to prepare HIPO diagrams for your own programs, you'll probably find that a number of minor questions are raised. For instance, should you plan all modules or only the critical modules? And to what level of detail should you go to in your HIPO diagrams? So let me try to answer some of these questions.

Which modules you should develop HIPO diagrams for If you have shop standards for module planning, they should specify which modules you should plan for each program. In most cases, a shop's standards will say that you should develop them for all of the modules of a program.

If you don't have shop standards, I think the same recommendations that I made for pseudocode apply to the use of HIPO diagrams. Develop the HIPO diagrams for all of the critical modules of a program, but don't develop them for trivial modules. If your HIPO diagrams are going to be reviewed by other members of your staff, of course, you had better develop HIPO diagrams for all modules that might come into question when they are reviewed.

How detailed your HIPO diagrams should be When you develop a HIPO diagram, you can easily get into a lot of detail. Not only must you ask yourself how far you should go when you develop the pseudocode for a module, but you must also ask how detailed your listings of input and output requirements should be. Should you list every input field, no matter how trivial? Or should you just list the major inputs or outputs?

In the module in figure 8-8, for example, do you really need to show that VALID-TRAN-SW is both an input to and an output from this module? In fact, what do you gain by showing it in either the input or the output box? And what about VALID- and INVALID-RETURN-COUNT? Should they be shown as both input and output fields?

My point is that the detail on a HIPO diagram can easily get out of hand. So we recommend this simple rule. Develop as much detail as you think a professional programmer would need in order to code the module for you from the HIPO diagram.

When you should type and when you should handwrite your HIPO diagrams Although the diagrams in this book are typed, you shouldn't have to type them in a production environment. Since HIPO diagrams are working papers, neat handwriting should be more than adequate, even if they are going to be reviewed. Your goal should be to create the HIPO diagrams as rapidly as possible. On the other hand, if you can create HIPO diagrams faster using a typewriter rather than handwriting, there's no reason why you shouldn't type them.

Why you shouldn't use HIPO diagrams for final documentation I've mentioned this before so I won't dwell on it. The only documentation you can be sure of is the actual COBOL listing of the working program or documents generated from the COBOL listing. So there's no point in trying to update your HIPO diagrams when you modify your program. Once you have a working version of the complete COBOL program, you can throw your HIPO diagrams away.

When you should use pseudocode instead of HIPO diagrams I think the major benefit of HIPO diagrams is that they represent a formal method for planning the modules of a program. As a result, they can easily be reviewed by other members of a programming staff, before the programmer actually starts to code the program. On the other hand, if you don't have reviews of module plans, I can see no reason for using HIPO diagrams instead of pseudocode.

Paul Noll doesn't agree with this, though. He thinks that most programmers can use the forced formality of HIPO diagrams. He says they force a planning discipline on most people that they wouldn't otherwise have. So, we leave it up to you.

If I were to make a recommendation, I would say start with HIPO diagrams if you are new to structured programming and uncomfortable with some of the new methods. Then, when you start to feel that HIPO diagrams are more trouble than they're worth, switch to pseudocode alone. Finally, when you realize that you can code a program directly from the structure chart without using pseudocode at all, you will be to the point of maximum productivity.

Discussion

If you have the kind of shop that could use more discipline and more standardization, HIPO diagrams as presented in this topic can help you go in that direction. In this case, though, we recommend that you combine the use of HIPO diagrams with a formal program of design walkthroughs as presented in chapter 17.

Before we go on, I want to make sure you realize that the methods for HIPO diagramming shown in this topic are simplified methods developed by Paul Noll. In contrast, as you will see in topic 4, IBM's recommendations for HIPO diagrams lead to diagrams that are much more cumbersome. As a result, we feel that creating those HIPO diagrams is too time-consuming to be practical for program development.

Terminology

HIPO diagram
IPO diagram
IPO

Objective

Given the specifications for a program module, plan the module using a HIPO diagram.

Topic 3 The principles of module planning

Whether you use pseudocode or HIPO diagrams to plan the modules of a program, there are some basic principles you should remember. These principles will help you to decide in what modules you should put control code and subfunctions. They will also help you decide when you should revise your structure chart. By following these principles, you will improve the quality of your programs because you will make them easier to read and understand.

Four principles of module planning

If you're an experienced COBOL programmer, you should be able to plan the code for any of the modules in a structure chart. After all, you can think of pseudocode as an abbreviated form of COBOL.

On the other hand, you can defeat the purposes of structured programming if you plan and code the modules incorrectly. That's why I'd like to present the four principles of module planning that follow. If you obey these principles and you've developed effective structure charts in the first place, you will end up with high-quality programs.

To illustrate the four principles, I'm going to use the model report-preparation program that I introduced in the last chapter. You can find the structure chart for this program in figure 8-10. And you can find pseudocode for three of its modules in figure 8-11.

Before I present the four principles of module planning, I want you to realize that you can code most modules of a program in more than one way. In general, the more complicated the module is, the more ways you can code it. What you want to do, then, is to plan and code a module so it is as easy to read and understand as possible. This, of course, is in keeping with the goals of structured programming.

With that in mind, look at the pseudocode in figure 8-12. This is another way that module 200 of the report-preparation program could be coded. Although I don't think it's as clear as the code in figure 8-11, that's often a matter of opinion. In this case, though, the code in figure 8-12 doesn't obey one of the four principles. That's why it's not as clear as I would like it to be.

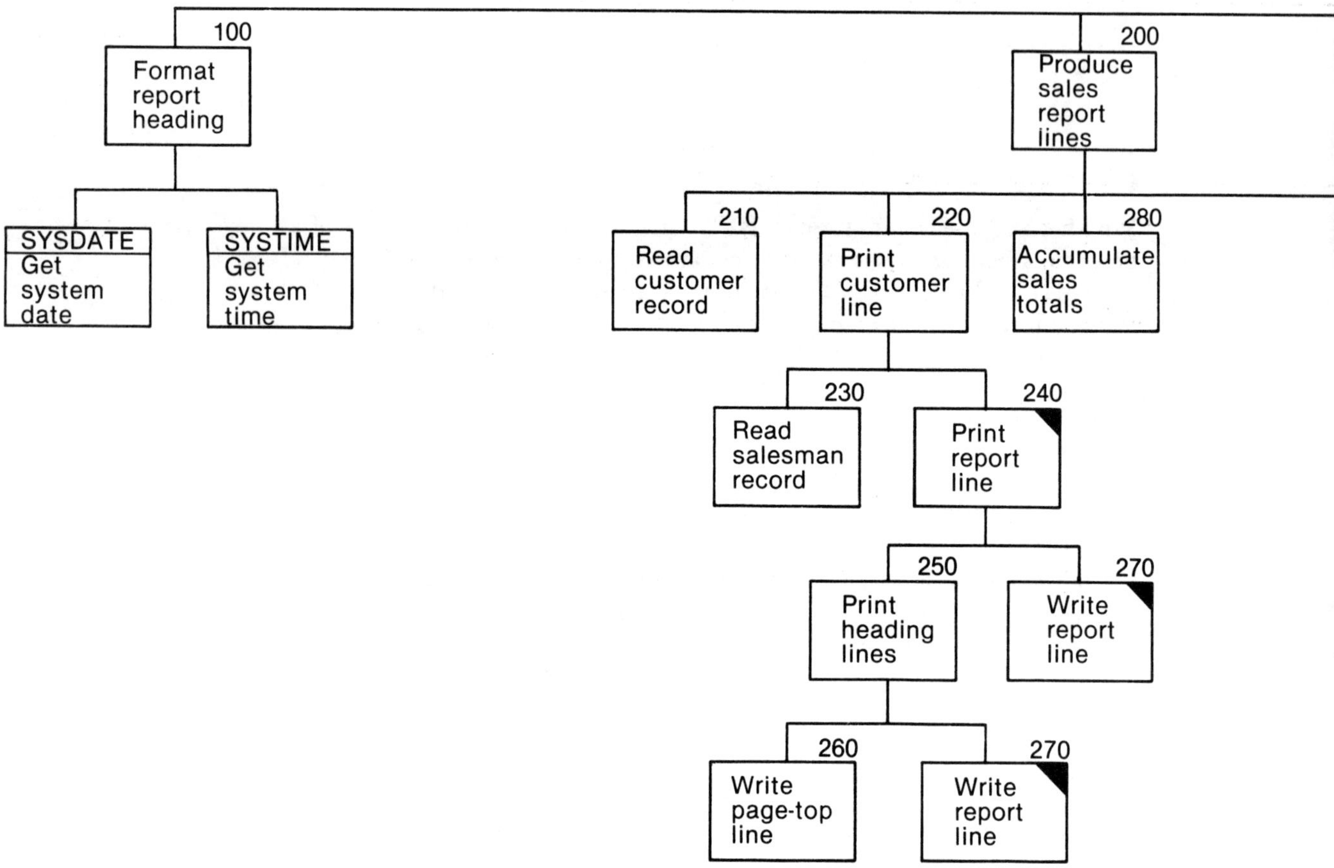

Figure 8-10 The structure chart for the model report-preparation program

Principle 1: Keep the modules independent I talked about this in the chapter on program design. When you design a program, you should try to keep the modules as independent as possible. In theory, then, you should be able to plan the code for one module without referring to the pseudocode or HIPO diagrams for other modules. But what does that mean in practice?

In practice, as you plan or code one module of a program, you will sometimes want to check other modules to see whether you remembered to set a switch or move a control field or something like that. If that's the only kind of checking you do, no problem. But if you find that you continually need to refer to the processing steps in one module in order to

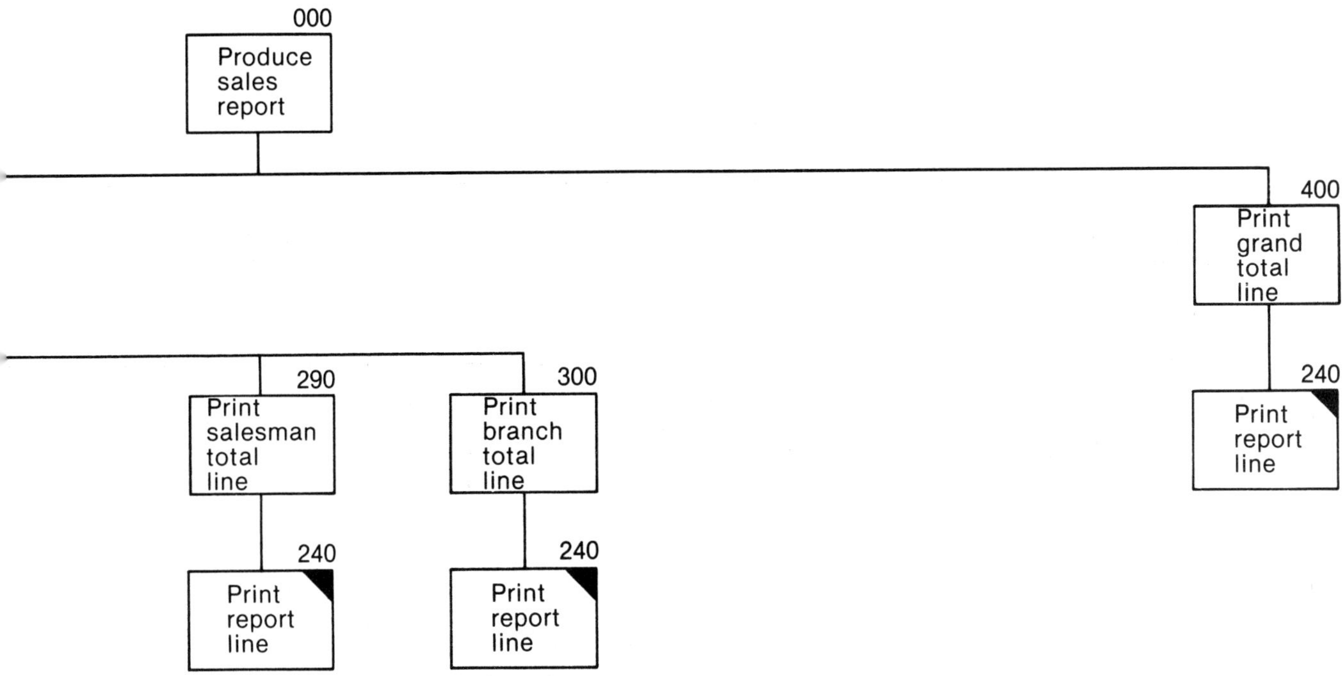

create the pseudocode or HIPO diagram for another module, something's wrong. Either your modules aren't independent or your functions aren't clearly defined.

As you code module 290 of the report-preparation program, for example, you may want to check the code for module 200 to make sure that it moves the new salesman-number field to the old salesman-number field. Similarly, as you code module 300, you may want to check module 200 to make sure that it moves the new salesman-key field (salesman number and branch number) to the old salesman-key field. In both of these cases, you're checking the code in a higher-level module to make sure it does something as you code a lower-level module.

```
000-produce-sales-report.

    Open files.
    DO 100-format-report-heading.
    DO 200-produce-sales-report-lines
        UNTIL customer-eof.
    DO 400-print-grand-total-line.
    Close files.
    Stop run.

200-produces-sales-report-lines.

    DO 210-read-customer-record.
    IF NOT customer-eof
        IF first-record
            MOVE cm-salesman-key to old-salesman-key
            DO 220-print-customer-line
            DO 280-accumulate-sales-totals
            MOVE 'N' to first-record-sw
        ELSE
            IF cm-salesman-key NOT GREATER old-salesman-key
                DO 220-print-customer-line
                DO 280-accumulate-sales-totals
            ELSE
                IF cm-branch-number GREATER old-branch-number
                    DO 290-print-salesman-total-line
                    DO 300-print-branch-total-line
                    DO 220-print-customer-line
                    DO 280-accumulate-sales-totals
                    MOVE cm-salesman-key to old-salesman-key
                ELSE
                    DO 290-print-salesman-total-line
                    DO 220-print-customer-line
                    DO 280-accumulate-sales-totals
                    MOVE cm-salesman-number to old-salesman-number
    ELSE
        DO 290-print-salesman-total-line
        DO 300-print-branch-total-line.

210-read-customer-record.

    READ CUSTMST
        AT END
            move 'Y' to customer-eof-sw.

NOTE:  To understand this pseudocode you must realize that the
       salesman key consists of both salesman number and branch
       number.  Also, the input file of customer records is in
       sequence by customer number within salesman number
       within branch number; in other words, it's in sequence
       by customer number within salesman key.
```

Figure 8-11 Pseudocode for some of the primary modules of the model report-preparation program

```
200-produces-sales-report-lines.

    DO 210-read-customer-record.
    IF NOT customer-eof
        IF first-record
            MOVE cm-salesman-key to old-salesman-key.
    IF NOT customer-eof
        IF cm-salesman-key NOT GREATER THAN old-salesman-key
            DO 220-print-customer-line
        ELSE
            IF cm-branch-number GREATER THAN old-branch-number
                DO 290-print-salesman-total-line
                DO 300-print-branch-total-line
                DO 220-print-customer-line
                MOVE cm-salesman-key to old-salesman-key
            ELSE
                DO 290-print-salesman-total-line
                DO 220-print-customer-line
                MOVE cm-salesman-number to old-salesman-number.
    IF NOT customer-eof
        DO 280-accumulate-sales-totals
    ELSE
        DO 290-print-salesman-total-line
        DO 300-print-branch-total-line.
```

Figure 8-12 Pseudocode for another way of coding module 200 of the report-preparation program

In contrast, you shouldn't have to make notes about what you want to put in a lower-level module as you plan or code a higher-level module. If you do, this usually indicates that the modules aren't independent. In other words, if you have to code two or more modules at the same time, they obviously aren't independent. I'll give you an example of this in a moment.

One way to determine how independent a module is, is to analyze the switches, flags, and control fields that are being passed to or from the module. In the pseudocode in figure 8-11, for example, the salesman-number and branch-number fields are control fields. The salesman-key field, which is made up of the salesman-number and branch-number fields, is also a control field.

Because HIPO diagrams list the switches, flags, and control fields in the input and output boxes, they can help you spot problems with module independence. In general, you should try to keep the number of switches, flags, and control fields used by a module to a minimum. If, for example, a module requires four different switches and eight control fields to determine what it will do, you can most likely improve the independence of the module by redesigning the structure chart or rethinking the code.

When you check a module for independence, you should also make sure that you don't pass switches and flags to lower-level modules. As I said earlier, it's all right to pass switches up to a calling module. There's no way around that. But when you pass switches down to a called module, it usually means that neither calling module nor called module are as independent as they could be.

```
200-produces-sales-report-lines.

    DO 210-read-customer-record.
    IF NOT customer-eof
        IF first-record
            MOVE cm-salesman-key to old-salesman-key
        ELSE
            IF cm-branch-number GREATER old-branch-number
                MOVE 'Y' to branch-change-sw
                MOVE 'Y' to salesman-change-sw
            ELSE
                MOVE 'Y' to salesman-change-sw.
    IF NOT customer-eof
        DO 290-print-salesman-total-line
        DO 300-print-branch-total-line
        DO 220-print-customer-line
        DO 280-accumulate sales-total
        MOVE cm-salesman-key to old-salesman-key
    ELSE
        DO 290-print-salesman-total-line
        DO 300-print-branch-total-line.

290-print-salesman-total-line.

    IF salesman-change
        format salesman total line and prepare it for printing
        DO 240-print-report-line
        MOVE zeros to salesman totals
        MOVE 'N' to salesman-change-sw.

300-print-branch-total-line.

    IF branch-change
        format branch total line and prepare it for printing
        DO 240-print-report-line
        MOVE zeros to branch totals
        MOVE 'N' to branch-change-sw.
```

Figure 8-13 Pseudocode for the report-preparation program that shows how passing switches to lower-level modules can reduce module independence

To illustrate this point, look at the code in figure 8-13. Here, module 200 is coded so it passes switches to the print modules. Then, each print module starts by testing a switch to see whether it should perform its function. But that means you have to know how you're going to code the print modules when you plan the code for module 200. And that means the print modules aren't independent of module 200. Then, to test and maintain the program, you have to be aware of the close relationships between the print modules and module 200. In short, program quality suffers when you pass switches to called modules.

In conclusion, you should realize that no module is completely independent. Since each module of a program operates on switches, flags, control fields, or data fields, each module has some relationship to the entire program and to one or more other modules in the program. On the other hand, if you want to produce programs that are easy to develop and maintain, you must try to keep each module as independent as is practical.

Principle 2: Document only the function specified by the module name As you implement a program, you are likely to discover some lines of code that the program requires that don't seem to fit in any of the modules of your program design. For some subfunctions like this, you and the other members of your programming group will have agreed upon certain conventions for handling them. In our shop, for example, we have agreed that certain verbs can include certain subfunctions as recommended in our verb list in figure 7-5. Thus, a print module can include the subfunction of resetting total fields.

In the absence of conventions like this, however, you should obey this principle: Document only the function specified by the module name. In other words, never place a subfunction in a module where it doesn't belong just because you can't find a good place for it. It is better to add another module to the structure chart for a subfunction like this, even if it is only a few coding lines long, than it is to place it where you won't be able to find it later on. When you can't tell from the structure chart in which module you might find the code for a subfunction, program quality suffers.

To illustrate this point, suppose the structure chart in figure 8-10 didn't have a module 280 for accumulating the totals from each input record. Then, you would have to put the code for this subfunction (only a few lines long) in some other module. In this program, though, this code can logically be placed in either module 200 or module 220. However, neither module name implies that it should do this subfunction. As a result, when you test or maintain the program, your structure chart isn't a precise index to the COBOL code. Instead, you have to look at the code for both modules in order to find the one that contains the code. In a simple program like this, that isn't too bad. But in a typical production program, this can have a serious effect on program quality.

In summary, if you took the time to create good module names when you designed your program, you should make effective use of the names when you plan and code the modules. You do this by putting only the named function in each module of a program.

Principle 3: In general, move subfunctions down the line Some subfunctions, like counting records or resetting total fields, are trivial enough that they don't require separate modules, yet they're hard to place in the existing modules. For instance, you know from experience that a report-printing program must count lines and reset the LINE-COUNT field to zero after page overflow. But which modules should do these subfunctions? Since subfunctions like these are usually just a line or two of code, you don't want to create separate modules for them. So you should try to place them in existing modules.

For subfunctions like this, we recommend that you move the subfunctions *down the line* in the structure chart and make them part of some low-level module. For example, we suggest that you count records in read or write modules and that you reset totals in print modules. This is in line with the inclusive verb meanings we recommended in our verb list in figure 7-5.

```
200-produces-sales-report-lines.

    DO 210-read-customer-record.
    IF NOT customer-eof
        IF first-record
            MOVE cm-salesman-key to old-salesman-key.
    IF NOT customer-eof
        IF cm-salesman-key NOT GREATER THAN old-salesman-key
            DO 220-print-customer-line
        ELSE
            IF cm-branch-number GREATER THAN old-branch-number
                DO 290-print-salesman-total-line
                ADD salesman-total-this-YTD to
                    branch-total-this-YTD
                ADD salesman-total-last-YTD to
                    branch-total-last-YTD
                MOVE zero to salesman-total-this-ytd
                             salesman-total-last-ytd
                DO 300-print-branch-total-line
                ADD branch-total-this-YTD to
                    total-sales-this-YTD
                ADD branch-total-last-YTD to
                    total-sales-last-YTD
                MOVE zero to branch-total-this-ytd
                              branch-total-last-ytd
                DO 220-print-customer-line
                MOVE cm-salesman-key to old-salesman-key
            ELSE
                DO 290-print-salesman-total-line
                MOVE zero to salesman-total-this-ytd
                             salesman-total-last-ytd
                DO 220-print-customer-line
                MOVE cm-salesman-number to old-salesman-number.
    IF NOT customer-eof
        DO 280-accumulate-sales-totals
    ELSE
        DO 290-print-salesman-total-line
        ADD salesman-total-this-YTD to
            branch-total-this-YTD
        ADD salesman-total-last-YTD to
            branch-total-last-YTD
        DO 300-print-branch-total-line
        ADD branch-total-this-YTD to
            total-sales-this-YTD
        ADD branch-total-last-YTD to
            total-sales-last-YTD
```

Figure 8-14 Pseudocode for module 200 of the report-preparation program with subfunctions moved up the line

When I created the pseudocode in figure 8-11, I used this principle when I had to decide in which modules I should reset the branch and salesman totals. If you review the structure chart in figure 8-10, you can see that I could have coded these subfunctions in modules 290 and 300, or I could have put them in module 200. As you can see from the pseudocode in figure 8-11, I moved these subfunctions down the line into modules 290 and 300.

In contrast, figure 8-14 shows the pseudocode of figure 8-12 with all subfunctions moved up the line. As you can see, module 200 is about twice as long in this form so it isn't as easy to read and understand. In a case like this, then, you're better off moving the subfunctions to the lower-level modules, which are less complicated than module 200 is.

Sometimes, however, it's illogical to move subfunctions down the line. This is often true in interactive programs. For instance, it's often better to clear a terminal screen in a control module for getting an interactive transaction than it is to clear it in a lower-level module. So we're not saying that you should always follow this down-the-line principle. Nevertheless, it is a useful principle that can be applied effectively in many programs.

Perhaps the main thing is to strive for consistency. Whenever possible, handle the same type of subfunction in the same way. If you develop a pattern for your decisions, you will minimize clerical errors and simplify debugging. And if you adopt this principle of moving code down the line *whenever placement is debatable*, you will take an important step towards consistency.

Principle 4: In general, move control code up the line When I speak of *control code*, I mean any code that affects the logic of a module. This includes code that compares two control fields. It includes code that tests the value of a switch or flag. And it includes code that sets the value of a switch, flag, or control field.

If you look again at the pseudocode for module 200 of the report-preparation program in figure 8-11, you can see that this module contains all of the control code that affects its logic. Specifically, it turns the first-record switch off after it controls the processing of the first record. It compares the control fields that determine when lines are to be printed. And it resets the values of the old control fields when the control fields change.

On the other hand, some of this code could be placed in modules 290 and 300. So the pseudocode for module 200 could be shortened as shown in figure 8-15. In this case, the old salesman number field is reset in module 290 and the old branch number field is reset in module 300. Now which is the better way to code module 200...as in figure 8-11 or as in figure 8-15?

The advantage of moving the control-code up into the control modules is that the control modules are more complete. That is, they show all the code that will affect their logic so there is little chance of omitting any critical code. The advantage of moving the control-code changes down into the work modules is that the control modules are shorter. That is, the IF conditions and module calls are not cluttered up by other code.

Although this is somewhat debatable, the consensus in our shop is that the first version is preferable to the second. As a result, our fourth principle is to move code that affects the logical operation of a module up the line. This is consistent with our first principle because that way the control module becomes more independent; you don't have to look at other modules to understand its operation.

```
200-produces-sales-report-lines.

    DO 210-read-customer-record.
    IF NOT customer-eof
        IF first-record
            MOVE cm-salesman-key to old-salesman-key
            DO 220-print-customer-line
            DO 280-accumulate-sales-totals
            MOVE 'N' to first-record-sw
        ELSE
            IF cm-salesman-key NOT GREATER old-salesman-key
                DO 220-print-customer-line
                DO 280-accumulate-sales-totals
            ELSE
                IF cm-branch-number GREATER old-branch-number
                    DO 290-print-salesman-total-line
                    DO 300-print-branch-total-line
                    DO 220-print-customer-line
                    DO 280-accumulate-sales-totals
                ELSE
                    DO 290-print-salesman-total-line
                    DO 220-print-customer-line
                    DO 280-accumulate-sales-totals
    ELSE
        DO 290-print-salesman-total-line
        DO 300-print-branch-total-line.
```

Figure 8-15 Pseudocode for module 200 of the report-preparation program with control code moved down the line

With this in mind, look again at the alternative coding for module 200 in figure 8-12. Can you tell how it violates this fourth principle? It's a minor point, but when you code the module in this way, you can't turn the first-record switch off until after it's used by module 220. That means that you must remember to turn the switch off in module 220 when you plan its code. Since it's easy to forget to do this, this may mean a program bug and an additional test run later on.

In general, then, I think this fourth principle will help you avoid problems that will reduce the quality of your programs. So, *when in doubt*, move control code up the line into its logical control module.

How to revise a structure chart as you plan the modules of a program

If you follow the principles of this topic, you will sometimes find that you have to modify a structure chart as you plan the modules of a program. Sometimes, you will find that you can't code a module in a readable form because it's dependent on some other module; then, the solution may be to revise the structure chart. Sometimes, you will find that a subfunction requires its own module so you have to add a module to a program. Sometimes, you will find that you have to divide a module into two or more modules because it is too long or complex to code in a practical manner. Sometimes, you will find that a subfunction module consists of only one line of code, so it's tempting to absorb it into its calling module. At this time, then, let me give you some ideas about handling conditions like this.

Before I start, though, I want you to realize that, generally speaking, there's nothing wrong with making changes to a structure chart as you plan its modules or even as you code its modules. One of the benefits of the design method we recommend is that you can easily revise the design. In fact, you can revise one portion of a structure chart without affecting the names or numbers of any of the other modules. Furthermore, because we have a rather rigid method for designing the top two levels of a structure chart, most of the changes you will make will be at the lower levels. And changes at the lower levels can be made quickly and easily.

So having to revise a structure chart, particularly at the lower levels, doesn't mean that you didn't do an adequate job of planning. As I think you'll see in a moment, you should expect to make a few changes to a program's design as you plan and code the program. And you should be able to make these changes with little or no cost in terms of programmer productivity.

When to add a module to a structure chart In principle 2 in this topic, we said that you should only provide for the function specified by a module's name. So when you realize that you're trying to put a subfunction in a module where it doesn't belong and that no module on the structure chart logically includes the subfunction, then it's time to add a module to the structure chart. As we said, it's better to add a module than it is to put a subfunction in a module where it will be difficult to find later.

When to divide one module into two or more modules When you have continuing difficulty in the planning or coding of a module, the solution may be to design some subordinates for the module. In other words, you simplify the module by dividing its function among some subordinates. Then, each subordinate does a subfunction of the original module. This in turn simplifies the code of the original module.

Although this may sound difficult, this type of design revision is easy to make. For instance, figure 8-16 shows the actual COBOL code for module 220 of the report-preparation program charted in figure 8-10. As you can see, this module requires a total of 56 lines of COBOL code. Not only is that longer than the recommended maximum for a paragraph in a COBOL program, but the code isn't that easy to follow.

Now look at the revised version of this module in figure 8-17 after some subordinates have been added to the structure chart. Here, the designer has one subordinate module for each format that a customer line may take. Module 221 formats a customer line in the form that is required for the first line of a new branch. Module 222 formats a customer line in the form that is required for the first line of a new salesman. And module 223 formats a customer line when neither branch nor salesman is new.

```
 220-PRINT-CUSTOMER-LINE.
*
     IF FIRST-RECORD
         MOVE CM-BRANCH-NUMBER    TO CL-BRANCH-NO
         MOVE CM-SALESMAN-NUMBER  TO CL-SALESMAN-NO
         MOVE CM-SALESMAN-KEY     TO SM-SALESMAN-KEY
         MOVE 'Y'                 TO RECORD-FOUND-SW
         PERFORM 230-READ-SALESMAN-RECORD
         IF RECORD-FOUND
             MOVE SM-SALESMAN-NAME TO CL-SALESMAN-NAME
         ELSE
             MOVE 'SALESMAN RECORD NOT FOUND'
                 TO CL-SALESMAN-NAME
     ELSE
         IF CM-SALESMAN-KEY GREATER OLD-SALESMAN-KEY
             IF CM-BRANCH-NUMBER GREATER OLD-BRANCH-NUMBER
                 MOVE CM-BRANCH-NUMBER    TO CL-BRANCH-NO
                 MOVE CM-SALESMAN-NUMBER  TO CL-SALESMAN-NO
                 MOVE CM-SALESMAN-KEY     TO SM-SALESMAN-KEY
                 MOVE 'Y'                 TO RECORD-FOUND-SW
                 PERFORM 230-READ-SALESMAN-RECORD
                 IF RECORD-FOUND
                     MOVE SM-SALESMAN-NAME TO CL-SALESMAN-NAME
                 ELSE
                     MOVE 'SALESMAN RECORD NOT FOUND'
                         TO CL-SALESMAN-NAME
             ELSE
                 MOVE SPACE               TO CL-BRANCH-NO
                 MOVE CM-SALESMAN-NUMBER  TO CL-SALESMAN-NO
                 MOVE CM-SALESMAN-KEY     TO SM-SALESMAN-KEY
                 MOVE 'Y'                 TO RECORD-FOUND-SW
                 PERFORM 230-READ-SALESMAN-RECORD
                 IF RECORD-FOUND
                     MOVE SM-SALESMAN-NAME TO CL-SALESMAN-NAME
                 ELSE
                     MOVE 'SALESMAN RECORD NOT FOUND'
                         TO CL-SALESMAN-NAME
         ELSE
             MOVE SPACE TO CL-SALESMAN-NAME
                           CL-SALESMAN-NO
                           CL-BRANCH-NO.
     MOVE CM-CUSTOMER-NUMBER TO CL-CUSTOMER-NO.
     MOVE CM-CUSTOMER-NAME   TO CL-CUSTOMER-NAME.
     MOVE CM-SALES-THIS-YTD  TO CL-SALES-THIS-YTD.
     MOVE CM-SALES-LAST-YTD  TO CL-SALES-LAST-YTD.
     COMPUTE CHANGE-AMOUNT = CM-SALES-THIS-YTD
                           - CM-SALES-LAST-YTD.
     MOVE CHANGE-AMOUNT TO CL-CHANGE-AMOUNT.
     IF CM-SALES-LAST-YTD NOT EQUAL ZERO
         COMPUTE CHANGE-PERCENT ROUNDED = CHANGE-AMOUNT
                                        / CM-SALES-LAST-YTD
                                        * 100
         MOVE CHANGE-PERCENT TO CL-CHANGE-PERCENT
     ELSE
         MOVE 'N/A' TO CL-CHANGE-PERCENT-R.
     MOVE CUSTOMER-LINE TO NEXT-REPORT-LINE.
     PERFORM 240-PRINT-REPORT-LINE.
     MOVE 1 TO SPACE-CONTROL.
*
```

Figure 8-16 The COBOL code for module 220 of the report-preparation program

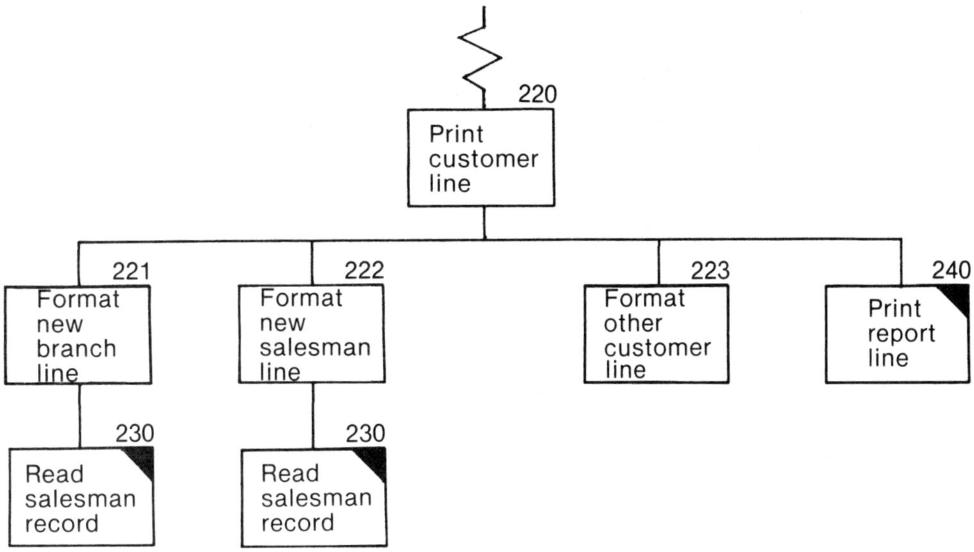


```
220-print-customer-line.

    IF first-record
        DO 221-format-new-branch-line
    ELSE
        IF cm-salesman-key GREATER old-salesman-key
            IF cm-branch-number GREATER old-branch-number
                DO 221-format-new-branch-line
            ELSE
                DO 222-format-new-salesman-line
        ELSE
            DO 223-format-other-customer-line.
    MOVE customer-line to next-report-line.
    DO 240-print-report-line.
    MOVE 1 to space-control.

221-format-new-branch-line.

    Format output line using module 230 to get the required salesman
    record.

222-format-new-salesman-line.

    Format output line using module 230 to get the required salesman
    record.

223-format-other-customer-line.

    Format output line clearing branch number, salesman number, and
    salesman name to spaces.
```

Figure 8-17 Revised structure and code for module 220 of the report-preparation program

By making this revision to the structure, the code for module 220 is simplified considerably. Instead of 56 lines, the module now requires 13 lines. Similarly, since the other code is divided between modules 221, 222, and 223, these modules should be easy to code too.

When to delete modules from a structure chart Sometimes, when you plan or code a module, you realize that it is only going to be one or two lines long. Then, the temptation is to absorb it into the calling module and to delete the module from the structure chart. In fact, some people recommend that you do this for all modules that are less than four lines.

To illustrate, consider the code for module 280 of the report-preparation structure chart in figure 8-10. Since it only has to accumulate two totals for each customer record, it can be coded in as little as two lines of code. So is module 280 necessary? Or should it be deleted from the structure chart?

As a general guideline, you should only delete a module from a program when you realize that it isn't a function or a subfunction. In other words, you should only delete a module when you realize that it logically belongs in some other module. Otherwise, you start to question the validity of every short module you encounter. So if a module makes sense where it is, keep it there, no matter how short it is.

Discussion

Although we feel that designing the program is the most critical task in the development of a COBOL program, how you code the modules is important too. In particular, you must do your best to make sure that each module does only one function and that it does it as independently as possible. In this topic, then, I've tried to give you some principles for planning the code of a module.

Although some people may feel that revising a program's design as you plan and code its modules indicates that you didn't design adequately in the first place, we disagree. In fact, we think some shops have gone from too little design in the GOTO era of programming to too much design in the structured programming era. As a result, they spend so much time in the design phase that it becomes counterproductive...and they still find that they have to make design revisions as they go along.

As we see it, no design method can insure that you will provide for every condition that comes up during the implementation of a program. So what you really want is a design method that allows you to make design revisions with little or no cost in terms of programmer productivity. That way you can continue to improve a program's design as you implement the program.

Terminology

control code

Objective

Given program specifications and a structure chart for a program's design, plan effective code for any module of the program using either pseudocode or a HIPO diagram.

Topic 4 Other methods for module planning

Earlier in this chapter, I told you that about one-third of the people who responded to our COBOL survey said they used pseudocode for module planning. And about one-fifth of the respondents said they used the simplified form of HIPO diagrams we presented in topic 2 of this chapter. Furthermore, we strongly feel that using pseudocode or simplified HIPO diagrams is the most effective way to plan the modules of a structured program.

However, our COBOL survey also showed that about one-fifth of the shops use HIPO diagrams in a more cumbersome form than the one I showed you in topic 2. And about one-third of the shops use some form of flowcharting to plan the modules of a program. Otherwise, no other method of module planning was used in even 5 percent of the shops. At this time, then, I'd like to say something about IBM's form of HIPO diagrams and program flowcharting as devices for module planning.

HIPO diagrams as presented by IBM As I said at the time, the HIPO diagrams presented in topic 2 are a simplified version of the HIPO diagrams presented in IBM's literature on HIPO documentation. In contrast, the IBM diagrams tend to be much more elaborate in terms of graphics.

Figure 8-18, for example, presents a HIPO diagram done in IBM style. Here, black arrows are used to indicate the flow of control to and from the module. White arrows are used to show the relationships between I/O items and processing steps. And boxes are placed around data items in the input and output portions of the form.

If you go to this level of detail on a HIPO diagram, I think HIPO diagrams are way too cumbersome to be practical. By using the fancy arrows and additional boxes, the HIPO diagram is more difficult to create and more difficult to change. In addition, the extra detail doesn't make the diagram easier to understand; and it doesn't make the diagram a better guide for coding.

To give you some idea of how the use of HIPO diagrams in this form can affect productivity, let me tell you that it took me about 45 minutes to create the HIPO diagram in figure 8-18 in rough, handwritten form. That was after the program had been coded and tested so I knew exactly what the input, output, and processing requirements were. About 30 minutes of that time was devoted to the graphics portion of the job: drawing the arrows and boxes without making a total mess.

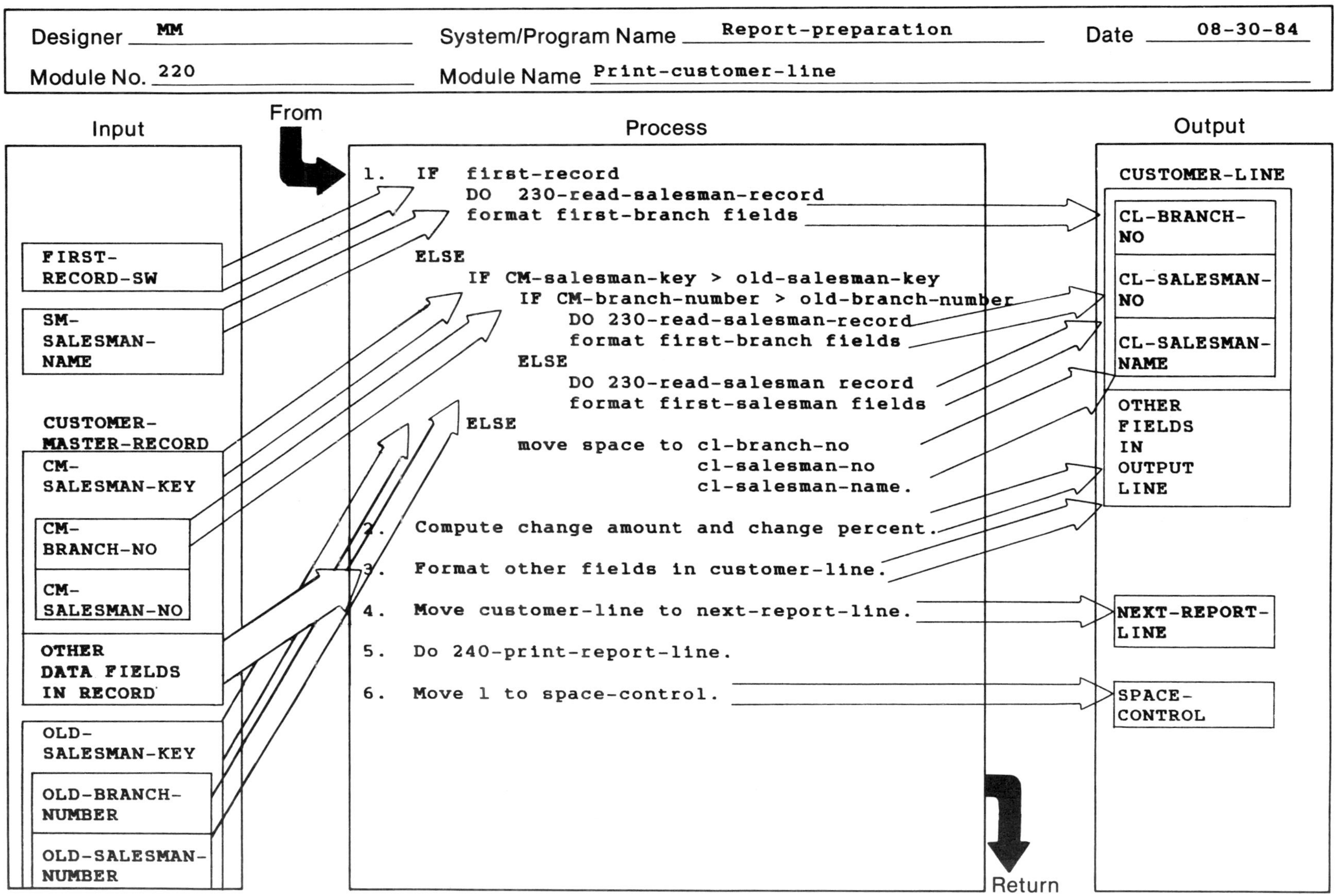

Figure 8-18 A HIPO diagram for module 220 of the report-preparation program with an emphasis on graphics

With this in mind, you can imagine how the use of HIPO diagrams can affect productivity. If, for example, you write a program of 16 modules and each HIPO diagram only takes you 30 minutes to create, you've used up one 8 hour day ...and you haven't written one line of code. Worse, you don't know anything more about the program than you would have discovered if you hadn't used any graphics on your HIPO diagram, if you had used pseudocode instead of HIPO diagrams, or if you had just started to code the program in COBOL using the structure chart as a guideline.

Structured flowcharts

I've already mentioned the problems with the program flowcharts of the GOTO era of programming. Briefly, they're difficult to create and maintain, they don't help you simplify the programming problem, and they are no more meaningful than the code itself. With that as background, I would have thought that no one would use flowcharts in conjunction with structured programming. But I was wrong. About one-third of the shops we surveyed still use flowcharts for planning the code of program modules. Apparently, old habits die hard.

Unfortunately, if you plan the modules of a program using the old type of program flowchart, you defeat the purposes of structured programming. Because the flowcharts lead you to the use of GOTO statements, you can't code each module on the structure chart as a single COBOL paragraph. Then, each paragraph of your program doesn't have a single entry and exit. And so on.

But what about *structured flowcharts*? When I presented the theory of structured programming, I used flowcharts to show you the basic structures. So it's certainly possible to draw a structured flowchart for a module that has only one entry and exit point. In fact, figure 8-19 shows a structured flowchart for module 000 of the edit program. This, at the least, is what I hope the one-third of the people who plan the modules of a program with flowcharts are using. And this is what a number of books and trainers recommend. So what's wrong with structured flowcharts?

Unfortunately, structured or not, program flowcharting is counterproductive. The flowcharts are still difficult to create and maintain so they reduce productivity. But the key point is that they are no more easy to understand than pseudocode or the COBOL code itself. A study in the mid-1970s established this to my satisfaction. And I think most programmers know this intuitively. So why take the time to draw flowcharts if pseudocode or COBOL will do the job just as well in a fraction of the time?

Simply stated, you've got to stop flowcharting if you want to get the benefits of structured programming. Perhaps more than any other single technique, flowcharting keeps us from developing reliable programs at a satisfactory rate of production.

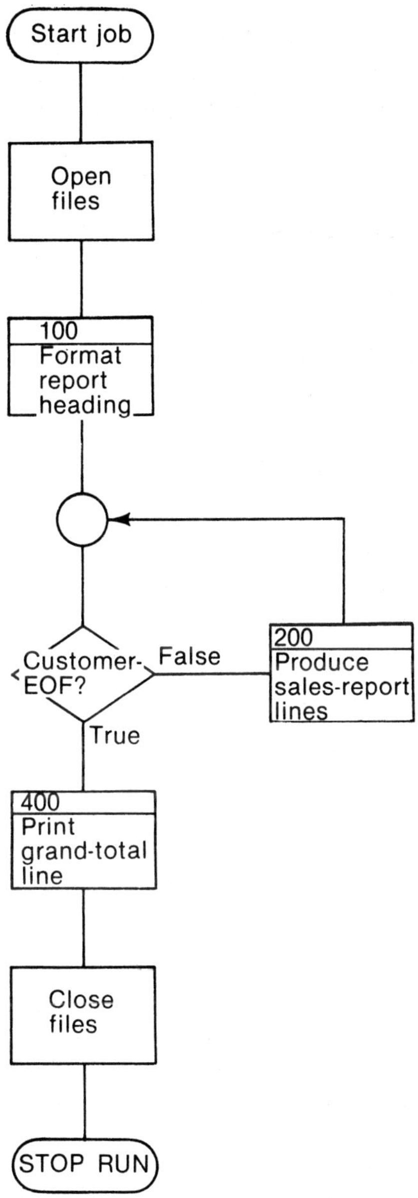

Figure 8-19 A structured flowchart for module 000 of the report-preparation program

Discussion

As we see it, IBM's HIPO diagrams and structured flowcharts are counterproductive because the emphasis is on graphics rather than on programming. To be a productive programmer, you need to be able to plan a program module as rapidly as possible. And our experiences have proven that the way to do this is to use pseudocode or HIPO diagrams or COBOL code itself, but in any case to avoid the use of graphics.

Terminology

structured flowchart

Objectives

None. This topic is for information only.

Chapter 9

How to code a structured program in COBOL

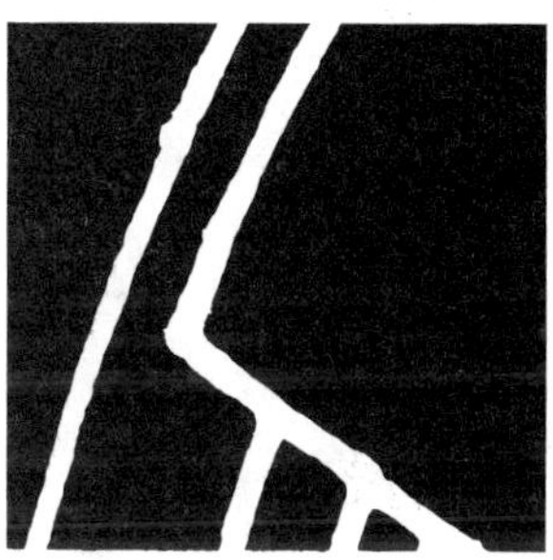

When it comes to coding, structured programming implies three things. First, it implies that you have a structured design for the program. Second, it implies that the program will be coded using only the accepted structures of structured programming. And third, it implies a style of coding that is designed to increase the readability of a program.

This chapter explains how the principles of structured programming are implemented in COBOL. In topic 1, you will learn how to code the basic structures in COBOL. In topic 2, you will be given some guidelines for using COBOL in a readable manner. Once you master the material in this topic, you will know how to code programs that will be both reliable and easy to maintain. Then, in topic 3, I'll show you how to improve your productivity as you code a COBOL program by reusing code from old programs. Finally, in topic 4, I'll present some other coding practices including one that you should definitely avoid.

Topic 1 The basic structures in COBOL

As you may recall, the basic structures of structured programming are the sequence, iteration, and selection structures. The iteration structure can also be referred to as the DO-WHILE, DO-UNTIL, or PERFORM-UNTIL structure; the selection structure can be referred to as the IF-THEN-ELSE structure. In addition to these structures, structured programming requires a facility for calling subordinate modules; this can be referred to as a DO structure.

In COBOL, any non-conditional, non-branching statement is a sequence structure. Similarly, a succession of two or more of these statements is a sequence structure. Thus, a series of MOVE statements is a sequence structure; and a series of arithmetic statements without ON SIZE ERROR options is a sequence structure.

In other words, the sequence structure is traditional COBOL code without GOTO statements or conditional statements. As a result, it doesn't require any special considerations for structured programming. The major emphasis of this topic, then, will be on three COBOL statements that do require special handling in a structured program: the PERFORM statement, which is used to call a module; the PERFORM-UNTIL statement, which corresponds to the DO-UNTIL (or PERFORM-UNTIL) structure; and the IF statement, which corresponds to the IF-THEN-ELSE structure.

The PERFORM statement

The PERFORM statement is used to call subordinate modules. For instance, the statement

```
PERFORM 100-FORMAT-REPORT-HEADING
```

calls the procedure named 100-FORMAT-REPORT-HEADING. After the statements in this procedure are executed, program control returns to the statement following the PERFORM. Although the PERFORM statement doesn't represent one of the basic structures of structured programming, it does correspond to the DO structure. As such, it is used for calling subordinate modules.

If you use modular programming techniques, you probably make frequent use of the PERFORM statement in your unstructured programs. However, you probably are used to coding the THRU clause as part of the PERFORM, as in this example:

```
PERFORM TABLE-LOOKUP THRU TABLE-LOOKUP-EXIT
```

Note, therefore, that the THRU clause isn't needed in structured programs since none of the called modules should contain GOTO statements. Instead, each called module should have only one entry and one exit point, and each should consist of a single paragraph. In fact, using the THRU clause can reduce the quality of a COBOL program as I'll discuss in topic 4.

The PERFORM-UNTIL statement

The PERFORM-UNTIL statement corresponds to the DO-UNTIL (or PERFORM-UNTIL) structure of structured programming. As a result, you code a DO-UNTIL structure in pseudocode with a PERFORM-UNTIL statement in COBOL. The PERFORM-UNTIL statement is commonly used in the top-level module of a structured program, but it may be used in other control modules as well.

To appreciate the use of the PERFORM-UNTIL statement, consider this statement:

```
PERFORM 300-EDIT-INVENTORY-TRAN
    UNTIL TRAN-EOF-SW = 'Y'.
```

Its logic is shown in figure 9-1. Here, module 300 will be executed repeatedly until TRAN-EOF-SW is equal to Y. Since the PERFORM-UNTIL statement tests to see whether the condition has been met *before* the module is called, the module will *not* be called the first time TRAN-EOF-SW is found to be equal to Y. Instead, the program will continue with the next statement after the PERFORM-UNTIL.

Figure 9-2 gives the format and logic of the PERFORM-UNTIL statement when the VARYING option is used. This option is commonly used to vary the value of a subscript or index each time a module is called. Note again that the condition is tested *before* the module is called. So in the statement

```
PERFORM 200-LOAD-PART-NUMBER-TABLE
    VARYING PN-TABLE-INDEX FROM 1 BY 1
    UNTIL PART-NUMBER-EOF
       OR PN-TABLE-INDEX > 100
```

the procedure named 200-LOAD-PART-NUMBER-TABLE will not be called if PART-NUMBER-EOF or PN-TABLE-INDEX is greater than 100.

COBOL example

```
PERFORM 300-EDIT-INVENTORY-TRAN
    UNTIL TRAN-EOF-SW = 'Y'.
```

Statement format

```
PERFORM procedure-name-1 UNTIL condition-1
```

Logic flow

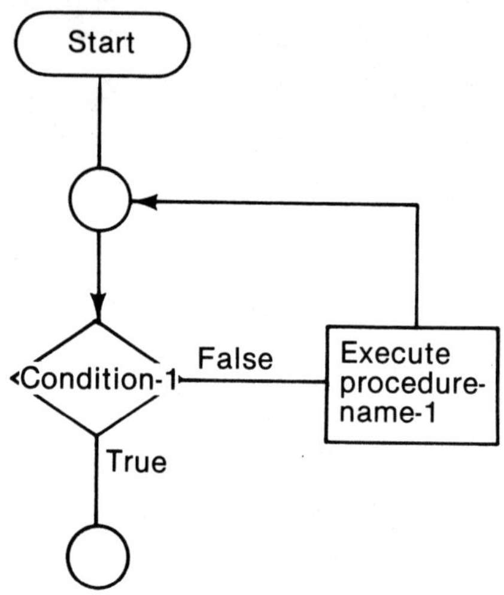

Figure 9-1 The execution of the PERFORM-UNTIL statement

Although COBOL allows three levels of VARYING clauses in a PERFORM-UNTIL statement, only one or two levels are recommended in structured COBOL. As more levels are used, the program becomes more difficult to read and understand. So you can often improve program readability by keeping the number of levels to a minimum.

The IF statement

The selection structure is coded in COBOL using the IF statement. Its format is this:

```
IF condition
    statement-1 ...
    NEXT SENTENCE
ELSE
    statement-m ...
    NEXT SENTENCE
```

COBOL example

```
PERFORM 200-LOAD-PART-NUMBER-TABLE
    VARYING PN-TABLE-INDEX FROM 1 BY 1
    UNTIL PART-NUMBER-EOF
       OR PN-TABLE-INDEX > 100.
```

Statement format

```
PERFORM procedure-name-1

   VARYING {index-name-1}
           {identifier-1}

           {index-name-2}
      FROM {literal-2   }  BY  {literal-3   }
           {identifier-2}      {identifier-3}

UNTIL condition-1
```

Logic flow

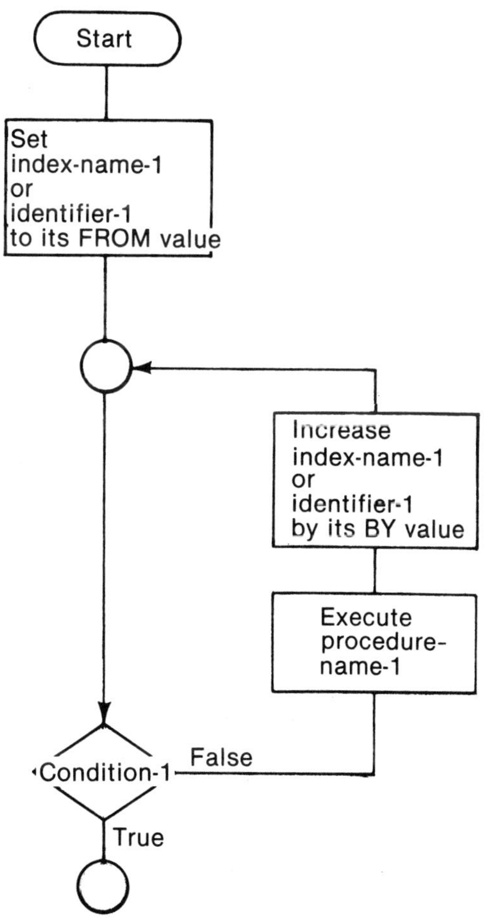

Figure 9-2 The PERFORM-UNTIL statement with the VARYING option

```
350-PROCESS-INVENTORY-TRAN.
*
     IF MT-DELETION
         IF IM-ITEM-NUMBER = MT-ITEM-NUMBER
             IF NOT MASTER-DELETED
                 PERFORM 360-APPLY-DELETION-TRANSACTION
             ELSE
                 PERFORM 410-WRITE-ERROR-TRANSACTION
         ELSE
             PERFORM 410-WRITE-ERROR-TRANSACTION
     ELSE
         IF MT-ADDITION
             IF IM-ITEM-NUMBER = MT-ITEM-NUMBEP
                 IF MASTER-DELETED
                     PERFORM 420-APPLY-ADDITION-TRANSACTION
                 ELSE
                     PERFORM 410-WRITE-ERROR-TRANSACTION
             ELSE
                 PERFORM 420-APPLY-ADDITION-TRANSACTION
         ELSE
             IF MT-CHANGE
                 IF IM-ITEM-NUMBER = MT-ITEM-NUMBER
                     IF NOT MASTER-DELETED
                         PERFORM 440-APPLY-CHANGE-TRANSACTION
                     ELSE
                         PERFORM 410-WRITE-ERROR-TRANSACTION.
```

Figure 9-3 The COBOL code for module 350 of the sequential file-maintenance program showing the use of nested IF statements

Here, the statements following the condition are executed if the condition is true; the statements following ELSE are executed if the condition is false. When NEXT SENTENCE is used, it means continue with the first statement after the period that marks the end of the IF statement. In effect, then, NEXT SENTENCE is a GOTO statement that goes to the next COBOL sentence. As a result, you should avoid using NEXT SENTENCE because it can reduce readability.

Although *nested IF statements* were often discouraged in the traditional COBOL shop, they are necessary in structured programs. In fact, you will often find IF statements nested three and four levels deep in structured programs. Nevertheless, if you don't use nested IF statements too much right now, I think you'll find that they are quite easy to master. And once mastered, they will improve the clarity of your programs and reduce debugging problems.

To illustrate the use of nested IF statements, consider the code in figure 9-3. This is the code for module 350 of the sequential file-maintenance program that I presented in chapter 7. This code is nested five levels deep. It determines which of four subordinate modules to call based on transaction type, a comparison of the control codes, and whether or not the last master record was deleted. Since code this complicated is necessary in many production programs, a professional programmer should be able to write it in a readable manner.

Indentation error:

```
IF condition-a
    PERFORM procedure-1
    IF condition-b
        PERFORM procedure-2
ELSE ◄──────────────────────── Improperly aligned ELSE clause
    IF condition-c
        PERFORM procedure-3
    ELSE
        PERFORM procedure-4.
```

Indentation corresponds to compilation:

```
IF condition-a
    PERFORM procedure-1
    IF condition-b
        PERFORM procedure-2
    ELSE
        IF condition-c
            PERFORM procedure-3
        ELSE
            PERFORM procedure-4.
```

Figure 9-4 Improper and proper use of indentation in a nested IF statement

The key to clarity when using nested IF statements is the use of indentation to show the levels of nesting. Thus, in figure 9-3, the ELSE that goes with the first IF is found directly beneath it. In addition, all statements that are done if the condition is true are indented four spaces from the IF; and the statements that are done if the condition is false are indented four spaces from the ELSE. This process continues for subsequent levels of nesting, so you can see that the last PERFORM statement in figure 9-3 is only executed if the transaction is a change, the item number in the transaction record is equal to the item number in the master record, and the master record is deleted. In other words, the transaction is invalid so module 410 is called to write the error transaction.

When coding IF statements, remember that each ELSE will be paired with the first IF that precedes it that doesn't already have an ELSE paired with it. So watch out. Since indentation doesn't affect the compilation, it is possible to pair IF and ELSE clauses through indentation even though the compiler will treat them differently. In the first part of figure 9-4, for example, the compiler will pair the first ELSE clause with the second IF statement, even though the programmer apparently means it to be paired with the first IF statement. In the second part of figure 9-4, the indentation represents the way the code will be interpreted by the compiler.

Since ELSE clauses are optional, nested IF statements can be coded in a variety of different forms. In all cases, however, indentation should

Example 1:

```
IF condition-a
    statement-group-a
    IF condition-b
        statement-group-b
        IF condition-c
            statement-group-c.
```

Example 2:

```
IF condition-a
    statement-group-a
    IF condition-b
        statement-group-b
        IF condition-c
            statement-group-c
        ELSE
            statement-group-d
    ELSE
        statement-group-e
ELSE
    statement-group-f.
```

Example 3:

```
IF condition-a
    statement-group-a
ELSE
    IF condition-b
        statement-group-b
    ELSE
        IF condition-c
            statement-group-c
        ELSE
            statement-group-d.
```

Figure 9-5 Proper use of indentation in some common forms of nested IF statements

be used to indicate which level of nesting a clause represents. In figure 9-5, some common variations are given for three levels of nesting. Note that in all cases the indentation corresponds to the way the compiler will interpret these statements.

If a string of nested IF statements merely checks a single field for a succession of independent values, the IF statements can be written without indentation as shown in the example in figure 9-6. As you can see, this code performs one module if the transaction code is equal to 1, performs another module if it is equal to 2, and executes some default code if it isn't equal to either 1 or 2. I hope you will agree that this code is just as clear as it would be with indentation (if not clearer). This method of coding IF statements is sometimes referred to as *linear nesting* since the IF conditions are tested in line, one right after the other.

```
 320-EDIT-TRANSACTION-FIELDS.
*
     MOVE 'Y'   TO VALID-TRAN-SW.
     MOVE SPACE TO INVALID-TRANSACTION-LINE.
     IF ITR-TRAN-CODE=1
         PERFORM 330-EDIT-CODE-1-FIELDS
     ELSE IF ITR-TRAN-CODE=2
         PERFORM 350-EDIT-CODE-2-FIELDS
     ELSE
         MOVE ERROR-INDICATOR TO ITL-TRAN-CODE-ERROR
         MOVE 'N'             TO VALID-TRAN-SW
         ADD 1                TO INVALID-TRAN-CODE-COUNT.
```

Figure 9-6 Nested IF statements in linear form—a linear nest

Discussion

If you're a COBOL programmer, I'm sure you already make frequent use of PERFORM, PERFORM-UNTIL, and IF statements. What structured coding asks of you, then, is not the use of new statements. Instead, it asks that you use the old statements in new ways.

Perhaps the two most difficult changes to make when using structured COBOL are (1) eliminating GOTO statements and (2) using nested IF statements. However, if you develop your structure chart properly, you will find that your need for GOTOs will largely disappear. In most cases, you will only be tempted to use GOTOs in some of the major control modules and in some of the more complex work modules. Then, if you can resist the urge to use a GOTO for a couple of weeks in a row, you should be able to break the GOTO habit altogether. And this will make an immediate improvement in the quality of your programs.

As for nested IF statements, you should adapt to them with little trauma. To eliminate errors when using them, you should use indentation to show your intention. And you should be sure that your ELSE clauses are properly paired with your IF clauses.

Is there a point where too many levels of nesting becomes confusing? Definitely. Once you get beyond four or five levels of nesting, the code becomes difficult to follow. And eight or nine levels of nesting is likely to be incomprehensible. As a result, you may want to reexamine your program design when you are forced to go beyond five levels of nesting. In many cases, you will find that you can reduce the complexity of your nested IF statements by redesigning your structure chart.

In any event, when you convert from GOTO or modular programming to structured programming, you should use only the control constructs shown in this topic. If you do that, the quality of your programs should improve somewhat right away. But you can still create programs that are difficult to read and modify using only these constructs. That's why GOTOless coding by itself isn't enough. In the next topic, then, I'll show you some COBOL conventions that will help you make dramatic improvements in the quality of your programs.

Terminology

nested IF statements
linear nesting

Objective

Given pseudocode or a HIPO diagram for a module requiring DO, DO-UNTIL, or IF-THEN-ELSE structures, code it in structured COBOL.

Topic 2 COBOL conventions for structured programs

If you use only the COBOL structures presented in topic 1, you will end up with properly structured modules that have only one entry and one exit point. But this isn't enough if you want to create programs that are easy to read, test, and modify. In this topic, then, you will be introduced to COBOL conventions that will help you make dramatic improvements in the quality of your programs.

General considerations

The sequence of code In some structured coding systems, the programmer decides the sequence of the modules in the Procedure Division. In our opinion, however, that's inefficient. If the sequence of modules is arbitrary both the original programmer and the subsequent maintenance programmers will have a difficult time locating modules in the program listing.

In contrast, we say that all paragraph names in the Procedure Division should be preceded by a sequence number taken from the structure chart. These paragraphs should then be placed into the program in the sequence dictated by the sequence numbers. This is illustrated by the edit program in appendix A. When you use this method of sequencing, it is easy to locate the modules of a structure chart, no matter how large the program is.

If declaratives are used, these paragraphs should be placed in sequence by module number within the declaratives section. If you remember, we recommend that declarative modules be numbered in the same way that other modules are numbered, but the numbers for the declarative modules should be preceded by the letter D. As a result, all paragraphs within the Procedure Division should be easy to locate.

We also recommend that all of the programmers in a shop use standard coding sequences in the Environment and Data Divisions. For instance, we recommend that SELECT statements be coded in this sequence: (1) input files, (2) I-O files, (3) output files with print files last, (4) sort files, and (5) if your compiler treats a terminal screen as a file, the screen file. Then, the FD statements in the file section of the Data Division should be coded in the same sequence used for the SELECT statements.

Finally, the group descriptions in the working-storage section should be coded in a regular pattern. In general, this pattern should consist of:

1. Groups of work fields such as switches, flags, and counters

2. Record descriptions in the same order as the related files are listed in the SELECT statements

3. Screen handling fields if they are defined within the COBOL program

In addition, we recommend that you code line descriptions for print files in this order: (1) heading lines, (2) body lines, (3) total lines. If you use regular coding sequences like these, it will be easier for you to locate code as you go from one program to another.

If you are likely to refer frequently to some of the working-storage definitions, you may want to put them at the start of the working-storage section. If, for example, you are writing a program that creates and processes a related set of tables, you may want to put the table definitions at the start of working storage. That way you will be able to find them easily.

If you review the code for the edit program in appendix A, you can see that all of the elements of the program are placed in a logical sequence. If you use standard coding sequences like these throughout your shop, one programmer can easily locate code in another programmer's program without using cross-reference listings. And it's easier for you to locate your own code as you test and maintain a program.

Blank comment lines in the source listing Although there are many ways to achieve vertical spacing in a source listing, we recommend that blank comment lines be used for this purpose. A blank comment line has an asterisk in column 7 and blanks in the remainder of the line. If you review the code for the edit program in appendix A, you can see how blank comment lines have been used to make the program easier to read.

Note, however, that there's a difference between a blank line and a blank comment line. Specifically, a blank line doesn't have an asterisk in column 7. Although you can use a blank line on some systems for vertical spacing in the source listing, this leads to inefficient compilation of the program. When the compiler encounters a blank line, it checks each of the columns to see whether or not it has any compilable code. In contrast, the compiler checks only column 7 of a blank comment line. Once it determines that the line is a comment, it ignores the rest of the line. So be sure to use blank comment lines, not blank lines, to vertically space your program listings.

Skipping in the source listing In some cases, you may want to skip to the top of a page to make your program listing more readable. For instance, you may want to skip to the top of the page at the start of the Procedure Division. Although an occasional use of skipping is all right, you should avoid the unnecessary use of skipping because it wastes paper. So skip to the top of a page only when it improves readability.

Data Division

Data names Structured or unstructured, the names used in a COBOL program should make sense. We've all said that for years. But I still find programs with fields named BOB, COUNTER, and SUBSCRIPT. So now more than ever before, don't save keystrokes by shortening names. COBOL allows up to thirty characters per name; why not use them to make your data names understandable?

When fields are all part of the same record, the relationships should be shown by giving the same two- or three-character prefix to all fields within the record. For instance, an employee's time card might make up a record named EMPLOYEE-TIME-CARD. Then, the fields within this record should be given names with the prefix ETC, such as ETC-EMP-NO, ETC-HRS-WORKED, and ETC-JOB-CODE. Using prefixes for related fields helps to show structure and cuts down coding errors.

Using hyphens in data names can also cut down coding errors and help prevent confusion. For example, suppose you decide to refer to various detail lines as LINEA, LINEB, and so on. The trouble is that when you get to LINED, your data name becomes a word and is no longer a logical name. And when you get to LINES, the problem is even more complicated because LINES is a COBOL reserved word. This type of problem should be avoided entirely by hyphenating the names as in LINE-A, LINE-B, LINE-D, and LINE-S. So use the hyphen in your naming schemes to make your data names understandable.

If you're coding a routine that directly relates to a user function, try to use the same names that the user uses. Then, if the routine doesn't work, you will be able to discuss it with the user using his terminology. If, for example, a user calls a certain value "the shrinkage factor," your name should be something like SHRINKAGE-FACTOR. Don't call the field WEIGHT-LOSS because it is likely to be confusing later on.

Indentation Indentation should be used in the Data Division to show the structure of related data items and to make the code easier to read. You should be using it now whether or not you are coding structured programs. It is simply an efficient coding practice.

Figure 9-7 illustrates the proper use of indentation in the Data Division. As you can see, there should always be two spaces between the level number and the data name, and each successive level should be indented four spaces more than the preceding level. Also, whenever possible, PICTURE, VALUE, and USAGE clauses should be vertically aligned.

Defining constant lines To define a constant line, I recommend this technique. Start the VALUE clause for the first 20 characters of the line in column 44 (or before). Then, there's room for the word VALUE, one space, a starting quote mark, a 20-character value, an ending quote mark, and a period before the end of the line. To continue the constant line, code successive lines like this with 20-character literals until the

```
 DATA DIVISION.
*
 FILE SECTION.
*
 FD  TRANSACTION-FILE
     LABEL RECORDS ARE STANDARD
     RECORD CONTAINS 28 CHARACTERS.
*
 01  TR-INPUT-AREA              PIC X(28).
*
 FD  PRINTER-FILE
     LABEL RECORDS ARE OMITTED
     RECORD CONTAINS 132 CHARACTERS.
*
 01  PRINT-AREA                 PIC X(132).
*
 WORKING-STORAGE SECTION.
*
 01  PRINT-FIELDS               COMP            SYNC.
*
     05  LINE-COUNT             PIC S999        VALUE +57.
     05  LINES-ON-PAGE          PIC S999        VALUE +56.
     05  SPACE-CONTROL          PIC 9.
*
 01  COUNT-FIELDS               COMP-3.
*
     05  VALID-RECORD-COUNT     PIC S9(5)       VALUE ZERO.
     05  INVALID-RECORD-COUNT   PIC S9(5)       VALUE ZERO.
*
 01  TOTAL-FIELDS               COMP-3.
*
     05  CUSTOMER-TOTAL         PIC S9(7)V99    VALUE ZERO.
     05  SALESMAN-TOTAL         PIC S9(8)V99    VALUE ZERO.
     05  GRAND-TOTAL            PIC S9(9)V99    VALUE ZERO.
*
 01  SUBSCRIPT-FIELDS           COMP            SYNC.
*
     05  COMMISSION-LEVEL-SUB   PIC S99.
     05  YEARS-SERVICE-SUB      PIC S99.
```

Figure 9-7 Proper use of indentation in the Data Division (part 1 of 2)

entire line is complete. That way you'll avoid the need for continuation lines, which, in Paul's opinion, should never be used due to the problems they can cause during compilation.

In the last record in figure 9-7, you can see the use of 20-character literals. Here, the 132-character line named HDG-LINE-2 is divided into six FILLER fields of 20 characters each and one of 12 characters. Then, the literals for the heading are simply placed wherever the programmer wants them to print in the line. The rest of the spaces are left blank, and no continuation lines are needed. I recommend this technique for all constant lines because it is easy to code and modify.

Grouping data items At one time, it appeared that the 77 level was going to be dropped from future COBOL standards and compilers. After all, what does this level do? It simply shows that a data item isn't related to any other data item. But since one of the goals of structured

```
*
 01   TR-RECORD.
*
      05   TR-TRAN-CODE              PIC X.
           88 TR-DELETE                                       VALUE 'D'.
           88 TR-ADD                                          VALUE 'A'.
           88 TR-CHANGE                                       VALUE 'C'.
      05   TR-BRANCH-NO              PIC XX.
      05   TR-SALESMAN-NO            PIC XXX.
      05   TR-CUSTOMER-NO            PIC X(5).
      05   TR-TRAN-DATE.
           10 TR-TRAN-MONTH          PIC 99.
           10 TR-TRAN-DAY            PIC 99.
           10 TR-TRAN-YEAR           PIC 99.
      05   TR-QUANTITY               PIC 9(5).
      05   TR-ITEM-NO                PIC X(6).
*
 01   HDG-LINE-1.
*
      05   FILLER              PIC X(20)    VALUE SPACE.
      05   FILLER              PIC X(18)    VALUE 'SALES SUMMARY FOR '.
      05   FILLER              PIC X(13)    VALUE 'MONTH ENDING '.
      05   HDG1-DATE           PIC 99/99/99.
      05   FILLER              PIC X(73)    VALUE SPACE.
*
 01   HDG-LINE-2.
*
      05   FILLER              PIC X(20)    VALUE '                    '.
      05   FILLER              PIC X(20)    VALUE '   SLSMN. NO.   CUST'.
      05   FILLER              PIC X(20)    VALUE '. NO.    SALES AMOUNT'.
      05   FILLER              PIC X(20)    VALUE '                    '.
      05   FILLER              PIC X(20)    VALUE '                    '.
      05   FILLER              PIC X(20)    VALUE '                    '.
      05   FILLER              PIC X(12)    VALUE '
*
 01   CUSTOMER-TOTAL-LINE.
*
      .
      .
      .
```

Figure 9-7 Proper use of indentation in the Data Division (part 2 of 2)

programming is to show relationships, the 77 level is more of a hindrance than a help.

It now appears that the 77 level will be retained, but that doesn't mean you should use it in your structured programs. Instead, you should try to group the data items. For instance, you can group all switches and flags as shown in figure 9-8. You can group all print fields, counters, total fields, and subscripts as shown in figure 9-7. You can group all fields required by a subprogram you are calling. And so on.

By using group items in this way, your working-storage section will have a structure of its own, and it will be much easier to locate data items in your program listing. Also, when all the items in a group have the same usage, you can save yourself some coding by simply assigning COMP or COMP-3 at the group level instead of doing it for each elementary item. This is shown in figure 9-7.

```
 WORKING-STORAGE SECTION.
*
 01  SWITCHES.
*
     05  TRAN-EOF-SW               PIC X          VALUE 'N'.
         88  TRAN-EOF                             VALUE 'Y'.
     05  ITEM-FOUND-SW             PIC X.
         88  ITEM-FOUND                           VALUE 'Y'.
     .
     .
*
 01  FLAGS.
*
     05  COMMISSION-LEVEL-FLAG     PIC X.
         88  COMMISSION-LEVEL-1                   VALUE '1'.
         88  COMMISSION-LEVEL-2                   VALUE '2'.
         88  COMMISSION-LEVEL-3                   VALUE '3'.
         88  COMMISSION-LEVEL-4                   VALUE '4'.
     .
     .
*
 PROCEDURE DIVISION.
*
 000-PREPARE-SALES-SUMMARY.
*
     .
     .
     PERFORM 200-PREPARE-SALES-LINE
         UNTIL TRAN-EOF.
     .
     .
*
 200-PREPARE-SALES-LINE.
*
     .
     .
     PERFORM 220-SEARCH-ITEM-TABLE.
     IF ITEM-FOUND
         PERFORM 230-CALCULATE-SALES-COMMISSION
     ELSE
         ...
     .
     .
*
 230-CALCULATE-SALES-COMMISSION.
*
     .
     .
     IF COMMISSION-LEVEL-1
         PERFORM 260-CALC-LEVEL-1-COMMISSION
     ELSE IF COMMISSION-LEVEL-2
         PERFORM 270-CALC-LEVEL-2-COMMISSION
     ELSE IF COMMISSION-LEVEL-3
         PERFORM 280-CALC-LEVEL-3-COMMISSION
     ELSE IF COMMISSION-LEVEL-4
         PERFORM 290-CALC-LEVEL-4-COMMISSION.
     .
     .
     .
```

Figure 9-8 Using condition names for program switches and flags

Using VALUE clauses to initialize fields We recommend that you use VALUE clauses to give working-storage fields starting values whenever starting values are required. In figure 9-7, for example, the count fields and the total fields are initialized to zeros using VALUE clauses. I mention this only because some structured programming practitioners recommend that you only use VALUE clauses in the Data Division if the values won't be changed during the execution of the program.

If you don't initialize fields using VALUE clauses, though, you must initialize the fields in the Procedure Division using MOVE statements. But this means many more lines of code in a typical program so productivity is reduced. It increases the likelihood that you'll forget to initialize a field so an extra test run or two is likely. It clutters up the module that initializes the fields so it is more difficult to read and maintain. In short, you should use VALUE clauses to initialize fields in working-storage and you should question the judgement of anyone who advises you not to.

Condition names Because condition names increase the clarity of a program, they should be used whenever practical in structured programs. In particular, they should be used for most switches and flags.

Figure 9-8 illustrates the proper use of condition names for the switches and flags in a structured program. For a *switch* (a field that has only two possible conditions), the codes used should be Y for "yes" and N for "no". For a *flag* (a field that has more than two possible conditions), the codes should be successive integers starting with 1 (1, 2, 3, etc.) or meaningful one-letter codes like W for "worker", S for "supervisor", and M for "manager".

To keep the names consistent, the condition names should be related to the data names whenever practical. For a switch, the condition name should be meaningful like TRAN-EOF, which stands for the transaction end-of-file. And the switch name should be the condition name followed by SWITCH or just SW. Thus, the switch name for the TRAN-EOF condition should be TRAN-EOF-SWITCH or TRAN-EOF-SW. (You should be consistent in your use of SWITCH or SW—always use one or the other.)

For a flag, the condition names may or may not be closely related to the flag name. For a flag like COMMISSION-LEVEL-FLAG in figure 9-8, it makes sense to relate the names as shown. For other types of flags, it makes more sense to give meaningful condition names like TRAINEE, ASSOCIATE, SENIOR-ASSOCIATE, and MANAGER and to use a general flag name like SALESMAN-STATUS-FLAG.

Condition names should also be used for any codes that are likely to be changed during the life of a program. This makes it easier to modify the program if the codes are changed. Without condition names, you have to change every statement in the Procedure Division that refers to the codes. With condition names, only the 88-levels need to be changed.

Figure 9-9 illustrates the use of condition names for codes that are part of input records. Note that more than one value is given for the

```
 WORKING-STORAGE SECTION.
*
 01   TR-RECORD.
*
     05   TR-TRAN-CODE                 PIC X.
          88   ISSUE                   VALUE   '1'.
          88   RECEIPT                 VALUE   '2'.
          88   RETURNS                 VALUE   '3'.
          88   SCRAP                   VALUES 'D'  'P'  'R'.
     05   TR-BRANCH-NO                 PIC XX.
     .
     .
*
 PROCEDURE DIVISION.
*
     .
     .
     IF ISSUE
         PERFORM 280-PROCESS-ISSUE-RECORD
     ELSE
         IF RECEIPT
             PERFORM 290-PROCESS-RECEIPT-RECORD
         ELSE
             IF RETURNS
                 PERFORM 300-PROCESS-RETURN-RECORD
             ELSE
                 IF SCRAP
                     PERFORM 310-PROCESS-SCRAP-RECORD
                 ELSE
                     PERFORM 320-PROCESS-INVALID-RECORD.
```

Figure 9-9 Using condition names for input codes

condition named SCRAP. In this example, you can see how condition names can increase program clarity. Without them,

```
IF ISSUE
```

would be

```
IF TR-TRAN-CODE EQUAL TO '1'
```

and

```
IF SCRAP
```

would be something like

```
IF TR-TRAN-CODE EQUAL TO 'D' OR 'P' OR 'R'
```

(Incidentally, RETURNS is used as one of the condition names because RETURN is a COBOL reserved word.)

Procedure Division

The STOP RUN statement As you might guess, a structured program should have only one statement that ends the program and returns control to the operating system. This statement should be in the first module of the program. This is illustrated in the coding for module 000 of the edit program in appendix A. If a program has more than one STOP RUN statement, it has more than one exit, so it isn't properly structured.

Section names Since we recommend that each module in a program should be coded as a single COBOL paragraph, section names should *not* be used unless they are required. However, sections are required when you use the sort feature or declaratives.

When you use section names for either of these functions, you shouldn't refer to the section names in your PERFORM statements. Instead, your PERFORM statements should refer to the paragraph names that represent the modules of the program. This leads to consistency throughout your program.

Indentation In topic 1, you saw how indentation should be used to clarify the intent of nested IF statements. Similarly, indentation should be used throughout the Procedure Division to show the relationships between the phrases and clauses within a statement.

Figure 9-10 illustrates the proper use of indentation in the Procedure Division. In general, the first word in each sentence starts in column 12. If a statement requires more than one coding line, the succeeding lines are indented four spaces. In statements like the OPEN, CLOSE, and MOVE (examples 1, 2, and 3), similar elements like file and data names should be aligned. If one or more statements are part of a conditional clause within another statement, conditional statements should be indented four more spaces. For instance, the two statements following the AT END condition in example 4 of figure 9-10 are indented four more spaces to show they're part of the AT END condition.

In general, nested IF statements are indented by four spaces for each level as shown in example 9 in figure 9-10. However, if several levels of nesting are used, you may run out of coding space. In this case, you can indent by only two spaces for each level. Whether indented by twos or fours, related IF and ELSE clauses should be aligned.

Since you will undoubtedly encounter statements that are not covered by this simple set of examples, always remember that the goal of indentation is clarity. If you encounter a special situation, code it in the way that is most understandable and most consistent with the rest of your code.

Compound conditions Although COBOL allows compound conditions to be expressed by using the words AND and OR, unstructured programs have often tried to avoid them. That's not necessarily good. If the problem description can best be stated using compound conditions, then

Example 1:

```
OPEN INPUT  TRANSACTION-FILE
            OLD-MASTER-FILE
     OUTPUT NEW-MASTER-FILE
            REPORT-FILE
            ERROR-FILE.
```

Example 2:

```
CLOSE TRANSACTION-FILE
      OLD-MASTER-FILE
      NEW-MASTER-FILE
      REPORT-FILE
      ERROR-FILE.
```

Example 3:

```
MOVE SPACE          TO PR-RECORD.
MOVE TP-ITEM-NO     TO PR-ITEM-NO.
MOVE TP-ITEM-DESC TO PR-ITEM-DESC.
```

Example 4:

```
READ TRANSACTION-FILE
    INTO TR-INPUT-AREA
    AT END
        MOVE 'Y'        TO TRAN-EOF-SW
        MOVE HIGH-VALUE TO TR-ITEM-NO.
```

Example 5:

```
WRITE PR-OUTPUT-AREA
    AFTER ADVANCING SPACE-CONTROL LINES.
```

Example 6:

```
WRITE NM-OUTPUT-AREA
    INVALID KEY
        PERFORM 420-PRINT-ERROR-MESSAGE.
```

Example 7:

```
MULTIPLY TR-QUANTITY BY TB-UNIT-PRICE
    GIVING IL-SALES-AMOUNT
    ON SIZE ERROR
        PERFORM 360-PROCESS-INVALID-TRAN.
```

Example 8:

```
PERFORM 110-READ-ITEM-CODE-TABLE
    VARYING TABLE-SUB FROM 1 BY 1
    UNTIL TABLE-EOF.
```

Figure 9-10 Proper use of indentation in the Procedure Division (part 1 of 2)

Example 9:

```
IF CR-CUST-CODE EQUAL TO 1
    MOVE .020 TO DISCOUNT-PERCENT
ELSE
    MOVE .000 TO DISCOUNT-PERCENT.
```

Example 10:

```
SEARCH ITEM-CODE-TABLE-ENTRY
    AT END
        PERFORM 320-PRINT-ERROR-MESSAGE
    WHEN IT-ITEM-NO (IT-INDEX) EQUAL TO TR-ITEM-NO
        MOVE IT-UNIT-PRICE (IT-INDEX) TO TP-UNIT-PRICE.
```

Figure 9-10 Proper use of indentation in the Procedure Division (part 2 of 2)

it's best to use compound conditions in the program too. In fact, the use of compound conditions will improve program clarity because the code will correspond to the problem definition.

To illustrate, suppose the decision table in figure 9-11 is used to document the processing required by a credit-processing module. If you attempt to code this processing without compound conditions, the code will be difficult to interpret because it won't correspond to the decision table. In contrast, look at the coding in figure 9-11. Though it is lengthy, it is as easy to follow because it follows the decision table right down the line. For each rule in the decision table, there is one IF statement with compound conditions. In addition, the programmer has used comment lines to indicate how each statement relates to the table. These comments not only clarify what's going on in the code, but they also space the code so you can easily read the IF statements and discover any missing periods.

Incidentally, we used the example in figure 9-11 in the earlier version of this book, and quite a few people found fault with it. Specifically, they say that this coding leads to inefficient object code. Here again, we feel that program quality and programmer productivity are more important than object-program efficiency. We also say that a systems product like the Capex optimizer can make the object code efficient so you can get both program clarity in the source code and efficiency in the object code.

When using compound conditions in either an IF statement or a PERFORM statement, you should align the parts of the compound condition as shown in figure 9-12. As you can see, the conditions in an IF statement are given extra indentation to set them off from the statements that are to be executed when the compound condition is true.

Another technique for adding to the readability of your code when you use compound conditions is to use parentheses to clarify or dictate how the compiler will interpret a compound condition. Without parentheses, the compiler will evaluate NOT conditions first, AND conditions second, and OR conditions third. With parentheses, the compiler will start with the innermost set of parentheses and work outward.

A decision table for credit processing

	Credit rules	Decision rules					
		1	2	3	4	5	6
Conditions	If over credit limit	Y	Y	Y	Y	N	N
	If times dunned is less than 4 and customer history is greater than 2 years	Y	N	Y	N	—	—
	If any invoices are over 60 days old	N	Y	Y	N	Y	N
Actions	Then process order (module 550)	X					X
	Then refuse credit (module 560)		X				
	Then refer to credit manager (module 570)			X	X	X	

COBOL code for the decision table

```
*
* CODING FOR THE CREDIT PROCESSING DECISION TABLE
*
* DECISION RULE 1
 IF         CM-BAL-OWED GREATER THAN CM-CREDIT-LIMIT
       AND (CM-TIMES-DUNNED LESS THAN 4
            AND CM-CUST-YEARS GREATER THAN 2)
       AND CM-OVER-60-BAL-OWED EQUAL TO ZERO
     PERFORM 550-PREPARE-SHIPPING-ORDER.
* DECISION RULE 2
 IF         CM-BAL-OWED GREATER THAN CM-CREDIT-LIMIT
       AND (CM-TIMES-DUNNED GREATER THAN 3
            OR CM-CUST-YEARS NOT GREATER THAN 2)
       AND CM-OVER-60-BAL-OWED GREATER THAN ZERO
     PERFORM 560-PRINT-REFUSE-CREDIT-LINE.
* DECISION RULE 3
 IF         CM-BAL-OWED GREATER THAN CM-CREDIT-LIMIT
       AND (CM-TIMES-DUNNED LESS THAN 4
            AND CM-CUST-YEARS NOT GREATER THAN 2)
       AND CM-OVER-60-BAL-OWED GREATER THAN ZERO
     PERFORM 570-PRINT-REFER-TO-MGR-LINE.
* DECISION RULE 4
 IF         CM-BAL-OWED GREATER THAN CM-CREDIT-LIMIT
       AND (CM-TIMES-DUNNED GREATER THAN 3
            OR CM-CUST-YEARS NOT GREATER THAN 2)
       AND CM-OVER-60-BAL-OWED EQUAL TO ZERO
     PERFORM 570-PRINT-REFER-TO-MGR-LINE.
* DECISION RULE 5
 IF         CM-BAL-OWED NOT GREATER THAN CM-CREDIT-LIMIT
       AND CM-OVER-60-BAL-OWED GREATER THAN ZERO
     PERFORM 570-PRINT-REFER-TO-MGR-LINE.
* DECISION RULE 6
 IF         CM-BAL-OWED NOT GREATER THAN CM-CREDIT-LIMIT
       AND CM-OVER-60-BAL-OWED EQUAL TO ZERO
     PERFORM 550-PREPARE-SHIPPING-ORDER.
*
```

Figure 9-11 Coding a decision table

Example 1:

```
PERFORM procedure-name
    UNTIL condition-1
      AND condition-2
       OR condition-3
      AND condition-4.
```

Example 2:

```
IF          condition-1
       OR condition-2
      AND condition-3
    statement-group-1
ELSE
    statement-group-2.
```

Figure 9-12 Proper indentation when using compound conditions

As a standard, then, I suggest that indentation always be used with compound conditions. In addition, I recommend that parentheses be used whenever NOT, AND, and OR are mixed in a compound condition. Rather than worry about how the compiler will interpret your code, use parentheses to dictate the interpretation that you want.

What about using implied subjects and implied relational operators as in the condition that follows?

```
J LESS THAN K AND GREATER THAN L AND M
```

I think common sense is your best guide here. If the code is easy to understand even though subjects and operators are omitted (implied), by all means omit them. But if the code becomes confusing, you should state the complete condition using indentation and parentheses. In our shop, we avoid the use of implied subjects and operators because two of the compilers we've used have had bugs related to their use. (Incidentally, when a subject or relational operator is omitted, the last-stated subject or operator is assumed to be in effect.)

If you encounter problems when using compound conditions, remember that you can write any compound condition as a series of nested IF statements. For instance,

```
IF CONDITION-1
    IF CONDITION-2
        PERFORM ROUTINE-A
```

is the same as

```
IF CONDITION-1 AND CONDITION-2
    PERFORM ROUTINE-A
```

So don't hesitate to use nested IFs if they can help you avoid a compiler bug or if they improve the clarity of your code.

Comments In unstructured programs, comments or comment lines were recommended throughout the program to explain what the paragraphs did. Without comments, the unstructured program was difficult to follow. In other words, comments were often used as a crutch because the code wasn't readable.

In contrast, the structured program should be relatively easy to follow by virtue of its structure alone. In addition, the structured programmer should use the conventions described in this topic so his coding becomes largely self-documenting. As a result, the code should make sense even without comments.

With this in mind, I want to point out a couple of instances when it's helpful to use comment lines. The first is to relate a block of code to other documentation such as a decision table. You've seen this in figure 9-11. A second is to explain an abstruse segment of code that just cannot be coded in a straightforward, easy-to-understand manner due to language restrictions (these should be rare).

Otherwise, comments should only be used when they actually contribute to the clarity of the program. Above all, don't use them to document something that is made clear by the code itself. That simply wastes time and reduces productivity.

The case structure In addition to the sequence, selection, and iteration structures, the COBOL programmer can sometimes make use of the *case structure*. It is an acceptable structure since it has only one entry and one exit point. But it should only be used when the coding situation is right for it.

The flowchart at the top of figure 9-13 gives the logic of the case structure. As you can see, it can be used for an indefinite number of cases: one function will be performed for each case depending on the value of the integer field that is tested at the start of the structure. If the integer field contains a 1, the function for case 1 will be performed; if the integer field contains a 2, the function for case 2 will be performed; and so on.

In the past, it was common to code the case structure using the GOTO DEPENDING statement. However, this requires an EXIT paragraph at the end of the case structure and a GOTO statement at the end of each of the other paragraphs within the case structure. As a result, we feel it is better to code the case structure with a *linear nest* of IF statements as shown in figure 9-13. (Incidentally, the 198X COBOL standards promise an EVALUATE statement that should make it easier to code the case structure as described in chapter 15.)

The case structure

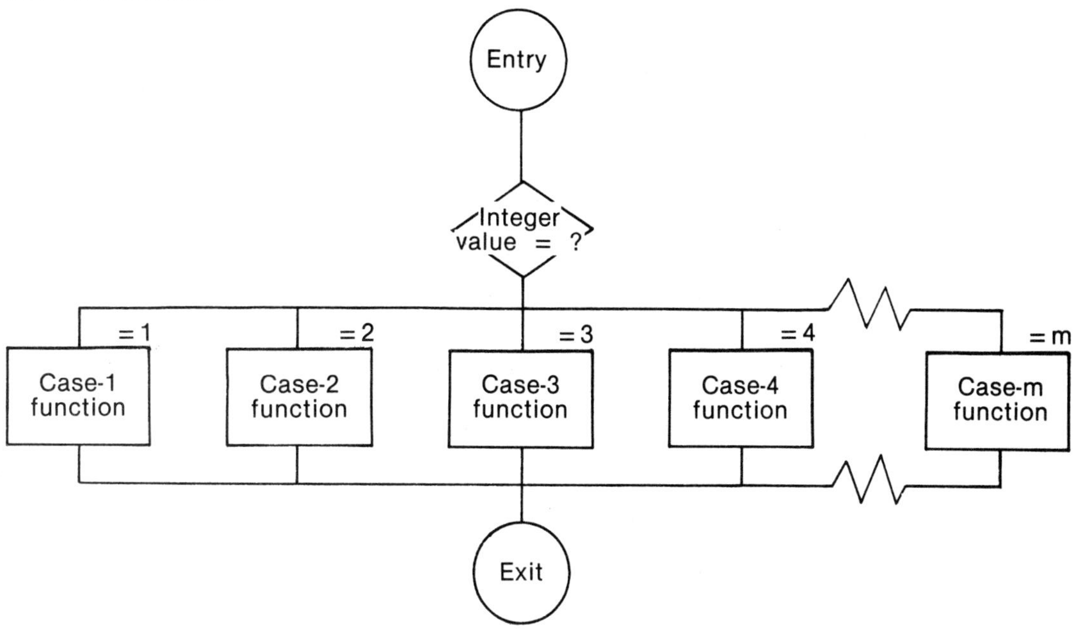

Coding for a case structure with 9 cases

```
IF TR-ACTIVITY-CODE EQUAL TO 1
    PERFORM CODE-1-FUNCTION
ELSE IF TR-ACTIVITY-CODE EQUAL TO 2
    PERFORM CODE-2-FUNCTION
ELSE IF TR-ACTIVITY-CODE EQUAL TO 3
    PERFORM CODE-3-FUNCTION
ELSE IF TR-ACTIVITY-CODE EQUAL TO 4
    PERFORM CODE-4-FUNCTION
ELSE IF TR-ACTIVITY-CODE EQUAL TO 5
    PERFORM CODE-5-FUNCTION
ELSE IF TR-ACTIVITY-CODE EQUAL TO 6
    PERFORM CODE-6-FUNCTION
ELSE IF TR-ACTIVITY-CODE EQUAL TO 7
    PERFORM CODE-7-FUNCTION
ELSE IF TR-ACTIVITY-CODE EQUAL TO 8
    PERFORM CODE-8-FUNCTION
ELSE IF TR-ACTIVITY-CODE EQUAL TO 9
    PERFORM CODE-9-FUNCTION
ELSE
    PERFORM DEFAULT-FUNCTION.
```

Figure 9-13 Coding the case structure

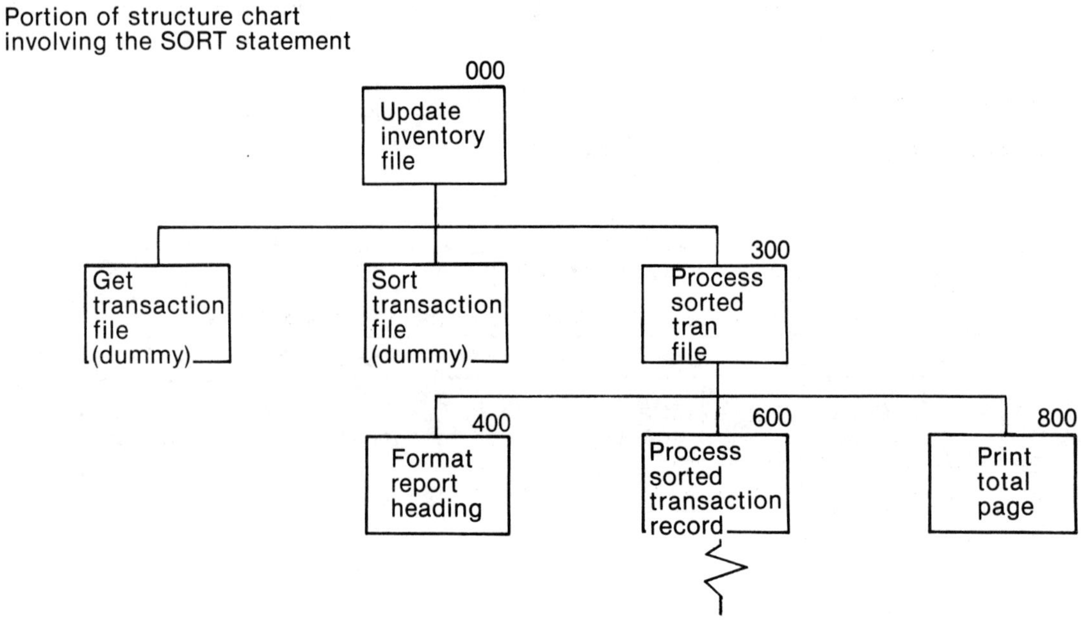

Figure 9-14 Proper use of the COBOL SORT statement in the random update program (part 1 of 2)

The sort feature The sort feature, which is used in many COBOL programs, forces you to use sections and a GOTO statement in a structured program. This is illustrated by figure 9-14, which shows the structure and some of the code for the model random-update program. For the complete structure chart and more of the code, please refer to figures 7-33 and 7-34.

The SORT statement in this program is found in module 000. It causes the input file to be read and sorted. Then, the SORT statement refers to an output procedure, which, by COBOL rules, must be a section rather than a paragraph name. As a result, module 300 in this program is coded as a section. This in turn means that the other parts of the program must also be contained in sections, so all modules before module 300 are included in a section named 000-UPDATE-INVENTORY-FILE.

Another requirement of COBOL is that the RELEASE statement must be contained in the input-procedure section when a SORT statement is used, and the RETURN statement must be contained in the output-procedure section. As a result, the section that starts with module 300 can't end without including the RETURN statement. But this statement is found in module 620. As a result, I have used a GOTO statement in module 300 that branches around the paragraphs for modules 400 through 800 after module 800 has been performed. This means the entire output procedure is found in the 300-PROCESS-SORTED-TRAN-FILE section. The last paragraph of this section is the EXIT paragraph as shown in figure 9-14.

Sample of sort coding

```
 PROCEDURE DIVISION.
*
 000-UPDATE-INVENTORY-FILE     SECTION.
*
        .
        .
        SORT SORTFILE
            ON ASCENDING KEY SF-ITEM-NUMBER
            USING RCPTTRAN
            OUTPUT PROCEDURE IS 300-PROCESS-SORTED-TRAN-FILE.
        .
        .
*
 300-PROCESS-SORTED-TRAN-FILE     SECTION.
*
        PERFORM 400-FORMAT-REPORT-HEADING.
        PERFORM 600-PROCESS-SORTED-TRAN-RECORD
            UNTIL TRAN-EOF.
        PERFORM 800-PRINT-TOTAL-PAGE.
        GO TO 300-EXIT.
*
 400-FORMAT-REPORT-HEADING.
*
        .
        .
        .
*
 620-RETURN-SORTED-TRANSACTION.
*
        RETURN SORTFILE INTO RECEIPT-TRANSACTION
            AT END
                MOVE HIGH-VALUE TO RT-ITEM-NUMBER
                MOVE 'Y' TO TRAN-EOF-SW.
*
        .
        .
        .
*
 300-EXIT.
*
        EXIT.
*
```

Figure 9-14 Proper use of the COBOL SORT statement in the random update program (part 2 of 2)

If you use the sort feature frequently, this coding should be clear to you right now. Otherwise, you may have to study the coding for a while before it becomes clear. In any event, the sort feature is of interest because its language forces restrictions upon the programmer that are not in the best interests of structured programming. And the 198X COBOL standards don't promise any improvements here.

Discussion

If you follow all of the recommendations presented in this topic, your COBOL code will be easier to read, debug, and maintain. Because of the structure in the Data Division, you will be able to locate fields more easily. Because of the structure in the Procedure Division, your program will be easier to read and understand.

On the other hand, if you don't follow the conventions in this topic (or conventions like them), the quality of your programs won't improve much even if you avoid the use of GOTO statements. So I think this basic set of conventions is one of the important contributions Paul Noll has made to the literature of structured programming. And yet, people who have been exposed to these conventions often continue to use their ineffective coding practices of the past. For instance, our survey of COBOL users showed that 80 percent of the shops still allow PERFORM THRUs, 61 percent still use GOTOs, and 59 percent still use 77 levels in the Data Division. Is it any wonder that we're not solving the program development problems of our industry?

Terminology

switch
flag
case structure
linear nest

Objective

Given program specifications and a structure chart, code the program in readable, structured COBOL using the guidelines presented in this topic.

Topic 3 How to improve your coding productivity

If you follow the recommendations made in topic 1 and topic 2, you will definitely improve your program quality. But you won't necessarily improve your productivity by much. Not if you still write every program from scratch.

In chapter 6, I gave you some ideas for reusing code from old programs when you develop new programs. I said that this could dramatically improve your productivity. And now, to emphasize this point, let me give you some specific ideas about reusing code.

After that, I'll give you some ideas on coding the short, long, and complicated modules that you encounter as you code a program. And then I'll show you why it's often more effective to just code a program from a structure chart than it is to plan it first using pseudocode or HIPO diagrams.

If you follow the suggestions given in this topic, I think you'll dramatically improve your coding productivity. And I'm not thinking in terms of 20 or 30 percent increases. I believe you can increase your productivity 200 percent and more when you do an effective job of reusing code from old programs.

What to copy from other programs

When I talk about reusing code from old programs, I mean actually copying portions of code from an old program into your new program. In most cases, of course, you will have to modify this copied code somewhat so it suits your program. But this is far more efficient than starting from scratch.

As I see it, most of the code that you create for each program should be copied from other programs. When you think of it, most of the modules you create are similar to modules in other programs. And most of the groups of data names you use are similar to groups in other programs. So why start them from scratch? But let me give you some specific ideas by division.

```
 IDENTIFICATION DIVISION.
*
 PROGRAM-ID.            INV2100.
*AUTHOR.                ANNE PRINCE.
*INSTALLATION.          MMA.
*DATE.                  SEPTEMBER 10, 1984.
*
 ENVIRONMENT DIVISION.
*
 CONFIGURATION SECTION.
*
 SOURCE-COMPUTER.       IBM-370.
 OBJECT-COMPUTER.       IBM-370.
*
 INPUT-OUTPUT SECTION.
*
 FILE-CONTROL.
*
     SELECT PARTNUM   ASSIGN TO SYS005-AS-PARTNUM.
     SELECT INVTRAN   ASSIGN TO SYS008-AS-INVTRAN.
     SELECT VINVTRN   ASSIGN TO SYS007-AS-VINVTRN.
     SELECT IINVTLST  ASSIGN TO SYS006-UR-1403-S.
```

Figure 9-15 Reusable code from the first two divisions of the edit program

Identification and Environment Divisions Figure 9-15 gives the code for the first two divisions of the edit program. Here, you can see that much of this code is the same from one program to the next. Change the program-id and date in the Identification Division, delete the SELECT statements that you don't need in the Environment Division, change the names in the SELECT statements that you do need ...and you're on your way.

Data Division Figure 9-16 gives the code for the file section of the Data Division of the edit program. These 18 lines of code describe three sequential files and one print file. So if your new program uses one or more sequential files, you can copy the portion of this code that you need. And if it requires a print file, you can copy the FD for the print file. Yes, you'll change file names, the number of characters in the RECORD CONTAINS clause, etc. But you should save many keystrokes by copying the code in the first place.

Figure 9-17 shows fields in the working-storage section of the edit program that can be reused from one program to the next. No, I don't

```
DATA DIVISION.
*
FILE SECTION.
*
FD  PARTNUM
    LABEL RECORDS ARE STANDARD
    RECORD CONTAINS 25 CHARACTERS.
*
COPY PARTNUM.
*
01  PART-NUMBER-RECORD.
*
    05  PNR-PART-NO              PIC X(5).
    05  PNR-PART-DESCRIPTION     PIC X(20).
*
FD  INVTRAN
    LABEL RECORDS ARE STANDARD
    RECORD CONTAINS 42 CHARACTERS.
*
01  INVENTORY-TRANSACTION        PIC X(42).
*
FD  VINVTRN
    LABEL RECORDS ARE STANDARD
    RECORD CONTAINS 42 CHARACTERS.
*
01  VALID-INVENTORY-TRANSACTION       PIC X(42).
*
FD  IINVTLST
    LABEL RECORDS ARE OMITTED
    RECORD CONTAINS 132 CHARACTERS.
*
01  PRINT-AREA        PIC X(132).
```

Figure 9-16 Reusable code from the file section of the edit program

mean that all of these fields will be used in any one program. But almost all programs require one or more switches, one or more count fields, the print fields, one or more total fields, and so on. So you can copy what you need into your new program.

If your new program uses a one-level table, you can find one defined in figure 9-17. Even if you never actually use the part-number table again, isn't the code the same for any one-level table with only one element in it? So why start a one-level table from scratch? By changing the names, number of occurrences, and pictures, you can adapt this code to suit any one-level table your new program may be using. In this case, although you may not save that many keystrokes, you will at least be sure that you have the syntax right.

```
 WORKING-STORAGE SECTION.
*
 01  SWITCHES.
*
     05  PART-NUMBER-EOF-SW         PIC X     VALUE 'N'.
         88  PART-NUMBER-EOF                  VALUE 'Y'.
     05  TRAN-EOF-SW                PIC X     VALUE 'N'.
         88  TRAN-EOF                         VALUE 'Y'.
     05  VALID-TRAN-SW              PIC X.
         88  VALID-TRAN                       VALUE 'Y'.
     05  PART-NUMBER-FOUND-SW       PIC X.
         88  PART-NUMBER-FOUND                VALUE 'Y'.
     05  VALID-DATE-SW              PIC X.
         88  VALID-DATE                       VALUE 'Y'.
*
 01  COUNT-FIELDS                   COMP-3.
*
     05  TRANS-PROCESSED-COUNT      PIC S9(5)     VALUE ZERO.
     05  INVALID-TRAN-CODE-COUNT    PIC S9(5)     VALUE ZERO.
     05  INVALID-SALES-COUNT        PIC S9(5)     VALUE ZERO.
     05  VALID-SALES-COUNT          PIC S9(5)     VALUE ZERO.
     05  INVALID-RETURN-COUNT       PIC S9(5)     VALUE ZERO.
     05  VALID-RETURN-COUNT         PIC S9(5)     VALUE ZERO.
     05  INVALID-COUNT              PIC S9(5)     VALUE ZERO.
     05  VALID-COUNT                PIC S9(5)     VALUE ZERO.
*
 01  PRINT-FIELDS.
*
     05  SPACE-CONTROL      PIC S9                     COMP    SYNC.
     05  LINE-COUNT         PIC S999     VALUE +999    COMP    SYNC.
     05  LINES-ON-PAGE      PIC S999     VALUE +57     COMP    SYNC.
     05  PAGE-COUNT         PIC S999     VALUE ZERO    COMP-3.
*
 01  DATE-FIELDS.
*
     05  TODAYS-DATE        PIC 9(6).
*
 01  PART-NUMBER-TABLE.
*
     05  PN-TABLE-ENTRY          OCCURS 100 TIMES
                                 INDEXED BY PN-TABLE-INDEX
                                 PIC X(5).
     05  PN-ENTRY-COUNT          INDEX.
*
 01  MISCELLANEOUS-FIELDS.
*
     05  ERROR-INDICATOR         PIC X     VALUE '*'.
*
```

Figure 9-17 Reusable code from the working-storage section of the edit program

Figure 9-18 shows reusable code for the heading of a report that is taken from the edit program. Here, you can see that a COPY statement is used to copy standard code for the first three heading lines of a report. So when you copy all of this code, you have all of the Data Division entries for a five-line heading. Then, you change the values in the report title and in heading lines 4 and 5, and this code is complete.

```
 01   COMPANY-NAME.
*
      05  FILLER       PIC X(10)    VALUE SPACE.
      05  FILLER       PIC X(20)    VALUE 'MIKE MURACH & ASSOCI'.
      05  FILLER       PIC X(20)    VALUE 'ATES, INC.' .
*
 01   REPORT-TITLE.
*
      05  FILLER       PIC X(11)    VALUE SPACE.
      05  FILLER       PIC X(20)    VALUE 'INVALID SALES AND RE'.
      05  FILLER       PIC X(29)    VALUE 'TURN TRANSACTIONS'.
*
 COPY RPTHDG14.
*
 01   HEADING-LINE-4.
*
      05  FILLER       PIC X(20)    VALUE 'TRAN   UPDATE   REFE'.
      05  FILLER       PIC X(20)    VALUE 'RENCE               '.
      05  FILLER       PIC X(20)    VALUE 'BRANCH    SALESMAN  '.
      05  FILLER       PIC X(20)    VALUE 'CUSTOMER            '.
      05  FILLER       PIC X(20)    VALUE '    PART     RETURN '.
      05  FILLER       PIC X(20)    VALUE '                    '.
      05  FILLER       PIC X(12)    VALUE '            '.
*
 01   HEADING-LINE-5.
*
      05  FILLER       PIC X(20)    VALUE 'CODE     CODE    NUM'.
      05  FILLER       PIC X(20)    VALUE 'BER         DATE    '.
      05  FILLER       PIC X(20)    VALUE 'NUMBER     NUMBER   '.
      05  FILLER       PIC X(20)    VALUE ' NUMBER     QUANTITY '.
      05  FILLER       PIC X(20)    VALUE '  NUMBER      CODE  '.
      05  FILLER       PIC X(20)    VALUE '                    '.
      05  FILLER       PIC X(12)    VALUE '            '.
*
```

Figure 9-18 Reusable code for the heading lines of a report

I'm sure you get the idea by now. You shouldn't spend hours entering Data Division code into the system from scratch. You can reduce your keystrokes dramatically by copying whatever type of Data Division entry you need from an old program and editing it so it suits your program. This also improves the likelihood that the code will compile without error.

Procedure Division Look at the code in figure 9-19. This is the code for the first two modules in the Procedure Division of the edit program. But this is very close to the code that is required for any program developed using the design method presented in this book. Change the file names, change the paragraph names, delete or modify a PERFORM or two, and you're on your way. If you code the Data Division entries for the heading lines as we've just suggested, module 100 can be used in any program that prepares a report by changing only the report number.

```
 000-EDIT-INVENTORY-TRANS.
*
     OPEN INPUT  PARTNUM
                 INVTRAN
          OUTPUT VINVTRN
                 IINVTLST.
     PERFORM 100-FORMAT-REPORT-HEADING.
     PERFORM 200-LOAD-PART-NUMBER-TABLE
         VARYING PN-TABLE-INDEX FROM 1 BY 1
         UNTIL PART-NUMBER-EOF.
     PERFORM 300-EDIT-INVENTORY-TRAN
         UNTIL TRAN-EOF.
     PERFORM 500-PRINT-TOTAL-PAGE.
     CLOSE PARTNUM
           INVTRAN
           VINVTRN
           IINVTLST.
     STOP RUN.
*
 100-FORMAT-REPORT-HEADING.
*
     CALL 'SYSDATE' USING TODAYS-DATE.
     MOVE TODAYS-DATE    TO HDG1-DATE.
     MOVE COMPANY-NAME   TO HDG1-COMPANY-NAME.
     CALL 'SYSTIME' USING   HDG2-TIME-DATA.
     MOVE 'INV2100'      TO HDG2-REPORT-NUMBER.
     MOVE REPORT-TITLE   TO HDG3-REPORT-TITLE.
*
```

Figure 9-19 Reusable code for the first two paragraphs of most programs

Figure 9-20 gives some code that can be reused whenever your program has to load a table from a sequential input file. Figure 9-21 gives some code that can be reused if your program reads a sequential input file. And figure 9-22 gives some code that can be reused if your program has to search a one-level table.

Again, I'm sure you get the idea. Most functions in a business program can be found in many other business programs. So why code each module from scratch? If you can reuse portions of a program's design from one program to the next, you can surely reuse portions of a program's code. And when you do, you reduce the number of keystrokes needed to create the program and you increase the likelihood that the syntax will be correct.

How to copy and edit code from other programs

I realize that some systems are much better than others when it comes to copying code from an old program into the one you're working on and modifying it (or editing it) so it suits your program. On our Wang VS system, for example, it's easy to copy code from another program whenever you need it in your new program. Then, after the code has been copied, our system makes it easy for you to edit it. If, for example, I

```
 200-LOAD-PART-NUMBER-TABLE.
*
     PERFORM 210-READ-PART-NUMBER-RECORD.
     IF NOT PART-NUMBER-EOF
         MOVE PNR-PART-NO TO PN-TABLE-ENTRY (PN-TABLE-INDEX)
     ELSE
         SET PN-TABLE-INDEX DOWN BY 1
         SET PN-ENTRY-COUNT TO PN-TABLE-INDEX.
*
 210-READ-PART-NUMBER-RECORD.
*
     READ PARTNUM
         AT END
             MOVE 'Y' TO PART-NUMBER-EOF-SW.
*
```

Figure 9-20 Reusable code for loading any one-level table from a sequential input file

```
 310-READ-INVENTORY-TRAN.
*
     READ INVTRAN INTO INVENTORY-TRANSACTION-RECORD
         AT END
             MOVE 'Y' TO TRAN-EOF-SW.
     IF NOT TRAN-EOF
         ADD 1 TO TRANS-PROCESSED-COUNT.
*
```

Figure 9-21 Reusable code for reading any sequential input file

```
 340-SEARCH-PART-NUMBER-TABLE.
*
     SET PN-TABLE-INDEX TO 1.
     SEARCH PN-TABLE-ENTRY
         AT END
             MOVE 'N' TO PART-NUMBER-FOUND-SW
         WHEN ITR-PART-NO = PN-TABLE-ENTRY (PN-TABLE-INDEX)
             MOVE 'Y' TO PART-NUMBER-FOUND-SW
         WHEN PN-TABLE-INDEX GREATER PN-ENTRY-COUNT
             MOVE 'N' TO PART-NUMBER-FOUND-SW.
*
```

Figure 9-22 Reusable code for searching any one-level table

want to reuse the code from a few modules taken from a sequential update program, I can easily copy the modules into my program wherever I need them. Then, if I want, I can globally replace the names in the old code with the required names in the new code. In a global replace, you only enter the old name once and the new name once; the system finds all occurrences of the old name and replaces it with the new name.

As far as I know, all modern systems allow you to copy code from another program and to edit it in your program. But if your system doesn't provide for this, it probably provides for some form of block copying that will at least let you create your starting source file. For example, on our first system, we could specify segments of code from one or more source files that we wanted to be merged into a single source file. Although this took more planning (you had to know the exact line numbers of the portions of code that you wanted to use), it still saved us countless hours of program entry.

Even if your copying capabilities are so inefficient that they're not worth using, it's still worth working from old programs when you create a new program. In this case, you re-enter the code into the system, but you copy it from old source listings. Although you don't save entry keystrokes this way, you still save the time it takes to create a segment of code and you still have the assurance that the syntax of the code is correct.

Fortunately, I think systems that don't provide adequate copying and editing functions are just about a thing of the past. But not enough programmers make adequate use of the facilities that they have.

With that in mind, let me make one final point: The programmer, himself or herself, should enter the source code into the computer system. You shouldn't code a program on coding forms and pass it to the key-entry department for entry into the system. You should code, copy, and edit your program based on your structure chart for the program, any module plans you have created, and any related source listings you have selected for your program. If you work in this way using a visual-display workstation, you should be able to create the initial version of your source program in a fraction of the time it takes to create handwritten code.

When to modify a structure chart based on coding discoveries

I covered this point somewhat in topic 3 of the last chapter so I won't dwell on it here. In general, however, three things may surprise you as you code a program. First, you may code short modules consisting of only a line or two that you expected to be longer. Second, you may code long modules consisting of dozens or hundreds of lines of code. And, third, you may code modules that are so complex in terms of logic that they are extremely difficult to understand. In any of these cases, you may want to modify your code and the structure chart by deleting modules from the program or adding modules to it.

How to handle short modules It's tempting to delete a module when it consists of only a line or two by absorbing it up into its calling module. To repeat what I said in the last chapter, though, this usually isn't worth doing. If you thought a module on your structure chart represented a function when you designed the program, don't delete it unless you decide that it isn't a function when you code the program. In other words, don't delete it just because it's short.

How to handle long modules Sometimes, modules like print modules or editing modules can be extremely long. But that by itself isn't reason enough to change your program's design. If, for example, a print module consists of dozens of MOVE statements in sequence, it should be easy enough to understand. So why change it?

Our recommendation on long modules, then, is to only divide them up into two or more modules when this division helps improve the clarity of the program. Sometimes, though, rather than making new modules, you can simply divide the code into its logical parts using blank comment lines. For instance, figure 9-23 presents module 330 of the edit program after it has been divided up in this way. Here, the code for each field that is being edited is separated from the other code by blank comment lines. Using this technique, you can make a module of 50 lines or more easy to read...provided that the code is straightforward.

How to handle complicated modules Sometimes, you code a module that is so complicated that you have continuous difficulties with it. In other words, you struggle with the module every time you encounter it during coding, testing, and maintenance. So how can you expect another programmer to take over the maintenance of your program?

At a time like this, you should see what you can do to simplify the module. In most cases, you will be able to modify the structure of your program in a way that will simplify the requirements of the difficult module. I gave you an example of this in the last chapter. By creating subordinates for a complicated module, you can often reduce the amount of code in the module. And by redesigning a program's structure, you can often reduce the complexity of the module.

On the other hand, most programs have only a few modules that are complicated. That's one of the benefits of structured programming. So it's not that bad if one of them is particularly complicated. At least, you can concentrate on this module knowing that the entire program will probably work if you can get this one module running right.

Why COBOL can be more effective than pseudocode when planning modules

In the chapter on module planning, I pointed out that some of our programmers believe that you should code a program right after you design it. In other words, you shouldn't bother to plan the coding of the modules using pseudocode or HIPO diagrams. You should just make a test plan as described in the next chapter and start to copy, edit, and code the program using a visual-display workstation.

```
 330-EDIT-CODE-1-FIELDS.
*
     IF ITR-UPDATE-CODE NOT = 'C'
         MOVE 'N'                TO VALID-TRAN-SW
         MOVE ERROR-INDICATOR TO ITL-UPDATE-CODE-ERR.
*
     CALL 'DATEDIT' USING ITR-REF-DATE, VALID-DATE-SW.
     IF NOT VALID-DATE
         MOVE 'N'                TO VALID-TRAN-SW
         MOVE ERROR-INDICATOR TO ITL-REF-DATE-ERR.
*
     IF           ITR-BRANCH-NO NOT NUMERIC
              OR ITR-BRANCH-NO NOT GREATER ZERO
              OR ITR-BRANCH-NO NOT LESS 25
         MOVE 'N'                TO VALID-TRAN-SW
         MOVE ERROR-INDICATOR TO ITL-BRANCH-NO-ERR.
*
     IF           ITR-SALESMAN-NO NOT NUMERIC
              OR ITR-CUSTOMER-NO NOT GREATER ZERO
         MOVE 'N'                TO VALID-TRAN-SW
         MOVE ERROR-INDICATOR TO ITL-SALESMAN-NO-ERR.
*
     IF           ITR-CUSTOMER-NO NOT NUMERIC
              OR ITR-CUSTOMER-NO NOT GREATER THAN ZERO
         MOVE 'N'                TO VALID-TRAN-SW
         MOVE ERROR-INDICATOR TO ITL-CUSTOMER-NO-ERR.
*
     IF           ITR-QUANTITY NOT NUMERIC
              OR ITR-QUANTITY NOT GREATER ZERO
         MOVE 'N'                TO VALID-TRAN-SW
         MOVE ERROR-INDICATOR TO ITL-QUANTITY-ERR.
*
     PERFORM 340-SEARCH-PART-NUMBER-TABLE.
     IF NOT PART-NUMBER-FOUND
         MOVE 'N'                TO VALID-TRAN-SW
         MOVE ERROR-INDICATOR TO ITL-PART-NUMBER-ERR.
*
     IF NOT VALID-TRAN
         ADD 1 TO INVALID-SALES-COUNT
     ELSE
         ADD 1 TO VALID-SALES-COUNT.
*
```

Figure 9-23 Using blank comment lines in a long module to make the code easier to read

One reason they feel this way is that COBOL is so much like pseudocode that you do duplicate work when you use pseudocode or HIPO diagrams. By eliminating this duplication of effort, you increase productivity. The other reason they feel this way relates to the reuse of code from one program to another.

When you plan the code for the modules of a program, you should base your plans on the plans for similar modules in other programs. In other words, you should reuse module plans as well as portions of structure charts. Unfortunately, module plans are only working papers. So they shouldn't be kept for final documentation. And that means they're usually not available when you want to copy ideas from them. Furthermore, even if they are available, you can't copy coding from them electronically and edit it. At best, you can copy the pseudocode pages or HIPO diagrams using a copier and make handwritten modifications to them. But your final result is likely to be messy.

In contrast, if you forget pseudocode and HIPO diagrams, you can plan the modules of a program in COBOL by copying related modules from other programs and editing them to suit your purposes. In other words, you create the code for all of the critical modules in the Procedure Division before you even start to do the other Divisions. Then, this COBOL code for the Procedure Division will help you figure out what you need in the Data Division.

If reviews of module plans are required in your shop, what's wrong with reviewing the COBOL code for the Procedure Division? It should be just as easy to read as pseudocode or HIPO diagrams. And because it's machine printed, it's likely to be more legible. Finally, once the review is complete, you can edit the Procedure Division to correct the problems that were detected and you've got part of the program done...no wasted effort.

Discussion

If you don't code a new program by copying at least 50 percent of its code from other programs, you're not getting the benefits of structured programming that you should be getting. In the GOTO era of programming, you couldn't reuse code, because the code wasn't divided into independent functions. But today, that shouldn't be true.

In order to copy code efficiently, though, you have to follow our principle of one COBOL paragraph for each module on the structure chart. That means that your modules will be shorter than they will be if you use other coding methods, so the paragraphs are more likely to be reusable. That also means that you will be able to find the portions of code that you are looking for more easily. In contrast, if you code the modules of your programs as a series of paragraphs or as separately-compiled subprograms, you won't be able to maximize your productivity by reusing code. More about this in the next topic.

Oddly enough, some people refuse to reuse code because they say it reduces program quality. Their feeling is that when you reuse code the names and routines you use become less pertinent to the program you're working on. I can only say to this that we certainly haven't found this to be true in practice. The worst thing I've found is that some programmers leave fields in their Data Divisions that they copied from old programs even though their new program never used them. But this is easy to police and easy to correct.

So reuse old code whenever possible. If you reuse as much old code as you can and if you make as much use of COPY members and general-purpose subprograms as you can, you should be creating less than 30 percent of each new program from scratch. And this in turn should give you plenty of freedom to concentrate on the 5 or 10 percent of the code in each program that really counts.

Terminology

None

Objective

Given a new program's specifications, a structure chart for the design of the program, and a library of model programs, code the new program reusing as much code as possible from the old programs.

Topic 4 Other coding methods

In our COBOL survey, 43 percent of the respondents said that they coded each module of the structure chart as a single COBOL paragraph. And that, of course, is what we recommend.

However, 30 percent of the shops said they coded each module as a series of paragraphs called by a PERFORM-THRU statement. Another 17 percent of the shops said they coded each module as a COBOL section. And 10 percent of the shops said they coded each module as a subprogram. Although the first two alternatives aren't necessarily bad, they can lead to reduced productivity and program quality. And the third alternative, implementing each module as a subprogram, can have a devastating effect on programmer productivity and program quality. In this topic, then, I'd like to discuss these alternatives.

Implementing each module of a program as a series of paragraphs called by a PERFORM-THRU statement

Figure 9-24 shows the first six modules of the edit program when they are implemented as paragraphs called by a PERFORM-THRU statement. As you can see, you can implement a program in this way without affecting the program much. In this case, each module ends with an exit paragraph, so each module requires at least two more lines of COBOL code. And each PERFORM statement requires 14 or 15 extra keystrokes for the THRU clause.

The benefit of coding a program in this way is that you can sometimes simplify the logic of a module by using the EXIT paragraph. In module 300, for example, the programmer has used a GOTO statement to branch to the EXIT paragraph if the transaction end-of-file switch is on. Then, it's obvious that the remaining statements in the paragraph are only executed if the end-of-file record hasn't been read. If you compare this code with the code for module 300 in appendix A, you can see that the difference isn't that significant. But in some cases, I think coding in this way can improve the clarity of a module.

The problem with PERFORM-THRUs is that they also give a programmer the license to reduce program quality. If you're going to use one GOTO in a module, why not two? And if you're going to code one extra paragraph for a module, why not two? If this gets out of control, you can quickly end up with modules that remind us of the days of GOTO programming. So that's our biggest argument against PERFORM-THRUs. As soon as you allow one GOTO statement in a program, where

```
 PROCEDURE DIVISION.
*
 000-EDIT-INVENTORY-TRANS.
*
     OPEN INPUT  PARTNUM
                 INVTRAN
          OUTPUT VINVTRN
                 IINVTLST.
     PERFORM 100-FORMAT-REPORT-HEADING THRU 100-EXIT.
     PERFORM 200-LOAD-PART-NUMBER-TABLE THRU 200-EXIT
         VARYING PN-TABLE-INDEX FROM 1 BY 1
         UNTIL PART-NUMBER-EOF.
     PERFORM 300-EDIT-INVENTORY-TRAN THRU 300-EXIT
         UNTIL TRAN-EOF.
     PERFORM 500-PRINT-TOTAL-PAGE THRU 500-EXIT.
     CLOSE PARTNUM
           INVTRAN
           VINVTRN
           IINVTLST.
     STOP RUN.
*
 000-EXIT.
*
     EXIT.
*
 100-FORMAT-REPORT-HEADING.
*
     MOVE CURRENT-DATE TO HDG1-DATE.
     MOVE COMPANY-NAME TO HDG1-COMPANY-NAME.
     CALL 'SYSTIME' USING HDG2-TIME-DATA.
     MOVE 'INV2100'    TO HDG2-REPORT-NUMBER.
     MOVE REPORT-TITLE TO HDG3-REPORT-TITLE.
*
 100-EXIT.
*
     EXIT.
*
 200-LOAD-PART-NUMBER-TABLE.
*
     PERFORM 210-READ-PART-NUMBER-RECORD THRU 210-EXIT.
     IF NOT PART-NUMBER-EOF
         MOVE PNR-PART-NO TO PN-TABLE-ENTRY (PN-TABLE-INDEX)
     ELSE
         SET PN-TABLE-INDEX DOWN BY 1
         SET PN-ENTRY-COUNT TO PN-TABLE-INDEX.
*
 200-EXIT.
*
     EXIT.
```

Figure 9-24 The use of PERFORM-THRUs to implement the edit program (part 1 of 2)

do you draw the line? If you don't draw the line rather rigidly, this method of coding can defeat the purposes of structured programming.

If you're going to use PERFORM-THRUs, then, we make these recommendations. First, make sure that each module consists of only two

```
*
 210-READ-PART-NUMBER-RECORD.
*
     READ PARTNUM
         AT END
             MOVE 'Y' TO PART-NUMBER-EOF-SW.
*
 210-EXIT.
*
     EXIT.
*
 300-EDIT-INVENTORY-TRAN.
*
     PERFORM 310-READ-INVENTORY-TRAN THRU 310-EXIT.
     IF TRAN-EOF
         GO TO 300-EXIT.
     PERFORM 320-EDIT-TRANSACTION-FIELDS THRU 320-EXIT.
     IF NOT VALID-TRAN
         PERFORM 360-PRINT-INVALID-TRAN-LINE THRU 360-EXIT
     ELSE
         PERFORM 400-WRITE-VALID-TRANSACTION THRU 400-EXIT.
*
 300-EXIT.
*
     EXIT.
*
 310-READ-INVENTORY-TRAN.
*
     READ INVTRAN INTO INVENTORY-TRANSACTION-RECORD
         AT END
             MOVE 'Y' TO TRAN-EOF-SW.
     IF NOT TRAN-EOF
         ADD 1 TO TRANS-PROCESSED-COUNT.
*
 310-EXIT.
*
     EXIT.
*
```

Figure 9-24 The use of PERFORM-THRUs to implement the edit program (part 2 of 2)

paragraphs: the main paragraph and the EXIT paragraph. Second, make sure that GOTOs are only allowed to branch to the EXIT paragraph. Third, the name for the EXIT paragraph should be the module number followed by the word EXIT as in 000-EXIT. If you take this advice, the use of PERFORM-THRUs should have little effect on programmer productivity. And it may even improve the clarity of some modules.

Incidentally, I have heard that some compilers don't stop PERFORMs properly unless you end each module with an EXIT paragraph. In addition, some shops require the use of PERFORM-THRUs even if you don't use branching within a module. As a result, you may be forced to use PERFORM-THRUs by your compiler or your shop standards. In either case, this should be a trivial matter if you handle PERFORM-THRUs as we've suggested.

Implementing each module of a program as a COBOL section

Figure 9-25 shows three modules of the edit program when they are implemented as COBOL sections. Here again, you can implement a program in this way with little effect on programmer productivity or program quality. When you use sections, you can end each section with an EXIT paragraph if you like. But a section can also consist of only one paragraph.

The benefit of using sections is that you can sometimes clarify the code of a module by using a GOTO statement that branches to an EXIT paragraph. This is illustrated by module 300 in figure 9-25. The problem with sections is that coding quality can deteriorate rapidly once you allow the use of GOTOs along with modules that consist of more than one paragraph.

If you're going to use sections, then, we make these recommendations. First, code every module on the structure chart as a section. In other words, don't use sections for only a few modules of a program. In a COBOL program, if you use one section, the entire program has to be in sections, so the occasional use of sections can lead to debugging problems. Second, code each PERFORM statement so it refers to a section name, not a paragraph name. Third, if you want to use GOTOs in a section, code the section as two paragraphs: a main paragraph and an EXIT paragraph. Fourth, if you use a GOTO statement in a section, only branch to the EXIT paragraph.

Some programmers like to use sections only to divide a Procedure Division into parts so the section names are never used in the PERFORM statements of the program. Although we see no problem with this, we see no benefit in it either. After all, all COBOL programs are already divided into parts called paragraphs. So any other division is artificial.

As you will see in chapter 14, we recommend that you develop each module of a program as a section when you develop CICS programs in COBOL on an IBM mainframe. We make this recommendation because the syntax of CICS implies the use of GOTOs. As a general rule, then, if a program requires some feature of a compiler that forces you to use GOTOs or implied GOTOs, it's logical to implement all of the modules of the program as sections.

Implementing each module of a program as a subprogram

If it's good for a module to be independent, why not implement each module as a subprogram? That way, you can be sure each module is independent. That's the theory behind the use of subprograms as a way to implement each module of a COBOL program.

```
 PROCEDURE DIVISION.
*
 000-EDIT-INVENTORY-TRANS SECTION.
*
     OPEN INPUT  PARTNUM
                 INVTRAN
          OUTPUT VINVTRN
                 IINVTLST.
     PERFORM 100-FORMAT-REPORT-HEADING.
     PERFORM 200-LOAD-PART-NUMBER-TABLE
         VARYING PN-TABLE-INDEX FROM 1 BY 1
         UNTIL PART-NUMBER-EOF.
     PERFORM 300-EDIT-INVENTORY-TRAN
         UNTIL TRAN-EOF.
     PERFORM 500-PRINT-TOTAL-PAGE.
     CLOSE PARTNUM
           INVTRAN
           VINVTRN
           IINVTLST.
     STOP RUN.
*
 000-EXIT.
*
     EXIT.
*
     .
     .
     .
*
 300-EDIT-INVENTORY-TRAN SECTION.
*
     PERFORM 310-READ-INVENTORY-TRAN.
     IF TRAN-EOF
         GO TO 300-EXIT.
     PERFORM 320-EDIT-TRANSACTION-FIELDS.
     IF NOT VALID-TRAN
         PERFORM 360-PRINT-INVALID-TRAN-LINE
     ELSE
         PERFORM 400-WRITE-VALID-TRANSACTION.
*
 300-EXIT.
*
     EXIT.
*
 310-READ-INVENTORY-TRAN SECTION.
*
     READ INVTRAN INTO INVENTORY-TRANSACTION-RECORD
         AT END
             MOVE 'Y' TO TRAN-EOF-SW
             GO TO 310-EXIT.
     ADD 1 TO TRANS-PROCESSED-COUNT.
*
 310-EXIT.
*
     EXIT.
*
```

Figure 9-25 The use of sections to implement the edit program

```
 PROCEDURE DIVISION.
*
 000-EDIT-INVENTORY-TRANS.
*
     CALL "EDIT100" USING HEADING-LINE-1
                          HEADING-LINE-2
                          HEADING-LINE-3.
     CALL "EDIT200" USING PART-NUMBER-TABLE.
     PERFORM 300-EDIT-INVENTORY-TRAN
         UNTIL TRAN-EOF.
     CALL "EDIT500" USING HEADING-LINE-1
                          HEADING-LINE-2
                          COUNT-FIELDS.
     STOP RUN.
*
 300-EDIT-INVENTORY-TRAN.
*
     CALL "EDIT310" USING TRAN-EOF-SW
                          INVENTORY-TRANSACTION-RECORD.
     IF NOT TRAN-EOF
         CALL "EDIT320" USING VALID-TRAN-SW
                              PART-NUMBER-TABLE
                              COUNT-FIELDS
                              ERROR-FIELDS
                              INVENTORY-TRANSACTION-RECORD
         IF NOT VALID-TRAN
             CALL "EDIT330" USING ERROR-FIELDS
                                  INVENTORY-TRANSACTION-RECORD
                                  HEADING-LINE-1
                                  HEADING-LINE-2
                                  HEADING-LINE-3
         ELSE
             CALL "EDIT340" USING INVENTORY-TRANSACTION-RECORD.
*
```

Figure 9-26 The Procedure Division for the edit program with the main functions implemented as subprograms

To illustrate this implementation of a COBOL program, look at figures 9-26 and 9-27. These give the code for the Procedure Divisions of two modules of the edit program when its main functions are implemented as subprograms. Although the Data Divisions aren't shown, the top-level module (figure 9-26) requires a smaller Data Division than the complete edit program in appendix A does, because it doesn't have to operate on all of the data of the program; it simply has to provide for the fields that it requires and the fields it passes to the modules it calls. Similarly, the subprogram for module 200 (figure 9-27) requires fewer entries in the Data Division than the edit program in the appendix requires. On the other hand, any subprogram requires a linkage section in the Data Division that describes the fields that will be passed to it from a calling program which means that these fields are duplicated. And each CALL statement in the Procedure Division must identify the fields or records that it is passing to the subprogram.

```
 PROCEDURE DIVISION USING PART-NUMBER-TABLE.
*
 000-LOAD-PART-NUMBER-TABLE.
*
     OPEN INPUT PARTNUM.
     PERFORM 100-LOAD-PART-NUMBER-ENTRY
         VARYING PN-TABLE-INDEX FROM 1 BY 1
         UNTIL PART-NUMBER-EOF.
     CLOSE PARTNUM.
*
 000-EXIT.
*
     EXIT PROGRAM.
*
 100-LOAD-PART-NUMBER-ENTRY.
*
     PERFORM 110-READ-PART-NUMBER-RECORD.
     IF NOT PART-NUMBER-EOF
         MOVE PNR-PART-NO TO PN-TABLE-ENTRY (PN-TABLE-INDEX)
     ELSE
         SET PN-TABLE-INDEX DOWN BY 1
         SET PN-ENTRY-COUNT TO PN-TABLE-INDEX.
*
 110-READ-PART-NUMBER-RECORD.
*
     READ PARTNUM
         AT END
             MOVE "Y" TO PART-NUMBER-EOF-SW.
*
```

Figure 9-27 The Procedure Division for module 200 of the edit program when implemented as a subprogram

People who believe in implementing a program in this way say that it leads to the reuse of program modules from one program to the next. And to some extent this can be true. Without any modification, for example, you could reuse the modules for formatting a standard report heading, loading the part-number table, reading the part-number-table file, reading the transaction file, printing report headings, writing page-top lines, and writing report-lines. Unfortunately, these modules are all short, simple modules. And you pay a dear price for the benefit of reusing them.

As we see it, you encounter five significant problems when you implement the modules of a program as subprograms. First, you have to code many more lines when you develop a program in this way due the repetition of Identification and Data Division elements in the subprograms. If, for example, we had coded the edit program as 16 separate subprograms, we estimate that the program would have required a total of 1500 or more lines of code in contrast to the 505 lines it requires in appendix A. To increase productivity, though, you want to keep the number of lines of code that a program requires to a minimum. So this factor alone can significantly reduce programmer productivity.

Second, when you use subprograms, you have to be concerned about the linkage. If you don't describe the linkage correctly in both calling module and called module, the program won't work right. This added complexity means that it will take you longer to code a subprogram module than it will take you to code a module as a COBOL paragraph. It also means that you're likely to encounter more debugging problems with a subprogram module and that it will be more difficult to maintain one.

Third, when you implement each module of a program as a subprogram, you have to link-edit the modules together using the system's linkage-editor program. This means extra programmer time as the programmer enters the procedure statements for the link-editing. This means extra machine time as the system links the subprograms together. This can mean extra delays as the programmer debugs the procedure language to get the link-editing done right.

Fourth, when you use subprograms, you don't have one single listing for a program; you have one listing for each subprogram. As a result, the documentation for the program is fragmented. This in turn leads to problems in testing, debugging, and maintenance.

Fifth, when you code the modules of a program as subprograms, the modules aren't as easy to reuse as when you code them as COBOL paragraphs. Yes, I said earlier that you could reuse some of the small, general-purpose modules, but what about the control modules and the large modules? Obviously, since they apply to one specific program, they can't be reused without modification. In contrast, you can copy a COBOL paragraph for any module of an old program into your new program and modify it to suit your purposes. So *all* of the modules of a program are reusable when they are coded as COBOL paragraphs.

The first thing people who believe in the use of subprograms will say to this criticism is that you shouldn't design a program as we've recommended when you implement program modules as subprograms. Instead, you must be concerned with the fields passed between the subprograms. In short, a good design is one that reduces the number of fields required for linkage between the modules. If you reduce the linkage requirements, coding isn't as difficult as I just described it, and testing, debugging, and maintenance are improved too.

Figure 9-28, for example, illustrates a design for the edit program that will reduce linkage problems and make it easier for you to implement each module of the program as a subprogram. As you can see, the designer used a type of tree chart that let him analyze the linkage fields as he designed the program. I'm not saying this is the best possible design for this program, but it is one that a professional programmer suggested to us.

Unfortunately, although this design may simplify linkage requirements, it was still difficult to code and test this program using one subprogram for each of the five modules. When we coded the program as designed in figure 9-28 using subprograms, it still took 810 lines of code as compared with the 505 lines in the original edit program. The modules were still more difficult to code than COBOL paragraphs due to the

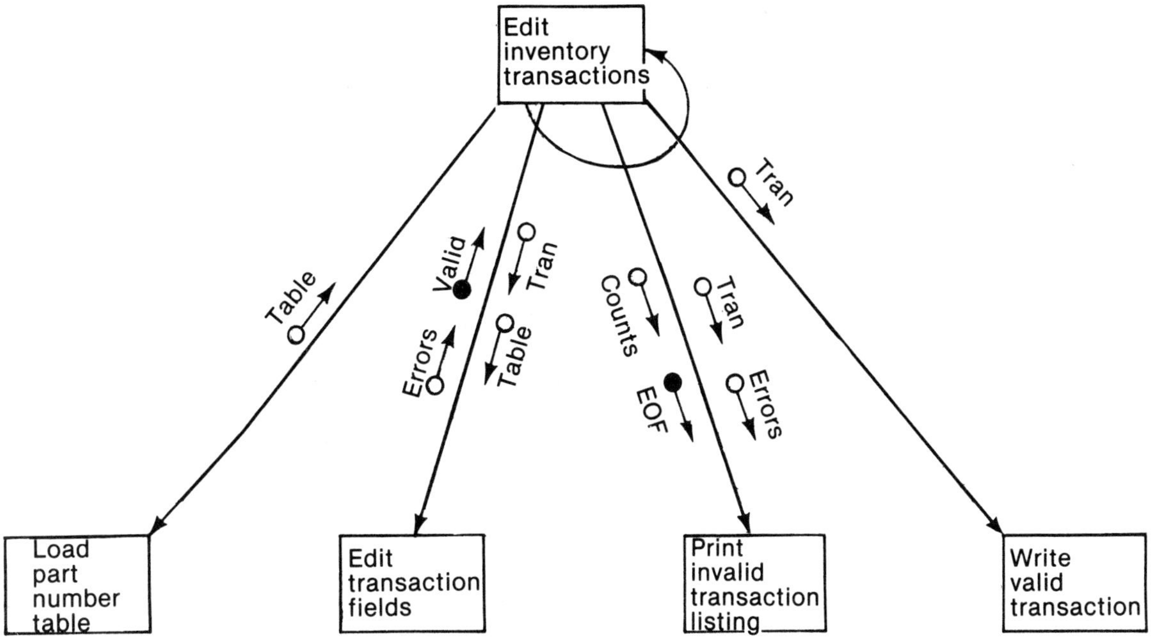

Figure 9-28 A tree chart for the edit program designed to reduce linkage problems when implementing each module as a subprogram

linkage considerations that remain. Link editing still took more time than simple compiling. The documentation was still fragmented. And now, because some of the simple modules have been absorbed into higher level modules, only two of the modules are reusable: the load-part-number-table module and perhaps the write-valid-transaction module.

Beyond all this, you create a new problem when you combine the modules of a program to reduce linkage problems. Specifically, as you reduce the number of modules in a program, the modules become longer and more complex. As a result, each module can become a development problem in itself. Then, the question is: How do you design and document each of the complex modules of the program? If you don't have an effective way to do this, you're back to where you started from...looking for an effective way to develop COBOL programs.

This isn't all just objective analysis either, because we liked the theory of subprograms enough to experiment with this method of coding. In fact, we developed a large production program in our shop using this method. In total, the program consisted of 18,500 lines of COBOL code divided among 19 subprograms. Since each of the subprograms was developed using the techniques presented in this book, we thought we would end up with a high-quality program. Unfortunately, that didn't happen because the linkage considerations made it difficult to develop and maintain the program. In fact, the program was so difficult to maintain that we eventually rewrote the program with one COBOL paragraph per module. Once we did this, we had no more problems with it.

Conclusion

If I accomplish one thing in this topic, I hope it's to get you to stop implementing each module of a program as a subprogram. For some types of systems programs, I'm sure it makes sense to treat each module as a subprogram. But when it comes to COBOL programs, we just don't see the benefits of it. If there are any, they sure don't compensate for the losses in programmer productivity.

On the other hand, if you want to use PERFORM-THRUs or PERFORM sections, we see no inherent problem with either. But don't let either method of coding take you back to the techniques of GOTO programming.

Terminology

None

Objectives

1. List three recommendations for use when you implement each module of a program as a series of paragraphs called by a PERFORM-THRU statement.

2. List four recommendations for use when you implement each module of a program as a section.

3. List five problems that result when you implement each module of a program as a subprogram.

Chapter 10

How to test a structured program

Once you have mastered the techniques of top-down design and structured coding, your productivity should increase significantly. And your programs should be more reliable and easier to maintain. But structured programming doesn't stop there.

In topic 1 of this chapter, I'm going to show you how structured programming should affect the testing tasks of program development. Then, in topic 2, I'm going to show you how top-down testing can improve your efficiency and morale as you code and test a program. When you complete this chapter, you should know how to apply the techniques of structured programming to all your testing tasks.

Topic 1 Some basic testing techniques

For some programs, you will use top-down design and structured coding, but you won't use top-down coding and testing as described in topic 2 of this chapter. Thus, the nine-task procedure presented in chapter 4 becomes the ten-task procedure shown in figure 10-1. In this case, coding and testing are handled as separate development tasks.

In general, you should only treat coding and testing as separate tasks when the program you are developing can be completed in one day. As a result, you should use top-down testing for most of the programs you develop. More about this in the next topic. For now, though, you should realize that all the techniques presented in this topic apply to testing whether or not you use top-down testing.

Up to this point, I've presented the four tasks for analyzing and designing a program. And I've presented techniques for coding a program in structured COBOL. Now, in this topic, I will present techniques that are related to the testing tasks of program development (steps 5 through 9 in figure 10-1). Specifically, I'll show you how to code job-control procedures in a structured style. I'll show you how to create a test plan for a program. I'll give you some ideas on creating test data for a program. I'll show you how to decide on the coding sequence for a program. And I'll give you some ideas on how to conduct a test run for a program.

Although I'm covering all of these tasks in a single topic, that doesn't mean that they aren't important. In fact, the failure to test programs adequately is still a major shortcoming in our industry. However, a complete presentation of testing techniques is beyond the intent of this book. So I'll only present those testing techniques that are related to the techniques of structured programming.

How to code job-control procedures in structured style

On some interactive systems today, you can test programs without coding job-control procedures. On other systems, you have to code procedures in some sort of procedure language or job-control language (JCL) for each test run you make. In either case, though, you often have to create the job-control procedure for the final test runs for your program. So you should know how to code a procedure in structured style.

Analysis

1. Get complete program specifications.
2. Get related programs, COPY members, and subprograms.

Design

3. Design the program using a structure chart.
4. If necessary, plan the modules of the program using pseudocode or HIPO diagrams.

Implementation

5. Plan the testing of the program by creating a test plan.
6. If necessary, code the job-control procedures for the test runs.
7. If necessary, create the test data for the test runs.
8. Code the program.
9. Test the program.
10. Document the program.

Figure 10-1 The preferred sequence of tasks for developing a program when you're not using top-down testing

When you code a procedure in structured style, you write it so it is as easy to read and modify as possible. To do this, we make these recommendations. First, try to code only one parameter per coding line so it's easier to distinguish one parameter from the next. Second, try to align the parameters in each statement so they're easier to read. And third, try to present the parameters for each statement in the same sequence every time so it's easier to locate a parameter if you should need to modify one.

Figure 10-2 shows both a structured and an unstructured procedure listing for a user of MVS JCL on an IBM mainframe. Although job-control language varies significantly from one system to the next, this illustrates the dramatic difference in readability that structuring your JCL can make. As you can see, the structured JCL is much easier to read and modify than the unstructured JCL.

How to create a test plan

Do you regularly develop *test plans* when you develop your programs? If you don't, you should. But time and again I find testing done in a disorganized manner. As in all phases of structured programming, the idea behind the test plan is to put the emphasis on planning.

But let's back up a minute. In general, you test programs in three phases: unit test, systems test, and acceptance test. The *unit test* is the programmer test in which you should make sure that all modules in your

A structured job-control procedure

```
//ARSTMTS   JOB   HE66YFNH,
//                'W. CLARY'
//EXTRACT1 EXEC   PGM=AGEDSEL,
//                REGION=120K,
//                PARM=010980
//STEPLIB   DD    DSN=MMA.USERLIB,
//                DISP=SHR
//ACCTREC   DD    DSN=ARMAST,
//                DISP=OLD
//AGEDACCT  DD    DSN=&&AGEDACCT,
//                DISP=(NEW,PASS),
//                UNIT=SYSDA,
//                SPACE=(TRK,(10,1),RLSE),
//                DCB=(LRECL=120,BLKSIZE=2400,RECFM=FB)
//DELSTMTS EXEC   PGM=ARSTMTS,
//                REGION=60K
//STEPLIB   DD    DSN=MMA.USERLIB,
//                DISP=SHR
//AGEDACCT  DD    DSN=&&AGEDACCT,
//                DISP=(OLD,DELETE)
//STMTS     DD    SYSOUT=A,
//                DCB=BLKSIZE=133
//
```

An unstructured job-control procedure

```
//ARSTMTS   JOB  HE66YFNH,'W. CLARY'
//EXTRACT1 EXEC  PGM=AGEDSEL,REGION=120K,PARM=010980
//STEPLIB   DD   DSN=MMA.USERLIB,DISP=SHR
//ACCTREC   DD   DSN=ARMAST,DISP=OLD
//AGEDACCT   DD   DSN=&&AGEDACCT,DISP=(NEW,PASS),UNIT=SYSDA,
//   SPACE=(TRK,(10,1),RLSE),DCB=(LRECL=120,BLKSIZE=2400,RECFM=FB)
//DELSTMT   EXEC  PGM=ARSTMTS,REGION=60K
//STEPLIB   DD   DSN=MMA.USERLIB,DISP=SHR
//AGEDACCT   DD   DSN=&&AGEDACCT,DISP=(OLD,DELETE)
//STMTS   DD   SYSOUT=A,DCB=BLKSIZE=133
//
```

Figure 10-2 Examples of structured and unstructured job-control procedures

program function properly. Since you know your program better than anyone else, you are best qualified to create the test plan for the unit test.

The *systems test* is designed to test the interfaces between the programs within a system. For instance, if you're writing an update program, the systems test will determine whether or not the edit programs create transaction files that are acceptable to your program. But if the test data used for the edit programs is incomplete, the output from the edit programs will be an inadequate test of your update program. So you can't rely on the systems test to test all aspects of your program.

The *acceptance test* is designed to determine whether the programs in a system can be run without any help from the developers. Although the data for the acceptance test should be developed by a creative person with plenty of testing experience, this isn't always the case. So you can't count on this phase of testing to test all aspects of your program either.

To a large extent, then, the burden of proof is on the programmer in the unit test. As a result, the test plan should be made with a maximum of planning. In general, if your test plan is good, you are likely to do an adequate job of testing. If it isn't, you most likely won't do an adequate job of testing. The test plan is that important.

Before you start your test plan, you should review each of the modules of your program. For each module that you review, you should list all of the conditions that you must test. When you're finished, you will have a list of all of the test conditions for all of the modules. As a result, if you create data that tests all of these conditions, you increase the likelihood that each module will be adequately tested.

If you created pseudocode or HIPO diagrams for your modules, you can use them to help you create the condition list. Similarly, if you code a program before you start to create the test plan, you can use the COBOL listing to help you create the condition list. If you haven't done any module planning or coding, you create the condition list by asking yourself what conditions each of the modules on the structure chart must handle.

Figure 10-3 is a list of conditions that I developed for the edit program that is presented in the appendix. It gives all of the conditions that should be tested for each module in module-number sequence. Although making a list like this can be a laborious job if the program is large and the modules are many, what choice do you have? If your job as programmer is to prove that your program works for all possible conditions, you must know what the conditions are. As you will see, however, your test data usually won't have to be extensive just because your list of conditions is long.

One of the fringe benefits of making a list like this is discovering conditions that your program didn't provide for. For instance, look at the condition for module 210 in figure 10-3. What happens if the table file is empty? Granted the possibility is obscure, but all transactions will be invalid if this happens. Depending on the way the part-number file is created, then, you may want to change module 000 so the program ends if the entry count is zero after module 200 is executed. Since the cost of correcting an error increases as you progress in the program-development sequence, finding one condition that hasn't been provided for can more than pay for the time you spend listing the conditions.

After you have made your list of conditions, you are ready to create the test plan. Specifically, you want to decide in what sequence the conditions should be tested. The intent here is to discover the major problems first. So you don't want to start by testing to see whether the branch-number field is edited properly. You want to start by testing to see whether the major modules are entered properly and whether control passes from one major module to another as intended.

Program: INV2100 EDIT INVENTORY TRANSACTIONS	Page: 1
Designer: Anne Prince	Date: 08-18-84

Module	Conditions
000	Is the maximum table size okay?
200	Are the first and last part-number records stored in the table properly? Is the entry count correct for the table so the table lookup will proceed without error?
210	What happens if the table file is empty?
310	Is the last record in the file processed? What happens if the transaction file is empty? Is the transaction count correct?
320	Are invalid transaction codes detected and counted properly?
330	Are all invalid conditions for all fields in code-1 transactions detected and asterisked? Are invalid part numbers detected by the table lookup routine? Are sales transactions counted properly, both valid and invalid?
350	Same ideas as module 330.
360	Does page overflow work for invalid-line printing? Are error fields asterisked as intended?
370	Do heading lines print properly? Is the spacing proper?
390	Does the correct number of lines print on each page of the transaction listing?
500	Are all total counts correct?

Figure 10-3 Module-by-module listing of conditions that should be covered by the edit program

In general, your test plan should have four main parts to it. First, the major modules of the program should be tested using only valid data; that is, no error conditions should be tested. Second, independent error conditions should be tested, one at a time (I call these *single errors*). Third, error conditions should be tested together to see whether one error condition has an effect upon another (I call these *contingencies*). In general, these three types of tests can be made with a low volume of input data. Then, in the fourth phase of testing, conditions that depend upon volume can be tested. I'm thinking now of things like page overflow and maximum table size. If testing a volume condition is impractical in the unit test and you know it will be tested in the systems or acceptance test, you may simply want to review your code for these conditions, perhaps with an associate, and then make sure the condition actually is tested later on.

As you create your test plan, you should also decide where the test data will come from. Will you code the data yourself and create the proper input files using utilities? Will you use a test data generator? Can you copy some "live" data for your volume test? Does another program create test data that you can use? Here again, you should make these decisions in a thoughtful, controlled manner since they can have a significant effect on the efficiency and effectiveness of your unit test.

Figure 10-4 gives a test plan for the edit program in this book. Although the program is limited, I think it will give you an idea of what a test plan should look like. As I've just described, this plan starts by testing with only good data, then adds single errors, then adds contingencies, and ends up by testing the volume conditions of page overflow and maximum table size. Notice that I haven't provided for every condition that is listed in figure 10-3, because some proved to be unnecessary. But I considered each condition when I made the test plan.

How to create test data

Too often in the past, test data was created without any test plan. Is it any wonder, then, that programs were put into production with dozens and even hundreds of bugs? In contrast, it is relatively easy to create test data when you have a test plan as a guide. Furthermore, your test plan will give you a solid basis for believing that your program is bug-free after it proves itself on the data you have created.

As you create the test data, you should also determine what output to expect. It still amazes me that programmers don't always know what output they are looking for as they test a program. I remember one time in particular when a programmer asked me to help him with a debugging problem. When I asked him what output he expected, he gave an embarrassed shrug and said he wanted the output to look like a report...no particular values in the report, just a report. So as part of this task, be sure to determine what the output should be. In some cases, doing this will help you uncover problems in your specifications, design, or module plans.

Program: INV2100 EDIT INVENTORY TRANSACTIONS		Page: 1
Designer: Anne Prince		Date: 08-18-84
Test phase	Data	Data source
1. Valid transactions	Three valid part-number records: two valid transactions, one for each transaction code, and one with the first part number in the table, one with the last part number	Self
2. Single error	Invalid transactions that will test all possible causes of invalid fields	Self
3. Contingencies	Mixed data from test runs 1 and 2; any new records that might cause a contingent error	Self
4. Page overflow and maximum table size	As many part number records as the program is supposed to provide for; 150 transactions, with enough invalid transactions to cause page overflow	Test data generator

Figure 10-4 A test plan for the edit program

As a general rule, the test data you use in your early test runs for a program should be low in volume, often just a couple of records for each input file. That way, it's relatively easy to determine the expected output for a batch of test data. For instance, in the test plan for the edit program in figure 10-4, two valid transactions are enough for the first testing step. Then, for step 2, a dozen or so transactions should be enough to test all of the invalid conditions that are possible in both transaction types. By using low-volume test files, you will keep your early test runs manageable and help to simplify the debugging process. Larger test files should only be introduced after all of the major bugs have been corrected.

If you are developing an interactive program, you can't actually create a file of test data that your program can read for the interactive entries that are required. But you can make a list of the entries that you want to make during the interactive test session. Then, during the test run, you can work directly from this list, entering the fields shown as they are required. In an interactive program, as in a batch program, you should still use a low volume of entries during the early test runs. And you should still know what output to expect from each test run.

How to decide on the coding sequence of your Procedure Division paragraphs

As I mentioned in chapter 9, the paragraphs in your COBOL program should be in sequence by module number. That doesn't mean, however, that you should code them in module-number sequence. Although a structured program is always coded from the top down, the programmer has considerable leeway as to the sequence in which he will actually code the modules.

As you decide on a coding sequence, the basic rule is this: Never code a module before you code its calling module. As a result, one of the most common coding sequences is level-by-level from the top down. On the other hand, you may prefer to code down the legs of the program. That is all right too. Figure 10-5 illustrates two different sequences in which the edit program could be coded: the first is level-by-level, the second is leg-by-leg. And, of course, the legs could be coded in many other sequences too. In general, as long as you code each module after you have coded its calling module, you can code the modules in whatever sequence you prefer.

How to test a program

If you're developing a short program like the edit program, you'll probably want to test all of the modules at once. In the next topic, however, I'm going to show you a better way to code and test a program. Nevertheless, testing all modules at once is acceptable, particularly on programs that take less than one day to develop.

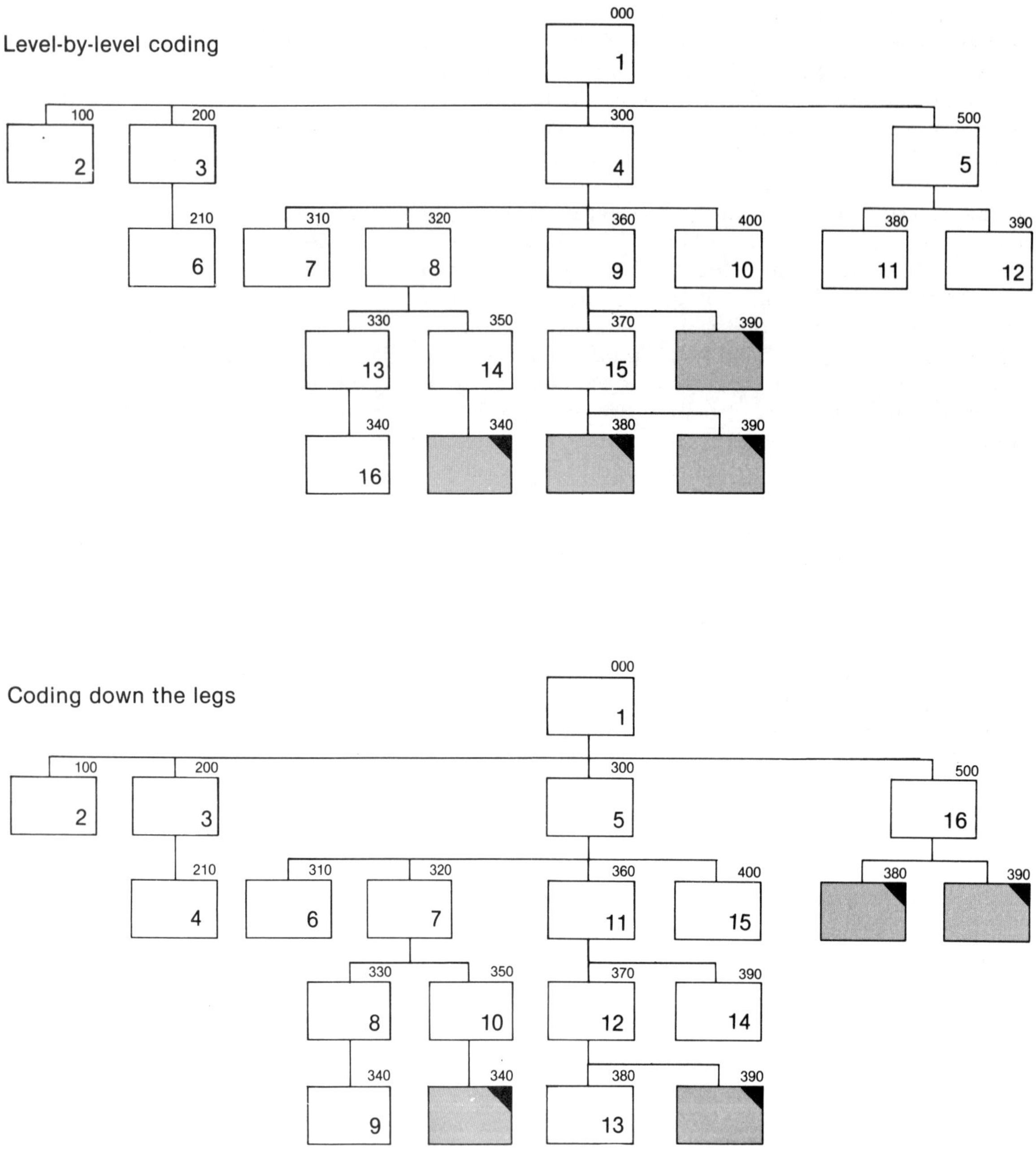

Figure 10-5 Alternative coding sequences for the edit program

In preparation for a test run, you will sometimes want to place debugging statements in your program. For instance, you may want to know which modules are executed during a test run and the sequence in which they are executed. So you can place a DISPLAY statement in each module or use one of the debugging statements like the TRACE statement if it is available on your system. When DISPLAY statements are used, you can simply place the statement at the start of each module using a literal to give the module name. For example, this statement could be used for module 200 of the edit program:

```
DISPLAY '200-LOAD-PART-NUMBER-TABLE'.
```

When you've completed this preparation, you're ready for the next test run indicated by your test plan.

If you are working on an interactive system, you probably won't need to use debugging statements much. As you probably know, many interactive systems today provide sophisticated debugging aids that can significantly improve your efficiency during testing. These aids usually include a way to trace the paragraphs that are executed during a test run. So if you're using a modern system, be sure you are familiar with all of the testing and debugging tools that are available to you.

Discussion

Some of the major benefits of structured programming become obvious during the testing phase of program development. First, because you've taken the time to design your program correctly, your program just won't have as many bugs as it would have had otherwise. Second, because you are using structured (GOTOless) COBOL, all modules will have only one entry and one exit point, so your program will be executed in a controlled manner from the top down. As a result, if there is a bug, it should be relatively easy to isolate the module in which it can be found. (Compare this with code that branches from page 7 of your source listing to page 31, back to page 15, and so on.) Third, because you have created a test plan based on conditions developed from your program's design, all of the modules in the program should be tested. This will contribute to the reliability of the program after it goes into production.

In my experience, in fact, testing a structured program is simply not the same problem as testing an unstructured program. Instead of a nightmarish month of test runs in which surprises are the norm, structured testing proceeds in an orderly fashion. Often, then, testing is a relatively minor task in a structured development procedure; design and coding are the critical tasks.

Terminology

test plan
unit test
systems test
acceptance test
single errors
contingencies

Objectives

1. Given an unstructured listing of a job-control procedure, rewrite it in structured style.

2. Given a program's specifications, design, and module plans (if any), create an acceptable test plan for the program.

3. Explain why you should use low volumes of test data in your early test runs for a program.

4. Give the basic rule that you should follow when you decide on the coding sequence for a program.

Topic 2 How to use top-down coding and testing

Although you will sometimes code and test all of the modules of a structured program at once, as described in topic 1, there's a better way to do it. This better way is called *top-down coding and testing*. In fact, we recommend that you use top-down coding and testing on any program that takes more than a day to develop.

In this topic, I'll start by introducing you to the theory and advantages of top-down coding and testing. Then, I'll present some techniques related to the effective use of top-down coding and testing. When you finish this topic, you should know how to use top-down coding and testing. And I hope you'll be motivated to use it for most of the new programs you develop.

An introduction to top-down coding and testing

When you use top-down coding and testing, you don't code the entire program and then test it. Instead, you code and test in phases. You normally start by coding and testing the level-0 module and one or more of the level-1 modules. Then, after correcting any bugs, you add one or more modules to this coding and test again. When this much of the program runs without bugs, you code a few more modules, add them to what you have, and test again. You continue in this way until all of the modules have been coded and you are testing the entire program. Because top-down coding and testing always go together, the phrase *top-down testing* implies top-down coding as well.

To illustrate top-down testing, figure 10-6 gives a test plan for the edit program. Rather than test all 16 modules at once, however, the programmer has decided to code and test only modules 000, 200, and 300 in the first phase of testing. This is illustrated by the structure chart in figure 10-7. Although the shaded modules will be called during the test run, they won't be tested as I'll explain later. After modules 000, 200, and 300 run without error, the programmer continues with the next phase of the test plan.

As you will see later, the programmer has considerable choice as to the modules that he codes and tests next. For instance, he could code module 210 next, or modules 310 and 320, or modules 360, 370, 380, and 390. And whether he adds one, two, or more modules at a time depends on the length and complexity of the modules.

Program: INV2100 EDIT INVENTORY TRANSACTIONS		Page: 1
Designer: Anne Prince		**Date:** 08-18-84
Test phase	**Data**	**Data source**
1. Modules 000, 200, and 300	None	Not applicable
2. Add modules 210, 310, 320, 330, 340, and 350	Three part-number records; Two valid transactions: one for each transaction code, and one with the first part number in the table, one with the last part number	Self
3. Add modules 100, 360, 370, 380, 390, 400, and 500	Invalid transactions that will test all possible causes of invalid fields	Self
4. Contingencies	Mixed data from steps 2 and 3; any new records that might cause contingent errors	Self
5. Page overflow and maximum table size	As many part-number records as the program is supposed to provide for; 150 transactions with enough invalid transactions to cause page overflow	Test data generator

Figure 10-6 A test plan for the edit program using top-down testing to test the major modules first

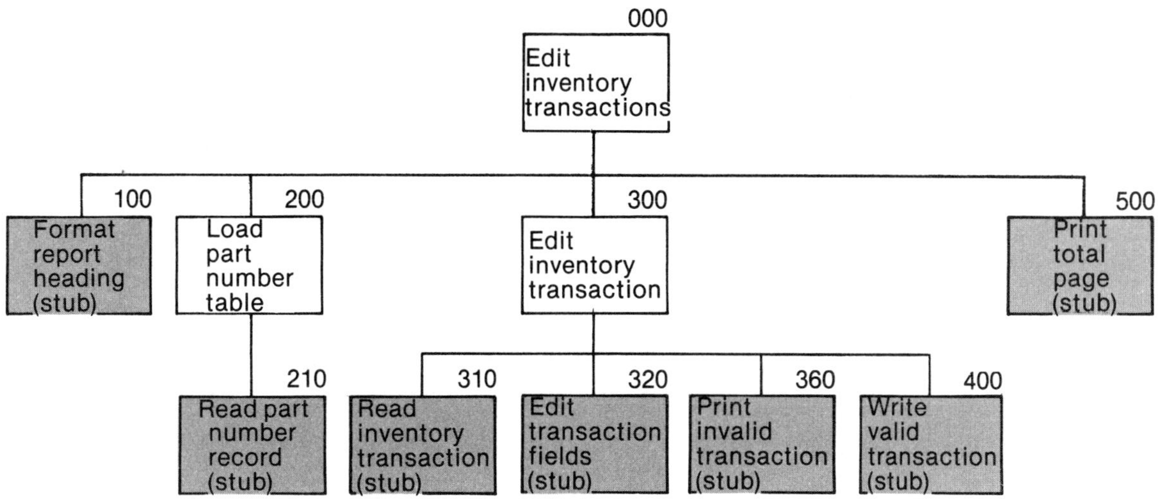

Figure 10-7 The first phase of coding and testing for the edit program using the test plan in figure 10-6

In the test plan in figure 10-6, the programmer has decided to add six modules to the program in the second phase of testing. This is illustrated by the structure chart in figure 10-8. Then, when all of these modules run without error, the programmer adds the remaining modules of the program.

In order to use top-down coding and testing, the programmer must code *program stubs*, or *dummy modules*, for all modules called by the modules that are being tested. In figure 10-7, for example, the shaded modules are program stubs. The coding for program stubs, as you will see, varies depending on whether the modules supply input, process data, or give output.

The benefits of top-down testing The primary benefit of top-down testing is improved testing efficiency (or improved productivity). To illustrate this benefit, imagine a program of 2000 lines or more with 1000 statements in the Procedure Division. If you test the entire program at once with all of its bugs, there is a good possibility that the first few days of testing will be very inefficient. If, for example, a couple of minor clerical errors cause some part of the program to execute improperly, it may be difficult to determine just where in the program the bug originates. And this in turn can lead to wasted effort: the addition of debugging statements in the source code, an unnecessary test run or two, and so on.

But if a program like this is tested from the top down, testing proceeds in increments of a few modules, perhaps 150 statements or less, at a time. As a result, it should be easy to locate the source of any bugs that are discovered during testing. They almost have to be in the modules just added or in the interfaces between the old modules and the new modules. Then, by the time all 1000 statements are tested together, all of the major control modules should be error free, so any additional errors

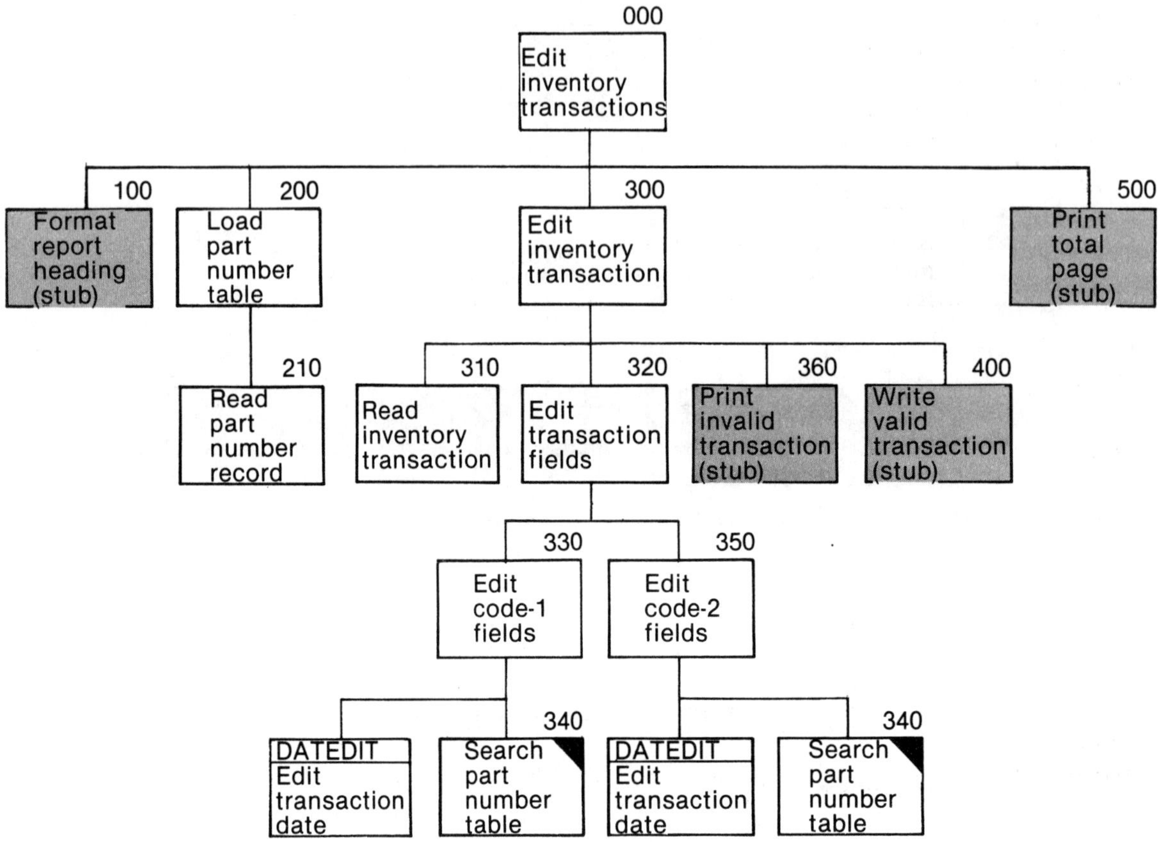

Figure 10-8 The second phase of coding and testing for the edit program using the test plan in figure 10-6

should be relatively trivial. In short, an unwieldy test run is turned into a series of easily-managed steps when you use top-down testing.

After improved testing efficiency, I think the second biggest benefit you get from using top-down testing is improved programmer morale. To me, variety is the spice of life, so it gets depressing to be involved in a large project in which the coding task alone will take a couple of weeks or more. While you are coding, you have to wonder whether you have made any major omissions or logical errors. And because you're not getting any feedback, your mind tends to get jumbled up as thoughts about one module interfere with thoughts about another.

How much better it is to code a couple hundred lines of COBOL and to test them before going any further. Besides giving a little variety to the project, it clears the mind. Once you know the top levels of the program are okay, you have confidence that you're on the right track. Furthermore, by proceeding in this way, you know that you won't be facing the task of debugging the entire program when you complete the coding.

A third benefit of top-down testing is improved program quality; in particular, improved program reliability. Although we don't have any data to prove this, we feel that a program is more likely to be reliable if it is tested on a top-down basis. Because a programmer is only concerned with a few modules each test run, it seems more likely to us that each module will actually be tested, thus making the resulting program more reliable. In contrast, it's easy to forget to test a module or two when you test all of the modules at once.

Later on, I'll present some minor benefits of top-down testing, but these are the important ones. If you use top-down testing, you should improve your productivity along with your program quality...and you should enjoy programming more than ever before.

Some related ideas

With this as background, we hope that you'll want to start using top-down testing right away. To use it well, however, you need to know (1) how to code program stubs, (2) when to use top-down testing, and (3) in what sequence to code and test the modules of a program. At this time, then, I'd like to give you some ideas in these areas.

How to code program stubs In general, there are three types of program stubs: input stubs, processing stubs, and output stubs. An *input stub* replaces a module that is supposed to supply data to a program. For instance, modules 210 and 310 in figure 10-7 are input modules, so their replacements are input stubs. A *processing stub* replaces a module that operates upon the data within a program such as module 320 in figure 10-7. And an *output stub* replaces a module that produces output in a program such as module 360, 400, or 500 in figure 10-7. How you code any of these three types of stubs will depend upon the requirements of the program and upon your test plan.

To illustrate some typical program stubs, I have coded the stubs that I would use for the first test phase of the edit program shown in figure 10-7. These stubs are shown in figure 10-9. When I code the modules later on, I delete these stubs and replace them with the actual code. Notice that I didn't even bother to code a stub for module 100. Since it isn't needed until I actually print a report line, I can put off coding it until then.

The minimum amount of code that an input stub should contain is shown in figure 10-9 for module 210. This stub simply displays the module number and indicates that the last record in the file has been read. A step up from this is the code shown for module 310. This simulates the reading of one input record the first time the module is executed and sets the end-of-file switch the second time the module is executed. Beyond this level, you may want to use a counter to simulate the reading of several records before setting the end-of-file switch. Or you may want to take records one at a time from a table that you created for the stub and pass them back to the calling module. At some point, of course, it becomes more practical to code the actual module and use actual input data than to code an extensive stub that will be thrown away

Input stubs

```
 210-READ-PART-NUMBER-RECORD.
*
     DISPLAY '210-READ-PART-NUMBER-RECORD'.
     MOVE 'Y' TO PART-NUMBER-EOF-SW.

 310-READ-INVENTORY-TRANSACTION.
*
     DISPLAY '310-READ-INVENTORY-TRANSACTION'.
     IF FIRST-RECORD
         MOVE 'C1AAAAAAAAAA09118411222333334444455555
             TO INVENTORY-TRANSACTION-RECORD
         MOVE 'N' TO FIRST-RECORD-SW
     ELSE
         MOVE 'Y' TO TRAN-EOF-SW.
```

Processing stubs

```
 320-EDIT-TRANSACTION-FIELDS.
*
     DISPLAY '320-EDIT-TRANSACTION-FIELDS'.
     MOVE 'N' TO VALID-TRAN-SW.
```

Output stubs

```
 360-PRINT-INVALID-TRANSACTION.
*
     DISPLAY '360-PRINT-INVALID-TRANSACTION'.
     DISPLAY INVENTORY-TRANSACTION-RECORD.

 400-WRITE-VALID-TRANSACTION.
*
     DISPLAY '400-WRITE-VALID-TRANSACTION'.
     DISPLAY INVENTORY-TRANSACTION-RECORD.

 500-PRINT-TOTAL-PAGE.
*
     DISPLAY '500-PRINT-TOTAL-PAGE'.
     DISPLAY VALID-SALES-COUNT.
     DISPLAY VALID-RETURN-COUNT.
     DISPLAY INVALID-SALES-COUNT.
     DISPLAY INVALID-RETURN-COUNT.
     DISPLAY INVALID-TRAN-CODE-COUNT.
     DISPLAY TRANS-PROCESSED-COUNT.
```

Figure 10-9 Program stubs for the first test phase of the edit program

later. So you must have solid reasons for going beyond the levels of detail shown in figure 10-9.

A processing stub should supply the codes or answers that the calling modules look for, but they don't have to be the right codes or answers. For instance, the code for module 320 in figure 10-9 moves an N into the valid-transaction switch. It will do this whether the transaction is valid or invalid. Nevertheless, this is all that module 300 needs in order to continue processing. Similarly, a calculate module may pass a constant value back to the program each time it is executed. For instance, a stub for a gross-pay calculation may return a constant value of $100.00 each time it is entered. Since this will allow the calling module to continue, it is acceptable.

For an output stub, you will generally use a DISPLAY statement to show what the output data is. This is illustrated in the code for modules 360, 400, and 500 in figure 10-9. For modules 360 and 400, the DISPLAY statement is used to print the contents of the entire transaction record. For module 500, DISPLAY statements are used to print the values of the fields named. Since the DISPLAY statements won't print the data in a neatly edited format, an output stub should only be used for a low-volume test run.

In some cases, due to the test data used, a program stub should never be reached at all. If, for example, only good transaction data is used in phase 2 of the test plan in figure 10-6, module 360 should never be executed during this test run. In a case like this, the stub should consist of a single statement that displays the module number so the error will be obvious if the module is called.

In figure 10-9, you can see that each program stub displays the paragraph name before doing any dummy processing. This helps the programmer determine whether all modules were called as intended. Although we recommend a DISPLAY statement for this purpose in each dummy module, you should realize that this isn't essential and creating these statements can be unnecessary work. So, to some extent, this use of DISPLAY statements should depend on your program's complexity and your personal preferences.

When to use top-down testing I've already presented the main benefits of top-down testing so I hope you'll want to use it for most of the programs you develop. At this time, though, let me present a couple of other reasons why you might want to use it. Then, let me give you a guideline for deciding when a program is long enough to warrant the use of top-down testing.

In some cases, you can use top-down testing to help you get around incomplete specifications. As you get the specifications for the edit program, for example, suppose you can't find out what the editing rules are going to be for each field of the transaction records. By using top-down design, this omission in the specifications shouldn't stop you from designing the program and coding all of the modules except the ones with incomplete specifications. In addition, though, by using top-down testing, you can test all of the modules except modules 330 and 350. So you can all but complete the program without knowing the editing rules.

You may also want to use top-down testing to help you get around a module or a group of modules that seem overwhelming to you. Suppose, for example, that you're a trainee and you haven't really mastered the table-handling feature of COBOL. As a result, modules 200 and 210 in the edit program bother you. To clear the air, then, you code a stub for module 200 using code with subscripts that you understand as shown in figure 10-10. This lets you forget about these modules until you have time to research the table-handling feature of COBOL and code them properly.

```
 200-LOAD-PART-NUMBER-TABLE.
*
     DISPLAY '200-LOAD-PART-NUMBER-TABLE'.
     MOVE 00001 TO PN-TABLE-ENTRY (1).
     MOVE 55555 TO PN-TABLE-ENTRY (2).
     MOVE 99999 TO PN-TABLE-ENTRY (3).
     MOVE 3 TO PN-ENTRY-COUNT.
     MOVE 'Y' TO PART-NUMBER-EOF-SW.
```

Figure 10-10 A program stub that simulates the functions of modules 200 and 210 in the edit program

When a program is getting more attention than it deserves because the user is concerned about it, you may have another good reason for using top-down testing. In this case, you can stub off all of the modules that the user isn't worried about, and test the ones he is worried about. If, for example, he's worried about the format of a printed report, you can code the print modules early in your development sequence. Then, you can show the user a sample of the output he will be getting and get reactions to it early in the development of the program. As always, the earlier you discover problems in specification or design, the better off you are.

In summary, then, there are many reasons for using top-down testing. So the real question is this: When is a program long enough to justify the use of top-down testing?

As a guideline here, our basic rule is this: If a program takes longer than a day to develop, it's worth using top-down testing when you develop it. That way, you'll produce a measurable amount of tested code each day. And you'll improve your productivity and your program's quality as you code and test the program.

How to decide on the coding sequence when using top-down testing

As you may have realized by now, you can develop the modules in a program in many different sequences when you use top-down coding and testing. If there are no outside influences, your goal should be to use the sequence that will be most efficient in terms of coding and testing. When you develop your test plan, then, you should ask questions like: Where are the major module interfaces in the program? Where, if anywhere, in the structure chart do I have doubts about the design? In what modules do I have doubts about how the coding should be done? Once again, you should attempt to detect the major errors first.

If you have no particular concerns about your program or module designs, you have great flexibility as to your development sequence. After you test the first two or three levels, it becomes a case of mop up. Eventually, you have to code and test all of the modules, so you may as well take them one leg at a time, introducing data that applies to each leg as you go along.

To illustrate another sequence for developing the modules of the edit program, look at the test plan in figure 10-11. In contrast to the one in figure 10-6, the programmer planned this coding sequence with his own efficiency in mind. In the first phase, he codes the top-level module and some of the trivial formatting and printing modules. He knows when he tests these modules that only the summary page should print with zeros in the total areas. But he also knows that he can spend most of his time in this phase developing the code in the first three divisions of the program. So it's all right if the coding in the Procedure Division is trivial.

Then, in the second testing phase, he can concentrate on the coding that will load the part-number file, print invalid transaction records, and write valid transaction records on the output file. Note that the modules that do the actual editing aren't going to be tested, but the one transaction with the invalid transaction code should be listed by the program and the two valid transactions should be written on the output file. This coding should go quite easily, because the programmer coded most of the entries in the first three divisions of the program during the first phase of coding and testing. As a result, there will be no doubt about the names to use in the Procedure Division statements.

Finally, in phase 3, the programmer adds the modules that actually edit the fields in the two types of transaction records. These, of course, are the most difficult modules of the program. But now that most of the trivial modules have already been developed, this coding and testing should proceed quite easily too.

Is the sequence of testing in figure 10-11 better than the one in figure 10-6? Not necessarily. I only present it to show you that there is more than one way to code and test the modules of a program from the top down. In the test plan in figure 10-6, the programmer decided to test the most difficult modules first and the trivial modules last; in the test plan in figure 10-11, the programmer took the opposite approach. As I see it, both plans are acceptable, so the approach you take will often depend on your own working style.

Incidentally, in case it isn't obvious, you have considerable flexibility when it comes to coding the first three divisions of a program on a top-down basis. Normally, you will code the entries in the Identification Division when you code the modules for the first phase of testing. But you don't have to code the entries in the Environment and Data Divisions until they are needed by the modules in the Procedure Division. For instance, you don't have to code the Data Division entries for the part-number table in the edit program until you code the modules that load the table. Similarly, you don't have to code the SELECT statement, FD statement, or record description for the part-number file until you code an I/O statement for the file.

Since you normally issue OPEN and CLOSE statements for all files in the top-level module of a program though, it is common to code the entries for all files and records in the first phase of testing, even if you don't operate on them in this phase. Otherwise, you have to omit them

Program: INV2100 EDIT INVENTORY TRANSACTIONS		Page: 1
Designer: Anne Prince		Date: 08-18-84
Test phase	Data	Data source
1. Modules 000, 100, 380, 390, and 500	None	Not applicable
2. Add modules 200, 210, 300, 310, 320, 360, 370, and 400	Three part-number records; two valid transaction records: one with each transaction code, and one with the first part number in the table and one with the last; one invalid transaction due to an invalid transaction code	Self
3. Add modules 330, 340, and 350	Same data as in phase 2	
4. Invalid transactions	Invalid transactions that will test all possible causes of invalid fields	Self
5. Contingencies	Mixed data from steps 2 and 4; any new records that might cause contingent errors	Self
6. Page overflow and maximum table size	As many part-number records as the program is supposed to provide for; 150 transactions with enough invalid transactions to cause page overflow	Test data generator

Figure 10-11 Another test plan for the edit program using top-down testing with the emphasis on coding efficiency

from your OPEN and CLOSE statements in module 000 until a later phase of testing. But this too is up to the individual programmer.

Discussion

As I have said, the primary benefits of top-down testing are improved productivity, improved program quality (reliability), and improved programmer morale. As the size of a program increases, these benefits take on more and more significance. As a manager, then, I would insist that top-down testing be used for all non-trivial programs. As a programmer, I would make top-down testing a way of life. It is simply a more enjoyable way to develop programs.

In our COBOL survey, though, only 20 percent of the shops said they used top-down testing for all programs. Another 30 percent said they used it "often." And about half of the shops said they didn't use it very much. So for those shops that don't use it frequently, top-down testing is another structured programming technique that can have a significant impact on the effectiveness of your development efforts.

Terminology

top-down coding and testing
top-down testing
program stub
dummy module
input stub
processing stub
output stub

Objectives

1. Given a program's specifications, design, and module plans (if any), create an effective top-down test plan for it.

2. Given a program's specifications, design, and test plan, code acceptable program stubs for any phase of the test plan.

Chapter 11

How to document a structured program

I don't think anyone likes to put together program documentation. It's tedious and time-consuming. So the more your documentation results from the program development process, the happier you'll be. And the more productive you'll be.

In addition, we recommend that your program documentation consist of only the essentials. All too often in the past, documentation binders bulged with items that no one ever used. Perhaps the most extreme example of this was the use of program flowcharts as required documentation in the GOTO era of programming. When Paul worked at Pacific Telephone, for example, they kept stacks of flowcharts as program documentation. But when Paul locked the files containing these documents for six months...and nobody asked for the key...it became apparent that no one ever used this documentation.

With this in mind, I'd like to present the primary components of effective program documentation. Then, I'll present some related ideas.

The primary components of program documentation

The primary pieces of your program documentation should be the program specifications, the structure chart, and the program listing. In appendix A, for example, I've shown you the primary documentation for the edit program. Although we've documented programs for six years now using only these documents, we have never had a problem with program maintenance. So I can assure you these components alone are adequate for most shops.

As we see it, this method of documenting programs is the most productive one because all three items are by-products of the development methods. When you finish a program, you refine the program specifications and structure chart somewhat, put it together with the program listing, and you're done. The result: useful documentation in a minimum of time.

Some related ideas

If we agree that these are the primary components of program documentation, there are still some questions to be answered. What other components are acceptable? How should program documentation be filed? And so on. At this time, then, I'd like to present some ideas related to the task of program documentation. Perhaps you will find some of them useful.

Other components of program documentation Traditionally, it has been tempting to include other items as part of the documentation for a program. For instance, some companies have kept listings of the procedures, test data, and output data used for each of the test runs for a program. Then, if a bug was detected later on, you could use the test run data to decide whether the program had been adequately tested before it was put into production. Although this documentation is easy enough to develop since it results from the testing phase of programming, I think it's unnecessary for the typical COBOL shop. What we want to do is reduce the likelihood of programming error, not assign blame for errors.

On the other hand, it's often useful to keep a copy of sample reports generated by a program as part of the program documentation. In contrast to the related print charts, they are always accurate since they are prepared by the system. In addition, every shop should have a file of reports in report-number sequence as part of its system documentation. So a sample report (or a copy of a page from one of the early production runs) should find its way into this file.

In some shops, the programmer may be required to prepare a user's guide for each program he writes. This guide is supposed to give any critical operating information to the intended user of the program. For a batch program, the user is normally the operations group. So in some cases, the user's guide isn't necessary. For an interactive program, though, the user's guide may be important.

In any event, COBOL shops vary substantially in terms of what program documentation is to include and who is to prepare it. For instance, user's guides for interactive programs are prepared in the system department in some companies. The best advice, then, is to find out what's required in your shop and to follow these standards.

When to use a structure listing instead of a structure chart for program documentation In chapter 3, I showed you a *structure listing* for the edit program. I'm repeating this listing in figure 11-1. In our shop, we use a structure listing instead of a structure chart as one of the primary items of program documentation. The structure listing is prepared by a program we call LISTMODS that uses the COBOL source program as input. In other words, the structure listing is prepared as an automatic by-product of the coding process. After a program has been completely tested, the programmer runs LISTMODS to create the structure listing for final documentation.

There are several benefits to using a structure listing:

1. You can be sure the structure listing shows all of the modules used in a program. In contrast, because structure charts are prepared manually, you can't be sure they're up-to-date. Too often, a programmer changes the program, but doesn't change the structure chart. This can happen during program development or program maintenance.

2. The structure listing can be prepared by the system in a fraction of the time it takes to create or modify a manually-prepared chart.

3. The structure listing shows many more modules on a single page than can be done using a structure chart. As a result, the structure of most programs can be listed on just a page or two. This makes it easier for the programmer to review the structure of a program.

As you can see, then, it's probably worth your time to convert from structure charts to structure listings as one component of final documentation. Although the listings may be a little more difficult to read than the charts, the benefits should more than offset this difficulty.

The question, then, is when to switch from structure charts to structure listings. If you've been using structured programming for several years, my recommendation is to switch as soon as possible. Using structure listings will improve your productivity with no loss in program quality. On the other hand, if you're just starting to experiment with structured programming, I think you should wait until you feel comfortable with the new methods. Once you're starting to produce programs so efficiently that refining structure charts becomes a frustration for you, you're ready for structure listings. In our shop, it only took us about three months before we felt a need for a better way to document the structure of a program.

If you don't have a structure listing program like LISTMODS, you can write one in about a week using the methods presented in this book. Otherwise, you can buy one from us for a modest price. Since ours is written in structured COBOL, you can easily modify it to run on your system. And if you're using an IBM mainframe, we can supply a version that you won't have to modify at all.

```
*
 000-EDIT-INVENTORY-TRANS
*
      100-FORMAT-REPORT-HEADING
     *
           'SYSDATE'
           'SYSTIME'
     *
      200-LOAD-PART-NUMBER-TABLE
     *
           210-READ-PART-NUMBER-RECORD
     *
      300-EDIT-INVENTORY-TRAN
     *
           310-READ-INVENTORY-TRAN
           320-EDIT-TRANSACTION-FIELDS
          *
                330-EDIT-CODE-1-FIELDS
               *
                     'DATEDIT'                          C
                     340-SEARCH-PART-NUMBER-TABLE       C
               *
                350-EDIT-CODE-2-FIELDS
               *
                     'DATEDIT'                          C
                     340-SEARCH-PART-NUMBER-TABLE       C
               *
          *
           360-PRINT-INVALID-TRANSACTION
          *
                370-PRINT-HEADING-LINES
               *
                     380-WRITE-PAGE-TOP-LINE            C
                     390-WRITE-REPORT-LINE              C
               *
                390-WRITE-REPORT-LINE              C
          *
           400-WRITE-VALID-TRANSACTION
     *
      500-PRINT-TOTAL-PAGE
     *
           380-WRITE-PAGE-TOP-LINE            C
           390-WRITE-REPORT-LINE              C
     *
*

C = COMMON MODULE
```

Figure 11-1 A structure listing for the edit program generated from the COBOL code

How to store program documentation Once you decide what items you're going to include in your program documentation, the next question is how to store these items. Traditionally, all of the documentation for one program has been kept in a single folder or binder of some sort. In fact, you can buy elaborate binders that will help you keep all of the documentation for one program together. Unfortunately, when the documentation system is elaborate, keeping it in order can become a major task in itself. That's why you may want to consider some alternatives as you convert to new development methods.

In our shop, we experimented with several different ways of storing program documentation. Now, we keep the program specifications for all programs in 3-ring binders that are meant for 8-1/2 x 11-inch papers. We don't keep the specifications for each program in a single binder; we keep the program specifications for all of the programs in a single system or subsystem in a single binder. For instance, the program specifications for all of the programs in our order-handling system are kept in one binder. Since the program specifications are the link between the systems documentation and the program documentation, the specification binders can be used when you are making a modification to a system or to a single program. Within each specification binder, programs are kept in sequence by program number.

To store the structure charts (or structure listings) and program listings, we use 11 x 14-inch data binders. Again, we use one binder for all of the programs in a system or subsystem, and we keep the programs in sequence by program number.

Using this system, it's easy to find the program specifications, structure chart, and program listing—the primary items of documentation—for any one program. In the past, we sometimes kept the structure charts in the binder with the program specifications, but this seemed to separate two pieces of documentation that naturally go together since the structure chart is the guide to the program listing.

Since structure charts are normally made on paper that isn't meant for data binders, we taped our structure charts on continuous-form paper so they could be filed in the data binders with the program listings. But now that we use structure listings that are printed on the same paper as the program listings, it's easier to file the structure listings with the program listings.

Perhaps you're saying that we can document programs this way because our programs are simpler than yours or because we run a smaller shop than yours. If so, I won't argue with you; large shops often have different requirements than small shops. But in our experience with program maintenance, the only documentation you can be sure of is documentation that is generated by the source code itself. Anything else, including the program specifications, may have been changed by a member of the maintenance staff who didn't bother to update the related documentation. Programmers seem to know this, because once they figure out which programs need to be changed by analyzing the systems documentation, they make the program modifications using only the structure charts (or listings) and the program listings. So in our shop, these are stored in the same binder.

Quite frankly, it takes time to put a modified program listing in a data binder that contains several hundred pages of listings. So our method of storing listings isn't perfect. As a result, you may want to continue to use a separate binder for each program's documentation. On the other hand, programmers shouldn't file program listings and structure charts in documentation binders; clerical workers should.

How do you file other items of program documentation? Or, more specifically, what do you do with all of the other items you created or collected during the development of your program? If you think they might be useful sometime in the future (or you just hate to throw them away), file all the remaining items in a single 8-1/2 x 11-inch manilla folder for the program. Then, file this extra documentation in a standard file cabinet in sequence by program number (or by program number within subsystem). Although you probably won't ever use this documentation, you'll be sure that you didn't throw away something that was useful. Then, when your file cabinets are completely filled, you can clean them out by throwing out the folders that haven't been used.

I hope you realize that these aren't supposed to be formal recommendations. I'm simply trying to give you ideas. Perhaps the way you're storing documentation is inefficient right now, so it's worth considering some simple changes.

How your system documentation should relate to your program documentation In chapter 3, I said that one of the critical factors you can't control when it comes to programming effectiveness is the systems methods of your shop. This is often quite obvious when you review all of the documentation for a system: both the systems documentation and the program documentation. In my experience, in fact, the program documentation is usually in better shape than the systems documentation. At the least, you can usually get a current copy of the source code for a program by recompiling the source program stored on the system. But the systems documentation may be hopelessly out-of-date. And, often, it's not that good to start with.

In chapter 20, I'll give you some ideas on how to design systems that are easier to develop and maintain. For now, though, let me just try to show you how systems documentation should relate to program documentation. Quite simply, one of the items of systems documentation should be an index to the programs of the system. In other words, this document should (1) identify all of the programs of the system by name, (2) identify the functions of all of the programs of the system, and (3) show the relationships between the programs of the system. In our method, we use a *system structure chart* to do this just as we use a *program structure chart* as an index to the modules (paragraphs) of each program.

Figure 11-2 shows the relationships between the system structure chart, the program structure chart, and the paragraphs of a program. So when a maintenance programmer is assigned a maintenance job, he can identify the program or programs that need to be modified by using the system structure chart and the related system documentation. Then, using the program numbers of the system structure chart, he can find the related program documentation. Finally, using a program structure chart, he can identify the modules that have to be changed in a program, and

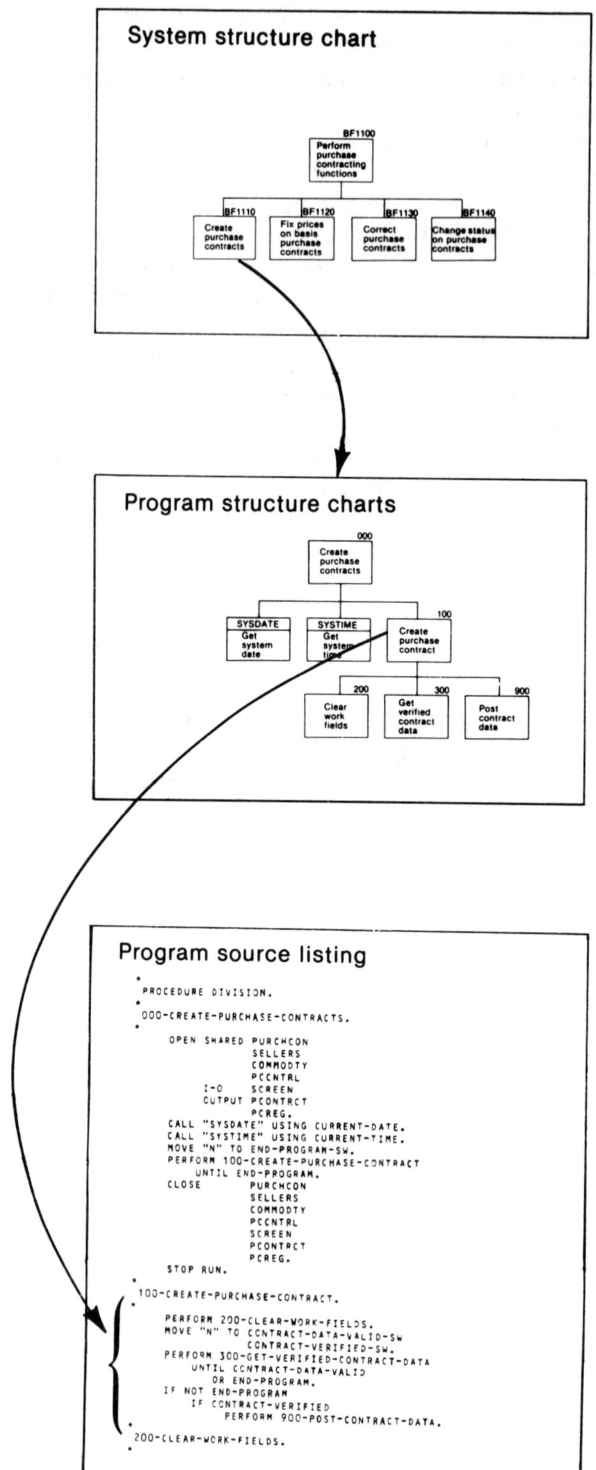

Figure 11-2 The relationships between the system documentation and the program documentation

using these module numbers, he can find the related paragraphs in the source code. In other words, the final documentation is a complete directory to every module of source code in the system.

I hope your system documentation relates to your program documentation in this way so you too have a directory to every module of source code in your system. But I've rarely seen this done in other shops. Often, in fact, because the systems documentation is so poor, one of the major jobs of the maintenance programmer is figuring out what programs need to be modified.

Summary

I hope this has given you some ideas for improving the documentation in your shop. As we see it, if you cut down on the amount of documentation you keep on the theory that most of it won't be used, you'll start to improve your program documentation. Then, if you rely more on machine-created documents and less on manually-prepared documents, you will improve your documentation some more. Finally, if you make sure your systems documentation provides a directory to your program documentation, you will ease your maintenance burden.

Terminology

structure listing
system structure chart
program structure chart

Objectives

1. List the three primary components of program documentation.

2. Explain how system documentation should relate to program documentation.

Section 3

Interactive COBOL considerations

This section shows you how to apply the procedures and techniques of section 2 to interactive programs. Although different computer systems and COBOL compilers force you to develop interactive programs in different ways, this section tries to show you how to develop interactive programs for any system or compiler.

To start, chapter 12 gives some general information that applies to the development of all interactive programs. Next, chapter 13 shows you specific techniques for developing interactive programs using internally-defined screens and COBOL extensions. Then, chapter 14 shows you specific techniques for developing interactive programs when you use CICS on an IBM mainframe; in this case, you don't use COBOL extensions for screen-handling.

Although you should read chapter 12 no matter what kind of compiler you use, you should only read chapter 13 or 14 if it applies to the type of system you're using. If, for example, you develop programs using CICS on an IBM mainframe, you need only read chapter 14. Similarly, if you develop programs using Microsoft COBOL on an IBM PC, you need only read chapter 13 because this version of COBOL uses interally-defined screens and COBOL extensions to support screen handling. On the other hand, if your system uses some combination of externally-defined screens and COBOL extensions, you should probably read both chapters 13 and 14 to get ideas on how you can develop programs using a combination of techniques.

Chapter 12

An introduction to program development for interactive programs

An interactive program is one that interacts with the user of the program by way of a computer terminal. The program displays messages, data, and questions on the screen of the terminal; the computer user sends commands, data, and responses back to the program by entering them on the keyboard of the terminal.

Before you can develop an interactive program in COBOL, you must know how your system and COBOL compiler provide for the interactive capabilities. On some systems, for example, the COBOL compiler itself provides statements that give your program the ability to send data to and receive data from a terminal. On other systems, one or more systems programs, not the COBOL compiler, give your program the ability to interact with a terminal. Since there is no standard way of providing for interactive capabilities, I'll present some common ways of providing this support in topic 1 of this chapter.

Then, in topic 2, I'll show you how developing an interactive program differs from developing a batch program. Although you do the same basic development tasks for either type of program, there are some differences that you should be aware of.

By the time you complete this chapter, you should be able to apply the development techniques of chapters 4 through 11 to any interactive program. Then, in chapters 13 and 14, you will learn how to apply these general techniques to interactive programs developed for specific systems.

Topic 1 An introduction to interactive COBOL

If you're familiar with COBOL standards, you know that there aren't any standards for interactive capabilities. And none are expected in the 198X ANSI standards for COBOL. As a result, you develop interactive programs differently from one type of system to the next.

Because interactive programs always operate on data received from one or more interactive *screens*, the code that relates to these interactive functions is often referred to as *screen-handling* code. Because this code is non-standard, you can say that interactive systems differ in the screen-handling code that they offer. For instance, the screen-handling code provided by Microsoft COBOL on the IBM PC differs from the code provided by VS COBOL on a Wang VS system. And IBM COBOL on an IBM mainframe doesn't even provide screen-handling code; on this system, you use a systems program called CICS to interact with a terminal.

Since differences in screen-handling code and screen-handling capabilities can affect the way in which you design an interactive program, I will first show you how different systems provide for interactive capabilities. Once you understand this, you will have a better idea of how the information in this part of this book applies to your system. For instance, chapter 13 applies to systems with COBOL compilers that provide screen-handling code for all interactive capabilities. And chapter 14 applies to IBM systems using CICS for interactive capabilities.

Although screen-handling capabilities can be provided in several different ways, I'm only going to present three ways in this topic. First, I'm going to show you how systems can provide for screen-handling using screens defined within the COBOL program. Second, I'm going to show you how systems can provide for screen-handling using screens defined outside the COBOL program. And third, I'm going to show you how CICS provides for screen-handling on an IBM mainframe.

Interactive COBOL using internal screen definitions

Most minicomputer and microcomputer systems today were intended for interactive use. In other words, they were designed to support users working at terminals. Accordingly, the COBOL compilers supplied for most small systems directly support screen handling. They do this by allowing the programmer to define a screen the program will use in the Data Division of the COBOL program. This can be referred to as an *internally-defined screen*, or an *internal screen*. Then, the program can send a screen to a terminal or receive data from a terminal using COBOL I/O statements in the Procedure Division of the program.

Figure 12-1 is a schematic illustration of a COBOL program with an internally-defined screen. It's schematic because the figure illustrates an executing COBOL program as source code. Obviously, though, it's not the source code, but the object code, that interacts with the operating system's facilities to do screen I/O. With this in mind, however, I hope this illustration will help you understand how a COBOL program on a system like this works.

A programmer who develops a program on a system like this codes all screens used by the program in the Data Division of the program. The screen description is written using COBOL extensions that allow the programmer to state where and how data is supposed to be sent to or received from a screen. In addition, the extensions allow the programmer to relate screen fields to work fields that are somewhere else in the Data Division. To pass data back and forth between the program and the terminal screen, the programmer codes Procedure Division statements that refer to the screen descriptions in the Data Division.

In a COBOL program like this, you can think of the terminal as a file open for input and output. Some systems actually treat the terminal as a file, and require that you define it as such (with a SELECT statement and an FD) and that you open and close it in the Procedure Division. Treating a terminal as a file, one COBOL compiler I've used allows the programmer to code READ and WRITE statements for a terminal operation. It's more common, however, to see extensions of DISPLAY and ACCEPT used for terminal operations in a compiler that uses internal screens.

If you haven't used an interactive compiler before, it's not difficult to learn the COBOL extensions that support screen handling. That's because they're logical developments of standard COBOL programming features. And once you write programs for one system like this, it's relatively easy to adapt your experiences to another one.

Interactive COBOL using external screen definitions

In contrast to a compiler that provides for internal screens, some COBOL compilers provide for the use of *externally-defined screens*, or *external screens*. This is schematically illustrated in figure 12-2. Here, the programmer creates one external definition, or *physical map*, for each screen used by a program. He does this using one of the other programs of the operating system, not the COBOL compiler.

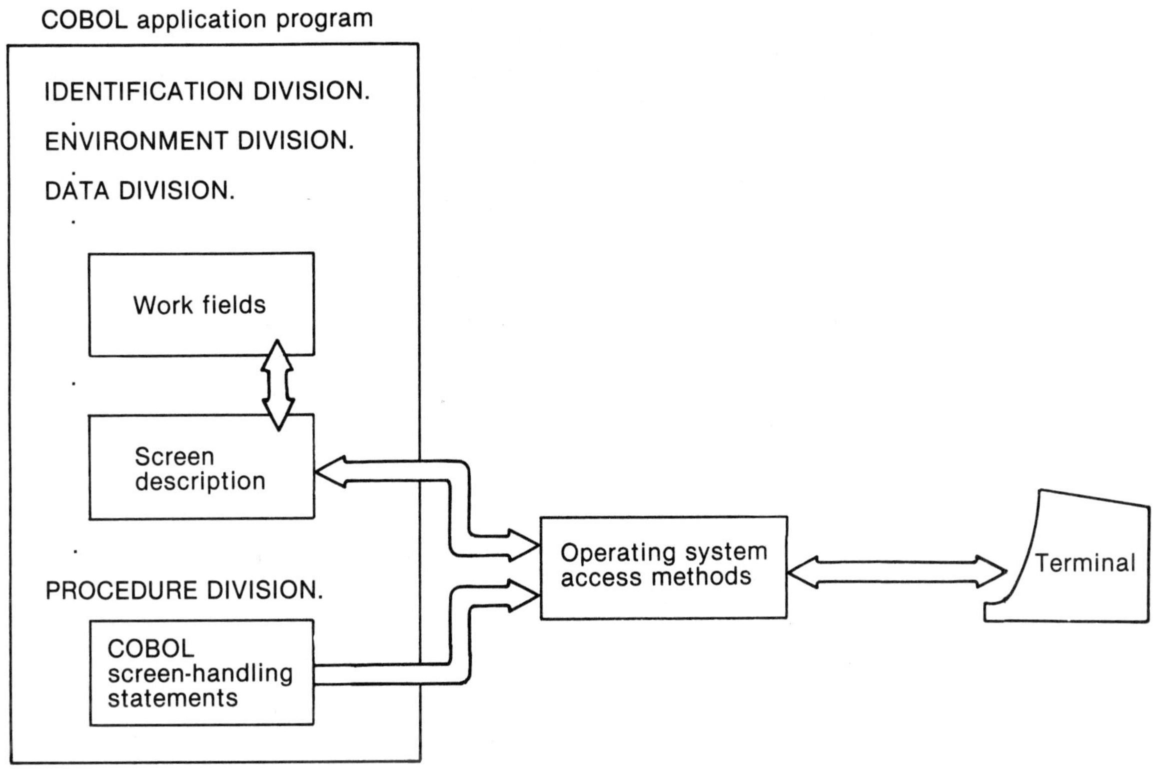

Figure 12-1 Schematic illustration of interactive COBOL with internal screen definition

To link the physical map to the COBOL program, the COBOL program contains a *symbolic map*. This map is usually created by the same program that created the physical map; then, it is copied into the COBOL program. Otherwise, the programmer creates the symbolic map that corresponds to the physical map.

To send data to or receive data from a terminal, the programmer uses an I/O statement in the Procedure Division that is an extension of standard COBOL. Depending on the compiler, this can be a READ or WRITE statement, or an ACCEPT or DISPLAY statement. When the I/O statement is executed, the access methods program of the operating system coordinates the physical map with the symbolic map. When an output statement is executed, the data stored in the symbolic map is sent to the terminal and displayed in the format specified by the physical map. When an input statement is executed, the data entered by the terminal operator in the format specified by the physical map is stored in the symbolic map.

To learn how to use a system like this, you don't have to learn much COBOL. Normally, there are just a few extensions that allow you to use the maps created outside of the COBOL program. However, you do have to learn how to create the physical and symbolic maps for each screen.

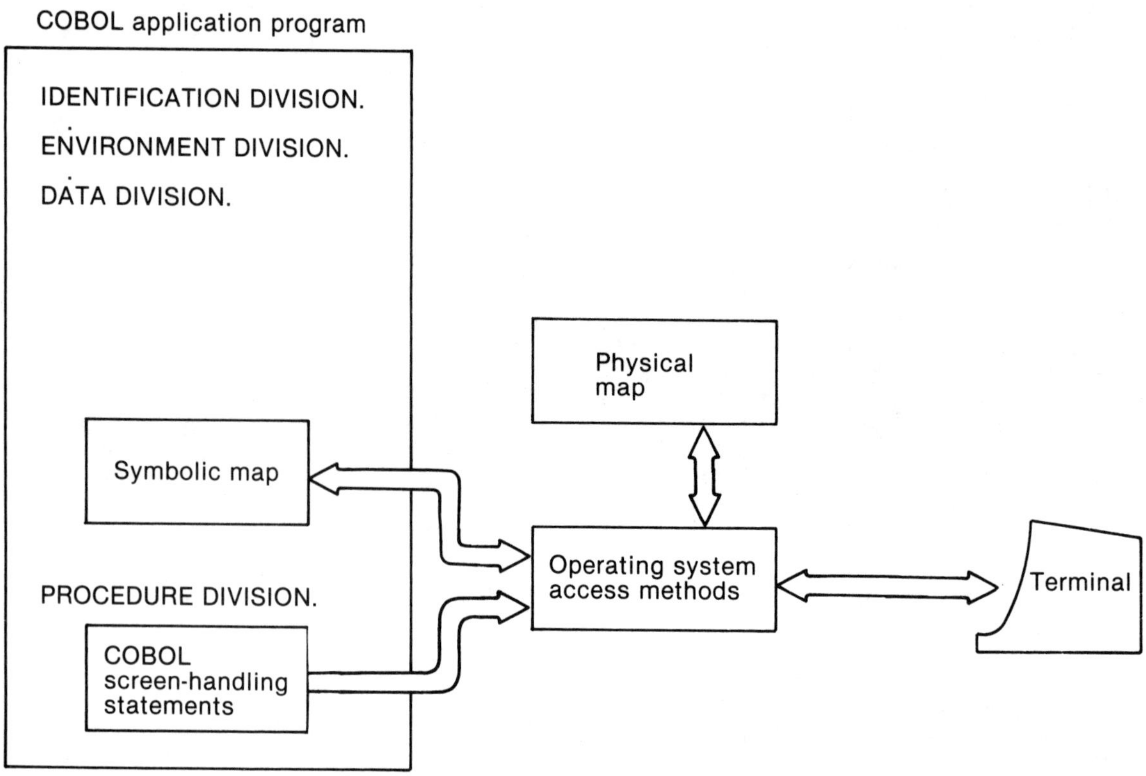

Figure 12-2 Schematic illustration of interactive COBOL with external screen definition

Interactive COBOL using CICS on an IBM mainframe

Most contemporary minicomputer and microcomputer systems (and their COBOL compilers) were designed to support sophisticated screen handling. In contrast, an IBM mainframe is a direct descendant of the batch-oriented systems of the mid-1960s. As a result, an interactive program on an IBM mainframe typically executes in an environment that is fundamentally a batch environment.

Most interactive programs that run on IBM mainframes today do so through IBM's *CICS (Customer Information Control System)*. In this case, the interactive COBOL program executes within and under the control of CICS. Each screen is defined to CICS, and the program requests CICS services to perform both screen and file input and output.

To understand better how CICS works, look at figure 12-3. As you can see, the COBOL program executes within CICS. (Although CICS can support many COBOL programs at once, figure 12-3 shows only one.) Then, to do screen-handling operations, the COBOL program doesn't issue screen-handling statements directly. Instead, it issues CICS commands that cause CICS to do the screen-handling operations.

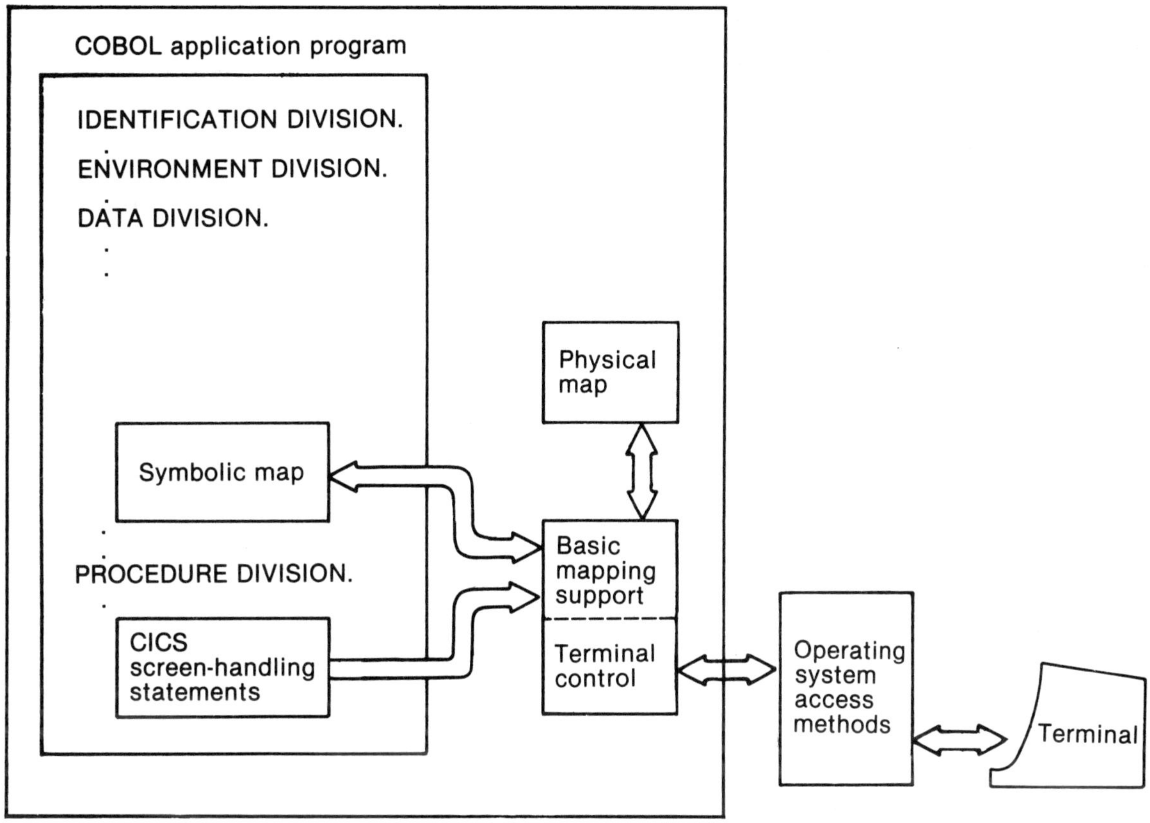

Figure 12-3 Schematic illustration of interactive COBOL with external screen handling under CICS

CICS is initiated like any other batch job and runs in one of a system's regions or partitions. During operation, it serves as an interface between the batch-oriented operating system and the interactive application programs. Running in a single partition, CICS can support hundreds of terminals simultaneously through a process called *multitasking*.

When you use CICS, it performs some of the functions you'd expect to code in COBOL. Consequently, a programmer who develops a COBOL program that will execute under CICS writes a source program that's a combination of COBOL statements and CICS commands. The result is a source program that has a different look than an IBM batch COBOL program and a different look than an interactive program written for a COBOL compiler that directly supports screen-handling.

When you use CICS, you use external screen definitions. As you can see in figure 12-3, each screen requires a physical map and a symbolic map. In contrast to the physical map, the symbolic map within the COBOL program is not a complete screen definition; it only defines the variable fields that are used in the screen. To cause a screen to be displayed, the COBOL program must request the CICS services that coordinate the physical and symbolic map definitions.

As more and more terminals are added to a CICS system, performance becomes more and more of a problem. In a large shop, this usually means that object-program efficiency is a critical consideration for CICS programmers. In fact, it's so important that it usually forces you to use a programming technique called *pseudo-conversational programming*. You'll see this illustrated in chapter 14.

Discussion

If you work on an IBM mainframe system, the odds are that you'll be working with CICS. If you work in a shop that uses a minicomputer or microcomputer system, you'll probably write your interactive COBOL programs for a compiler that uses internal screens. Otherwise, you're likely to use some combination of external screens and COBOL extensions.

Fortunately, you develop an interactive program using similar techniques no matter how your system supports interactive capabilities. In the next topic, then, I'll present general techniques for developing interactive COBOL programs. These will be of use to you no matter what system you're working on.

Once you understand these general techniques for developing interactive programs, I'll show you some specific techniques. Chapter 13 shows you specific design and coding techniques for developing programs on a system that provides screen handling using internal screens and COBOL extensions. And chapter 14 shows you specific design and coding techniques for developing programs using external screens on a CICS system. If you work on a system that uses some combination of external screens and COBOL extensions, you may have to read both chapters 13 and 14 to develop a hybrid development method that will be effective for your system.

Terminology

screen
screen handling
internally-defined screen
internal screen
externally-defined screen
external screen
physical map
symbolic map
CICS
Customer Information Control System
multitasking
pseudo-conversational programming

Objective

Describe the differences between systems that support interactive capabilities (1) by using internal screens and COBOL extensions, (2) by using external screens and COBOL extensions, and (3) by using CICS.

Topic 2 How to develop an interactive program

When you develop an interactive program, you do the same tasks that you do when you develop a batch program. So the development procedure I presented in figure 4-1 applies to interactive programs as well as to batch programs. And everything I presented in chapters 4 through 11 applies to interactive programs.

On the other hand, how you do a task varies somewhat depending on whether you are developing a batch or an interactive program. So in this topic, I will go through each of the nine tasks I presented in chapter 4 and relate them to interactive programming. Although how you do some of these tasks will vary depending on how your system supports interactive programming, the material in this topic applies in general to any interactive system.

Task 1: Get complete program specifications

The specifications for a batch COBOL program and an interactive program have much in common: program overviews, COPY members for record layouts, print charts, and so forth. In addition to these components, however, the specifications for an interactive program should include screen layouts. And if the flow from one screen to another in the program is complicated, the specifications should include a screen flow diagram.

Figure 12-4 shows a program overview for a typical interactive program. This program accepts wholesale order transactions from the entry operator and processes them. As you can see, the overview refers to the screen layouts that are part of the specification. If the program specifications had included a screen flow diagram, the overview might also refer to it.

As a programmer, your job is to make sure that you get complete specifications before you start to implement your program. If they're not given to you, this may mean that you have to develop the missing information. In practice, this often means that you have to develop your own screen layouts and your own screen flow diagrams. So I'd like to show you how to develop these items right now.

Program: ORD1100 PROCESS WHOLESALE ORDERS	Page: 1
Designer: Mike Murach	Date: 08-17-84

Input/output specifications

File	Description	Use
CUSTMAST	Customer master file	Input
INVMAST	Inventory master file	I-O
OPENITEM	Open item file	I-O
INVTRAN	Wholesale invoice transaction file	Output
INVREG	Print file: Wholesale invoice register	Output

Process specifications

Accept wholesale orders from the terminal user using the ORDER-ENTRY screen. As part of the editing routine, look up the customer number in the customer master file and each item number in the inventory master file. For a valid order, all related master records must be found.

Whenever an order has passed the editing routines, let the operator visually verify the order via the ORDER-VERIFICATION screen. If the operator accepts the order, process it.

To process an order:

1. Prepare an invoice record that can be used to print an invoice later on. Write this record on INVTRAN.
2. Update the related inventory records in INVMAST.
3. Add the invoice record to the open-item file, OPENITEM.
4. Prepare the appropriate lines for the invoice register and write them on INVREG.

If the operator presses the PF16 key when the ORDER-ENTRY screen is active, end the program.

Figure 12-4 A program overview for an interactive program

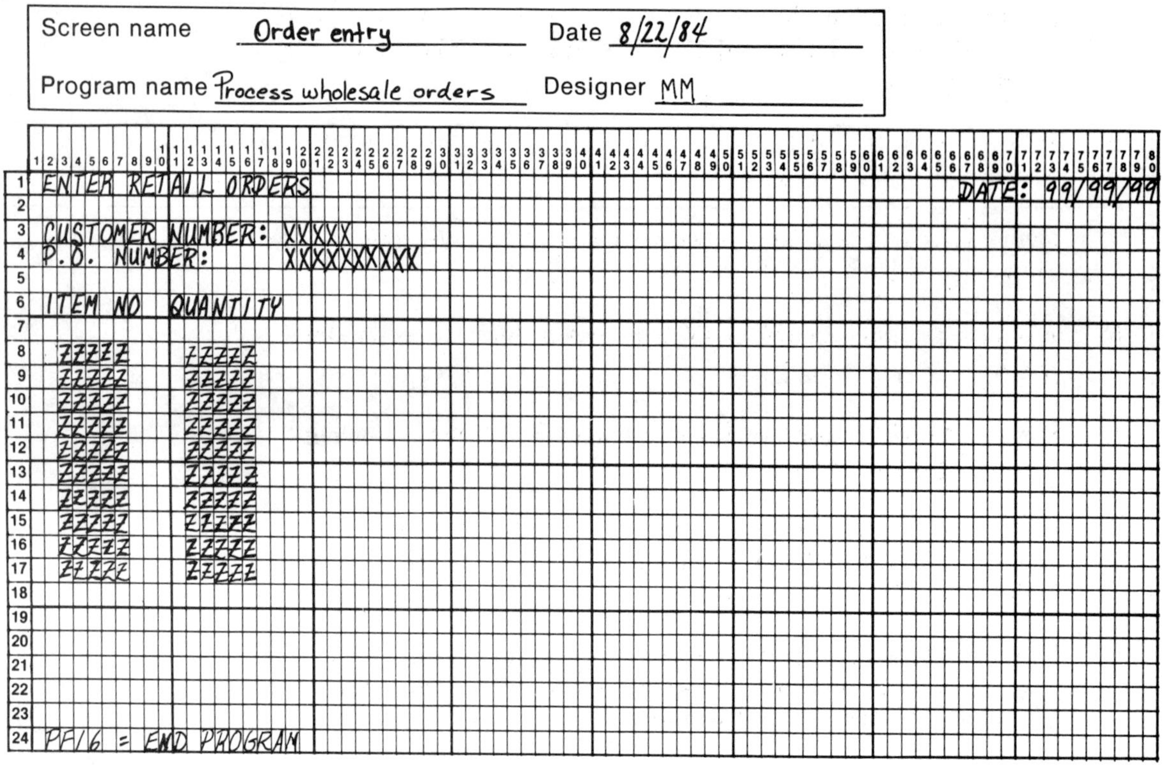

Figure 12-5 A screen layout form for an order-entry screen

How to create screen layouts Figure 12-5 shows a *screen layout* for the order-entry screen referred to by the program overview in figure 12-4. As you can see, it simply shows where constant and variable data will appear on a screen. As a result, it is similar to a print chart.

If you have to design a screen layout, you should try to design each screen in a standard way. If you do this, two benefits will result. First, the terminal users will find that the interactive programs are easier to use. Second, it will be easier to create and maintain the programs that display and accept the screens.

With this in mind, here are some ideas for preparing screen layouts:

1. Divide your screens into three zones: the heading zone, the data zone, and the communication zone. The *heading zone* (usually, lines 1 and 2 of a screen) should be used to display information like the program name, the date, and the screen number. As much as possible, this should follow a standard format. The *data zone* should display all data relevant to the program. And, the *communication zone* (usually, lines 23 and 24 of a screen) should be used to display error messages and operator instructions.

2. As much as possible, the screens should be self-explanatory. In other words, the user shouldn't require an extensive user manual in order to use a program.

3. Whenever possible, data elements should be aligned vertically to make them easier to read.

4. Data elements should be grouped logically to make the screen easier to understand.

5. A screen shouldn't be unnecessarily crowded. Instead, use multiple screens.

6. If you use highlighting, use it consistently within the program and from one program to another.

7. Indicate errors in a useful and consistent way. At the least, an error message for a user entry should identify the field in error and indicate what's wrong with it.

8. If an operator uses a special source document for making entries to a program (that is, a *dedicated source document*), the screen should be patterned after the source document.

9. When an entry program doesn't have a dedicated source document, you should try to pattern the screen after a related output document or a primary input document.

These ideas are taken from our book on systems design, *How to Design and Develop Business Systems* by Steve Eckols. So if you would like to get more information on screen design, we refer you to Steve's book.

Figure 12-6 shows a screen layout for another interactive program. The heading zone of this screen is just line 1; it displays the program function and the date. The communication zone is lines 23 and 24 of the screen with line 23 used for error messages and line 24 used for standard operator instructions. If you review this screen layout and the one in figure 12-5, you can see that they follow the guidelines for screen layout that I just gave you.

How to develop screen flow diagrams *Screen flow* refers to the sequence in which a program will move from one screen of a program to another. A *screen flow diagram* shows the screen flow of a program along with the conditions that affect screen flow during the execution of a program.

To illustrate, figure 12-7 shows a screen flow diagram for a simple interactive program that uses only one interactive screen. As you can see, the operator enters a transaction into the entry screen after which the program edits the fields in the transaction. If one or more fields is invalid,

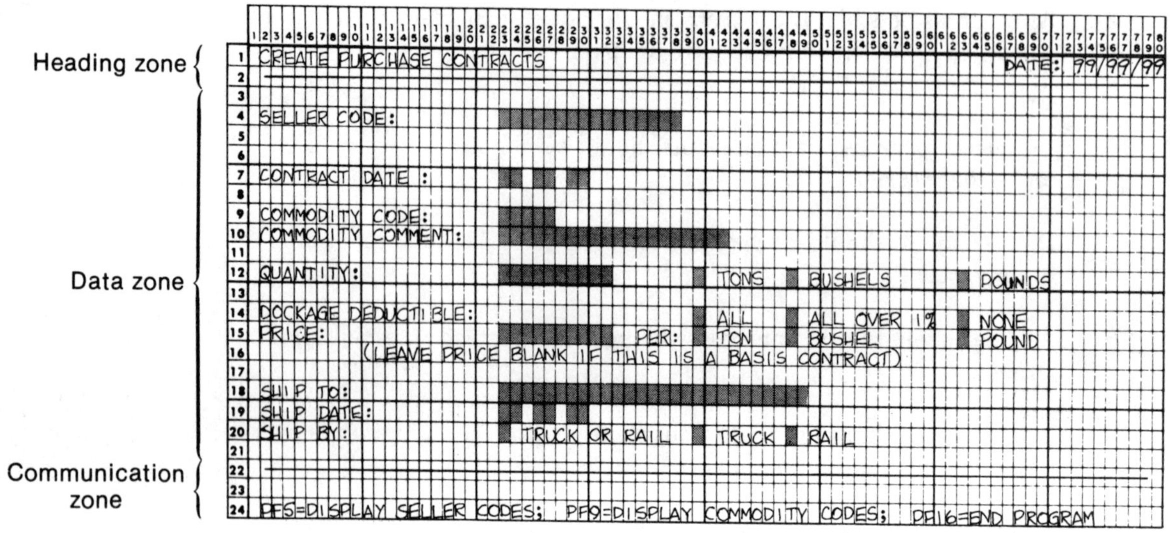

Figure 12-6 A screen layout designed for consistency and readability

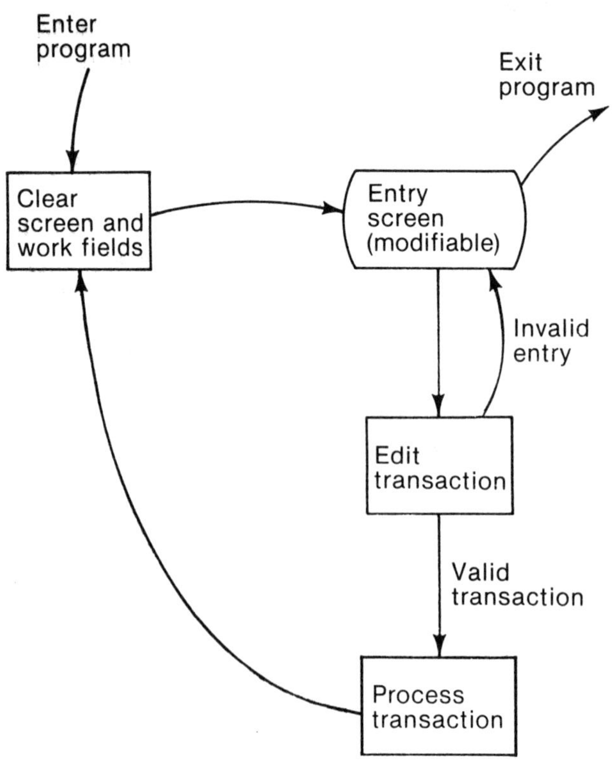

Figure 12-7 A screen flow diagram for a single entry-screen program

the program returns to the entry screen with an appropriate message displayed in the communication area of the screen. If the transaction is valid, the program processes it after which it clears the screen and work fields for the next transaction. Then, the program sends a fresh entry screen to the operator. To relate the screen flow diagram to the screen layout forms, you should use the same screen names in the diagram that you use on the forms.

For a simple program like the one in figure 12-7, you don't really need a screen flow diagram. In fact, you don't normally show the edit box on a screen flow diagram because you assume that all interactive programs edit all the entries for a transaction and return to the entry screen if one or more is invalid. When a program requires two or more screens, though, a screen flow diagram can help you understand the program. And it can help you design the program as you'll see in a moment. As a general rule, then, you should prepare a screen flow diagram for any program in which the screen flow isn't obvious.

Although one-screen programs are common, there is a problem with them. In brief, they don't give the entry operators a chance to *sight-verify* the data they have entered. As a result, the accuracy of the data depends entirely on how good the editing routines for the entries are. But this usually means that some invalid data will be accepted by the system. It also means that an operator can be frustrated when he releases an incorrect transaction by accident, it is accepted as valid by the editing routines, and he can't get it back to correct it. This is a particular problem when the data is entered by non-technical personnel in the user department rather than by trained data-entry operators.

Whenever possible, then, a program should give the operators a chance to sight-verify the data they have entered. In general, this requires one *verification screen* for each *entry screen* used by a program. In figure 12-8, for example, you can see the entry and verification screens used by an order-entry program. In the top portion of this figure, you can see the entry screen that lets the operator enter customer number, purchase order number, and the item numbers and quantities for each of the items ordered by a customer. As you can imagine, it's possible for these entries to pass the editing routines of a program and still be incorrect.

But in the bottom portion of this figure, you can see a verification screen for these entries. Before displaying this screen, the program looks up the related records and gets the data needed to expand the entries of the operator. As a result, the operator can see more completely the effect of the entries he has made. By sight verifying this data, the operator can make sure the data is correct. Then, when he indicates that the data is acceptable, the transaction is processed.

When you write an interactive program that provides for sight verification of the entries for a single screen, the screen flow will be something like that shown in figure 12-9. Like most screen flow diagrams, this one doesn't show when the editing will take place, because it's assumed that editing will be done for each screen used by a program, both entry screens and verification screens. Then, if an editing routine

Layout of entry screen

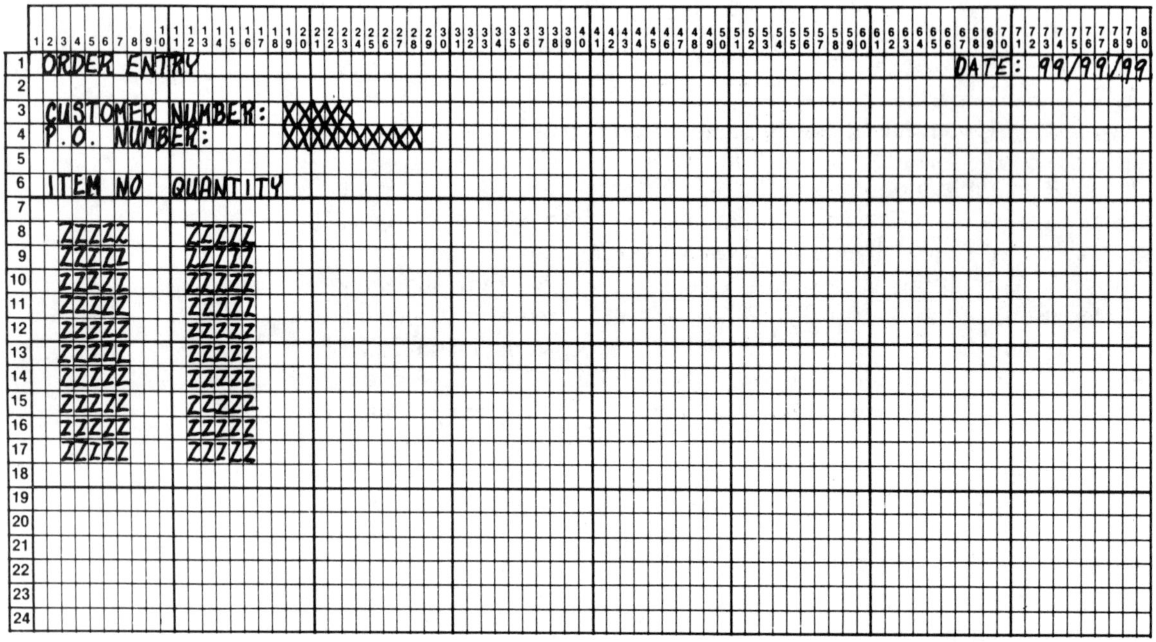

Layout of verification screen

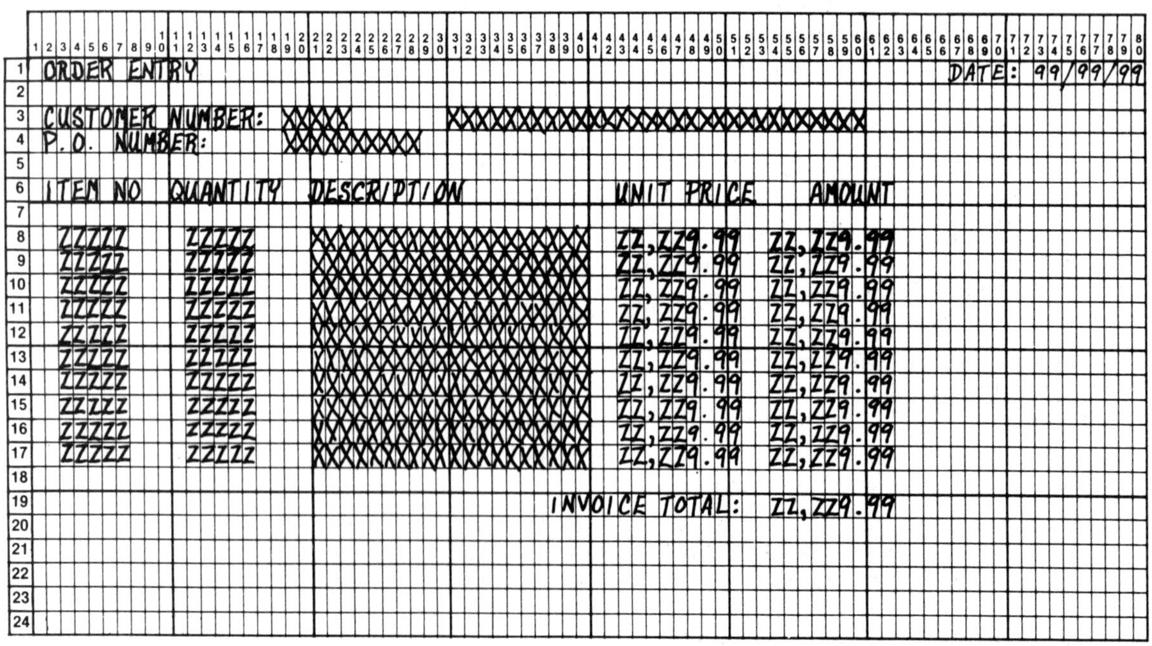

Figure 12-8 Screen layouts for the entry and verification screens of an order-entry program

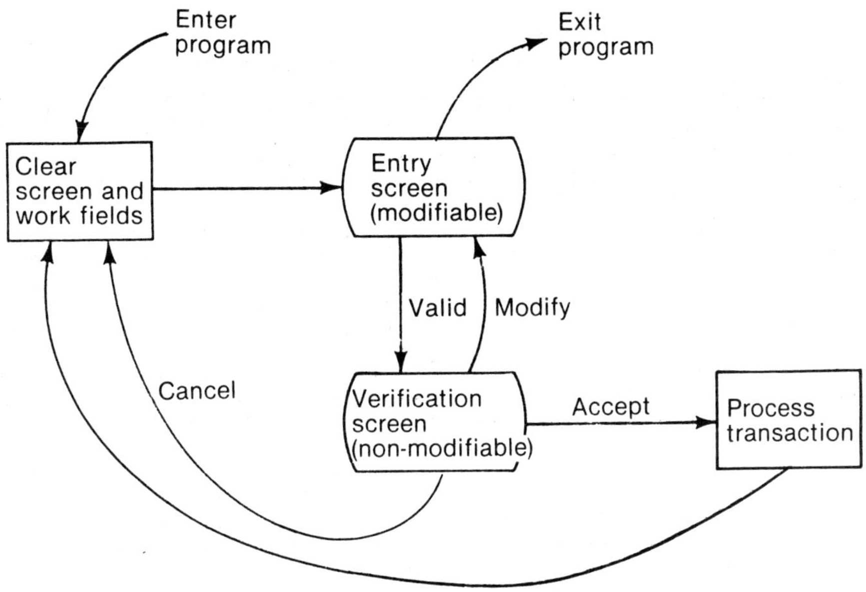

Figure 12-9 A screen flow diagram for a single entry-screen program with verification

detects errors, the program returns the operator to the entry screen or verification screen with an appropriate error message.

If you study the screen flow diagram in figure 12-9, you can see that the program displays a verification screen after the editing routines have validated the data for an entry screen. Then, when an operator makes an entry on the verification screen, the editing routines check to make sure that it's valid. For this diagram, the entry must indicate that the operator accepts, cancels, or wants to modify the current transaction.

If the entry for the verification screen is valid, the program proceeds based upon the entry. If the operator accepts the transaction, the program processes it. If the operator wants to modify the transaction, the program lets him modify the data by returning him to the entry screen. If the operator cancels the transaction, the program clears the screen and work fields and returns the operator to the entry screen so he can start over.

If you write a program with more than one entry screen and you want to allow for sight verification by the operator, you must provide one verification screen for each entry screen. In addition, if you want to give the operator a chance to go back to an earlier screen after entering the data in all of the screens, you must provide a final verification screen. This is illustrated by the screen flow diagram in figure 12-10, which provides for three entry screens. If the operator decides on the final verification screen that he wants to modify something he entered, the program returns to the first entry screen so the operator can review his entries from the start and correct whatever needs to be corrected.

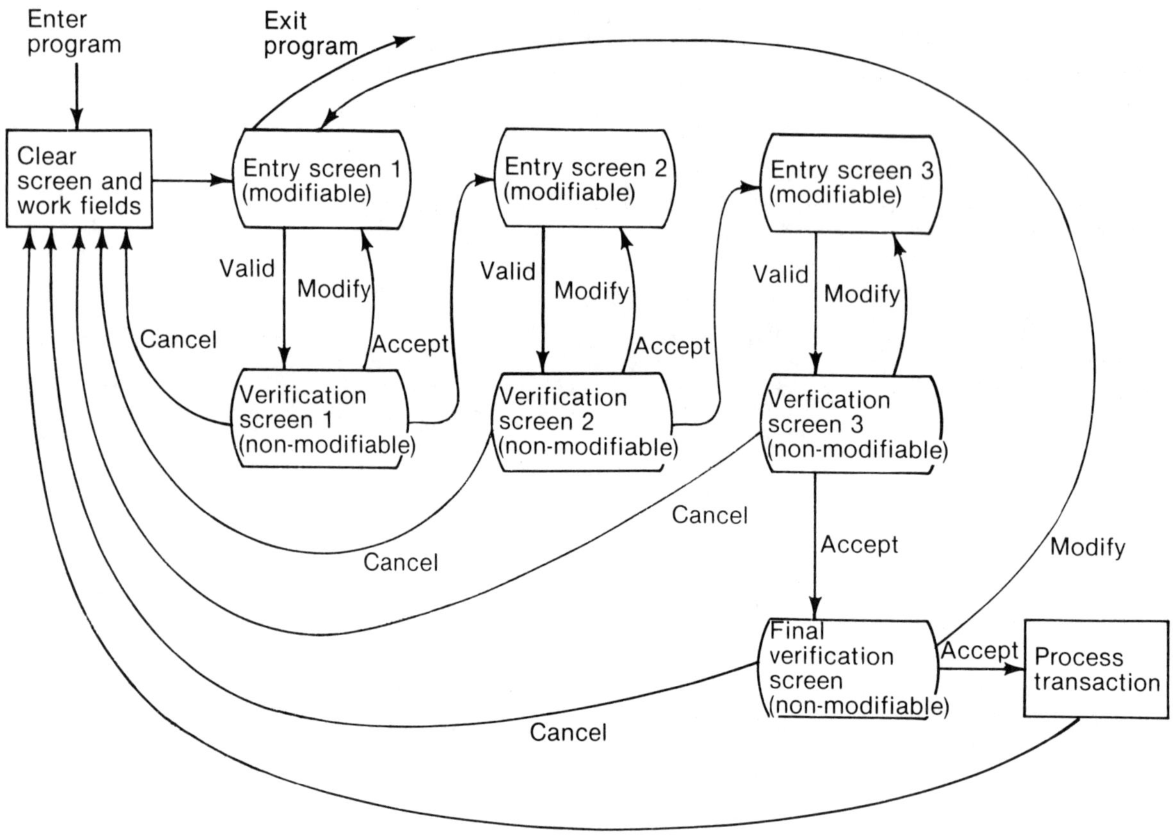

Figure 12-10 A screen flow diagram that provides for complete verification of a transaction that requires three entry screens

When you provide for sight verification by the operator, your system becomes easier to use. Or, to use the current jargon, it becomes more "user friendly." One of the most frustrating entry problems is to enter data that you know is incorrect and not be given the chance to correct it by the program. So we recommend that you provide for sight verification whenever it is practical.

When you design the screen flow for a program, you should try to make it consistent throughout a system or application. If you can do this, the operators will get used to the standard flow that you use. And this too will make the system easier to use.

Of course, most programs require only one or two entry screens. So screen flow usually isn't much of a problem. If you find yourself planning a program that requires many screens, you should probably review what you're trying to do, discuss the application with the system designer, and make sure it's a reasonable function. That's not to say, though, that a program shouldn't have many screens. One critical program in a system I'm familiar with uses 28 separate screens, and it works logically and effectively. But, it's the exception, not the rule.

Although we recommend the screen-flow models shown in figures 12-9 and 12-10, we realize that they may be impractical in your shop. For instance, they may require more internal storage during execution than your system can provide. Or, operations management may feel that sight-verification slows down entry to a point that isn't justified by the application. When the accuracy of transaction data is critical, however, we feel that these are the most effective data-entry models that you can follow. This is particularly true when the data is to be entered by operators in a user department.

Task 2: Get related programs, COPY members, and subprograms

After you have complete specifications for your program, you should gather any related materials you can use. These can be related programs, COPY members, or subprograms.

As in a batch programming assignment, if you have access to programs that are similar to the one you're working on, you should use them as models for your new program. In general, regardless of the application, if the screen-flow of an old program is similar to the one you're working on, it should be of use to you. As you will see, two programs with similar screen flows should have similar program designs. And you should be able to reuse much of the old code in your new program. So don't create new code from scratch if you don't have to.

When you get the related COPY members for an interactive program, you should be able to find some that provide standard screen-handling code. In our shop, for example, we have a COPY member that provides mnemonic names for the field-attribute characters that our system requires for screen-handling functions. Similarly, you might have a COPY member that provides standard heading descriptions for the screens your programs will use. In the next two chapters, I'll give you some examples of what I mean, but you should realize now that this code will vary from one compiler to the next.

When you get the related subprograms for an interactive program, you should be able to find some that are related to screen-handling. For example, you may find a subprogram that formats a standard screen heading. Or, you may find subprograms that perform generalized screen-handling functions. But your use of subprograms in interactive programs will vary somewhat based on the compiler you're using.

Task 3: Design the program

When you design an interactive program, you do so in the same general way that you design a batch program. For instance, figure 12-11 shows the basic structure of a program that gets data from only one entry screen and does not provide for sight verification of the entered data. Here, the

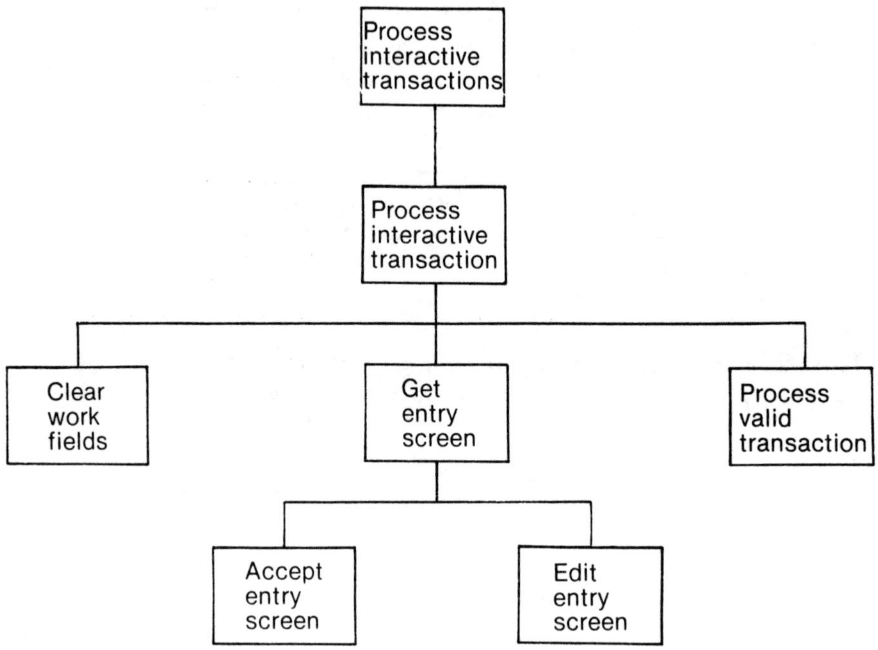

Figure 12-11 The basic structure of a single entry-screen program without verification

level-0 module executes the primary level-1 module of the program until the operator indicates that there are no more transactions. And the primary level-1 module does everything required for the processing of one transaction.

To create a structure chart for an interactive program, as for a batch program, you start with a top-level module that represents the entire program. Then, you decide on the one level-1 module that will be performed repeatedly during the execution of the program; it will represent the processing for one interactive transaction. Next, you decide what functional modules need to be performed before and after the primary level-1 module and you show these on the chart. After that, you divide each of the level-1 modules into component functions. You continue to identify subordinate modules in this way, one level at a time, until you reach the point where you're confident that you can code each module in a single COBOL paragraph.

To determine the subordinates for your primary level-1 module, you can use the screen flow diagram for an interactive program. To illustrate this, look back to the screen flow diagram in figure 12-7. To develop the structure chart for this program, you first need to realize that the screen flow diagram represents the processing that will be done for one transaction. And that means that the primary level-1 module of the program must provide for this processing. For the flow in figure 12-7, then, the primary module must (1) clear work fields, (2) accept the entry screen, (3) edit the entry screen, and (4) process the entered transaction.

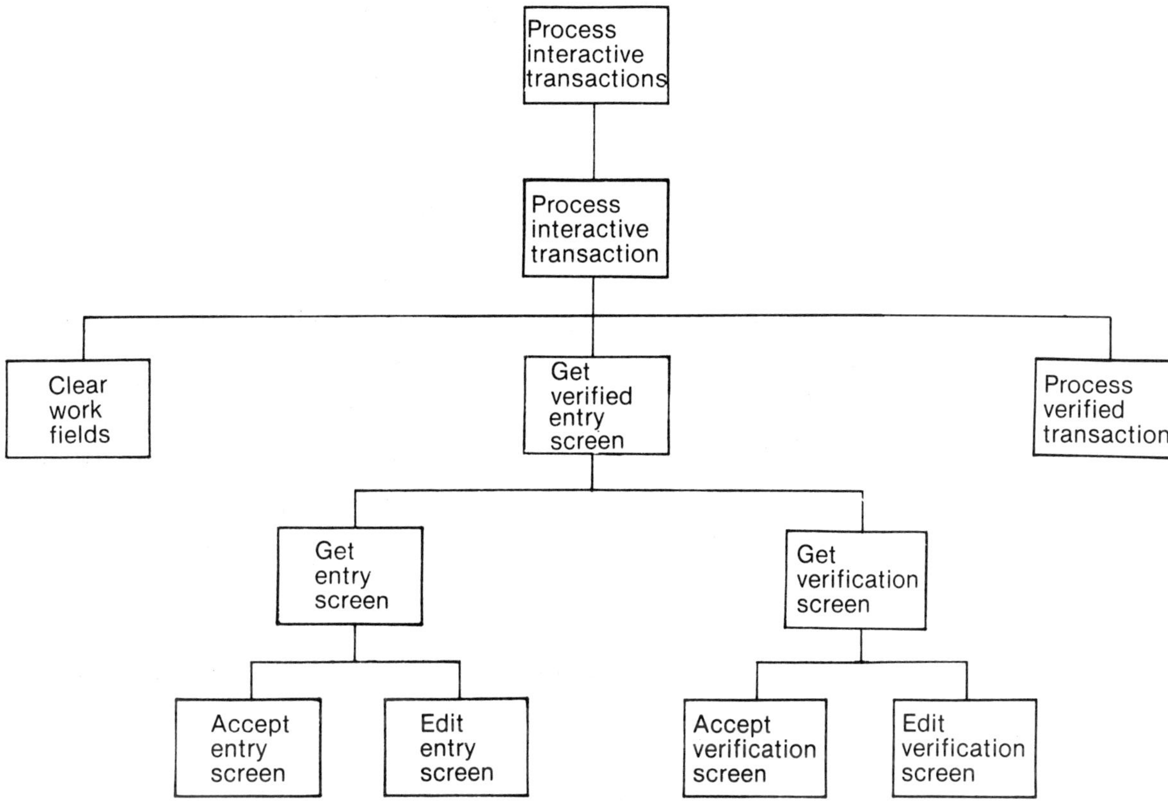

Figure 12-12 The basic structure of a single entry-screen program with verification

A program based on the screen flow diagram in figure 12-7 requires a structure chart like the one in figure 12-11. If you compare the diagram with the structure chart, you can see the relationships between the two. In brief, the level-2 subordinates for the primary level-1 module (1) clear the work fields, (2) get an entry screen (or an edited entry screen), and (3) process a valid transaction (a transaction that passes the editing routines). Then, the level-3 subordinates for the module that gets an entry screen (1) accept the entry screen (which means to get the unedited data) and (2) edit the data of the entry screen.

Once you understand this relationship between the screen flow diagram and the structure chart for a program, you can design an interactive program quite mechanically. For instance, the structure chart in figure 12-12 gives the basic structure for a program with the screen flow shown in figure 12-9. This program gets a transaction using a single entry screen, but it gives the operator a chance to sight verify the screen before processing takes place. In effect, then, this program operates upon the data in two screens: the entry screen and the verification screen.

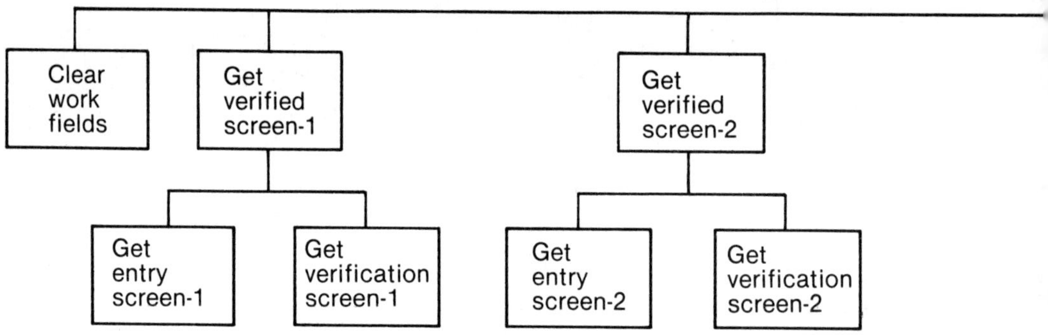

Figure 12-13 The basic structure of a three entry-screen program with complete verification that processes only one type of transaction

In the structure chart in figure 12-12, you can see that the level-3 modules (1) get an entry screen and (2) get a verification screen. Then, each of these modules calls subordinates that (1) accept the screen and (2) edit the data in the screen. After the data in the entry screen passes the editing routines, the operator gets a chance to sight verify it.

An acceptable verification entry for this program indicates that the transaction should be (1) accepted, (2) cancelled, or (3) modified. So the editing routine for the verification screen checks to make sure the verification entry is one of these three choices. Then, if the entry is valid, the program proceeds based on the verification entry. If the operator has accepted the transaction, the program processes the verified transaction. If the operator has cancelled the transaction, the program lets him enter a new transaction. If the operator has indicated that he wants to modify the old transaction, the program lets him do that.

Figure 12-13 gives the basic structure of a program that has the screen flow given by the diagram in figure 12-10. This, as you may recall, is the flow for a program that requires three entry screens for one transaction. It also provides one verification screen for each entry screen and a final verification screen for the entire transaction. Although the

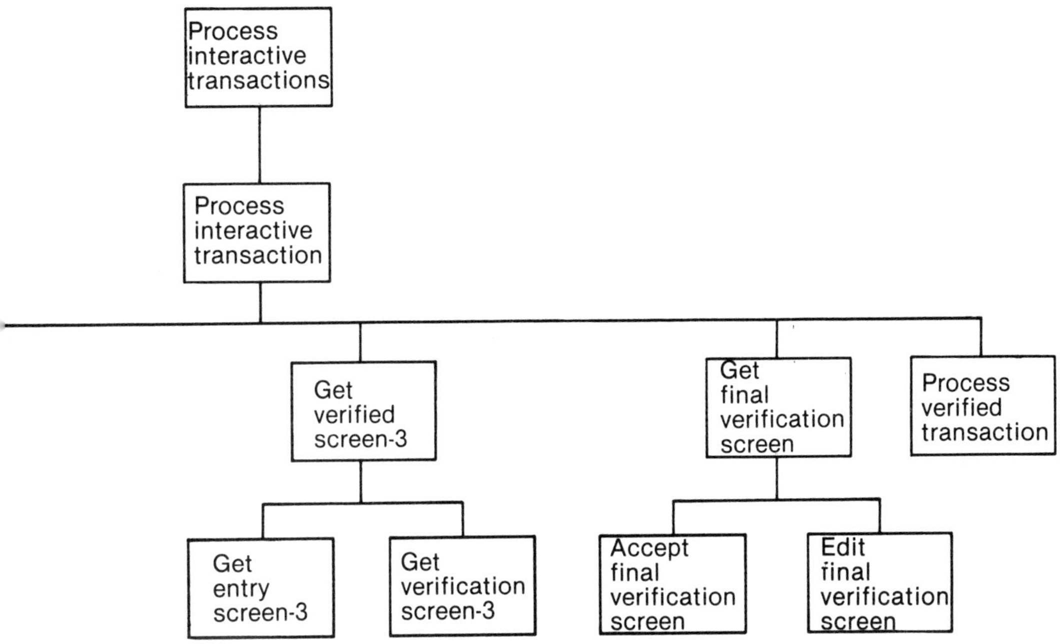

structure in figure 12-13 is complicated, you should recognize that it's just three groups of modules that correspond to the get-verified-entry-screen modules in figure 12-12, plus a group of modules for the final verification screen.

Although most interactive programs process only one type of transaction, some process more than one type. A common example of this is a file-maintenance program that lets the operator enter an addition transaction, a deletion transaction, or a change transaction. Although this changes the flow and structure of an interactive program somewhat, you can still design the program using the screen flow diagram as a guideline. For instance, figures 12-14 and 12-15 give a general screen flow diagram and structure chart for a program that processes two types of transactions.

Although the design ideas I've just given apply to most interactive computer systems, system details do affect the design of an interactive program. This is particularly true when you design the lower-level modules of a program, the ones I've left out of the basic designs I've presented in this chapter. In the next two chapters, then, I'll give you examples of complete program designs for specific computer systems.

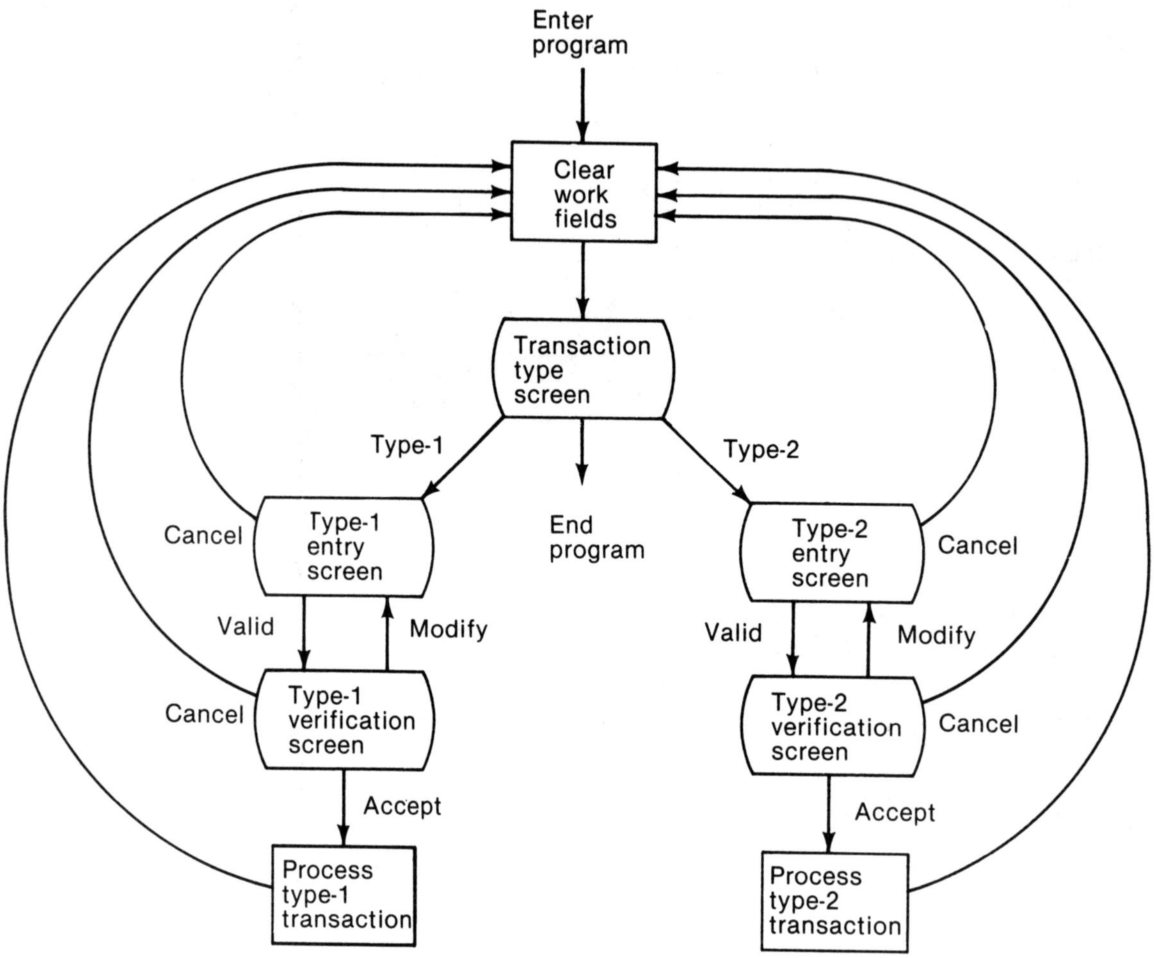

Figure 12-14 A screen flow diagram for a program that processes two types of transactions with verification

Task 4: Plan the modules of the program

As I explained in chapter 8, you may or may not use pseudocode or HIPO diagrams to plan the coding of the modules in your programs. This depends on your shop standards as well as your personal preferences. In many cases, if you have free choice, you may prefer to plan only the critical modules of a program or none of them at all.

If you're new to interactive programming, though, we recommend that you use pseudocode to plan the critical modules of a new program.

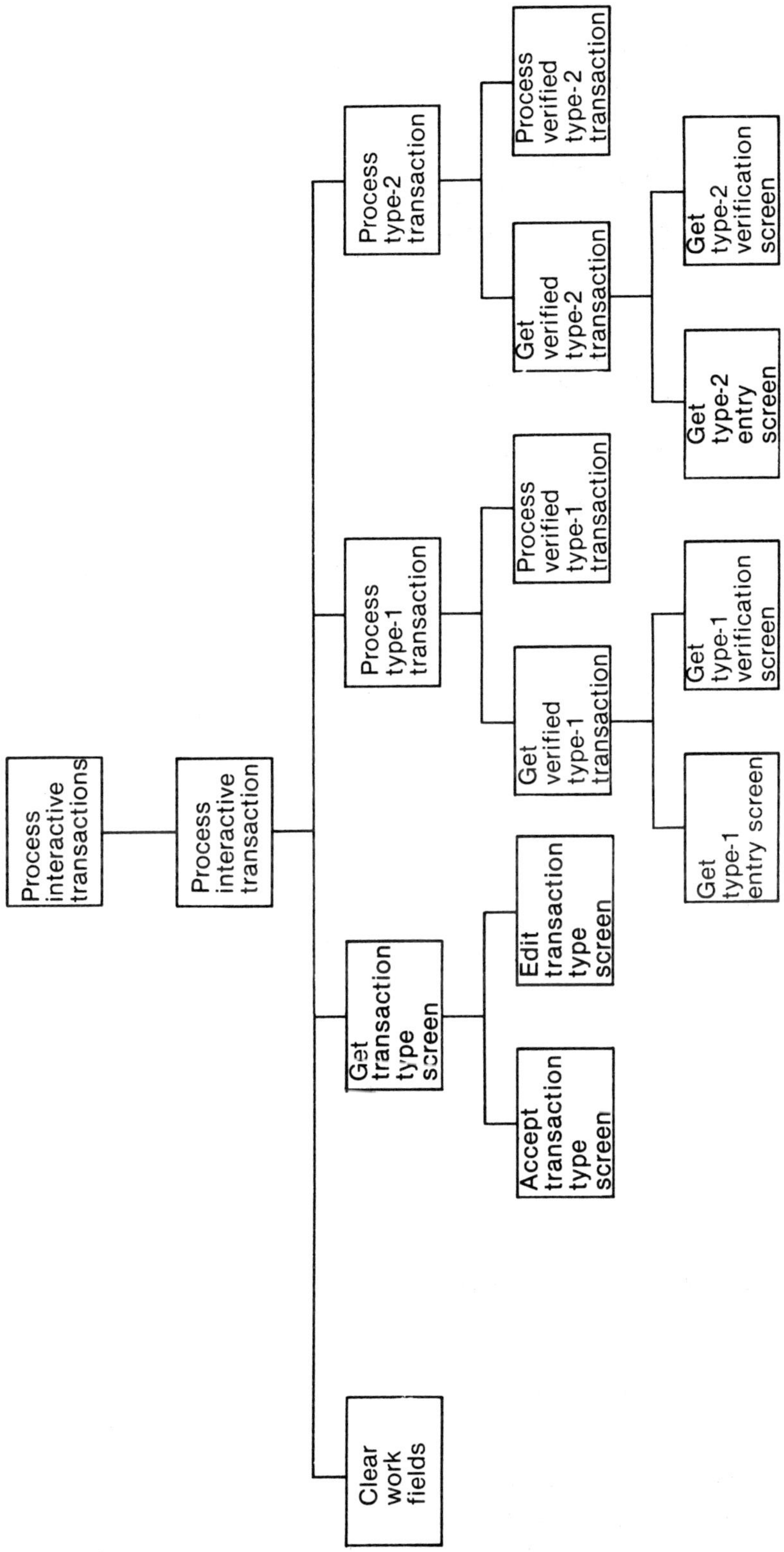

Figure 12-15 The basic structure of a program that processes two types of transactions with verification using the screen flow in figure 12-14

```
000-process-interactive-transactions.

    Open files.
    DO 100-process-interactive-transaction
        until end-program.
    Close files.
    Stop run.

100-process-interactive-transaction.

    DO 110-clear-work-fields.
    Set switch for not valid-type.
    DO 120-get-transaction-type-screen.
        UNTIL valid-type
           OR end-program.
    IF not end-program
        IF transaction-type-1
            DO 150-process-type-1-transaction
        ELSE IF transaction-type-2
            DO 200-process-type-2-transaction.

120-get-transaction-type-screen.

    DO 130-accept-transaction-type-screen.
    DO 140-edit-transaction-type-screen.

150-process-type-1-transaction.

    Set switch for not transaction-cancelled.
    Set switch for not transaction-accepted.
    DO 160-get-verified-type-1-transaction
        UNTIL transaction-accepted
           OR transaction-cancelled.
    IF transaction-accepted
        DO 190-process-verified-type-1-transaction.

160-get-verified-type-1-transaction.

    DO 170-get-type-1-entry-screen
        UNTIL transaction-accepted
           OR transaction-cancelled.
    IF transaction-accepted
        set switch for not transaction-accepted
        DO 180-get-type-1-verification-screen
            UNTIL transaction-accepted
               OR transaction-cancelled.
```

Figure 12-16 Pseudocode for the critical modules of the program designed in figure 12-15

For instance, figure 12-16 illustrates pseudocode for the critical modules of the program charted in figure 12-15. By using pseudocode, you can assure yourself that your design will work before you start to code the modules. Keep in mind, however, that once you're familiar with the coding for interactive programs, you may find that you can work more efficiently by going directly from the design to the COBOL code.

Task 5: Create a test plan for the program

When you create a test plan for an interactive program, you do so just as you do for a batch program. In our experience, though, it's always best to test an interactive program from the top down. Even more so than for batch programs, top-down testing seems to fit the development environment for an interactive program. When you use top-down testing, the problems that arise during testing are almost certain to be in the modules just added to the program or in the interfaces between the new modules and the calling modules. When that's the case, testing is a manageable process. In contrast, when you test an interactive program all at once, it can be difficult indeed to isolate the cause of a program bug.

Figure 12-17 lists some items you should check when you test an interactive program. If you review this list, you can see that not all of the items are the kind that will show up in a test plan. Nevertheless, you should be aware of them when you create your plan, when you create your interactive test data, and when you observe the interactive results during a test run.

Task 6: If necessary, code the job-control procedures for the program

On many interactive systems, you don't have to code job-control procedures to test an interactive program. On some systems, however, you do have to. And in some shops, you have to create them for systems and acceptance tests, even if you don't have to create them for unit tests. Remember, then, if you do have to create job-control procedures, that you should structure them as much as your procedure language permits.

Task 7: If necessary, create the test data for the test runs

If an interactive program requires tape or disk master files, you may have to create test data for these files. If so, you create this data just as you would for a batch system.

In addition, for any interactive program, you have to create test data for the transactions that the operator will enter during a test run. In most cases, these can be simple, handwritten lists of data to be entered. Remember, however, that you should know what results to expect for each transaction that you enter. Otherwise, you won't know whether your program executed successfully during the test run.

As you create interactive test data, you may want to refer again to the listing in figure 12-17. It may give you some ideas for data entries that you might otherwise omit. At the least, your test data should make sure that your program provides for all of the conditions listed.

What to check for as you examine the appearance of the screen:

Are all headings and captions placed correctly?
Is there any garbage on the screen?
Are there any misspellings?
Do all the fields have the correct attributes?
Is the cursor in the correct initial location?
Does the cursor move correctly from field to field?

What to check for as you enter valid data:

Are all program screens displayed in the correct sequence?
Do all control keys work correctly?
Are the operator messages always correct?
Are the functions of all control keys shown?
Does the program properly acknowledge receipt of valid data?
Are work fields properly cleared after each valid transaction?
Are control totals accumulated properly?
Are files updated properly?

What to check for as you enter single errors:

Does each case of invalid data for each field yield a correct error message?
Do lookup routines work properly?
When you correct the error, does the error message go away?
Does the program post transactions even though errors are detected?

What to check for as you enter compound errors:

Are all errors detected, or does the program only detect the first error in a transaction?
Are all errors properly indicated?

Figure 12-17 A checklist for testing an interactive program

Task 8: Code and test the program using top-down testing

In the next two chapters, I'll present some specific suggestions for coding interactive COBOL programs. For now, though, I want to make a few general comments that apply to the coding of interactive COBOL programs on all systems. These are consistent with the principles of structured coding that we presented in chapter 9.

First, you should adopt a shop standard for grouping and sequencing screen-handling fields in the Data Division. If you do, all Data Divisions in your shop will have the same organization, so it will be easier for you to find fields in your own programs or in someone else's. Depending on your compiler, of course, the screen-handling groups will vary. So I'll make some specific recommendations in chapters 13 and 14.

Second, the paragraphs in your Procedure Division should correspond directly to the program structure chart. As a result, the structure chart will serve as a directory to the source code. Ideally, this means coding each module as a separate COBOL paragraph. But under CICS, it means coding each module as a separate section as you will see in chapter 14.

Third, when you code the Procedure Division, you should only use the proper structures. In most cases, this means that you should code an interactive program without GOTOs and with only the accepted constructs of structured programming. But in CICS, you have to use GOTOs in some instances as you will see in chapter 14.

During the testing of a program, you must work in a carefully controlled manner using the test plan and test data you created earlier. In particular, you must make sure that the interactive output provides the expected results. Too often, though, interactive programs fail early in their production lives because a programmer didn't check the interactive results closely enough. Not only must the displayed results look right (be in the right format), but they must be right (provide accurate data).

Task 9: Document the program

The documentation for a structured interactive program is easy to assemble. For the most part, it consists of the original program specifications (including the screen layouts and screen flow diagram), plus the program structure chart and the compiler listing.

If a program uses external screens, though, you will have some additional documentation for each screen. And if your system doesn't provide for screen handling using COBOL extensions, you may have some sort of translator listing in addition to your COBOL listing.

Discussion

Throughout this topic, I've pointed out the similarities between batch and interactive program development. In general, if you can develop batch programs using the techniques in part 2, you can develop interactive programs using the same basic techniques. In fact, we created our own shop standards for interactive programs based on the first version of this book, which only showed how to develop batch programs.

If you're new to interactive programming, you may find that it is more difficult than batch programming for two reasons. First, interactive programs typically combine functions that in a batch system are likely to be in separate programs. For example, a single data-entry program is likely to combine data capture, editing, and updating. So if you're used to working on single-function batch programs, multi-function interactive programs might seem complicated to you at first. However, if you develop an interactive program from the top down as we have recommended in this topic, you should minimize your problems.

Second, interactive programs use terminal devices that can provide sophisticated display features. As a result, making use of these features can be more difficult than using the I/O operations in a batch program. In the next two chapters, then, I'll give you some ideas on how to code the screen-handling functions of an interactive program with a minimum of difficulty.

Terminology

screen layout
heading zone
data zone
communication zone
dedicated source document
screen flow
screen flow diagram
sight verification
verification screen
entry screen

Objectives

1. Given the program specifications for an interactive program, design the screens required by the program using screen layout forms.

2. Given the program specifications for an interactive program and the screen layouts required by the program, plan the screen flow using a screen flow diagram.

3. Given complete specifications for an interactive program, including screen layouts and a screen flow diagram, develop a basic structure chart for it. This chart does not have to be designed to a level that requires a knowledge of the system's compiler details.

Chapter 13

How to design and code interactive programs that use internal screen definitions

In the last chapter, I explained the differences between COBOL compilers that use internally-defined screens and those that use externally-defined screens. I also showed you a general procedure for developing any interactive program. But I warned you that the way in which a system supports interactive programming can affect the way in which you design and code a program.

In this chapter, then, I'm going to show you some specific techniques for designing and coding programs when your system uses internally-defined screens. In topic 1, I'll show you some specific design techniques. In topic 2, I'll show you some specific coding techniques. The two compilers that I'll use for illustrating these techniques are (1) the Microsoft COBOL compiler as used on an IBM PC and (2) the VS COBOL compiler as used on a Wang VS system. When you complete this chapter, though, you should be able to apply these design and coding techniques to any system that uses internally-defined screens.

If you develop programs for an IBM mainframe using CICS, you can skip this chapter because chapter 14 presents specific techniques for CICS users. On the other hand, if you don't use CICS but your system uses externally-defined screens, you should read this chapter as well as the next chapter. Although the process of creating and coding the screen definitions will differ when you use external screens, you should be able to use many of the same design and coding techniques that are presented in this chapter. Then, the next chapter will give you some ideas for defining your external screens. By combining the techniques presented in both chapters, you should be able to create a hybrid development method for interactive programs that will be specific to your own system.

Topic 1 How to design interactive programs that use internal screen definitions

In general, there are two types of compilers that use internally-defined screens. The first type gets data from a screen, one field at a time. A compiler of this type can be called a *field-oriented compiler*. The second type gets all of the data in a screen at the same time. A compiler of this type can be called a *screen-oriented compiler*. As you will see, you design and code programs for a field-oriented compiler somewhat differently than you do for a screen-oriented compiler.

Some compilers allow you to get data from screens either field by field or screen by screen. In this case, you can use either field-oriented design and coding techniques or screen-oriented techniques when you develop a program. However, because screen-oriented techniques are usually more efficient, both in terms of programming and operations, we recommend that you use screen-oriented techniques if your compiler supports them. This will also make it easier for you to convert to a more sophisticated computer system and compiler later on.

In this topic, I'm going to show you how to design a program for either type of compiler. In fact, I'm going to show you two program designs for the same program specifications. One design is for a field-oriented program that uses the Microsoft COBOL compiler on the IBM PC. Although Microsoft COBOL also provides a screen-oriented compiler, I have chosen to develop a field-oriented program here as an example. The other design is for a screen-oriented program that uses the VS COBOL compiler on a Wang VS system. When you finish this topic, you should clearly see how an interactive compiler can affect program design. You should also be able to apply the techniques presented in this topic to any program that uses internal screens, whether it is field-oriented or screen-oriented.

Program specifications for an interactive file-maintenance program

Figures 13-1, 13-2, and 13-3 give the program overview, the screen flow diagram, and the three screen layouts for an interactive program that maintains a file of customer records. To start, the program gets an action code (or transaction-type code) from the action screen, but it also gets a customer code. The action can be to add a record to the customer file, to

Program: MNT2100 Maintain customer file	**Page:** 1
Designer: Steve Eckols	**Date:** 08-26-84

Input/output specifications

File	Description	Use
CUSTMAST	Customer master file	Update

Process specifications

Until the operator indicates end of program by using a function key in step 1:

1. Get a valid combination of action code and customer code from the ACTION SCREEN. Use the operator-entered customer code as the primary key for a random read on CUSTMAST. If the action is addition, there shouldn't be a record for the customer code in the customer file; if the action is deletion or change, there should be a record for the customer code in the customer file.

2. For an addition transaction, get the valid customer entries from the CUSTOMER ENTRY SCREEN. Then, get a valid verification entry from the TRANSACTION VERIFICATION SCREEN. If the transaction is accepted, write the addition record onto the customer file. If the transaction is to be modified, repeat this step so the operator can modify the entries for the new customer. If the transaction is to be cancelled, cancel this transaction and continue with step 1.

3. For a change transaction, get the valid change entries from the CUSTOMER ENTRY SCREEN. Then, get a valid verification entry from the TRANSACTION VERIFICATION SCREEN. If the transaction is accepted, write the changed record back onto the customer file. If the transaction is to be modified, repeat this step. If the transaction is to be cancelled, cancel this transaction and continue with step 1.

4. For a deletion transaction, get a valid verification entry from the TRANSACTION VERIFICATION SCREEN. If the transaction is accepted, delete the record from the customer file. If the transaction is to be cancelled, cancel this transaction and continue with step 1.

Figure 13-1 A program overview for an interactive file-maintenance program

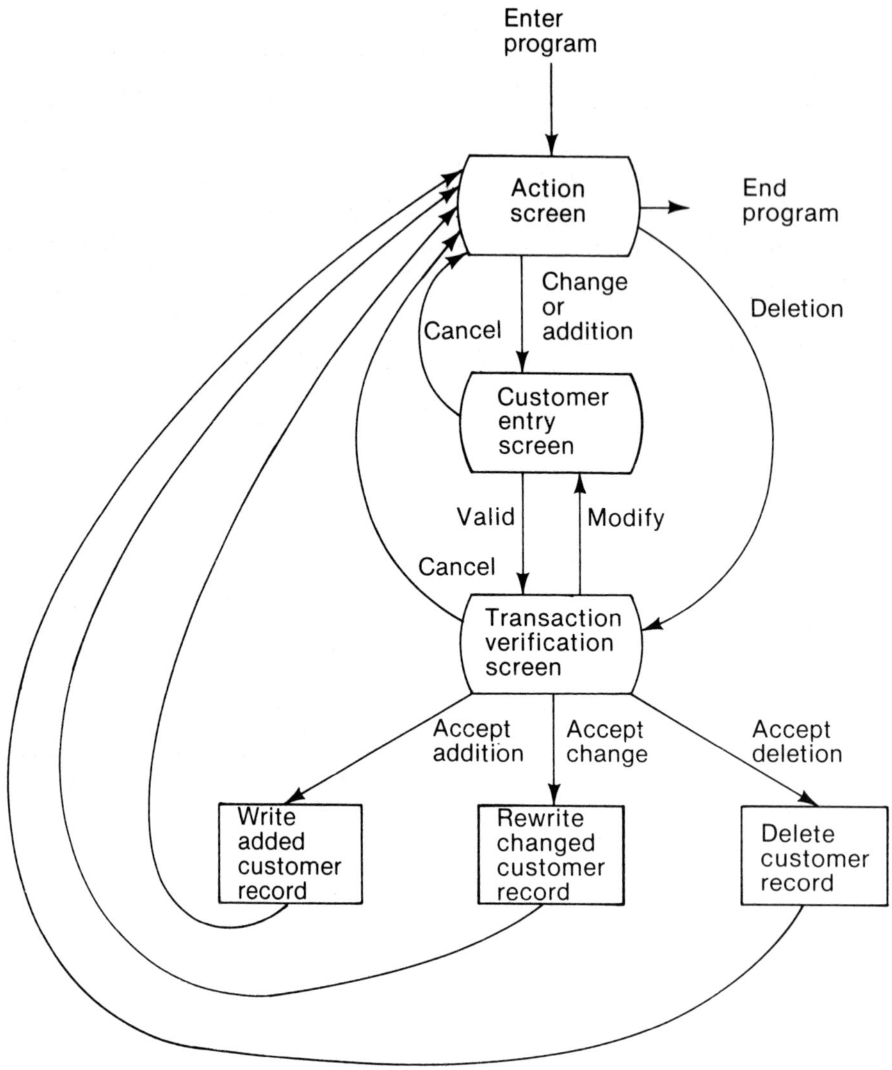

Figure 13-2 A general screen flow diagram for the interactive file-maintenance program

change a record in the file, or to delete a record from the file. Then, if the combination of the customer code and action code are valid, the program continues with the next screen.

If the transaction is a change or an addition, the program gets the data from the customer-entry screen. This screen allows the operator to change data taken from a master record that already exists or to enter data for a new record that is to be added to the file. After the program gets valid data from this screen, it gets a response from the transaction-verification screen. This response tells the program whether the operator wants to accept the transaction, modify the transaction using the

Action screen

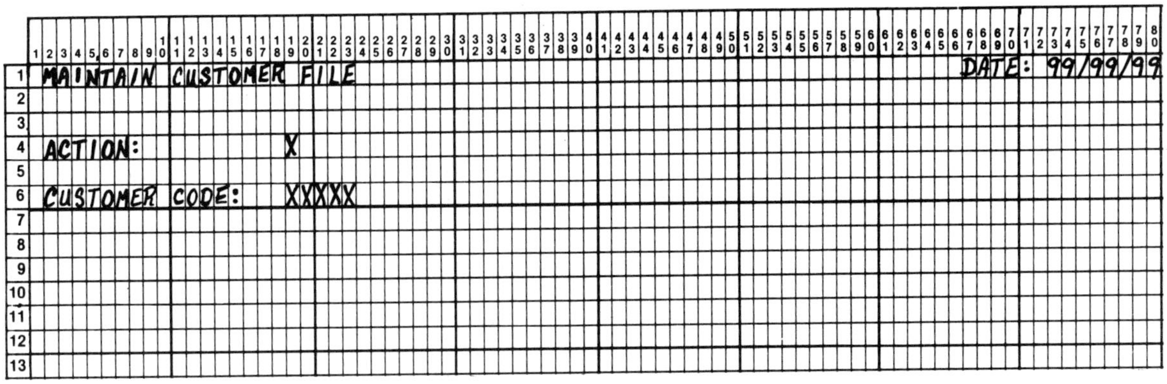

Customer entry screen

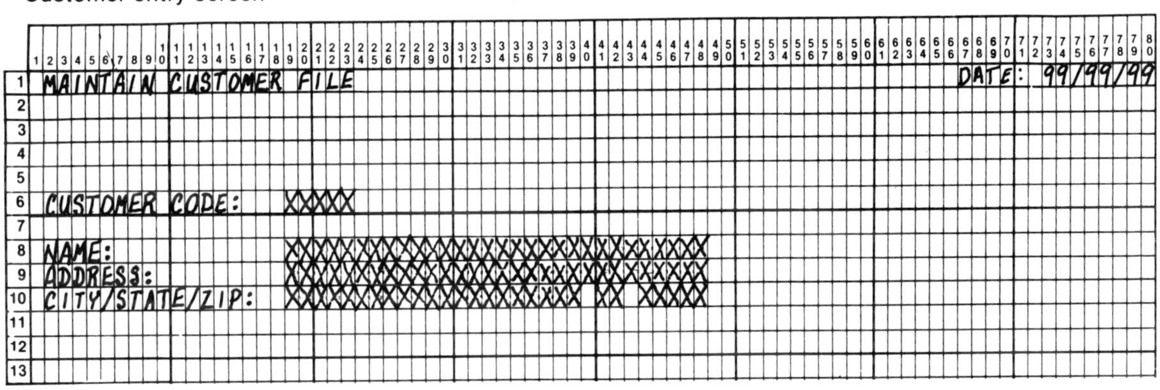

Transaction verification screen

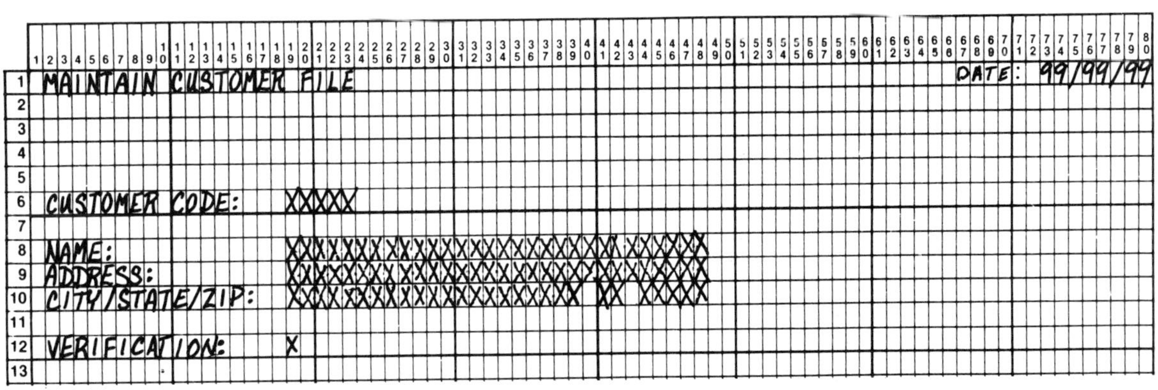

Figure 13-3 The heading and data areas used by the three screens of the interactive file-maintenance program

customer-entry screen, or cancel the transaction altogether and start again with the action screen.

If the transaction is a deletion, the program skips the customer-entry screen. Instead, it gets the data from the transaction-verification screen. Then, the operator can indicate whether he wants to accept the deletion transaction or cancel it. In other words, the operator has only two choices for a deletion (accept or cancel), but he has three choices for a change or an addition (accept, modify, or cancel).

If you look at the layout of the screens in figure 13-3, you can see that the customer-entry and the transaction-verification screens are almost identical in the heading and data zones. The only difference is that the transaction-verification screen accepts a code to verify the transaction. They also differ in the communication zone of the screens. For the customer-entry screen, the communication zone will display a continuous message that tells the operator how to cancel the transaction. For the transaction-verification screen, the communication zone will display a message that tells the operator how to accept, cancel, or modify a transaction.

The screen layouts in figure 13-3 could be used to develop this program on any interactive system. However, because VS COBOL on the Wang VS system provides for easy use of its function keys, some minor modifications have been made to the screens for that program. In particular, rather than entering an action code on the action screen and a verification code on the transaction-verification screen, function keys are used to indicate the appropriate codes. You will see how the function keys work when I discuss the Procedure Division code for screen-oriented compilers.

If you've written programs like this before, you know that you won't always let the operator enter the desired customer code for a new customer (an addition). Instead, you'll let the computer system assign the next available code to the addition record. In this case, however, we're assuming that the user wants to assign mnemonic codes for his customers. Thus, DELTA might be the customer code for Delta Lithograph Company and IBM might be the code for International Business Machines. That way, if the number of customers in the file is relatively low, the user can remember most of the codes of his key customers.

Similarly, if the transactions for a program like this are entered in batches by transaction type, you probably wouldn't make the operator enter the action code for each transaction. Instead, you would have the operator enter the action code only once for each batch of transactions. If, for example, the operator was going to enter a batch of additions, he would only enter the action code for additions at the start of the batch. Then, the program would only ask for the customer codes and field entries for the addition records until all of them had been processed. At that time, the operator would indicate that he wanted to enter a different type of transaction and the program would respond accordingly.

You can see, then, that the screen layouts and screen flow for a program like this depend to a large extent on the user's specifications. If the user is going to enter the transactions in large batches sorted by transaction type, you can improve upon the screen flow given in figure 13-2. On the other hand, if only a few transactions are going to be entered at a time and they aren't going to be sorted by transaction type, the screen flow for this program is quite efficient.

Program design 1: A field-oriented structure

The five pages of figure 13-4 present an acceptable structure chart for a field-oriented version of this program when using Microsoft COBOL on the IBM PC. If you look at the top three levels of this program, you can see that it is similar to the basic structure I gave you in the last chapter for a program that processes two types of transactions (figure 12-15). The difference is that this program processes three types of transactions: additions, changes, and deletions.

In level 1 of figure 13-4, you can see module 100 will be performed before the primary level-1 module and module 900 will be performed after it. As you can tell from the module names, both of these are interactive modules: one displays the screen constants of the heading area; the other clears the screen after all transactions have been processed. Since screen-handling modules like these will vary from one interactive system to another, the best way to find out what they should be is to get advice from other programmers in your shop and to study their interactive programs. In general, you should look for housekeeping functions like clearing the screen at the start of a program to remove data displayed by the last program, displaying constant data (such as headings or captions that won't change during the interactive session), or clearing the screen at the end of the session.

Once you understand the top three levels of the structure chart in figure 13-4, you are ready to study the remaining levels. For most programs, it's the modules at the fourth level and below that are affected by the way in which a compiler handles screens. At this time, then, let me describe the design of this structure chart, one leg at a time.

The get-valid-action-screen leg This leg of the program (on page 1 of figure 13-4) gets the data from an action screen until the data is valid or the operator indicates that the program should end by pressing the appropriate function key. For the entries in this screen to be valid, not only must the action code and customer code be valid, but they must be consistent with each other. If, for example, the operator indicates an addition, the program must *not* be able to find a record in the customer file that has the customer code entered by the operator. Similarly, if the operator indicates a change or deletion, the program must be able to find a customer record that has the customer code entered by the operator. When the programmer realized this during coding, she added module 315 to the program and moved modules 320 through 380 down one level in the structure chart. That way, module 390 and its subordinates can check

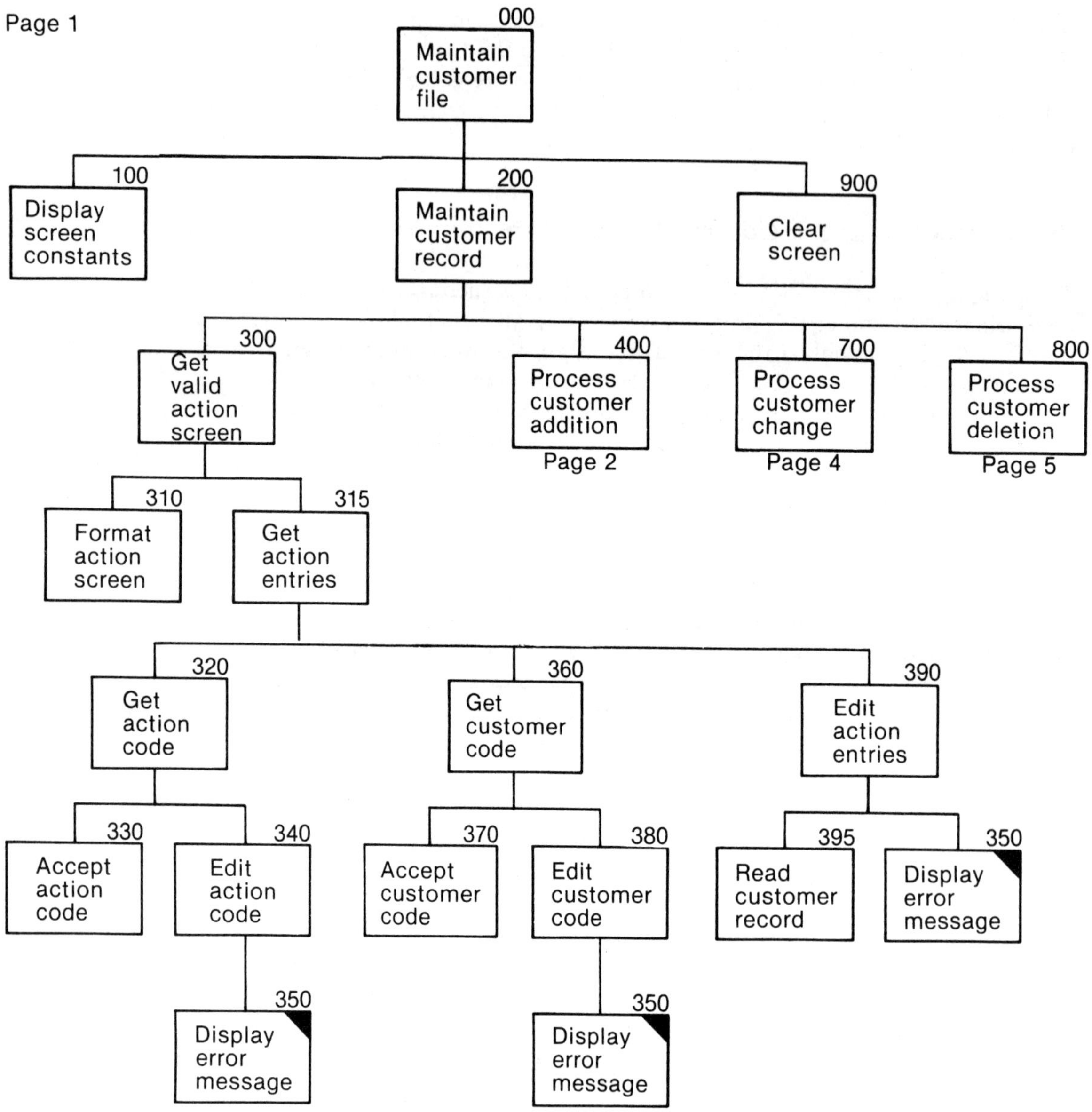

Figure 13-4 Structure chart for the interactive file-maintenance program using a field-oriented compiler on the IBM PC (part 1 of 5)

to make sure that the action code and the customer code are consistent after they are edited independently.

Because this program is going to be implemented on a field-oriented basis, the get modules that are subordinate to module 315 get only one field. Thus, module 320 gets only the action code. And module 360 gets only the customer code. As you can see, each module that gets the data

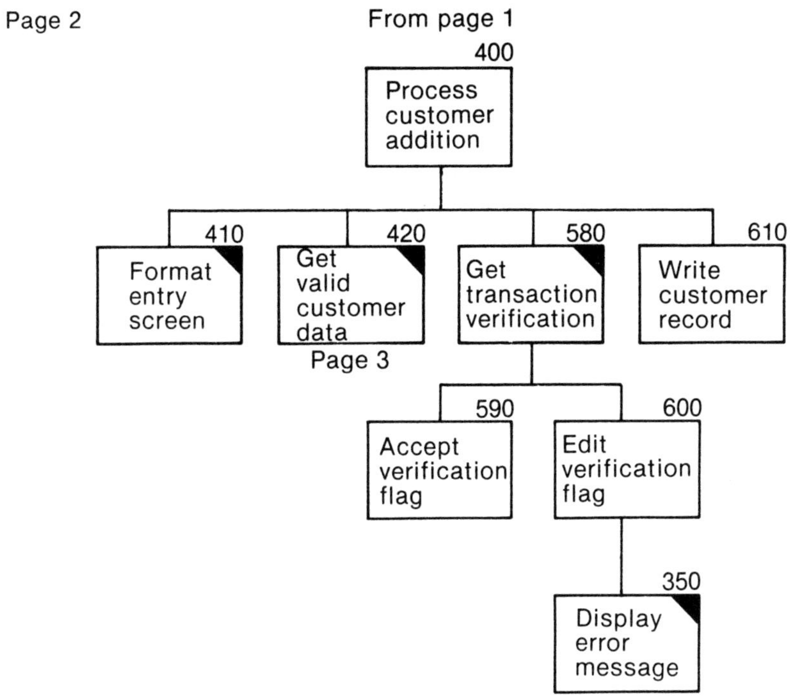

Figure 13-4 Structure chart for the interactive file-maintenance program using a field-oriented compiler on the IBM PC (part 2 of 5)

from a single field calls two subordinates: one to accept the field, the other to edit it. Then, if the edit module determines that the field is invalid, it calls common module 350 to display an appropriate error message for the field.

The process-customer-addition leg This leg of the program (page 2 of figure 13-4) processes an addition transaction. As you can see, module 400 calls four modules to (1) format the customer-entry screen, (2) get valid data from the customer-entry screen, (3) get the operator's verification of the data in the customer-entry screen, and (4) write the addition record on the customer file if the operator accepts the transaction.

To get the transaction verification, module 580 calls two modules: one to accept the operator's response, the other to edit it to make sure it's valid. If the response isn't valid, module 600 calls module 350 to display an appropriate error message.

The get-valid-customer-data leg This leg of the program (page 3 of figure 13-4) gets the data from a customer-entry screen until the data is valid or the operator cancels the entry. When you're writing a field-oriented program, the top-level module of a leg that gets a screen full of data calls one module for each entry field in the screen. In this case,

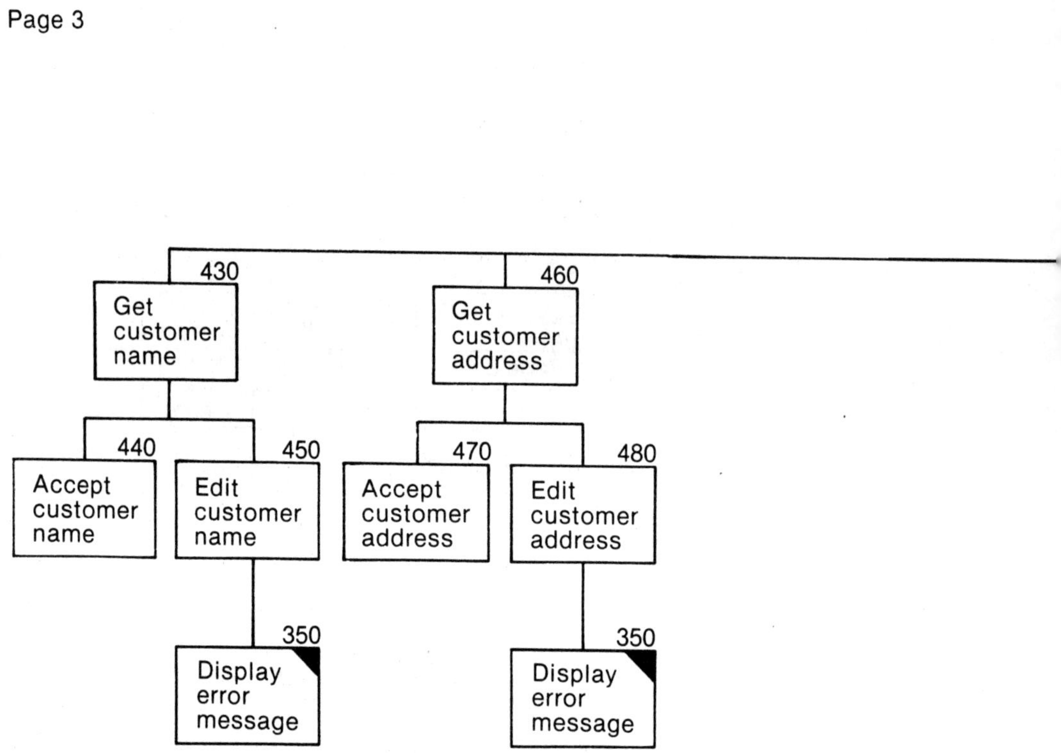

Figure 13-4 Structure chart for the interactive file-maintenance program using a field-oriented compiler on the IBM PC (part 3 of 5)

module 420 calls five modules that each get one field. Then, these modules each call two modules: one to accept the field, the other to edit it. If an edit module detects invalid data, it calls module 350, a common module, to display an appropriate error message. As you can see in figure 13-4, edit modules 540 and 570 each call a subprogram to help with the edit function. This illustrates that an edit module can also call whatever modules it needs to support its function.

The process-customer-change leg In this leg of the program (page 4 of figure 13-4), module 700 calls three common modules. First, it calls module 410 to format the customer-entry screen. Then, it calls module 420 to get the customer data for a change transaction. After it gets the valid data, module 700 calls module 580, the last common module, to get the operator's verification response for the transaction. If the response is to accept the transaction, module 700 calls module 710 to rewrite the changed customer record on the customer master file.

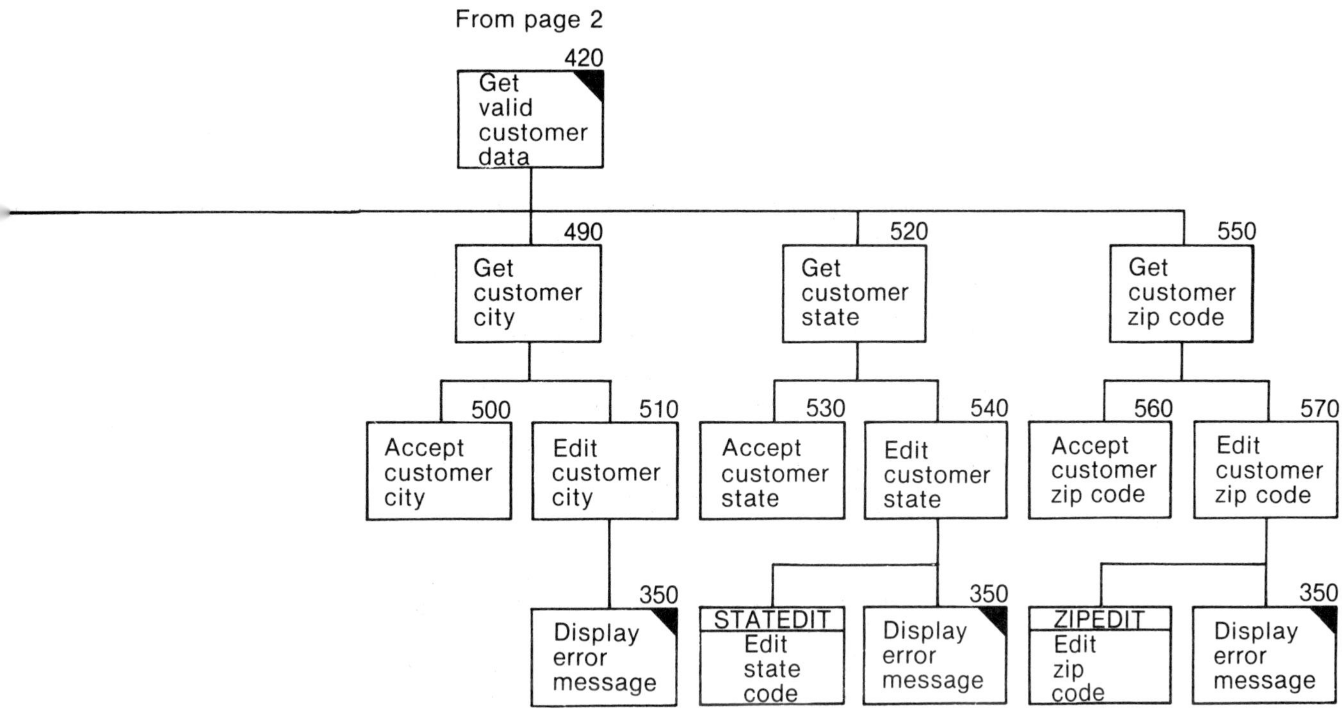

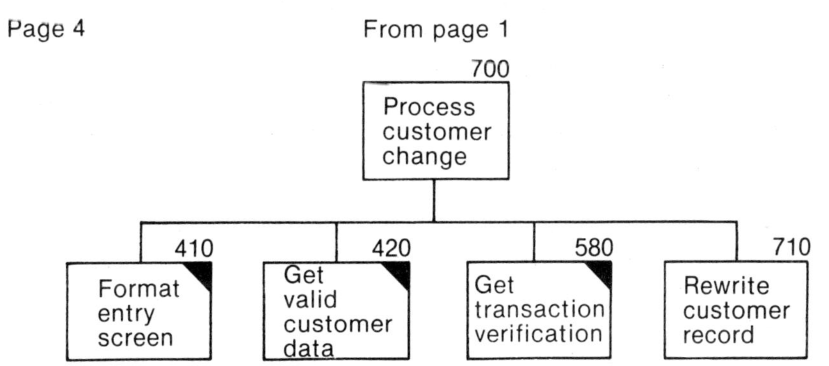

Figure 13-4 Structure chart for the interactive file-maintenance program using a field-oriented compiler on the IBM PC (part 4 of 5)

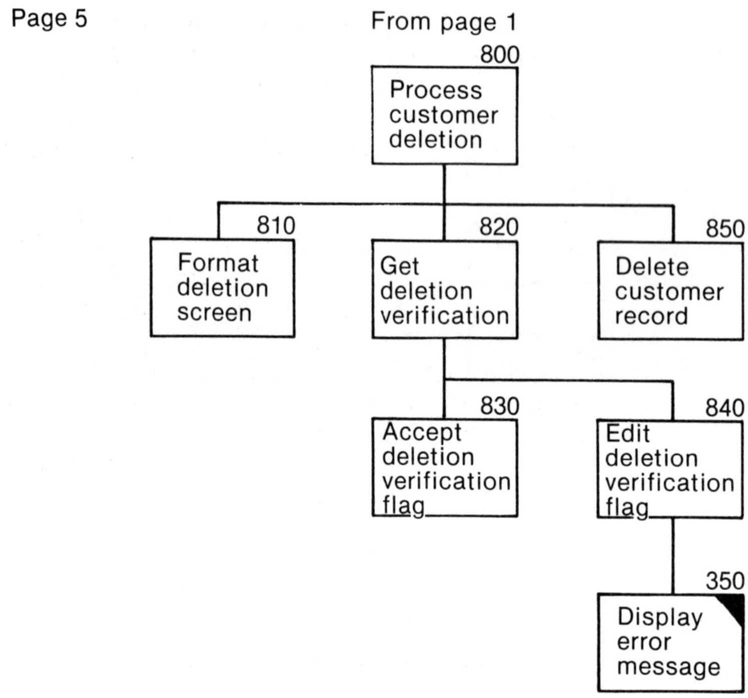

Figure 13-4 Structure chart for the interactive file-maintenance program using a field-oriented compiler on the IBM PC (part 5 of 5)

The process-customer-deletion leg Because the verification of a deletion is done somewhat differently than that for a change or an addition, the process-customer-deletion leg of this program (page 5 of figure 13-4) doesn't use module 580 to get a transaction verification. Instead, it uses module 820 to get a deletion verification. You should realize, however, that the data zone of the screen for deletion verification is the same as the one for transaction verification. But the message in the communication zone doesn't offer the choice of modifying the transaction. Although you could code module 580 and its subordinates so they would handle the verification for all three types of transactions, the use of new modules for verifying deletions simplifies the COBOL code.

Some additional perspective I hope by now you understand the structure of this program and can see the structural requirements that are common to programs that are developed for field-oriented compilers. Typical subordinates for a module that controls the processing for one screen are (1) a module that formats the screen and (2) a module that gets the fields within the screen. Typical subordinates for a module that gets one field within a screen are (1) a module to accept the field and (2) a module to edit the field. Whenever one of the edit modules in a program detects an invalid field, it calls a common module that displays an error message so the operator can reenter the field.

As a standard design practice, we recommend that you isolate screen-handling code in separate modules of a field-oriented program. If you do this, your programs will be easier to develop and maintain. As you can see in figure 13-4, then, each format, accept, and display function is a separate module of the program. For instance, modules 310, 330, and 350 are all screen-handling modules.

Since the code for a module that accepts or edits a single field is normally quite simple, you may feel that the field-editing code should be included in the accept modules. Since this reduces the number of modules in the structure chart for a program, there certainly is some benefit to doing this. As a result, we feel that either method of handling field-editing is all right. If your accept modules include the editing, though, you should make sure that the other programmers in your shop understand this expanded use of the *accept* verb.

On the other hand, we recommend that you always isolate the code for modules that display error messages when using a field-oriented compiler. Thus, module 350 in figure 13-4 is called by all of the field-editing modules. Although you could code the display functions within the edit modules, this would mean many separate DISPLAY statements for the same line on the screen. And this can lead to problems on a small system when the object program becomes larger than the system can support.

A couple of years ago, for example, we developed interactive COBOL programs for a Datapoint ARC system that limited the size of a COBOL object module to 48K. Although that may sound like plenty for most applications, another constraint of the system was that each DISPLAY or ACCEPT statement for screen handling used 2K. As a result, we had to keep the number of screen I/O statements we coded to a minimum in all but the smallest of programs. We did so by placing common interactive functions in common modules, such as module 350 in figure 13-4. Then, those routines could be called by PERFORM statements throughout the program.

If you compare the structure of the chart in figure 13-4 with the basic structure in figure 12-15, you can see some variations in levels 4 and 5. In particular, the designer of the Microsoft program took out one level of subordination. Also, the designer used names for some of the modules that take away the screen orientation of the design in figure 12-15. If, for example, the designer had followed the structure of figure 12-15 more diligently, the design for the process-customer-addition leg of the program would be more like the one in figure 13-5. Here, you can see another level of subordination caused by the addition of module 405 to the structure. You can also see that the names for modules 410, 420, and 580 refer directly to the screens used by the program.

Which design is better? I leave that up to you. If you like the formality of a design like the one in figure 12-15 or 13-5, by all means keep the extra level of subordination and refer directly to the screen names in your module names. On the other hand, I want you to realize that a design like the one in figure 13-4 is an effective one. Since the code

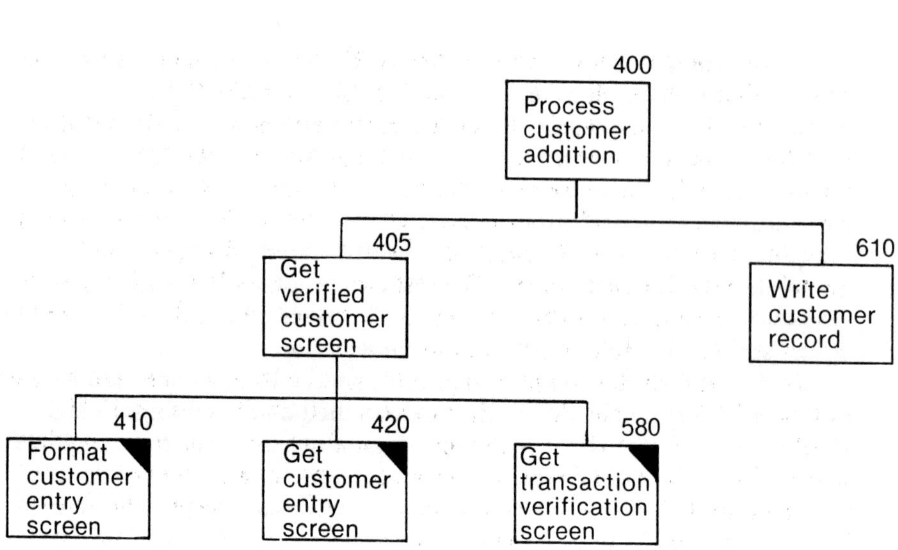

Figure 13-5 An alternate structure for the process-customer-addition leg of the interactive file-maintenance program using a field-oriented compiler

for module 400 isn't complicated (as you can see in figure 13-15 of the next topic), the extra level of subordination isn't really needed. And since the module names are both functional and specific, the references to the screen names aren't really needed. In our shop, then, our programmers use the less formal design style shown in figure 13-4.

Program design 2: A screen-oriented structure

Figure 13-6 presents an acceptable structure chart for the interactive program I presented at the start of this topic when using VS COBOL on the Wang VS system. If you look at the top three levels of this program, you can see that it is similar to the basic structure I gave you in the last chapter for a program that processes two types of transactions (figure 12-15). The difference is that this program processes three types of transactions: additions, changes, and deletions.

In level 1 of figure 13-6, you can see that module 100 will be performed before the primary level-1 module. This module, which sets the field attributes, is a module that depends upon the screen-oriented compiler you're going to use. In contrast, the other modules in the top three levels of the program will be the same no matter what screen-oriented compiler you use.

If you compare this structure chart with the one in figure 13-4, you can see that it is simpler than the one for Microsoft COBOL. In particular, it doesn't require all of the accept and edit modules for the individual fields of each screen. Since a single screen-handling statement (called DISPLAY AND READ) can display an entire screen (heading, captions, messages, and values) and accept many fields, it uses one accept module for each screen. In addition, if editing is required, one edit module is used for each screen. For instance, module 410, which gets the customer-entry screen, calls one module to accept all the data from this screen and one module to edit all the data.

In contrast to the design in figure 13-4, the get-customer-data module in figure 13-6 also calls the verify-customer-data module (module 440). Furthermore, due to the way the screen-handling code for this compiler works, this verify module doesn't have any subordinates. Since you can code module 440 on the Wang system so it will only accept valid function keys, no editing of the verification response is required. Therefore, the coding can be simplified by making the verify-customer-data module subordinate to the get-customer-data module. Then, this module is performed only if the data entered is valid.

In the process-customer-deletion leg of the program in figure 13-6, the module that verifies the deletion is different than the one that verifies an addition or a change. That is similar to the way this is handled in the Microsoft COBOL program. Simply stated, because the responses for a deletion are different than those for an addition or change, it's easier to handle the verification with two modules than one.

Some additional perspective I hope by now you understand the structure of this program and can see the structural requirements that are common to programs that use screen-oriented compilers. Typical subordinates for a module that gets one screen are (1) a module to accept the screen, (2) a module to edit the fields in the screen and, in some cases, (3) a module to verify the data entered. Whenever an edit module detects an invalid field, it puts an error message in the communication zone of the entry screen so it will be displayed the next time the accept module is performed.

As a standard design practice, we recommend that you isolate screen-handling code in separate modules of a screen-oriented program. If you do this, your programs will be easier to develop and maintain. As you can see in figure 13-6, then, each accept function is a separate module of the program. For instance, modules 310, 420, 440, and 610 are all screen-handling modules.

If you compare the structure of the chart in figure 13-6 with the basic structure in figure 12-15, you can see some variations in levels 4 and

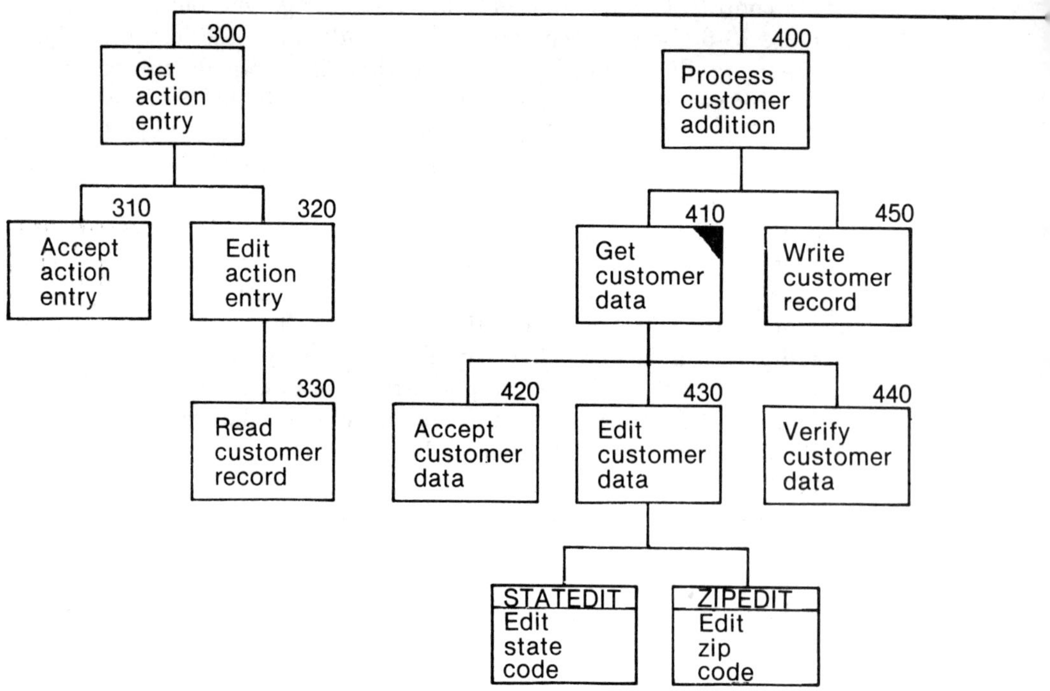

Figure 13-6 Structure chart for the interactive file maintenance program using a screen-oriented compiler on the Wang VS system

5. In particular, the designer of the Wang program took out one level of subordination. Also, the designer used names for some of the modules that take away the screen orientation of the design in figure 12-15. If, for example, the designer had followed the structure of figure 12-15 more diligently, the design for the process-customer-addition leg of the program would be more like the one in figure 13-7. Here, you can see another level of subordination caused by the addition of module 405 to the structure. You can also see that the module names for modules 410 through 440 refer directly to the screens used by the program.

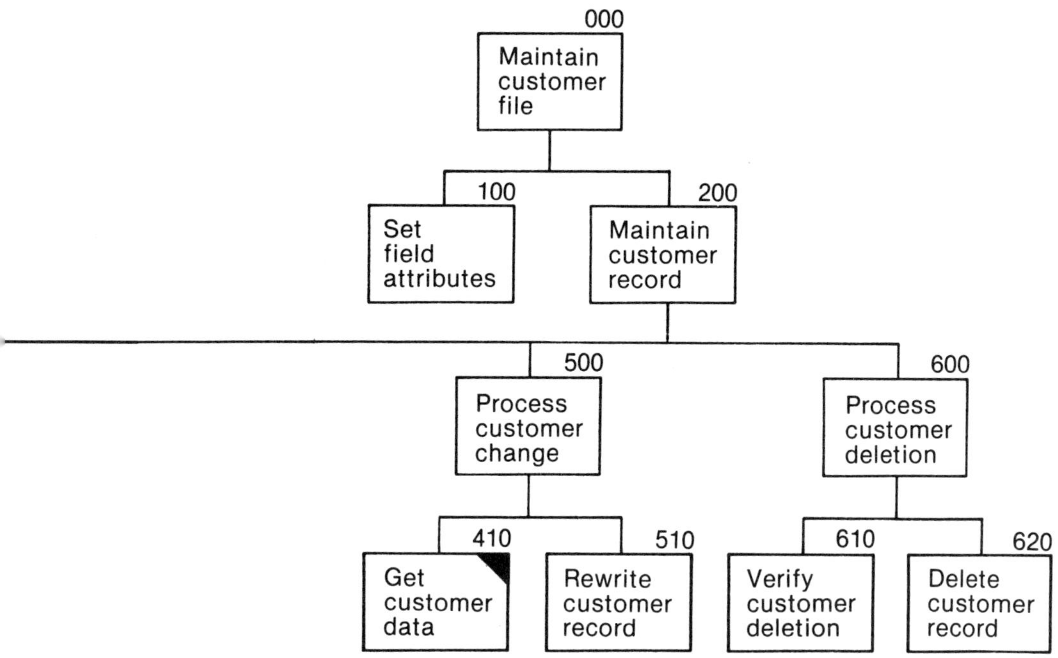

Which design is better? Again, I leave that up to you. If you like the formality of a design like the one in figure 12-15 or 13-7, by all means keep the extra level of subordination and refer directly to the screen names in your module names. On the other hand, I want you to realize that a design like the one in figure 13-6 is an effective one. Since the code for module 400 isn't complicated (as you can see in figure 13-16 of the next topic), the extra level of subordination isn't really needed. And since the module names are both functional and specific, the references to the screen names aren't really needed. In our shop, then, our programmers use the less formal design style shown in figure 13-6.

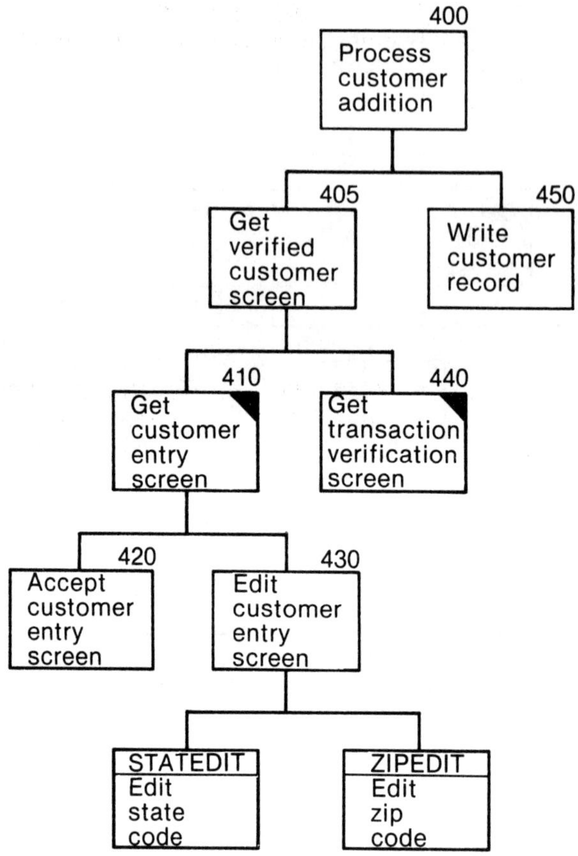

Figure 13-7 An alternate structure for the process-customer-addition leg of the interactive file-maintenance program using a screen-oriented compiler

Discussion

You should realize by now that you need to be familiar with the screen-handling code of your compiler before you can design your own interactive programs. In general, you need to know whether you're going to use a field-oriented or a screen-oriented compiler. But you also need to know in detail how to code all of the screen-handling functions that are used in your shop.

Once you know the coding details of your compiler, you can design interactive programs using the principles presented in chapter 7 along with the interactive examples given in this topic and in chapter 12. If you have our *COBOL Programmer's Handbook*, you will find the complete file-maintenance programs for the Microsoft and Wang compilers in it so you can use one of these as your first model program. Otherwise, you can design and code your own model program based on the ideas given in this text. Then, after you've developed a few interactive programs, you'll be ready to improve upon your first model program and to develop a complete set of interactive model programs for your compiler.

Terminology

field-oriented compiler
screen-oriented compiler

Objective

Given the specifications for an interactive COBOL program that uses internal screens, create an acceptable structure chart for its design.

Topic 2 How to code interactive programs that use internal screen definitions

Once you learn how to use the screen-handling code for an interactive COBOL compiler, you need to learn how to code it in structured style. When your compiler uses internally-defined screens, however, this is quite easy. Since the screen-handling code consists of logical extensions to standard COBOL code, you simply apply the principles presented in chapter 9 to the screen-handling code.

In this topic, then, I'll show you how you can apply the principles of structured coding to screen-handling code. In case you're not familiar with screen-handling code, I'll start this topic by presenting some typical examples. Since there are no COBOL standards for this type of code, I'll show you examples for both field-oriented and screen-oriented compilers. Once you're familiar with this type of code, I'll present some guidelines for coding it in a structured style.

Types of screen-handling code

As I said in the first topic of this chapter, there are two types of compilers that use internally-defined screens. The first type provides field-oriented code for screen-handling; the second type provides screen-oriented code. At this time, then, I'd like to show you some examples of code for each type of compiler.

Screen-handling code for field-oriented compilers Figure 13-8 shows some examples of field-oriented code when using the Microsoft COBOL compiler. As you can see, all of this code is in the Procedure Division. The three paragraphs shown are for the display, format, and accept modules in the structure chart in figure 13-4.

In the display and format modules, you can see that DISPLAY statements are used to erase a screen, to display a constant like MAINTAIN CUSTOMER FILE, and to display the contents of a field like DISPLAY-DATE. In the accept module, you can see that ACCEPT statements are used to get a value from the screen and to determine which function key the operator has pressed (if any). The numbers in the parentheses after a DISPLAY or ACCEPT verb give the row and column at which a display or accept operation should start.

```
 PROCEDURE DIVISION.
*
      .
      .
      .
*
 100-DISPLAY-SCREEN-CONSTANTS.
*
     DISPLAY (1, 1)  ERASE.
     DISPLAY (1, 2)  "MAINTAIN CUSTOMER FILE".
     DISPLAY (1, 66) "DATE:".
     DISPLAY (6, 2)  "CUSTOMER NUMBER:".
     CALL "SYSDATE" USING CURRENT-DATE.
     MOVE CURRENT-DATE TO DISPLAY-DATE.
     DISPLAY (1, 72) DISPLAY-DATE.
*
      .
      .
      .
*
 310-FORMAT-ACTION-SCREEN.
*
     DISPLAY (4, 2)  "ACTION:".
     DISPLAY (6, 2)  "CUSTOMER CODE:".
     DISPLAY (6, 16) ERASE.
     DISPLAY (24, 2) ACTION-OPTIONS-MESSAGE.
*
      .
      .
      .
*
 370-ACCEPT-CUSTOMER-CODE.
*
     ACCEPT (6, 19) CM-KEY WITH UPDATE.
     ACCEPT FUNCTION-KEY FROM ESCAPE KEY.
     IF F10
         MOVE "Y" TO END-PROGRAM-SW.
*
```

Figure 13-8 Field-oriented screen-handling code in Microsoft COBOL

Another way in which a field-oriented compiler can work is shown in figure 13-9. In this example of Datapoint COBOL, the ACCEPT verb refers to a Data Division definition for a field on a screen. And the data definition gives the location of the field on the screen. Also, the data definition tells where the default value of the field is to come from (FROM CM-KEY) and where the entered value is to be stored (INTO CM-KEY). Although the actual syntax of the data definition for a screen field will vary from one system to another, this example is typical of many field-oriented compilers.

Whether a field-oriented compiler provides its screen-handling functions via Procedure Division code or a combination of Data and Procedure Division code, most compilers provide for functions other than those I've just illustrated. For example, most compilers provide for editing a displayed field so it's easier to read. And some compilers provide code that allows you to specify left and right justification, display intensity,

```
 DATA DIVISION.
*
      .
      .
      05   AS-CUST-CODE        LINE 6
                               COLUMN 19
                               PIC X(5)
                               FROM CM-KEY
                               INTO CM-KEY.
      .
      .
*
 PROCEDURE DIVISION.
*
      .
      .
      ACCEPT AS-CUST-CODE.
      .
      .
```

Figure 13-9 Field-oriented screen-handling code using Datapoint COBOL

blinking, reverse video, underlining, display suppression...even colors. Since my point here is not to teach you interactive coding, I'm not going to present any of these functions in this book. But you should become familiar with the code for all of the screen-handling functions that are used in your shop.

Screen-handling code for screen-oriented compilers Figure 13-10 shows an example of screen-handling code when using the Wang VS COBOL compiler. Specifically, this shows the code related to module 310 in the structure chart in figure 13-6. As you can see, the entire action screen is defined in the Data Division. Then, the DISPLAY AND READ statement is used in the Procedure Division to display the entire screen and to accept data from all of the entry fields defined for the screen. In this case, however, only one field is accepted from the screen (the customer code field) along with one function key indicating the action to be taken.

In this example, you can see that the syntax for the screen definitions differs somewhat from that in figure 13-9. Instead of FROM and INTO, the Wang compiler uses SOURCE and OBJECT to tell where the default value of a field is to come from and where the entered value is to be stored. You can also see that the entire screen definition is given a usage of DISPLAY-WS, which is a COBOL extension that indicates a screen definition.

In the Procedure Division, you can see some screen-handling code related to the use of program function keys (PF keys). The phrase

```
ONLY PFKEYS 1, 2, 3, 16
```

means that only these keys are active when this screen is displayed. So when the operator presses one of these four keys, the program continues;

```
 01  ACTION-SCREEN          DISPLAY-WS.
*
     05  FILLER             LINE 1
                            COLUMN 1
                            PIC X(80)
                            SOURCE DSP-HEADING-LINE.
     05   FILLER            LINE 6
                            COLUMN 2
                            PIC X(14)
                            VALUE "CUSTOMER CODE:".
     05  AS-CUST-CODE       LINE 6
                            COLUMN 19
                            PIC X(5)
                            SOURCE CM-KEY
                            OBJECT CM-KEY.
     05  FILLER             LINE 22
                            COLUMN 1
                            PIC X(80)
                            SOURCE DSP-LINE-22.
     05  FILLER             LINE 23
                            COLUMN 1
                            PIC X(80)
                            SOURCE DSP-ERROR-LINE.
     05  FILLER             LINE 24
                            COLUMN 1
                            PIC X(80)
                            SOURCE DSP-MESSAGE-LINE.
*
     .
     .
 310-ACCEPT-ACTION-ENTRY.
*
     MOVE "PF1 = ADD; PF2 = CHANGE; PF3 = DELETE; PF16 = END PROGR
-         "AM" TO DSP-MESSAGE-AREA.
     MOVE SCREEN-ORDER-AREA
         TO ORDER-AREA OF ACTION-SCREEN.
     DISPLAY AND READ ACTION-SCREEN ON SCREEN
         ONLY PFKEYS 1, 2, 3, 16.
     IF FUNCTION-KEY EQUAL 16
         MOVE "Y" TO END-PROGRAM-SW.
     SET WCC-BEEP IN SOA-WCC OFF.
*
```

Figure 13-10 Screen-oriented screen-handling code in Wang VS COBOL

otherwise, the program waits for a valid response. The last statement in this module is screen-handling code that turns off the beeper on the operator's workstation. The beeper is turned on when an invalid field is entered, as you will see later.

Like a field-oriented compiler, a typical screen-oriented compiler provides screen-handling functions other than those I've just illustrated. For example, most compilers provide for editing a displayed field so it's easier to read. And some compilers provide code that allows you to specify left and right justification, display intensity, blinking, reverse video, underlining, display suppression...even colors. Since my point here is not to teach you interactive coding, I'm not going to present any of these functions in this book. Here again, though, you should become familiar with the code for all of the screen-handling functions that are used in your shop.

Coding guidelines for interactive programs

If you're comfortable with the ideas for coding structured COBOL for batch programs as presented in chapter 9, you won't have any trouble coding an interactive program. Frankly, the difficult part of developing an interactive COBOL program is designing it. Once that's done, the coding is easy.

At this time, then, I'll present some coding guidelines for interactive programs that use internally-defined screens. As you will see, all of these are logical extensions to the ideas I presented in chapter 9.

Environment Division

If your compiler requires screen-handling code in the Environment Division, make sure that it is organized so your programs are as easy to develop as possible. When using Wang COBOL, for example, you have to use hexadecimal codes to position the cursor of a screen, change the intensity of a field, protect a displayed field from being modified by an operator, and so on. But if you use these codes in their hex form, your programs will be difficult to read, develop, and maintain. Fortunately, however, the compiler lets you give symbolic names to these values in the Environment Division. Then, by using these names, you can create programs that are much easier to develop and maintain.

Figure 13-11 is a COPY member that gives symbolic names to the hex values that are required for screen-handling on the Wang VS. We use it in all of our interactive programs. If you look ahead to figures 13-13, 13-16, and 13-17, you can see how these figurative constants are used in the Data Division and Procedure Division of a program. You can also imagine how difficult the programs would be to understand if we didn't use symbolic names for this purpose.

Data Division

Most interactive COBOL programs will require some Data Division fields that are directly associated with screen-handling. To make your programs consistent throughout your shop, then, you should adopt a standard way to code these data descriptions. In particular, you should adopt standards for sequencing these descriptions and standards for formatting them.

The sequence of screen-handling descriptions In general, you should group all screen-handling fields at the end of the working-storage section

```
BIT-0                  IS "80"
BIT-1                  IS "40"
BIT-2                  IS "20"
BIT-3                  IS "10"
BIT-4                  IS "08"
BIT-5                  IS "04"
BIT-6                  IS "02"
BIT-7                  IS "01"
HEX-1                  IS "01"
HEX-2                  IS "02"
HEX-3                  IS "03"
HEX-4                  IS "04"
HEX-5                  IS "05"
HEX-6                  IS "06"
.
.
.
FAC-BLI-PRO-ALL        IS "94"
FAC-BLI-PRO-ALL-UL     IS "B4"
FAC-BLI-PRO-UC         IS "95"
FAC-BLI-PRO-UC-UL      IS "B5"
FAC-BLI-PRO-NUM        IS "96"
FAC-BLI-PRO-NUM-UL     IS "B6"
FAC-BLA-MOD-ALL        IS "98"
FAC-BLA-MOD-ALL-UL     IS "B8"
FAC-BLA-MOD-UC         IS "99"
FAC-BLA-MOD-UC-UL      IS "B9"
FAC-BLA-MOD-NUM        IS "9A"
FAC-BLA-MOD-NUM-UL     IS "BA"
FAC-BLA-PRO-ALL        IS "9C"
FAC-BLA-PRO-ALL-UL     IS "BC"
FAC-BLA-PRO-UC         IS "9D"
FAC-BLA-PRO-UC-UL      IS "BD"
FAC-BLA-PRO-NUM        IS "9E"
FAC-BLA-PRO-NUM-UL     IS "BE"
FAC-DISPLAY-DIM        IS "8C"
FAC-DISPLAY-BRIGHT     IS "84"
FAC-ALPHA-ENTRY        IS "81"
FAC-NUMERIC-ENTRY      IS "82"
FAC-BLINK              IS "91"
FAC-BLANK              IS "9C"
WCC-POSITION-CURSOR    IS "A0"
WCC-ALARM              IS "E0"
WP-RETURN-CHAR         IS "03"
WP-MERGE-CHAR          IS "0D".
```

Figure 13-11 A COPY member for the figurative constants used for screen-handling in the Environment Division of a Wang VS COBOL program

of the Data Division. On some compilers, screen descriptions are coded in their own Data Division section that immediately follows working storage. For example, Microsoft COBOL has a SCREEN SECTION, and Datapoint COBOL has a FORMS SECTION. On other systems, screen-handling code is contained entirely within working storage. Regardless of the program organization forced on you by your compiler, though, if you group all screen-related fields at the end of working storage, they'll be in the same place in all of your installation's programs.

Screen-control fields

Standard screen-control fields (COPY member)
Program-specific screen-control fields

Screen constants

Standard heading-zone constants (COPY member)
Standard communication-zone constants (COPY member)
Standard captions (COPY member)
Program-specific captions
Standard operator instructions (COPY member)
Program-specific operator instructions
Standard error messages (COPY member)
Program-specific error messages

Screen descriptions

These should be coded in the normal sequence in which they appear when the program is executed.

Figure 13-12 Suggested coding sequence for screen-handling code in the Data Division

Within the screen-handling code, you should use a standard sequence for coding groups of fields in the Data Division. For instance, we use the sequence shown in figure 13-12. Here, we've grouped the screen-handling code into three major groups: (1) screen-control fields, (2) screen constants, and (3) screen descriptions. Note that this sequence will work even if the screen descriptions have to be coded in their own section.

To improve your programming efficiency, you should use COPY members for the fields within these groups whenever possible. For example, figure 13-13 presents two COPY members that we use with Wang COBOL in our shop. The first is for some screen-control fields. The second is for some screen constants that define the heading line and the communication lines of a standard screen.

Depending on your compiler, you may or may not have to code *screen-control fields*. Of the three types of screen-handling fields, control fields vary the most from one compiler to the next. For example, on the Wang VS compiler, the position of the cursor is controlled by manipulating the values of fields in a group item called the *screen order area* as defined by the COPY member in figure 13-13. In contrast, other systems handle cursor positioning in a completely different way.

Screen constants consist of data elements that will be used for headings, captions, and messages throughout your program. Like screen-control fields, many screen constants should be treated as COPY members since all screens in an installation should be formatted in the same way and should use similar error messages. For example, figure 13-13 shows a

```
 01   SCREEN-ORDER-AREA.
*
      05   SOA-RECORD-NO        PIC X     VALUE HEX-1.
      05   SOA-WCC              PIC X     VALUE LOW-VALUE.
      05   SOA-COLUMN-NO        PIC X     VALUE HEX-1.
      05   SOA-ROW-NO           PIC X     VALUE HEX-1.
```

```
 01   DSP-HEADING-LINE.
*
      05   FILLER             PIC X          VALUE FAC-DIM-PRO-UC-UL.
      05   DSP-PROGRAM-NAME   PIC X(50).
      05   FILLER             PIC X(15)      VALUE SPACE.
      05   FILLER             PIC X(6)       VALUE "DATE: ".
      05   DSP-SYSTEM-DATE    PIC 99/99/99.
*
 01   DSP-LINE-22.
*
      05   FILLER             PIC X          VALUE FAC-DIM-PRO-UC-UL.
      05   FILLER             PIC X(79)      VALUE SPACE.
*
 01   DSP-MESSAGE-LINE.
*
      05   DSP-MESSAGE-FAC    PIC X          VALUE FAC-BRT-PRO-ALL.
      05   DSP-MESSAGE-AREA   PIC X(79)      VALUE SPACE.
*
 01   DSP-ERROR-LINE.
*
      05   DSP-ERROR-FAC      PIC X          VALUE FAC-BRT-PRO-ALL.
      05   DSP-ERROR-MESSAGE  PIC X(79)      VALUE SPACE.
```

Figure 13-13 Two COPY members used for screen-handling code in the Data Division of a Wang VS COBOL program

COPY member that defines constants in the heading and communications zones of a standard screen. So if you haven't set up COPY members for common screen constants, you should do so soon.

In most interactive programs, *screen descriptions* make up the largest portion of the screen-handling code in the Data Division. For instance, the Data Division code in figure 13-10 is a screen description for the action screen of the file-maintenance program. In general, you should code screen descriptions in the normal sequence in which the screens appear when the program is executed. Since screen descriptions vary from one program to another, you normally can't use COPY members for them. But if one program uses the same screen that another program uses, by all means copy the screen description from the old program into the new one.

Formatting guidelines for screen descriptions Because screen descriptions can make up a significant portion of an interactive COBOL program, here are some general guidelines for formatting them. To start, you should (1) code each screen description as an 01-level item; (2) give each screen the name assigned to it on the screen-layout form; (3) define each screen field as an 05-level item; and (4) code the screen fields in the sequence in which they appear on the screen, from top to bottom and left to right. If you do these things, it's easy to locate a screen or field description when you need to refer to one later on.

In some cases, it's appropriate to define component parts of an 05-level item. For example, you might code a date field at the 05-level and want to break it down into month, day, and year. When you do, number the lower-level items in increments of 5. In this case, the month, day, and year fields would be coded at level 10. When coding screen descriptions, it's rarely necessary to code levels below 10.

If you'll need to refer to a screen field in a Procedure Division statement, give that field a name. In this case, create the name just as you would if the field were part of a record description: first, form a suffix from the first letters of the screen name; then, name the field within the record. In figure 13-10, for example, the customer code field is named AS-CUST-CODE with AS standing for Action Screen. For fields that won't be referred to, name them FILLER if your system allows it (most do).

In addition to a field name (or FILLER), most screen elements require five clauses: (1) row location, (2) column location, (3) picture, (4) value, either literal (VALUE) or variable (SOURCE/FROM), and (5) receiving field (OBJECT/INTO). In addition, some fields may require clauses for special features. To make these clauses as readable as possible, you should code each clause on a separate line in a standard sequence like the one above and you should align the clauses.

You can see these coding guidelines illustrated by the screen description in figure 13-14. This is the description for the customer-entry screen of the file-maintenance program as it is coded in Wang VS COBOL. As you can see, this description is easy to read so it makes the program easier to develop and maintain.

Procedure Division

If my recommendations for the Data Division differ little from batch coding standards, my suggestions for the Procedure Division differ even less. If you've understood the program designs presented in the last topic, coding the Procedure Divisions should present no problems for you. If you apply the batch coding principles of chapter 9 to your interactive Procedure Divisions, they'll be well structured, easy to develop, and easy to maintain.

As in a batch program, you should code each module of a structure chart as a separate COBOL paragraph. If your structure chart is organized as I recommended in topic 1, each module will usually be of a reasonable size and screen I/O functions (as well as file I/O functions) will be isolated in their own modules. In addition, you'll be able to code the entire program without using GOTO statements.

```
 01   CUSTOMER-ENTRY-SCREEN  DISPLAY-WS.
*
      05   FILLER               LINE 1
                                COLUMN 1
                                PIC X(80)
                                SOURCE DSP-HEADING-LINE.
      05   FILLER               LINE 6
                                COLUMN 2
                                PIC X(14)
                                VALUE "CUSTOMER CODE:".
      05   CES-CUST-CODE        LINE 6
                                COLUMN 19
                                PIC X(5)
                                SOURCE CM-CUSTOMER-CODE.
      05   FILLER               LINE 8
                                COLUMN 2
                                PIC X(5)
                                VALUE "NAME:".
      05   CES-NAME             LINE 8
                                COLUMN 19
                                PIC X(30)
                                SOURCE CM-NAME
                                OBJECT CM-NAME.
      05   FILLER               LINE 9
                                COLUMN 2
                                PIC X(8)
                                VALUE "ADDRESS:".
      05   CES-ADDRESS          LINE 9
                                COLUMN 19
                                PIC X(30)
                                SOURCE CM-ADDRESS
                                OBJECT CM-ADDRESS.
      05   FILLER               LINE 10
                                COLUMN 2
                                PIC X(8)
                                VALUE "CITY:".
      05   CES-CITY             LINE 10
                                COLUMN 19
                                PIC X(21)
                                SOURCE CM-CITY
                                OBJECT CM-CITY.
      05   CES-STATE            LINE 10
                                COLUMN 41
                                PIC XX
                                SOURCE CM-STATE
                                OBJECT CM-STATE.
      05   CES-ZIP-CODE         LINE 10
                                COLUMN 44
                                PIC X(5)
                                SOURCE CM-ZIP-CODE
                                OBJECT CM-ZIP-CODE.
      05   FILLER               LINE 22
                                COLUMN 1
                                PIC X(80)
                                SOURCE DSP-LINE-22.
      05   FILLER               LINE 23
                                COLUMN 1
                                PIC X(80)
                                SOURCE DSP-ERROR-LINE.
```

Figure 13-14 A screen description in structured style for the customer-entry screen of the file-maintenance program as coded in Wang VS COBOL

Figures 13-15 and 13-16 give examples of Procedure Division coding for typical control modules in interactive programs. The first example is in Microsoft COBOL; the second is in Wang VS COBOL. Both examples are for the file-maintenance program presented in topic 1, so the coding in figure 13-15 is for the structure chart in figure 13-4. And the coding in figure 13-16 is for the structure chart in figure 13-6. If you review this code, I'm sure you'll see how similar interactive control code is to batch code. Although the code in figure 13-16 includes a few screen-handling statements, the code in figure 13-15 has none.

When you code the Procedure Division for an interactive program, you sometimes run into problems that you don't often encounter in a batch program. Two common problems are (1) that you can't always move subfunctions down the line as recommended in chapter 8; and (2) that you can't always code an interactive module in the most straightforward manner possible. Before closing, then, let me briefly discuss these problems.

When you shouldn't move subfunctions down the line If you remember from chapter 8, one general principle of module planning for a batch program is to code a subfunction in the lowest-level module possible. In other words, you should move subfunctions down the line. Although that's also a good general rule for interactive programs, it doesn't always work. In some interactive programs, you'll find that you have to code trivial subfunctions in high-level modules if the program is to work properly.

In an interactive program that edits all entry fields, for example, an operator should be allowed to return to an entry screen and correct any errors the program detects. In terms of coding, that means that a get-screen module should be performed until the data it gets is error-free. In addition, however, the logical place to put code that sets entry fields to their initial values (normally, spaces or zeros) is in this get-screen module. After all, initializing screen values is a subfunction. So it should be moved down the line into the get-screen module, or perhaps into an even lower module.

Unfortunately, though, your program won't work right if you initialize entry fields in the get-screen module of a program. In this case, whenever an operator wants to correct some of his entries, the variables will be reset to their starting values. As a result, the data the operator has already entered is lost. But this means that the operator has to reenter all of the fields in the screen, not just those he wants to correct. Since this reduces operator efficiency, this obviously isn't the way you want an interactive program to work. As a result, the entry fields must be set to their initial values in a module above the get-screen module. In this case, then, the subfunction must be moved up the line instead of down the line.

This basic idea is illustrated by the code in figure 13-16. Here, you can see that all of the fields in the customer master record are set to spaces in module 400, not in the module that gets the customer-entry screen (module 410). If the fields were cleared in module 410, the

```
 PROCEDURE DIVISION.
*
 000-MAINTAIN-CUSTOMER-FILE.
*
     OPEN I-O CUSTMAST.
     PERFORM 100-DISPLAY-SCREEN-CONSTANTS.
     PERFORM 200-MAINTAIN-CUSTOMER-RECORD
         UNTIL END-PROGRAM.
     PERFORM 900-CLEAR-SCREEN.
     CLOSE CUSTMAST.
     CHAIN "MNT2000.EXE".
     STOP RUN.
*
     .
     .
     .
*
 200-MAINTAIN-CUSTOMER-RECORD.
*
     MOVE SPACE TO CM-KEY
                   ACTION-FLAG.
     PERFORM 300-GET-VALID-ACTION-SCREEN.
     IF NOT END-PROGRAM
         MOVE "N"    TO CANCEL-ENTRY-SW
         MOVE SPACE TO VERIFICATION-FLAG
         IF ADD-RECORD
             MOVE SPACE  TO CUSTOMER-MASTER-RECORD
             MOVE CM-KEY TO CM-CUSTOMER-CODE
             PERFORM 400-PROCESS-CUSTOMER-ADDITION
                 UNTIL ACCEPT-ENTRY
                    OR CANCEL-ENTRY
         ELSE IF CHANGE-RECORD
             PERFORM 700-PROCESS-CUSTOMER-CHANGE
                 UNTIL ACCEPT-ENTRY
                    OR CANCEL-ENTRY
         ELSE IF DELETE-RECORD
             PERFORM 800-PROCESS-CUSTOMER-DELETION
                 UNTIL ACCEPT-ENTRY
                    OR CANCEL-ENTRY.
*
     .
     .
     .
*
 400-PROCESS-CUSTOMER-ADDITION.
*
     PERFORM 410-FORMAT-ENTRY-SCREEN.
     PERFORM 420-GET-VALID-CUSTOMER-DATA.
     IF NOT CANCEL-ENTRY
         MOVE SPACE TO VERIFICATION-FLAG
         MOVE "N"    TO VALID-ENTRY-SW
         PERFORM 580-GET-TRAN-VERIFICATION
             UNTIL VALID-ENTRY
         IF ACCEPT-ENTRY
             PERFORM 610-WRITE-CUSTOMER-RECORD.
*
```

Figure 13-15 Procedure Division code for the file-maintenance program in Microsoft COBOL

```
 PROCEDURE DIVISION.
*
 000-MAINTAIN-CUSTOMER-FILE.
*
     CALL "SYSDATE" USING CURRENT-DATE.
     MOVE CURRENT-DATE              TO DSP-SYSTEM-DATE.
     MOVE "MAINTAIN CUSTOMER FILE" TO DSP-PROGRAM-NAME.
     OPEN SHARED CUSTMAST
          I-O    SCREEN.
     PERFORM 100-SET-FIELD-ATTRIBUTES.
     PERFORM 200-MAINTAIN-CUSTOMER-RECORD
         UNTIL END-PROGRAM.
     CLOSE CUSTMAST
           SCREEN.
     STOP RUN.
*
     .
     .
     .
*
 200-MAINTAIN-CUSTOMER-RECORD.
*
     MOVE SPACE  TO CM-KEY
                    DSP-ERROR-MESSAGE.
     MOVE HEX-6  TO SOA-ROW-NO.
     MOVE HEX-19 TO SOA-COLUMN-NO.
     MOVE "N"    TO VALID-ACTION-SW.
     PERFORM 300-GET-ACTION-ENTRY
         UNTIL VALID-ACTION.
     IF NOT END-PROGRAM
         MOVE "N" TO CANCEL-ENTRY-SW
         IF FUNCTION-KEY EQUAL 1
             PERFORM 400-PROCESS-CUSTOMER-ADDITION
         ELSE IF FUNCTION-KEY EQUAL 2
             PERFORM 500-PROCESS-CUSTOMER-CHANGE
         ELSE IF FUNCTION-KEY EQUAL 3
             PERFORM 600-PROCESS-CUSTOMER-DELETION.
*
     .
     .
     .
*
 400-PROCESS-CUSTOMER-ADDITION.
*
     MOVE SPACE  TO CUSTOMER-MASTER-RECORD.
     MOVE CM-KEY TO CM-CUSTOMER-CODE.
     MOVE HEX-8  TO SOA-ROW-NO.
     MOVE HEX-19 TO SOA-COLUMN-NO.
     MOVE "N"    TO VALID-ENTRY-SW.
     PERFORM 410-GET-CUSTOMER-DATA
         UNTIL VALID-ENTRY.
     IF NOT CANCEL-ENTRY
         PERFORM 450-WRITE-CUSTOMER-RECORD.
*
```

Figure 13-16 Procedure Division code for the file-maintenance program in Wang VS COBOL

operator would have to reenter all of the fields in the customer-entry screen each time the editing module detected an error.

Of course, there are other ways to code an initialization subfunction like this. If you prefer to move the subfunction down the line, you can do so. If you do, though, you need to code additional conditions at the lower level and set switches properly above. So the result is a more complicated program, one in which the called module isn't properly independent of the calling module. In a case like this, then, it makes more sense to move the subfunction up the line, not down the line.

Why you shouldn't code a screen-oriented edit module in the most straightforward manner possible Batch programming standards encourage you to code each module of a program in the most obvious and straightforward way. That makes a program easier to maintain. And, of course, you should also do this in an interactive program. At times, though, it's better to write a segment of interactive code in a way that isn't straightforward.

To illustrate this, look at the code in figure 13-17. This is the code for the edit module in the screen-oriented version of the file-maintenance program. This module edits all of the customer data fields, highlights those that are in error, turns the workstation beeper on, positions the cursor to the first field in error, and displays an appropriate error message. But if you look closely, you can see that the fields are edited in the reverse order from the way they appear on the screen. And this isn't the most straightforward way to code the module.

We coded the module this way so the cursor will point to the first field in error when control is passed back to the entry operator and so the error message will apply to this first field. In contrast, if we had coded the field edits in the sequence in which the fields appear on the screen, the program would work all right if only one field was in error. But if the operator made two or more errors, the program would display an error message for the last incorrect field and position the cursor at it. Since that isn't what we want if we want to maximize operator efficiency, we edited the fields in the reverse order from the way in which they appear on the screen.

Since this is efficient code for an edit module, we recommend that you code your own edit modules as in figure 13-17. Even though the fields are edited in the reverse sequence from the way you would expect them to be edited in a batch program, that's the right way to code a module like this. Although it is possible to edit the fields in the order they appear and have the error display work properly, it's a more complicated and less efficient method.

Discussion

Once you understand the screen-handling code for an interactive compiler that uses internal screens, you should develop standards for

```
 430-EDIT-CUSTOMER-DATA.
*
     IF CM-ZIP-CODE = SPACE
         MOVE HEX-10     TO SOA-ROW-NO
         MOVE HEX-44     TO SOA-COLUMN-NO
         MOVE FAC-BLINK TO FAC OF CES-ZIP-CODE
         MOVE "ZIP CODE:  YOU MUST ENTER A ZIP CODE."
             TO DSP-ERROR-MESSAGE.
     IF CM-STATE = SPACE
         MOVE HEX-10     TO SOA-ROW-NO
         MOVE HEX-41     TO SOA-COLUMN-NO
         MOVE FAC-BLINK TO FAC OF CES-STATE
         MOVE "STATE:  YOU MUST ENTER A STATE."
             TO DSP-ERROR-MESSAGE
     ELSE
         CALL "STATEDIT" USING CM-STATE
                               VALID-STATE-SW
         IF NOT VALID-STATE
             MOVE HEX-10     TO SOA-ROW-NO
             MOVE HEX-41     TO SOA-COLUMN-NO
             MOVE FAC-BLINK TO FAC OF CES-STATE
             MOVE "STATE:  INVALID STATE CODE"
                 TO DSP-ERROR-MESSAGE.
     IF DSP-ERROR-MESSAGE = SPACE
         CALL "ZIPEDIT" USING CM-STATE
                              CM-ZIP-CODE
                              VALID-ZIP-CODE-SW
         IF NOT VALID-ZIP-CODE
             MOVE HEX-10     TO SOA-ROW-NO
             MOVE HEX-44     TO SOA-COLUMN-NO
             MOVE FAC-BLINK TO FAC OF CES-ZIP-CODE
             MOVE "ZIP CODE:  ZIP CODE DOESN'T AGREE WITH STATE CO
-                "DE." TO DSP-ERROR-MESSAGE.
     IF CM-CITY = SPACE
         MOVE HEX-10     TO SOA-ROW-NO
         MOVE HEX-19     TO SOA-COLUMN-NO
         MOVE FAC-BLINK TO FAC OF CES-CITY
         MOVE "CITY:  YOU MUST ENTER A CITY."
             TO DSP-ERROR-MESSAGE.
     IF CM-ADDRESS = SPACE
         MOVE HEX-9      TO SOA-ROW-NO
         MOVE HEX-19     TO SOA-COLUMN-NO
         MOVE FAC-BLINK TO FAC OF CES-ADDRESS
         MOVE "ADDRESS:  YOU MUST ENTER AN ADDRESS."
             TO DSP-ERROR-MESSAGE.
     IF CM-NAME = SPACE
         MOVE HEX-8      TO SOA-ROW-NO
         MOVE HEX-19     TO SOA-COLUMN-NO
         MOVE FAC-BLINK TO FAC OF CES-NAME
         MOVE "NAME:  YOU MUST ENTER A NAME."
             TO DSP-ERROR-MESSAGE.
     IF DSP-ERROR-MESSAGE NOT = SPACE
         MOVE "N" TO VALID-ENTRY-SW
         SET WCC-BEEP IN SOA-WCC ON.
*
```

Figure 13-17 An edit module in Wang VS COBOL in which the fields are edited in reverse order from the way they appear on the screen

using the code. As this topic points out, these standards should be simple extensions to the standards you use for coding batch programs.

With few exceptions, then, you should be able to design and code programs for compilers that use internal screens using the same design and coding principles that you use for batch programs. In contrast, as the next chapter illustrates, you can't always do that when you use a compiler that uses external screens.

Terminology

screen-control field
screen constant
screen description

Objective

Given program specifications and an acceptable design for an interactive program, code the program using the structured coding guidelines given in chapter 9 and in this topic.

Chapter 14

How to design and code interactive programs using CICS on an IBM mainframe

If you're a CICS programmer who isn't using structured techniques to develop your programs, this chapter is for you. Because it's difficult to adapt some of the principles of structured programming to the requirements of CICS, structured techniques aren't widely used in CICS shops. But they should be. By applying the techniques of structured programming to CICS programs, you can improve both program quality and programmer productivity. So the benefits of using structured programming techniques for CICS programs far outweigh the difficulties of using them.

If you don't know CICS, this chapter will introduce you to it from the COBOL programmer's point of view. However, this chapter is an introduction only. If you want to master CICS, we recommend our CICS books by Doug Lowe, *CICS for the COBOL Programmer* (*Part 1* and *Part 2*). In fact, you should know that Doug developed the structured programming standards for CICS programs that are presented in this chapter.

If you don't use CICS but your system does use external screens, we recommend that you read this chapter as an introduction to one type of system that uses external screens. Our hope, then, is that this chapter will give you some ideas that you can apply to the development of programs on your system. By combining the ideas in this chapter with those from the previous chapter, you should be able to develop your own standards for interactive programs. As you read this chapter, though, you should realize that CICS places more restrictions on the programmer than most other systems that use external screens. And this has a significant effect on the way you design and code your programs. So it's probably easier to develop programs for your system than it is to develop them for a CICS system.

Topic 1 How to design interactive programs using CICS on an IBM mainframe

Before you can develop a structure chart for a CICS program, you need to understand a technique that's required for most CICS programs. It's called pseudo-conversational programming. I'll start this topic, then, by presenting this technique. After that, I'll present program specifications for a typical interactive program. I'll finish by showing you how to design a CICS program that meets these specifications. By the time you complete this topic, you should be able to design an effective structure chart for any CICS program.

The pseudo-conversational programming technique

If you're an experienced CICS programmer, you're probably familiar with pseudo-conversational programming. If so, you can skip ahead to the program specifications for the interactive file-maintenance program. Otherwise, you need to know what pseudo-conversational programming is.

As I said in chapter 12, CICS manages networks of terminals attached to IBM mainframe computer systems. Because many users normally use a CICS system at the same time, program efficiency is often a critical consideration on a system like this. In fact, performance is so important in most shops that it dictates how the CICS programs are designed. In particular, most CICS shops require that all programs be designed so they support pseudo-conversational programming as opposed to conversational programming.

Conversational programming When a terminal user executes an interactive program, the program appears to wait for the user to enter data. In fact, the programs I described in the last chapter actually do wait for the user to respond. Programs like this are called *conversational programs*.

Because a computer works so much faster than an operator, you can imagine that a conversational program spends nearly all of its time waiting. On a single-user system (like the IBM PC) or a several-user system (like the Wang VS), that's usually not a problem. But on a CICS system with dozens or hundreds of users, it can be a serious problem.

To illustrate, figure 14-1 shows a CICS system with five users, four of them running conversational programs. As you can see, two of the

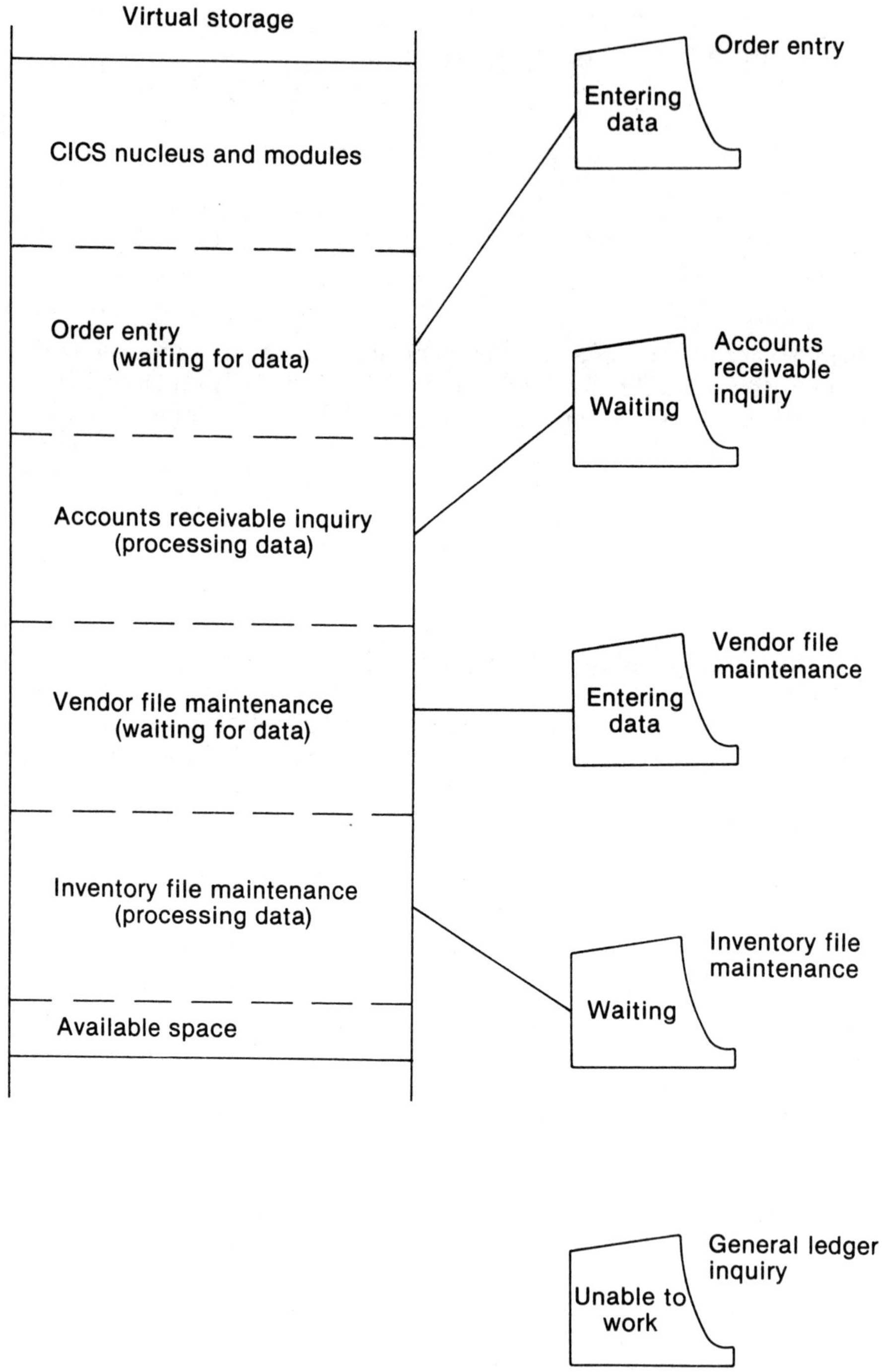

Figure 14-1 Conversational programs under CICS

programs are waiting for data, while the other two are processing data. Because the four programs occupy nearly all of the storage available for interactive programs, a fifth user can't work because there isn't enough storage left to load his program.

In the illustration in figure 14-1, only half of the programs are waiting for input data. That's pretty good. But consider a more typical system with 30 users. If an operator averages 30 seconds to enter a transaction and the system takes one second to process it, then only one of the 30 users' programs is processing data at any given moment. The other 29 are taking up space in storage as they wait for a transaction. And what if the system supports 300 users instead of 30? I think you'll agree that conversational programs can be horribly inefficient on large systems.

Pseudo-conversational programming The solution to this performance problem is to remove a program from storage when it's waiting for data from a terminal. And that's what happens with a *pseudo-conversational program* under CICS. After a pseudo-conversational program processes the data from a screen, it sends another screen to the terminal and ends so it is no longer in storage. However, the operator can continue to key in data at the terminal, because that function is controlled by the terminal, not the program. Then, when the operator has entered the required data, the program is restarted to process it. The result is that the program is in storage only when it needs to be: when it's processing data.

Figure 14-2 shows what happens if the programs in figure 14-1 are pseudo-conversational. Here, only the two programs that are actually processing data take up main storage. As a result, all five operators can work, and storage is available for additional operators. Because pseudo-conversational programs use storage more efficiently than conversational programs, almost all CICS installations require CICS programs to be pseudo-conversational.

How a pseudo-conversational program works To understand how a pseudo-conversational program works, you need to know how a CICS program is restarted. In brief, an operator signals CICS to restart a pseudo-conversational program by pressing one of the terminal's *AID (attention identifier) keys*. AID keys on a 3270-type terminal are the enter key, the clear key, the PF (program function) keys, and the PA (program attention) keys. Of course, most operators don't think in terms of restarting their programs when they press an AID key. Usually, an operator just knows that he presses specific AID keys to get his program to do specific things. On the other hand, as a CICS programmer, you *do* need to think of an AID key as causing a program to be reloaded and executed.

With this as background, you can understand that the typical processing sequence in most CICS programs has six steps. First, the operator keys in data and presses the enter key (one of the AID keys), which restarts the program. Second, CICS reloads the program. Third, the program issues a CICS command, RECEIVE MAP, to retrieve the

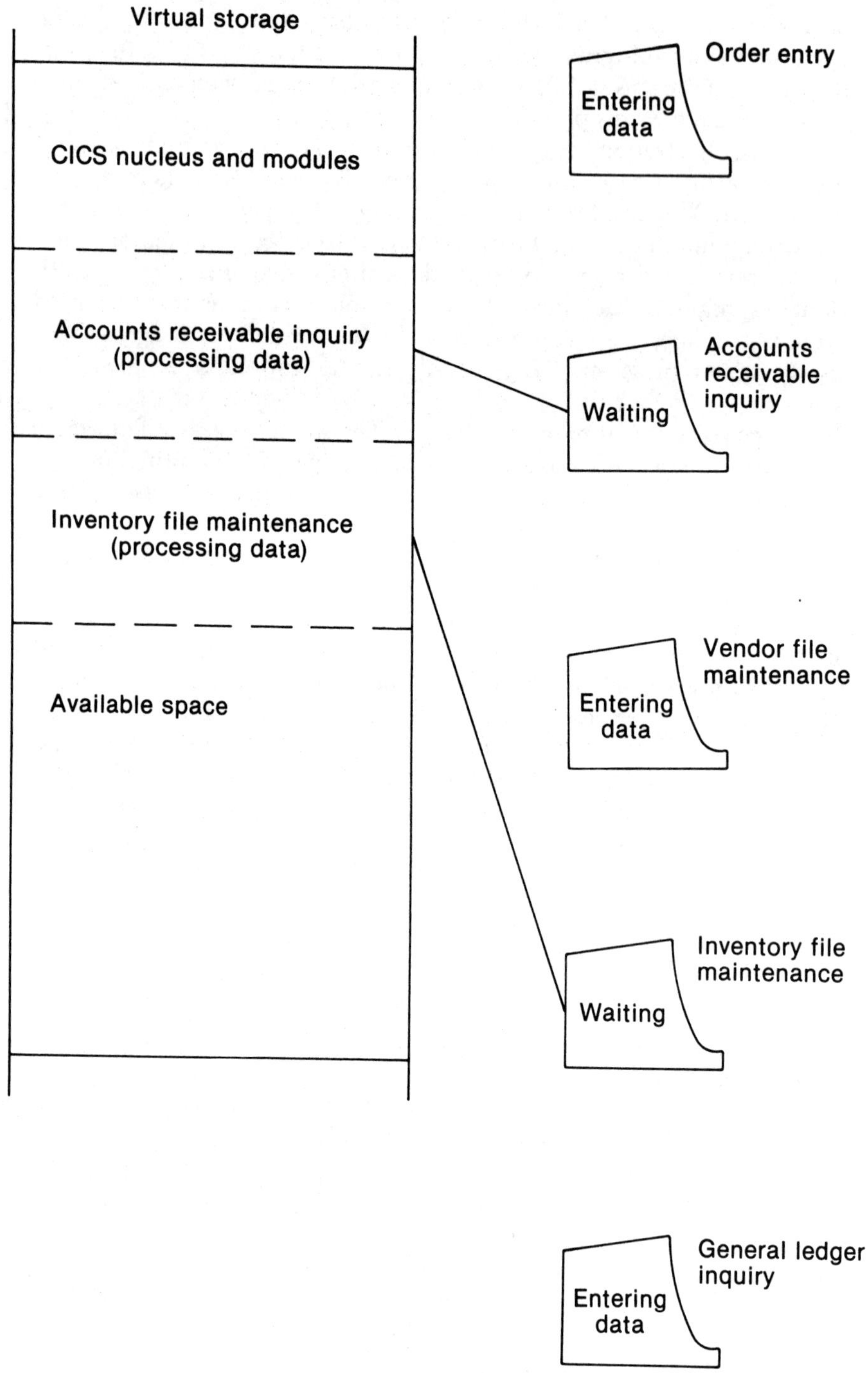

Figure 14-2 Pseudo-conversational programs under CICS

data from the screen. Fourth, the program processes the data it gets from the screen. Fifth, the program issues a CICS command, SEND MAP, to display the next screen (often with processing results displayed on it). Sixth, the program ends by issuing a RETURN command that tells CICS that the program is to be restarted the next time the operator presses an AID key. When the program ends, the terminal still displays the screen image and the operator can enter data on the screen.

To end a pseudo-conversational session, the operator presses a specified AID key (often, the clear key). Then, when the program is restarted, it first determines whether this AID key was pressed. If it wasn't (as is the case during most of the pseudo-conversational session), the program continues through the typical processing sequence. But if the program detects that the operator *did* signal the end of the session, it ends by issuing a RETURN command that does *not* specify that the program is to be restarted. As a result, the pseudo-conversational session ends.

If you're not already familiar with this technique, it may seem strange to you. However, it's quite manageable once you get used to it. In fact, creating a structure chart for a pseudo-conversational CICS program is a relatively simple process.

Program specifications for a CICS file-maintenance program

To illustrate how to design a structure chart for a CICS program, I'll present the design for a typical interactive program. The program overview, the screen flow diagram, and the three screens used by this program are presented in figures 14-3 through 14-7. If you've read chapter 13, you can see that this is the same basic program that I used to illustrate design and coding techniques for systems that use internal screens.

To start, the program gets a customer code from the action screen. But it also determines the transaction type by determining which AID key the operator uses to release the action screen for processing. PF1 (program function key 1) indicates an addition transaction; PF2 indicates a change transaction; PF3 indicates a deletion transaction; and the CLEAR key means that the program should end (no more transactions). Then, if the combination of the customer code and transaction type are valid, the program continues with the next screen.

If the transaction is a change or an addition, the program gets the data from the customer-entry screen. This screen allows the operator to change data taken from a master record that already exists or to enter data for a new record that is to be added to the file. After the program gets valid data from this screen, it gets a response from the transaction-verification screen. This response tells the program whether the operator wants to accept the transaction, modify the transaction using the customer-entry screen, or cancel the transaction altogether and start again with the action screen.

Program: MNT2100	Maintain customer file IBM VS COBOL using CICS	Page: 1
Designer: Steve Eckols		Date: 09-06-84

Input/output specifications

File	Description	Use
CUSTMAST	Customer master file	Update

Process specifications

Until the operator indicates end of program by using the CLEAR key in step 1:

1. Get a valid combination of action code and customer code from the ACTION SCREEN. Use the operator-entered customer code as the primary key for a random read on CUSTMAST. If the action is addition, there shouldn't be a record for the customer code in the customer file; if the action is deletion or change, there should be a record for the customer code in the customer file.

2. For an addition transaction, get the valid customer entries from the CUSTOMER ENTRY SCREEN. Then, get a valid verification entry from the TRANSACTION VERIFICATION SCREEN. If the transaction is accepted, write the addition record onto the customer file. If the transaction is to be modified, repeat this step so the operator can modify the entries for the new customer. If the transaction is to be cancelled, cancel this transaction and continue with step 1.

3. For a change transaction, get the valid change entries from the CUSTOMER ENTRY SCREEN. Then, get a valid verification entry from the TRANSACTION VERIFICATION SCREEN. If the transaction is accepted, write the changed record back onto the customer file. If the transaction is to be modified, repeat this step. If the transaction is to be cancelled, cancel this transaction and continue with step 1.

4. For a deletion transaction, get a valid verification entry from the TRANSACTION VERIFICATION SCREEN. If the transaction is accepted, delete the record from the customer file. If the transaction is to be cancelled, cancel this transaction and continue with step 1.

Figure 14-3 A program overview for the CICS file-maintenance program

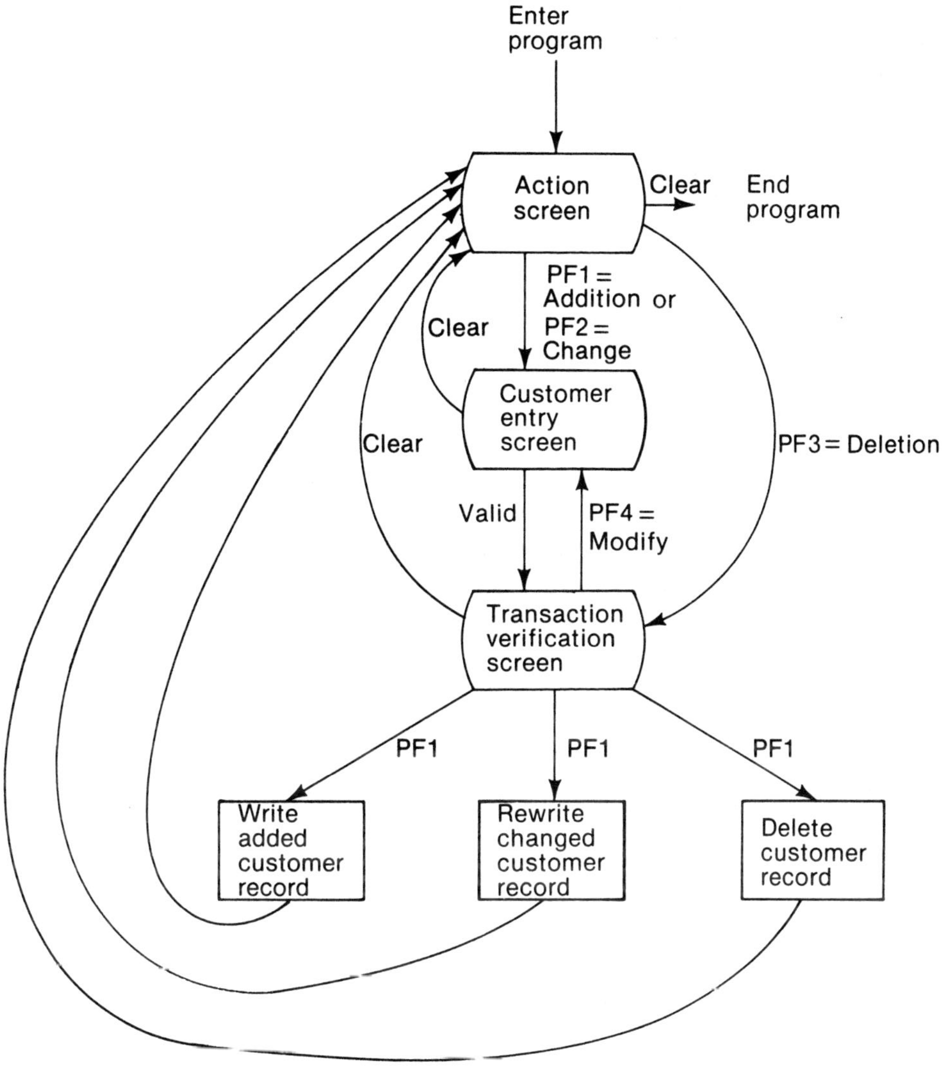

Figure 14-4 A screen flow diagram for the CICS file-maintenance program

If the transaction is a deletion, the program skips the customer-entry screen. Instead, it gets the data from the transaction-verification screen. Then, the operator can tell the program whether he wants to accept the deletion transaction or cancel it. In other words, the operator has only two choices for a deletion (accept or cancel), but he has three choices for a change or an addition (accept, modify, or cancel).

If you look at the layout of the screens in figures 14-5 through 14-7, you can see that the customer-entry and the transaction-verification screens are the same in the heading and data zones. They only differ in the communication zone of the screens. Because of this, as you will see in topic 2, the programmer decided to code them as one external CICS screen.

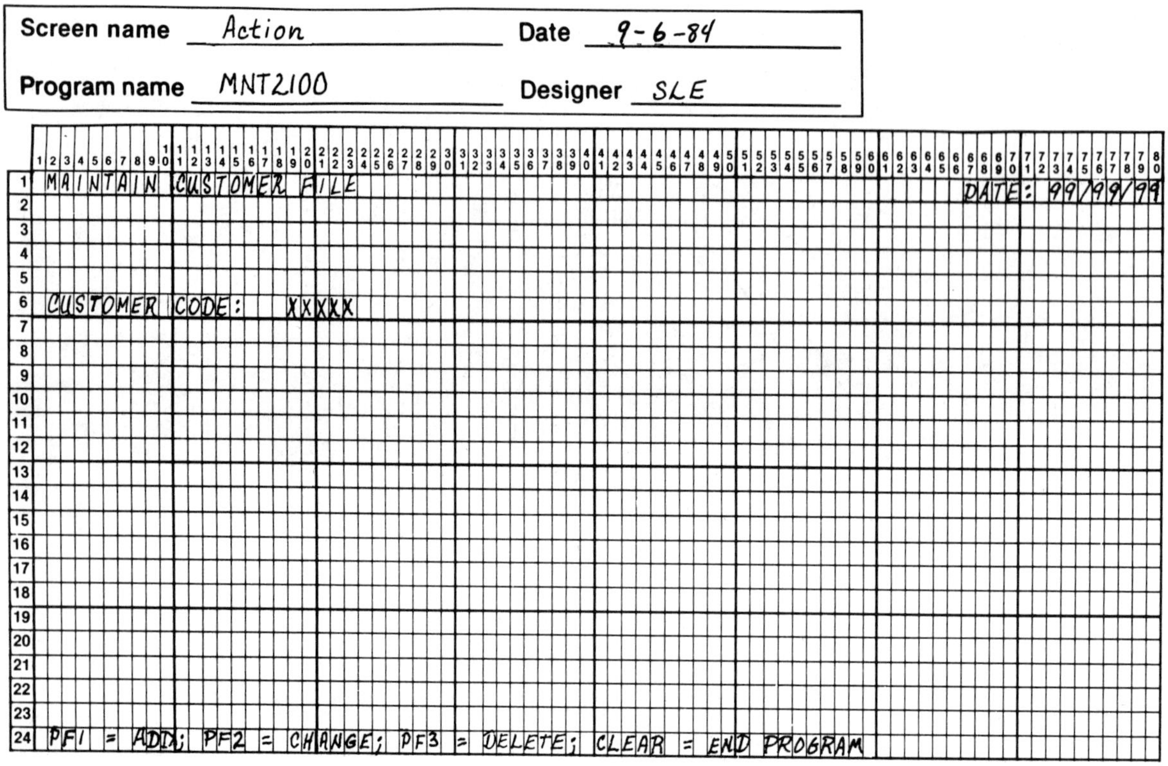

Figure 14-5 The action screen for the CICS file-maintenance program

If you've written programs like this before, you know that you won't always let the operator enter the desired customer code for a new customer (an addition). Instead, you'll let the computer system assign the next available code to the addition record. In this case, however, we're assuming that the user wants to assign mnemonic codes for his customers. Thus, DELTA might be the customer code for Delta Lithograph Company and IBM might be the code for International Business Machines. That way, if the number of customers in the file is relatively low, the user can remember most of the codes of his key customers.

Similarly, if the transactions for a program like this are entered in batches by transaction type, you probably wouldn't make the operator indicate the transaction type for each transaction. Instead, you would have the operator indicate the type only once for each batch of transactions. If, for example, the operator was going to enter a batch of additions, he would only indicate that the transactions are additions at the start of the batch. Then, the program would only ask for the customer codes and field entries for the addition records until all of them had been processed. At that time, the operator would indicate that he wanted to enter a different type of transaction and the program would respond accordingly.

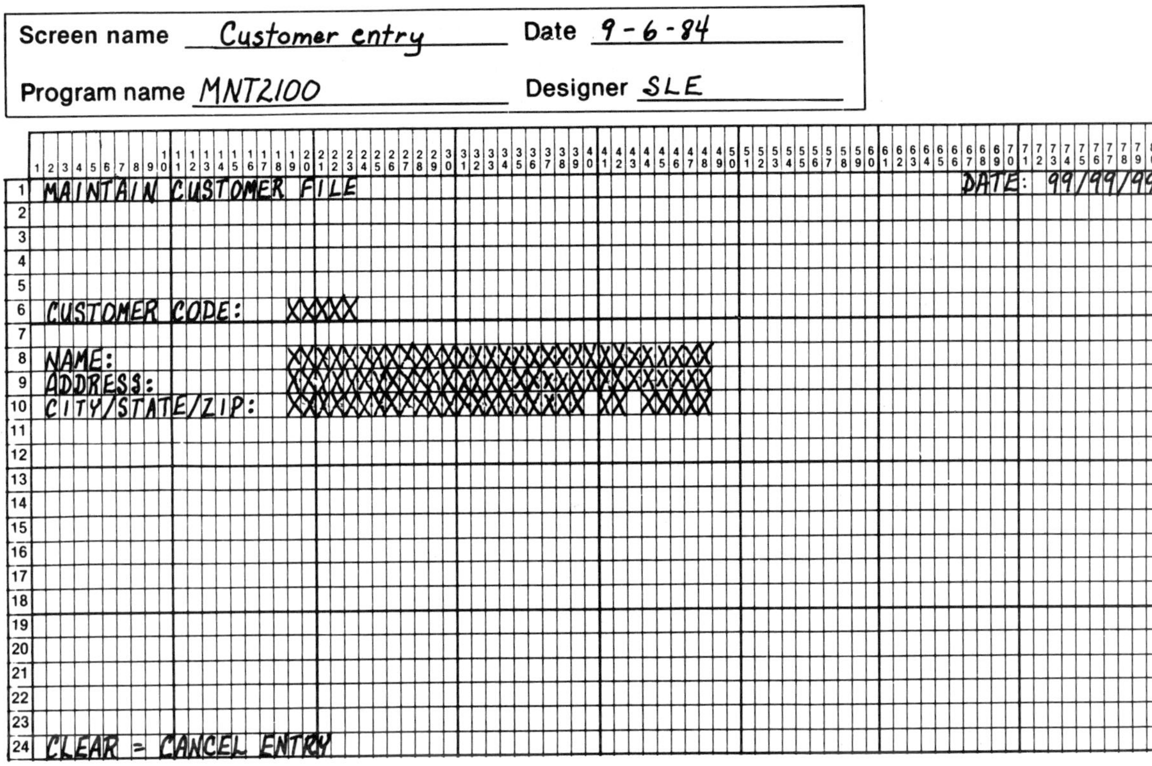

Figure 14-6 The customer-entry screen for the CICS file-maintenance program

You can see, then, that the screen layouts and screen flow for a program like this depend to a large extent on the user's specifications. If the user is going to enter the transactions in large batches sorted by transaction type, you can improve upon the screen flow given in figure 14-4. On the other hand, if only a few transactions are going to be entered at a time and they aren't going to be sorted by transaction type, the screen flow for this program is quite efficient.

How to develop a structure chart for a CICS program

Because of the requirements of a pseudo-conversational program, you use some new techniques when you design a CICS program. In particular, you design the first three levels of a CICS program in a way that is quite different from the way the other programs in this book are designed. You also number the modules of a CICS program in a slightly different way.

How to design the top two levels of a CICS program To start the design of a CICS program, you draw the top-level, or level-0, module.

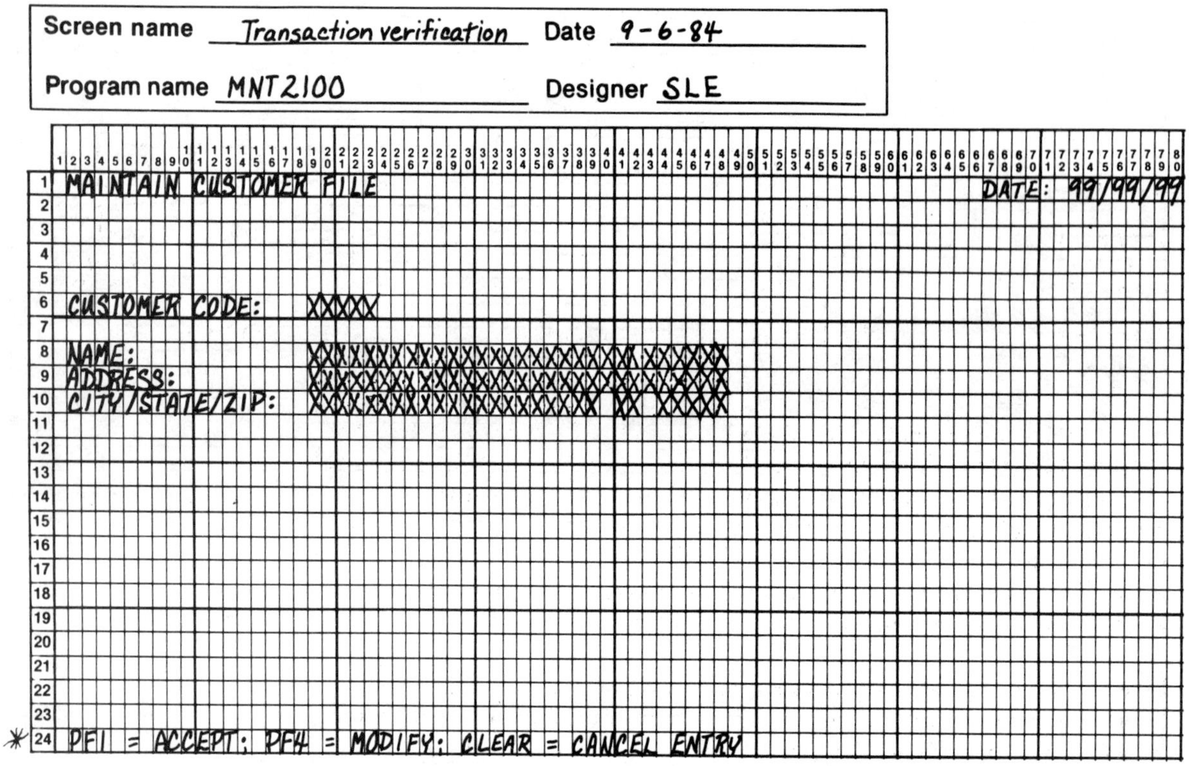

* For a deletion verification the operator message is
PF1 = DELETE THIS RECORD; CLEAR = CANCEL ENTRY

Figure 14-7 The transaction-verification screen for the CICS file-maintenance program

This module represents the entire program, so you should give it an appropriate functional name. For the CICS file-maintenance program, MAINTAIN CUSTOMER FILE is an acceptable name. In other words, you design the top-level module just as you design the top-level module in any other program.

To derive the level-1 modules, you use a somewhat mechanical process. To begin, you draw a start-terminal-session module like the one in figure 14-8. All pseudo-conversational programs need a module like this to properly format the first screen. Then, you add one level-1 module for each screen the program processes. Because the CICS file-maintenance program processes three screens, there are three screen-processing modules in level-1 in figure 14-8. Similarly, if a program processes six screens, you draw six level-1 modules after the start-terminal-session module. Finally, if your program must display an ending message when the session ends, you add a send-termination-message module to level-1 of the program. Since the CICS file-maintenance program doesn't require one, you won't find this module in figure 14-8.

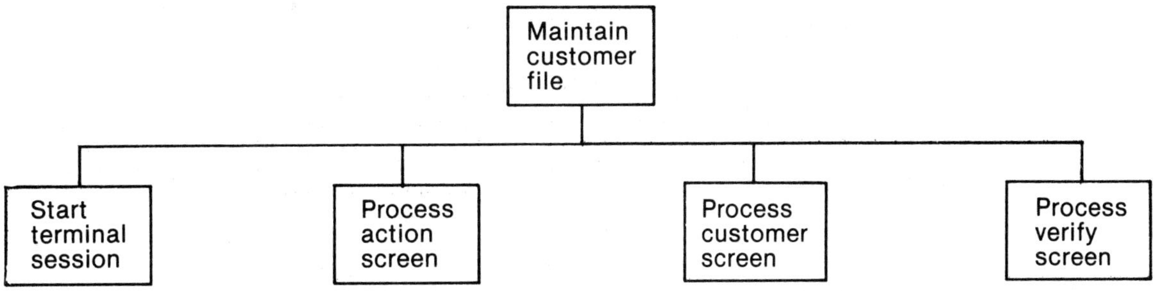

Figure 14-8 The top two levels of the structure chart for the CICS file-maintenance program

If you analyze the two levels shown in figure 14-8, you can see that the structure for a CICS program differs considerably from the structure of the programs in the previous chapter. When you use pseudo-conversational programming, the program structure chart represents the processing for a single transaction, not for an entire terminal session. In a sense, then, it corresponds to the structure charts in chapter 13 from level-1 down, rather than from level-0 down.

How to design the screen-processing legs of a program When you design the level-2 modules for a program, you should realize that each screen-handling module must provide for at least three functions : (1) receiving the screen, (2) editing or processing the data received from the screen, and (3) sending the next screen. As a result, most of your programs will have level-2 modules like those in the structure chart in figure 14-9. This is the complete structure chart for the file-maintenance program.

As you can see in figure 14-9, the leftmost level-2 subordinate for each screen-processing module is a receive module. The rightmost module or modules are send modules. And modules that either edit or process the data received from a screen are drawn between the receive and send modules.

To simplify program design and coding, we recommend that you create only one send module for each screen your program processes. In figure 14-9, then, you will find three send modules, one for each screen of the program. If the field attributes and messages for a screen need to be varied from one execution of the program to the next, these variables can be changed in the module that calls the send module.

To determine which send modules a screen-handling leg requires, you can analyze your screen flow diagram. In figure 14-4, for example, you can see that the flow can go from the customer-entry screen to either the action screen or the transaction-verification screen. In addition, if the editing routines detect invalid data, the flow may go from the customer-entry screen to the editing routine and back to the customer-entry screen for corrections. So the process-customer-screen leg of the program requires all three send modules as you can see in part 2 of figure 14-9.

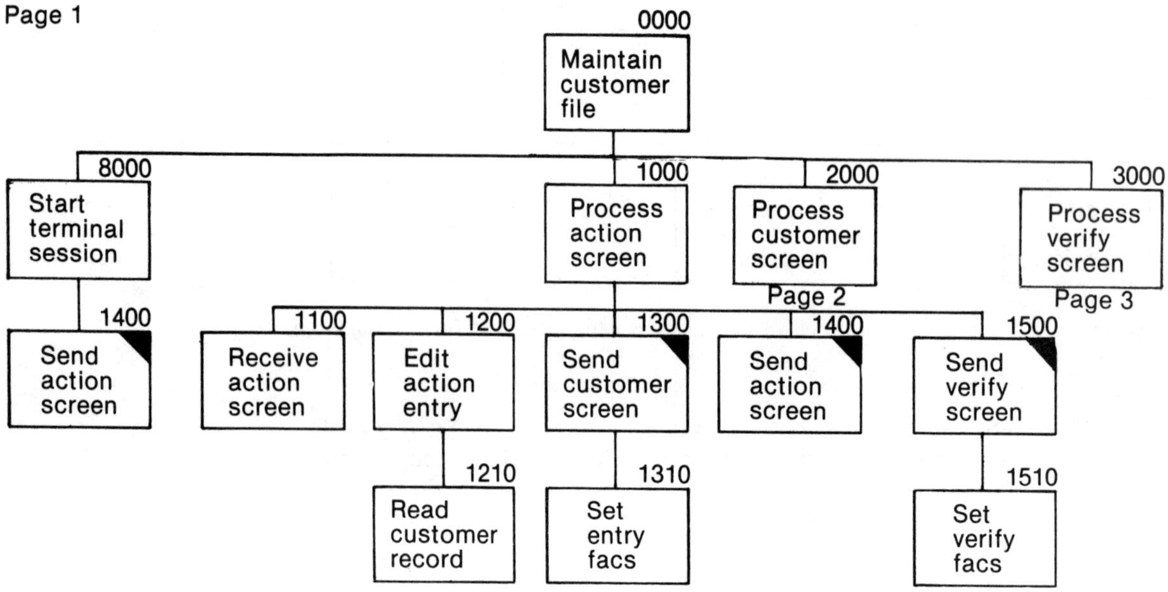

Figure 14-9 The complete structure chart for the CICS file-maintenance program (part 1 of 3)

Similarly, you can tell from the screen flow diagram that the start-terminal-session module needs to send only one screen, the action screen. And you can tell that the process-verify-screen module needs to send either the action-screen or the customer-entry screen depending on whether the operator cancels or accepts the transaction or whether he wants to modify it. In addition, if the operator presses an invalid AID key, the process-verify-screen module must send the transaction-verification screen back to the terminal with an appropriate error message.

Subordinate to a send module, you may need to use modules that set the field attribute characters (facs) for a screen. In general, facs do not need to be set at all since they are defined in the mapset. However, there are cases in which you will need a module to set the facs, particularly if a screen is used for more than one purpose. In the customer file-maintenance program, for example, one external screen is used for both the customer-entry and transaction-verification screens. So, both modules 1300 and 1500 call modules to set the facs accordingly.

As you might guess, receive and send modules are much the same from one program to the next. So the major variations are in the editing and processing modules. As you can see in figure 14-9, you can have any number of processing modules in level-2 for a screen-processing module. Thus, module 3000 calls three different processing modules. And, module 1000 calls only one module, module 1200, to edit the screen data.

The modules at the fourth level of the program and below depend, of course, on the program specifications. Since these subordinates have nothing to do with screen-handling, you design them just as you do for

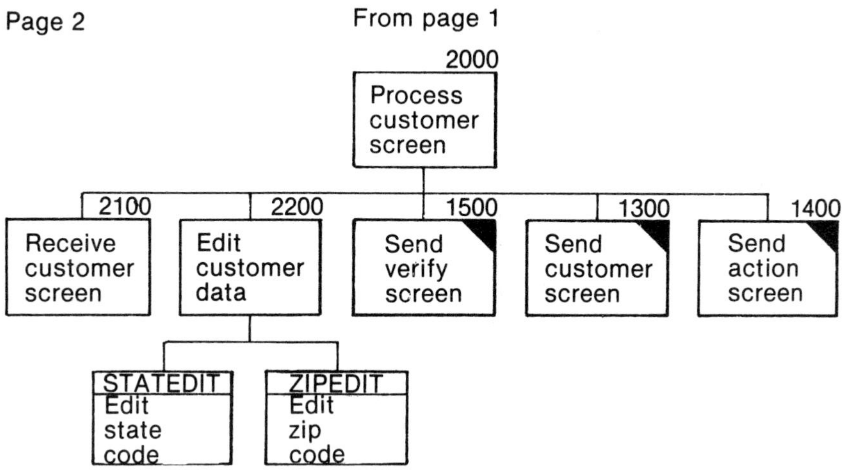

Figure 14-9 The complete structure chart for the CICS file-maintenance program (part 2 of 3)

any other program. Thus, module 2200 in figure 14-9 calls two subprograms that support the editing function. And module 3200 calls module 3210 to write a new record on the customer file. Since you use CICS commands for all I/O operations in a CICS program, the code for module 3210 will be a CICS command, not a COBOL statement. Nevertheless, you name the I/O modules just as you do in a standard COBOL program.

Subordinate to module 3300, you can see a read module, module 3310, which reads a customer record with the intent to update it. This is different than the function of module 1210, which simply reads a record. Since more than one user may be using the customer master file, module 3310 reads a record and holds it so no other program can modify it. Then, when the record is deleted or rewritten, it is released so it can be modified by other programs.

This program has both read and read-for-update modules for the customer record because CICS doesn't provide for a way to hold a record for update between executions of a program. Instead, a held record is automatically released when the program ends. Therefore, the customer record is only read-for-update when the program knows that it is going to rewrite or delete the record before sending a screen back to the terminal and ending.

You should be aware that there is another minor problem associated with updating records of shared files. It is possible that between the time a record is read initially and the record is read again for update, another user could access the same record and modify or even delete the record. However, if this is a problem for a particular application, there are a couple of solutions for it. One involves saving the record in the communication area between program executions and comparing it with the record that is read for update to be sure that the record hasn't been modified. The other involves placing a flag in the record itself that would

Page 3

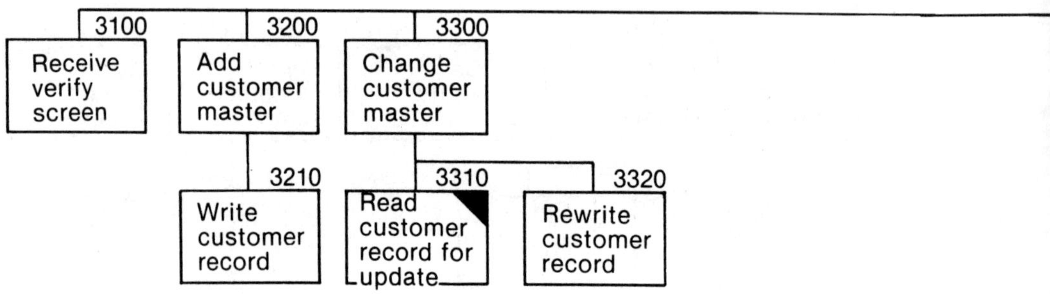

Figure 14-9 The complete structure chart for the CICS file-maintenance program (part 3 of 3)

indicate when a record was being updated so another user wouldn't modify it at the same time.

Why you should isolate I/O functions in their own modules As in all programs, we recommend that you isolate I/O functions, including screen-handling functions, in their own modules. That's why all I/O functions are in separate modules in the chart in figure 14-9.

As we see it, you should isolate I/O functions for two reasons. First, they have a significant effect on the structure of your programs. As a result, if you isolate the I/O functions, your structure charts will be easier to read and understand because they will show which I/O functions must be done and where these functions fit into the overall structure of the program.

Second, in most cases, CICS requires you to use branching logic within an I/O module to process exceptional conditions. I'll have more to say about this in the next topic. For now, though, you should realize that it's easier to control the branching logic if you isolate the code in a single module.

As you may know, some people object to isolating I/O functions in a CICS program. They say this degrades program performance because it increases the number of PERFORM statements required by a program. We feel, however, that you should keep your perspective on this. Yes, it's true that the use of PERFORM statements can slightly degrade program performance as I'll explain in the next topic. But in this case, we feel that the development benefits you gain more than justify the marginal reduction you may experience in program performance.

How to number the modules of a CICS program Once you've decided that your structure chart is correct, you should number its modules. When you code the program, as you'll see in the next topic, you'll

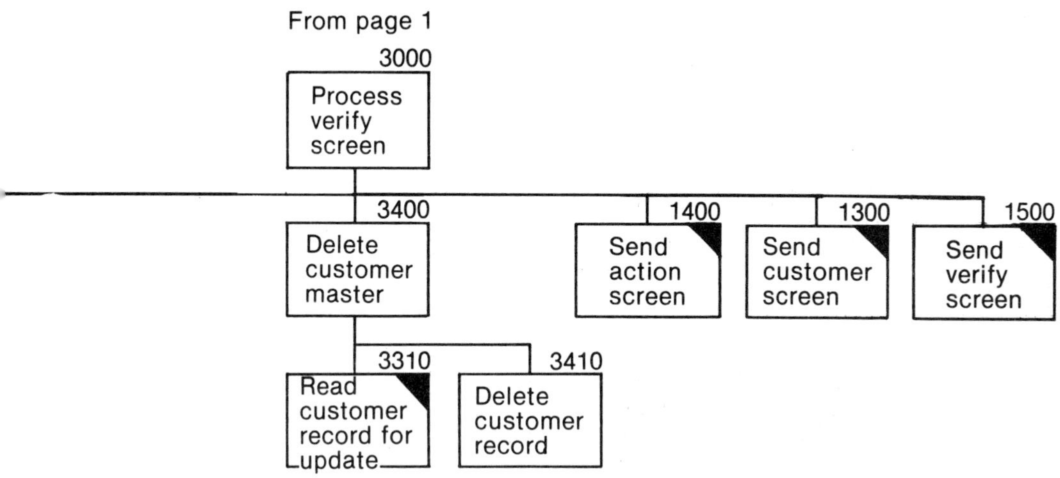

combine these numbers with the module names to form COBOL section names. Since you'll code the sections in numeric sequence in your program, the structure chart becomes a directory to the sections of the Procedure Division.

Although you can use complicated numbering schemes, I recommend that you number the modules as shown in figure 14-9. Here, the top-level module is number 0000, and the start-terminal-session module is number 8000. If the program required a send-termination-message module, it would be number 9000. The other level-1 modules are numbered by 1000 starting with 1000.

You give numbers 8000 and 9000 to your start-session and send-termination-message modules so they appear at the end of your Procedure Division. This leads to improved program performance. If these modules were at the start of your program, your system would have to page them in and out each time a terminal session is restarted. But since they're only executed once for each terminal session, this would be inefficient. When they're at the end of your program, though, they will be paged into storage only once for each terminal session.

As you can see in figure 14-9, we usually number the level-2 modules by 100s. Below that we number by tens. But once you're below level 1, the numbering is largely a matter of personal preference.

Discussion

If you understand the design of the file-maintenance program, you should be able to adapt it to other CICS programs. In fact, because of the rigid design principles that we recommend for the first three levels of a CICS program, you may find that designing a CICS program is easier than designing a program for other systems.

Terminology

conversational program
pseudo-conversational program
AID key
attention identifier key

Objective

Given the specifications for an interactive COBOL program that's to be developed for an IBM mainframe using CICS, create an acceptable structure chart for its design.

Topic 2 How to code interactive programs using CICS on an IBM mainframe

When you code a CICS program, you do so in two stages. First, you create the mapset for the external screens using Basic Mapping Support. Second, you code the program in COBOL. In this topic, then, I'll first show you how to create the mapset for a program in a way that is consistent with the principles of structured programming. After that, I'll give you some ideas for coding a CICS program in a structured style.

Since this isn't a book on CICS, this topic assumes that you already know how to code CICS programs. But if you don't, this topic will give you a general understanding of how you code CICS programs in COBOL. Then, if you want to learn more about CICS, we recommend our CICS books by Doug Lowe called *CICS for the COBOL Programmer* (*Part 1* and *Part 2*).

Guidelines for defining external screens using Basic Mapping Support

When you develop CICS programs, you use *Basic Mapping Support* (*BMS*), which is a component of CICS. To use BMS, you have to write an assembler-language program called a *mapset*. This program defines the external screens used by your program.

After you've coded the mapset in assembler language, it must be assembled. When it's assembled, it transforms your mapset into two mapsets, a *physical mapset* and a *symbolic mapset*. The physical mapset is a load module that is used by BMS. The symbolic mapset is a COPY member that you use in your COBOL program.

In keeping with the principles of structured programming, you should create your mapsets in as organized a fashion as possible. At this time, then, I'd like to give you some guidelines for coding an assembler language mapset. I'd also like to tell you when and how you should create your own symbolic mapsets.

If your shop has a mapset generator, you will probably want to use it. Once you get used to it, it should help you increase your productivity. In this case, you may not need these guidelines for creating mapsets. On the other hand, if your mapset generator creates symbolic maps that are difficult to read, you may want to read the material on symbolic mapsets so you can create your own.

How to code an assembler-language mapset Figure 14-10 illustrates the first page of the assembler-language mapset required by the CICS file-maintenance program. Since I assume that you know how to create BMS mapsets, I won't go into the coding of the mapset in this book. Briefly stated, though, the assembler-language coding defines the characteristics of the screens that are going to be used. It also defines the attributes of each field used in each screen of the program. If you compare the code in figure 14-10 with the screen layout in figure 14-5, I'm sure you can see the relationship between the mapset coding and the action screen.

Incidentally, although the program specifications for this program give three separate screen layouts, the programmer treated them as only two screens. Since the customer-entry screen and the transaction-verification screen are the same in both the heading and data zones, it's reasonable to code them as one screen. In figure 14-10, then, the action screen is defined with the name MT21MP1 (an abbreviation of MNT2100, the program name, and map 1); the customer-entry and transaction-verification screens are defined with the name MT21MP2.

To make a mapset as easy to read as possible, we recommend that you give it as much structure as possible. For instance, the mapset in figure 14-10 was coded using guidelines like these:

1. Separate the coding for each screen by two full lines of asterisks (comment lines); and separate the coding for each field or related group of fields in a screen by one full line of asterisks.

2. Code only one parameter per line in each statement, and align the parameters vertically.

3. Within the limits of assembler language, give each record and field a meaningful name. Since a name can only be seven characters long, it is difficult to make the names easy to read. But do the best you can.

Although you may want to modify these guidelines somewhat to fit the requirements of your shop, I think you'll agree that the code in figure 14-10 is about as readable as you can make the coding for an assembler-language mapset.

When to create your own symbolic mapset A symbolic mapset is a COPY member used in a COBOL program that defines the format of the data sent to or received from the screens used by the program. When an application program requests that a screen be sent to a terminal, BMS takes data from the symbolic map within the COBOL program. After it formats the data according to the physical map, it sends it to the terminal. Likewise, when an application program requests that data be received from a terminal, BMS uses the physical map to format the data from the screen according to the requirements of the symbolic map.

```
MT21SET  DFHMSD TYPE=&SYSPARM,                                         X
               LANG=COBOL,                                             X
               MODE=INOUT,                                             X
               TERM=3270-2,                                            X
               CTRL=FREEKB,                                            X
               STORAGE=AUTO,                                           X
               TIOAPFX=YES
***********************************************************************
***********************************************************************
MT21MP1  DFHMDI SIZE=(24,80),                                          X
               LINE=1,                                                 X
               COLUMN=1
***********************************************************************
         DFHMDF POS=(1,1),                                             X
               LENGTH=22,                                              X
               ATTRB=(BRT,PROT),                                       X
               INITIAL='MAINTAIN CUSTOMER FILE'
***********************************************************************
         DFHMDF POS=(1,66),                                            X
               LENGTH=5,                                               X
               ATTRB=(BRT,PROT),                                       X
               INITIAL='DATE:'
DATE1    DFHMDF POS=(1,72),                                            X
               LENGTH=8,                                               X
               ATTRB=(BRT,PROT)
***********************************************************************
         DFHMDF POS=(6,1),                                             X
               LENGTH=14,                                              X
               ATTRB=(BRT,PROT),                                       X
               INITIAL='CUSTOMER CODE:'
CODE1    DFHMDF POS=(6,18),                                            X
               LENGTH=5,                                               X
               ATTRB=(UNPROT,IC,FSET)
         DFHMDF POS=(6,24),                                            X
               LENGTH=1,                                               X
               ATTRB=PROT
***********************************************************************
ERROR1   DFHMDF POS=(23,1),                                            X
               LENGTH=79,                                              X
               ATTRB=(BRT,PROT)
MESSAG1  DFHMDF POS=(24,1),                                            X
               LENGTH=77,                                              X
               ATTRB=(BRT,PROT)
DUMMY1   DFHMDF POS=(24,79),                                           X
               LENGTH=1,                                               X
               ATTRB=(DRK,PROT,FSET),                                  X
               INITIAL=' '
***********************************************************************
***********************************************************************
MT21MP2  DFHMDI SIZE=(24,80),                                          X
               LINE=1,                                                 X
               COLUMN=1
***********************************************************************
         DFHMDF POS=(1,1),                                             X
               LENGTH=22,                                              X
               ATTRB=(BRT,PROT),                                       X
               INITIAL='MAINTAIN CUSTOMER FILE'
***********************************************************************
         DFHMDF POS=(1,66),                                            X
```

Figure 14-10 The first page of the mapset listing for the CICS file-maintenance program

Unfortunately, the symbolic mapset BMS generates isn't easy to use. For instance, figure 14-11 presents the first page of the symbolic mapset BMS generated from the assember-language code in figure 14-10. Since the mapset doesn't follow the principles of structured programming when it comes to naming, indentation, or alignment, I think you'll agree that this mapset is difficult to read. As a result, if you use this mapset in your program, the quality of your program is reduced. That's why we recommend that you create your own symbolic mapsets when using CICS.

Before you create your own, though, be sure to check your shop's standards for CICS programming. In some shops, programmers aren't allowed to create their own symbolic maps because of the chance that this will introduce errors into the program-development process. As we see it, though, there's little chance for error if you create your maps carefully. Also, the benefits of having symbolic maps that are easy to read justifies any development problems that result from errors in the symbolic maps.

How to create your own symbolic mapset Before you can create your own symbolic mapset, you must understand the symbolic mapset created by BMS. In figure 14-11, then, you can see that BMS generated two 01-level items (MT21MP1I and MT21MP1O) for the first map in the mapset (the map for the action sceen). Because the second 01-level item for the map contains a REDEFINES clause, these items overlay each other. The fields in the first 01-level group are intended for use in input operations (suffix I); the fields in the second group are meant for output operations (suffix O). When BMS generates a symbolic mapset, it generates two 01-level descriptions like this for each screen that is defined.

If you check the code for each 01-level description, you can see that each one begins with a 12-byte FILLER that CICS uses for its own purposes. Then, five data names are created for each DFHMDF macro you coded with a label in the assembler-language mapset. The names for these fields are created by adding a one-character suffix to the seven-character label coded on the DFHMDF macro. If a label isn't coded on the macro, the corresponding field isn't coded in the symbolic map.

The shaded areas in figure 14-11 show the code generated for the data-entry field labelled CODE1 in figure 14-10. As you can see, five data names have been generated for this one entry field: CODE1L, CODE1F, CODE1A, CODE1I, and CODE1O. The first field generated (CODE1L) is a two-byte binary field that contains the length (suffix L) of the data entered by the operator into that field. The next two fields generated in the symbolic map are redefinitions of a single byte of storage. On an input operation, this is used for the flag byte (suffix F) that indicates if the operator entered data into the field. On an output operation, this byte can be used to override the field attributes specified in the physical map (suffix A). After these first three fields, the actual data field has two names in the symbolic map, one for input (CODE1I) and one for output (CODE1O). This allows the field's PICTURE clauses to differ on input and output (although they're the same for this field).

```
  BKEND
01   MT21MP1I.
     02  FILLER PIC X(12).
     02  DATE1L      COMP   PIC   S9(4).
     02  DATE1F      PICTURE X.
     02  FILLER REDEFINES DATE1F.
       03 DATE1A      PICTURE X.
     02  DATE1I   PIC X(8).
     02  CODE1L      COMP   PIC   S9(4).
     02  CODE1F      PICTURE X.
     02  FILLER REDEFINES CODE1F.
       03 CODE1A      PICTURE X.
     02  CODE1I   PIC X(5).
     02  ERROR1L      COMP   PIC   S9(4)
     02  ERROR1F      PICTURE X.
     02  FILLER REDEFINES ERROR1F.
       03 ERROR1A      PICTURE X.
     02  ERROR1I   PIC X(79).
     02  MESSAG1L      COMP   PIC   S9(4
     02  MESSAG1F      PICTURE X.
     02  FILLER REDEFINES MESSAG1F.
       03 MESSAG1A      PICTURE X.
     02  MESSAG1I   PIC X(77).
     02  DUMMY1L      COMP   PIC   S9(4)
     02  DUMMY1F      PICTURE X.
     02  FILLER REDEFINES DUMMY1F.
       03 DUMMY1A      PICTURE X.
     02  DUMMY1I   PIC X(1).
01   MT21MP1O REDEFINES MT21MP1I.
     02  FILLER PIC X(12).
     02  FILLER PICTURE X(3).
     02  DATE1O   PIC X(8).
     02  FILLER PICTURE X(3).
     02  CODE1O   PIC X(5).
     02  FILLER PICTURE X(3).
     02  ERROR1O   PIC X(79).
     02  FILLER PICTURE X(3).
     02  MESSAG1O   PIC X(77).
     02  FILLER PICTURE X(3).
     02  DUMMY1O   PIC X(1).
01   MT21MP2I.
     02  FILLER PIC X(12).
     02  DATE2L      COMP   PIC   S9(4)
     02  DATE2F      PICTURE X.
     02  FILLER REDEFINES DATE2F.
       03 DATE2A      PICTURE X.
     02  DATE2I   PIC X(8).
     02  CODE2L      COMP   PIC   S9(4)
     02  CODE2F      PICTURE X.
     02  FILLER REDEFINES CODE2F.
       03 CODE2A      PICTURE X.
     02  CODE2I   PIC X(5).
     02  NAMEL      COMP   PIC   S9(4)
     02  NAMEF      PICTURE X.
     02  FILLER REDEFINES NAMEF.
       03 NAMEA      PICTURE X.
     02  NAMEI   PIC X(30).
```

Figure 14-11 The first page of the symbolic mapset generated by BMS for the CICS file-maintenance program

Once you understand what these fields do and where they must be, it's relatively easy to create your own symbolic mapset. For instance, figure 14-12 presents the first page of the symbolic mapset the programmer created for the CICS file-maintenance program as a replacement for the one in figure 14-11. To create a symbolic mapset like this, you work from your assembler-language mapset (like the one in figure 14-10). In general, you create a group of three 05-level data names for each field you labelled in the assembler-language mapset.

As you create your own symbolic mapset, we recommend that you follow these guidelines:

1. Code only one 01 item for each map, and choose a name for it that corresponds to the screen name you used on the layout form for the screen. In figure 14-12, for example, the programmer used ACTION-MAP for the action screen and CUSTOMER-DATA-MAP for the map that is used for both the customer-entry and the transaction-verification screens.

2. Start each map with a 12-byte FILLER item.

3. For each map field, code three data names using these rules:
    a. Start each data name with a two- or three-character prefix that's an abbreviation of the map name. For instance, CDM could be the prefix for the CUSTOMER-DATA-MAP.
    b. Include one character to define the field's function: L for length, A for attribute, or D for data.
    c. Create a meaningful name for each field such as CDM-L-CUSTOMER-CODE. To do so, you should separate each component of the field with a hyphen.

4. Separate each set of three data names from other sets with a blank comment line.

5. Align the elements in each symbolic map so they're easy to read.

If you follow these guidelines or ones like them, we believe you'll end up with symbolic mapsets that improve both program quality and programmer productivity.

Guidelines for coding CICS programs in COBOL

Because you can't apply the principles of structured coding to CICS programs as easily as you can to non-CICS programs, most CICS programs today aren't written in a structured style. But it is possible to code CICS programs using the principles of structured coding. And if you

```
 BKEND    C.MT21SET

*
01   ACTION-MAP.
*
     05   FILLER                             PIC X(12).
*
     05   AM-L-DATE                          PIC S9(4)    COMP.
     05   AM-A-DATE                          PIC X.
     05   AM-D-DATE                          PIC 99/99/99.
*
     05   AM-L-CUSTOMER-CODE                 PIC S9(4)    COMP.
     05   AM-A-CUSTOMER-CODE                 PIC X.
     05   AM-D-CUSTOMER-CODE                 PIC X(5).
*
     05   AM-L-ERROR-MESSAGE                 PIC S9(4)    COMP.
     05   AM-A-ERROR-MESSAGE                 PIC X.
     05   AM-D-ERROR-MESSAGE                 PIC X(79).
*
     05   AM-L-OPERATOR-MESSAGE              PIC S9(4)    COMP.
     05   AM-A-OPERATOR-MESSAGE              PIC X.
     05   AM-D-OPERATOR-MESSAGE              PIC X(77).
*
     05   AM-L-DUMMY                         PIC S9(4)    COMP.
     05   AM-A-DUMMY                         PIC X.
     05   AM-D-DUMMY                         PIC X.
*
01   CUSTOMER-DATA-MAP.
*
     05   FILLER                             PIC X(12).
*
     05   CDM-L-DATE                         PIC S9(4)    COMP.
     05   CDM-A-DATE                         PIC X.
     05   CDM-D-DATE                         PIC 99/99/99.
*
     05   CDM-L-CUSTOMER-CODE                PIC S9(4)    COMP.
     05   CDM-A-CUSTOMER-CODE                PIC X.
     05   CDM-D-CUSTOMER-CODE                PIC X(5).
*
     05   CDM-L-NAME                         PIC S9(4)    COMP.
     05   CDM-A-NAME                         PIC X.
     05   CDM-D-NAME                         PIC X(30).
*
     05   CDM-L-ADDRESS                      PIC S9(4)    COMP.
     05   CDM-A-ADDRESS                      PIC X.
     05   CDM-D-ADDRESS                      PIC X(30).
*
     05   CDM-L-CITY                         PIC S9(4)    COMP.
     05   CDM-A-CITY                         PIC X.
     05   CDM-D-CITY                         PIC X(21).
*
     05   CDM-L-STATE                        PIC S9(4)    COMP.
     05   CDM-A-STATE                        PIC X.
     05   CDM-D-STATE                        PIC XX.
*
     05   CDM-L-ZIP-CODE                     PIC S9(4)    COMP.
     05   CDM-A-ZIP-CODE                     PIC X.
```

Figure 14-12 The first page of the symbolic mapset created by the programmer for the CICS file-maintenance program

Communication area
  Switches
  Flags
  Control total fields
  Record descriptions

Field attribute characters (COPY member)

Symbolic maps (COPY member)

Linkage section
  DFHCOMMAREA
  Execute Interface Block

Figure 14-13 The recommended coding sequence for the CICS fields in the Data Division of a CICS program

want to improve CICS program development, you should make every effort to do so. With that in mind, here are our recommendations for the coding of CICS programs.

Data Division

CICS programs will normally have some fields in the Data Division that are like those in batch programs and some that are unique to CICS. Like a batch program, a CICS program will normally require switches, flags, report lines, record descriptions, and so forth. In addition, however, a CICS program requires fields to define and manipulate screens and to communicate between program executions during a pseudo-conversational terminal session.

Sequence of code In general, you should code the elements in the Data Division in the same sequence that you would use for a non-CICS program: (1) groups of work fields, (2) record descriptions, and (3) screen-handling fields. Then, after these fields, you should code the CICS fields that your program requires in the sequence shown in figure 14-13. As you can see, I've divided the CICS fields into four groups: the fields of the communication area, the field attribute characters, the symbolic maps, and the fields of the linkage section.

The communication area When a pseudo-conversational program ends after sending a screen to a terminal, the data in its Working-Storage Section is lost unless it's explicitly saved. In most programs, however, you will want to pass some data from one execution of the program to the next. One way to do this is to save fields in the communication area.

```
 01   COMMUNICATION-AREA.
*
      05  CA-PROCESS-FLAG                  PIC X.
          88  PROCESS-ACTION-SCREEN                  VALUE '1'.
          88  PROCESS-CUSTOMER-SCREEN                VALUE '2'.
          88  PROCESS-VERIFY-SCREEN                  VALUE '3'.
      05  CA-ACTION-FLAG                   PIC X.
          88  ADD-RECORD                             VALUE '1'.
          88  CHANGE-RECORD                          VALUE '2'.
          88  DELETE-RECORD                          VALUE '3'.
*
```

Figure 14-14 The communication area for the CICS file-maintenance program

Often, for example, a flag is defined in the communication area that the program evaluates to determine what screen it should display next. The communication area can also be used to store data that's accumulated from execution to execution, such as control totals. As you can see, then, the functions of fields defined in the communication area can closely parallel those of other working-storage fields.

In a batch program, you should code all fields with similar functions (such as switches, flags, and total fields) together under an 01-level item. But you can't do that in a CICS program. In a CICS program, if fields are going to be passed from one program execution to another, they need to be grouped together in the communication area. As a result, you can expect to combine a variety of field types in the communication area. A typical combination is a flag, a control-total field, and a record description.

When you use a communication area in your program, you should name it COMMUNICATION-AREA and code it at the 01 level. For instance, figure 14-14 presents the communication area for the CICS file-maintenance program. Below level 01, you should code the major groups of the communication area starting at the 05 level in the same sequence that you would use in a non-CICS program: switches, flags, and so on. All field names in the communication area should start with CA-, but otherwise you follow the basic rules for naming any field in the Data Division. In figure 14-14, the two flags aren't grouped because the area consists of only these two fields.

Field attribute characters If your CICS program will need to change any field attributes (and most will for functions such as highlighting fields in error), you'll probably need to include a working-storage group that contains values of commonly used attribute bytes. Although I didn't explain it when I presented the assembler-language mapset, you should realize that the attributes of a field are determined by the bits in its attribute byte. So if you change the value of the attribute byte, you change the attributes of the field.

```
BKEND     C.DFHBMSCA

01        DFHBMSCA.
  02      DFHBMPEM   PICTURE X    VALUE   IS   ' '.
  02      DFHBMPNL   PICTURE X    VALUE   IS   ' '.
  02      DFHBMASK   PICTURE X    VALUE   IS   '0'.
  02      DFHBMUNP   PICTURE X    VALUE   IS   ' '.
  02      DFHBMUNN   PICTURE X    VALUE   IS   '&'.
  02      DFHBMPRO   PICTURE X    VALUE   IS   '-'.
  02      DFHBMBRY   PICTURE X    VALUE   IS   'H'.
  02      DFHBMDAR   PICTURE X    VALUE   IS   '<'.
  02      DFHBMFSE   PICTURE X    VALUE   IS   'A'.
  02      DFHBMPRF   PICTURE X    VALUE   IS   '/'.
  02      DFHBMASF   PICTURE X    VALUE   IS   '1'.
  02      DFHBMASB   PICTURE X    VALUE   IS   '8'.
  02      DFHSA      PICTURE X    VALUE   IS   ' '.
  02      DFHCOLOR   PICTURE X    VALUE   IS   ' '.
  02      DFHPS      PICTURE X    VALUE   IS   ' '.
  02      DFHHLT     PICTURE X    VALUE   IS   ' '.
  02      DFH3270    PICTURE X    VALUE   IS   ' '.
  02      DFHVAL     PICTURE X    VALUE   IS   'A'.
  02      DFHALL     PICTURE X    VALUE   IS   ' '.
  02      DFHERROR   PICTURE X    VALUE   IS   ' '.
  02      DFHDFT     PICTURE X    VALUE   IS   ' '.
  02      DFHDFCOL   PICTURE X    VALUE   IS   ' '.
  02      DFHBLUE    PICTURE X    VALUE   IS   '1'.
  02      DFHRED     PICTURE X    VALUE   IS   '2'.
  02      DFHPINK    PICTURE X    VALUE   IS   '3'.
  02      DFHGREEN   PICTURE X    VALUE   IS   '4'.
  02      DFHTURQ    PICTURE X    VALUE   IS   '5'.
  02      DFHYELLO   PICTURE X    VALUE   IS   '6'.
  02      DFHNEUTR   PICTURE X    VALUE   IS   '7'.
  02      DFHBASE    PICTURE X    VALUE   IS   ' '.
  02      DFHDFHI    PICTURE X    VALUE   IS   ' '.
  02      DFHBLINK   PICTURE X    VALUE   IS   '1'.
  02      DFHREVRS   PICTURE X    VALUE   IS   '2'.
  02      DFHUNDLN   PICTURE X    VALUE   IS   '4'.
  02      DFHMFIL    PICTURE X    VALUE   IS   ' '.
  02      DFHMENT    PICTURE X    VALUE   IS   ' '.
  02      DFHMFE     PICTURE X    VALUE   IS   ' '.

BKEND
```

Figure 14-15 The IBM-supplied COPY member DFHBMSCA for field attribute characters

To make it easier for you to modify attribute bytes, IBM supplies a standard COPY member called DFHBMSCA. This member, shown in figure 14-15, defines many attribute characters, but has some serious limitations. First, the names assigned to the various characters are cryptic. Second, DFHBMSCA doesn't include some of the most commonly used characters. And third, many of the characters it does include are almost never used in a typical shop.

Rather than DFHBMSCA, then, we recommend that you develop your own COPY member for field attribute characters. For instance, figure 14-16 shows the one we use in our shop. It includes a more useful selection of field attribute characters than the IBM-supplied member, and

```
 BKEND    C.FACDEFN

*
 01  FIELD-ATTRIBUTE-CHARACTERS.
*
     05  FAC-UNPROT                    PIC X          VALUE ' '.
     05  FAC-UNPROT-MDT                PIC X          VALUE 'A'.
     05  FAC-UNPROT-BRT                PIC X          VALUE 'H'.
     05  FAC-UNPROT-BRT-MDT            PIC X          VALUE 'I'.
     05  FAC-UNPROT-DARK               PIC X          VALUE '<'.
     05  FAC-UNPROT-DARK-MDT           PIC X          VALUE '('.
     05  FAC-UNPROT-NUM                PIC X          VALUE '&'.
     05  FAC-UNPROT-NUM-MDT            PIC X          VALUE 'J'.
     05  FAC-UNPROT-NUM-BRT            PIC X          VALUE 'Q'.
     05  FAC-UNPROT-NUM-BRT-MDT        PIC X          VALUE 'R'.
     05  FAC-UNPROT-NUM-DARK           PIC X          VALUE '*'.
     05  FAC-UNPROT-NUM-DARK-MDT       PIC X          VALUE ')'.
     05  FAC-PROT                      PIC X          VALUE '-'.
     05  FAC-PROT-MDT                  PIC X          VALUE '/'.
     05  FAC-PROT-BRT                  PIC X          VALUE 'Y'.
     05  FAC-PROT-BRT-MDT              PIC X          VALUE 'Z'.
     05  FAC-PROT-DARK                 PIC X          VALUE '%'.
     05  FAC-PROT-DARK-MDT             PIC X          VALUE ' '.
     05  FAC-PROT-NUM                  PIC X          VALUE '0'.
     05  FAC-PROT-NUM-MDT              PIC X          VALUE '1'.
     05  FAC-PROT-NUM-BRT              PIC X          VALUE '8'.
     05  FAC-PROT-NUM-BRT-MDT          PIC X          VALUE '9'.
     05  FAC-PROT-NUM-DARK             PIC X          VALUE '@'.
     05  FAC-PROT-NUM-DARK-MDT         PIC X          VALUE QUOTE.

 BKEND
```

Figure 14-16 An improved COPY member for field attribute characters

the names it assigns them are easier to understand when they appear in the Procedure Division. For instance, FAC-UNPROT-NUM-BRT means that the field is unprotected (so data can be entered into it), numeric (so the shift is numeric, not alphabetic), and bright.

Symbolic maps I've already described how you can create your own symbolic maps so they're easier to read and use. But whether or not your shop allows you to code your own symbolic maps, you should group the descriptions you use at the end of the Working-Storage Section after the definitions for the field attribute characters. Because symbolic maps are COPY members, all you need to code is one COPY statement for each mapset your program requires.

Linkage Section fields All CICS programs have a Linkage Section. So at the least, you need to code a field called DFHCOMMAREA in the Linkage Section as illustrated in figure 14-17. CICS uses this area in conjunction with the communication area in the Working-Storage Section of the program. The working-storage communication area is used to pass data to the next execution of a pseudo-conversational program; DFHCOMMAREA is used to receive the data. In other words, two versions of the communication area exist for each program.

```
*
 LINKAGE SECTION.
*
 01  DFHCOMMAREA                    PIC X(2).
*
 01  BLL-CELLS.
*
     05  FILLER                     PIC S9(8)    COMP.
     05  BLL-CWA                    PIC S9(8)    COMP.
*
 01  COMMON-WORK-AREA.
*
     05  CWA-DATE                   PIC 9(6).
*
```

Figure 14-17 The Linkage Section for the CICS file-maintenance program

If you don't include an entry for DFHCOMMAREA, the CICS command translator automatically inserts a definition for a one-byte communication area. We recommend, however, that you always code your own definition so you won't forget to do so if your program requires an area of more than one byte. For the CICS file-maintenance program, DFHCOMMAREA is defined as two bytes to match up with the communication area defined in figure 14-14.

Similarly, the CICS command translator automatically inserts an item in the Linkage Section called the *Execute Interface Block* (*EIB*). The Execute Interface Block is a CICS area that contains information related to the current task. In this case, though, you can't code your own definition for the EIB because its fields are the same in all CICS programs. You will see how one of its fields, EIBCALEN, is used in the section on coding.

Command-level COBOL also allows you to access areas of storage that are owned by CICS rather than by your program. The *Common Work Area* (CWA) is one such area that's available to all tasks in a CICS system. The CWA is defined by each installation and typically contains information that can be useful to many programs in the installation, such as the current date and company name.

When CICS loads and executes your program, it expects to find two fields defined in the Linkage Section: the Execute Interface Block and DFHCOMMAREA. As a result, CICS automatically establishes addressability to these two fields. However, if you define any other field in the Linkage Section, such as the CWA, you must establish addressability to it yourself.

To establish addressability to a field in the Linkage Section, you use a convention called *Base Locator for Linkage* (or BLL). Figure 14-17 illustrates how this convention is used in the file-maintenance program. The 01 level item named BLL-CELLS stores the addresses of Linkage Section fields. The first field contains the address of the BLL-CELLS item itself and the second field contains the address of the Common Work Area, whose definition follows. You will see how these fields are used in the section on coding.

Procedure Division

When you code the Procedure Division of a CICS program, you have to adapt the principles we presented in chapter 9 to the CICS environment. Among other things, this means coding the modules of a program as sections, not paragraphs. It also means that you should have more concern for program performance than you normally have when you work on other systems. So here are our guidelines for coding this division.

Why you should code the modules of a CICS program as sections Throughout this book, I've stressed the importance of coding each structure chart module as a separate COBOL paragraph. That way, the structure chart becomes an index to the paragraphs in the Procedure Division of the COBOL program. Unfortunately, though, you can't follow this practice when you develop a CICS program.

Because some CICS commands cause branching, you should code modules that include those commands as sections, not as paragraphs. That way, you can confine the branching to a single section. But if you code part of a COBOL program in sections, you have to code all of it in sections. So the best way to code a CICS program is to code each module on the structure chart as a section.

Fortunately, for most modules in a CICS program, there's little difference between a paragraph and a section. Both are named by combining the module number and name of the structure chart. And both are called by PERFORM statements. The only coding difference is that you need to code the word SECTION after a procedure name to create a section name. For instance, this is a paragraph name:

```
0000-MAINTAIN-CUSTOMER-FILE.
```

But this is a section name:

```
0000-MAINTAIN-CUSTOMER-FILE SECTION.
```

In either case, though, you call the module with a statement like

```
PERFORM 0000-MAINTAIN-CUSTOMER-FILE.
```

As a result, the use of sections has little effect on the COBOL code when each section consists of only one paragraph.

On the other hand, if a module in a CICS program requires either a HANDLE AID or a HANDLE CONDITION command, it's going to be coded as three or more paragraphs within a single section. That, of course, is why we recommend the use of sections for CICS programs. By using sections, you can code a module like this so it has only one entry and one exit point. In a moment, then, I'll show you how to code this type of module.

Format

```
EXEC CICS
    command option(value)
            option(value)
            .
            .
            .
END-EXEC.
```

Example

```
EXEC CICS
     SEND MAP('MT21MP1')
          MAPSET('MT21SET')
          FROM(ACTION-MAP)
          ERASE
END-EXEC.
```

Figure 14-18 The recommended format of a CICS command

How to code CICS commands When you code a CICS command, you should format the command as illustrated in figure 14-18. When a CICS command requires more than one option, you should use blank spaces to separate them, not commas. And to make your programs easier to read, you should code each option on a separate line.

How to code modules that include HANDLE CONDITION or HANDLE AID commands The HANDLE CONDITION and HANDLE AID commands don't actually do any processing; they just tell your program what paragraph to branch to when it encounters certain conditions. Usually, a statement like this is coded so it handles the conditions raised by another CICS command. For instance, a HANDLE AID command is used to direct the processing when certain AID keys are pressed. It's associated with the RECEIVE MAP command.

When you code a HANDLE CONDITION or HANDLE AID command, we recommend the coding structure shown in figure 14-19. As you can see, the first paragraph in the section contains the HANDLE AID or HANDLE CONDITION command and the CICS command associated with it. After this, the first paragraph may contain other CICS commands or COBOL statements. Then, the last statement in the first paragraph is a GOTO statement that passes control to the last paragraph in the section, which should be named xxxx-EXIT where xxxx is the structure chart module number. For example, the section for module 1100-RECEIVE-ACTION-SCREEN should end with a paragraph named 1100-EXIT. Since the only statement in the last paragraph is EXIT, that's the module's one exit point.

Between the first and last paragraphs in the section, you code one paragraph for each option you coded on the HANDLE AID or HANDLE CONDITION command. Each of these paragraphs is named using the module number and the name of the condition or key being processed.

```
xxxx-module-name SECTION.

     HANDLE AID or HANDLE CONDITION command.
     CICS command that requires
          the HANDLE AID or HANDLE CONDITION command.
     GO TO xxxx-EXIT.

xxxx-routine-1.

     COBOL statements for key-or-condition-1.
     GO TO xxxx-EXIT.

xxxx-routine-2.

     COBOL statements for key-or-condition-2.
     GO TO xxxx-EXIT.

     .
     .
     .

xxxx-routine-n.

     COBOL statements for key-or-condition-n.
     GO TO xxxx-EXIT.

xxxx-EXIT.

     EXIT.
```

Figure 14-19 The general structure of a module containing a HANDLE AID or a HANDLE CONDITION command

For instance, in a module named 1210-READ-CUSTOMER-RECORD, you code a paragraph named 1210-NOTFND to process the NOTFND condition. The last statement in each of these intermediate paragraphs is a GOTO statement that branches to the EXIT paragraph. However, a GOTO statement in the last intermediate paragraph is optional since control falls through to the EXIT paragraph anyway.

Figures 14-20 and 14 21 give examples of modules that include HANDLE AID and HANDLE CONDITION commands. These are for modules 1100 and 1210 of the CICS file-maintenance program charted in figure 14-9. As you can see, each module has only one entry and exit point. And the branching within each module is controlled. So if you use standards like these in your shop for your CICS I/O modules, you can quickly improve the quality of your CICS programs.

In certain cases it is beneficial to place a HANDLE CONDITION command outside of its related I/O module. This is particularly true when sequential file processing is involved. For example, consider the case in which a read module is performed repeatedly within a PERFORM-UNTIL loop. If the HANDLE CONDITION command is coded in the read module, the processing related to the HANDLE CONDITION command is performed every time the read module is performed. In contrast, if the HANDLE CONDITION command is coded outside of the read module just before the related PERFORM-UNTIL statement, the

```
 1100-RECEIVE-ACTION-SCREEN SECTION.
*
     EXEC CICS
         HANDLE AID CLEAR(1100-CLEAR-KEY)
                    PF1(1100-PF1-KEY)
                    PF2(1100-PF2-KEY)
                    PF3(1100-PF3-KEY)
                    ANYKEY(1100-ANYKEY)
     END-EXEC.
     EXEC CICS
         RECEIVE MAP('MT21MP1')
                 MAPSET('MT21SET')
                 INTO(ACTION-MAP)
     END-EXEC.
     MOVE 'N'                     TO VALID-ACTION-SW.
     MOVE 'INVALID KEY PRESSED'   TO AM-D-ERROR-MESSAGE.
     GO TO 1100-EXIT.
*
 1100-CLEAR-KEY.
*
     MOVE 'Y' TO END-SESSION-SW.
     GO TO 1100-EXIT.
*
 1100-PF1-KEY.
*
     MOVE '1' TO CA-ACTION-FLAG.
     GO TO 1100-EXIT.
*
 1100-PF2-KEY.
*
     MOVE '2' TO CA-ACTION-FLAG.
     GO TO 1100-EXIT.
*
 1100-PF3-KEY.
*
     MOVE '3' TO CA-ACTION-FLAG.
     GO TO 1100-EXIT.
*
 1100-ANYKEY.
*
     MOVE 'N'                     TO VALID-ACTION-SW.
     MOVE 'INVALID KEY PRESSED'   TO AM-D-ERROR-MESSAGE.
*
 1100-EXIT.
*
     EXIT.
*
```

Figure 14-20 Module 1100 of the CICS file-maintenance program showing typical coding for a CICS receive-screen module

processing related to the HANDLE CONDITION command is performed only once. And this can have a tremendous effect on program efficiency. I mention this only to show you that the HANDLE CONDITION command doesn't always have to be in the same module as the related CICS command. However, the paragraphs that handle the conditions should always be in the same module as the I/O command.

```
 1210-READ-CUSTOMER-RECORD SECTION.
*
     MOVE 'Y' TO CUSTOMER-FOUND-SW.
     EXEC CICS
         HANDLE CONDITION NOTFND(1210-NOTFND)
     END-EXEC.
     EXEC CICS
         READ DATASET('CUSTMAS')
              INTO(CUSTOMER-MASTER-RECORD)
              RIDFLD(AM-O-CUSTOMER-CODE)
     END-EXEC.
     GO TO 1210-EXIT.
*
 1210-NOTFND.
*
     MOVE SPACE TO CUSTOMER-MASTER-RECORD.
     MOVE 'N'   TO CUSTOMER-FOUND-SW.
*
 1210-EXIT.
*
     EXIT.
*
```

Figure 14-21 Module 1210 of the CICS file-maintenance program showing typical coding tor a CICS file- handling module

How to code the level-0 module Because the level-0 modules of your CICS programs contain the code required to implement pseudo-conversational programming, you should code them in a consistent fashion. For instance, figure 14-22 gives our coding for the level-0 module of the CICS file-maintenance program. Please refer to this coding as I explain the basic coding structure that you should use for a module like this.

As discussed earlier, you use the Common Work Area to access areas of storage owned by CICS. But, before you can use any of these fields, you must load their addresses into the appropriate areas in the Linkage Section. And, you must do this each time the program is executed.

Figure 14-22 illustrates how this is accomplished in the file-maintenance program using the ADDRESS command. Quite simply, the ADDRESS command loads the address of the Common Work Area into the field named BLL-CWA. Then, the program can access the fields defined in the Common Work Area, in this case, the current date.

The first time a program is executed during a terminal session, there's no previous screen to process. As a result, the first thing the level-0 module must do is determine if the current execution of the program is the first one of the session. To do this, the module should test the value of one of the fields in the Execute Interface Block of the Linkage Section called EIBCALEN. It contains the length of the communication area passed to the program. If the length is zero, it indicates that nothing is being passed to this execution of the program so the current execution is the first of the session. If the length isn't zero, it means that this isn't the first execution of the program.

```
 000-MAINTAIN-CUSTOMER-FILE SECTION.
*
     EXEC CICS
         ADDRESS CWA(BLL-CWA)
     END-EXEC.
     IF EIBCALEN = ZERO
         PERFORM 8000-START-TERMINAL-SESSION
     ELSE
         MOVE DFHCOMMAREA TO COMMUNICATION-AREA
         IF PROCESS-ACTION-SCREEN
             PERFORM 1000-PROCESS-ACTION-SCREEN
         ELSE IF PROCESS-CUSTOMER-SCREEN
             PERFORM 2000-PROCESS-CUSTOMER-SCREEN
         ELSE
             PERFORM 3000-PROCESS-VERIFY-SCREEN.
     IF END-SESSION
         EXEC CICS
             XCTL PROGRAM('MNT2000')
         END-EXEC
     ELSE
         EXEC CICS
             RETURN TRANSID('MT21')
                    COMMAREA(COMMUNICATION-AREA)
                    LENGTH(2)
         END-EXEC.
*
```

Figure 14-22 The top-level module of the CICS file-maintenance program

If the current execution is the first one of the session, the program performs module 8000 to send the first screen to the terminal. If it's not the first execution, the program moves the communication area in the Linkage Section (DFHCOMMAREA) to the communication area in working-storage. It then uses condition names associated with a flag in the communication area to determine what screen to process. This flag was set by the previous execution of the program. So each time the program executes, it performs either module 8000 or one of the process-screen modules.

After the appropriate screen-processing module has been performed, the program ends its current execution. If the operator has indicated that the terminal session should end, the program terminates by issuing an XCTL command that passes control to the next program (MNT2000 in figure 14-22). Otherwise, it ends by issuing a RETURN command that specifies that the program should be restarted the next time the operator presses an AID key and that the communication area should be saved for the next execution of the program.

How to code edit modules Figure 14-23 gives a general structure for an edit module in a CICS program. Basically, you edit each field with a series of nested IF statements. When you detect an error, you (1) modify the attribute field so the error is highlighted, (2) move -1 to the length field so the cursor will be placed under the field in error, and (3) move an appropriate error message to the error-message field. In general, you

```
IF error-condition-1 for field-1
    MOVE attribute-character TO attribute-field for field-1
    MOVE -1                  TO length-field for field-1
    MOVE error-message       TO error-message-field
ELSE IF error-condition-2 for field-1
    .
    .
    .
IF error-condition-1 for field-2
    .
    .
    .
If error-message-field NOT = LOW-VALUE
    MOVE 'N' TO VALID-DATA-SW.
```

Note: Fields should be tested in the reverse order of how they appear on the screen.

Figure 14-23 An effective coding structure for an edit module in a CICS program

should edit the fields from the bottom of the screen to the top, so the error message will relate to the first error field on the screen and the cursor will be moved to this field. Naturally, if the editing you're doing is complicated, your edit module can call subordinate modules that support the editing function.

Figure 14-24 shows the application of these coding recommendations to module 2200 of the CICS file-maintenance program. Here, you can see that the module uses the CICS LINK command to call subprograms that edit the state and zip code fields. It also moves the field attribute character FAC-UNPROT-BRT-MDT to the attribute byte of any field in error. This highlights each of the error fields by showing them in bright (BRT) intensity on the screen.

How to optimize program performance Because program performance is often critical in a CICS environment, you normally have to be concerned with it when you develop a CICS program. Although you can optimize your program's performance using several different coding techniques, you should realize that the technique of pseudo-conversational programming is by far the most important one. Beyond that, you can (1) reduce the size of your program's working-storage section, (2) code subfunctions in-line whenever it's practical, and (3) place infrequently used sections of code near the end of your program.

If you're familiar with the CICS literature, you've probably encountered the terms *working set* and *locality of reference*. A program's *working set* is the number of virtual-storage pages normally required in main storage as the program executes. In general, the smaller the working set, the more efficient the program. *Locality of reference* means that a program shouldn't refer unnecessarily to data that isn't in the working set. If it does, the page containing the required data must be moved into main storage. And that degrades the entire system. The three efficiency

```
2200-EDIT-CUSTOMER-DATA SECTION.
*
    MOVE LOW-VALUE        TO CDM-D-ERROR-MESSAGE.
    MOVE FAC-UNPROT-MDT   TO CDM-A-NAME
                             CDM-A-ADDRESS
                             CDM-A-CITY
                             CDM-A-STATE
                             CDM-A-ZIP-CODE.
    IF        CDM-D-ZIP-CODE = SPACE
           OR CDM-L-ZIP-CODE = ZERO
        MOVE FAC-UNPROT-BRT-MDT TO CDM-A-ZIP-CODE
        MOVE -1                 TO CDM-L-ZIP-CODE
        MOVE 'YOU MUST ENTER A ZIP CODE'
            TO CDM-D-ERROR-MESSAGE.
*
    IF        CDM-D-STATE = SPACE
           OR CDM-L-STATE = ZERO
        MOVE FAC-UNPROT-BRT-MDT TO CDM-A-STATE
        MOVE -1                 TO CDM-L-STATE
        MOVE 'YOU MUST ENTER A STATE'
            TO CDM-D-ERROR-MESSAGE
    ELSE
        MOVE CDM-D-STATE TO WS-STATE-CODE
        EXEC CICS
            LINK PROGRAM('STATEDIT')
                 COMMAREA(WS-STATE-EDIT-FIELDS)
                 LENGTH(3)
        END-EXEC
        IF NOT WS-VALID-CODE
            MOVE FAC-UNPROT-BRT-MDT TO CDM-A-STATE
            MOVE -1                 TO CDM-L-STATE
            MOVE 'STATE CODE IS INVALID'
                TO CDM-D-ERROR-MESSAGE.
*
```

Figure 14-24 Module 2200 of the CICS file-maintenance program showing efficient coding for an edit module (part 1 of 2)

techniques that I mentioned are designed to optimize a program's working set and locality of reference.

The first efficiency technique is to reduce the size of a program's working storage section. If several users in a CICS system are running the same program, each has his own copy of the program's working storage, but all share the same procedural code. As a result, if you can reduce the size of your program's working storage, you reduce it for each user of the program. So this has a multiplying effect: the more people that use a program at one time, the more benefit you get from reducing the size of a program's working storage. In some cases, then, this can have a dramatic effect on the overall response time of a CICS system.

Of course, you can't eliminate data that's required by your program. But you can reduce the size of your working-storage section by coding constant data as literals in the Procedure Division rather than as fields in the working-storage section. Here, I'm thinking especially of error messages. If your program edits 15 fields, each field has three edit checks, and the error messages average 20 characters each, your program may

```
           IF CDM-D-ERROR-MESSAGE EQUAL LOW-VALUE
               MOVE CDM-D-ZIP-CODE TO WS-ZIP-CODE
               EXEC CICS
                   LINK PROGRAM('ZIPEDIT')
                        COMMAREA(WS-ZIP-EDIT-FIELDS)
                        LENGTH(8)
               END-EXEC
               IF NOT WS-VALID-CODE
                   MOVE FAC-UNPROT-BRT-MDT TO CDM-A-ZIP-CODE
                   MOVE -1                 TO CDM-L-ZIP-CODE
                   MOVE 'ZIP CODE DOES NOT AGREE WITH STATE CODE'
                       TO CDM-D-ERROR-MESSAGE.
      *
           IF         CDM-D-CITY = SPACE
                   OR CDM-L-CITY = ZERO
               MOVE FAC-UNPROT-BRT-MDT TO CDM-A-CITY
               MOVE -1                 TO CDM-L-CITY
               MOVE 'YOU MUST ENTER A CITY'
                   TO CDM-D-ERROR-MESSAGE.
      *
           IF         CDM-D-ADDRESS = SPACE
                   OR CDM-L-ADDRESS = ZERO
               MOVE FAC-UNPROT-BRT-MDT TO CDM-A-ADDRESS
               MOVE -1                 TO CDM-L-ADDRESS
               MOVE 'YOU MUST ENTER AN ADDRESS'
                   TO CDM-D-ERROR-MESSAGE.
      *
           IF         CDM-D-NAME = SPACE
                   OR CDM-L-NAME = ZERO
               MOVE FAC-UNPROT-BRT-MDT TO CDM-A-NAME
               MOVE -1                 TO CDM-L-NAME
               MOVE 'YOU MUST ENTER A NAME'
                   TO CDM-D-ERROR-MESSAGE.
      *
           IF CDM-D-ERROR-MESSAGE NOT = LOW-VALUE
               MOVE 'N' TO VALID-DATA-SW.
      *
```

Figure 14-24 Module 2200 of the CICS file-maintenance program showing efficient coding for an edit module (part 2 of 2)

have as many as 900 bytes of error messages. Then, if you place this data in working storage, each user is given his own copy of it. As a result, if 30 users run the program at the same time, error messages occupy 27K of virtual storage. On the other hand, if you code the error messages as literals in the Procedure Division, only one copy is in storage, no matter how many users run the program.

The second efficiency technique is to code the subfunctions of a module in-line, rather than coding them as modules called by PERFORM statements. In a CICS system, whenever you call a module using a PERFORM statement, a page fault may occur. And paging is one of the major factors affecting the response time of a CICS system.

Unfortunately, this technique is not in keeping with the principles of structured design and structured coding. In brief, the more you use in-line coding, the less structure your program has, and the more difficult it is to code, test, and maintain. As a result, you should strive for a balance between program performance and development efficiency. As a general rule, we feel that you should only use in-line coding when it won't have much effect on program quality.

The third efficiency technique is to place infrequently-used sections of code at the end of your source program. In the CICS file-maintenance program, for example, module 8000 is executed only once. That's why we numbered it so it is coded last in the Procedure Division of the program. When you place a module like this at the end of the program, rather than at the start where you'd expect it, your program experiences fewer page faults while the main sections of the program are executing. As a result, response time is improved with no loss in program quality.

Discussion

Quite frankly, CICS wasn't designed with structured programming in mind. If it were, BMS would provide better documentation and COBOL code for the mapsets required by a program. And the CICS commands wouldn't branch to procedure names to handle exceptional conditions. Beyond this, the coding required for screen-handling would be easier to read and understand. I guess these shortcomings explain why the principles of structured coding generally have *not* been applied to CICS programs.

As I said at the start of this chapter, though, it's high time to start developing CICS programs on a structured basis. And now that you've completed this chapter, you can see that it's possible to do so without much difficulty. So why wait? The sooner you apply the principles of structured programming to your CICS programs, the sooner you'll improve your program quality and your productivity.

Terminology

Basic Mapping Support
BMS
mapset
physical mapset
symbolic mapset
communication area
Execute Interface Block
EIB
Common Work Area
CWA
Base Locator for Linkage
BLL
working set
locality of reference

Objectives

1. Given the screen layouts for a program, create an assembler language mapset for the program in structured style.

2. Given an assembler language mapset for a program, create a symbolic map that satisfies the COBOL coding standards recommended in this book.

3. Given the specifications, structure chart, and mapsets for a CICS program, code the program in COBOL using the techniques presented in this topic.

4. Describe three techniques for improving the performance of a CICS program, not including the technique of pseudo-conversational programming.

Section 4

Related subjects

This section consists of seven chapters that present subjects that are related to the procedures and techniques presented in sections 2 and 3. For instance, chapter 15 shows you how the 198X COBOL standards may affect your development techniques. And chapter 16 compares other methods of program development with the methods recommended in this book.

Although you should read section 2 before you read the chapters in this section, you don't have to read section 3 first. Furthermore, you can read the chapters in this section in whatever sequence you prefer.

Chapter 15

How the 198X COBOL standards will affect your development methods

In 1968, the American National Standards Institute published the first ANS COBOL standards. In 1974, the institute published a revised version of these standards. Today, most COBOL shops use compilers based on the 1974 ANS COBOL standards.

As I write this, though, a new version of the standards is in the process of being approved. At one time, these standards were expected to be approved and published by 1981. Later on, this date was pushed back to 1982. And now, we don't really know when these standards will be approved and published. As a result, most people in the COBOL industry refer to them as the 198X standards.

The difficulty, of course, is getting people to agree on the new standards. Of particular concern are those changes that would affect the thousands of programs already in use. As a result, though the new standards will probably be released in 1985, further delays are possible. And even if the new standards are released in 1985, it will be a year or two after that before companies start converting to the 198X COBOL compilers.

Meanwhile, IBM has announced a new compiler for its mainframes that supports the 198X COBOL standards. This compiler is referred to by IBM as the VS COBOL II compiler. Planned availability for this compiler is the fourth quarter of 1984 under a controlled release plan. Initially, it will only run on MVS systems, but we expect it to be available on all IBM mainframes eventually. As we understand it, this is the first COBOL compiler for mainframes that IBM has developed from scratch since the mid-1960s. And there is considerable interest in it.

Although we don't know exactly what the final version of the 198X standards will be, it's clear that some new Procedure Division constructs will be a part of those standards. It's also clear that these constructs will have some effect on the way you design and code COBOL programs. We know from preliminary versions of the standards what these constructs will look like. And we know from the manuals for VS COBOL II exactly how IBM intends to implement them.

In this chapter, then, I will familiarize you with the new constructs. I will show you how they work and give you recommendations for their use. So when you have finished this chapter, you should know what to expect in the future. And, you should be assured that the 198X standards and compilers won't have much effect on the way you develop programs.

Structured delimiters

Figure 15-1 shows the *structured delimiters* that are expected to be a part of the 198X standards. And all of these plus an END-CALL delimiter are going to be supported by the VS COBOL II compiler. Simply stated, the purpose of a structured delimiter is to show where a statement ends. As a result, these delimiters can sometimes be used to improve the readability of your COBOL code.

In general, structured delimiters are only useful when one conditional statement is used within another one. This is illustrated by the examples in figure 15-1. If a statement isn't used within another statement, it doesn't need a structured delimiter, because the period at the end of the statement is the delimiter. As a result, structured delimiters should have only a minor effect on your coding and no effect at all on the way you design programs.

Of all the structured delimiters, you'll probably use the END-IF statement the most. Because structured programming makes extensive use of nested IF statements, the END-IF can help you improve the readability of your modules as illustrated in figure 15-2. In the top example, the programmer had to code the IF NOT EMPLOYEE-EOF condition twice because the only way he could end the preceding IF statement was with a period. In the bottom example, the programmer ends the IF statement with an END-IF so the code for the module is easier to read.

You should notice in figure 15-2 that the structured delimiter in the second example is aligned with the IF statement it ends. This makes it obvious which IF statement it is associated with. Whenever you use structured delimiters, then, you should align them in this way.

With the exception of the END-IF delimiter, I don't think you'll use delimiters much when you convert to a 198X compiler. If you isolate I/O statements in their own modules as we recommend in this book, you won't ever need the delimiters for the I/O verbs. And you should have only an occasional need for delimiters on the computational verbs and the other miscellaneous verbs. As a general rule, you should only use structured delimiters when they improve readability...and this should be infrequently.

Input/Output verbs

READ	REWRITE	RETURN
WRITE	DELETE	START

Example:

```
IF CONDITION-A
    READ TRANREC
        INVALID KEY
            MOVE 'Y' TO INVALID-KEY-SW
    END-READ
    MOVE TR-RECORD-KEY TO OLD-RECORD-KEY.
```

Computational verbs

ADD	MULTIPLY	COMPUTE
SUBTRACT	DIVIDE	

Example:

```
IF CONDITION-A
    ADD B TO C
        ON SIZE ERROR
            MOVE ZERO TO C
    END-ADD
    ADD C TO D.
```

Miscellaneous verbs

IF	EVALUATE	STRING
PERFORM	SEARCH	UNSTRING

Example:

```
IF CONDITION-A
    IF CONDITION-B
        PERFORM 100-PROCESS-CONDITION-B
    ELSE
        PERFORM 200-PROCESS-OTHER-CONDITION
    END-IF
    PERFORM 300-PROCESS-CONDITION-A.
```

Figure 15-1 Verb list for structured delimiters

The inline PERFORM

The *inline PERFORM* is a construct that many structured programming advocates have wanted for years. When you use an inline PERFORM, you code the performed function right after the PERFORM statement, and you end the function with the END-PERFORM delimiter. In other words, the performed function is not coded in a separate paragraph. This is illustrated by the example in figure 15-3.

Coding without END-IF

```
*
 100-PRODUCE-EMPLOYEE-LINE.
*
     PERFORM 110-READ-EMPLOYEE-RECORD.
     IF NOT EMPLOYEE-EOF
         IF SR-ACTIVE-EMPLOYEE
             PERFORM 120-PRINT-ACTIVE-LINE
         ELSE
             PERFORM 130-PRINT-INACTIVE-LINE.
     IF NOT EMPLOYEE-EOF
         PERFORM 140-ACCUMULATE-GRAND-TOTAL.
*
```

Coding with END-IF

```
*
 100-PRODUCE-EMPLOYEE-LINE.
*
     PERFORM 110-READ-EMPLOYEE-RECORD.
     IF NOT EMPLOYEE-EOF
         IF SR-ACTIVE-EMPLOYEE
             PERFORM 120-PRINT-ACTIVE-LINE
         ELSE
             PERFORM 130-PRINT-INACTIVE-LINE
         END-IF
         PERFORM 140-ACCUMULATE-GRAND-TOTAL.
*
```

Figure 15-2 How END-IF can improve the readability of a module

When the inline PERFORM is used as shown in figure 15-3, we agree that it is useful. Here, module 000 simply calls module 200 to load the part-number table. Then, module 200 uses an inline PERFORM-VARYING statement to load the table. Without the inline PERFORM, module 000 must call module 200 with a PERFORM-VARYING statement. In this case, though, module 200 doesn't really load the table, it loads one entry of the table, so its name is somewhat misleading. For functions like this, we believe that the coding with the inline PERFORM is preferable to the coding without it.

The problem with the inline PERFORM is that it makes it relatively easy for you to code more than one function as a single COBOL paragraph. And this has an effect on our design principle that says you should design your program so that each of its modules can be coded in a single paragraph. As a result, when the 198X compilers become available, you must revise this principle so it says: Design your program so that each of its modules can be coded in a single paragraph *without using inline PERFORMs*. In addition, you should only use inline PERFORMs when they simplify the structure and coding of a program.

Coding without inline PERFORM

```
 000-EDIT-INVENTORY-TRANS.
*
      .
      .
      PERFORM 200-LOAD-PART-NUMBER-TABLE
          VARYING PN-TABLE-INDEX FROM 1 BY 1
          UNTIL PART-NUMBER-EOF.
      .
      .
*
 200-LOAD-PART-NUMBER-TABLE.
*
      PERFORM 210-READ-PART-NUMBER-RECORD.
      IF NOT PART-NUMBER-EOF
          MOVE PNR-PART-NUMBER
              TO PN-TABLE-ENTRY (PN-TABLE-INDEX)
      ELSE
          SET PN-TABLE-INDEX DOWN BY 1
          SET PN-ENTRY-COUNT TO PN-TABLE-INDEX.
*
```

Coding with inline PERFORM

```
 000-EDIT-INVENTORY-TRANS.
*
      .
      .
      PERFORM 200-LOAD-PART-NUMBER-TABLE.
      .
      .
*
 200-LOAD-PART-NUMBER-TABLE.
*
      PERFORM
          VARYING PN-TABLE-INDEX FROM 1 BY 1
          UNTIL PART-NUMBER-EOF
              PERFORM 210-READ-PART-NUMBER-RECORD
              IF NOT PART-NUMBER-EOF
                  MOVE PNR-PART-NUMBER
                      TO PN-TABLE-ENTRY (PN-TABLE-INDEX)
      END-PERFORM.
      SET PN-TABLE-INDEX DOWN BY 1.
      SET PN-ENTRY-COUNT TO PN-TABLE-INDEX.
*
```

Figure 15-3 How an inline PERFORM can improve the code of a load-table module

As a result, we don't think you should use inline PERFORMs much. As we see it, you should only use inline PERFORMs when 1974 COBOL forces you to divide a function in a way that you wouldn't otherwise divide it. Then, the use of an inline PERFORM can help you consolidate the code in a single module so you improve both the structure and coding of your program.

Incidentally, the END-PERFORM in figure 15-3 isn't needed for the inline PERFORM to work correctly. I only included it to show you how it can be coded. In practice, an END-PERFORM is only needed if the inline PERFORM is coded within some other statement like an IF statement.

Coding with test before

```
 100-GENERATE-DEPT-STATISTICS.
*
         .
         .
         PERFORM 130-SEARCH-DEPT-TABLE
             VARYING DT-INDEX FROM 1 BY 1
             UNTIL DT-ENTRY-FOUND
                OR DT-INDEX GREATER THAN DT-TABLE-LIMIT.
         SET DT-INDEX DOWN BY 1.
         .
         .
*
 130-SEARCH-DEPT-TABLE.
*
         IF DEPT-LOOKUP = DT-ENTRY (DT-INDEX)
             MOVE 'Y' TO DT-ENTRY-FOUND-SW.
```

Coding with test after

```
 100-GENERATE-DEPT-STATISTICS.
*
         .
         .
         PERFORM 130-SEARCH-DEPT-TABLE
             WITH TEST AFTER
             VARYING DT-INDEX FROM 1 BY 1
             UNTIL DT-ENTRY-FOUND
                OR DT-INDEX EQUAL DT-TABLE-LIMIT.
         .
         .
*
 130-SEARCH-DEPT-TABLE.
*
         IF DEPT-LOOKUP = DT-ENTRY (DT-INDEX)
             MOVE 'Y' TO DT-ENTRY-FOUND-SW.
```

Figure 15-4 How WITH TEST AFTER can improve the code of a search function

The PERFORM-UNTIL WITH TEST AFTER statement

As I mentioned in chapter 9, the condition stated in a PERFORM-UNTIL statement is tested before the performed module is called. Then, if the condition is true, the module isn't called. Although this is acceptable for most uses of the PERFORM-UNTIL, there are times when it would be nice to have the statement test the condition after the module is called. And that is what the WITH TEST AFTER language of the 198X standards is intended to provide for.

Figure 15-4 illustrates how this statement can be useful. Without this clause, the search module derives an index that is one larger than the index of the desired table entry. As a result, the search module has to set the index down by 1 before passing control back to its calling module. But when the WITH TEST AFTER clause is used, the index has the desired value when the table entry is found.

```
EVALUATE ITR-TRAN-CODE
    WHEN 1          PERFORM 240-EDIT-CODE-1-FIELDS
    WHEN 2          PERFORM 250-EDIT-CODE-2-FIELDS
    WHEN 3          PERFORM 260-EDIT-CODE-3-FIELDS
    WHEN 4          PERFORM 270-EDIT-CODE-4-FIELDS
    WHEN 5          PERFORM 280-EDIT-CODE-5-FIELDS
    WHEN 6 THRU 10  PERFORM 290-EDIT-COMMON-FIELDS
    WHEN OTHER      MOVE MARK TO ITL-TYPE-CODE-ERROR
                    MOVE 'N' TO VALID-TRAN-SW
                    ADD 1 TO INVALID-TRAN-CODE-COUNT.
```

Figure 15-5 An EVALUATE statement that operates on a single field

This same logic applies to the example in figure 15-3. If WITH TEST AFTER is used in the PERFORM-VARYING statement, you don't have to set PN-TABLE-INDEX down by 1 after the table is loaded to get the proper entry count. The WITH TEST AFTER clause can be used whether or not the function is performed inline.

Because the WITH TEST AFTER clause has limited application, you probably won't use it much. In fact, you can do anything with the traditional PERFORM statement that you can do WITH TEST AFTER. Nevertheless, you should use this clause whenever it improves the clarity of your code.

The EVALUATE statement

In chapter 9, we recommended that you implement a case structure as a succession of nested IF statements coded in linear form. When the 198X standards become available, though, you'll be able to implement this structure using the EVALUATE statement as shown in figure 15-5. Notice that by using the word OTHER, you can perform a function if the field has a value other than those specified. And by using THRU, you can code conditions that would be more difficult to code in a nested IF statement.

You can also use the EVALUATE statement to handle more complex sets of conditions as shown in the example in figure 15-6. Here, three fields are tested simultaneously and a function is performed only if all three conditions are satisfied. In addition, you can use ANY to indicate that any value will satisfy the condition for the associated field. Using code like this, you can use the EVALUATE statement to code the requirements of some types of decision tables.

I think you can tell from these examples that the EVALUATE statement can help you improve the readability of some programming functions. On the other hand, it has limited application so you probably won't use this statement much. Furthermore, this statement has no effect on the design of your programs.

One danger in using the EVALUATE statement is that you can create code with it that is extremely difficult to read. In fact, I haven't begun to show you all the different ways that this statement can be coded. Our general recommendation, then, is to use this statement when it improves

```
 WORKING-STORAGE SECTION.
*
 01   APPLICANT-CATEGORY-FIELDS.
*
      05   EXPERIENCE-CATEGORY            PIC X.
           88   NO-EXPERIENCE                      VALUE '1'.
           88   UNDER-5-YEARS                      VALUE '2'.
           88   5-AND-OVER-YEARS                   VALUE '3'.
      05   COLLEGE-DEGREE-CATEGORY        PIC X.
           88   NO-DEGREE                          VALUE 'N'.
           88   BACHELORS-DEGREE                   VALUE 'B'.
           88   MASTERS-DEGREE                     VALUE 'M'.
           88   DOCTORAL-DEGREE                    VALUE 'P'.
      05   SALARY-REQUIREMENT-CATEGORY PIC X.
           88   UNDER-20-THOUSAND                  VALUE '1'.
           88   20-30-THOUSAND                     VALUE '2'.
           88   OVER-30-THOUSAND                   VALUE '3'.
*
      .
      .
      .
*
 PROCEDURE DIVISION.
*
      .
      .
      .
*
 300-EVALUATE-APPLICANT-DATA.

      EVALUATE EXPERIENCE-CATEGORY
               COLLEGE-DEGREE-CATEGORY
               SALARY-REQUIREMENT-CATEGORY
          WHEN 1       B        1      PERFORM 310-ACTION-1
          WHEN 1       M        2      PERFORM 320-ACTION-2
          WHEN 1       P        3      PERFORM 330-ACTION-3
          WHEN 2       NOT P    NOT 3  PERFORM 340-ACTION-4
          WHEN 2       P        ANY    PERFORM 350-ACTION-5
          WHEN 3       NOT P    ANY    PERFORM 360-ACTION-6
          WHEN 3       P        ANY    PERFORM 370-ACTION-7
          WHEN OTHER                   PERFORM 380-DEFAULT-ACTION.
```

Figure 15-6 An EVALUATE statement that operates on three fields so it can direct the processing of a decision table

the clarity of your code. But use nested IF statements when the EVALUATE statement becomes confusing.

The SET-TO-TRUE statement

The SET-TO-TRUE statement is designed to be used with conditional variables. By using this statement, you can set a condition to true without knowing the value required by the condition. This is illustrated in figure 15-7. As you can see, using the SET-TO-TRUE statement is equivalent to moving the value of a condition to a field.

If you use the recommendations in this book for the coding and testing of switches and flags, your coding for switches and flags will be

Field description with condition names

```
 DATA DIVISION.
*
        .
        .
        05  COMMISSION-STATUS          PIC X.
            88  TRAINEE                VALUE '1'.
            88  ASSISTANT              VALUE '2'.
            88  ASSOCIATE              VALUE '3'.
            88  MANAGER                VALUE '4'.
*
        .
        .
        .
```

Turning a condition on with a MOVE statement

```
 PROCEDURE DIVISION.
*
        .
        .
        MOVE '3' TO COMMISSION-STATUS.
        .
        .
*
```

Turning a condition on with a SET-TO-TRUE statement

```
 PROCEDURE DIVISION.
*
        .
        .
        SET ASSOCIATE TO TRUE.
        .
        .
*
```

Figure 15-7 The SET-TO-TRUE statement

quite readable. As a result, the SET-TO-TRUE statement won't do much to improve the clarity of your code. But it may make it easier for you to write the code in your Procedure Divisions.

In particular, you may want to use the SET-TO-TRUE statement when the value assigned to a condition name is not directly related to the condition name. In figure 15-7, for example, numeric values are assigned to the conditions even though mnemonic codes could be used to relate the codes and the conditions. In a case like this, it's easier for you to remember a condition name than the value assigned to it. So it's somewhat easier for you to code the program if you use SET-TO-TRUE statements for turning conditions on. And this can also make your code somewhat easier to follow.

Discussion

In this chapter, I haven't covered all of the Procedure Division code that will be available in the 198X compilers. For instance, a CONTINUE statement, which does nothing, and an INITIALIZE statement, which sets fields to starting values, are expected to be a part of the new standards. However, I did cover all of the statements that are related to the structure of your programs.

I have presented this material so you know what to expect in the future. But I also presented it to show you that the 198X standards and the VS COBOL II compiler will have little or no effect on the way you design your programs. And they won't have much effect on the way you code your programs either. Yes, you'll use END-IFs in most of your programs; and you'll use an occasional inline PERFORM, PERFORM-UNTIL WITH TEST AFTER, EVALUATE, or SET-TO-TRUE statement. But you won't be coding anything you couldn't have coded almost as well with a 1974 COBOL compiler.

In conclusion, then, I want you to realize that the 198X compilers aren't going to have much effect on your program quality or your productivity. I have read optimistic reports that the new language in the 198X standards is going to make it easier to develop structured programs, but I see nothing in the standards to support this belief. As we see it, you can develop high-quality programs right now using the 1974 compilers So the sooner you start using 1974 COBOL the way it ought to be used, the better off you'll be. Then, you can make an easy transition to a 198X compiler later on.

Terminology

structured delimiter
inline PERFORM

Objective

Explain how each of the following will affect the way in which you design and code COBOL programs:

- structured delimiters
- inline PERFORMs
- the WITH TEST AFTER clause of the PERFORM-UNTIL statement
- the EVALUATE statement
- the SET-TO-TRUE statement

Chapter 16

What you should know about other development methods

In our survey on development methods, we found that 73 percent of the people were familiar with IBM's HIPO documentation, 32 percent were familiar with Warnier-Orr diagrams, and 38 percent were familiar with the methods of Yourdon inc. In terms of use, 10 percent of the people used Warnier-Orr diagrams to design programs, 15 percent used Yourdon techniques to design programs, and 20 percent used HIPO diagrams to plan the modules of a program. With that many people knowing about these methods and using these methods, I thought you ought to know something about them too.

In this chapter, then, I'll try to show you what these methods are. I'll try to show you what's right with them...and also what's wrong with them. When you complete this chapter, you should know whether or not you want to do additional research on these methods.

These are the only other methods that I'm going to present because our survey showed that no other methods are used enough to be significant. Specifically, our survey showed that less than 15 percent of the respondents were familiar with any method other than our method and the three I just mentioned. And less than 5 percent of the respondents actually used any other methods. So I don't think any other methods are worth mentioning in this chapter.

Before I start, I think I should tell you that I'm going to make every effort to be objective in this chapter. But I definitely have my biases. If I didn't think the methods I've already presented are the best ones for developing COBOL programs, I wouldn't be writing this book at all. In this chapter, however, my purpose is not to criticize someone else's ideas;

it's to try to show you what to use and what to avoid if you want to improve program quality and programmer productivity in your shop.

IBM's HIPO documentation

HIPO stands for Hierarchy plus Input-Process-Output. The three basic HIPO documents are (1) the hierarchy, or structure, chart, (2) the HIPO diagram, and (3) the extended description form. In general, the *hierarchy chart* is used to chart the modules within a system or a program; the *HIPO diagram* is used to describe the input, processing, and output of one of the modules in the hierarchy chart; and the extended description form is used to provide detail on the processing requirements of a module.

To illustrate, figure 16-1 shows a hierarchy chart for the edit program as it might be shown in a HIPO manual. A chart like this is also known as a *visual table of contents* in the HIPO literature. The complete HIPO documentation for a program consists of the hierarchy chart plus one HIPO diagram for each module of the program. In addition, whenever needed, you can use one or more extended description forms to give more detail for the documentation of a module.

If you look at the chart in figure 16-1, you can see that is it similar to the structure charts that we've used throughout this book. A trivial difference is that common modules are indicated by shading in the lower righthand corner of a module box rather than in the upper corner. A more significant difference is the numbering system used in most HIPO literature. Also, module names are given in capital letters in the bottom of all but the top-level box so each module can be implemented as a subprogram under that name.

Since I've covered HIPO diagrams in some detail in chapter 8, I'm not going to show you examples of HIPO diagrams and extended descriptions right now. If you are interested in them, though, figure 8-18 gives an example of a typical HIPO diagram as presented in a HIPO manual. And figure 8-9 gives an example of an extended description form.

HIPO documentation at the system and program level Since HIPO is a flexible documentation system, you can use it to document system requirements, the design of a system, or the design of a program. In addition, it provides facilities that let you document both a structured program and an unstructured program. In short, you can use HIPO to document the structure and modules of a complete system or any part of a system. Theoretically, at least, you can create HIPO documentation for a system from the top down ending up with one hierarchy chart per program and one HIPO diagram for each module in each program.

To some extent, Paul's structure charts were based on the HIPO hierarchy chart. We've already shown you how Paul's HIPO diagrams are based on a structured subset of the techniques used for creating IBM's HIPO diagrams. And if you check the chapter on systems design and analysis, you'll see that we recommend a system structure chart to

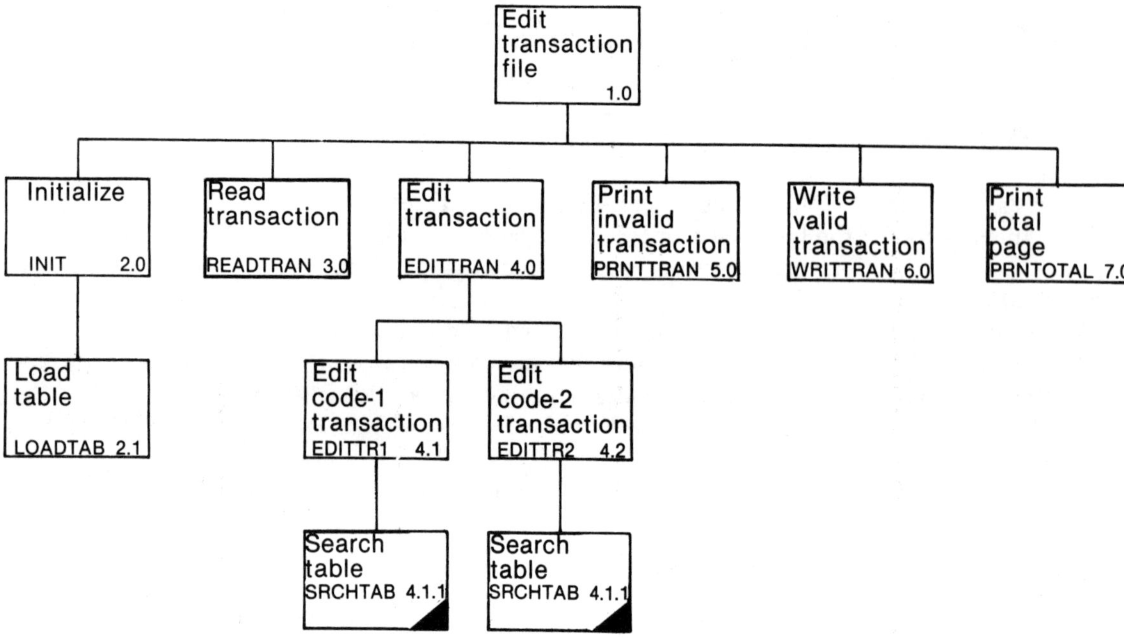

Figure 16-1 A visual table of contents for the edit program as used in HIPO documentation

document the programs used within a system. So there's no doubt that HIPO documentation has had an influence on us and on many people in our industry.

On the other hand, HIPO is a documentation method; it is not a design method. It doesn't tell you how to decide what modules a system should consist of. And it doesn't tell you how to decide what modules a program should consist of. If you use HIPO, the burden is on you to develop design techniques that help you make these decisions.

The effect of HIPO on program design and documentation Back in the 1970s, we felt HIPO documentation had a good chance of becoming an industry standard for program design and documentation because IBM was promoting it. But this hasn't happened.

The main problem is that HIPO manuals and books show you how to document everything; but they don't show you how to design anything. So when Paul decided to use hierarchy charts and HIPO diagrams to document the design of a program, he still had to develop a design method. But that, of course, is the trick: developing an effective design method. Anyone can draw boxes and connect them with lines.

Beyond this, as I explained in topic 4 of chapter 8, I think HIPO diagrams as promoted by IBM have proven to be too cumbersome for documenting program modules. They take too long to create; they're too difficult to modify; and they don't really represent anything that pseudocode or COBOL code doesn't represent as well.

In summary, I think HIPO's day has passed. IBM doesn't seem to promote it much any more. And I think fewer people and companies will be using it five years from now than are using it today.

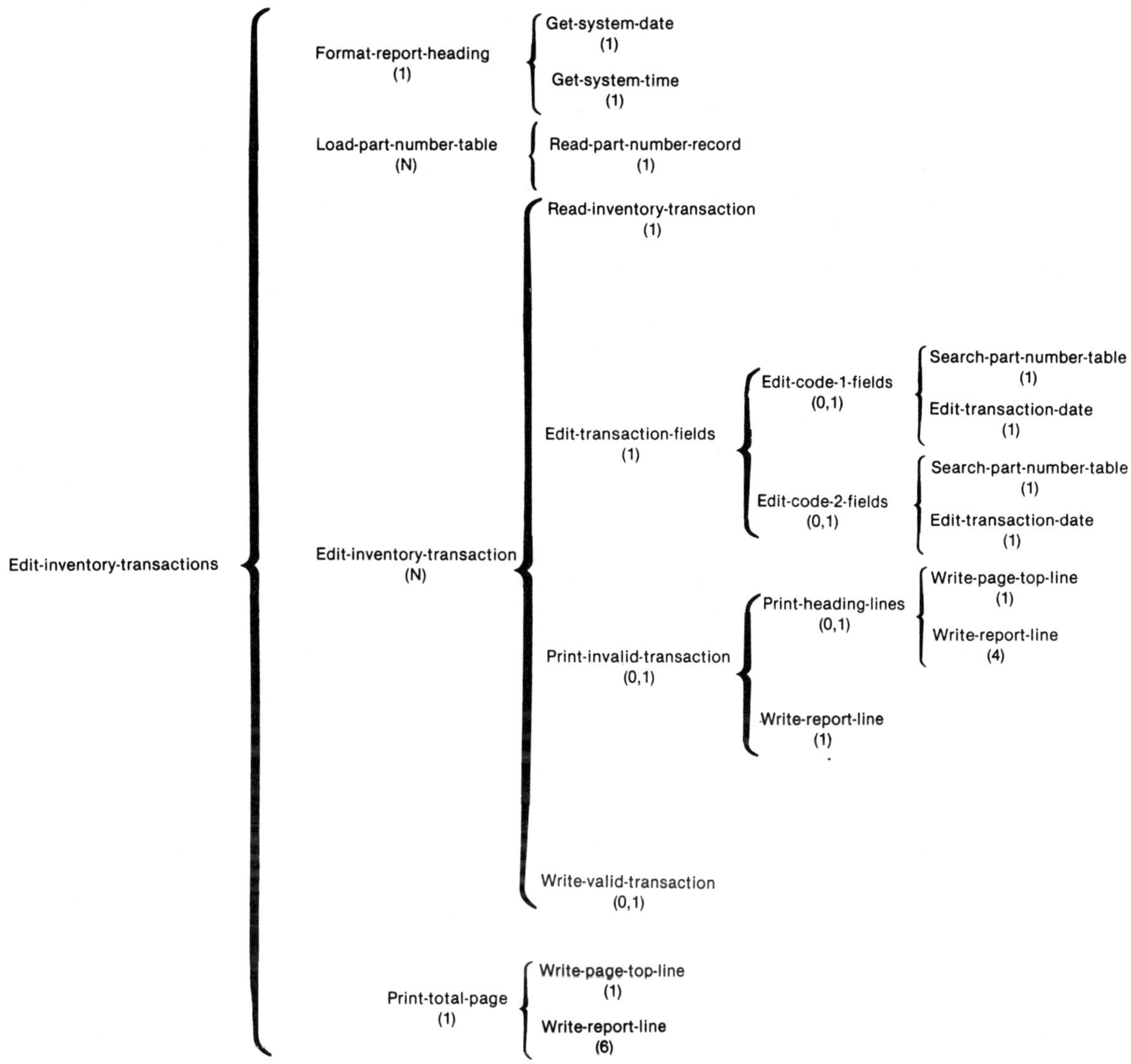

Figure 16-2 A Warnier diagram for the edit program

Warnier-Orr diagrams

A *Warnier diagram* is a series of brackets that represents the structure of something. Within the brackets, you can use other symbols to show the logic, repetition, and sequencing of the structural components. For example, figure 16-2 presents a Warnier diagram for the edit program. As you can see, the brackets show in a left-to-right structure what a structure chart shows in a top-down structure. The numbers in the parentheses below a module name indicate how many times a module may be executed by its calling module.

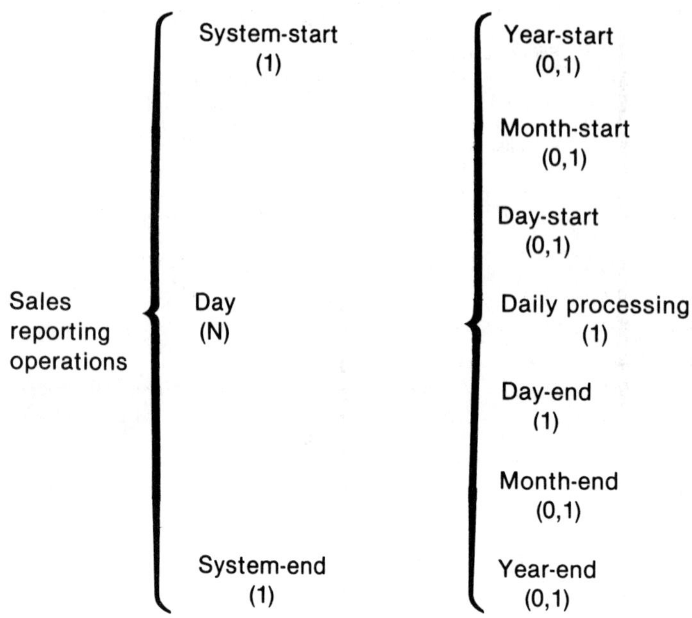

Figure 16-3 A Warnier diagram for the periodic operations of a sales reporting system

Warnier diagrams are named after their French developer, Jean-Dominique Warnier. But they are also known as *Warnier-Orr diagrams*, because an American, Kenneth Orr, has been the primary promoter of these diagrams in the United States. In fact, Mr. Orr made a complete presentation of Warnier diagrams in a book called *Structured Systems Development*, which was published in 1977 by Yourdon inc.

Warnier diagrams for different design tasks Because Warnier diagrams are a graphics device, you can use them to design many different aspects of a system. In his book, for example, Mr. Orr shows how you can use them to document data structures, system structures, program structures, and operational structures. For instance, figure 16-3 shows you how a Warnier diagram can be used to represent the structure of a system's operations (this is a modification of one of the book's illustrations).

The effect of Warnier diagrams on program design I was surprised to find in our survey that 10 percent of the respondents used Warnier diagrams to design their programs. When I talked with Paul about it, he said this didn't bother him. After all, you can think of Warnier diagrams as structure charts laid on their side. In fact, you may be able to draw a Warnier diagram faster than you can draw a structure chart because you don't have to draw all the boxes and lines.

So, I think we have to keep an open mind about Warnier diagrams. In order to use them for program structures, I think you need to develop a notation for common modules and module numbering. But that shouldn't be hard to do. Then, if you find it's easier to draw Warnier diagrams than structure charts, they're worth a try. Once you develop the COBOL program, you can redraw the Warnier diagram for final documentation. If this isn't acceptable in your shop, you can draw a structure chart from the Warnier diagram for the final documentation. Or, perhaps your shop has structure listing software that will create final structure documentation from the COBOL source code as we recommended in chapter 11.

With this in mind, I think we can say that Warnier diagrams can have a minor effect on program design. Perhaps by using these diagrams you can speed up the design phase of program development. And that's a step in the right direction.

On the other hand, like HIPO documentation, Warnier diagrams are a documentation method, not a design method. Sure, you can use them to document your designs. But the literature on Warnier diagrams doesn't tell you how to decide what programs a system should consist of or what modules a COBOL program should consist of. So whether or not you use Warnier diagrams, you still need an effective design method if you want to improve program quality and programmer productivity.

Yourdon inc.'s structured analysis and design

Since the early 1970s, Ed Yourdon has been a major promoter of structured techniques. Ed is president of Yourdon inc., a company that specializes in training seminars on structured analysis and design. In 1975, his book called *Techniques of Program Structure and Design* was published by Prentice Hall. Since then, his company has published many other books on structured systems design and structured programming.

Since Yourdon inc. is a company of many people and since the company has published many books written by these people and others, it's difficult to say exactly what the Yourdon method of structured analysis and design is. To some extent, I'm sure, the theory and practice of Yourdon inc. is still evolving. So it's natural that the Yourdon seminars and books aren't always consistent in their recommendations. Nevertheless, I think it's generally clear as to what the Yourdon methods are. So let me try to show you how these methods are applied at the system and program levels.

Structured analysis and design at the system level In general, the Yourdon approach to analysis and design at the system level centers around the *data flow diagram*. A data flow diagram (or *DFD*) is used both to document an existing system and to design a new system. For instance, figure 16-4 presents a data flow diagram for one level of a workers' compensation system. In a DFD like this, the circles represent *processes*; the parallel lines represent *data stores* (which are usually files); and the arrows represent *data flows*. Perhaps the best Yourdon book on the use of DFDs is *Structured Analysis and System Specification* by Tom De Marco published in 1978.

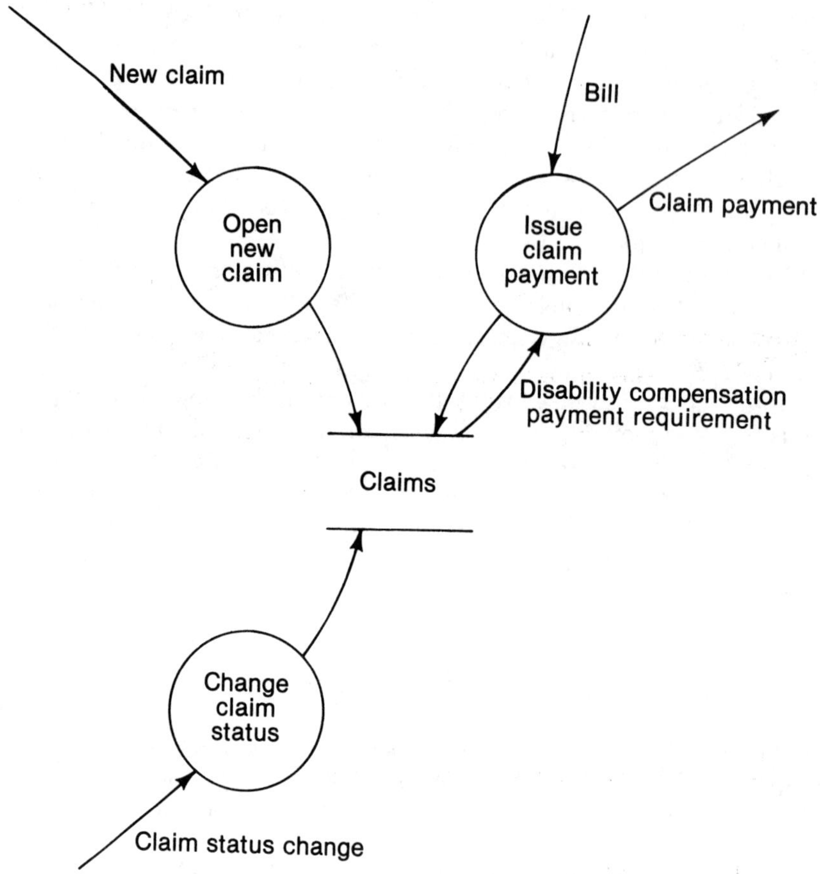

Figure 16-4 A data flow diagram for a workers' compensation system

When you design a new system using structured analysis and design, you do so in four stages: physical analysis, logical analysis, logical design, and physical design. In each stage, you create a set of DFDs. You start by creating one DFD for the entire system. You then expand this DFD into several new DFDs at the next level down. These in turn can be expanded down another level. And so on until an entire system is documented by a collection of DFDs. In the physical design stage, as we understand it, you continue to design down to the point at which each DFD represents one module in a program. And, eventually, you combine these modules to identify the programs of the system.

Since this book is about program development and not system development, I won't try to explain what's right or wrong about this method of system design. In brief, though, we believe that DFDs are useful for system analysis and design. Although we don't use the same analysis or design theory, we use DFDs when we design our own systems. In fact, we recommend them for the analysis and logical design phases of system development. You'll learn more about this in chapter 21.

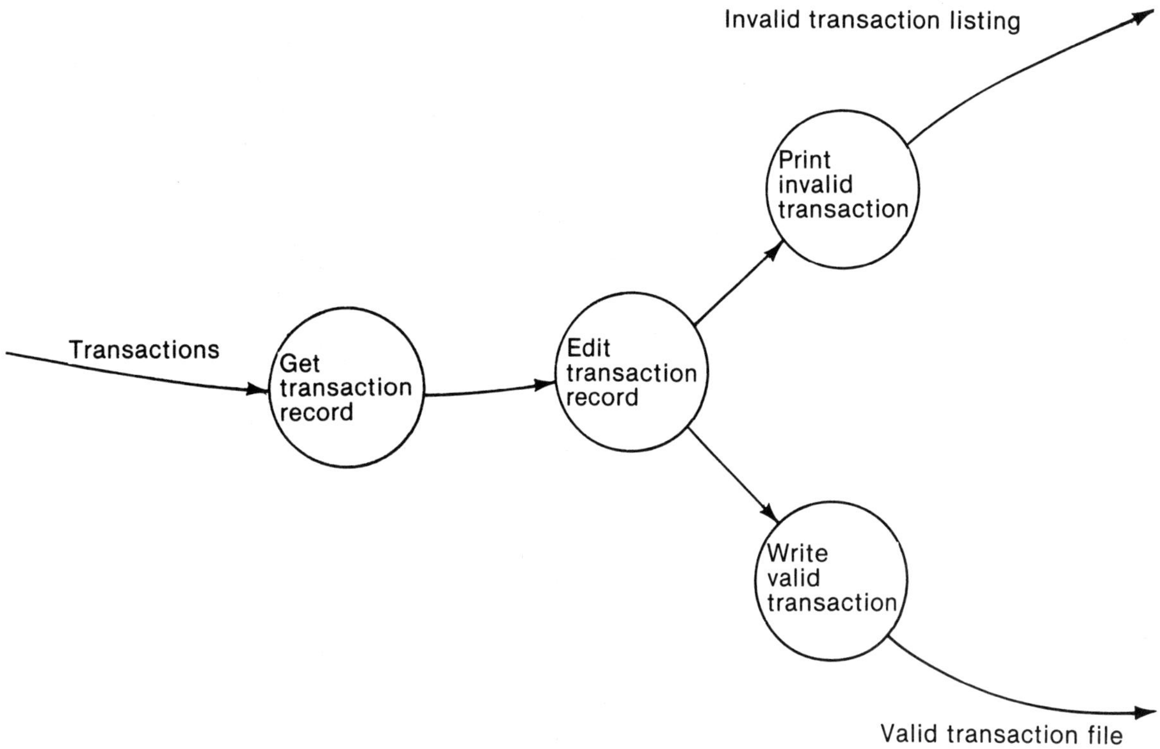

Figure 16-5 A bubble chart for the edit program

Structured analysis and design at the program level The people and books of Yourdon inc. offer many ideas and theories on program design and development. Their definitive work on the subject of program design is *Structured Design* by Ed Yourdon and Larry L. Constantine published in 1975 by Yourdon inc. Unfortunately, this 599-page book is extremely academic and theoretical. And the book doesn't try to show you how to apply its theory to the design of COBOL programs. So I can't recommend this book for someone who develops COBOL programs. Fortunately, though, the Yourdon principles of program design are repeated in two other Yourdon books, *The Practical Guide to Structured Systems Design* by Meilir Page-Jones and *Learning to Program in Structured COBOL (Part 2)* by Timothy R. Lister and Edward Yourdon.

As I understand these books, you start the process of program design by creating a DFD like the one in figure 16-5 for the program. A program DFD like this can also be called a *bubble chart* or a *program graph*. The bubble chart in the example is a chart created for our edit program. Here, each of the circles represents a process within the program.

Using the bubble chart, you go through a mental process called *transform analysis* that will help you derive a structure chart for the program like the one in figure 16-6. In addition, by using transform analysis, the modules of your resulting program are supposed to have

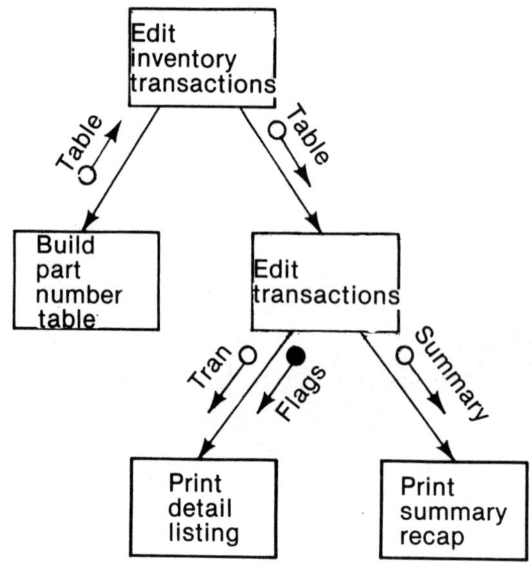

Figure 16-6 A tree chart for the edit program that shows a concern for coupling and cohesion

acceptable degrees of what the people at Yourdon inc. call coupling and cohesion.

Coupling refers to the degree of dependence that two modules have on each other. Two modules are highly coupled when there is a strong degree of interdependence. Two modules are loosely coupled with there is a low degree of interdependence.

Cohesion, on the other hand, refers to the degree to which all of the code in a module relates to the purpose of the module. If, for example, all of the code in a module relates to a single function, the module is said to be highly cohesive. Conversely, if the code in a module is only loosely related, the module is said to have a low degree of cohesiveness.

To emphasize their points, the Yourdon literature describes seven types of cohesiveness and five types of coupling. These are summarized in figure 16-7. As we read it, then, the goal of the Yourdon design method is to create program designs in which the modules have the lowest possible degree of coupling and the highest possible degree of cohesiveness.

After you create the first structure chart for a program using the Yourdon approach to program design, you analyze its modules for coupling and cohesion. Based on this analysis, you modify the program design to try to achieve more optimum degrees of coupling and cohesion. When you're satisfied that the design works and that the modules are optimized, you are ready to implement the program.

The effect of Yourdon inc. on program design As you can probably tell by now, the people at Yourdon inc. have much to say about program design. Since the mid-1970s, they have been effective promoters of their design methods. Without Yourdon inc., I'm sure many companies would

Five types of coupling

1. Data coupling	Loose	Good
2. Stamp coupling		
3. Control coupling		
4. Common coupling		
5. Content coupling	Tight	Bad

Seven types of cohesion

1. Functional cohesion	Highest cohesion	Good
2. Sequential cohesion		
3. Communicational cohesion		
4. Procedural cohesion		
5. Temporal cohesion		
6. Logical cohesion		
7. Coincidental cohesion	Lowest cohesion	Bad

Figure 16-7 Types of coupling and cohesion

still be struggling with unstructured design methods. So, at the least, we have to give Yourdon inc. much credit for its role as an agent of change.

In addition, both Paul and I agree in general with the Yourdon concepts of coupling and cohesion. When Paul says you should design independent, functional modules, he's also saying that you should do your best to optimize the coupling and cohesion of your modules. As a result, we encourage you to read the Yourdon literature on these concepts because it may help you design modules with improved independence and functionality.

In the context of this book, however, we have to ask whether the Yourdon design techniques are the best ones for COBOL shops and COBOL programmers. Do these design techniques lead to effective program designs for COBOL programs? And do these design techniques lead to maximum programmer productivity in a typical COBOL shop? As we see it, the Yourdon design techniques have two serious shortcomings.

First, the Yourdon techniques are difficult to learn because of the large amount of new terminology that they introduce and because they are so theoretical. In seems, in fact, that many COBOL programmers are either unwilling or unable to master the Yourdon theories and techniques. In Paul's consulting experience, for example, he finds that few programmers ever complete the multimedia training courses that are available on the Yourdon methods. And it's unusual to find a shop in which a majority of the programmers have converted to the Yourdon techniques. So, if you want your programmers to convert to Yourdon techniques, your first problem is likely to be a training problem.

Second, the Yourdon design techniques do not lead to programs in which each module can be coded as a single COBOL paragraph. And this is a critical shortcoming of the design method. As I've said throughout this book, both program quality and programmer productivity deteriorate when the design modules of a program require more than a paragraph. We feel, in fact, that the more COBOL paragraphs a program requires per module on the structure chart, the worse the program is.

To illustrate the shortcomings of the Yourdon design method, look again at the design for our edit program that is shown in figure 16-6. This design was created by the programming manager of a staff of more than 200 programmers in a large insurance company. This man had gone to the Yourdon seminars and considered himself an expert on Yourdon techniques. He started by creating the bubble chart in figure 16-5 for the program, and he followed this by doing a transform analysis. After he created the preliminary structure chart for the program, he analyzed it for degrees of coupling and cohesion after which he revised the initial design. When he was finished, he was convinced that this was the best possible design for the edit program.

Now, in terms of coupling and cohesion, I'm sure you can argue that the design in figure 16-6 is an effective program design for the edit program. But in terms of COBOL programming, it's ineffective to the extreme. In particular, all of the critical code in the program is still in one module, the edit-transactions module, so none of the critical design decisions have even been dealt with. And they won't be dealt with until the programmer plans or codes this module.

In fairness, you must remember that the design in figure 16-6 is *not* a design by any member of the Yourdon staff. So the people at Yourdon might recommend a more effective design for this program. On the other hand, the design in figure 16-6 is typical of the designs shown in the Yourdon literature. And the person who created it considered himself an expert on Yourdon methodology. So, at the least, this design highlights the training problem you're likely to encounter with the Yourdon methods.

The effect of Yourdon inc. on COBOL coding In general, Yourdon inc. has been far more concerned with program design than with COBOL coding. So most of their books and courses say little about COBOL coding. Nevertheless, I think they've had an effect on COBOL coding that should be mentioned.

Learning to Program in Structured COBOL (Part 2) and *How to Manage Structured Programming* by Ed Yourdon (1975, Yourdon inc.) both say that the building block for the modules of a COBOL program should be the paragraph. More specifically, they rule out the COBOL section and a series of paragraphs called by a PERFORM-THRU statement as acceptable implementations of a program module. Since a COBOL paragraph has only one entry point and one exit point, they believe it is a legitimate COBOL construct for the modules of a structured program. Needless to say, we agree with this.

In addition, however, both of these books indicate that a separately-compiled subprogram is also a legitimate implementation of a module of a program. In fact, they seem to prefer this implementation because then you know for sure what the data interfaces of the module are. In contrast, a COBOL paragraph has access to all of the data in the Data Division. Unfortunately, however, this support for subprograms has led some people to believe that the best way to develop a program is as a collection of subprograms. And that can lead to serious development problems.

For instance, when we asked the manager who created the program design of figure 16-6 how he would code the modules, he said each of the five modules would be coded as a subprogram. When we asked him what he gained by doing this, he said that the modules have a better chance of being reused by other programs if they're coded as subprograms. "But," we said, "your top-level module consists of only two calls to the level-2 modules. Certainly, no one would reuse a module like that. And no other program will print the same detail listing, edit the same transactions, or print the same summary recap. In fact, the only module that might be reused is the build-part-number-table module. So why should any of the other modules be treated as subprograms?" His answer: "To avoid pathological coupling."

Here, then, you can see that the Yourdon design theory supports impracticality, because there's simply no point in creating subprograms that are only going to be used in one program. Although they may help you reduce coupling, they compound your linkage problems so testing and maintenance become more difficult. But I've already mentioned the problems with subprograms in topic 4 of chapter 9.

In fairness, the Yourdon literature doesn't specifically say that you should implement each module of a COBOL program as a subprogram. But you can see how the goal of data coupling could lead you to that conclusion. Theoretically, at least, if each module of a program is a subprogram, the only kind of coupling you can have is data coupling, and that's what the literature says you should strive for.

Discussion

When you analyze other development methods, you have to consider the superficial aspects like the graphic conventions as well as the theoretical and practical aspects such as the design principles and techniques. As we see it, then, HIPO documentation and Warnier-Orr diagrams are relatively harmless since they are primarily documentation methods, not design or development methods.

In contrast, the focus of Yourdon inc. is on theory and techniques for analyzing and designing systems and programs. So before you adopt their programming techniques, you should make sure that they are the best ones for you in terms of program quality and programmer productivity.

In this chapter, I've tried hard to be fair in my presentation of other methods, but now I'm wondering if I overdid it. Since that wouldn't be right either, I want you to know that Paul and I don't believe in any of the methods presented in this chapter. If we thought that HIPO documentation, Warnier diagrams, or Yourdon methods were of any value to the COBOL programmer, we would have presented them in detail elsewhere in this book. We only present them at all because programmers are often curious about them. When I first met Paul, he referred to some of these other methods as "academic poppycock." I agreed with him then, and neither Paul nor I have changed our opinions.

Terminology

HIPO
hierarchy chart
HIPO diagram
visual table of contents
Warnier diagram
Warnier-Orr diagram
data flow diagram
DFD
process
data store
data flow
bubble chart
program graph
transform analysis
coupling
cohesion

Objective

Describe the characteristics of each of the following:

HIPO documentation
Warnier-Orr diagrams
Yourdon inc.'s structured analysis and design

Chapter 17

What you should know about structured walkthroughs

Historically, most programmers have worked alone. Once a programmer was assigned a program, he was left on his own to design, code, and test it. Although his manager may have asked him frequently when he was going to complete the program, no one reviewed his progress, measured his productivity, or analyzed the quality of his code. His work was his own.

Naturally, some major errors resulted from this isolation. Often, for example, programmers working on related programs did so under different sets of assumptions. As a result, when the programs came together during the system test, they discovered that the interfaces didn't work properly. And, sometimes, a manager who hadn't checked a programmer's work for three or more months would find that the programmer who had reported for weeks that the program was 90 percent complete, hadn't done anything of value on the program. So it would have to be reassigned and restarted.

To avoid disasters like this, there has been a considerable push to convert programming from a job done by individuals working in private to a job done by groups working in public. Two of the catch phrases that express this goal are "from private art to public practice" and "from private works to corporate assets." One of the techniques that has helped to accomplish this in many companies is the structured walkthrough.

In this chapter, I am going to present structured walkthroughs as they are taught by Paul Noll in his seminars and as they are used in many COBOL shops today. Then, I'll relate some of the experiences we've had with walkthroughs in our own COBOL shop, and I'll question two traditional walkthrough practices. When you finish this chapter, I think you'll know whether or not you want to try walkthroughs in your shop. And, if you're already using them, I think you may pick up some ideas that will lead you to change your walkthrough policies.

An introduction to structured walkthroughs

In simple terms, a *structured walkthrough* is a group review of some phase of a program's development for the purpose of detecting errors. In other words, the reviewers are asked to "walk through" the functions of the program, sometimes using test cases prepared by the program's developer. Because the programmer himself is usually too close to the problem to discover all errors by himself, this public review will often uncover problems that the programmer would never have thought of.

The major objective of a walkthrough is to detect errors early...errors in program specifications, design errors, coding errors, testing errors, and so on. Theoretically, at least, the later in the development of a program that an error is discovered, the more it costs to correct it. So a specification error that costs $50 to correct during the specification stage may cost $500 or more to correct if it isn't found until the systems test for the application.

The format of a walkthrough To increase the effectiveness of the group review, structured walkthroughs have been given a rather specific format. Although this format will vary somewhat from one company to another, the following characteristics apply to all walkthroughs:

1. The programmer initiates (or originates) the walkthrough when he is ready for public review of some phase of his work.

2. The programmer (or originator) invites from two to six associates to participate in the walkthrough.

3. No managers attend walkthroughs since the emphasis is on finding errors, not on programmer evaluation.

4. The programmer states the objectives of the walkthrough in writing before the meeting.

5. The programmer distributes all materials pertinent to the walkthrough to each participant before the meeting.

6. A list of errors or questions (an *action list*) is compiled during the structured walkthrough, but no attempt is made to correct these errors during the meeting.

7. The programmer takes action on each item on the action list and lets the participants know what actions were taken.

Walkthrough type	Walkthrough materials
Specification	Program overview, record descriptions (COPY members), print charts, screen layouts, and screen flow diagram
Design	Program specifications plus structure chart or program specifications plus structure chart and HIPO diagrams
Test plan	Program specifications, structure chart, and test plan; or program specifications, structure chart, test plan, and test data
Coding	Program specifications, structure chart, and one of the following: program listing before compilation, program listing after clean compilation but before testing, or program listing after testing
User guide	Specifications plus user guide

Figure 17-1 Types of walkthroughs and required materials for each type

When to use structured walkthroughs In general, a walkthrough can be conducted any time a programmer completes a phase of work that is likely to contain errors. Figure 17-1, for example, gives some typical times at which walkthroughs can be conducted. In our survey, the most common kinds of walkthroughs were: program specifications (49% of the companies that used walkthroughs did these), program designs (31%), test plans (40%), and COBOL coding (49%). Less common walkthroughs were pseudocode walkthroughs (11%) and user guide walkthroughs (23%).

As indicated in figure 17-1, a design walkthrough can be conducted on the structure chart alone or on the structure chart plus HIPO diagrams. Most of the companies in our survey did their design walkthroughs on structure charts alone. But this can depend on the complexity of the problem.

Although a coding walkthrough can be conducted before or after the coding is compiled, I think reviewing code after compilation leads to maximum productivity. That way you don't spend time finding errors that the compiler is going to catch anyway. Also, the cross-reference listing can make it easier to review the code.

As you progress in the sequence of development, of course, the value of a walkthrough diminishes. For instance, finding an error in a coding walkthrough is likely to be far less valuable than finding an error in a structure chart walkthrough. As a result, I think the two most important walkthroughs are the specification and design walkthroughs. After that, test plan walkthroughs are useful because they help to make sure that programs are tested thoroughly. And coding walkthroughs are valuable

Walkthrough agenda

Notice date: May 25, 1984

Originator: Paul Noll

Meeting date and time: Wednesday
May 30
1:30 P.M.

Location: Room 578

Program: Produce sales report

Type of walkthrough: Design

Materials:

1. Program specifications
2. Structure chart

Objectives:

Please review for

1. Completeness and logic
2. Meaningful names

Figure 17-2 Typical agenda for a design walkthrough

because they help to promote the use of coding standards throughout a shop.

How to prepare for the walkthrough meeting As I mentioned earlier, the programmer is responsible for arranging the walkthrough. She also has to distribute an agenda to each of the participants along with all related materials. This should be done at least 48 hours before the meeting so the participants have adequate time to prepare.

Figure 17-2 shows a typical agenda for a design walkthrough. Here, as stated under "objectives," the programmer wants the participants to review the structure chart for (1) completeness and logic, and (2) meaningful names. In other words, the programmer wants to know (1) if all of the functions indicated by the specifications are logically provided for, and (2) if all of the module names make sense.

Figure 17-3 shows a typical agenda for a coding walkthrough. Here, the programmer wants the participants to check for (1) missing code, (2) coding errors, (3) meaningful names, and (4) consistent names. He says to simply note the inconsistent names in red so mentioning them won't take up time at the meeting. Since the walkthrough is to be done after the

Walkthrough agenda

Notice date: June 11, 1984

Originator: Doug Lowe

Meeting date and time: Tuesday
June 12
9:00 A.M.

Location: Conference room

Program: Update inventory file

Type of walkthrough: Coding

Materials:

1. Specifications
2. Structure chart
3. Compiled COBOL listing

Objectives:

Please review for

1. Missing code
2. Coding errors
3. Meaningful names
4. Consistent names (note in red)

Figure 17-3 Typical agenda for a coding walkthrough

COBOL program has compiled cleanly, the walkthrough participants don't have to worry about syntax errors.

If the participants are to prepare properly for the meeting, the programmer must send them complete information relating to the type of walkthrough that will be held. Before a design walkthrough for structure chart only, for example, the programmer must distribute a packet consisting of program specifications and structure chart. Before a coding walkthrough, she must prepare packets that contain program specifications, structure chart, and program listing.

If you are a participant in a walkthrough, you too must prepare for the meeting. The idea is for you to study the materials on your own and to mark possible errors for discussion at the meeting. If you don't have time to prepare due to conflicting demands, you should cancel out or ask for a change in the meeting time. If you go to the meeting unprepared and hope to discover errors while you're there, you'll end up wasting your own time, and you'll be little help to the programmer who asked you to participate in the walkthrough.

How to conduct the meeting Before a meeting begins or sometimes at the start of a meeting, a *moderator* and a *recorder* should be appointed. In general, neither should be the programmer who initiated the walkthrough, but this isn't essential. The moderator will be in charge of conducting the meeting and keeping the meeting on track. The recorder will be in charge of recording errors and problems detected during the walkthrough. Quite often, you will find that one person on a programming staff does a better-than-average job as a moderator, so he or she is repeatedly appointed to that position.

Once a meeting begins, it normally progresses in three distinct phases. First, the programmer presents an overview of what the walkthrough materials consist of and what the walkthrough is intended to accomplish. Second, the programmer and participants walk through the materials in an attempt to detect errors. During this phase, the recorder lists all questions raised on the action list. Third, the participants review the action list to see whether or not something really has to be done about each item on the list. If not, the item is deleted.

The most important phase of the walkthrough, of course, is the one in which the participants try to detect errors. This phase may be conducted formally or informally. Often, the best results are achieved when the discussion proceeds informally. If you're the moderator, you should remember that your job is to get as many ideas as possible from each participant, so you should conduct the meeting in a way that will achieve that end.

To illustrate how this phase of the walkthrough might proceed, suppose you are the moderator for a design walkthrough for the sequential file-maintenance program that is presented in this book. The materials for the walkthrough consist of specifications, a structure chart, and HIPO diagrams. Quite simply, you might start by asking if anyone had any questions about the specifications, proceed by asking for questions about the structure chart, and end up by asking for questions about each HIPO diagram taken in sequence. Rather than rigidly adhere to this sequence, however, you might let the discussion go uncontrolled until it becomes unproductive, at which time you should intervene and get the group back on track. If, for example, a participant wants to examine how the structure chart relates to HIPO diagram number 200 when you're talking about the specifications, let it go as long as it relates to the purpose of the walkthrough. When the discussion gets personal or trivial, however, by all means intervene.

When a question is raised, the programmer should be given a chance to dispense with it right away. If he doesn't have a good answer, the other participants should be given the chance to give their opinions. If there is agreement that the question indicates a real problem, the recorder should list the point on the action list. Then, the walkthrough should go on to the next question.

By far the most important job of the moderator is to keep all participants focused on error detection, *not* error correction. Unfortunately, it's all too tempting for a programmer who has detected an error to want to correct it too. As moderator, though, you can't let the person correct the error because (1) it detracts from the purpose of the walkthrough, (2) it can be an affront to the originating programmer, and (3) instant-methods work has a good chance of being sloppy-methods work.

The second most important job of the moderator is to avoid discussions of trivial details. For instance, you don't want to take up the group's time by letting one of the participants point out spelling errors in pseudocode or syntax errors in COBOL. Instead, you should suggest that this type of error be passed on to the programmer by marking the errors on his (the participant's) materials in red and giving them to the programmer after the meeting. In the agenda in figure 17-3, for example, the originator himself has asked that this be done.

Although I have said that walkthroughs are normally done in three phases, I question the value of the normal first and third phases. The overview phase, for example, is likely to be a time waster. Too often, it seems, the programmer takes this opportunity to try to sell the participants on what he has done. Besides, the walkthrough materials should be self-explanatory and the purpose of the walkthrough should be stated on the agenda. So what does the overview accomplish?

Similarly, the review of the action list (the normal third phase) can waste time. In addition, it can cause dissension. In this phase, the recorder normally reads the action list to see if there is agreement that action must be taken on each item listed. In some cases, a question may have been resolved later on in phase 2, so it can be deleted from this list. Nevertheless, Paul says that if an item was important enough to put on the list in the first place, it's important enough for the programmer to resolve in his followup to the meeting. At best, further discussion can only eliminate an item or two from the list. At worst, it can lead to serious conflict that creates a bad atmosphere for future walkthroughs.

In Paul's opinion, then, most walkthroughs should consist of only one phase, the error-detection phase. Although an overview can be useful in some cases, a review of the action list rarely justifies the time it takes.

How to follow up the meeting If walkthroughs are going to be successful in your company, followup is critical. If at any time the participants in a walkthrough get the feeling that nothing is going to be done about the questions they raised, the motivation for active participation in future walkthroughs is destroyed. So Paul recommends that the programmer follow up the walkthrough in two phases.

First, within one hour after the end of the meeting, copies should be made of the action list and one copy should be given to each of the participants. I put the arbitrary time limit of one hour on this part of the followup so there isn't time to type or rewrite the action list in order to make it a thing of beauty. If it is redone, there is always a chance that an

Action list

Originator: Paul Noll

Program: Produce sales report

Type of walkthrough: Design

Questions:	Resolution:
1. Is there an unnecessary level in the Structure chart? Can modules 130, 140, and 150 be moved from level 3 to level 2?	Changed. The modules have been moved to level 2. See attached structure chart.
2. Will module 120 process the first record in the file?	Changed. It didn't work. See attached HIPO diagram.
3. Should control field changes be made in module 120 (the major control module) rather than in the print modules?	Changed. I moved the control field changes from the print modules to module 120. See attached HIPO diagram.
4. Is the module name for module 120 meaningful?	Changed. From "process sales record" to "produce sales line."
5. Inconsistency in use of TR and TRAN in several HIPO diagrams (marked in red and returned).	Changed. All references are now TRAN.

Figure 17-4 An action list for a design walkthrough including the resolution of the questions

item will be omitted. And refining the list just doesn't add anything to the effectiveness of the walkthrough.

Second, within two days following the meeting, the programmer should have an answer for each question on the action list. Furthermore, these answers should be passed on to the participants of the walkthrough so they know their work wasn't in vain. The simplest way to return the answers is to write them on the action list itself, make one copy for each participant, and distribute them. But if the answers are detailed, they might be prepared on separate pages. In some cases, the questions will lead to a major design change, in which case the best answer is a request for another walkthrough.

To illustrate proper followup for an action list, figure 17-4 shows the action list that we developed when we did a walkthrough on one of Paul's programs several years ago. Even though Paul had given a lot of thought to this program and felt that his design was complete and proper, the walkthrough still led to two significant changes. And the two people who detected these problems were in their early 20s, just recently graduated from college. So I hope this gives you some idea of the potential structured walkthroughs have for detecting errors.

When an item on the action list doesn't lead to a change, the programmer must still explain how the item was resolved. For instance, a programmer may write: "I've checked with systems and they say the preceding program will sort the transactions, so sequence checking isn't necessary" or "The credit department is trying to establish a fixed policy for this condition and they will have specifications for me within two weeks." In some cases, you will want to discuss an item like this with the participant who raised the question about it to make sure he's satisfied with the way you resolved it.

From management's point of view, the followup for a walkthrough should include a report to management that indicates that the walkthrough was conducted and all problems were resolved. For this purpose, Paul recommends a form like the one in figure 17-5. In fact, this form can also be used to announce the walkthrough and to present its agenda. After the meeting is over and the questions have been resolved, each participant initials the form indicating that he or she is satisfied, and the form is passed on to management. In addition, the programmer should keep a copy of the completed form for her own records.

Notice that the form in figure 17-5 doesn't indicate whether errors were uncovered or not, it only indicates that in the end everyone was satisfied. So why would a manager want a record with such a minimal amount of information? First, because it is a record of the project's progress...it tells what phase of program development has been completed. Second, if structured walkthroughs are a part of the installation's standards, it is a record that the standards are being adhered to. Third, it is a management tool. If, for example, major design problems are discovered during the testing of a program, a manager might well ask why five members of his staff signed off on a design walkthrough for it six weeks earlier.

Eight keys to effective walkthroughs

Although walkthroughs have the potential to make a significant contribution to program quality, there are a number of practices and attitudes that can make them ineffective. As a result, I have listed eight keys to walkthrough effectiveness in figure 17-6.

No manager present If a manager is present, the effectiveness of a walkthrough can deteriorate. Instead of a friendly interaction between peers, the walkthrough can turn into an evaluation session. Who has uncovered the most errors? Who participates the most? Why hasn't the originating programmer spotted some of these errors himself? Even if the manager doesn't intend to judge the participants, the atmosphere will change and the results will be less valuable.

Error detection only I've mentioned this before, but it's worth repeating. The time to correct errors is after the meeting. Don't allow error correction to interfere with the walkthrough.

Walkthrough Agenda

Notice date: May 26, 1978

Originator: Paul Noll

Meeting date and time: Wednesday May 31 1:30 P.M.

Location: Room 578

Program: Produce sales report

Type of Walkthrough: Design

Materials:

1 Specifications

2 Structure chart

3 HIPO diagrams for all control modules

4

5

Objectives:
Please review for

1 Completeness and logic

2 Meaningful names

3 Naming consistency

4

5

Team:

	Name	Present	Resolution Initials	Resolution Date
Moderator	Mike Murach	Yes		
Recorder	Doug Lowe	Yes		
Member 1	Judy Taylor	Yes		
Member 2				
Member 3				
Member 4				

Date of resolution June 2, 1978 **Originator's signature** ____________

Figure 17-5 A walkthrough form that serves as an agenda and as a record of followup

1. No manager present
2. Error detection only
3. Two hour time limit
4. The right participants
5. Vested interests
6. Show results
7. No counting
8. Professional behavior only

Figure 17-6 A checklist for effective walkthroughs

Two hour time limit An effective walkthrough requires intense concentration. And the personal interactions can be emotionally exhausting. So try to complete the walkthrough in an hour or an hour-and-a-half. Beyond this time limit, the results deteriorate, and two hours should be the absolute limit. If you're only halfway through the materials after two hours, just arrange to meet again the next day.

The right participants If there is one main reason why walkthroughs fail, it's personality problems. If one participant is a rival of the originator, the personality clashes can be troublesome. Or if two of the participants don't get along, this friction can continually force the meeting off track. Apart from being free of rivalries, each participant must have the proper capabilities and motivation. So selecting the right participants can make or break a walkthrough.

Vested interests If all of the participants in a walkthrough really care about the project, the results are sure to be good. Unfortunately, each programmer's primary concerns are his own projects and their deadlines, so it's easy to treat someone else's walkthrough as an obstacle to your own progress.

If possible, then, a manager should make sure that each programmer has a vested interest in the programs that he will be invited to walk through. This can be done by creating teams as described in the next chapter. It can also be done by creating walkthrough groups so that each member is always a participant in the walkthroughs of the other group members. Then, one programmer has a vested interest in the programs done by his team or group members because he knows the roles will soon be reversed. In small shops, the ties of friendship are often strong enough to give each programmer a genuine interest in the other programs that are being developed. In any event, if the feeling of vested interests isn't present, something must be done to create it.

Show results I've mentioned this before, but it too bears repeating. Vested interests or not, the participants in walkthroughs will soon lose their motivation if they don't feel that their efforts are getting results. So the action list should be distributed right after the meeting, and the actions taken should be distributed within a couple of days thereafter.

Of course, it's not enough just to distribute the action list and the actions taken. The walkthrough participants have to feel that the items recorded on the list are significant. If the action list consists of trivial items that the programmer should have been able to find by himself in the first place, the belief in walkthroughs quickly wanes. So you can't just start a ritual of walkthroughs and forget about them; you have to check the results periodically. You may even find that walkthroughs aren't right for your shop.

No counting As I've already mentioned, one of the main things to guard against is personality problems. Unfortunately, it's all too easy for antagonist A to point out that he found eight errors in B's design, but B only found three in his. Then, the walkthrough turns into a counting game, and its effectiveness decreases.

Managers too can contribute to this unproductive atmosphere by keeping score. Although the walkthrough form in figure 17-5 doesn't give any indication of how many errors were found, I've seen other forms that do. One form not only has a place to record error counts by classification, but also has a place to record the number of personality clashes that came up. Now with a management form like this, how can you keep the programmers from counting? So, again, no counting...unless it's the number of bug-free programs that you put into production.

Professional behavior only I'm including this to remind you to avoid personality conflicts, whether you're the originator, the moderator, or one of the other participants. Sure, we all need praise, and the walkthrough tends to focus on the negative rather than the positive. But be professional about it. Just because someone found eight errors in your HIPO diagrams during your last design walkthrough doesn't mean you should seek revenge the next time he invites you to one of his walkthroughs. Similarly, be patient; don't trample on someone else's ideas just because you think they're trivial. If you react too strongly (and negatively) to one idea, you can easily drive away the motivation to present the next idea. Finally, if you do find an error, don't bore in. Don't say, "How can you overlook something like that?" or "You missed the same thing the last time." If you detect the error, you've done your job.

The benefits of walkthroughs

As I've indicated before, the primary benefit resulting from structured walkthroughs is that errors are detected early in the development cycle. As a result, walkthroughs are intended to improve program quality, not programmer productivity. When walkthroughs are used effectively, they will not only detect errors earlier than they would be detected otherwise, but they will also detect some errors that wouldn't be caught at all until a program is put into production. In fact, one proponent of walkthroughs predicts that you can cut down production bugs by a factor of five if you conduct walkthroughs after each of the major phases of program development.

Three other benefits of structured walkthroughs are improved program maintainability, improved on-the-job training, and improved programmer morale. If you're looking for design and coding bugs, you simply can't overlook modules that aren't functional, names that aren't meaningful, illogical module subordination, and so on. So these are the types of problems that become part of the action list. Once these problems are corrected, of course, the program becomes more logical and easier to read. As a result, the program becomes easier to maintain.

Training often improves when structured walkthroughs are used because the trainees and junior programmers have a formal reason for exchanging ideas with their senior associates. Under other conditions, the trainee is often made to feel like he is a bother when he asks a senior associate for help. Furthermore, the senior programmers are likely to pick up ideas from their more recently trained juniors as a result of the walkthrough discussions.

As for the effect on morale, it has to do with reduced anxiety and the feeling of belonging. Because each programmer will have some assurance via the walkthroughs that his program is progressing as planned, there is less cause for concern; the chance that something major has been overlooked is greatly reduced. Because each programmer has a clearly defined reason for cooperating with other programmers, a team spirit develops. Although some programmers apparently enjoy the isolation of traditional programming practices, I think the majority appreciate the group interaction that walkthroughs encourage.

The objections to walkthroughs

Initially, as you might guess, there is considerable resistance to walkthroughs in the average programming shop. In most shops, walkthroughs mean changing from "private art to public practice." And change is always difficult. As you might guess, this can be particularly irksome to the programmer who has been free to work independently over the years. As a result, senior programmers are likely to be outspoken opponents of walkthroughs. When this happens, a manager has to ask whether or not walkthroughs are so valuable that they're worth the personality conflicts.

Our answer to this is that programming has become too important to be left to its unmanaged, unprofessional, private self. In our experiences, many project failures have come about because programmers were in over their heads, were afraid to admit it, and were not called upon to display their work in a public review. So even though change is always difficult, there doesn't seem to be much choice about it. Programming has to go public.

The most common objection to walkthroughs that comes from management is that they tie up programming manpower. For instance, a critic may well question how finding a half dozen errors can justify the two or more programmer-hours of work done by each member of a six-programmer walkthrough team. Paul's answer is that detecting just one major error in an early stage of development can justify 12 hours of work.

On the other hand, there is a balance to be reached between the number of errors found and the number of programmer-hours devoted to a walkthrough. Although we have no data to support it, we intuitively feel that four to six participants is too many for optimum productivity. Instead, we think that a group of three good programmers with vested interests and good rapport can accomplish as much and more than six other programmers might accomplish. We know for certain that the more participants in the group, the less efficient the discussions are.

Our experiences with walkthroughs

Our experiences with walkthroughs at Mike Murach & Associates are mixed. When we first started using them, we seemed to derive all of the benefits I listed above. We discovered bugs and programming problems early. We improved program designs and coding quality so our programs were easier to maintain. The walkthroughs forced our trainees to interact with our experienced programmers so training improved. And everyone seemed to enjoy the walkthrough process.

In a relatively short time, however, the effectiveness of our walkthroughs started to deteriorate. We had more and more dissension and personality problems. We discovered fewer and fewer errors of significance. And our best programmers complained that walkthroughs were completely undermining their productivity as well as their enjoyment of their jobs.

When I analyzed what was happening, I came to these conclusions. Like most companies, we had programmers of varying capabilities. At the time I did my analysis, we had three programmers who were outstanding, six that were average or better than average, and three that were definitely below average. We had some good programmers with less than two years experience, and we had some marginal programmers with more than ten years experience. So trying to create effective teams or walkthrough groups out of these diverse backgrounds was a difficult task in the first place.

What actually happened, then, was this. The outstanding programmers ended up carrying the walkthrough meetings. They usually detected the most errors and made the most useful suggestions for improving the quality of a programmer's design and code. In contrast, the marginal programmers made few comments of significance, and often slowed down meetings with trivial comments and needless questions. To complicate matters, most of the programmers became frustrated by the process so personality problems came to the fore.

After I finished my analysis, I decided that the only way to solve the problem was to make walkthroughs voluntary. Because walkthroughs are informal, they depend on mutual trust and cooperation. So you just can't say that all programmers must participate in walkthroughs. Once we made walkthroughs voluntary, however, only four of our programmers said they wanted to continue them. In general, our outstanding programmers wanted to work alone so they could maximize their productivity. And our marginal programmers also wanted to work alone so they didn't have to submit their work to public review. As a result, the walkthrough group we ended up with consisted of average or better than average programmers, and I think all of them benefitted by the walkthrough interaction.

With only four of 12 programmers participating in walkthroughs, though, we could no longer depend on the walkthrough process to insure program quality. So we had to develop other ways to do this. But that's a management problem I'll discuss in chapter 21.

Two walkthrough principles to question

Since walkthroughs didn't work out for us the way they're described in most textbooks, I reevaluated the walkthrough process after I made walkthroughs voluntary in our shop. As part of this reevaluation, I discussed the failure of our walkthrough procedures with my best programmers. When I completed the reevaluation, I ended up questioning two of the principles of walkthroughs that are widely accepted throughout the programming industry. First, I question whether managers should be prohibited from attending the walkthrough meetings (no managers present). Second, I question whether the participants should be prohibited from solving problems at a walkthrough meeting (error detection only).

Should managers be present? When walkthroughs fail, it's usually because the participants aren't cooperating. An outstanding programmer gets to feeling that she always does all the work at the walkthroughs so she arrives for one walkthrough completely unprepared. A programmer who has been roundly criticized by an associate in his last walkthrough comes prepared for revenge and points out every trivial problem in the programmer's code. And so on.

If no manager is present, of course, management may never find out about these problems. And walkthrough after walkthrough may be a complete waste of time. In fact, they may contribute to employee dissatisfaction and high turnover.

I think the main reason managers aren't welcome at walkthroughs is that programmers don't trust them. They know that if a manager comes, they're going to be judged and that's going to be true most of the time. On the other hand, who better than a manager can put an end to personality conficts and make sure that everyone will do their best job at a walkthrough? In addition, if a manager participates in the walkthroughs, she will have a much better idea about who on her staff is competent, who is frustrated, and so on.

With this as background, I'd like to suggest that managers attend walkthroughs every now and then. As I see it, this can improve the effectiveness of the walkthroughs. And it can improve a manager's effectiveness. I'm not suggesting that managers attend all walkthroughs, but occasional management participation has to help the effectiveness of a walkthrough program.

In the past, I occasionally participated in our walkthroughs. And I think it was worthwhile. Yes, I might have put additional pressure on my staff members during those walkthroughs, but at least we kept a professional tone to the meetings. In addition, I always learned something from my programmers by attending the meetings. And I think they learned something from me too.

Should you correct some errors? Another accepted principle of walkthroughs is that errors should be detected only; they should not be corrected. Overall, I think that's a good rule, but some of our best programmers object to it. After all, they say, if you're going to take the time to find a problem, you should also have the satisfaction of correcting it. At the least, they say, the programmer who has requested the walkthrough should write down the suggestions that he gets for a solution so he can analyze them later on.

With this in mind, I think we should modify the principle of error-detection only. When there is a critical design problem, I think solutions should be solicited. If they are, I think you're likely to end up with a better solution than you would have come up with otherwise. I'm certainly not saying that you should solicit solutions for trivial problems. But why not get all the ideas you can for the solution of a critical problem?

Discussion

In our COBOL survey, we found that 78 percent of our respondents used walkthroughs, at least occasionally, with 29 percent using them "often" and 6 percent using them "always." Furthermore, 63 percent of our respondents felt walkthroughs were "important" or "very important" when it came to improving programmer productivity. And 68 percent felt walkthroughs were "important" or "very important" when it came to improving program quality.

I think this data shows that both programmers and managers like walkthroughs. Not only do they use them, but they also think they're important. In the interest of truth, however, I'd like to say that I think our respondents are wrong when it comes to the effect of walkthroughs on programmer productivity. Because each programmer must devote part of his productive time to the programs of other programmers when walkthroughs are used, I don't think walkthroughs help to improve productivity. In fact, any improvements in program quality that result from walkthroughs are likely to be offset by reductions in programmer productivity.

Nevertheless, if you haven't yet used walkthroughs in your shop, I think you should experiment with them. In particular, I recommend that you use walkthroughs when you first convert to structured programming. Later on, if you decide you're no longer getting the benefits you want from walkthroughs, you can drop them from your development procedures. By that time, though, everyone should be comfortable with the structured techniques.

So if you're a programming manager whose staff is just converting to structured methods, I'd like to recommend a minimum plan that you can experiment with. In this plan, you start with only two types of walkthroughs: design walkthroughs and coding walkthroughs. Also, instead of the four to six members recommended by most books and articles, use groups of only three members (or two if you're a two-programmer shop). Because you are likely to uncover one or more major errors or omissions in your first couple of design walkthroughs, I think you'll quickly be convinced that walkthroughs can contribute to program reliability. Then, after your first coding walkthroughs, I think you'll also realize how walkthroughs can help you improve the maintainability of your code.

So you can get a better understanding of the benefits of walkthroughs, I suggest that you attend about one walkthrough a week...even though you're the manager. In fact, I recommend that you participate in the walkthroughs you attend. But don't assume that you will be the moderator just because you're the boss. Instead, just be a participant. If they ask you to be the recorder, fine, but let someone else be the moderator. If you're the moderator, you won't learn as much from the meeting.

If you are a programmer and it doesn't look like walkthroughs will be implemented in your shop for a while, I recommend that you experiment with walkthroughs on an informal basis. Get a friend to review your work and do the same for him. If you do, I think it will have an immediate effect on your program quality. And I think you'll find that your work will become more interesting and enjoyable.

Terminology

structured walkthrough
action list
moderator
recorder

Objectives

1. List five types of structured walkthroughs.

2. Describe the proper methods of preparing for, conducting, and following up on a structured walkthrough.

3. Describe the primary benefit of structured walkthroughs.

Chapter 18

What you should know about programming teams

Teams of one kind or another are used in most COBOL shops. Some of these are formal teams like chief programmer teams; some are informal teams. Some teams are assembled to develop a single program; some are assembled to develop all of the programs in a system or subsystem.

In terms of program quality or programmer productivity, most people don't think teams are very important. In our survey, for example, only 6 percent of the respondents felt that chief programmer teams were "very important" in terms of their effect on programmer productivity. And only 3 percent felt they were "very important" in terms of their effect on program quality.

From a management point of view, however, you often have to assign several people to a single programming or systems project if you want to get it done on time. If, for example, it's going to take one programmer six months to complete a program but the program is needed in three months, a team effort may solve the problem. Similarly, if a systems project is needed in six months but the project requires two programmer-years of work, you have little choice but to approach the problem with a team effort.

Types of teams

In the mid-1970s, two types of teams received considerable publicity. One type is called a chief programmer team. The other type is called an egoless team. In case you're not familiar with the concepts behind these types of teams, I'd like to introduce you to them at this time. In addition, I'd like to present what I call the traditional programming team.

The chief programmer team If you analyze the tasks done by a programmer, I think you'll find that some are very demanding, while others are clerical. For instance, designing the structure of a program or debugging an abstruse interface problem are difficult intellectual tasks. On the other hand, redrawing a structure chart or coding a record description in working storage are relatively low-level tasks.

The idea behind a *chief programmer team* (or *CPT*) is to increase programmer productivity by assigning members of the team to tasks that match their capabilities and specialties. This team is headed by a *chief programmer*, or *superprogrammer*. Thus, we might find a chief programmer team consisting of the chief programmer who designs and controls the entire project; a backup chief programmer who is the chief's righthand man and who takes the chief's place if he is unable to complete the project; a librarian who submits jobs for compilation and testing; two programmers for the primary tasks of program development; a junior programmer for the less demanding tasks of program development; a technical writer for preparing user guides, and a secretary for the clerical tasks of typing and filing.

The organization chart in figure 18-1 illustrates the general structure of a chief programmer team. It also shows how a team like this usually fits into the traditional organization of a COBOL shop. As you can see, the chief programmer reports to the project director who in turn reports to the programming manager. In other words, the chief programmer isn't the manager of the people who report to him although he does direct their activities.

Although chief programmer teams were often intended to work on one program at a time, there's no reason why a team like the one in figure 18-1 can't be assigned to an entire project. In this case, you would expect the chief programmer to develop the most difficult portions of the programs within the system, while assigning tasks of appropriate difficulty to other members of the team.

As we see it, the primary duties of a chief programmer should be (1) to design the program or set of programs to be developed, (2) to plan the implementation of the programs so they can be developed most efficiently, and (3) to review the work done by the members of the team so the implementation is carried out as planned. At some time during a project, then, you might find a chief programmer designing structure charts, creating pseudocode or HIPO diagrams for critical modules of a program, coding critical modules, creating test plans, reviewing the test data, reviewing code, reviewing test results, and so on. You might also find him in conference with user, management, programming, or operations personnel. When walkthroughs are conducted, the chief programmer is often the moderator.

Because it is difficult to hire people with all the talents required of a chief programmer, this alone can make the concept of a chief

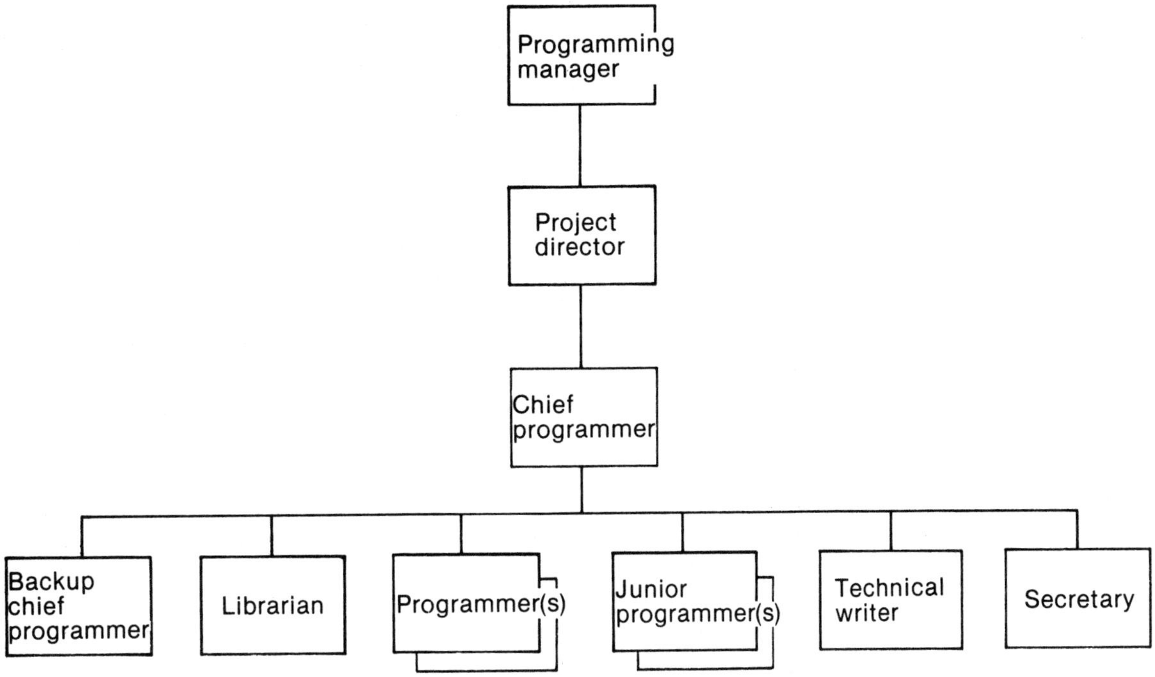

Figure 18-1 The organizational structure of a chief-programmer team

programmer team difficult to implement. In general, the chief programmer must not only be an outstanding technician, but he must also be good at dealing with people. In the long run, the effectiveness of the team will usually depend on the effectiveness of the chief programmer.

Egoless teams I've tried to illustrate the concept of *egoless teams* in figure 18-2. Here, the programming manager has divided her staff into three teams, but there's no management hierarchy on any team. In other other words, the members of the team are supposed to work together as equals without any specific management intervention to force them to get along.

Teams like this are called "egoless" teams because the team members can't be overly concerned with their own problems if this concept is to work. They must be able to review the designs and coding of others without letting their ego get in the way of their objectivity. Similarly, they must allow their own work to be reviewed by the other members of the team without getting their feelings hurt by the others' comments and suggestions.

I don't particularly like the term *egoless* because it implies a forsaking of self that probably isn't healthy. Instead of "egoless," I prefer that members of a programming team think of themselves as professionals. As a professional programmer, you should be able to review the work of a peer or a subordinate with reasonable objectivity. And you should be able

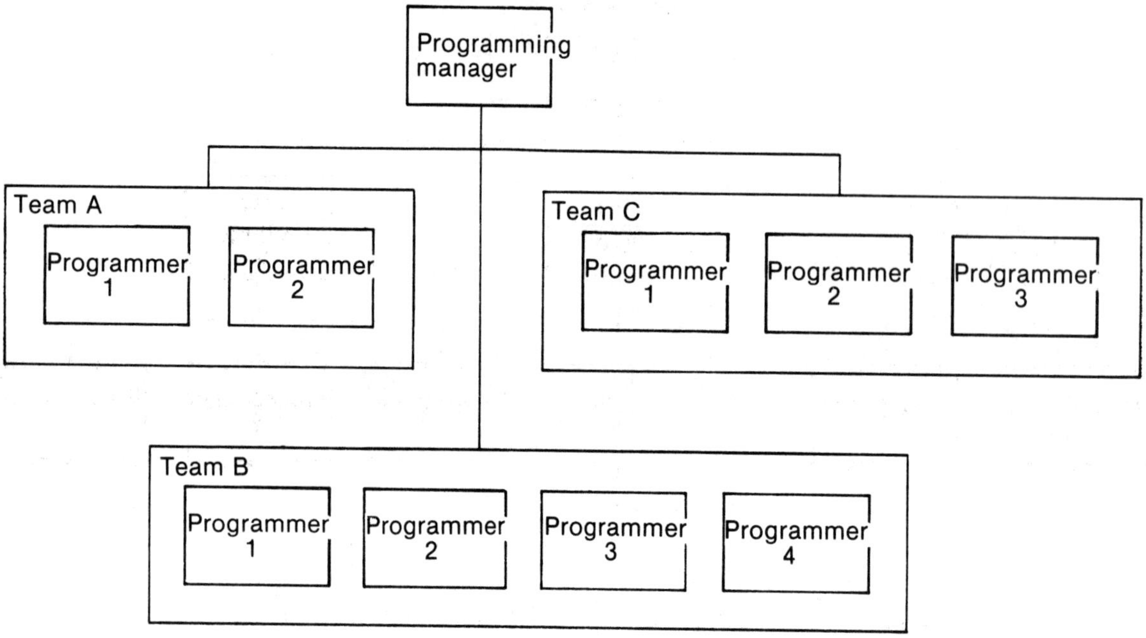

Figure 18-2 The conceptual structure of an egoless team

to accept reviews of your own work in the spirit of learning how to do your job better. This is true whether you are part of a team or not.

The traditional programming team Figure 18-3 gives the organizational structure of what I think of as the *traditional programming team*. In this case, programmers are assigned to a project manager who in turn reports to the programming manager. There's no question on a team like this as to who's the boss or who a programmer has to please in order to get a raise or promotion. And since the project manager is the one who assigns programs or programming tasks to the programmer, there shouldn't be much doubt as to what a programmer has to do in order to please the boss.

In contrast, although the chief programmer is the boss of his team in terms of training and assignments, someone else is usually the boss in terms of performance reviews, pay increases, and promotions. Similarly, egoless teams are usually encouraged to work on their own with limited management involvement. As a result, the manager of a chief programmer team or an egoless team may not know enough about the team members to do an adequate job of judging their performance, authorizing pay raises, and recommending promotions.

The benefits of teams

As I mentioned earlier, teams are used to shorten the development time of a program, subsystem, or system. That's the primary benefit you get from

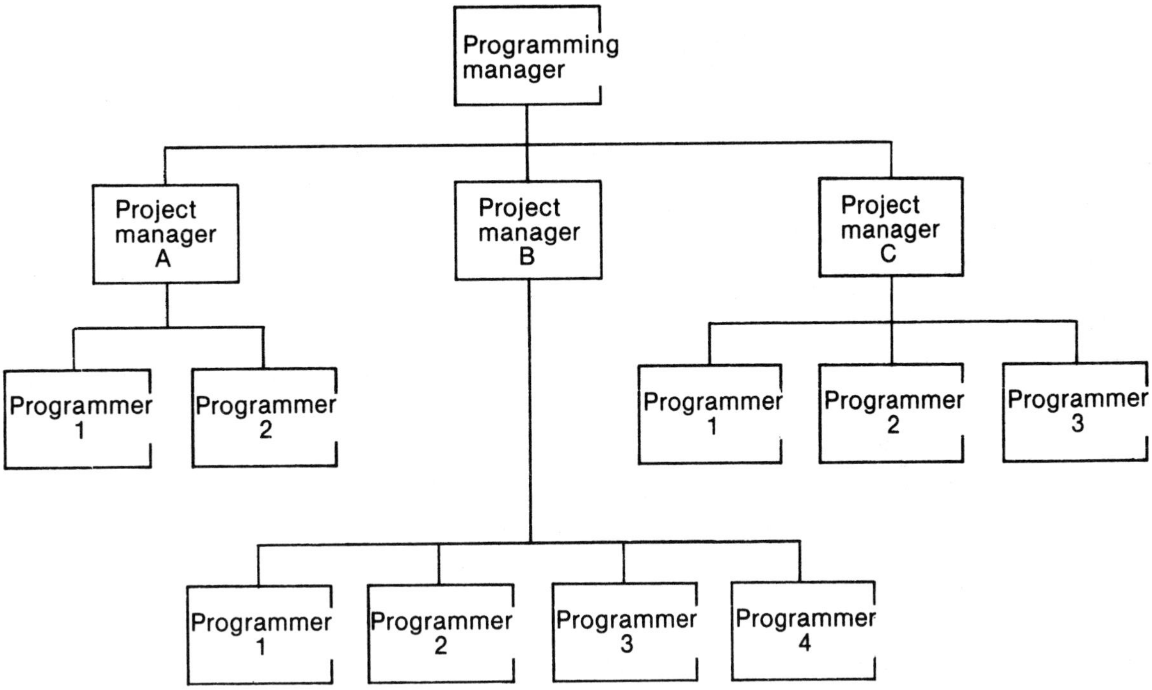

Figure 18-3 The organizational structure of a traditional programming team

using teams. If you want to finish a two-year project in six months, perhaps a team of five programmers can make this possible.

There are also three other benefits that can result from using teams. First, the use of teams can improve program quality. When you use a chief programmer team, for example, one of the chief programmer's main jobs is to control program quality. When you use egoless teams, the team members review each other's designs and code in an attempt to improve program quality. And when you use traditional programming teams, one of the project manager's responsibilities should be to review and control program quality.

Second, the use of teams can improve on-the-job training. Specifically, a team can give programmers a formal structure within which they can share ideas. Furthermore, trainees and junior programmers are more likely to come into contact with specialists and senior programmers in a team environment, so they can pick up information they wouldn't pick up otherwise.

Third, the use of teams can improve the morale of a group of programmers (although, as you will see in a moment, teams can also destroy morale). I don't think there's any question about the fact that some people prefer working on teams. And working on an efficient team can be an exhilarating experience. In my experience, morale is usually high when people have the feeling that their capabilities are being used to maximum advantage and that they're learning by their associations with others.

The problems with teams

The most obvious problem associated with teams is the problem of communication. If, for example, one programmer develops a program, his only communication problem is to make sure that the program is coordinated with the other programs of the system. But if two people work on the same program, they have to be concerned that the modules they are developing will coordinate properly with the other modules of the program. And the more people that work on a program or system, the more communication problems you have.

Unfortunately, as the communication problems go up, productivity goes down. That's why three people working on one project may only be able to produce as much work as two people working on two separate projects. So a major disadvantage of teams is the reduced productivity resulting from increased communication problems.

The second major problem with teams is reduced morale (in contrast to the benefit I mentioned above) due to personality problems. In my experience, some people like to work alone, some like to work in groups, and the two don't mix very well. In addition, some people are much more competent than others and the good programmers don't like to feel that they're carrying the poor programmers. So personality problems are quite common.

When you use chief programmer teams, you are likely to experience some additional problems. First, these teams are difficult to create due to conflicts with the policies of unions and personnel departments. Second, in order to be effective, they often require some disrupting organizational changes. Third, they are often difficult to staff because of the shortage of people who are qualified to be chief programmers. Fourth, since the personnel requirements of a chief programmer team change as a project progresses, it is difficult to coordinate the personnel requirements of a chief programmer team with those of the other projects in a programming department.

Our suggestions for using teams

Quite frankly, our experiences with teams haven't been that positive. In fact, we've had most of the problems that I mentioned above. My hope, then, is that you can learn from our experiences. Although I don't know all the answers, I do think I can give you some ideas on what to watch out for. So here are my suggestions for using teams.

Suggestion 1: Don't insist that every programmer be on a team Perhaps our worst experiences were with our two best programmers. As we staffed up, it seemed natural to make these two people the heads of programming teams. In technical terms, both were in the superprogrammer category, so we created two modified versions of chief programmer teams and went to work.

Within a short time, though, it became obvious that our teams were not working effectively. Finally, completely frustrated, one of the superprogrammers came to me with the suggestion that he do the entire project himself. In fact, he was willing to bet that he could do the entire project twice as fast alone as he could with his five person team. Based on this conversation, we dismantled the team, gave the project to him alone, and he made good on his word...he did the project in three months by himself with little or no frustration.

When the second superprogrammer realized what had happened, it gave him the courage to come to me with a similar request. He said that only one person on his team was actually making a contribution, so he suggested that the two of them take over the entire project and that I reassign the other three programmers on his team. After I did this, the project took off and the subsystem was installed six months later.

My point is that some people, often your best people, don't really like to work on teams. In fact, if you force them to, they are likely to cause personality problems. Even if you make them team leaders, they may destroy the effectiveness of a team because they don't really like to lead people. So why not get the maximum productivity from these outstanding producers by letting them work alone?

Suggestion 2: Don't use a team to develop a single program unless there's no reasonable alternative As programmer productivity goes up, there's less reason to use a team to develop a single program. If, for example, a programmer can produce 10,000 lines of COBOL code per month, he can probably develop a 25,000 line program in about three months. So why bother to assign a team to a program like this? Nevertheless, some 40 percent of the respondents in our survey indicated that they sometimes use teams to develop single programs.

Unfortunately, it seems that communication problems are compounded when a team is used to develop a single program, because the interfaces between program modules are more complicated than the interfaces between programs. That's why we recommend that you avoid using a team to develop a single program whenever possible. And the easiest way to do this is to assign your superprogrammers to the large programs.

If you are developing a program that is so large that it simply can't be done by one programmer in the required time, the next thing to consider is dividing the program up into two or more programs. If you can do this, you can reduce communication problems so you can increase the productivity of your staff.

Of course, you can't always divide one program into two or more programs for several reasons. Sometimes, this kind of program packaging will conflict with user requirements; sometimes, it will lead to hardware inefficiency; sometimes, it will conflict with operational requirements; and so on. Often, however, repackaging one program into two or more programs will allow you to deliver the product on time with a maximum of programmer productivity. Then, later on, you can combine the two or more programs into one to meet the other requirements of the system. And you can usually do this with a minimum of reprogramming. As we see it, then, you have a better chance of satisfying the user's requirement this way than you do by assigning several programmers to a single program, which is a risky process at best.

In our programming survey, over half the installations indicated that they never wrote programs over 25,000 lines long. So these installations should never need to use a team to develop a single program if they can get one or more of their programmers to maximize their productivity by using the techniques presented in this book. On the other hand, if you absolutely feel that you need to write a program of more than 25,000 lines and you must assign a team to it, make sure that the program is completely designed before you turn the team loose on its development.

Suggestion 3: Don't experiment with chief programmer teams or egoless teams unless they seem especially suited to your projects and your staff Although the idea of chief programmer teams or egoless teams can be appealing, neither idea seems to have worked out well in practice. In Paul's opinion, chief programmer teams are all but dead in large businesses and egoless teams never caught on at all. After our experiments with both types of teams, we feel that it's almost impossible to staff either type of team effectively. And if either type of team isn't staffed properly, communication difficulties and personality conflicts can create more problems than any team can solve.

Furthermore, you don't really have that much to gain by experimenting with either type of team. As I said earlier, less than 10 percent of the people that answered our survey thought that teams had a significant effect on either programmer productivity or program quality. And this is consistent with our experiences. So unless you feel that you have just the right project and the right team members for a chief programmer or egoless team, I wouldn't bother experimenting with either.

Suggestion 4: Put the emphasis on management when you use traditional programming teams Because of the continuing requirement to deliver programs, subsystems, and systems on time, most shops have to use teams and will continue to use them in the future. In general, though, they use traditional programming teams in one form or another. That is, several people are assigned to a single project and they report to the project manager, at least for the life of the project.

If that's the way you use teams in your shop, I have only one suggestion. Make sure that the project managers are managers. In other words, make it clear that the project managers are responsible for the quality of the code produced by their team and also for the productivity of the team members. Unless they evaluate their programmers in terms of productivity and program quality, program development will be a largely unmanaged process.

In our survey, only 17 percent of the respondents said that they made any attempt to measure programmer productivity, and only 43 percent said they made any attempt to measure program quality. Worse, only a few of those who said they did measure productivity and program quality could say how they measured it. For instance, two respondents said they measured productivity as the percent of time devoted to productive work, which is hardly a measure of productivity. And several of those who said they measured program quality said they based it on user satisfaction, even though this says nothing about program maintainability.

My point is that we have to put more emphasis on the management of program development. And we can start by doing this at the project level. So the manager of a programming project should be more than just the senior member of the team. She should be the first level of programming management. In chapter 21, then, I'll give you some ideas on how to manage at the project level.

Discussion

To a large extent, teams are a necessary evil in a programming department. You often have to assign a team to a project if you want to complete it on time. But at the same time you know that the more members you add to a team, the more communication and personality problems you will have. And this in turn will reduce the productivity of each of the team members.

With this in mind, the design and development methods presented in this book can help you in two ways when it comes to using teams. First, because the productivity of your programmers may jump severalfold by using our methods, you may find that you won't need to use teams as frequently. Second, if you do have to assign a team to a single program, our design methods will help reduce communication problems because they clearly indicate the functions of and the relationships between the modules of a program.

Terminology

chief programmer team
CPT
chief programmer
superprogrammer
egoless team
traditional programming team

Objectives

1. Describe the organization of each of the following types of teams:

   chief programmer team
   egoless team
   traditional programming team

2. Explain how the use of each of the three types of teams can affect program quality.

3. Explain how the use of each of the three types of teams can affect programmer productivity.

Chapter 19

What you should know about development support libraries

The idea behind a development support library is to keep current documentation on the programs that are in development, just as you should keep current documentation on the programs that have already been put into production. In other words, the development libraries and documentation should be as organized as the production libraries and documentation.

Most COBOL shops, however, don't maintain their development support libraries as well as they do their production libraries. So if a programmer quits, his development work may be lost because no one can tell where it is or what phase it's in. Similarly, if a programmer wants to review the most recent listing of a program that interfaces with the one he's working on, he may have trouble finding it. In a typical COBOL shop, only the programmer who's developing a program knows where the most recent listing for it is. In fact, he may be the only one who knows in which user library the source file is kept in case you want to compile it to get a new listing.

Fortunately, improvements in computer systems in the last ten years have made it easier to create and maintain development support libraries. In general, development libraries today are much more organized than they were in the 1970s. As a result, development support libraries probably aren't that important in terms of programmer productivity or quality control. On the other hand, if you are going to improve your program development procedures, you may as well improve every aspect of your procedures. And your development support libraries are probably an item that can stand some reorganization.

In this chapter, then, I am first going to present development support libraries as they were used in the 1970s. In those days, most development systems weren't interactive. After that, I'll give you some ideas for implementing development support libraries on a modern computer system.

Development support libraries in the 1970s

The original idea behind a *development support library* (or *DSL*) was to keep centralized libraries that contained the essential documentation for all programs that were being developed. This helped change programming from private art to public practice. With centralized files, the current documentation for each program could easily be found and reviewed by anyone associated with a project.

In general, development support libraries were divided into two parts. One part was an *internal library* (or machine library) that contained current files of job-control language (procedures), source code, object code, and load modules. The other was an *external library* that contained current listings of everything stored in the internal library plus related information like program specifications, drafts of user guides, and so on.

As part of the concept of development support libraries, a staff member called a *librarian* was responsible for keeping the libraries up-to-date. In other words, the programmers were no longer responsible for this. Because the librarian took some of the clerical load away from each programmer, this usually contributed to programmer productivity. Some people, for example, felt that two programmers with the help of a librarian could do the work of three programmers working without clerical help.

In the 1970s, of course, most computer systems were only partly interactive, if at all. So programmers usually submitted development jobs to the system in batches. If a company still used punched cards for job requests and source programs, the programmer would submit coding forms to the librarian who would make sure that the procedure decks and source decks got keypunched by the keypunch department. The librarian would also make sure that the decks were submitted to the computer system after they were keypunched.

If the computer system provided for on-line entry of procedures and source programs, the programmers were sometimes responsible for making some of these entries themselves. In general, though, there weren't enough entry stations to go around so the programmers didn't do any key entry.

In any event, figure 19-1 schematically illustrates the concept of the development support library in the 1970s. As you can see, the librarian is the only interface between the programmers and the external and internal libraries so he was the key to a successful implementation of this concept.

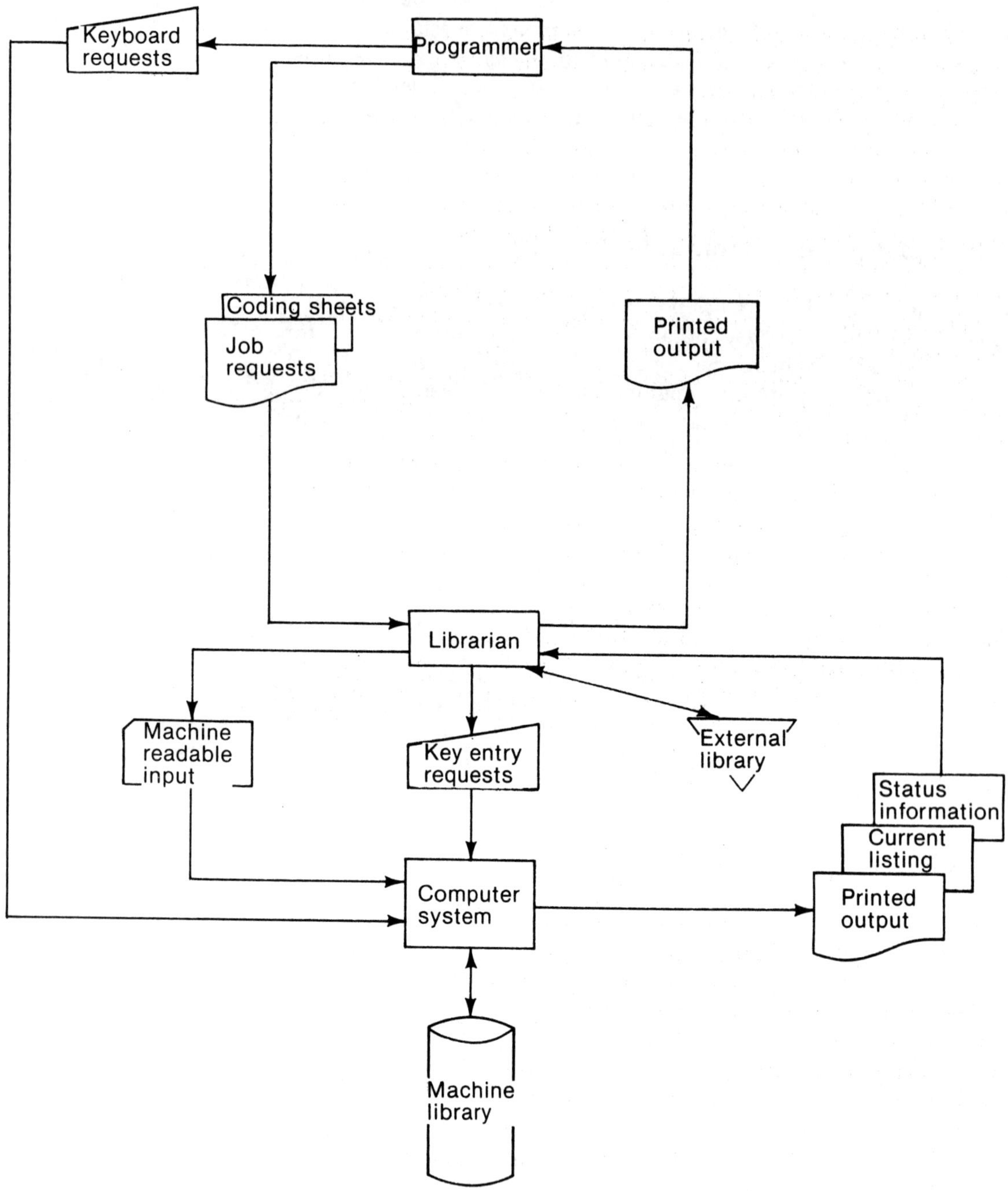

Figure 19-1 The concept of development support libraries in the 1970s

Not only could the librarian reduce the clerical burden of the programming staff, but he had the major responsibility of keeping the development libraries organized.

In the 1970s, the first step toward the successful implementation of a development support library was to develop or buy software for maintaining the machine libraries. On large IBM systems, for example, you could buy or lease library software such as Pansophic's *Panvalet* or Applied Data Research's *Librarian*. Among other things, software products like these made it easier for you to create and update libraries and library members, to retrieve source files for compilation, to initiate test runs, and to backup and restore libraries. So, if you had the budget for it, it was worth getting effective librarian software.

Once you had adequate software and procedures for development support libraries, the next step was to staff the position of librarian...and this usually wasn't easy. First, the title itself had negative connotations so few people wanted the job. Second, management had a hard time deciding whether the librarian should be a clerical worker, an operator on the way up, a programmer trainee, or what. Third, in a large company, the personnel department often had to develop a job description for this position.

As you might imagine, then, development support libraries in the 1970s were something less than ideal. Although improvements in computer systems led to continual improvements in the use of internal libraries, most external libraries were not well managed. And the average librarian, if a company had one at all, failed to provide the clerical support that might have had a significant effect on programmer productivity.

Development support libraries today

In contrast to the 1970s, it's relatively easy to implement a development support library today on a modern computer system. In a modern COBOL shop, each programmer should have her own computer terminal or at least access to one as often as she needs it. And this terminal should provide library functions that make it easy to create, modify, and test a program. If possible, the terminal should also provide word processing capabilities, or at least text processing capabilities.

If you are using a modern computer system, figure 19-2 gives you an idea of how we think development support libraries should be implemented on it. As you can see, the programmers should be responsible for their own interaction with the computer system so much of the need for a librarian is eliminated. In fact, clerical support should only be needed to keep the external library up-to-date. In addition, you should use the internal libraries to store the critical files and documents of a system so you can be sure you're always working with the most up-to-date version of an item. As a result, you should keep the documents stored in an external library to a minimum.

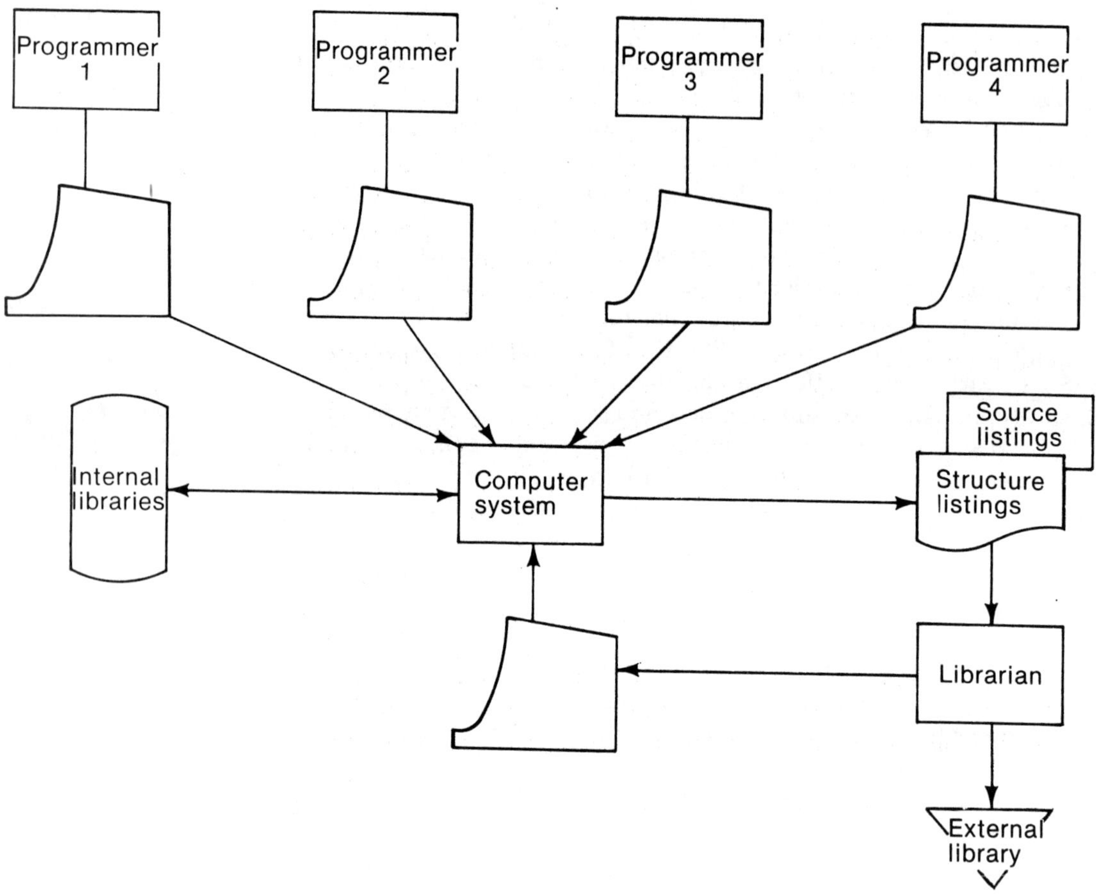

Figure 19-2 The concept of development support libraries today

With this as background, I'd like to give you some ideas on the use of development support libraries. Keep in mind, however, that your specific implementation of them will depend on the size of your staff, the capabilities of your computer system, and so on.

The system documentation In order to keep an organized development support library, you need to start with organized system documentation. In particular, the system documentation must provide a directory to all of the programs in the system that is being developed. In our analysis and design method, for example, we use a system structure chart as described in chapter 20. The system structure chart, which is comparable to a program structure chart, identifies the programs and procedures of a system. Just as each box on a program structure chart names and numbers one module of a program, each box on a system structure chart names and numbers one procedure or program of a system.

You can use a system chart in many ways to facilitate the use of development support libraries. In our shop, for example, we put the system structure chart for each system in development on a bulletin board that is available to all members of the development staff. When a program is assigned to a programmer, we put his or her name in the box representing the program. And when the program is finished, we record that fact on the system structure chart using colored pencils. At any time, then, the system structure chart is a complete directory to the programs in development. It shows the names of each program to be developed, the name of the programmer who has been assigned to each program, and whether or not the program has been completed.

If you don't use a system structure chart, you should use something that gives the same information. At the least, you need to provide a document that shows the relationships between all of the programs of a system as well as the names of all of the programs of the system. If you do this, the programmers have any easy way to find things in the internal libraries for the system.

Internal libraries Since all programmers in a modern COBOL shop have access to interactive terminals, they have access to any documents or files kept on the computer system. That's why you should try to keep as much of your documentation as possible in the internal libraries of the system. How you organize these libraries and files depends a lot on the size of your staff and the limitations of your system, but here are a few ideas.

In our shop, we start by keeping one word processing library for each system in development. In this library, we keep the program overviews for each program in the system. Then, if a programmer has to modify or expand a program overview, he can do it without getting any external documentation. Also, once the modifications are made, the program overview library is up-to-date and any other programmer who accesses this library will find the up-to-date overview.

Similarly, we keep one COPY library for each system in development. Here again, we don't try to keep an external library for COPY members, because we want to make sure that each programmer only has access to the most current versions of the COPY members. If all COPY members are kept in one COPY library, you won't have two different people working with two different versions of program specifications.

As for source libraries, we keep one for each system in development. Then, by using the system structure chart as a directory to the programs of the system, each programmer can find any source listing that he's interested in. For instance, the source listing for program ORD1100 will be source file ORD1100 in the source library for the system.

When you use libraries in this way, a programmer or manager can easily get any document she wants from the system itself. That includes the program overviews, COPY members, and source listings for any program in the system. And these libraries will always hold the most current version of a program document.

How you handle libraries for test data depends a lot on your own development practices. In our shop, each programmer has his own library for test data. That way he can develop test data for unit tests in any way he sees fit. In addition, we keep one library for the system test data of each application.

Subprogram libraries can be handled in several ways. For instance, we keep one subprogram source library and one subprogram object library for our entire installation. That way there's no question about which library a subprogram is in. This also makes the procedure for link editing easier to use. On the other hand, you may want to keep your general purpose subprograms separate from subprograms that are specific to particular systems or subsystems. And this is okay too.

With internal libraries like these available to all of the programmers, we've found that we've reduced the need for communication between programmers. In many cases, for example, a programmer can interactively review another programmer's overviews, COPY members, and source listings without ever getting listings for these items. And he can get the answers to his questions without ever interrupting the other programmer's work. So the extra cost of providing terminals for all programmers and disk storage for the many internal libraries is justified by increased programmer productivity.

Needless to say, this also changes programming from private art to public practice. With as much program information as possible stored on the computer system, all of it can be open to review by peers or management. And I think that's as it should be. As professional programmers, we should be proud of our work so we shouldn't be afraid to have it open to review at all times.

External libraries In a modern COBOL shop, I think the external development libraries should be as slim as possible. In our shop, for example, we keep only two pieces of documentation in our external libraries for development support. And these items are only placed in the external library after a program has been completed by a programmer. The two items are (1) the structure listing (or structure chart) and (2) the source listing. In practice, then, our programmers rarely use the external library because the source listing is always available to them via their terminals. And since we use structure listing software, the structure listing is available to them too.

Why, then, have an external library? Because the items in this library become the eventual program documentation for the system. In other words, when all of the programs for an application are stored in the external library, the system and its program documentation are done. Also, the external library can be used by management at any time (1) to audit the quality of the completed programs and (2) to verify how much work has been done on a system.

Should you bother to place interim development documents such as compiler or test run listings in the external library before a program is completed? I don't think so for several reasons. First, it's almost impossible to keep the interim documents up-to-date since they are changing continually. Second, using our development methods, a program shouldn't be in development for weeks at a time so there's little reason to want to review interim documentation. Third, the interim documentation doesn't usually mean anything anyway; somehow a program can stay "90 percent complete" for months no matter what the interim documentation indicates.

Clerical support When using a modern computer system, the programmers themselves should enter all of their programs, job procedures, and data into the system. This is simply the most efficient way to get ideas and code from the programmer's head into the system. No one should be hand coding anything and turning it over to a clerical person for entry into the system. That's an obsolete procedure because you can enter data and code into a system yourself at least five times faster than you can code it by hand; and you eliminate the middle man at the same time.

With this in mind, the only clerical support a programming staff should need is in preparing final documentation and filing it in the external library. And a person can provide this clerical support with little or no technical background and only a minimum of training. As a result, you shouldn't have trouble finding and training a librarian for a project team.

In our shop, for example, we found that our programmers didn't like to redraw their revised structure charts after they completed their programs. Normally, a programmer made a few handwritten modifications to a structure chart as he coded and tested the program. But rather than redraw the chart, he would submit this somewhat messy chart as final documentation. Worse, a typical programmer would sometimes forget to show all of the modifications made to the chart so the chart really didn't correspond to the COBOL code of the program.

To solve this problem, we decided to provide clerical support for our programmers. Not only would these clerks redraw the structure charts for final documentation, but they would check the COBOL code to make sure that the structure on the charts corresponded to the code. This simple step helped to increase programmer productivity as well as the quality of our final documentation. Eventually, however, we decided to use structure listings generated by the computer system from the COBOL code instead of structure charts as final documentation. So this need for clerical help was eliminated. Now, we only provide clerical support for filing the documents of the external library.

Discussion

As you can see, it's relatively easy to keep a useful development support library today...if you let the computer system maintain most of your libraries. Then, if you let your programmers do their own entry work, you increase their productivity at the same time that you eliminate most of the need for clerical support. This in turn makes it easy to staff the position of librarian, because you don't need a technical person for it. And productivity is improved at all levels in your shop.

Terminology

development support library
DSL
internal library
external library
librarian

Objective

In general terms, explain how a development support library should be implemented on a modern computer system.

Chapter 20

How your system development method can affect program development

In chapter 3, I pointed out how a company's systems analysis and design methods can affect program development...negatively. If, for example, a systems designer omits an important field in a record of the system, it can mean many hours of reprogramming when the omission is discovered. Similarly, if the systems documentation doesn't make it easy to tell which programs do which functions, the system can be difficult to maintain. Then, if one of the programs that needs to be modified isn't modified, the system will fail. In short, an ineffective system development method can defeat the purposes of an effective program development method.

In this chapter, though, I'd like to show you how systems methods can affect program development positively. If, for example, your system documentation makes it easy to identify the programs in a system that need to be changed due to a maintenance request, program maintenance is easier. And if the program specifications that come from the systems group include COPY members for all record descriptions required in the system, it will improve programmer productivity. In short, an effective systems development method goes hand in hand with an effective program development method. In fact, you should think of the systems development process as a continuous process that includes program development.

Rather than speak in general terms in this chapter, I'm going to show you how the system development method we use can help you improve program development. We developed our system development method when we realized that traditional methods of system development were going to defeat us. Although we wanted to develop reliable systems that were easy to use, we also wanted to develop them at a rate of productivity that was unheard of. As you might guess, we soon realized that we couldn't do either using traditional development methods. Just as the program flowchart had proven to be ineffective for programming, we realized that the systems flowchart was ineffective for systems design and that it was particularly ineffective for the design of interactive systems.

Like our program development method, our system development method is based on techniques taken from several different sources. For instance, our use of data flow diagrams is a simplification of the techniques promoted by Yourdon inc. Our system structure charts are a simplification of the systems documentation used in HIPO. Our use of data dictionary notation and database design documents is based on similar tools taken from the field of database administration. And so forth. As I see it, our strength in developing methods is that we're good at creating consistent, practical procedures from a collection of unrelated techniques.

At this time, then, I'd like to introduce you to our system development method. As you read this introduction, please remember that I'm not presenting our method because I think it's the last word on systems analysis and design. I'm presenting it to show you how an effective systems method can make your program development methods work better. My hope is that this introduction will give you some ideas for changes that you can make to your own system development procedures. In particular, I'm thinking of changes that will make your system development and your program development efforts more cohesive.

The eight phases of our system development method

Figure 20-1 lists the eight phases of our system development method. As you can see, the phases are divided into three groups: analysis, design, and implementation. Although the first two phases must be done in sequence, the remaining phases are usually overlapped. The reasons for this will become clear as I present the phases.

Phase 1: Create an analysis data flow diagram for the existing system In recent years, system developers have come up with a simple yet effective tool for systems analysis: the *data flow diagram*, or *DFD*. The DFD is a drawing that shows what information comes into a system, what information goes out, and where that information is transformed in between. Although the DFD forces you to break a system down into manageable parts, it doesn't let you lose track of the relationships between the parts.

Analysis

1. Create an analysis data flow diagram for the existing system.
2. Create a model data flow diagram for the new system.

Design

3. Define the data requirements.
4. Create a system structure chart.
5. Design the database.
6. Create the program specifications.

Implementation

7. Develop the programs of the system using structured programming techniques.
8. Document the system.

Figure 20-1 The eight phases of our system development method

An *analysis DFD* shows how an existing system functions. Even if you've never been exposed to an analysis DFD, I think you'll understand what one represents. For instance, look at figure 20-2. This is an analysis DFD for a retail distribution system. In fact, this is a simplified subset of our own retail distribution system as it was in the late 1970s.

As you can see by reading the names assigned to the arrows, circles, and paired lines in this diagram, it represents everything from processing customer orders to preparing an aged-trial balance for accounts receivable. In brief, the circles represent *processes*; the parallel lines represent *data stores* (which are usually files or database views); and the arrows represent *data flows* to or from a process or data store. In this example, then, the fourth process has five data flows: two input and three output. It combines information taken from the customer orders and the inventory data store to produce four copies of an invoice, which are distributed to three different destinations.

When you use a DFD, you can clarify, in a few strokes of a pen or pencil, concepts that might remain ambiguous using traditional analysis techniques. And the more complex the situation under study, the more valuable the DFD becomes. Perhaps most important, however, is that the DFD is meaningful to users. In our experience, most users welcome the use of DFDs because it's easy for them to recognize their own functions and data elements on the DFDs.

When you realize that the analysis DFD is the only essential document that we create when we analyze an existing system, you can see how our method differs from traditional analysis methods. Instead of developing dozens (or hundreds) of pages of documentation for an existing

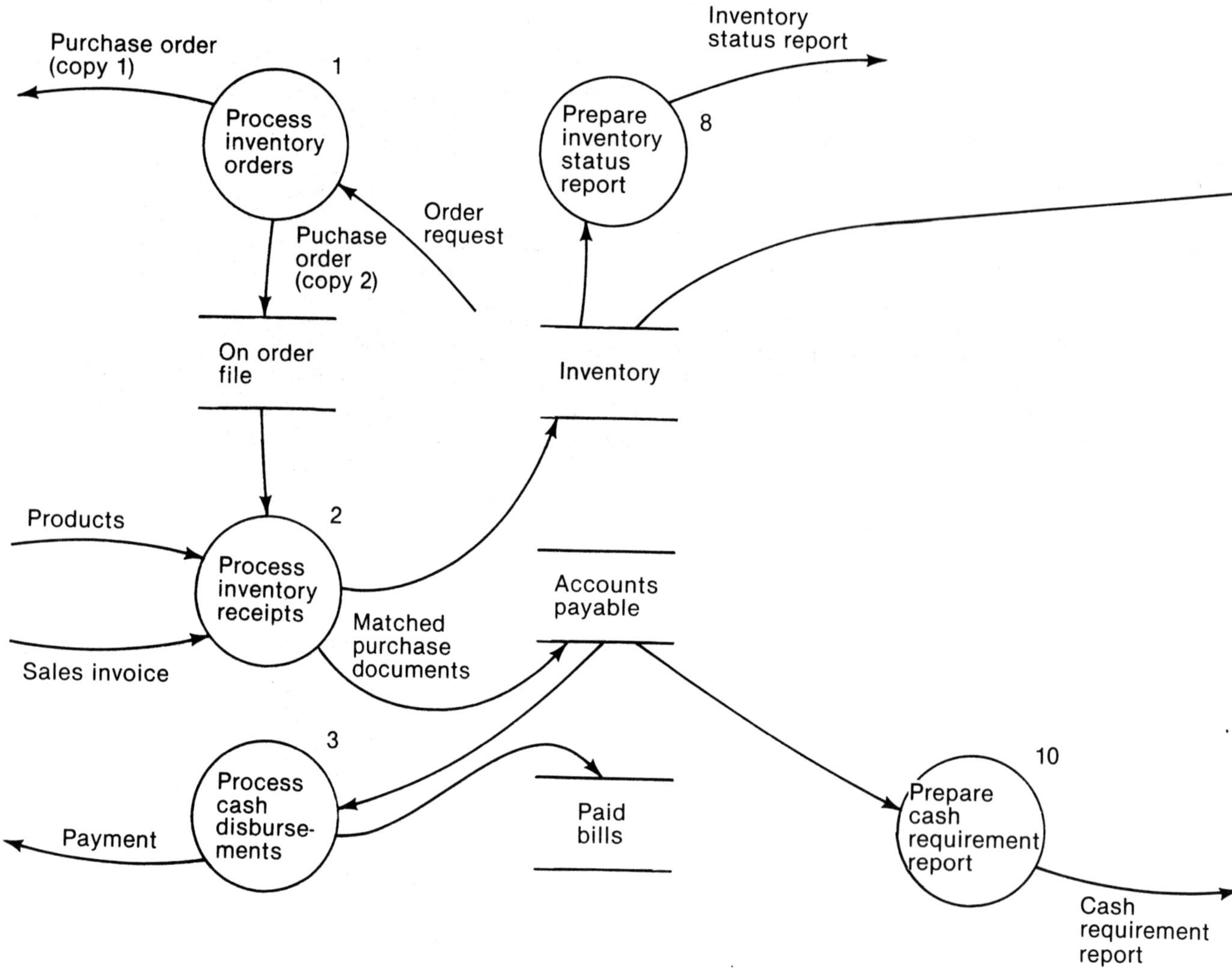

Figure 20-2 An analysis DFD for a simplified version of a retail distribution system

system, we try only to understand what data it uses, what information it produces, and how the processes and data stores are related.

Phase 2: Create a model data flow diagram for the new system In contrast to an analysis DFD, a *model DFD* shows how a new system will function. When you create a model DFD, you work from the analysis DFD. In figure 20-3, for example, you can see the model DFD derived from the analysis DFD in figure 20-2. If you compare the two DFDs, you can see that the model DFD is simpler than the analysis DFD.

As you will see in a moment, the model DFD provides the starting point for your system and database design. As a result, when you create it, you must emphasize the critical processes and data stores and not let yourself be distracted by details. Therefore, some of the nonessential

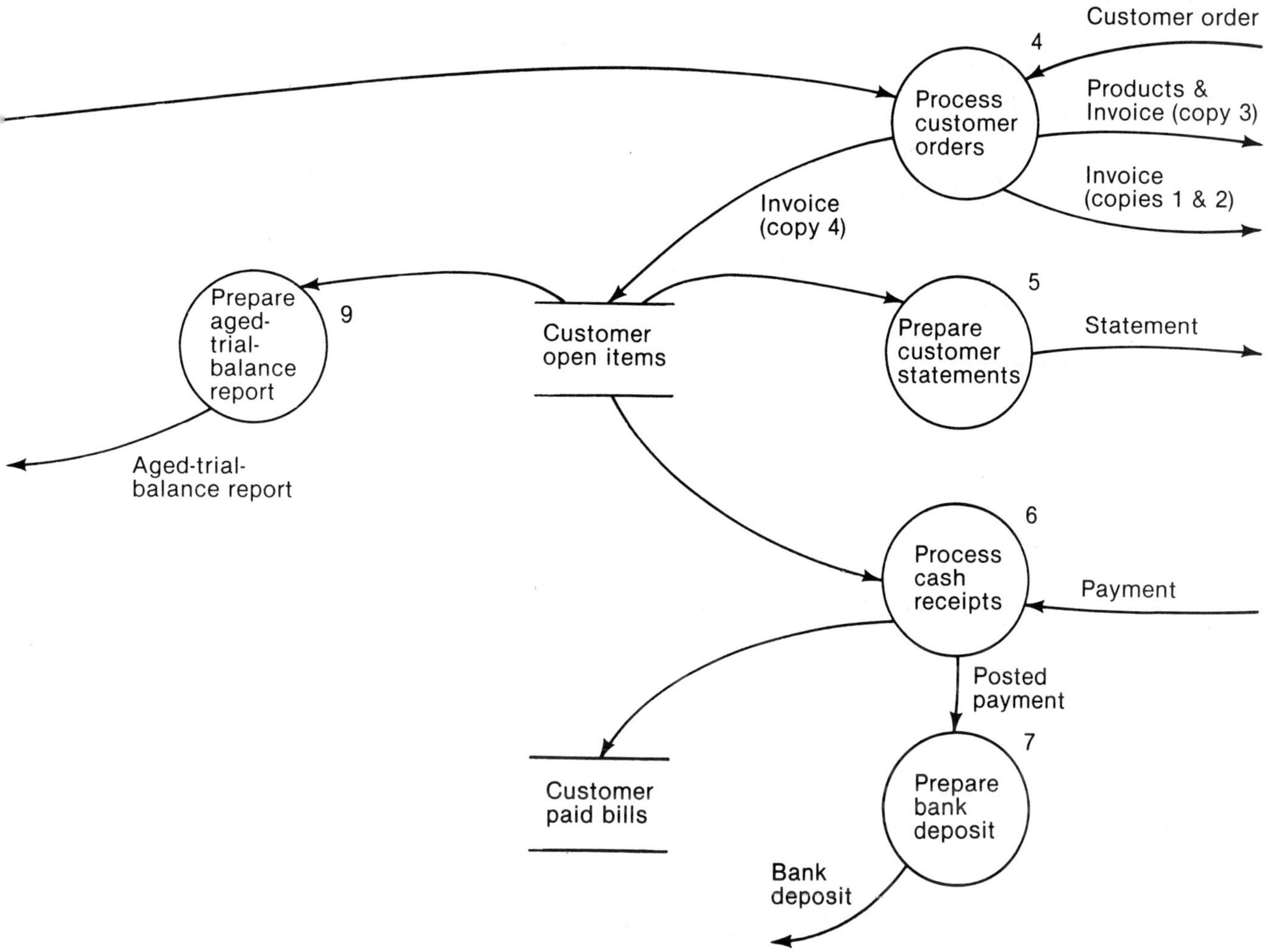

detail is omitted from a model DFD. This makes it easier for you to focus on the critical parts of the system.

If you review the model DFD in figure 20-3, you can see that all of the processes are connected by data stores. In fact, when you create the model DFD, one of your main concerns is to design the data stores so this linkage between processes is as logical and manageable as possible. In general, the use of analysis and model DFDs helps you identify and analyze the use of data stores in the old and new systems, so the database in the new system is usually more efficient than the one in the old system.

Phase 3: Define the data requirements After you have modelled the new system, you start to identify the data that you will need to perform

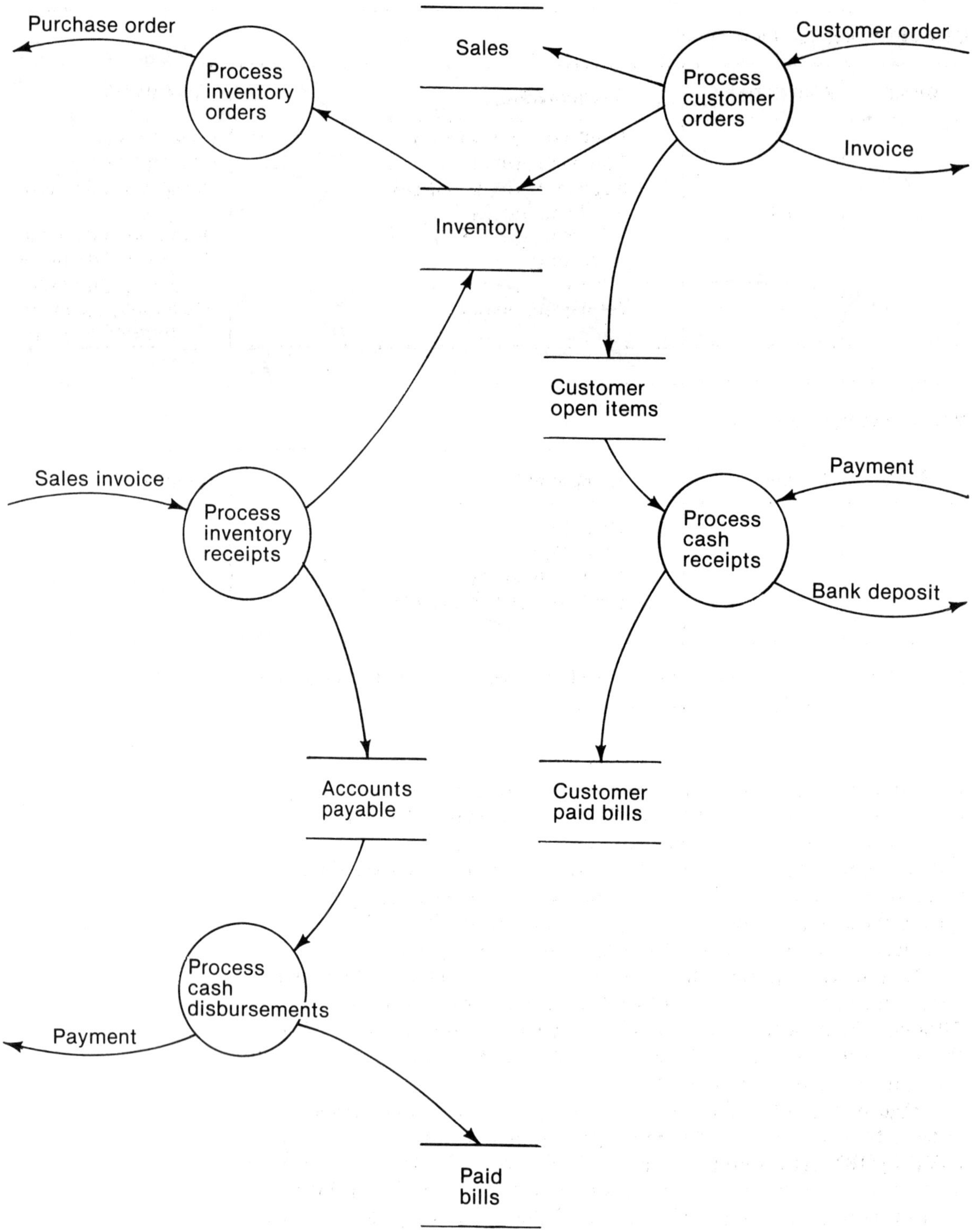

Figure 20-3 The model DFD for the retail distribution system

Data structure: Purchase Order

Group	Repetitions	Components	Comments
		Purchase order number	Control item
		Purchase order date	Control item
Y		Supplier name & address	Inventory data store
	1-10	Purchase details	
		Product	Inventory data store
		Quantity	Inventory data store
		Price	Inventory data store
		Total order amount	Calculated (Total of quantity × price)

Data structure: Inventory

Group	Repetitions	Components	Comments
		Product	
		Unit price	
		Reorder quantity	
Y		Supplier name & address	

Figure 20-4 The contents list for the purchase order along with the preliminary contents list for the INVENTORY data store

each process in the new system. As I mentioned earlier, though, this phase of system development is overlapped with other phases of system development. On the one hand, you can't completely define a new system's data requirements until you have a complete understanding of what all of its processes do. On the other hand, you can't completely specify the system's processes until you know how its data will be organized. As a result, these phases have to be overlapped.

In any event, to start this phase of system development, you create *preliminary contents lists* for the critical data stores of the system. Although the data stores are often files, they can also be database views. But you decide that later. For now, you simply try to identify the contents required by the data stores.

Figure 20-4 shows the *contents list* we prepared for the purchase order output document and the preliminary contents list for the INVENTORY data store that was prepared from it. In these lists, we have used our own version of *data dictionary notation*. For each element of a data structure, we indicate whether the element is a group element, how many repetitions it contains, and any comments pertaining to it. For an output entry, the comment should indicate where the element comes from

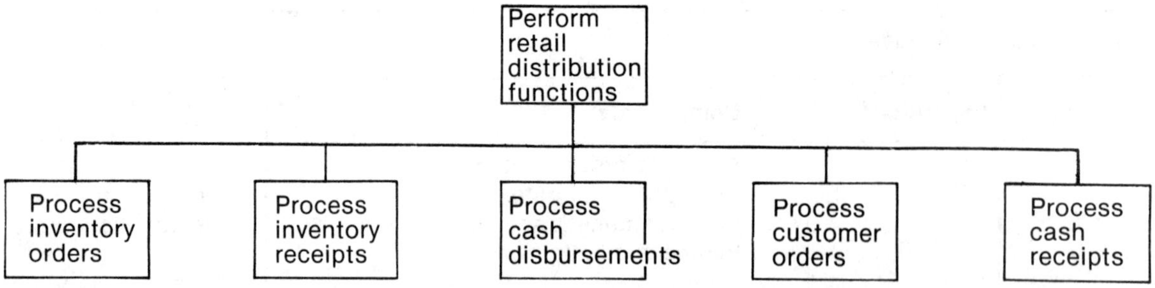

Figure 20-5 The system structure chart for the retail distribution system based on the model DFD in figure 20-3

so you can be sure to include that element in the proper data store. Although the notation we use consists of just a few symbols and a few conventions for using them, the resulting entries provide a solid basis for designing the files or database of your system.

As you refine a systems' processes, you add to the preliminary contents lists. For instance, as you refine the processes required to maintain inventory, you will find that you need to include additional fields in the INVENTORY data store such as quantity on hand and quantity on order. Then, when you have completely defined all of the processes, your content lists should be complete.

Phase 4: Create a system structure chart The model DFD shows the relationships between the critical processes and data stores in a system. After you've established those relationships, you need to examine and organize *all* of the system's processes. For this purpose, we develop a *system structure chart.* A system structure chart is similar to the program structure chart in that it shows the control relationships among the programs of the system by indicating levels of subordination.

You begin developing the system structure chart by drawing one module for each process on your model DFD. These modules are subordinate to a module that represents the entire system. For instance, figure 20-5 illustrates this preliminary version of the structure chart for the simplified retail system. As you can see, the five boxes in the second level of the chart correspond to the five processes in figure 20-3.

From this point, you expand each of the processes showing all functions that are subordinate to them. Next you must add all of the processes that were left out of the model DFD in order to simplify it. Finally, you must group all related processes together. For instance, figure 20-6 shows a partial expansion of the system structure chart for the retail distribution system. Here, you can see that the designer has moved the second-level boxes of figure 20-5 to the third level of the structure chart. In addition, she has added other modules at the second level for functions not shown on the model DFD. She knows, for example, that all systems are going to have to maintain files, prepare documents on demand for some users, and perform periodic functions like month-end and year-end procedures. In addition, since this is an interactive system, the designer has added a second-level box that will control the processing of interactive inquiries.

After your structure chart is complete, you number the modules of the chart. Using our method, you number each module using a prefix of from one to four characters that indicates the system or subsystem. This is followed by a four-digit number. Thus, SLS0000 is the top-level module in the sales processing leg of the system in figure 20-6. And INV2000 is the top-level module in the perform-inventory-receipts-function leg of the system.

The system structure chart is a critical document in our development method because it becomes the major planning document for the physical system. In most instances, each box at the lowest level of each leg on the structure chart will become a program in the new system. Some of the higher level modules will become procedures, and, if you are designing an interactive system, some of them will become menu programs. In other words, the system structure chart identifies every procedure, menu, and program that needs to be developed in the entire system. As a result, it is valuable in planning the sequence of development of the system and for monitoring progress during the implementation of the system.

When you develop interactive systems, the system structure chart becomes the best design tool I've seen for developing a sensible menu structure. Since the structure chart shows the hierarchy of the program functions that make up a system, it can correspond to the accesses of a menu-driven system. For instance, SLS1000 in figure 20-6 could be a menu program with four selections: one for each of the three programs it controls and one to return to the previous menu.

If you compare a system structure chart with a traditional systems flowchart, you can see how structure charts can improve system development. In contrast to the flowchart, you can review a structure chart with a user to make sure that it provides for all of the functions he anticipates having. In addition, you can easily revise the structure chart during the development process to correspond to the way the user envisions the hierarchy of his system. When you revise a structure chart, it doesn't affect any of the programs in the chart, so this doesn't mean reprogramming. At most, it means a change to a menu or a procedure.

Phase 5: Design the database Because the model DFD identifies the critical data stores of a new system, it provides the starting point for the design of a system's database. In addition, however, you must identify the data stores that you deliberately excluded from the model DFD. After you've identified all of the files or database views your system will require, you need to determine how they will be accessed. To accomplish this, you examine each module of your system structure chart and decide how each file that it uses must be accessed.

After you've defined the access paths for each data structure, you should prepare a *data access diagram* showing the relationships between

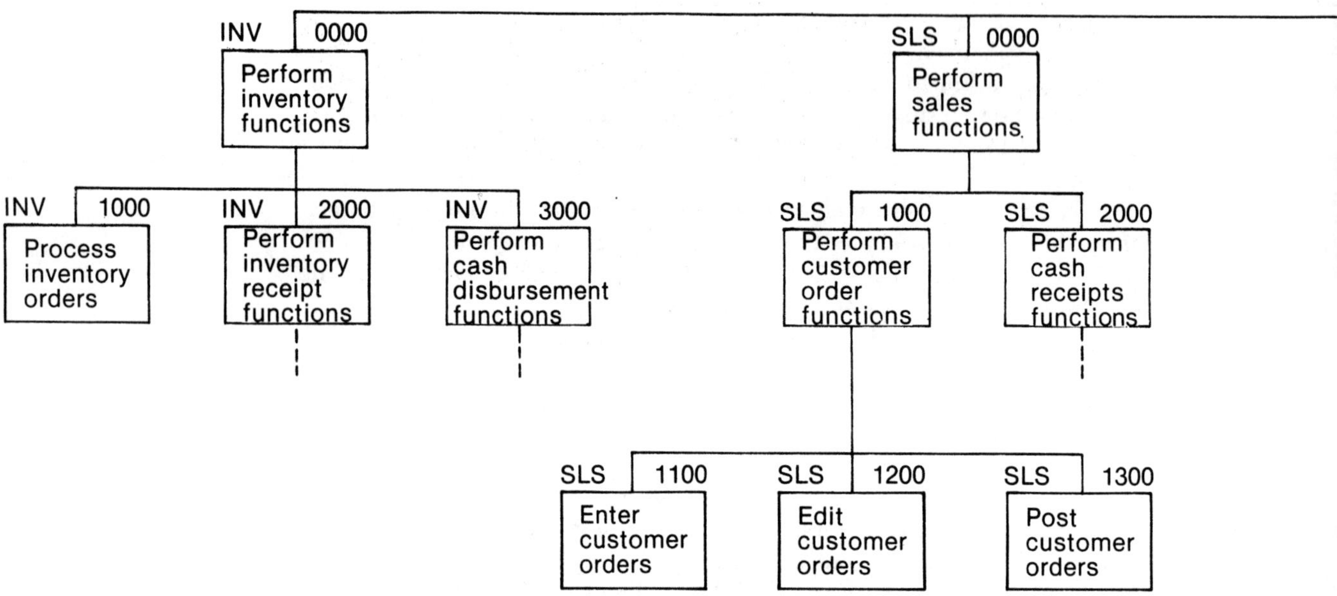

Figure 20-6 A partial structure chart showing the final organization of the retail distribution system

the access paths and the data structures. For instance, figure 20-7 shows part of the data access diagram for our actual retail system. In a diagram like this, the circles represent keys, the boxes represent files or database views, and the arrowheads indicate whether a file may contain one or more than one record for a specific key. By using a data access diagram, you can make sure that you are providing for all of the accesses that a system requires. You can also make sure that these accesses are logical and efficient.

Another useful tool in database design is the *data hierarchy diagram*. For instance, figure 20-8 is the diagram for our actual retail distribution system. As the name implies, a data hierarchy diagram shows the hierarchical relationships among data structures. The arrowheads in a diagram like this again indicate whether a record in one file can access one or more than one record in another file. By recognizing these relationships, you will have a better understanding of how to implement your database.

Phase 6: Create the program specifications As you're deciding how the system's database will be organized, you also begin to develop program specifications. As discussed in chapter 5, these specifications generally

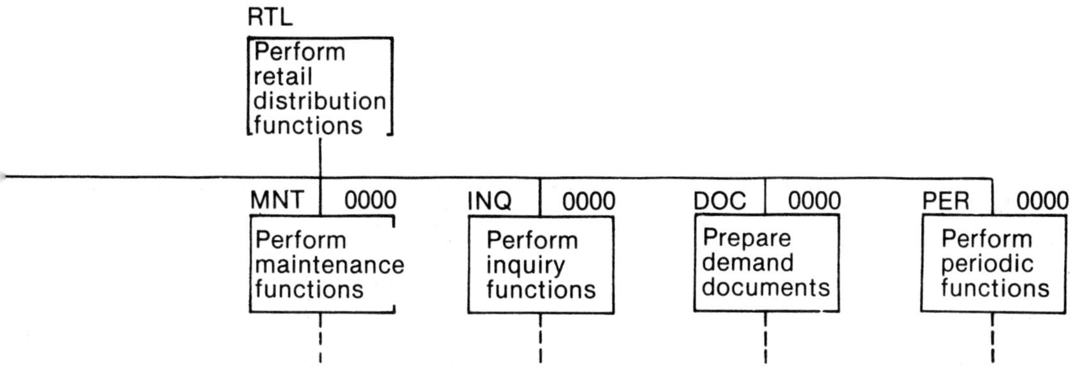

include a program overview, COPY members for the record descriptions in each of the files to be used in the program, and any related report layouts. If you are working on an interactive system, you will also need to include related screen layouts and perhaps a screen flow diagram as discussed in chapter 12. As I mentioned in chapter 5, if the systems designer doesn't develop complete specifications for each program, the programmer must take on this responsibility.

In our system, the primary document of the program specification is the program overview. In fact, if the systems designer creates a system structure chart and one overview for each box on the chart, any programmer or analyst should be able to understand what the system does and how it does it. As a result, the program specifications don't have to be as wordy as traditional specifications have often been. Also, if questions come up about the interface between two programs, the system structure chart and the overviews should provide the answers.

Phase 7: Develop the programs of the system using structured programming techniques This book, of course, tells you how to develop the programs of a system. In other words, this book presents the program development method that is phase 7 of our system development

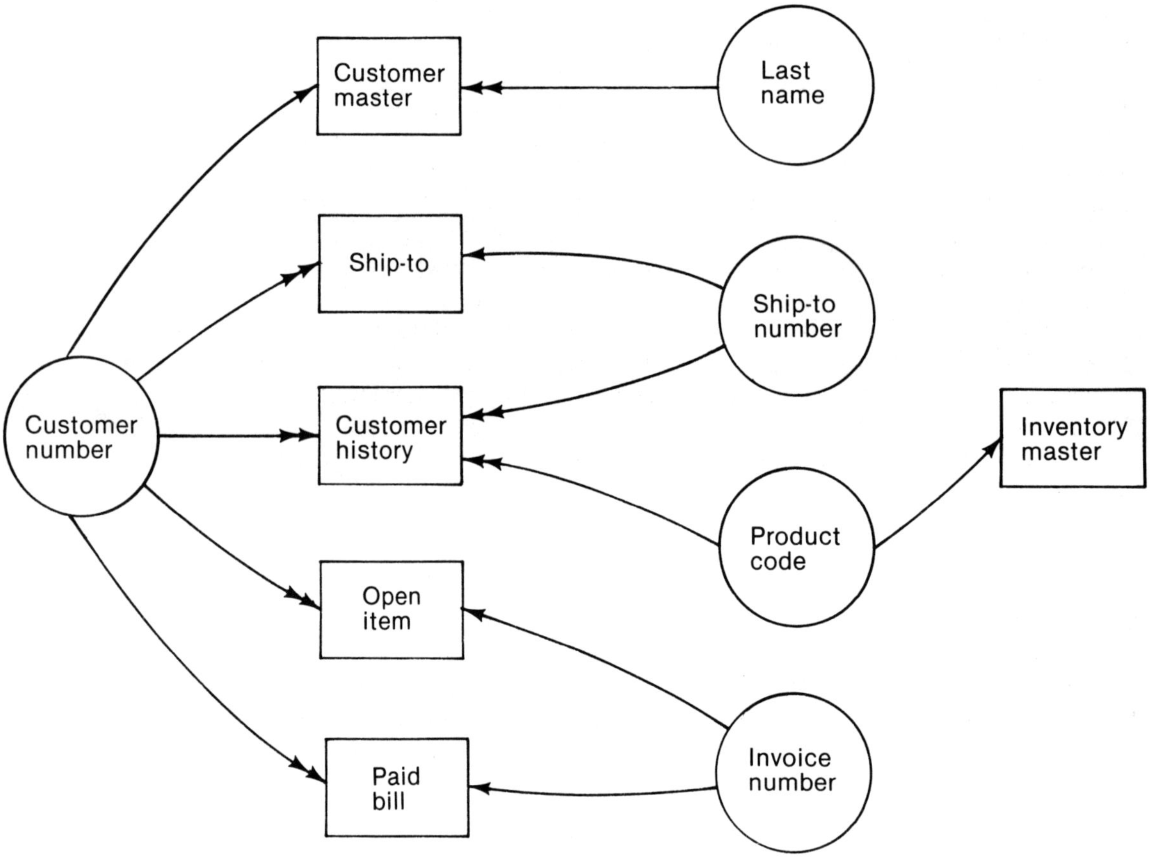

Figure 20-7 A data access diagram for an actual retail distribution system

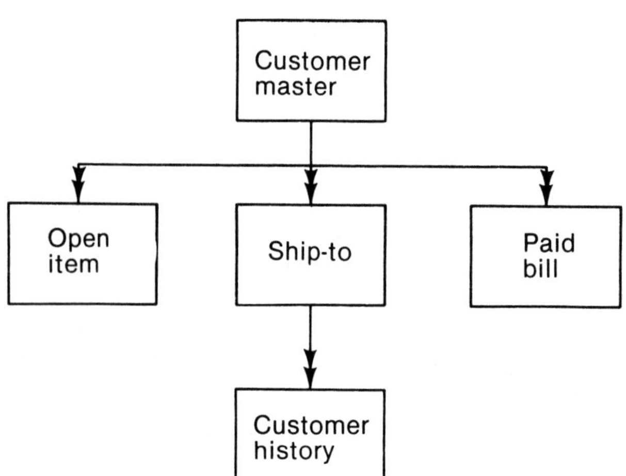

Figure 20-8 A data hierarchy diagram for an actual retail distribution system

method. Needless to say, this phase of system development often takes longer than all of the other phases combined.

Phase 8: Document the system Because businesses change, almost all systems require maintenance as they age. In addition, almost all systems have bugs, some that may not be found until months or years after the installation of the system. Then, when modifications have to be made to a system, it's essential that the persons doing that maintenance have access to complete, accurate, up-to-date documentation for the entire system.

If you use our methods for system analysis and design, you will have most of the documents needed for complete system documentation when you complete the development of the system. Although data flow diagrams and the system structure chart are critical for understanding a system development problem, they are also valuable as documentation. Similarly, program overviews, program structure charts, and the program code itself are excellent documentation at the program level.

Figure 20-9 lists our suggested contents for final system documentation. As you can see, we have divided it into three groups: system documentation, database documentation, and program documentation. Although you probably aren't familiar with some of the items of documentation, I won't go into a detailed explanation of them here. However, I would like to point out the clear relationship between the three documentation groups. Figure 20-10 illustrates this relationship.

Briefly stated, the model DFD and the system structure chart direct you to the database and program documentation. The program documentation in turn refers to the database documentation and the program implementation documents (the program structure chart and the program source listing). As a result, the documentation of the system is both complete and integrated.

The benefits of our system development method

I have already mentioned some of the benefits of our system development method. But let me be more specific. When you use our method or one like it, you experience four main benefits.

Increased development productivity Although structured programming techniques can make dramatic improvements in programmer productivity, there's more to development productivity than this. If program development is only one phase out of eight as it is in our shop, you must also be concerned with productivity in the other seven phases. In my opinion, though, the productivity of the average analyst or designer in these other phases of system development is low, and the problem is often the system development method. Obviously, if you use inefficient methods, your productivity is going to be low.

In contrast, our system development method is efficient because it is a top-down development method. In other words, system development progresses by considering the most critical factors first, then the next most

Section 1: System documentation

- Model data flow diagram
- System structure chart
- Security concepts and implementation
- Backup concepts and implementation
- User instructions

Section 2: Database documentation

- File concepts narrative
- Data access diagram
- Data hierarchy diagram
- File and record descriptions in source code
- File-usage cross-reference listing
- File-update cross-reference listing

Section 3: Program documentation

- Subprogram documentation
    - Programmer instructions
    - Subprogram listings
    - Subprogram-usage cross-reference listing
- Standard segments of source code
- Procedure listings
- Program specifications
    - Program overview
    - Report layouts
    - Screen layouts
- Program implementation documents
    - Program structure chart or structure listing
    - Program source listing

Figure 20-9 Suggested contents for final system documentation

critical factors, and so on. Throughout the development process, we are able to defer trivial decisions because our method clearly proceeds from the top down. As we see it, too many development methods try to gather all system information at once and then work with it. This is inefficient, and it leads to ineffective systems.

One of the most obvious ways that our method helps improve development productivity is by shortening the analysis process. Using traditional methods, many analysts collect far more data when they analyze the old system than is necessary. After all, if you're going to replace the old system, you don't need to know exactly how it works. You only need to know what its inputs are, what its outputs are, and what functions it performs. Most of the information about how it performs its functions is irrelevant during the analysis phase. And it's easy to get this information if it's needed in a later development phase.

In contrast to the traditional analysis phase, then, we usually can develop an analysis DFD for an existing system in a matter of days, not weeks or months. And this document is all that we need for doing the subsequent phases efficiently and effectively. So in this phase alone, you can make dramatic gains in productivity by using our method.

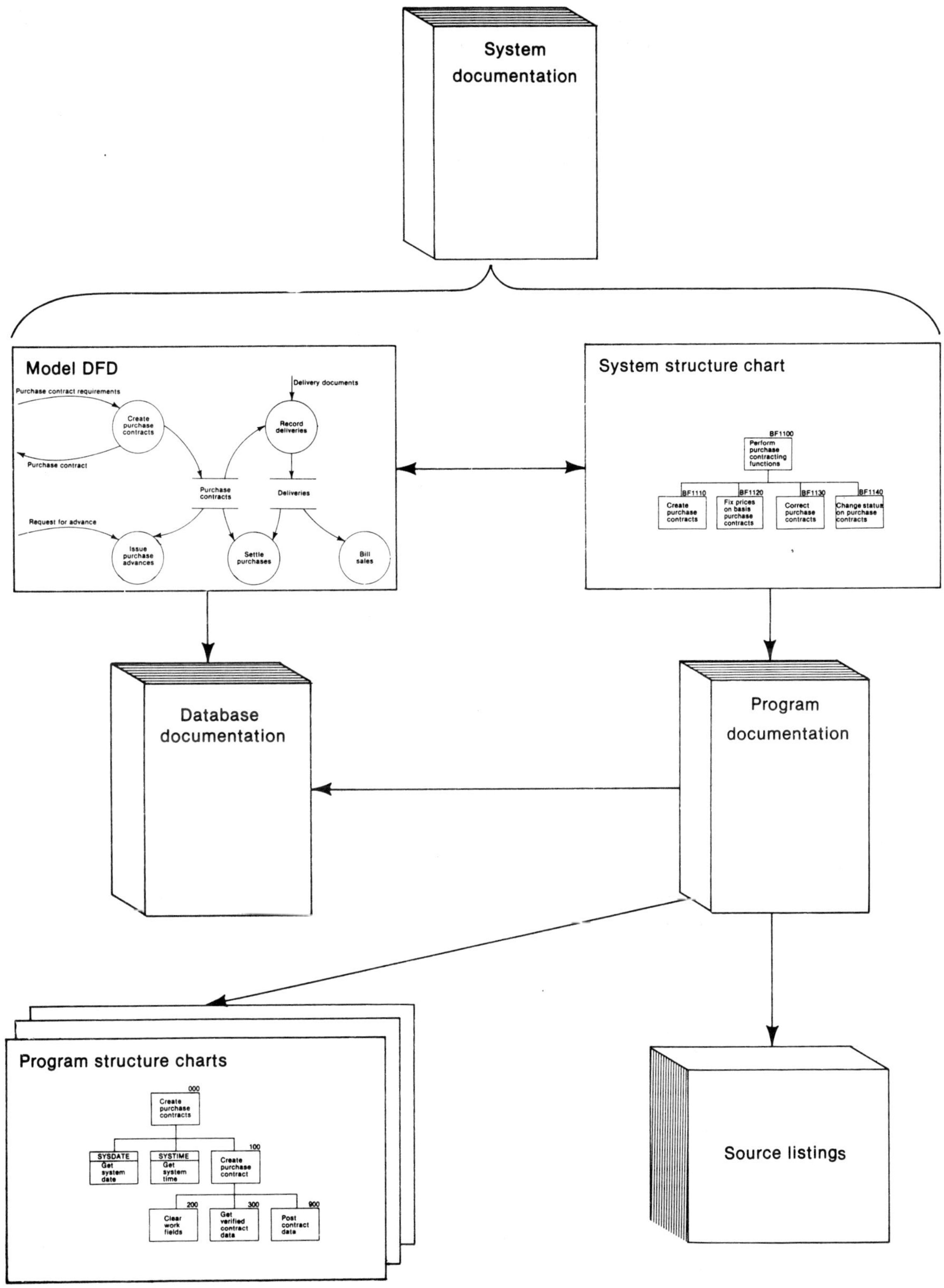

Figure 20-10 The relationships between the major components of final documentation

A few years ago, for example, we were hired to do a preliminary design of a complete new system for a company with 90 employees. Because the job was extensive, we assigned three analysts to the first phase of the job, the analysis of the existing system. One week later, we had a complete set of analysis DFDs for the company. From that point on, one designer worked on the job to create the model DFD, the first version of the system structure chart, some preliminary contents lists, and some preliminary access diagrams for the database. At this point, five weeks after the start of the job, we felt we had enough information to identify the programs and procedures required by the entire system and to bid on the program development portion of the job.

Meanwhile, the consulting group of a nationally-known accounting firm had been hired to do the same job. So, before the company accepted our bid, they wanted to evaluate the accounting firm's design and bid. Four months later, the accounting firm presented four 3-ring binders full of detail that they said represented their analysis of the existing system; this had been prepared by a four-man team during the four-month period. They also estimated that they would need six more months (or 24 more man-months) to do a preliminary design of the new system. At that point, I asked to review the contents of their four binders. When I did, I found that they had documented the flow of every piece of paper in the company, but they had nothing that showed them the relationships between the processes and the data stores...nothing that would help them in the next phase of development. Using their methods, it seemed that the analysis and design phases could go on indefinitely. And they did.

User satisfaction through user involvement Many times I've listened to users complain about the systems that have been developed for them. And I have to feel that the main problem is that the user hasn't been involved throughout the development process. In traditional system development, it seems that the user is forgotten once the analysis portion of the job is done and the user has agreed upon a system specification. Then, six months or more later, the user is asked to review the completed system. And for the first time, the user realizes that the development group had an incomplete understanding of what he wanted.

In our development method, though, you review the development documents with the user. This is possible because the documents are developed with the user in mind. They use his language; they represent his current system; and they represent his future system. The DFDs and the system structure chart in particular are ideal for communicating with the user. In contrast, the traditional design documents tend to be in data processing rather than user language so they aren't useful for this purpose. Or, they tend to be so overwhelming that the user doesn't feel that he has the time to adequately review them, so he doesn't review them at all.

In our development method, we also recommend early implementation of critical portions of the system. Then, the user can review these portions of the system while it is still relatively inexpensive to make design changes. By improving your program development methods as described in this book, you can implement these portions in a short period of time. And, if you have to change them, you can make the changes with a minimum of effort.

Early implementation of selected subsystems When you finish the design phase for a system, you will often find that your development schedule disappoints the user. For instance, the user requests a system for installation in six months, but you realize that the system will require 18 months of work and you only have two programmers you can assign to the project. So the best you can do is deliver a system in nine months, but that leaves no room for estimating errors.

By using our methods, however, you will often be able to provide a usable subsystem within the time period requested by the user. This ability to select and implement usable subsystems depends to a large extent on the system structure chart. Because it identifies all of the functions of a system, it makes it easy for you to select the functions that make a useful subsystem for the user. After the subsystem is developed, the programming staff can complete the entire system and phase in new subsystems as they become available. In contrast, this type of phased implementation is often difficult to plan and control using traditional development methods.

Simplified system maintenance through improved documentation As I've explained, the documentation you develop when using our method is complete and understandable, but it isn't overwhelming. The critical system document is the system structure chart, because it is a directory for all of the programs and procedures in the system. Then, the program structure chart for each module on the system chart is a directory to each paragraph in the COBOL program. This relationship is illustrated in figure 20-11. As a result, it's relatively easy to identify the COBOL paragraphs within a system that need to modified for a maintenance request.

In contrast, traditional system documentation is often a nightmare. Several times in the past, I have been asked to review a system's documentation to see whether we would want to make enhancements to the software on a contract basis. On all of the occasions, I found that the program documentation wasn't too bad, but the system documentation was impossible to work with. If it existed at all, it was likely to be incomplete. So you could make changes to the programs without too much trouble, but it was almost impossible to determine which programs needed to be modified.

How our systems methods can help you improve program development

By now, you should have a general understanding of how a system development method can affect program development. But, again, I'd like

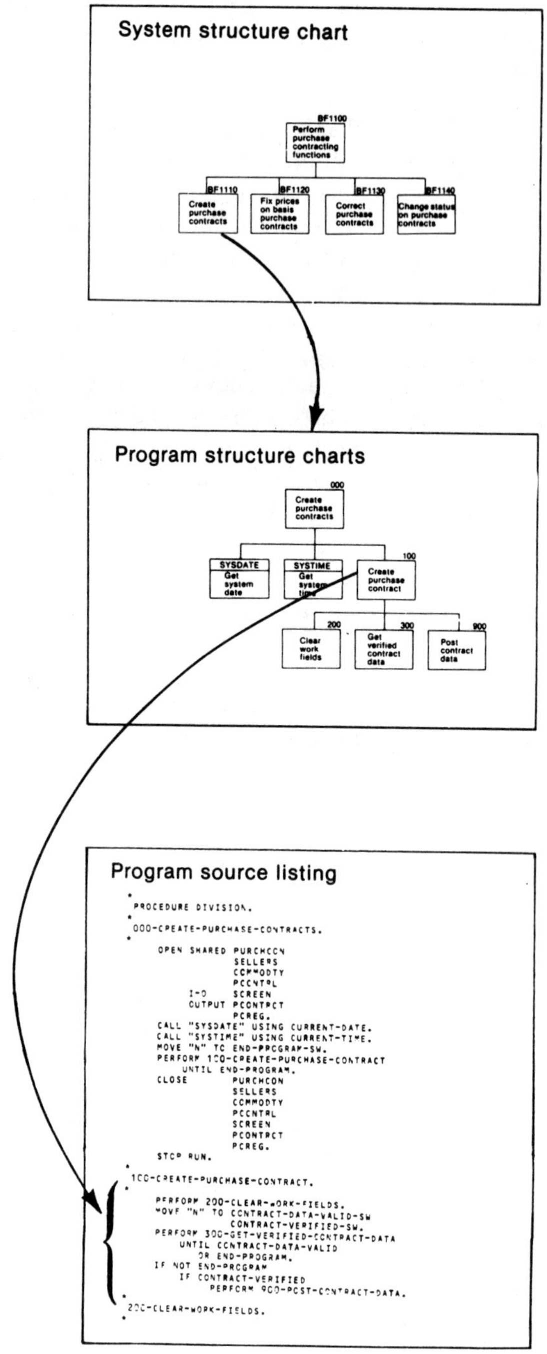

Figure 20-11 The relationships between the system structure chart, the program structure chart, and the source code

to be as specific as possible. As I see it, our system development method can help you improve program development in three main ways.

Improved programmer productivity due to reduced reprogramming Reprogramming can have a devastating effect on programmer productivity. If a late system change means changes to 20 programs that have already been tested, programmer productivity deteriorates. In fact, an ineffective systems development method can make it impossible for your programmers to achieve high rates of productivity.

In contrast, our method lets your programmers maximize their productivity by eliminating most of the reprogramming that is common to systems development. It does this in several ways. First, it reduces or eliminates changes in specifications due to user dissatisfaction. I've already mentioned user involvement throughout the development process. And this of course helps. In addition, though, details aren't lost when you use our method because you proceed in a highly organized fashion from the top down. As a result, the user should receive no surprises.

Second, if you use our methods, you are more likely to produce a well-structured database that provides for all of the system's functions. This means no more reprogramming because a necessary data element was left out of a file or a file requires an additional access path. To start, the model DFD forces you to identify the data stores that are central to the system. Then, by focusing on the functional requirements of each process on the system structure chart, you are able to identify the fields needed in every file, how each file needs to be accessed, and how the files are related. To make sure you have a complete and efficient accessing structure, you use data access and data hierarchy diagrams.

Third, reprogramming is reduced by better packaging of the programs in the first place. In our system, remember, you move from the model DFD to the system structure chart. And this chart identifies all of the programs in the system. Since it is a flexible documentation tool, you can experiment with different forms of packaging in this design phase and select the optimum packaging. As a result, you shouldn't have late programming changes due to a repackaging of programs.

In summary, our method helps reduce or eliminate programming changes due to the three most common causes of change. As we see it, user requests are the most common cause of reprogramming. Database changes are the second most common cause. And program repackaging is the third most common cause.

Improved program reliability through improved program specification Although I've talked about program reliability throughout this book, that's a little misleading. What you're really after is system reliability because you can't have reliable programs and an unreliable system. If a system fails, it's due to a program failure whether or not all of the programs in the system do what they're supposed to do. If a system fails, someone didn't specify something right or someone didn't read a program specification right.

As we see it, then, our system development method can improve program reliability because it improves system reliability. In general, when you use our method, you improve your chances that the programs of the system will interface properly. Then, it's less likely that a system bug will slip through the systems test.

Now, we're not saying that our method will eliminate all system bugs forever. But ours is a top-down method that helps you keep system failures to a minimum. In particular, the system chart helps you understand the relationships between the programs so you can specify them properly. And the programmers can refer to the system chart and program specifications so they can correct the interface problems that they discover. In the long run, this means that the system as well as its programs are going to be more reliable.

Improved program maintenance through improved system documentation I've already mentioned this when I listed the four main benefits of our system development method. But the point is worth making again. In brief, it is possible to have programs that are easy to maintain and a system that is difficult to maintain. So your system documentation must make it easy for your maintenance department to identify the programs that need to be modified when a request for maintenance is made. And, as figure 20-11 shows, that's what our system documentation does.

Our documentation method is so effective in fact that some maintenance departments use it to document the old systems that they are called upon to maintain. If, for example, you are asked to maintain a system with inadequate documentation, you can start by drawing a system structure chart for it. You can normally develop this structure chart from the job-control procedures stored on the system. Then, when you're done, you have a directory to the programs of the system that will help you on your current maintenance task as well as on future tasks. If the programs are unstructured, of course, you've still got a major job on your hands, but at least you'll be able to tell what programs must be maintained.

Discussion

I hope you see by now how closely related system development and program development are. That's why an ineffective system development method can be a continuing frustration for a programming group. On the other hand, an effective system method supports and improves program development.

If you'd like to know more about our system development method, I recommend our book by Steve Eckols called *How to Design and Develop Business Systems*. Steve was the primary developer of our system development method, and his book is easy to read and understand. At the least, I think his book will give you many ideas that you can incorporate into your current procedures for system development.

Terminology

data flow diagram
DFD
analysis data flow diagram
analysis DFD
process
data store
data flow
model data flow diagram
model DFD
preliminary contents list
contents list
data dictionary notation
system structure chart
data access diagram
data hierarchy diagram

Objectives

1. List the eight phases of our system development method.

2. List the four main benefits of our system development method.

3. Explain how an effective system development method can improve programmer productivity, program reliability, and program maintainability.

Chapter 21

How to manage programmers and programming projects

At the start, let me say that we don't have all the answers for programming managers. In fact, I don't think anybody does. But Paul and I have had some experiences that you might be interested in. And we do have three recommendations that we think are difficult to ignore.

So I don't misrepresent myself, I want you to know that I'm certainly not an expert on the management of program development. My only experiences in programming management took place about three years ago when one of our project teams ran into serious problems. By that time, the project manager was totally frustrated; the programmers on the team were all behind schedule; and the interactive programs they had developed were not up to my standards of reliability or ease-of-use. To deal with the problems, I released the project manager to work on a new project by himself. I also took over the management of the team. Since that experience, I have had nothing but respect for those programming and project managers who successfully manage program quality and programmer productivity.

When I started, my team consisted of six people: two trainees with less than one year's experience whom we had trained from scratch; two above average programmers who had been with us for more than two years; and two programmers with more than ten years experience whom we had just recently hired. Unfortunately, the two experienced programmers we had just hired were new to our methods and never completely accepted them. Furthermore, they had the firm notion that producing 1000 lines of tested code per month was quite an achievement.

But I felt that at their salaries they had to produce 1000 lines of code per week if they were to be as valuable to me as the recent trainees.

For six months, then, I devoted myself to managing this team and to getting the best possible results from the members of the team. At the start, I had the belief that I could develop a management system that would work for most companies. But by the time I finished, I had the distinct feeling that managing programmers is a difficult job that you'll never be completely successful at. On the plus side, during the last 3 months of the project, everyone on my team produced tested COBOL code at a rate of 500 or more lines per week. And there was no question that the quality of their code had improved in terms of ease-of-use, reliability, and maintainability. On the negative side, I still felt that all but two of the six programmers had much room for improvement in terms of productivity and program quality. Overall, I felt frustrated throughout the life of the project, and I felt that my efforts were at best a partial success.

Based on my experiences, I say unequivocally that management by itself is difficult. And programming management may just be an especially difficult form of management. So if you are a successful programming manager, you probably won't benefit much (if at all) by reading this chapter. But if, like most programming managers, you too are having trouble maintaining program quality and programmer productivity, maybe this chapter will give you some ideas that will help you do a better job.

Three recommendations for improved management

As Paul and I see it, program development in most companies is poorly managed. You might even say that it isn't managed at all. Less than 20 percent of the managers who responded to our survey said that they measured programmer productivity in their shop. And only a few of those who said they did could tell how they measured it. Similarly, less than 40 percent said that they made any attempt to audit or measure program quality. And again, only a few of those could tell you how they did it.

But if you don't measure the quality of the product you're developing or the productivity of the people who are developing it, you're not managing program development. So there's obviously room for improved management in most companies. With that in mind, let me present our three basic recommendations for improved management.

Recommendation 1: Establish standards for program development If you only adopt one of our three recommendations, this is the one to start with. Although most COBOL shops have standards for coding, testing, and documenting a program, less than half have standards for designing a program, planning the modules of a program, using COPY members, and so on. But these are some of the critical tasks of program development. Furthermore, in those companies that do have COBOL standards, the standards tend to be too loose to be useful. For instance, over 60 percent of the companies that responded to our COBOL survey allowed an unrestricted use of 77 levels, PERFORM-THRUs, and GOTOs. But all of these uses can reduce the quality of a COBOL program.

Our recommendation, then, is that you establish rigid standards for program development as soon as you can. These standards should describe how program specifications are to be developed, how subprograms are to be used, how COPY members are to be used, how programs are to be designed, and so on. Although you can't standardize the thought process, you should at least try to make sure that two people in your shop go about the development of a program in the same way.

If by now you have decided to adopt the development method presented in this book, you should know that we sell another book that can work as an instant standards manual for you. This book is called *The COBOL Programmer's Handbook*, and it summarizes the methods of this book in the form of programming standards. Then, if you provide each of your programmers with this handbook, you will be sure that they all know what your standards are. In the past, hundreds of companies have used our standards as a starting point for their own standards. After they use our standards for a while, they modify them somewhat to make them more appropriate for their own system, their own projects, and their own staff.

If you adopt effective development standards and let your programmers know about them, program quality and programmer productivity will improve in your shop whether or not you audit program quality and measure programmer productivity. True, not all of your programmmers will obey the standards unless they're forced to. But enough will obey the standards to improve things in your shop. On the other hand, if you audit quality and measure productivity, your results should be even better.

Recommendation 2: Audit program quality The companies who said they audited program quality in our survey said they did it in many different ways. Some, for example, put the emphasis on user sign offs, user evaluation forms, and user requests for program changes. In other words, if the user is happy, they assume the program has acceptable quality. In contrast, several other companies put the emphasis on object program efficiency as determined by diagnostic programs such as the Capex optimizer. Only a few, however, used internal audits that tried to evaluate the readability (and hence the maintainability) of a program.

Unfortunately, I don't think users are good judges of program quality. Although they can tell you that a program is bad (it doesn't work right), they can't tell you if it's good. On the other hand, judging a program by its object program efficiency is even worse. As we see it, a programmer shouldn't be concerned about object program efficiency unless a program fails to meet some performance standard that is related to program efficiency. At that time, the programmer can fine tune the program so it meets the performance standards, and he can usually do this quite easily. In most cases, though, a program like the Capex optimizer can do the fine tuning so the programmer doesn't even have to do it.

What, then, do I mean by auditing program quality? I mean that someone or some group should actually review the final documentation for a program and decide whether it meets the installation standards. Unfortunately, only a few companies that responded to our survey actually reviewed the final program documentation when they audited program quality. So that's something that has to change.

To audit the quality of a program, you must start with its program design as documented by its structure chart. If this design is good, the program quality down the line will probably be good. And if the design is illogical, the resulting program will probably be unreliable and hard to maintain. So go back to the check list in topic 2 of chapter 7. If the structure chart passes these tests, you have the start of a good program.

To illustrate the audit of a program's design, look at the structure chart in figure 21-1. In our shop, this program would not pass a quality review. For example, the names for many of the modules don't represent one independent function. And improper subordination is used in several portions of the chart. In addition, the programmer didn't put each I/O statement in its own module, and he used a prime read in the initialize module. But this design is based on an example given in a textbook on structured COBOL that was published by a company whose specialty is giving seminars on structured methods. So you can expect to find some of these problems in the programs designed by members of your staff.

After you have passed judgement on the structure chart for a program, you should page through the COBOL listing for the program. In particular, read the coding for the major control modules. Is it easy to read the program? And does the code follow the installation standards? If the program passes these tests, you have a good program.

Who should audit a program for quality? This depends on your organization. For instance, you might have an independent audit committee that does random audits of all programs. This group may report to the programming manager or the information director. In addition to this, though, we feel that the project manager should audit the programs of the programmers who report to her. Otherwise, she won't know who is doing good work and who isn't; she won't know who needs additional training and who doesn't; and she won't know who's ready for more demanding assignments and who isn't.

Should the project manager audit all of the programs produced by her staff? This depends on the staff. If all the programmers are experienced with reputations for producing high-quality programs, spot checks will probably be adequate. On the other hand, if one or more of the programmers isn't accustomed to producing high-quality programs, that's where the auditing and training time ought to go.

Yes, it's time-consuming to audit a program, and I suppose that's why so few companies do it. Auditing a 4000-line interactive program, for example, can take an hour or more, particularly if it isn't up to the

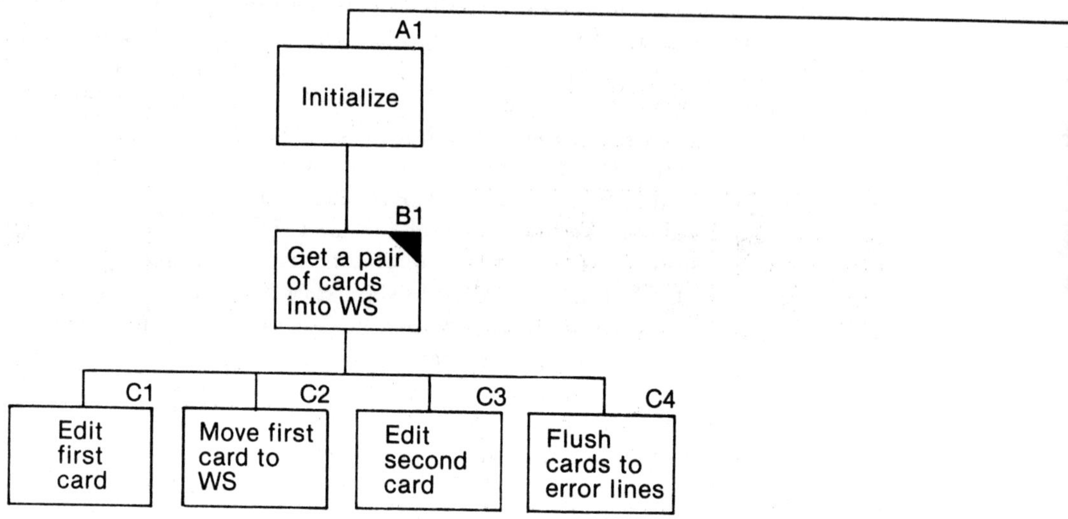

Figure 21-1 A program design that shouldn't pass a quality audit

installation's standards. In general, the worse a program is, the more time it takes to audit it. And after you audit a poor program, you usually have to take some corrective action. So if you regularly audit programs, you quickly realize that your most valuable programmers are the ones who do high-quality work with a minimum of management. Then, they not only save themselves time, but they save you time. If you don't audit programs, you may never realize who your most valuable programmers are.

Recommendation 3: Measure programmer productivity When Paul first consults in a company, the programming manager usually asks him something like this: "How much can we expect our productivity to increase if we use your methods?" To this, Paul replies: "What rate of productivity are you getting now?" After some embarassed shuffling, the manager usually admits that he doesn't know because they don't measure productivity. But if you don't measure productivity, how can you manage your staff? How do you know what pay increase a programmer deserves? How do you know whether a person is worth what you pay him? On what basis, do you recommend promotions? After all, the two most

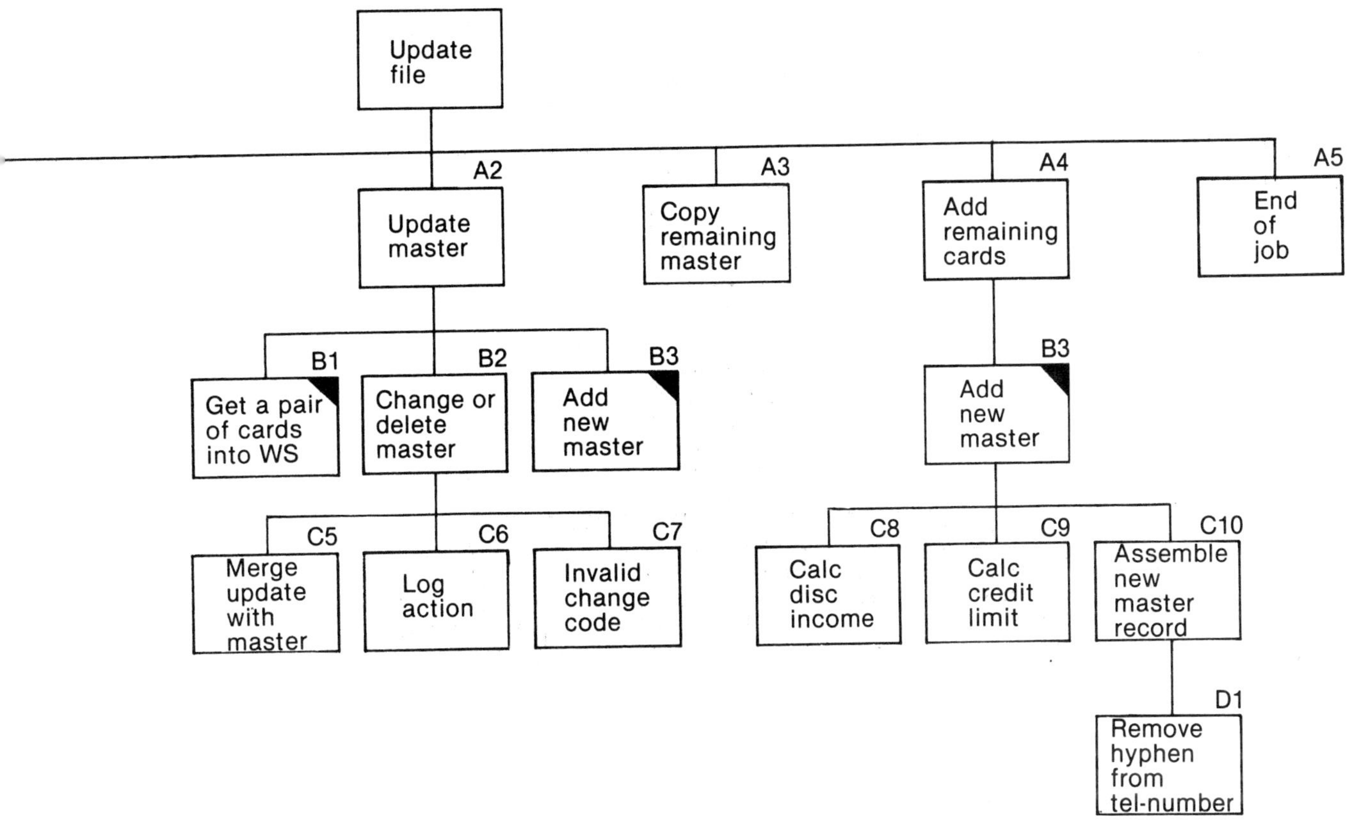

important measures of a programmer's worth are (1) the quality of his programs and (2) the amount of programming he produces.

Before you can measure productivity, though, you must decide what unit of measure to use. And this appears to put most people into a quandary that leads them to do nothing. The general reasoning is that whatever measure you use, it won't be completely fair and the wily programmers will figure out how to look good against this measure. If, for example, you decide to measure the number of lines of COBOL code produced by each programmer, some programmers will put in more comments or put in more MOVE statements or divide their statements over more lines or do something so they'll get a higher productivity rating.

My answer to this is that you have to combine productivity measures with quality audits. If, for example, you decide to measure lines of code, then you must do spot checks in your audits to make sure that no one is writing unnecessary code. When I managed my programming team, for example, I had absolutely no problem with this because I did the coding audits myself. If a programmer had put in unnecessary coding to increase his productivity rating, it would have been easy to spot. But no one ever tried it, and I don't think the majority of programmers are even tempted to try it. What the average programmer really wants is to do a good job and to get rewarded for it. As a result, only the marginal or poor programmer benefits when you don't measure productivity...the good ones appreciate measurement.

What, then, is the best unit of measure? In our shop, we've used lines of code and lines of code minus comments. But if everyone uses comments in the same way, both of these lead to the same relative measure of productivity. Paul recommends the count of the number of verbs used in the Procedure Division, but on our system you often get more Data Division statements and fewer verbs in an interactive program than you do in a comparable batch program so this isn't quite fair. Furthermore, the interactive program is usually more difficult to write than the batch program even if all of the above factors are equal. For a while, we experimented with productivity algorithms based on the number of files used by a program, the number of interactive screens, the number of statements in the Data Division, the number of statements in the Procedure Division, and so on. But when we finished experimenting, we decided to stay with lines of code minus comments.

With this as background, our recommendation is to start by measuring lines of code. You can easily get this number by looking at the last page of a program's compiler listing. And it's probably as fair as any other measure. Later on, if you feel you need a more sophisticated unit of measure, you can experiment with other program data.

The important thing to remember is that productivity measurement is only one indication of a programmer's worth so the unit of measure isn't that important. As a manager, you should know who you assigned the most difficult programs to. You should know who gets interrupted the most for technical questions. And you should know which programmers have adminstrative duties that take significant amounts of time away from their programming efforts. So lines of code or whatever productivity measure you're using is only one of the factors that you must consider when evaluating a programmer's productivity.

You can keep track of a programmer's productivity data quite easily by using a simple 3-ring binder with one page per programmer. Then, as each program is completed, you record the productivity measures for that program on one line of that programmer's page. If, for example, you want to keep track of lines of code and verbs, you can record the number of lines of code from the last page of the compiler listing and the number of verbs from the Procedure Division map. At the end of the measurement period, you can summarize the productivity measurements for all of your programmers.

If you want to keep more data on each program, you can write a statistics program that will generate most of the data you need from a COBOL source file. In our shop, for example, we used to generate the data shown in figure 21-2 from a program's source file whenever a program had passed its unit test. Note that this summary not only gives data that is related to productivity such as lines in the Procedure Division

```
PROGRAM NAME                    ORD1100
DATE STARTED                    03/23/85
DATE COMPLETED                  03/28/85

LINES OF CODE                   3436
LINES MINUS COMMENTS            3264
DD LINES MINUS COMMENTS         1506
PD LINES MINUS COMMENTS         1758
NUMBER OF FILES                    4
NUMBER OF MODULES                 61
LINES/MODULE                      29

NUMBER OF PERFORMS                75
NUMBER OF CALLS                    3
NUMBER OF GOTOS                    0

NUMBER OF READS                    3
NUMBER OF WRITES                   2
NUMBER OF REWRITES                 1
```

Figure 21-2 A statistical summary for a program that can be generated from the COBOL source file

and lines in the Data Division, but it also gives data related to program quality such as number of GOTOs and number of READs. When you use summaries like this, the project manager can file them in a 3-ring binder that has one section for each programmer. Then, at the end of an accounting period, the manager can summarize and review the productivity of each of his programmers.

If you have a microcomputer with spreadsheet software available to you, we recommend that you automate your statistics somewhat. For instance, figure 21-3 gives a summary by programmer for the first quarter of a year as prepared by a microcomputer. Here, several different productivity factors are recorded for each program including a type factor assigned by the project manager that gives each program a numeric value from 1 to 100 based on the functions it performs. If you keep data like this for a few months, it gives you a basis for changing your unit of measure to one that is more appropriate for your shop. Then, when you're sure you know what data you want to measure on a continuing basis, you may want to write a set of programs that keeps this data in a more sophisticated manner.

To give you some basis for comparison, it's also nice to summarize your statistics for all programmers in a single report like the one in figure 21-4. And, again, this can be done on a microcomputer using spreadsheet software. Or, you can develop a simple system for keeping this data for you.

No matter how you do it, though, it doesn't take much time to record some simple productivity measures. And the results certainly justify this time. In my experience as a project manager, for example, I found that the most productive programmer on my team was a trainee with six-months' experience. And she was outperforming the two experienced programmers we had just hired by a rate of more than 5 to 1. When I added in the fact that she was being paid about one-third as much as the

April 1, 1985
Year-to-date program completions by programmer
Programmer: Anne Prince

PROGYTD

Program Name	Program Type	Type Factor	No. of Files	No. of Screens	COBOL Verbs	Lines - Comments	COBOL Lines
ORD0000	Menu	1	0	1	65	301	418
ORD1100	Entry	20	4	9	859	3264	3426
ORD1200	Update	15	4	0	583	2215	2332
ORD1300	Procedure	2	0	0	0	0	0
ORD1310	Extract	10	2	1	324	1233	1298
ORD1320	Extract	10	3	0	363	1382	1455
ORD1330	Extract	10	3	0	205	781	823
INV0000	Menu	1	0	1	65	301	418
INV1100	Entry	20	3	5	696	2645	2785
INV1200	Update	15	3	0	527	2004	2110
INV1300	Extract	10	3	0	417	1586	1670
Totals		114	25	17	4104	15712	16735

Figure 21-3 A productivity summary for one programmer

April 1, 1985
Year-to-date programming summary by programmer

YTDSUM

Programmer Name	Type Factor	No. of Files	No. of Screens	COBOL Verbs	Lines - Comments	COBOL Lines	Lines/ Week
Steve Eckols	285	62	42	10,260	31,812	41,862	3,220
Doug Lowe	228	50	34	8,208	25,450	33,490	2,576
Anne Prince	114	25	17	4,104	15,712	16,745	1,288
Judy Taylor	93	22	15	3,576	13,602	14,318	1,101
Fred Winsome	12	3	1	476	1,527	1,909	147
Totals	732	162	109	26,624	88,103	108,324	8,332
Average	146	32	22	5,325	17,621	21,665	1,666

Figure 21-4 A productivity summary for a team of programmers

two experienced programmers, I realized I not only had a management problem, I had a moral dilemma. If I couldn't train the experienced programmers to reach her level of productivity, I either had to pay her much more or I had to pay them much less.

To give you more perspective on productivity measurement, let me compare program development to book development. At present, we have four people in our company who are writing books. Although we meet periodically to discuss the progress of their projects, I don't judge these writers on how many pages of manuscript they produce each year. On the contrary, a book's quality is far more important than the speed at which it is produced. So I evaluate my writers based on the quality of their writing, not their productivity.

On the other hand, I can't afford to ignore productivity. Because I've been in the publishing business for 17 years, I can tell you approximately how long a book should take to develop based on its length and complexity. So when a writer's project falls far behind schedule, I know that he isn't working at a speed that is consistent with professional writing standards. At that time, I try to help the writer overcome whatever problem is slowing him down. But if the writer never reaches a professional level of productivity, his value to the company can be marginal, even if the quality of his work is good. At that point, productivity becomes a major issue.

To put this in numeric terms, I think a professional writer should be able to produce at least ten single-spaced pages of technical manuscript per week. This assumes that the writer spends much of his time doing research and planning. Similarly, I think a COBOL programmer in our shop should be able to produce 500 lines of tested code per week. And that assumes that the programmer spends most of his time on research, planning, and design.

With guidelines like this, you don't become slaves to productivity measurement. If an employee produces at a rate that is below your minimum standards, you have identified a problem. But otherwise, you judge an employee by the quality of his programs, the complexity of the programs he produces, his contributions in non-programming functions, and so on. In an environment like this, you will have some programmers who regularly produce 5,000 lines of tested code per month. You will have some programmers who produce only 2500 lines of code per month but who make up for it by producing high-quality programs, by helping the trainees with technical problems, and by performing administrative duties. And you will have some programmers who produce 500 lines of unreadable, unreliable code per month. When you know the facts, you can justly reward the programmers who are doing good work for you, and you can retrain or reproach those who aren't.

Some related management ideas

Paul and I are confident that the three recommendations we just made are sound ones. They don't take much time to implement. And they yield some important results.

Needless to say, however, many problems and questions can come up when you implement a new program development method. At this time, then, let me give you some related management ideas.

Which techniques to implement first If it's possible, we think you should adopt and enforce all of the development procedures presented in section 2 of this book. In other words, as part of your development standards, we think you should include specifications for all nine tasks in our program development method. On the other hand, we realize that it's not always possible to get an entire shop to adopt a new method due to skepticism, habit, and departmental politics. In this case, you can implement a new development method by introducing a couple of tasks at a time.

I think you can tell which development techniques we feel are most important by the tone of the chapters in this book. As Paul and I see it, the two most important techniques are top-down program design as described in chapter 7 and structured COBOL coding as described in chapter 9. If you enforce the use of these techniques in your shop, your programming results will improve dramatically.

After you have established those techniques, you should add the other techniques presented in section 2 of this book. Each of these will make a contribution to your development efforts. In particular, the techniques of reusing code from old programs and top-down coding and testing will make important contributions to your development practices.

Although many companies feel that structured walkthroughs are important when it comes to improving program quality, I think there are other ways to do this. In particular, whether you use walkthroughs or not, I think you should audit program quality as a management practice. Our advice, then, is to use walkthroughs when you first implement the new techniques because it helps to promote consistent use of the techniques throughout your shop. On the other hand, you should reevaluate the benefits you're getting from walkthroughs after about six months. When you do, you may find that they no longer justify the time spent on them.

When to start with a pilot project If you can't get your staff to agree that they should adopt the method presented in this book, you may want to test the method on a pilot project. In this case, it's important that you select a useful project of three-programmer months or more. It's also nice if the project has been troublesome for a period of time. Then, if the development team produces a quality system in a short time, the results will be that much more dramatic.

A couple of years ago, for example, we were trying to get a large contract programming job. Unfortunately, the DP manager of the company didn't believe that we could develop programs as rapidly as we had promised. As a pilot project, then, we offered to do a system for them at our cost. The DP manager liked this idea and suggested a workers' compensation system that one of his programmers had already worked on for 22 months. We gladly accepted this project because it looked quite manageable. And when our lead programmer/analyst did the entire job by himself including the systems design in less than two months, some 22,000 lines of code, we had proven the effectiveness of our methods.

How to convince your programmers to use your new development techniques We hope, of course, that this book will convince your programmers that they should use our development method. So our first recommendation is that you make this book available to your staff members. But judging from our COBOL survey, the first edition of this book only convinced about half the readers to use our method. So it will probably take something more than this book to convince all of your programmers to use our method.

In Paul's experience, our programming methods have been accepted most readily when the managers themselves have believed in the new techniques. So we think it's important that the programming and project managers set the tone for a shop's development methods. In our shop, for example, we didn't have to convince our programmers to use our methods because the question never came up. We had our standards, and that was all there was to it. When an accounting firm hires an accountant, they don't have to convince him to use fair accounting practices; that's simply what a professional accountant uses. Similarly, I don't think you should have to convince programmers to use professional development methods; that's simply what a professional programmer should be using.

In a shop full of experienced programmers, of course, change is always difficult. And hard feelings can result if you simply command your programmers to use new standards for program development. As a result, Paul and I believe that you should try to get agreement on new development standards before they become official. On the other hand, program development is too important to leave to majority rule. As a manager, if you want to make dramatic changes in programmer productivity and program quality, you have to insist on the techniques you believe in.

When you try to get agreement on a new development method, a common objection is this: "That method takes all of the creativity out of our jobs." In other words, the experienced programmers feel that their creativity will be impaired by rigid development standards. But Paul's answer is that inefficiency isn't creativity. What we're suggesting is that you establish standards that let your programmers handle much of the detail of programming in a consistent and professional way. That way, they should have more energy to devote to the creative and analytical aspects of their jobs. So we just don't think this objection has any substance.

How to train your programmers in the new development techniques
Sometimes, when you adopt new development techniques, training becomes a problem. But if you adopt our techniques, this shouldn't be true. First, both *Case Studies* and an *Instructor's Guide* are available with this book. So you can run a complete course on our program development method in your own shop with a minimum of effort.

Second, all of the COBOL books that we publish use the same design and coding techniques that are presented in this book. If, for example, you want to teach COBOL to people who have no programming experience, we have a COBOL course for novices that uses the techniques presented in this book. When you use this course, your trainees will write high-quality programs from the start. Similarly, our courses on Report

Writer, VSAM, and CICS use the design and coding techniques presented in this book.

How to work with ineffective systems documentation In the last chapter, I tried to show you how important system development methods are to your program development efforts. But what if you have no power over the system development group? In this case, you have to take whatever systems documentation they give you, even if it is inadequate for your purposes.

In a case like this, we recommend that you create your own systems documentation before you start to develop the programs for a system. In particular, you can create your own system structure chart as described in the last chapter no matter what systems documentation they give you. If, for example, your systems group gives you system flowcharts, you can create a system structure chart from the flowcharts without too much trouble. Once you've done this, you can create your own program specifications as described in chapter 5.

Once you have a structure chart for a system and program overviews for each program on the chart, you're ready to develop the system. As I explained in the last chapter, you improve the reliability and maintainability of a system when you document it using system structure charts and program overviews. And these documents can also help you control and monitor the project.

How to maintain unstructured programs A question we're often asked is what to do about the hundreds of unstructured programs that still have to be maintained after you switch to structured development methods. In short, how do you apply structured methods to the maintenance of unstructured programs?

Since over 50 percent of the programming costs in many shops goes toward the maintenance of old programs, you can see that this is a significant problem. In fact, it's so significant that it deserves to be the subject of an entire book. Although Paul has many ideas about this, I'm only going to mention one that relates to pilot projects.

In brief, Paul says that a program that has been a continual maintenance problem is often an ideal pilot project. Because the program already exists, you know how many lines of code it is, how many files it uses, and so on. You may also know how long it took to develop and how many times it has failed in the last six months. As a result, you will have some basis for comparison when you rewrite this program using modern development methods. Then, when you rewrite the program, you should be able to prove the effectiveness of the new development methods at the same time that you solve a maintenance problem.

In the long run, in fact, the way to end the problem of maintaining unstructured programs is twofold. First, convert to structured methods today so your maintenance problem won't be any worse two years from now than it is today. Second, whenever you have to make a major modification to an unstructured program, consider rewriting it in structured style. Then, every time you do rewrite one, you'll have one less maintenance problem.

How to estimate the development time for a programming project Like the maintenance of unstructured programs, estimating the development time for a project continues to be a problem even after you convert to structured development methods. To estimate well, you have to develop an algorithm that expresses the work required by a program in terms of some unit of measure. You must be able to apply this algorithm to a program when all you have for it is its specifications. And you must know how many units of work each of the programmers who will be assigned to the project can do in a given period of time. In short, we feel that this subject is so complex that it's beyond the intent of this book. So all I'd like to do right now is give you a few ideas related to estimating procedures.

To start, I think we all know how poor our estimating techniques are right now. But to illustrate the foolishness of many of these techniques, let me tell an anecdote that took place when Paul worked for Pacific Telephone about ten years ago. At that time, a user of one of the accounting systems came to Paul directly to ask whether some enhancements could be made to the report-printing capabilities of the system he was using. When Paul analyzed the problem, he realized that the changes weren't that complicated even though the results made them appear to be. So he made the enhancements himself in an afternoon of work. Needless to say, the user was delighted.

"But now," Paul said, "I'd like you to go through the proper channels to request the programming modification I've already done for you. And don't tell them that you already have what you want." When the user did this, he was shocked to find that the programming manager estimated a development time of 9 months and a cost of $200,000 for the half day's work that had already been done.

This just illustrates that much of the estimating that we do has little basis in fact. Because we can't tell how large a system or program is going to be, we hedge a bit on the high side. And because we don't know how fast the programmers are going to work when they develop the system or program, we hedge some more. In fact, it's not uncommon for an estimator to make a hedged estimate and then double it for safe measure.

In the face of these difficulties, what do we suggest? Most important, I think, is to make sure your programmers are as productive as possible. If, for example, you can improve your programmers' productivity from 500 lines of tested code per month to 2500 lines of code per month, you have more room for error when you estimate program development times. If your programmers are only producing 500 lines of code per month and a 25,000 line project turns out to be 35,000 lines due to estimating errors, that means another 20 programmer-months of work. But if your programmers are producing 2500 lines per month, that error means only 4 more programmer-months of work. As a result, your estimates will at least appear to be better if you make a dramatic improvement in your productivity.

After you've improved programmer productivity, you can concentrate on improving your estimating procedures. But to do this, you must have data on the productivity of the programmers in your shop. So the sooner you start measuring productivity, the better off you'll be. If, for example, you measure the data shown in the summary in figure 21-4, you'll have some data that can help you when you try to improve your estimating procedures. Using data like this, you can develop an algorithm for estimating the number of work units a program will require based on program type, number of screens, and number of files. And once you've estimated the work units, you can estimate how long it will take your programmers based on the productivity of the programmers assigned to the project. In short, the sooner you start collecting productivity data, the sooner you'll be able to improve your estimating procedures.

Discussion

As I said at the start of this chapter, our intent in this chapter is to give you some ideas that may help you manage your programmers and projects more effectively. But we certainly don't know all the answers.

On the other hand, I don't think anyone has much basis for arguing with our three basic recommendations. First, to run a productive shop, you have to establish development standards for the entire shop; it's not enough that a few programmers use the new methods. Second, you have to enforce the use of the standards by doing quality audits of the programs developed in the shop. Third, you have to measure productivity because any professional must not only be judged by the quality of his work, but also by his productivity. If you accept these recommendations, we don't see how you can help but improve your effectiveness as a manager.

Terminology

None

Objective

List the three recommendations that we feel are essential if you are to improve program quality and programmer productivity in your shop.

Appendix A

The documentation for an edit program: specifications, structure chart, and COBOL listing

Program:	INV2100 EDIT INVENTORY TRANSACTIONS	Page:	1
Designer:	Anne Prince	Date:	08-17-84

Input/output specifications

File	Description	Use
INVTRAN	Inventory transaction file	Input
PARTNUM	Part number file	Input
VINVTRAN	Valid inventory transaction file	Output
IINVTLST	Print file: Invalid inventory transaction listing	Output

Process specifications

This program edits a file of transaction records consisting of two record types: sales transactions and return transactions. Although the formats for these records are similar, they are not exactly alike.

For efficiency, since the company has less than 100 inventory items, load a part-number table at the start of the program that can be used to check for valid part numbers throughout the program. The part numbers can be read from the part-number file. The records in this file are in order of transaction frequency; the first part number has the most activity, the last part number has the least.

Print the output listing in the same order that the transactions are read. And print the editing totals on a separate page on the invalid transaction listing.

The records in the valid transaction file have the same format as the records in the input transaction file.

Program:	**INV2100 EDIT INVENTORY TRANSACTIONS**	Page:	**2**
Designer:	**Anne Prince**	Date:	**08-17-84**

Process specifications

The basic processing requirements follow:

Load the part-number table.

Do until the end of the inventory transaction file:

1. **Read an inventory transaction record.**
2. **Edit the transaction fields.**
3. **If the transaction is invalid, print a line on the invalid transaction listing.**
4. **If the transaction is valid, write a record to the valid transaction file.**

After all transactions have been processed, print the total page.

Program:	INV2100 EDIT INVENTORY TRANSACTIONS	Page:	3
Designer:	Anne Prince	Date:	08-17-84

Process specifications

Editing rules for a sales transaction:

ITR-UPDATE-CODE	Must be "C"
ITR-TRAN-CODE	Must be 1
ITR-REF-NO	No restrictions
ITR-REF-DATE	Use DATEDIT subprogram; must be a valid date in the form MMDDYY
ITR-BRANCH-NO	Numeric, greater than zero, and less than 25
ITR-SALESMAN-NO	Numeric and greater than zero
ITR-CUSTOMER-NO	Numeric and greater than zero
ITR-QUANTITY	Numeric and greater than zero
ITR-PART-NO	Must match with a number in the part-number table that is loaded at the start of the program
ITR-RETURN-CODE	Not used

Editing rules for a return transaction:

ITR-UPDATE-CODE	Must be "C"
ITR-TRAN-CODE	Must be 2
ITR-REF-NO	No restrictions
ITR-REF-DATE	Use DATEDIT subprogram; must be a valid date in the form MMDDYY
ITR-BRANCH-NO	Not used
ITR-SALESMAN-NO	Not used
ITR-CUSTOMER-NO	Numeric and greater than zero
ITR-QUANTITY	Numeric and greater than zero
ITR-PART-NO	Must match with a number in the part-number table that is loaded at the start of the program
ITR-RETURN-CODE	Alphabetic

```
  BKEND    C.PARTNUM

*
 01  PART-NUMBER-RECORD.
*
     05  PNR-PART-NO                PIC X(5).
     05  PNR-PART-DESCRIPTION       PIC X(20).

  BKEND
```

```
 BKEND   C.INVTRAN

*
01  INVENTORY-TRANSACTION-RECORD.
*
    05  ITR-TYPE-CODE.
        10  ITR-UPDATE-CODE       PIC X.
        10  ITR-TRAN-CODE         PIC X.
    05  ITR-REF-NO                PIC X(10).
    05  ITR-REF-DATE              PIC X(6).
    05  ITR-BRANCH-NO             PIC XX.
    05  ITR-SALESMAN-NO           PIC XXX.
    05  ITR-CUSTOMER-NO           PIC X(5).
    05  ITR-QUANTITY              PIC X(5).
    05  ITR-PART-NO               PIC X(5).
    05  ITR-RETURN-CODE           PIC X(4).

 BKEND
```

Document name Invalid Sales and Return Listing **Date** 3-17-84

Program name INV2100 **Designer** Anne Prince

Record Name	Line	Print positions
Heading-Line-1	1	DATE: 99/99/99 MIKE MURACH & ASSOCIATES, INC. PAGE: ZZ9
Heading-Line-2	2	TIME: 99:99 XX INV2100
Heading-Line-3	3	INVALID SALES AND RETURN TRANSACTIONS
	4	
Heading-Line-4	5	TRAN UPDATE REFERENCE BRANCH SALESMAN CUSTOMER PART RETURN
Heading-Line-5	6	CODE CODE NUMBER DATE NUMBER NUMBER NUMBER QUANTITY NUMBER CODE
	7	
Invalid-Transaction-Line	8	*1 *X *XXXXXXXXXX *XX/XX/XX *XX *XXX *XXXXX *XXXXX *XXXXX
	9	*2 *X *XXXXXXXXXX *XX/XX/XX *XXXXX *XXXXX *XXXXX *XXXX
	10	X X XXXXXXXXXX XX/XX/XX XX XXX XXXXX XXXXX XXXXX XXXX
	11	
	12	
	13	
	14	
	15	
Error-Code-Line	16	* INDICATES ERROR FIELDS
	17	
	18	
	19	
Total page:	20	
	21	
Heading-Line-1	22	DATE: 99/99/99 MIKE MURACH & ASSOCIATES, INC. PAGE: ZZ9
Heading-Line-2	23	TIME: 99:99 XX INV2100
	24	
Summary-Heading	25	SUMMARY FOR SALES AND RETURN EDITING RUN
	26	
Total-Line	27	VALID SALES ZZ,ZZ9-
	28	RETURNS ZZ,ZZ9-
	29	TOTAL ZZ,ZZ9-*
	30	
	31	INVALID SALES ZZ,ZZ9-
	32	RETURNS ZZ,ZZ9-
	33	TOTAL ZZ,ZZ9-*
	34	
	35	INVALID TRAN CODES ZZ,ZZ9-*
	36	
	37	TRANSACTIONS PROCESSED ZZ,ZZ9-* *
	38	
	39	
	40	
	41	
	42	
	43	
	44	
	45	
	46	
	47	
	48	
	49	
	50	

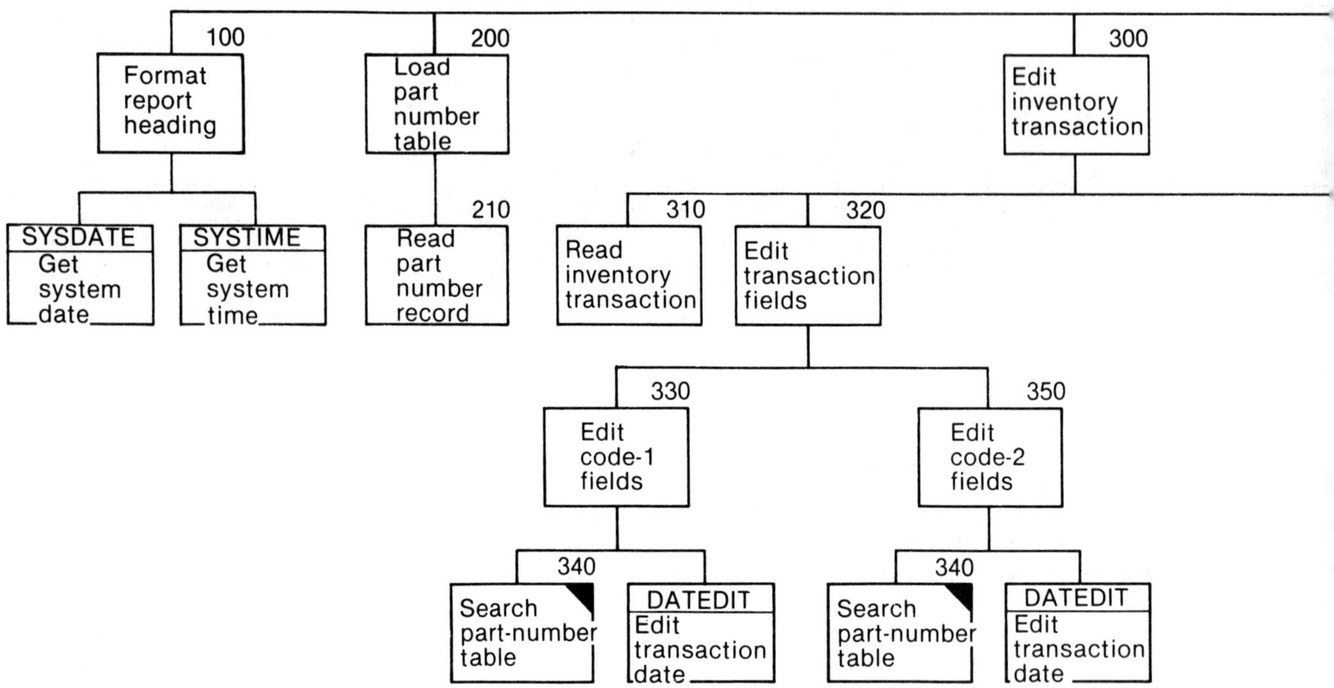

100
Format report heading
200
Load part number table
300
Edit inventory transaction
SYSDATE
Get system date
SYSTIME
Get system time
210
Read part number record
310
Read inventory transaction
320
Edit transaction fields
330
Edit code-1 fields
350
Edit code-2 fields
340
Search part-number table
DATEDIT
Edit transaction date
340
Search part-number table
DATEDIT
Edit transaction date

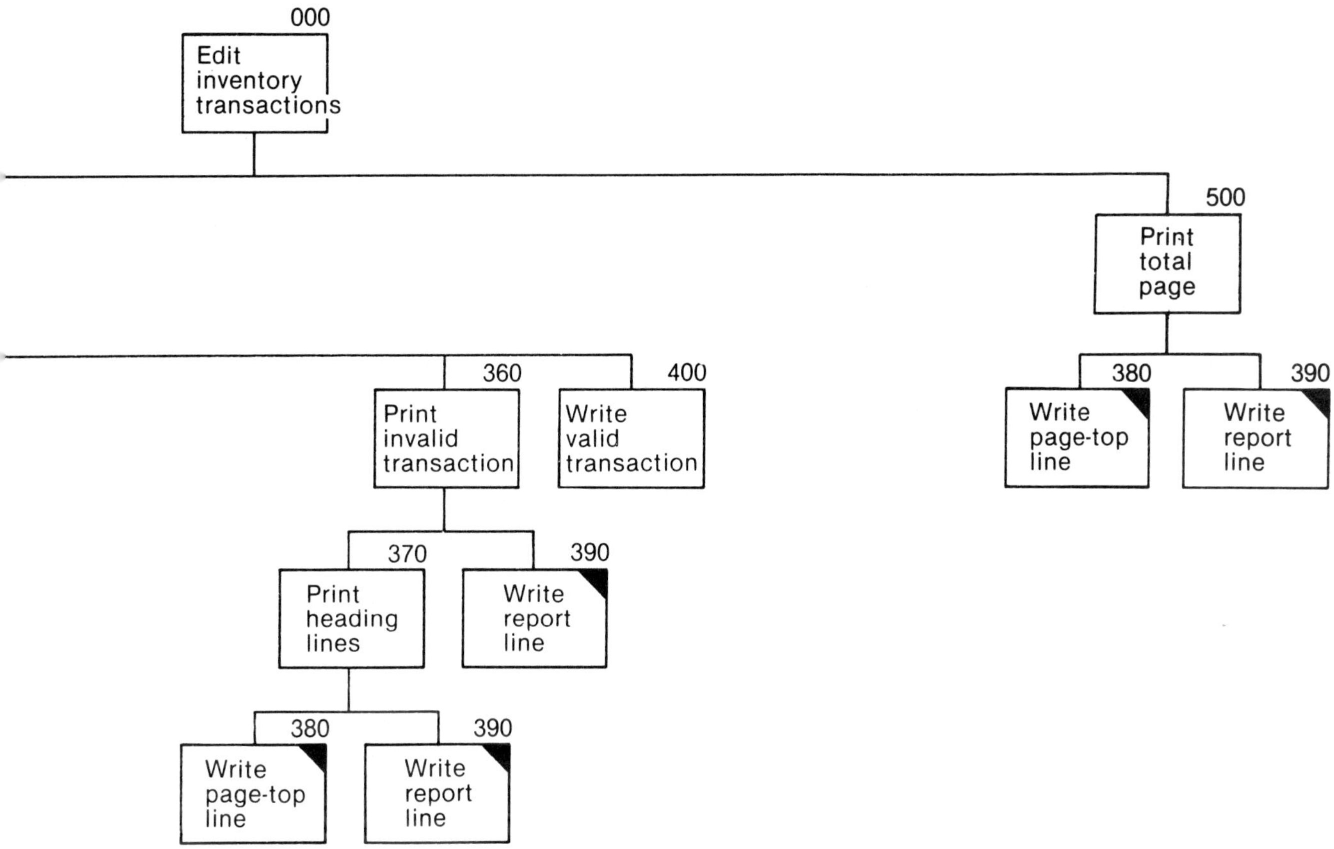
000
Edit inventory transactions
500
Print total page
360
Print invalid transaction
400
Write valid transaction
380
Write page-top line
390
Write report line
370
Print heading lines
390
Write report line
380
Write page-top line
390
Write report line

```
    1  IBM DOS/VS COBOL                                         REL 3.0

 CBL APOST,LANGLVL(1),LIB
        000100 IDENTIFICATION DIVISION.
        000200*
        000300 PROGRAM-ID.           INV2100.
        000400*AUTHOR.               ANNE PRINCE.
        000500*INSTALLATION.         MMA.
        000600*DATE.                 SEPTEMBER 10, 1984.
        000700*
        000800 ENVIRONMENT DIVISION.
        000900*
        001000 CONFIGURATION SECTION.
        001100*
        001200 SOURCE-COMPUTER.      IBM-370.
        001300 OBJECT-COMPUTER.      IBM-370.
        001400*
        001500 INPUT-OUTPUT SECTION.
        001600*
        001700 FILE-CONTROL.
        001800*
        001900     SELECT PARTNUM  ASSIGN TO SYS005-AS-PARTNUM.
        002000     SELECT INVTRAN  ASSIGN TO SYS008-AS-INVTRAN.
        002100     SELECT VINVTRN  ASSIGN TO SYS007-AS-VINVTRN.
        002200     SELECT IINVTLST ASSIGN TO SYS006-UR-1403-S.
        002300*
        002400 DATA DIVISION.
        002500*
        002600 FILE SECTION.
        002700*
        002800 FD  PARTNUM
        002900     LABEL RECORDS ARE STANDARD
        003000     RECORD CONTAINS 25 CHARACTERS.
        003100*
        003200 COPY PARTNUM.
      C       *
      C        01  PART-NUMBER-RECORD.
      C       *
      C            05  PNR-PART-NO              PIC X(5).
      C            05  PNR-PART-DESCRIPTION     PIC X(20).
        003300*
        003400 FD  INVTRAN
        003500     LABEL RECORDS ARE STANDARD
        003600     RECORD CONTAINS 42 CHARACTERS.
        003700*
        003800 01  INVENTORY-TRANSACTION        PIC X(42).
        003900*
        004000 FD  VINVTRN
        004100     LABEL RECORDS ARE STANDARD
        004200     RECORD CONTAINS 42 CHARACTERS.
        004300*
        004400 01  VALID-INVENTORY-TRANSACTION      PIC X(42).
        004500*
        004600 FD  IINVTLST
        004700     LABEL RECORDS ARE OMITTED
        004800     RECORD CONTAINS 132 CHARACTERS.
        004900*
        005000 01  PRINT-AREA      PIC X(132).
```

```
2                        14.23.04        10/25/84

005100*
005200 WORKING-STORAGE SECTION.
005300*
005400 01  SWITCHES.
005500*
005600     05  PART-NUMBER-EOF-SW        PIC X    VALUE 'N'.
005700         88  PART-NUMBER-EOF                VALUE 'Y'.
005800     05  TRAN-EOF-SW               PIC X    VALUE 'N'.
005900         88  TRAN-EOF                       VALUE 'Y'.
006000     05  VALID-TRAN-SW             PIC X.
006100         88  VALID-TRAN                     VALUE 'Y'.
006200     05  PART-NUMBER-FOUND-SW      PIC X.
006300         88  PART-NUMBER-FOUND              VALUE 'Y'.
006400     05  VALID-DATE-SW             PIC X.
006500         88  VALID-DATE                     VALUE 'Y'.
006600*
006700 01  COUNT-FIELDS                  COMP-3.
006800*
006900     05  TRANS-PROCESSED-COUNT     PIC S9(5)    VALUE ZERO.
007000     05  INVALID-TRAN-CODE-COUNT   PIC S9(5)    VALUE ZERO.
007100     05  INVALID-SALES-COUNT       PIC S9(5)    VALUE ZERO.
007200     05  VALID-SALES-COUNT         PIC S9(5)    VALUE ZERO.
007300     05  INVALID-RETURN-COUNT      PIC S9(5)    VALUE ZERO.
007400     05  VALID-RETURN-COUNT        PIC S9(5)    VALUE ZERO.
007500     05  INVALID-COUNT             PIC S9(5)    VALUE ZERO.
007600     05  VALID-COUNT               PIC S9(5)    VALUE ZERO.
007700*
007800 01  PRINT-FIELDS.
007900*
008000     05  SPACE-CONTROL     PIC S9                      COMP   SYNC.
008100     05  LINE-COUNT        PIC S999    VALUE +999      COMP   SYNC.
008200     05  LINES-ON-PAGE     PIC S999    VALUE +57       COMP   SYNC.
008300     05  PAGE-COUNT        PIC S999    VALUE ZERO      COMP-3.
008400*
008500 01  DATE-FIELDS.
008600*
008700     05  TODAYS-DATE       PIC 9(6).
008800*
008900 01  PART-NUMBER-TABLE.
009000*
009100     05  PN-TABLE-ENTRY          OCCURS 100 TIMES
009200                                 INDEXED BY PN-TABLE-INDEX
009300                                 PIC X(5).
009400     05  PN-ENTRY-COUNT          INDEX.
009500*
009600 01  MISCELLANEOUS-FIELDS.
009700*
009800     05  ERROR-INDICATOR         PIC X    VALUE '*'.
009900*
010000 COPY INVTRAN.
C          *
C           01  INVENTORY-TRANSACTION-RECORD.
C          *
C              05  ITR-TYPE-CODE.
C                  10  ITR-UPDATE-CODE       PIC X.
C                  10  ITR-TRAN-CODE         PIC X.
```

```
     3                          14.23.04          10/25/84

 C                 05  ITR-REF-NO                PIC X(10).
 C                 05  ITR-REF-DATE              PIC X(6).
 C                 05  ITR-BRANCH-NO             PIC XX.
 C                 05  ITR-SALESMAN-NO           PIC XXX.
 C                 05  ITR-CUSTOMER-NO           PIC X(5).
 C                 05  ITR-QUANTITY              PIC X(5).
 C                 05  ITR-PART-NO               PIC X(5).
 C                 05  ITR-RETURN-CODE           PIC X(4).
    010100*
    010200 01  COMPANY-NAME.
    010300*
    010400     05  FILLER        PIC X(10)   VALUE SPACE.
    010500     05  FILLER        PIC X(20)   VALUE 'MIKE MURACH & ASSOCI'.
    010600     05  FILLER        PIC X(20)   VALUE 'ATES, INC.' .
    010700*
    010800 01  REPORT-TITLE.
    010900*
    011000     05  FILLER        PIC X(11)   VALUE SPACE.
    011100     05  FILLER        PIC X(20)   VALUE 'INVALID SALES AND RE'.
    011200     05  FILLER        PIC X(29)   VALUE 'TURN TRANSACTIONS'.
    011300*
    011400 COPY RPTHDG14.
 C         *
 C          01  HEADING-LINE-1.
 C         *
 C              05  FILLER                   PIC X(7)    VALUE 'DATE:'.
 C              05  HDG1-DATE                PIC 99/99/99.
 C              05  FILLER                   PIC X(26)   VALUE SPACE.
 C              05  HDG1-COMPANY-NAME        PIC X(50).
 C              05  FILLER                   PIC X(31)   VALUE SPACE.
 C              05  FILLER                   PIC X(6)    VALUE 'PAGE:'.
 C              05  HDG1-PAGE-NUMBER         PIC ZZ9.
 C         *
 C          01  HEADING-LINE-2.
 C         *
 C              05  HDG2-TIME-DATA.
 C                  10  FILLER               PIC X(7)    VALUE 'TIME:'.
 C                  10  HDG2-HOURS           PIC XX.
 C                  10  FILLER               PIC X       VALUE ':'.
 C                  10  HDG2-MINUTES         PIC XX.
 C                  10  FILLER               PIC X       VALUE SPACE.
 C                  10  HDG2-TIME-SUFFIX     PIC X(8).
 C              05  FILLER                   PIC X(101)  VALUE SPACE.
 C              05  HDG2-REPORT-NUMBER       PIC X(10).
 C         *
 C          01  HEADING-LINE-3.
 C         *
 C              05  FILLER                   PIC X(36)   VALUE SPACE.
 C              05  HDG3-REPORT-TITLE        PIC X(60).
    011500*
    011600 01  HEADING-LINE-4.
    011700*
    011800     05  FILLER        PIC X(20)   VALUE 'TRAN   UPDATE   REFE'.
    011900     05  FILLER        PIC X(20)   VALUE 'RENCE               '.
    012000     05  FILLER        PIC X(20)   VALUE 'BRANCH   SALESMAN   '.
    012100     05  FILLER        PIC X(20)   VALUE 'CUSTOMER            '.
```

```
     4                     14.23.04          10/25/84

012200         05  FILLER        PIC X(20)    VALUE '    PART      RETURN    '.
012300         05  FILLER        PIC X(20)    VALUE '                    '.
012400         05  FILLER        PIC X(12)    VALUE '            '.
012500*
012600 01      HEADING-LINE-5.
012700*
012800         05  FILLER        PIC X(20)    VALUE 'CODE      CODE     NUM'.
012900         05  FILLER        PIC X(20)    VALUE 'BER            DATE  '.
013000         05  FILLER        PIC X(20)    VALUE 'NUMBER     NUMBER    '.
013100         05  FILLER        PIC X(20)    VALUE ' NUMBER     QUANTITY '.
013200         05  FILLER        PIC X(20)    VALUE '  NUMBER      CODE   '.
013300         05  FILLER        PIC X(20)    VALUE '                    '.
013400         05  FILLER        PIC X(12)    VALUE '            '.
013500*
013600 01      INVALID-TRANSACTION-LINE.
013700*
013800         05  ITL-TRAN-CODE-ERR        PIC X.
013900         05  ITL-TRAN-CODE            PIC X.
014000         05  FILLER                   PIC X(6).
014100         05  ITL-UPDATE-CODE-ERR      PIC X.
014200         05  ITL-UPDATE-CODE          PIC X.
014300         05  FILLER                   PIC X(5).
014400         05  ITL-REF-NO-ERR           PIC X.
014500         05  ITL-REF-NO               PIC X(10).
014600         05  FILLER                   PIC XX.
014700         05  ITL-REF-DATE-ERR         PIC X.
014800         05  ITL-REF-DATE             PIC XX/XX/XX.
014900         05  FILLER                   PIC X(4).
015000         05  ITL-BRANCH-NO-ERR        PIC X.
015100         05  ITL-BRANCH-NO            PIC XX.
015200         05  FILLER                   PIC X(6).
015300         05  ITL-SALESMAN-NO-ERR      PIC X.
015400         05  ITL-SALESMAN-NO          PIC XXX.
015500         05  FILLER                   PIC X(6).
015600         05  ITL-CUSTOMER-NO-ERR      PIC X.
015700         05  ITL-CUSTOMER-NO          PIC X(5).
015800         05  FILLER                   PIC X(7).
015900         05  ITL-QUANTITY-ERR         PIC X.
016000         05  ITL-QUANTITY             PIC X(5).
016100         05  FILLER                   PIC XX.
016200         05  ITL-PART-NUMBER-ERR      PIC X.
016300         05  ITL-PART-NUMBER          PIC X(5).
016400         05  FILLER                   PIC X(5).
016500         05  ITL-RETURN-CODE-ERR      PIC X.
016600         05  ITL-RETURN-CODE          PIC X(4).
016700         05  FILLER                   PIC X(42).
016800*
016900 01      ERROR-CODE-LINE.
017000*
017100         05  FILLER        PIC X(132)   VALUE '* INDICATES ERROR FIELDS'.
017200*
017300 01      SUMMARY-HEADING.
017400*
017500         05  FILLER        PIC X(20)    VALUE 'SUMMARY FOR SALES AN'.
017600         05  FILLER        PIC X(112)   VALUE 'D RETURN EDITING RUN'.
017700*
```

```
    5                          14.23.04          10/25/84

017800 01  TOTAL-LINE.
017900*
018000         05  TL-HEADING    PIC X(22).
018100         05  FILLER        PIC XX.
018200         05  TL-COUNT      PIC ZZ,ZZ9.
018300         05  FILLER        PIC X.
018400         05  TL-AST-1      PIC X.
018500         05  FILLER        PIC X.
018600         05  TL-AST-2      PIC X.
018700         05  FILLER        PIC X(98)  VALUE SPACE.
018800*
018900 PROCEDURE DIVISION.
019000*
019100 000-EDIT-INVENTORY-TRANS.
019200*
019300         OPEN INPUT  PARTNUM
019400                     INVTRAN
019500              OUTPUT VINVTRN
019600                     IINVTLST.
019700         PERFORM 100-FORMAT-REPORT-HEADING.
019800         PERFORM 200-LOAD-PART-NUMBER-TABLE
019900             VARYING PN-TABLE-INDEX FROM 1 BY 1
020000             UNTIL PART-NUMBER-EOF.
020100         PERFORM 300-EDIT-INVENTORY-TRAN
020200             UNTIL TRAN-EOF.
020300         PERFORM 500-PRINT-TOTAL-PAGE.
020400         CLOSE PARTNUM
020500               INVTRAN
020600               VINVTRN
020700               IINVTLST.
020800         STOP RUN.
020900*
021000 100-FORMAT-REPORT-HEADING.
021100*
021200         CALL 'SYSDATE' USING TODAYS-DATE.
021300         MOVE TODAYS-DATE    TO HDG1-DATE.
021400         MOVE COMPANY-NAME   TO HDG1-COMPANY-NAME.
021500         CALL 'SYSTIME' USING  HDG2-TIME-DATA.
021600         MOVE 'INV2100'      TO HDG2-REPORT-NUMBER.
021700         MOVE REPORT-TITLE   TO HDG3-REPORT-TITLE.
021800*
021900 200-LOAD-PART-NUMBER-TABLE.
022000*
022100         PERFORM 210-READ-PART-NUMBER-RECORD.
022200         IF NOT PART-NUMBER-EOF
022300             MOVE PNR-PART-NO TO PN-TABLE-ENTRY (PN-TABLE-INDEX)
022400         ELSE
022500             SET PN-TABLE-INDEX DOWN BY 1
022600             SET PN-ENTRY-COUNT TO PN-TABLE-INDEX.
022700*
022800 210-READ-PART-NUMBER-RECORD.
022900*
023000         READ PARTNUM
023100             AT END
023200                 MOVE 'Y' TO PART-NUMBER-EOF-SW.
023300*
```

```
6                    14.23.04        10/25/84

 300-EDIT-INVENTORY-TRAN.
*
     PERFORM 310-READ-INVENTORY-TRAN.
     IF NOT TRAN-EOF
         PERFORM 320-EDIT-TRANSACTION-FIELDS
         IF NOT VALID-TRAN
             PERFORM 360-PRINT-INVALID-TRANSACTION
         ELSE
             PERFORM 400-WRITE-VALID-TRANSACTION.
*
 310-READ-INVENTORY-TRAN.
*
     READ INVTRAN INTO INVENTORY-TRANSACTION-RECORD
         AT END
             MOVE 'Y' TO TRAN-EOF-SW.
     IF NOT TRAN-EOF
         ADD 1 TO TRANS-PROCESSED-COUNT.
*
 320-EDIT-TRANSACTION-FIELDS.
*
     MOVE 'Y'    TO VALID-TRAN-SW.
     MOVE SPACE TO INVALID-TRANSACTION-LINE.
     IF ITR-TRAN-CODE = 1
         PERFORM 330-EDIT-CODE-1-FIELDS
     ELSE IF ITR-TRAN-CODE = 2
         PERFORM 350-EDIT-CODE-2-FIELDS
     ELSE
         MOVE ERROR-INDICATOR TO ITL-TRAN-CODE-ERR
         MOVE 'N'             TO VALID-TRAN-SW
         ADD 1                TO INVALID-TRAN-CODE-COUNT.
*
 330-EDIT-CODE-1-FIELDS.
*
     IF ITR-UPDATE-CODE NOT = 'C'
         MOVE 'N'             TO VALID-TRAN-SW
         MOVE ERROR-INDICATOR TO ITL-UPDATE-CODE-ERR.
     CALL 'DATEDIT' USING ITR-REF-DATE, VALID-DATE-SW.
     IF NOT VALID-DATE
         MOVE 'N'             TO VALID-TRAN-SW
         MOVE ERROR-INDICATOR TO ITL-REF-DATE-ERR.
     IF         ITR-BRANCH-NO NOT NUMERIC
             OR ITR-BRANCH-NO NOT GREATER ZERO
             OR ITR-BRANCH-NO NOT LESS 25
         MOVE 'N'             TO VALID-TRAN-SW
         MOVE ERROR-INDICATOR TO ITL-BRANCH-NO-ERR.
     IF         ITR-SALESMAN-NO NOT NUMERIC
             OR ITR-SALESMAN-NO NOT GREATER ZERO
         MOVE 'N'             TO VALID-TRAN-SW
         MOVE ERROR-INDICATOR TO ITL-SALESMAN-NO-ERR.
     IF         ITR-CUSTOMER-NO NOT NUMERIC
             OR ITR-CUSTOMER-NO NOT GREATER ZERO
         MOVE 'N'             TO VALID-TRAN-SW
         MOVE ERROR-INDICATOR TO ITL-CUSTOMER-NO-ERR.
     IF         ITR-QUANTITY NOT NUMERIC
             OR ITR-QUANTITY NOT GREATER ZERO
         MOVE 'N'             TO VALID-TRAN-SW
```

```
     7                        14.23.04        10/25/84

029000             MOVE ERROR-INDICATOR TO ITL-QUANTITY-ERR.
029100         PERFORM 340-SEARCH-PART-NUMBER-TABLE.
029200         IF NOT PART-NUMBER-FOUND
029300             MOVE 'N'             TO VALID-TRAN-SW
029400             MOVE ERROR-INDICATOR TO ITL-PART-NUMBER-ERR.
029500         IF NOT VALID-TRAN
029600             ADD 1 TO INVALID-SALES-COUNT
029700         ELSE
029800             ADD 1 TO VALID-SALES-COUNT.
029900*
030000 340-SEARCH-PART-NUMBER-TABLE.
030100*
030200         SET PN-TABLE-INDEX TO 1.
030300         SEARCH PN-TABLE-ENTRY
030400             AT END
030500                 MOVE 'N' TO PART-NUMBER-FOUND-SW
030600             WHEN ITR-PART-NO = PN-TABLE-ENTRY (PN-TABLE-INDEX)
030700                 MOVE 'Y' TO PART-NUMBER-FOUND-SW
030800             WHEN PN-TABLE-INDEX GREATER PN-ENTRY-COUNT
030900                 MOVE 'N' TO PART-NUMBER-FOUND-SW.
031000*
031100 350-EDIT-CODE-2-FIELDS.
031200*
031300         IF ITR-UPDATE-CODE NOT = 'C'
031400             MOVE 'N'             TO VALID-TRAN-SW
031500             MOVE ERROR-INDICATOR TO ITL-UPDATE-CODE-ERR.
031600         CALL 'DATEDIT' USING ITR-REF-DATE, VALID-DATE-SW.
031700         IF NOT VALID-DATE
031800             MOVE 'N'             TO VALID-TRAN-SW
031900             MOVE ERROR-INDICATOR TO ITL-REF-DATE-ERR.
032000         IF          ITR-CUSTOMER-NO NOT NUMERIC
032100                  OR ITR-CUSTOMER-NO NOT GREATER ZERO
032200             MOVE 'N'             TO VALID-TRAN-SW
032300             MOVE ERROR-INDICATOR TO ITL-CUSTOMER-NO-ERR.
032400         IF          ITR-QUANTITY NOT NUMERIC
032500                  OR ITR-QUANTITY NOT GREATER ZERO
032600             MOVE 'N'             TO VALID-TRAN-SW
032700             MOVE ERROR-INDICATOR TO ITL-QUANTITY-ERR.
032800         PERFORM 340-SEARCH-PART-NUMBER-TABLE.
032900         IF NOT PART-NUMBER-FOUND
033000             MOVE 'N'             TO VALID-TRAN-SW
033100             MOVE ERROR-INDICATOR TO ITL-PART-NUMBER-ERR.
033200         IF          ITR-RETURN-CODE NOT ALPHABETIC
033300                  OR ITR-RETURN-CODE = SPACE
033400             MOVE 'N'             TO VALID-TRAN-SW
033500             MOVE ERROR-INDICATOR TO ITL-RETURN-CODE-ERR.
033600         IF NOT VALID-TRAN
033700             ADD 1 TO INVALID-RETURN-COUNT
033800         ELSE
033900             ADD 1 TO VALID-RETURN-COUNT.
034000*
034100 360-PRINT-INVALID-TRANSACTION.
034200*
034300         IF LINE-COUNT GREATER LINES-ON-PAGE
034400             PERFORM 370-PRINT-HEADING-LINES.
034500         MOVE ITR-TRAN-CODE               TO ITL-TRAN-CODE.
```

```
      8                    14.23.04        10/25/84

034600         MOVE ITR-UPDATE-CODE            TO ITL-UPDATE-CODE.
034700         MOVE ITR-REF-NO                 TO ITL-REF-NO.
034800         MOVE ITR-REF-DATE               TO ITL-REF-DATE.
034900         MOVE ITR-BRANCH-NO              TO ITL-BRANCH-NO.
035000         MOVE ITR-SALESMAN-NO            TO ITL-SALESMAN-NO.
035100         MOVE ITR-CUSTOMER-NO            TO ITL-CUSTOMER-NO.
035200         MOVE ITR-QUANTITY               TO ITL-QUANTITY.
035300         MOVE ITR-PART-NO                TO ITL-PART-NUMBER.
035400         MOVE ITR-RETURN-CODE            TO ITL-RETURN-CODE.
035500         MOVE INVALID-TRANSACTION-LINE TO PRINT-AREA.
035600         PERFORM 390-WRITE-REPORT-LINE.
035700         MOVE 1                          TO SPACE-CONTROL.
035800*
035900 370-PRINT-HEADING-LINES.
036000*
036100         ADD 1                 TO PAGE-COUNT.
036200         MOVE PAGE-COUNT       TO HDG1-PAGE-NUMBER.
036300         MOVE HEADING-LINE-1 TO PRINT-AREA.
036400         PERFORM 380-WRITE-PAGE-TOP-LINE.
036500         MOVE HEADING-LINE-2 TO PRINT-AREA.
036600         MOVE 1                TO SPACE-CONTROL.
036700         PERFORM 390-WRITE-REPORT-LINE.
036800         MOVE HEADING-LINE-3 TO PRINT-AREA.
036900         PERFORM 390-WRITE-REPORT-LINE.
037000         MOVE HEADING-LINE-4 TO PRINT-AREA.
037100         MOVE 2                TO SPACE-CONTROL.
037200         PERFORM 390-WRITE-REPORT-LINE.
037300         MOVE HEADING-LINE-5 TO PRINT-AREA.
037400         MOVE 1                TO SPACE-CONTROL.
037500         PERFORM 390-WRITE-REPORT-LINE.
037600         MOVE 2                TO SPACE-CONTROL.
037700*
037800 380-WRITE-PAGE-TOP-LINE.
037900*
038000         WRITE PRINT-AREA
038100             AFTER ADVANCING PAGE.
038200         MOVE 1 TO LINE-COUNT.
038300*
038400 390-WRITE-REPORT-LINE.
038500*
038600         WRITE PRINT-AREA
038700             AFTER ADVANCING SPACE-CONTROL LINES.
038800         ADD SPACE-CONTROL TO LINE-COUNT.
038900*
039000 400-WRITE-VALID-TRANSACTION.
039100*
039200         WRITE VALID-INVENTORY-TRANSACTION
039300             FROM INVENTORY-TRANSACTION-RECORD.
039400*
039500 500-PRINT-TOTAL-PAGE.
039600*
039700         ADD 1                  TO PAGE-COUNT.
039800         MOVE PAGE-COUNT        TO HDG1-PAGE-NUMBER.
039900         MOVE HEADING-LINE-1    TO PRINT-AREA.
040000         PERFORM 380-WRITE-PAGE-TOP-LINE.
040100         MOVE HEADING-LINE-2    TO PRINT-AREA.
```

```
9                    14.23.04        10/25/84

           MOVE 1                   TO SPACE-CONTROL.
           PERFORM 390-WRITE-REPORT-LINE.
           MOVE SUMMARY-HEADING TO PRINT-AREA.
           MOVE 3                   TO SPACE-CONTROL.
           PERFORM 390-WRITE-REPORT-LINE.
           MOVE SPACE TO TOTAL-LINE.
           COMPUTE VALID-COUNT = VALID-SALES-COUNT
                               + VALID-RETURN-COUNT.
           COMPUTE INVALID-COUNT = INVALID-SALES-COUNT
                                 + INVALID-RETURN-COUNT.
           MOVE 'VALID   SALES'              TO TL-HEADING.
           MOVE VALID-SALES-COUNT            TO TL-COUNT.
           MOVE TOTAL-LINE                   TO PRINT-AREA.
           PERFORM 390-WRITE-REPORT-LINE.
           MOVE SPACE                        TO TOTAL-LINE.
           MOVE '          RETURNS'          TO TL-HEADING.
           MOVE VALID-RETURN-COUNT           TO TL-COUNT.
           MOVE TOTAL-LINE                   TO PRINT-AREA.
           MOVE 1                            TO SPACE-CONTROL.
           PERFORM 390-WRITE-REPORT-LINE.
           MOVE SPACE                        TO TOTAL-LINE.
           MOVE '              TOTAL'        TO TL-HEADING.
           MOVE VALID-COUNT                  TO TL-COUNT.
           MOVE '*'                          TO TL-AST-1.
           MOVE TOTAL-LINE                   TO PRINT-AREA.
           PERFORM 390-WRITE-REPORT-LINE.
           MOVE SPACE                        TO TOTAL-LINE.
           MOVE 'INVALID SALES'              TO TL-HEADING.
           MOVE INVALID-SALES-COUNT          TO TL-COUNT.
           MOVE TOTAL-LINE                   TO PRINT-AREA.
           MOVE 2                            TO SPACE-CONTROL.
           PERFORM 390-WRITE-REPORT-LINE.
           MOVE SPACE                        TO TOTAL-LINE.
           MOVE '          RETURNS'          TO TL-HEADING.
           MOVE INVALID-RETURN-COUNT         TO TL-COUNT.
           MOVE TOTAL-LINE                   TO PRINT-AREA.
           MOVE 1                            TO SPACE-CONTROL.
           PERFORM 390-WRITE-REPORT-LINE.
           MOVE SPACE                        TO TOTAL-LINE.
           MOVE '              TOTAL'        TO TL-HEADING.
           MOVE INVALID-COUNT                TO TL-COUNT.
           MOVE '*'                          TO TL-AST-1.
           MOVE TOTAL-LINE                   TO PRINT-AREA.
           PERFORM 390-WRITE-REPORT-LINE.
           MOVE SPACE                        TO TOTAL-LINE.
           MOVE 'INVALID TRAN CODES'         TO TL-HEADING.
           MOVE INVALID-TRAN-CODE-COUNT      TO TL-COUNT.
           MOVE '*'                          TO TL-AST-1.
           MOVE TOTAL-LINE                   TO PRINT-AREA.
           MOVE 2                            TO SPACE-CONTROL.
           PERFORM 390-WRITE-REPORT-LINE.
           MOVE SPACE                        TO TOTAL-LINE.
           MOVE 'TRANSACTIONS PROCESSED'     TO TL-HEADING.
           MOVE TRANS-PROCESSED-COUNT        TO TL-COUNT.
           MOVE '*'                          TO TL-AST-1.
           MOVE '*'                          TO TL-AST-2.
           MOVE TOTAL-LINE                   TO PRINT-AREA.
           PERFORM 390-WRITE-REPORT-LINE.
```

Appendix B

Program specifications for an edit program that you should be able to develop in one day using the methods presented in this book

Program: AR2100 EDIT AR TRANSACTIONS	Page: 1
Designer: Anne Prince	Date: 10-16-84

Input/output specifications

File	Description	Use
ARTRAN	AR transaction file	Input
VARTRAN	Valid AR transaction file	Output
IARTLST	Print file: Invalid AR transaction listing	Output

Process specifications

This program edits a file of accounts receivable transaction records consisting of three record types: billing transactions, credit transactions, and payment transactions. Although the formats for these records are similar, they are not exactly alike.

Print the output listing in the same order that the transactions are read. And print the editing totals on a separate page on the invalid transaction listing.

Since the billing fields (code, charge, and cost) don't appear on the invalid transaction listing, if an error is detected in one of these fields the following message should be printed:

    INVALID ENTRY IN BILLING FIELDS

The records in the valid transaction file have the same format as the records in the input transaction file.

Program: AR2100 EDIT AR TRANSACTIONS	Page: 2
Designer: Anne Prince	Date: 10-16-84

Process specifications

The basic processing requirements follow:

Do until the end of the AR transaction file:

1. Read an AR transaction record.
2. Edit the transaction fields.
3. If the transaction is invalid, print a line on the invalid transaction listing.
4. If the transaction is valid, write a record to the valid transaction file.

After all transactions have been processed, print the total page.

Program: AR2100 EDIT AR TRANSACTIONS	Page: 3
Designer: Anne Prince	Date: 10-16-84

Process specifications

Editing rules for a billing transaction:

ART-TRANSACTION-CODE	Must be B
ART-CUSTOMER-NUMBER	Must be numeric and greater than zero
ART-INVOICE-NUMBER	Must be numeric and greater than zero
ART-PAYMENT-CREDIT-AMOUNT	Blank
ART-TRANSACTION-DATE	Must be a valid date in the form MMDDYY; use DATEDIT subprogram
ART-BRANCH-NUMBER	Must be numeric and greater than zero
ART-ACCOUNT-REP-NUMBER	Must be numeric and greater than zero
ART-SERVICE-CODE	At least the first code must be alphabetic
ART-SERVICE-CHARGE	Must be numeric and greater than zero if the related service code is not blank; must be blank if the related service code is blank
ART-SERVICE-COST	Must be numeric and greater than zero if the related service code is not blank; must be blank if the related service code is blank

Editing rules for a credit or payment transaction:

ART-TRANSACTION-CODE	Must be C or P
ART-CUSTOMER-NUMBER	Must be numeric and greater than zero
ART-INVOICE-NUMBER	Must be numeric and greater than zero
ART-PAYMENT-CREDIT-AMOUNT	Must be numeric and greater than zero
ART-TRANSACTION-DATE	Must be a valid date in the form MMDDYY; use DATEDIT subprogram
ART-BRANCH-NUMBER	Must be numeric and greater than zero
ART-ACCOUNT-REP-NUMBER	Must be numeric and greater than zero
ART-SERVICE-CODE	Blank
ART-SERVICE-CHARGE	Blank
ART-SERVICE-COST	Blank

```
*
 01  AR-TRANSACTION-RECORD.
*
     05  ART-TRANSACTION-CODE               PIC X.
         88  ART-BILLING                              VALUE 'B'.
         88  ART-CREDIT                               VALUE 'C'.
         88  ART-PAYMENT                              VALUE 'P'.
     05  ART-CUSTOMER-NUMBER                PIC X(5).
     05  ART-INVOICE-NUMBER                 PIC X(5).
     05  ART-PAYMENT-CREDIT-AMOUNT.
         10  ART-PAYMENT-CREDIT-DOLLARS     PIC X(5).
         10  ART-PAYMENT-CREDIT-CENTS       PIC XX.
     05  ART-TRANSACTION-DATE               PIC X(6).
     05  ART-BRANCH-NUMBER                  PIC X.
     05  ART-ACCOUNT-REP-NUMBER             PIC XX.
     05  ART-BILLING-DATA                   OCCURS 3 TIMES.
         10  ART-SERVICE-CODE               PIC XXX.
         10  ART-SERVICE-CHARGE             PIC X(7).
         10  ART-SERVICE-COST               PIC X(7).
```

Document name *Invalid Accounts Receivable Listing* Date *10-17-84*

Program name *AR2100* Designer *A. Prince*

Record Name	Line	Print chart content
Heading-Line-1	1	DATE: 99/99/99 MIKE MURACH & ASSOCIATES, INC. PAGE: ZZ9
Heading-Line-2	2	TIME: 99:99 XX AR2100
Heading-Line-3	3	INVALID ACCOUNTS RECEIVABLE TRANSACTIONS
	4	
Heading-Line-4	5	TRAN CUSTOMER INVOICE TRAN ACCOUNT PAYMENT OR
Heading-Line-5	6	CODE NUMBER NUMBER DATE BRANCH REP CREDIT AMOUNT BILLING FIELDS
	7	
Invalid-Transaction-Line	8	*X *XXXXX *XXXXX *XX/XX/XX *X *XX *XXXXX.XX XXXXXXXXXXXXXXXXXXXXXXXXXXXXXX
	9	B XXXXX XXXXX XX/XX/XX X XX INVALID ENTRY IN BILLING FIELDS
	10	C XXXXX XXXXX XX/XX/XX X XX XXXXX.XX
	11	P XXXXX XXXXX XX/XX/XX X XX XXXXX.XX
	12–15	
Error-Code-Line	16	* INDICATES ERROR FIELD
	17–19	
Total page data to be printed after first two lines of the standard heading	20–24	
Summary-Heading-Line	25	SUMMARY FOR ACCOUNTS RECEIVABLE EDITING RUN
	26	
Total-Line-1	27	VALID TRANSACTIONS ZZ,ZZ9
Total-Line-2	28	INVALID TRANSACTIONS ZZ,ZZ9
	29	
Total-Line-3	30	TOTAL TRANSACTIONS ZZ,ZZ9 **
	31–50	

Index

fold

fold

Comment Form

Your opinions count

Your opinions today will affect our future products and policies. So if you have questions, criticisms, or suggestions, I'm eager to get them. You can expect a response within a week of the time we receive your comments.

Also, if you discover any errors in this book, typographical or otherwise, please point them out. We'll correct them when the book is reprinted.

Thanks for your help!

Mike Murach, President
Mike Murach and Associates, Inc.

Book title: How to Design and Develop COBOL Programs

Dear Mike: ______________________________

Name and Title ______________________________
Company (if any) ______________________________
Address ______________________________
City, State, Zip ______________________________

fold

fold

Fold where indicated and staple.
No postage necessary if mailed in the U.S.

fold

fold

NO POSTAGE
NECESSARY
IF MAILED
IN THE
UNITED STATES

BUSINESS REPLY MAIL

First Class Permit No. 3063 Fresno, CA

POSTAGE WILL BE PAID BY ADDRESSEE

Mike Murach & Associates, Inc.

4222 West Alamos, Suite 101
Fresno, California 93711-9990

fold

fold

Order Form

Our Unlimited Guarantee

To our customers who order directly from us: You must be satisfied. Our books must work for you, or you can send them back for a full refund...no matter how many you buy, no matter how long you've had them.

Name & Title ______________________

Company (if any) ______________________

Address ______________________

City, State, Zip ______________________

Phone number (including area code) ______________________

Qty.	Product code	Title	Price
	CICS and VSAM		
___	CIC1	CICS for the COBOL Programmer: Part 1	$25.00
___	VSAM	VSAM for the COBOL Programmer	15.00
	COBOL Language Elements		
___	CAG	COBOL Advisor's Guide	$100.00
___	SAC1	Structured ANS COBOL: Part 1	20.00
___	SAC2	Structured ANS COBOL: Part 2	20.00
___	RW	Report Writer	13.50
	COBOL Program Development		
___	DDCP	How to Design and Develop COBOL Programs	$20.00
___	CPHB	The COBOL Programmer's Handbook	20.00
	Other (please specify)		
___	___		
___	___		

Qty.	Product code	Title	Price
	System Development		
___	DDBS	How to Design and Develop Business Systems	$20.00
___	SDCS	System Development Case Studies	6.00
___	SDIG	System Development Instructor's Guide	35.00
	OS Subjects		
___	TSO	MVS TSO	$22.50
___	OJCL	OS JCL	22.50
___	OSUT	OS Utilities	15.00
___	OSDB	OS Debugging for the COBOL Programmer	20.00
	Assembler Language		
___	ASMD	DOS Assembler Language	$22.50
___	ASMO	OS Assembler Language	22.50
	Other (please specify)		
___	___		
___	___		

☐ Bill me the appropriate price plus shipping and handling (and sales tax in California) for each book ordered.

☐ I want to **save** shipping and handling charges. Here's my check or money order for $________. California residents, please add 6% sales tax to your total. (Offer valid in the U.S. only.)

☐ Bill the appropriate book prices plus shipping and handling (and sales tax in California) to my
_____ Visa _____ MasterCard:

Card number ______________________

Valid thru (month/year) ______________________

Cardowner's signature ______________________
(not valid without signature)

Mike Murach & Associates, Inc.

4222 West Alamos, Suite 101
Fresno, CA 93711 • 209-275-3335

To order more quickly,

Call **toll-free** 1-800-221-5528
In California, call 1-800-221-5527

fold

fold

NO POSTAGE
NECESSARY
IF MAILED
IN THE
UNITED STATES

BUSINESS REPLY MAIL

First Class Permit No. 3063 Fresno, CA

POSTAGE WILL BE PAID BY ADDRESSEE

Mike Murach & Associates, Inc.

4222 West Alamos, Suite 101
Fresno, California 93711-9990

fold

fold